The American Society of International Law's First Century

1906–2006

THE AMERICAN SOCIETY OF INTERNATIONAL LAW

The American Society of International Law's First Century

1906–2006

FREDERIC L. KIRGIS

MARTINUS NIJHOFF PUBLISHERS
LEIDEN / BOSTON

A C.I.P. Catalogue record for this book is available from the Library of Congress.

Published by Martinus Nijhoff Publishers.

Printed on acid-free paper.

ISBN 90-04-15068-4

Koninklijke Brill NV incorporates the imprints Brill Academic Publishers, Martinus Nijhoff Publishers and VSP.
http://www.brill.nl

Printed and bound in The Netherlands

To all those for whom the establishment and maintenance of international relations on the basis of law and justice is a priority

FOREWORD

The purpose of the American Society of International Law is to "foster the study of international law and to promote the establishment and maintenance of international relations on the basis of law and justice." Rick Kirgis's centennial history illustrates how the Society has balanced, in various eras from 1906 to the present, the tricky task of both studying and promoting by talking more or less simultaneously to three separate audiences: government decision makers, a national and later an international community of scholars and, ultimately, a general educated public. It describes how a small group of leaders formed an organization with a somewhat messianic purpose, and how two world wars transformed it into a leading global scholarly study group. Now, as we look forward to the beginning of a second century, the Society has launched an effort to realize more fully its public education role.

A major theme of this history is how international law has played a part in the U.S. Government's foreign policy thinking and how citizens and scholars have sought to influence those policies over the past century. Another theme is the timelessness of the issues confronting an international legal society. Throughout the organization's history, certain themes appear, fade and then reappear. Will the Society take positions on controversial issues of the day? Can it effectively organize itself on a regional basis throughout the country? What are the pressing issues for scholarly research? How do practicing lawyers and political scientists fit in the picture? Where will the funds for all the projects come from? These are issues that remain with us.

A special birthday deserves a lasting commemoration, and the Society is fortunate to have this fine history to mark our centennial.

James H. Carter
President, American Society of International Law

CONTENTS

List of Illustrations

(To be found on pages 263 through to 278.)

PREFACE

When Edith Brown Weiss asked me in 1994 if I would write a history of the American Society of International Law, of which she was then the President, I was happy to accept. The Society has meant a very great deal to me throughout my professional career, and I looked forward to learning more about it as I researched its history.

A short history of the Society's first fifty years already exists. Written by George A. Finch, a fixture among the Society's leaders for many years, it appeared in 50 *American Journal of International Law* 293 (1956). I have drawn on Finch's effort, as will appear in the text and endnotes, but I have thought it important to provide a more thorough record of relevant decisions and events than he did, and of course to bring his history up to date.

I determined at the outset that I would approach the project as a scholar and (untrained) historian, rather than as a promoter for the Society. I set out to write an accurate, analytical record of its efforts through the years to live up to its stated object: "to foster the study of international law and to promote the establishment and maintenance of international relations on the basis of law and justice."

I have done my best to tie the Society's decisions and activities to the major events, and to some of the leading American public figures, of the relevant historical periods. I have tried, too, to assess the effectiveness of those decisions and activities, although it has not always been possible to reach clear conclusions on this score.

I have included some details that no doubt are of interest primarily to those who have had, or who in the future will have, some responsibility for administering or overseeing the Society's activities. In other words, the book should be a handy reference tool for those who need to know how things have been done in earlier times. To facilitate its use as a reference tool, I have provided endnote references for most of the historical material in the text. Textual footnotes have been kept to a minimum.

I hope, though, that the book is much more than a dry reference tome. I have tried to make it readable and interesting for those who simply want to know something about the Society and its place in the world. Hence, many details that would be likely to interest only a Society administrator or officer, or a member of the Journal's Board of Editors or staff, have been relegated to two memoranda that will be available in paper form at the Society's headquarters and, I hope, on line. The memoranda are "ASIL History: Details Relating to Budget, Finances and Membership" (2006), and "ASIL History: The Journal, Its Editors and Business Practices, with an Appendix: Recipients of the Francis Deak Prize" (2006).

I have not been above including some anecdotes that seemed to capture the personalities of the Society's leaders. For trivia buffs, the anecdotes should spice up the history a bit; for others, perhaps they will simply be amusing interludes.

In the end, the reader will have to make his/her own judgment about how well the Society has run the course it set out for itself in 1906. I hope this book will provide a basis for that judgment. And of course no judgment at this stage can be final. The American Society of International Law will carry on into its second century with new and continuing programs that take into account what it has done in its first one hundred years. It will continue to do its best to demonstrate not only what international law is or should be, but also that, in the words of former ASIL President Louis Henkin, international law matters.

I owe thanks to several prominent Society members, officers and Executive Directors who graciously consented to be interviewed on audio tape, or to provide me with written recollections, in connection with the preparation of this work. They include Richard Edwards, Eleanor Finch, Lawrence Hargrove, Charlotte Ku, Monroe Leigh, Myres McDougal, Christopher Merillat, James Nafziger, Covey Oliver, Seymour Rubin and Stephen Schwebel. Transcripts of the taped interviews are on file with the Society.

Thanks are owed as well to virtually everyone on the Society's staff during the years 1994 through 2005. The staff made me welcome as a virtual colleague during my many hours of research in Tillar House. Special thanks are owed to Charlotte Ku, Rick LaRue, Sandra Liebel, Jill Watson, Marilou Righini and Jennifer Krieger, all of whom pitched in when needed and all of whom offered encouragement and helpful advice. I relied on them, and they unfailingly came through.

The photographs in the book and the quotations at the beginning of each chapter are the result of the diligent efforts of ASIL interns Joseph Bertini, Elizabeth Drobnick, Eric Marfin, Ross Liemer and Allison Schultz. Many thanks are owed to them, as well.

An abridged version of Chapter One appeared under the title, "The Formative Years of the American Society of International Law," 90 *AJIL* 559 (1996).

Frederic L. Kirgis
(Rick Kirgis)

Lexington, Virginia
October 2005

Chapter One

THE FORMATIVE YEARS

This Society may serve as a collegium, in the true sense of the word, in which all who choose to seek a broader knowledge of the law that governs the affairs of nations may give each to the other the incitement of earnest and faithful study and may give to the great body of our countrymen a clearer view of their international rights and responsibilities.

—Elihu Root
Address by the President of the Society,
1 *ASIL Proceedings* 44 (1907)

A. GETTING STARTED

1. The Peace Movement at the Turn of the Twentieth Century

The United States at the dawn of the twentieth century was just beginning to comprehend the influence it could have on the international scene. It had no desire to become involved in the European power politics that had produced, in the lifetimes of many Americans then living, the Crimean War, the Franco-Prussian War, and the essentially European Boer War in South Africa. Nevertheless, there was a distinct strain of expansionism in American foreign policy. For those concerned with establishing a nonviolent world order, there was an awakening belief that American values, American economic dynamism and the lessons to be drawn from the American federal experience could beneficially affect the ways in which nation states interacted with each other. This belief, combined with a deep aversion to what was seen as essentially a European proclivity to settling disputes by resorting to war, motivated the efforts of some of the more influential participants in the American peace movement. That movement, in turn, gave birth to the American Society of International Law.

The American peace movement was an odd collection of visionaries, world federalists and "legalists."[1] The legalists included lawyers, diplomats and academics who placed their faith in formal dispute-settlement mechanisms as the means

---

1 See David S. Patterson, "An Interpretation of the American Peace Movement, 1898-1914," in *Peace Movements in America* 20, 23-24 (Charles Chatfield ed. 1973). For a slightly different taxonomy, see Ruhl J. Bartlett, *The League to Enforce Peace* 4 (1944).

for avoiding war. Before the first decade of the century had run its course, they would organize the ASIL in an effort to provide a forum that would promote practical (and essentially American) ways to attain the goal of peace.

The American legalists were part of a wider body of like-minded persons striving to develop international law as an instrument of peace. In England, the conditions attached by William Whewell when he established the Chair in International Law at Cambridge University directed the holder to aim in his work to lay down such rules and suggest such measures as might tend ultimately to extinguish war among nations.[2] The Institute of International Law, a European-based body of eminent legal experts, was founded in 1873 with the aim of becoming "the organ of the legal conscience of the civilized world."[3] Although it failed of that lofty purpose, it worked steadily to articulate principles of international law; in 1904 it was awarded the Nobel Peace Prize in recognition of its contribution to peaceful conflict resolution.[4] The International Law Association, based in London, sprang from the Conference for the Reform and Codification of International Law, organized by the peace movement and held in Brussels in 1873.[5]

The American peace movement was building up steam as the twentieth century began. The movement itself was nothing new. The American Peace Society had been organized in 1828, but had failed to make much of an impact on the shapers of American foreign policy.[6] By 1895, though, members of the American foreign policy establishment had begun to gather annually at Lake Mohonk, in upstate New York, to discuss the preservation of peace, and more particularly the perceived importance of international arbitration as an alternative to war. The first Hague Peace Conference had been held in 1899 and had seemed to offer hope for just that outcome.

American participants in the Hague Peace Conferences of 1899 and 1907 placed great faith in the concepts of arbitration and adjudication. This, it has been asserted, was an outgrowth of classical legal ideology: faith in the idea that maintenance of order depended more on a social norm – a realization that order served everyone's long-term interest – than on the use of state power. At the international level, what was therefore needed was a body of recognized law, and the creation of neutral institutions to interpret and apply it, so that

---

2 See Henry Sumner Maine, *International Law* 1 (1888; reprint 1979).

3 See Irwin Abrams, "The Emergence of the International Law Societies," 19 *Review of Politics* 361, 375 (1957).

4 See Irwin Abrams, *The Nobel Peace Prize and the Laureates* 52-53 (1988).

5 See Abrams, *supra* note 3, at 371-72, 376-79.

6 See C. Roland Marchand, *The American Peace Movement and Social Reform, 1898-1918*, at 5-6 (1972).

the goals of stability and reasoned dispute settlement could be achieved and be seen to be achieved.[7]

The American participants realized that the products of their efforts – the Permanent Court of Arbitration[8] and an International Prize Court[9] – were less than perfect: the Permanent Court because it was not really a court or even an arbitral body, but rather a roster of potential arbitrators, and the Prize Court because the subject matter over which it had jurisdiction was quite limited.[10] By the time of the second Hague Conference, the American emphasis had shifted from arbitration to the creation of a permanent judicial body that would apply established, neutral rules and principles of international law to the settlement of international disputes.[11] Differences of opinion among the 44 participating states about the method of selecting judges, and perhaps deeper differences as well, prevented the 1907 Conference from realizing that goal.

Nevertheless, the American legalists were optimistic. Joseph Choate, who led the American delegation to the second Peace Conference, said in 1913 of the first Conference:

> [H]ere, for the first time, it was unanimously agreed that respect for law must be fundamental in all international arbitration.
>
> ...
>
> War had been, from the beginning, the normal condition of the world, interrupted by fitful intervals of peace, but now we are coming in sight of the new doctrine, – the American doctrine, as it may well be called – that peace is and shall be the normal condition of mankind, and that war is only an occasional incident interrupting and disturbing it, for now all nations agree that arbitration is the most efficacious and equitable

---

7 See Jonathan Zasloff, "Law and the Shaping of American Foreign Policy: From the Gilded Age to the New Era," 78 *NYU L. Rev.* 239, 255-57, 308-09, 322-23, 361-65 (2003).

8 Convention for the Pacific Settlement of International Disputes, July 29, 1899, 1 Bevans 230, 187 Consol. Treaty Ser. 410, as amended, Oct. 18, 1907, 1 Bevans 577, 205 Consol. Treaty Ser. 233. See also 2 James Brown Scott, *The Hague Peace Conferences of 1899 and 1907*, at 80 & 308 (1909) (hereafter Scott, *The Hague Peace Conferences*).

9 Id. at 472.

10 The Prize Court never came into existence.

11 See Calvin DeArmond Davis, *The United States and the Second Hague Peace Conference* 253, 260-61 (1975); Elihu Root's Instructions to the American Delegates to the Hague Conference of 1907, in 1907 Foreign Rel. of the U.S., pt. 2, at 1128, 1135; 1 Scott, *The Hague Peace Conferences*, *supra* note 8, at 426-28 (1909).

> method of deciding controversies which have not been capable of settlement by diplomatic methods.[12]

James Brown Scott, the leader among the founders of the American Society of International Law and a delegate to the second Peace Conference, asserted that "the great work of the First Conference, indeed its chief title to remembrance, lies in the creation of a court, in reality a panel of judges, to which nations might freely and with confidence resort for the constitution of a tribunal for the judicial settlement of international disputes."[13] John W. Foster, a former Secretary of State, considered the "arbitration convention" to be "the most important and the crowning work of the [first] Hague Conference."[14]

Faith in arbitration stemmed largely from the outcome of the well-known *Alabama* claims, in which an international tribunal awarded the United States USD 15.5 million against Great Britain for the latter's failure to prevent the fitting out in Britain of Confederate warships during the American Civil War.[15] It was thought that the agreement to arbitrate the *Alabama* claims, and Britain's compliance with the award, may have averted a war between the United States and Great Britain.[16]

The *Alabama* arbitration was not the only source of faith for the true believers. In the three decades following the *Alabama* decision, almost a hundred cases were submitted to international arbitration.[17] Many of the ensuing awards were compatible with American interests. In 1914, James Brown Scott, as Director of the Division of International Law for the Carnegie Endowment, published a

---

12 Joseph H. Choate, *The Two Hague Conferences* 33 (1913). Choate recognized the inadequacies of the Permanent Court of Arbitration in the form it took at the Hague Conferences. Id. 77-80.

13 1 Scott, *The Hague Peace Conferences*, *supra* note 8, at 277 (1909). Like Choate, Scott was aware that the Permanent Court had its shortcomings, but he was optimistic about its development into a true permanent court of arbitration. Id. at 281, 311.

14 John W. Foster, *Arbitration and the Hague Court* 39 (1904).

15 The Treaty of Washington, May 8, 1871, 12 Bevans 170, 143 Consol. Treaty Ser. 145, established the tribunal and set out the rules of neutral conduct it was to apply. The award appears in 1 John Bassett Moore, *International Arbitrations* 653 (1898).

16 See the remarks of Henry B. Brown, 2 *ASIL Proc.* 132, 144 (1908). See also Gladstone's pronouncement in the British House of Commons on June 15, 1880:

> I regard the fine imposed on this country as dust in the balance compared with the moral value of the example set when two great nations ... went in peace and concord before a judicial tribunal rather than resort to the arbitrament of the sword.

Quoted in George A. Finch, "The American Society of International Law 1906-1956," 50 *AJIL* 293 (1956) (hereafter cited as Finch, "The ASIL 1906-1956").

17 See Manley O. Hudson, *International Tribunals, Past and Future* 5 (1944).

pamphlet summarizing 83 arbitrations and diplomatic settlements "in the nature of arbitral adjustments" to which the United States had been a party. This, he thought, "would advance the cause of arbitration by showing how frequently and successfully it has been resorted to." Scott appended a table indicating that 52 of the awards or settlements went in favor of the United States, 14 went the other way, and 17 favored "all parties."[18]

International arbitration among governments was the sole formal topic of discussion at the Lake Mohonk Conferences, held annually from 1895 until the outbreak of World War I.[19] Several of the individuals in attendance at these prestigious gatherings became influential figures in the formation and early years of both the American Society of International Law and the Carnegie Endowment for International Peace. Their enthusiasm for arbitration was unquestionably motivated in large part by their belief in it as the most promising available instrument of peace. Their ardor may have been helped along by the fact that several of them had been employed as counsel, or in some other capacity, in arbitral proceedings involving the United States.[20] Their faith in America, as the champion of what was just and right, was probably also a factor: since, in their view, the United States was very likely to have justice on its side in any dispute, there would be little to fear if an arbitral body were to decide the matter.[21]

The American legalists also had faith in the settlement of disputes among nation states by a permanent international court. Scott was influential in establishing the American Society for Judicial Settlement of International Disputes, and became its first President. That Society held its first conference in December 1910. Scott and Elihu Root, who was by then the President of the American Society of International Law, were two of the three keynote speakers. The conference was devoted to the proposition that a permanent international court, preferably modeled on the United States Supreme Court, would promote peaceful resolution of international disputes by applying recognized principles

---

18 James Brown Scott, "Introductory Note to Arbitrations and Diplomatic Settlements of the United States" (Carnegie Endowment for International Peace, Division of International Law Pamphlet No. 1, 1914). The table is in id. at 20. John Bassett Moore shared Scott's belief in arbitration, as evidenced by his monumental *History and Digest of the International Arbitrations to which the United States Has Been a Party* (6 vols. 1898).

19 See Larry L. Fabian, *Andrew Carnegie's Peace Endowment: The Tycoon, The President, and Their Bargain of 1910*, at 25-26 (1985); Finch, "The ASIL 1906-1956," *supra* note 16, at 295 (1956).

20 See Marchand, *supra* note 6, at 45-46.

21 See Fabian, *supra* note 19, at 17.

of international law.[22] The same theme carried through to its sixth and last conference, in 1916.[23]

2. The Birth of the American Society of International Law

At the eleventh Lake Mohonk Conference, held from May 31 to June 2, 1905, the American Society of International Law was conceived. By then, international lawyers had become a significant presence among the Conference participants. Thirteen members of the Conference in 1905 were international lawyers, up from one or two in 1901 and 1902.[24]

George W. Kirchwey, the Dean of the Columbia University Law School in 1905 and a first-time participant in the Conference, told the group on the final day that he longed "for some exhibition of a more definite purpose in the gathering than the threshing of the old straw of the Constitution or treading the wine press of ancient wars." The time had come, he said, to take "some definite step in the direction of organization of machinery for forwarding the purpose" of promoting peace through the use of international arbitration.[25]

An informal committee consisting of Kirchwey, Robert Lansing, later to become Secretary of State, and James Brown Scott, then a Columbia University law professor, had already met to discuss forming an international law society and a journal devoted to international law.[26] When Kirchwey's intervention with the other members of the conference met no opposition, the three men decided to proceed.[27] A group of 24 interested members then met and decided to appoint a committee "to draft a form of organization for an American international law society."[28] A committee of seven members was formed. It acted as a steering committee, eventually adding 14 more members. The members

---

22 See Proceedings of International Conference under the Auspices of the American Society for Judicial Settlement of International Disputes, Dec. 15-17, 1910.

23 See Proceedings of Sixth National Conference of the American Society for Judicial Settlement of International Disputes, Dec. 8-9, 1916. The focus of the sixth conference was entirely on the U.S. Supreme Court.

24 Marchand, *supra* note 6, at 40.

25 Report of the Eleventh Annual Meeting of the Mohonk Lake Conference on International Arbitration 128-29 (1905).

26 See James Brown Scott, "History of the Organizaton of the American Society of International Law," 1 *ASIL Proc.* 23 (1907), on which much of the narrative in this chapter regarding formation of the Society is based.

27 Kirchwey and Scott must have been very close. In later correspondence, Kirchwey addressed Scott by a homespun nickname and used one for himself as well. Letter from Kirchwey to Scott, Jan. 14, 1913, in the Society's files.

28 Id. at 26.

were principally professors of international law and diplomats with experience in matters involving international law.[29]

In the ensuing months, those members of the committee of seven who lived in New York City (Kirchwey, Scott, Oscar S. Straus, Chandler P. Anderson and John Bassett Moore) met several times to draw up a tentative constitution. James Brown Scott did much of the work.[30] It was later said of him:

> Those of us who began our association with this Society at the outset know that it was Dr. Scott's idea, this American Society of International Law. It was his vision, and it was due to his energy, his devotion, that his idea, his vision, became a reality.[31]

The religious metaphor to describe Scott's relationship with the Society and with international law occurred to others as well. Frederic Coudert, who became a member of the Executive Council in 1907 and much later became President of the Society, said in the year of Scott's death:

> As a Founder, as Secretary, as President through a decade, there was no activity of the Society that did not receive [Scott's] full-hearted, enthusiastic support and leadership. For him international law was more than a study or a profession; it was, in fact, a religion.[32]

* * *

Scott was born in 1866 and grew up in Philadelphia. He graduated *summa cum laude* from Harvard College, and went on to study international law in Berlin, Heidelberg and Paris until 1894. He then practiced law in Los Angeles until 1899, organizing the Los Angeles Law School – now the University of Southern California Law Center – in 1896. In 1899 he became the Dean of the University of Illinois College of Law.

A year after Scott took up his post at the University of Illinois, the United States Supreme Court handed down its opinion in *The Paquete Habana* with its now-famous dictum near the end of the opinion, "International law is part of our law, and must be ascertained and administered by the courts of justice of appropriate jurisdiction, as often as questions of right depending on it are duly presented for their determination."[33] Shortly thereafter Scott published the first

---

29 Report of the Eleventh Annual Meeting of the Mohonk Lake Conference, *supra* note 25, at 141.

30 See Ralph D. Nurnberger, "James Brown Scott: Peace Through Justice" 58 (Ph.D. dissertation, Georgetown University, 1975) (hereafter cited as Nurnberger dissertation).

31 Address by Jesse S. Reeves, Vice President of the Society, 32 *ASIL Proc.* 1 (1938).

32 Frederic R. Coudert, "An Appreciation of James Brown Scott," 37 *AJIL* 559 (1943).

33 *The Paquete Habana*, 175 U.S. 677, 700 (1900).

American casebook on international law.[34] *The Paquete Habana* appeared in the Introduction. Scott had edited out almost all of the Supreme Court's long opinion. He began his edited version with the dictum quoted above. His Preface left no doubt about how he interpreted the dictum or about his stance on the role of international law in the domestic law of the United States:

> The idea underlying this volume is that international law is part of the English common law; that as such it passed with the English colonists to America; that when, in consequence of a successful rebellion, they were admitted to the family of nations, the new republic recognized international law as completely as international law recognized the new republic. Municipal law it was in England; municipal law it remained and is in the United States. No opinion is expressed on the vexed question whether it is law in the abstract; our courts, State and Federal, take judicial cognizance of its existence, and in appropriate cases enforce it, so that for the American student or practitioner it is domestic or municipal law.[35]

In recent years, some scholars have taken a less generous view about the role of international law – at least as to customary international law – in U.S. domestic law.[36]

Scott left Illinois in 1903 to accept a professorship at Columbia. From there, he was appointed Solicitor of the State Department in 1906 by Secretary of State Elihu Root, having written what Root described as a nonchalant letter of application that so intrigued Root that he read it aloud at a Cabinet meeting. President Theodore Roosevelt was intrigued as well; he encouraged Root to pursue Scott. Next came a personal interview with Root that began with Scott tripping over his briefcase into Root's arms.[37] Miraculously, it seems, Scott got the job.

Following his stint as Solicitor of the State Department, Scott settled in as Secretary and Director of the Division of International Law at the Carnegie

---

34 James Brown Scott, *Cases on International Law*, published by the Boston Book Company in 1902 and reissued by West Publishing Company in 1906.

35 Id. at v. The same text appeared in Scott's preface to the 1922 edition. James Brown Scott, *Cases on International Law* xi (1922). For more on Scott's position, see Mark W. Janis, "International Law as Fundamental Justice: James Brown Scott, Harold Hongju Koh, and the American Universalist Tradition of International Law," 46 *St. Louis U. L.J.* 345, 348-52 (2002).

36 In particular, Curtis Bradley and Jack Goldsmith have written a series of articles challenging the judiciary's use of customary international law as law in the United States when it has not been adopted and enacted by Congress. See, e.g., Curtis A. Bradley & Jack L. Goldsmith, III, "The Current Illegitimacy of International Human Rights Litigation," 66 *Fordham L. Rev.* 319 (1997).

37 See Scott's Appreciation of Elihu Root, 31 *ASIL Proc.* 1, 6-7 (1937). Some of the information in this paragraph comes from an interview with Eleanor H. Finch, May 16, 1994.

Endowment for International Peace in 1911. At various times after he moved to Washington he held lectureships or professorships at George Washington, Johns Hopkins and Georgetown Universities. He was, of course, a prolific scholar throughout his career. He died in 1943.[38]

In 1905, it remained for Scott and his colleagues to make the Society a reality. When they felt that their proposed constitution and plan for a journal of international law were ready to be vetted by the organizing committee of 21, they invited the full committee, along with some other interested persons, to a dinner meeting on December 9, 1905, at the home of Oscar S. Straus, the committee chair and later the U.S. Secretary of Commerce and Labor. Ten committee members and ten others attended the meeting. The non-members in attendance included, not coincidentally, Andrew Carnegie, the industrialist/philanthropist with a known interest in international arbitration as a means of avoiding war. Carnegie, who was a close friend of Elihu Root, went on to establish the Carnegie Endowment in 1910.

Straus proposed the new constitution, explaining that specialists and other interested persons would form the nucleus of the new Society's membership. The Society's *raison d'être*, in his view, was "to popularize and develop international law."[39] This work, he later said, "is to secure the peace of justice."[40] (Similarly, James Brown Scott later described the Society as "a little band of workers whose only purpose is to popularize, in so far as we can, the principles of international law, and by concrete example to show how they apply to the settlement of questions between nations.")[41]

An annual meeting would draw the members together. It would feature papers and discussion – a format that proved to have considerable staying power. Straus noted, however, that the annual meetings would reach only a limited number of interested people. If that were to be the Society's sole activity, it might fail of its purpose. Thus he proposed that the Society publish a Journal devoted solely to international law. He saw a real need, since at that time there was no such journal in the English language.[42] The establishment of such a journal would,

---

38 This synopsis of Scott's career is based on George A. Finch, "James Brown Scott, 1866-1943," in 38 *AJIL* 183, 184-85 (1944) (hereafter cited as Finch, Biog. sketch of Scott). See also Christopher R. Rossi, *Broken Chain of Being: James Brown Scott and the Origins of Modern International Law* 5-7 (1998).

39 The quote is from James Brown Scott's paraphrase of Mr. Straus' remarks, 1 *ASIL Proc.* 28 (1907).

40 Letter from Oscar S. Straus to James Brown Scott, Apr. 27, 1916, reprinted in 10 *ASIL Proc.* 137 (1916).

41 Letter from Scott to Richard Olney, Apr. 24, 1913.

42 The first issue of the Journal listed ten "principal periodicals devoted wholly or in part to questions of international law." Only one, the American Political Science Review, was

he concluded, reflect credit upon the Society, as well as furnish the most efficient means of developing international law.[43]

Elihu Root later expanded on the reasons for establishing the new Journal. In its first issue, he noted that uninformed public sentiment sometimes pushed governments into wars that could have been avoided had the positions of the disputing states been more widely understood. Unnecessary wars had to be avoided. "One means to bring about this desirable condition," he said, "is to increase the general public knowledge of international rights and duties and to promote a popular habit of reading and thinking about international affairs." He conceded that "the whole body of any people" could not be expected to study international law, but enough of them could "become sufficiently familiar with it to lead and form public opinion in every community in our country upon all important international questions as they arise." Consequently he viewed the new Journal primarily as affording a practical benefit to the people of the United States.[44]

The December 1905 meeting endorsed the proposed constitution, with minor amendments. James Brown Scott then presented his plan for the contents of the new Journal. It was the fruition of an idea he had formed a few years earlier, when he was at the University of Illinois.[45] He proposed that the new Journal contain:

- Addresses and papers read at the Society's annual meetings;
- Articles "of an historical or critical nature dealing with the various phases of international law";
- Articles dealing with important international law of the day;

---

published in English, and its coverage of international law was limited to a section in each issue. 1 *AJIL* 135-36 (1907).

43 Again, the paraphrase is by James Brown Scott. 1 *ASIL Proc.* 29 (1907). At the 1905 Lake Mohonk Conference, the initial group of interested members had conceived of such a journal as a vehicle "to disseminate not only the proper ideas regarding peace and arbitration, but to disseminate instruction regarding the great principles of international law and those questions that lead to differences between nations." The group also believed that the Journal "would be most useful in stimulating the scholars who are devoting themselves to that subject." Report of the Eleventh Annual Meeting of the Mohonk Lake Conference, *supra* note 25, at 141.

44 Elihu Root, "The Need of Popular Understanding of International Law," 1 *AJIL* 1, 2-3 (1907). The New York Tribune reported that "the journal does not confine itself to academic essays on abstract topics of international law, but pays most attention to the issues which are at the present time of special interest." *N.Y. Tribune*, Feb. 9, 1907. A thorough synopsis of the articles in the first issue appeared in the *New York Sun*, Feb. 10, 1907.

45 See Finch, Biog. sketch of Scott, *supra* note 38, at 188; 25 *ASIL Proc.* 242-43 (1931).

- A chronicle of important international events, such as treaties and arbitral awards; governmental acts affecting the development of international law; and decisions of domestic and foreign courts affecting international law;
- A review of the literature of international law;
- A comprehensive bibliography of publications relating to international law;
- Book reviews of the more important international law publications;
- Editorial comments on international matters.

Scott contemplated that contributors to the new Journal would include not only academics, but also practitioners, diplomats and students of diplomatic history. Articles should be solicited, he said, from "the great foreign authorities and publicists" and translated into English if submitted in a foreign language.[46] The Journal should be issued quarterly. It would be under the editorial control of an Editor-in-Chief, assisted by a Board of Editors. Ultimate control would be in the Society's Executive Council.

At a meeting on January 12, 1906, in the offices of the Bar Association of the City of New York, the Constitution of the American Society of International Law was formally adopted. The Society was an unincorporated association. According to Article II, "The object of this Society is to foster the study of International Law and promote the establishment of international relations on the basis of law and justice. For this purpose it will cooperate with other societies in this and other countries having the same object."[47]

There was debate about the conditions, if any, that would be placed on eligibility for membership. Some favored limiting eligibility to members of the legal profession and former diplomats. Others wished to include corporate members.[48] Ultimately it was decided to exclude commercial entities. Unlike the Institute of International Law, which had been organized in 1873, the new Society would not limit membership to international law experts: "The value of men of affairs, and the broad experience they bring to the discussion of a question of theory, cannot be or should not be overlooked or rejected."[49]

In the event, of course, membership was extended beyond "men of affairs." Not only were other men included, but women eventually became eligible.

---

[46] 1 *ASIL Proc.* 30 (1907).

[47] 1 *ASIL Proc.* 5 (1907).

[48] The debate over admitting corporate members made the news. See *N.Y. Times*, Jan. 13, 1906.

[49] Editorial Comment, 1 *AJIL* 129, 134 (1907).

In fact, one woman, Mary Elizabeth Urch, Dean of Women at Lewiston State Normal School in Idaho, was included in the list of members at the time of the first Annual Meeting in April 1907.[50] Her name remained on the list in 1908, but then disappeared.

Dean Urch must have slipped onto the membership roll unnoticed. At the first meeting of the Executive Council on January 29, 1906, the question arose whether women would be eligible for membership. According to the minutes of the meeting, "After discussion ... it was moved and carried that 'any man of good moral character, interested in the objects of the Society, may be admitted to membership in the Society.'"[51] Women more prominent than Dean Urch – women such as Beva Ann Lockwood of the National Equal Rights Party and Jane Addams of Hull House – were denied membership.[52]

The Executive Council's decision in 1906 was a curious one, even for its time. Women were active in the Lake Mohonk Conferences and were striving to make their influence felt in the American peace movement.[53] The women at the Conferences were not lawyers, but a good many of the men were not lawyers either. At the 1905 Lake Mohonk Conference, Judge Stiness, reporting for the original group of members interested in forming an international law society, had said that "the secretary of this committee will welcome the names of any of the gentlemen here, and ladies also, who wish to unite with us and become members of this American International Law Society."[54]

As it happened, women did not become formally eligible for membership in the Society until 1920.[55] In fact, as late as 1917, women were not even allowed to attend the annual banquet as guests, although they could attend meetings of the Society.[56] The Journal did publish a book review by a woman in 1919, but it concealed her gender by identifying her as H.K. Thompson.[57]

---

50 See Alona E. Evans & Carol Per Lee Plumb, "Notes and Comments: Women and the American Society of International Law," 68 *AJIL* 290 (1974).

51 Précis of the First Meeting of Executive Council of the American Society of International Law, Jan. 29, 1906, at 3.

52 Evans & Plumb, *supra* note 50, at 290-91.

53 Précis, *supra* note 51, at 10.

54 Report of the Eleventh Annual Meeting of the Mohonk Lake Conference, *supra* note 25, at 141-42.

55 See Chapter Two, *infra*. The Society's files contain an application for membership from Isabelle Bridge, of New York City, in 1916, and a reply from James Brown Scott turning her down.

56 Letter from James Brown Scott to Ellery C. Stowell, Apr. 13, 1917, in which Scott expressed his regret that the custom of excluding women from the banquet still existed.

57 Evans & Plumb, *supra* note 50, at 295, identifying her as Hope K. Thompson. She reviewed Lassa Oppenheim, League of Nations (1919), in 13 *AJIL* 627 (1919).

Individuals were to be elected to membership by the Executive Council on the nomination of two members in regular standing. There were about 125 initial members, "most of them prominent men."[58] The founding membership represented predominately two groups: lawyers with diplomatic experience and legal academics.[59]

The full Executive Council soon found that it could not expeditiously consider each application for membership, so it created a committee on membership to do so. The committee was kept busy – by April 1907, the Society had 525 members.[60] Of these, only approximately eleven per cent appear to have been academics at the higher education level.[61] By way of contrast, in 1993, academics represented slightly more than 20 per cent of the membership[62] – a percentage that held roughly steady for many years.[63]

From the outset, the Society's Constitution has provided for the election of not more than one honorary member in any year. Eligible persons are those who are not citizens of the United States and who "have rendered distinguished service to the cause which this Society is formed to promote."[64] The first election was held at the first Annual Meeting in 1907; two honorary members were elected, one for 1906 and one for 1907. They were Thomas Erskine Holland, professor of international law and diplomacy at Oxford, and Henri Lammasch, professor of international law at the University of Vienna.[65] Other distinguished honorary members have followed in their footsteps, though not in every year. In some years the Society's Committee on Selection of Honorary Members has not agreed on anyone of significant stature to deserve nomination.

* * *

---

58 N.Y. Tribune, Jan. 13, 1906.

59 See Nurnberger dissertation, *supra* note 30, at 60-62. This of course reflected the membership of the initial organizing group. See text at note 29 *supra*.

60 See 1 ASIL Proc. 216 (1907).

61 The 1907 members are listed in 1 ASIL Proc. 11-22 (1907). Of the 525 listed members, 56 are identified as "Professor" or "Doctor." It is probable that a few others of that ilk did not identify themselves as such.

62 There were about 4,300 members in 1993. Approximately 880 of them were identified with institutions of higher learning. 1993 *ASIL Membership Directory* xi, 561-76.

63 In November 1933, George Finch, then the Secretary of the Society, wrote a letter to the Editor of the American Bar Association Journal rebutting an offhand assertion in the A.B.A. Journal that about 80 per cent of the Society's members were law professors. Finch pointed out that of the Society's 1100 members at that time, 235 (about 21 per cent) were connected with colleges and universities. See 20 *ABA J.* 59 (1934).

64 ASIL Constitution Art. III.

65 See 1 *ASIL Proc.* 261-62 (1907).

At first, the Society operated out of James Brown Scott's home in Washington. When Scott became the chief administrative officer of the newly established Carnegie Endowment for International Peace in 1911, the Endowment provided the Society with office space in its headquarters on Jackson Place, near the White House. From Jackson Place, Scott administered the day-to-day operations of the Society. He had help from George A. Finch, who became the Assistant Secretary of the Endowment in 1912. The Society stayed on Jackson Place until the Carnegie Endowment moved to New York City in 1950.[66]

The Society's membership at the Annual Meetings has always elected the President and Vice Presidents. A Nominating Committee, appointed annually by the Executive Council in the early years (more recently, elected at the Society's Business Meeting), proposes each slate of officers.

The first President of the Society was Elihu Root, then the Secretary of State and destined to be a Nobel Peace Prize laureate in 1912. Root was a person who inspired great admiration and loyalty from those who worked for him.[67] These admirers included Scott, who was the Solicitor of the Department of State under Root. Scott's service to Root has been described as "efficient and almost worshipping."[68] Root himself was a loyal person. When President Wilson ordered American troops to occupy Vera Cruz, Mexico in April 1914, Root (no longer the Secretary of State) had serious reservations about the justification for doing so; nevertheless, at the Society's annual banquet just four days after the troops had gone in, Root – with tears running down his cheeks – pledged his loyalty to the President.[69] He asked the assembled Society members to drink a toast to the President. They stood while the orchestra played the Star Spangled Banner.[70]

Root was also a person who, in accordance with the principles of the Society he headed, put justice before power – at least insofar as his responsibilities in the government and the realities he faced allowed him to do so.[71] For example, while Root was reviewing one of Scott's legal memoranda at the State Department, he is quoted as saying to Scott, "We must always be careful, and especially so in our relations with the smaller states, that we never propose a settlement which we

---

66 See Finch, "The ASIL 1906-1956," *supra* note 16, at 297-98; Finch remarks, 44 *ASIL Proc.* 65-66 (1950).

67 See 2 Philip C. Jessup, *Elihu Root* 505 (1938) (hereafter cited as Jessup, *Elihu Root*); Richard W. Leopold, *Elihu Root and the Conservative Tradition* 189 (1954).

68 1 Jessup, *Elihu Root*, *supra* note 67, at 456.

69 2 id. at 257-60.

70 See 8 ASIL Proc. 327 (1914).

71 See Zasloff, *supra* note 7, asserting that Root's classical legal ideology led him to err on the side of law and legal institutions, rather than the use of power, even when the realities of world politics should have led him to err on the other side.

would not be willing to accept if the situation were reversed."[72] Even when Root, as Secretary of War in 1903, defended Theodore Roosevelt's role in detaching Panama from Colombia – an event of which Root had no prior knowledge because he was in Europe tending to other matters – he did so in the belief that Panama had what in a later era would be called a right of self-determination.[73]

Root gave stature to the Society in its early days. One historian of the peace movement has said, "With Root as president, the American Society of International Law represented the emerging 'establishment status' of the peace movement in its purest form."[74] Root and Scott were both conservatives, though they came to be so in rather different ways. Root was the quintessential political conservative of his day, reflecting not only his faith in law as a necessary and sufficient force for order and justice, but also his social position and his views about the need to educate and lead the public. Scott's conservatism did not reflect so much social position as it did his firm belief in law and an ordered international system.[75]

Initially there were 12 Vice Presidents of the Society, including Chief Justice of the United States Melville W. Fuller, Associate Justices David J. Brewer and William R. Day, former Secretaries of State John W. Foster and Richard Olney, Secretary of War William H. Taft, and Andrew Carnegie. James Brown Scott was the first Recording Secretary. Charles Henry Butler, Reporter of the United States Supreme Court, was the Corresponding Secretary, and Chandler P. Anderson, special counselor to the State Department, was the Treasurer. The first Executive Council included former diplomats, other public servants, and distinguished academics.

In sharp contrast to the practice of the Society in recent years, turnover at the top was slow. Elihu Root remained President for 18 consecutive years, until 1924. James Brown Scott remained Recording Secretary for the same period. In 1924, Scott became a Vice President, and served as President from 1929 to 1939. He then was elected Honorary President and remained such until his death in 1943. George Grafton Wilson attended the Lake Mohonk Conference in 1905 and participated in the initial discussions that led to the Society's formation. He became a member of the first Executive Council and remained a member (eventually as a Vice President and then as an Honorary Vice President) until he died in 1951, the last survivor of those who were present at the Society's creation. Other founding members who held offices continuously throughout their lifetimes were Charles Noble Gregory, Robert Lansing, Oscar Straus and Theodore S. Woolsey.

---

72 James Brown Scott, "Elihu Root: An Appreciation," 31 *ASIL Proc.* 1, 8 (1937).

73 See 1 Jessup, *Elihu Root*, *supra* note 67, at 401-05, 518.

74 Marchand, *supra* note 6, at 52. Root, however, did not identify himself with the peace movement. See Zasloff, *supra* note 7, at 306.

75 See Hatsue Shinohara, "The Rise of a New International Law in America," 5 *Japanese J. Am. Studies* 85, 89-90 (1993-94).

Two other founders, Charles Henry Butler and John Bassett Moore, had long but not continuous tenures as officers. Much of Moore's tenure was as an Honorary Vice President, a post that made minimal demands on his time.

The first meeting of the Executive Council on January 29, 1906, approved the proposal to establish a Journal, and referred the matter to the Executive Committee. The Executive Council also decided to publish a prospectus setting out the aims and scope of the Society. The prospectus asserted "that Government and people are fundamentally and constitutionally interested in international law, and that a correct understanding of the system as a whole is an essential element of good citizenship." The Society thus "would count for much in the formation of a sound and rational body of doctrine concerning the true principles of international relations. It is equally certain that the publication of a journal devoted to the exposition of those principles would offer a ready and valuable means of communication between jurists and students of international law on the one hand, and the scientific and lay public on the other."[76]

At the next Executive Council meeting, on June 1, 1906, James Brown Scott was appointed Managing Editor (Editor-in-Chief) of the new American Journal of International Law. Scott was initially given authority to name the Editorial Board, though the Executive Council retained the ultimate responsibility and soon began electing the Board.[77] Members of the first Board of Editors, in addition to Scott, were Charles Noble Gregory of the University of Iowa, Robert Lansing of Watertown, New York, John Bassett Moore of Columbia University, William W. Morrow of San Francisco, Leo S. Rowe of the University of Pennsylvania, Oscar S. Straus of the District of Columbia, George Grafton Wilson of Brown University, Theodore S. Woolsey of Yale University and David J. Hill of The Hague, serving as the European Editor. Editors were to serve three-year terms, with the first Board serving until January 1, 1910.[78]

The formation of the Society was thus complete. It was conceived not primarily as a scholarly society, but as an instrument for peace in the world. Those who conceived it were brought together by their faith in arbitration as a means of avoiding war and serving American interests, but they broadened their focus to encompass the spectrum of international relations and to promote justice as well as peace.

The founders regarded the Journal as an integral organ of the Society from the outset. It was designed not just for discourse among scholars and diplomats, but also as a vehicle to bring international law into the public consciousness.

---

[76] "Prospectus: The Aim and Scope of the American Society of International Law," 1 *ASIL Proc.* 35, 36 (1907), reprinted in Appendix B, *infra*.

[77] The results of the Executive Council's election of Editorial Board members first appear in the Society's Annual Proceedings for 1910. See 4 *ASIL Proc.* 196 (1910).

[78] Letter from J.B. Scott to Oscar S. Straus, Dec. 12, 1908, p. 4.

Implicit in this was a conception of international law not as a process, but as a set of norms ascertainable through the use of "scientific" methods. Legal scholars, including those in the international law field, were thought to be scientists searching with the help of neutral principles to find and declaim the law. They were driven by the belief that international law could control, or at least significantly influence, the conduct of national governments if its rules were clearly identified using the tools of science, and if an appropriate, law-based dispute-settlement mechanism were available.

3. The Original Goals in Retrospect

With the benefit of hindsight, these premises seem naïve. Arbitration has hardly proved to be a substitute for war. In fact, it is surprising that the men of the world who founded the Society thought that it could be. As Professor Woolsey pointed out at the first Annual Meeting, the typical arbitration treaty of the day exempted from the duty to arbitrate those matters important enough to lead to war.[79] And as Sir Robert Jennings, the eminent British international law scholar and judge, pointed out 90 years later, "This notion [that resort to adjudication and resort to war are more or less alternative forms of dispute resolution] rested upon an egregiously mistaken assumption that wars and other resorts to force are about what international lawyers would recognize as legal 'disputes' which would answer to the adversarial procedures of a court of justice."[80]

Nor has it proved possible to put together a journal that is scholarly, in the sense that it reflects and conveys original ideas about norms and processes, and is at the same time a purveyor of international law directly to the public.[81] Although the Journal has from its inception been devoted in part to conveying information about international events and instruments, its stature has come instead from the depth of analysis in articles and comments that are not aimed at popular audiences. This should have been apparent early on, when both the Society and the Journal were closely identified with the American peace move-

79 1 *ASIL Proc.* 240, 241 (1907).

80 Robert Y. Jennings, "The Role of the International Court of Justice," 68 *Brit. Y.B. Int'l L.* 1, 53 (1997).

81 Interestingly, James Brown Scott carried over the goal of informing the public about international law into the Carnegie Endowment, where he was Director of the Division of International Law. One of his aims in persuading the Carnegie Institution – later the Endowment – to publish the *Classics of International Law* was to spread "the knowledge of a law of nations and [put] at the disposal of the general reader as well as the expert the process of its literary growth and development." 9 *Y.B. Carnegie Endowment for International Peace* 106 (1920). The importance of making the *Classics of International Law* accessible to experts is undeniable; that the general reader has taken advantage of the opportunity to read Gentili, Grotius, Pufendorf et al. is doubtful, to say the least.

ment. In the words of one commentator, the pre-World War I peace movement became elitist and thus

> never developed meaningful contacts with movements for social and political change. Its rhetoric reflected this elitism. While it was always lofty in tone, it became less warmly humanistic and more coldly intellectual. Its idealistic message could arouse the interest of high-minded individuals in the peace movement, but because it expressed no urgent social message it could not sustain the active involvement of a reform-minded generation in the cause.[82]

Nevertheless, the Society laid the groundwork at the outset for intensive work on conflict avoidance and conflict resolution, as well as on a myriad of other international law and world order issues. Moreover, the Society – if not the Journal as such – has at various times, particularly in the 1990s and into the 21st century, engaged in programs to try to enhance public awareness of international law as a force for justice and order in the world. From the beginning, individual Society members have tried to do the same thing.[83] The founders may not have had a clear vision of what the new Society could or would do, but they certainly cannot be said to have wandered off aimlessly.

B. GAINING MOMENTUM

1. The Early Annual Meetings

The Society's first Annual Meeting was held on Friday and Saturday, April 19 and 20, 1907, at the New Willard Hotel in Washington. It focused on five topics, each of them having considerable importance at that time for the United States:

- Would immunity from capture during war of non-offending private property upon the high seas be in the interest of civilization?
- Is trade in contraband of war unneutral, and should it be prohibited by international and municipal law?
- Is forcible collection of contract debts in the interest of international justice and peace?

---

82 Patterson, *supra* note 1, at 33.

83 For example, Charles Cheney Hyde gave "a popular course on International Law, as interpreted by the United States," consisting of 20 lectures at Northwestern University in the spring of 1916. The Society's files contain the printed announcement of the lecture series, but they do not show what the public turnout was.

- The rights of foreigners in the United States in case of conflict between federal treaties and state laws.
- The Second Hague Conference and the development of international law as a science.

The program for the meeting noted matter-of-factly that at an arranged time, "The President of the United States will receive the members of the Society at the White House."[84] This set the stage for similar announcements – and similar receptions – at other annual meetings in the early years. The men then in control of the Society had direct access to the White House.

Elihu Root, the President of the Society, began the first Annual Meeting with an analysis of Japan's claim that the decision by the San Francisco Board of Education in 1906 to send "all Chinese, Japanese, or Korean children to the Oriental Public School,"[85] rather than to the normal public schools, violated the 1894 Treaty of Commerce and Navigation between the United States and Japan.[86] Root gave a detailed analysis, focusing particularly on the treaty-making power in the United States and on the supremacy of a treaty over any contrary law of California or any municipality. Although he took a strong position in favor of the federal power to enter into treaties touching on the rights of aliens in the United States, he did plant a seed that gave rise for many years to controversy over the extent of the treaty-making power – a seed that Charles Evans Hughes was to nurture into full flower at a later Annual Meeting.[87] It concerned the possibility that some matters are not sufficiently "international" to be the subjects of treaties. Root said:

> It is, of course, conceivable, that, under pretense of exercising the treaty-making power, the President and Senate might attempt to make provisions regarding matters which are not proper subjects of international agreement, and which would be only a colorable – not a real – exercise of the treaty-making power ... Although there are no express limitations upon the treaty-making power granted to the National Government, there are certain implied limitations arising from the nature of our Government and from the other provisions of the Constitution; but those implied limitations do not in the slightest degree touch the making of treaty provisions relating to the treatment of aliens within our territory.[88]

---

84 1 *ASIL Proc.* 39 (1907).

85 Quoted in 1 *ASIL Proc.* 46 (1907).

86 Treaty of Commerce and Navigation, Nov. 22, 1894, Art. 1, 9 Bevans, *Treaties and Other Int'l Agreements of the United States of America 1776-1949*, at 387.

87 23 *ASIL Proc.* 194-96 (1929).

88 Address by Elihu Root, President of the Society, 1 *ASIL Proc.* 43, 49-50 (1907), reprinted

In later years the controversy shifted away from the federal treaty-based authority to control the treatment of aliens by local officials, and raged instead over the federal authority to enter into treaties controlling state or local restrictions on the asserted rights of citizens. In either form, it was and is an issue of particular importance for a federation such as the United States.

One could even see the origin of the mid-century Bricker Amendment debate in Root's comments at the first Annual Meeting. The Bricker Amendment would have amended the Constitution to provide that a treaty would be effective in U.S. domestic law only through legislation that would be valid in the absence of a treaty. George Finch, like James Brown Scott a disciple of Root and Scott's successor as the Society's Recording Secretary, was a leading proponent of the Bricker Amendment as protection against what he regarded as abuse of the treaty-making power to regulate matters of domestic concern.[89] For the proposition that some matters are not of international concern and therefore are not legitimate treaty subjects, Finch relied in part on the views of Chandler P. Anderson, the Society's first Treasurer and special counsel for Root when he was Secretary of State.[90] Finch began his international law career in the State Department in 1906, and served there under Anderson. It is quite possible that Anderson or Finch, or both, assisted Root in the preparation of the remarks quoted above, and one of them may even have written them.

That the scope of the federal treaty authority was the subject of the opening address at the Society's first Annual Meeting not only shows the longevity of the issue, but also demonstrates from the outset the "Americanness" of the Society. It was as understandable in 1907 as it is a century later that the Society would have a particular interest in what came to be called the foreign relations law of the United States, and in international law issues of particular interest to the United States.

In fact, one could view the Society at that time as being rather parochial. James Brown Scott, the guiding force of the Society, was a quintessentially American international lawyer. His unofficial biographer noted that Scott "tended to project America's traditions, democratic heritage and institutions upon other nations

---

in 1 *AJIL* 273, 279 (1907). The dispute was also the subject of Editorial Comments by James Brown Scott in id. at 150 and at 449.

89 See George A. Finch, "The Need to Restrain the Treaty-making Power of the United States Within Constitutional Limits," 48 *AJIL* 57 (1954); George A. Finch, "Observations on Proposed Amendments to the United States Constitution," 48 *ASIL Proc.* 128 (1954); George A. Finch, "The Treaty-Clause Amendment: The Case for the Association," 38 *ABA J.* 467 (1952).

90 See Finch, "Observations on Proposed Amendments," *supra* note 89, at 131; Finch, "The Treaty-Clause Amendment," *supra* note 89, at 468. For Anderson's views, see Chandler P. Anderson, "The Extent and Limitations of the Treaty-making Power under the Constitution," 1 *AJIL* 636, 639, 665 (1907).

regardless of their cultural backgrounds."[91] Other leading lights in the Society looked to Anglo-Saxon experience and values as prerequisites for a stable world order.[92] The United States Supreme Court was held up as the ideal model for a World Court.[93]

Some other themes that were to recur surfaced at the first Annual Meeting. When William J. Coombs, of Brooklyn, expressed his disappointment with the meeting's failure to work toward a common position on the codification of international law,[94] he gave voice to the tension between the intellectual discussion of current issues and the impulse to reach practical conclusions that might promote world order. It is a tension that has not gone away.

Related to that – and also in evidence at the first Annual Meeting – has been the question of whether the Society should adopt positions on controversial international law issues. As has been noted above, one of the topics discussed at the first Annual Meeting had to do with the forcible collection of debts. William Barnes, of Nantucket, proposed that the Society adopt a resolution disapproving the use of naval power to collect debts and approving the non-interventionist Calvo and Drago doctrines.[95] The draft resolution was referred to the Executive Committee,[96] from which it never emerged. Similar tactics were to be used in subsequent years.[97]

Even though the Society did not take a position on the Calvo and Drago doctrines, or on any other substantive issue, the press regarded the first Annual Meeting as newsworthy. At the last session, on April 20, 1907, former Secretary of State Richard Olney criticized the United States government for practically expropriating Colombian territory to build the Panama Canal without paying compensation to Colombia.[98] The press reported the gist of what he said, noting

91 Nurnberger dissertation, *supra* note 30, at 101.

92 See Marchand, *supra* note 6, 16, at 46.

93 Id. at 59-60. See the remarks of Wayne Mac Veagh, 3 *ASIL Proc.* 48, 51 (1909); remarks of A.J. Montague, id. at 227-35; remarks of N.W. Harris, id. at 236.

94 1 *ASIL Proc.* 96-97 (1907).

95 Id. at 141. For a contemporaneous discussion of the doctrines, see Amos S. Hershey, "The Calvo and Drago Doctrines," 1 *AJIL* 26 (1907).

96 1 *ASIL Proc.* 142-43 (1907).

97 See, e.g., 2 *ASIL Proc.* 129-30 (1908); 3 id. 235-36 (1909); 10 id. 169 (1916) (matters referred to the Executive Council rather than to the Executive Committee, but the effect was the same).

98 Address of Richard Olney, 1 *ASIL Proc.* 218, 227 (1907).

that he "created something of a sensation among his auditors."[99] The Washington press continued to cover the Society's Annual Meetings into the 1940s.

* * *

In those early twentieth-century days of optimism that law and legal process could be made to supplant war, the media in the United States paid more attention to the development of international law than it has in recent years. Not only did the press cover the Society's annual meetings, but it gave considerable play to law-making conferences, sometimes using experts as correspondents. A member of the Society, Professor Amos S. Hershey of Indiana University, served as a correspondent for the *New York Evening Post* and the *Boston Evening Transcript* at the Second Hague Peace Conference in 1907.[100]

The discussion of substantive issues at the Society's 1907 Annual Meeting had a look that remains familiar, though the issues have changed in the intervening years. Papers on opposite sides of issues were prepared and read. Some were a bit more lengthy than the program planners apparently contemplated. There was discussion of the papers, but it was not as wide-ranging as discussion from the floor often has been in more recent years.

Problems lurking in the nature of international law were commented upon then, as they are today. For example, John Bassett Moore's paper lamented that "the two chief defects in international law at the present day are, first, the lack of a ready mode of demonstrating that a certain rule, the validity of which may be asserted by one power and denied by another, is in reality a principle of international law; and, secondly, the lack of a fixed and definite method of assuring the observance of the system."[101] It is a refrain still heard.

One verse of the refrain led off the second Annual Meeting. Elihu Root opened the meeting with a presidential address, in accordance with what he said had already become the custom imposed on Presidents of the Society (thus establishing, presumably, that even in those days custom did not take years to develop). Root's theme was enforcement of international law through governments' sensitivities to international opinion, in the absence of effective third-party sanctions. He argued that similar sensitivities are the principal force behind compliance with municipal law, so the international and municipal systems were not nearly as different as was believed in some quarters.[102]

---

99 *Wash. Herald*, Apr. 21, 1907. The *N.Y. Herald*, Apr. 21, 1907, reported that Olney "caused a stir." His remarks were also reported by the *N.Y. Times* and *N.Y. Sun* of Apr. 21, 1907. These clippings are on file with the Society.

100 See 2 *AJIL* 29, n. 1 (1908).

101 Address of John Bassett Moore, 1 *ASIL Proc.* 252, 258-59 (1907).

102 Elihu Root, "The Sanction of International Law," 2 *ASIL Proc.* 14 (1908).

The second address was by Robert Lansing, the future Secretary of State, who elaborated on Root's topic of the previous year – state responsibility toward aliens. Among other things, he noted with approval a portion of an 1885 report made by Francis Wharton in which Wharton argued that a government was responsible not only for its own treatment of aliens, but also for any injury to them if the exercise of reasonable care could have averted it.[103] Like Root, Lansing had put his finger on a matter that would continue to capture the attention of decision-makers. A little more than a hundred years after Wharton's assertion, the Inter-American Court of Human Rights in the landmark *Velásquez Rodriguez* case found a similar duty (and extended it to a state's treatment of its own citizens) in Article 1(1) of the American Convention on Human Rights.[104] That Article calls on all states parties to "ensure" to all persons subject to their jurisdiction the full exercise of the Convention's rights and freedoms.[105] What had been asserted to be customary law benefiting aliens in the late nineteenth and early twentieth centuries became treaty law benefiting citizens as well as aliens, in the Americas and elsewhere,[106] in the late twentieth and early twenty-first centuries.

Yet another issue was discussed at the 1908 Annual Meeting that has resonance a century later. One of the topics was the establishment of an international prize court. James Brown Scott noted that if the United States were to participate in such a court, a large part of its municipal law would be "transferred from its national courts ... to an international court established at The Hague. It may seem to a certain extent a renunciation of sovereignty."[107] (Scott favored such a renunciation.) Had he lived so long, he might have witnessed U.S. non-ratification of the first Optional Protocol to the Covenant on Civil and Political Rights, which creates a procedure for individual petitions to the U.N. Human Rights Committee, or the U.S. decision not to participate in the International Criminal Court.

---

103 Address by Robert Lansing, in id. at 44, 47.

104 *Velásquez Rodriguez* case, Inter-Am. Ct. H.R. Judgment of July 29, 1988, Ser. C, No. 4, 1988 Ann. Rep. of the Court 35, paras. 161-75.

105 American Convention on Human Rights, Nov. 22, 1969, Art. 1(1), 1144 U.N.T.S. 123, OAS Treaty Ser. No. 36.

106 The International Covenant on Civil and Political Rights, Dec. 19, 1966, Art. 2(1), 999 U.N.T.S. 171, and the [European] Convention for the Protection of Human Rights and Fundamental Freedoms, Nov. 4, 1950, 213 U.N.T.S. 221, as amended most significantly by Protocol No. 11, E.T.S. No. 155 (1998), contain language quite similar to the language in American Convention Art. 1(1). The UN Human Rights Committee has found that governments have an affirmative duty to act when it is known that a citizen's life has been threatened. See *Delgado Páez v. Colombia*, 45 UN GAOR Supp. No. 40, Vol. II (A/45/40), at 43 (1990). Regarding the European System, see Jean-Paul Costa, "The European Court of Human Rights and Its Recent Case Law," 38 *Tex. Int'l L.J.* 455, 460 (2003).

107 2 *ASIL Proc.* 152, 155 (1908).

2. The Early Leaders

During the early years the Society remained under the effective control of well-connected men who were either intimately involved with public affairs or attached to the elite academic institutions of the land. The Society's President, Elihu Root, was the Secretary of State from 1905 to 1909 and had earlier served as Secretary of War. Other officers were, or would become, high public officials. That this would be so seems to have been taken for granted. Thus when one of the Society's Vice Presidents was elevated to the highest office in the land, the minutes of the next Executive Committee meeting reported drily: "Mr. Anderson [the Society's Treasurer] called attention to the probable vacancy in the office of vice president caused by the election of Mr. Taft to the Presidency of the United States."[108] Business in the Society then went on as usual.

James Brown Scott was not politically prominent. Nevertheless he was well-connected in high government circles, largely through his close association with Root. Among other things, he frequently attended intergovernmental conferences, typically as a legal adviser.

The early leaders had much in common, whether they were primarily practitioners, government officials or scholars. They were public spirited, and many of them – as in the case of Root and Scott – were identified with conservative principles. (Interestingly, these principles in the pre-World War I era encompassed support for a World Court, not just support for a permanent arbitral tribunal.) The Society's initial leaders had social stature, although not all of them were born into wealth. Many, but again not all, were the products of the most prestigious American colleges and universities.[109]

As we have seen, Scott was a *summa cum laude* graduate of Harvard College. Root, the source of much of the Society's stature in the early years, was the son of a mathematics professor at Hamilton College in upstate New York. Root stayed at home for college, and then got his law degree from New York University. Once he began his illustrious career, he seems to have been equally comfortable in the Washington establishment as back home in upstate New York.[110] His advice was sought by government officials at the highest levels virtually until his death.

3. The American Journal of International Law Takes Shape

While the Society was developing its substantive agenda, its flagship publication, the *American Journal of International Law*, was getting on its feet. It was, said James Brown Scott, "an organ of progressive and scientific thought" which would endeavor to "bring home to the English reader, layman or specialist, the theory

---

108 Minutes of the Executive Committee meeting, Dec. 12, 1908.

109 See Marchand, *supra* note 6, at 50-51, 55-56.

110 The definitive biography of Root is Jessup, *Elihu Root*, *supra* note 67 (2 volumes).

and practice of international law. The journal is the handmaid of science and its pages will be closed to the language of prejudice and bias."[111]

Scott was the Managing Editor – a title changed in 1909 to Editor-in-Chief. He personally advanced the funds needed to publish the first issue. These amounted to USD 1,700, which the Society later repaid in full.[112] Scott also paid for the second issue (April 1907), and the Society reimbursed him for that as well.[113] At about that time, the Society contracted with Baker, Voorhis and Company, of New York, to publish the Journal for ten years. The Society agreed to pay Baker, Voorhis half of the Society's annual dues; Baker, Voorhis agreed to pay the Society half of the proceeds from the sale of the Journal.[114]

The Society's Executive Committee decided on April 25, 1908, to invite subscriptions to a Special Publication Fund to support the continued publication of the Journal. Twenty-three members pledged amounts ranging from USD 10 (15 pledges) to USD 100 (one pledge).[115] Fund-raising does not appear to have been any easier then than in more recent times.

In the early years, and well into its maturity, the Journal had at least one influential institutional subscriber. Moreover, it was one that could be counted on to buy multiple copies. By Executive Order of the President of the United States, the State Department bought a copy of each Journal issue for each U.S. embassy, legation and consulate abroad, a total of about 450 copies.[116] The fact that the President of the Society was also the Secretary of State may have had something to do with this, but the subscription was renewed annually for many years after Root had left the State Department. The Department continued to purchase the Journal for its Foreign Service until at least 1950, though the number of copies it purchased declined over time.

Scott clearly had his hands full producing the Journal in the early years. He had a full-time job as Solicitor of the Department of State. He said of his situation, "As I am occupied during the day I have had to devote nights, holidays

---

111 James Brown Scott, Editorial Comment, 1 *AJIL* 134-35 (1907).

112 Letter from James Brown Scott to Oscar B. Straus, Dec. 12, 1908 (hereafter cited as Scott letter to Straus). The letter is an important chronicle of the start-up of the Journal. It is in the Society's Executive Council Minutes file for 1906-1937.

113 Finch, "The ASIL 1906-1956," *supra* note 16, at 298.

114 Scott letter to Straus, *supra* note 112. The contract with Baker, Voorhis was not renewed when its term expired. A new contract was then entered into with the American branch of Oxford University Press. Minutes of the Board of Editors meeting of Dec. 2, 1916, at 1-2; 11 *AJIL*, title page (1917). By 1920, four-fifths of the USD 5 annual dues were going toward publishing the Journal. 14 *ASIL Proc.* 6 (1921).

115 The list, with amounts pledged, is in the Society's files. See also 2 *ASIL Proc.* 130 (1908).

116 Scott letter to Straus, *supra* note 112.

and Sundays to the work."[117] He asked the Society for some help. The Executive Committee responded in December 1908, by appointing W. Clayton Carpenter as a full-time Business Manager of the Journal.[118] Carpenter resigned in 1909 and was replaced by George A. Finch, who began a long and prominent association with the Journal – an association that was to include ten years as Editor-in-Chief (1943 to 1953).

The fledgling Journal could not afford the luxury of sitting back and waiting for eminent authors to submit manuscripts for publication. Scott solicited articles from authors in the United States, Europe and Latin America. It did not take long, though, for the Journal to attract authors. By the end of 1908, international law specialists were beginning to send Scott unsolicited offers to write articles.[119]

Scott not only edited the Journal (and essentially ran the Society), he was a significant contributor to the Journal's pages. In the first two volumes, he contributed seven leading articles.[120] He also wrote most of the Editorial Comments in the early volumes.[121]

The Editorial Comments were based on current events. They were not of "an academic nature," because academic comments "would lose their interest to the readers."[122] The Editorial Comments thus were seen as purveyors of information, and in some cases as vehicles for explanation of the legal issues raised by current events, to an audience that was thought to be different from the readers interested in the more scholarly lead articles. They were precursors of the *ASIL Insight* series, which was to take form in 1996 not as a department of the Journal, but as an on-line service explaining to non-experts the international law aspects of current events.

The Journal contained other departments envisaged in Scott's original proposal.[123] The Chronicle of International Events, which ran in the Journal from the first issue until 1950, outlined significant events in chronological order. It mentioned such things as the signing, ratification or denunciation of treaties, various national decrees, regulations and proclamations, the convening of significant international conferences, some national elections, and other events

[117] Id.

[118] Minutes of Executive Committee meeting of Dec. 12, 1908, at 2.

[119] Scott letter to Straus, *supra* note 112.

[120] The first of these, The Legal Nature of International Law, 1 *AJIL* 831 (1907), was based on two articles Scott had previously published. The others, on topics ranging from the peace conferences to naval warfare to the proposed court of arbitral justice, appear to have been original contributions to the Journal.

[121] In the earliest years, Editorial Comments were unsigned. That Scott was the author appears in an appendix to the Scott letter to Straus, *supra* note 112.

[122] Scott letter to Straus, *supra* note 112.

[123] See text at note 45 *supra*.

that caught the compiler's eye. The events were not always directly connected with international law.[124]

The Chronicle usually gave only the most basic data about an event, unlike the fuller treatment given by Charles Rousseau in his "Chronique des faits internationaux," published in the *Revue Générale de Droit International Public*.[125] The compiler for the Journal was originally someone in the library of the State Department, but in 1913 the Carnegie Endowment took it over.[126]

Beginning with volume 1 in 1907 and ending in 1924, the Journal contained lists of public documents relating to international law. The lists included documents issued not only by the United States government, but also by other governments around the world, with prices if they were available.

Another department, now defunct, was called Periodical Literature of International Law. It contained citations to articles relating to international law in publications other than the Journal itself. Some of the articles were in non-law periodicals, and many were in languages other than English. The department was discontinued after 1964, because the *Index to Foreign Legal Periodicals* began publication and was thought to provide more comprehensive coverage than the Journal could.[127]

The Judicial Decisions and Book Reviews/Book Notes departments have appeared continuously from volume 1 to the present. The Judicial Decisions department focused heavily on decisions that would not be readily available in law libraries in the United States, such as decisions of foreign municipal courts and international arbitral decisions. Extensive quotations from the opinions were used, making the department a valuable research tool for those interested in foreign and international cases.

The Book Review department had much the same outlook in 1907 that it has a century later. From the outset, reviews of books in major continental European languages have been included occasionally, as well as reviews of books in English. The reviews, then as now, tended to be short, with exceptions for lengthy or particularly important books. The ubiquitous James Brown Scott wrote four of the five signed book reviews in the first issue of the Journal, and one suspects that he wrote most or all of the unsigned shorter reviews as well.

---

[124] For example, under date of Jan. 1, 1907, it was noted that Andrew Carnegie had donated USD 750,000 for a new building to be used by the Bureau of American Republics. Under date of Jan. 8, 1907, the death of the Shah of Persia was noted. "Chronicle of International Events," 1 *AJIL* 488, 493, 494 (1907).

[125] The "Chronique des faits internationaux" also contains maps where appropriate, and is organized by country rather than chronologically within the period covered.

[126] Letter from George A. Finch to Otis G. Stanton, July 31, 1913.

[127] Comment by John Hazard in 64 *ASIL Proc.* 269 (1970).

C. PERSONALITIES, PROGRAMS AND PROBLEMS

1. Attaining Maturity

As the Society moved from its third to its fourth year of existence in 1909, it could take modest pride in the fact that its income exceeded its expenditure in each of its first three years. The excess was modest at best, but the Society was nonetheless showing itself to be viable financially. From a meager net income for the first year (1906-1907) of USD 73.98, the Society's cash on hand in the income account increased to USD 1,119.66 in April 1908 and to USD 2,568.12 in April 1909.[128] So few were the Society's expenditures in those simpler times that each expense was identified in the published Treasurer's Reports by the number of the check that paid the bill.

When William Howard Taft took office as President of the United States in 1909, the officers of the Society looked for a way to maintain the Society's association with him. They struck upon the idea of making him the Honorary President.[129] This required an amendment of the Society's Constitution, which was accomplished at the Annual Meeting in 1909. Taft remained the Honorary President until he left his higher office in 1913. At that point, although the position of Honorary President remained in the Society's Constitution, it went unfilled until 1921.[130]

* * *

Elihu Root's opening remarks at the Annual Meeting in 1909 touched on an issue close to the hearts of the "legalists" in the peace movement: the creation of a permanent international court.[131] John W. Foster then developed the theme in some detail in his address to the Meeting,[132] and an entire session was devoted to it.[133] Root, Foster and the other "legalists" had come to believe that the typical international arbitration, though useful as a dispute-settlement mechanism, was insufficiently structured to apply and develop neutral rules of international law that could govern the conduct of nation states. The reason was that the arbitrators, typically selected by the disputing parties on an *ad hoc*, case-by-case

128 ASIL Treasurer's Reports of Apr. 18, 1907, Apr. 25, 1908, and Apr. 20, 1909. The Treasurer's Reports through April 1910 appear in 5 *ASIL Proc.* 372-82 (1911).

129 Letter from James Brown Scott to Elihu Root, Apr. 5, 1909.

130 When Warren Harding became President of the United States in 1921, he became the Honorary President of the Society, until his death in 1923. Elihu Root, who stepped down as the Society's President in 1924, succeeded Harding as Honorary President.

131 3 *ASIL Proc.* 13, 14-15 (1909).

132 Id. at 25.

133 Id. at 221-38.

basis with only one neutral umpire for each case, were very much inclined to reach settlements based on compromise and diplomatic acceptability. They could not be expected to rely on scientifically ascertainable rules of law. Far preferable to *ad hoc* arbitration, in the legalists' view, would be a permanent court staffed with professional, full-time judges whose duty would be to apply rules of law consistently and impartially.[134]

This was the goal Root had instructed the U.S. representatives to seek at the 1907 Hague Conference. James Brown Scott, the U.S. expert on international law at the Conference, worked indefatigably for the creation of a world court.[135] Although the effort failed, Root was able to announce at the 1909 Annual Meeting that two disputes involving the United States – one with Great Britain and the other with Venezuela – would be submitted to tribunals composed of neutral arbitrators who he thought would reach essentially judicial decisions.[136]

The 1909 Annual Meeting, like its predecessors, dealt with some subjects that have retained their topicality over the years. Among them were the political offense exception in extradition treaties and the development of international law by U.S. courts. Henry B. Brown, retired Justice of the United States Supreme Court, delivered the paper on the role of the Court. Among the interesting features of his paper is his discussion of sovereign immunity. In 1909, one could assume, as former Justice Brown did, that merchant ships would be privately owned and operated. Thus he was able to draw a tidy distinction between merchant ships (not immune) and naval vessels (immune),[137] without having to address the issues that would dominate sovereign immunity discussions later in the century: whether government-operated merchant ships (or other commercial activities) should be immune, and if not, how to distinguish commercial from non-commercial activities.

The 1909 Annual Meeting was the first to witness extensive remarks from the floor. The remarks followed delivery of a paper on the "equality of nations," large and small. The floor debate was largely a function of the absence of two of the three scheduled speakers on that topic. As John W. Foster remarked, this left the meeting "a little short on material and long on time."[138] Apparently the Annual Meeting organizers hoped that there would be time for floor debate even if all the speakers showed up, but the propensity of speakers to outlast their allotted

---

134 See 2 Jessup, *Elihu Root*, *supra* note 67, at 75-76.

135 See Nurnberger dissertation, *supra* note 30, at 147-49.

136 The cases were the *North Atlantic Coast Fisheries* case, later reported in James Brown Scott, The Hague Court Reports 141 (1916), 4 *AJIL* 948 (1910), and the *Orinoco Steamship Company* case, Hague Court Reports 226, 5 *AJIL* 230 (1911).

137 3 *ASIL Proc.* 166, 175 (1909).

138 Id. at 247.

time was at least as great then as it has been in later years.[139] In any event, the practice of engaging in floor debate caught on and has become an expected, if not always realized, feature of most panel discussions at Annual Meetings.[140]

The 1911 Meeting culminated with a noteworthy roster of annual banquet speakers. They included the President of the United States (Mr. Taft, who as Honorary President of the Society might have found it difficult to stay away), the Chief Justice of Canada and the Japanese and British Ambassadors to the United States. The Chief Justice of the United States, who had been asked to speak, had accepted what he thought was simply an invitation to attend the banquet and declined to speak.[141]

2. The Codification Project

At the Society's 1909 Business Meeting, held then as now during the Annual Meeting, the members voted to embark on an ambitious project close to James Brown Scott's heart. The Society adopted this resolution:

> Whereas the arbitration of questions of a legal nature between nations is recognized as the most effective and, at the same time, the most equitable means of settling disputes which diplomacy has failed to settle; and
>
> Whereas the establishment of a permanent court of international arbitration is predicated upon principles of justice universally recognized; therefore, be it
>
> Resolved, that the President of the American Society of International Law shall appoint a committee of seven members ... to report to the annual meeting of this society in 1911 a draft codification of those principles of justice which should govern the intercourse of nations in times of peace; and make a preliminary report, if possible [before the 1910 Annual Meeting].[142]

---

139 In 1910, the Society's Executive Council adopted a resolution requiring the Program Committee, in sending out invitations to speakers, to state the allotted time for the presentation (not more than 20 minutes for a principal presentation and not more than 10 minutes for a secondary one); an acceptance of the invitation was to be regarded as an agreement to limit the presentation to the time specified. No sanction was set forth. 4 *ASIL Proc.* 196 (1910).

140 Early Annual Meetings did not always feature animated debate when there was time for it. See the Chair's largely unsuccessful attempt to stimulate debate in 4 *ASIL Proc.* 77-78, 80 (1910). In 1911, after the Chair turned to the floor for discussion of papers on the rights of aliens, there was a "pause" followed by the next formal presentation. 5 *ASIL Proc.* 171 (1911).

141 See note 165 *infra*.

142 3 *ASIL Proc.* 268 (1909).

Scott, who introduced the resolution on behalf of Robert Lansing, pointed out that the first paragraph was copied from the 1899 Hague Convention for the Pacific Settlement of International Disputes.[143] Presumably he was trying to avoid any suggestion that the Society was taking a position on a controversial issue.

Scott accepted an interpretation offered by Crammond Kennedy, to the effect that the codification effort would focus on "rules or principles in view of the existing state of international law and of that ideal state which we expect to reach by the evolution of international law ..."[144] The Kennedy interpretation suited Scott perfectly. Scott heartily endorsed the idea of codification, which he thought was essential in order to give international arbitral and judicial bodies a consistent set of norms to apply in settling disputes. Furthermore, he also favored participation by private groups of international lawyers, and believed that it was not enough simply to codify existing practice; rules *de lege ferenda* should be articulated at the same time.[145]

Thus was born within the Society in 1909 the commingling of the codification and the progressive development of international law – a virtually irresistible phenomenon well known in later years to other codifiers, including the International Law Commission. That the Society's efforts eventually came to naught simply shows how ambitious, indeed how utopian, the project was.

The codification project was still in its formative stage at the time of the Society's 1910 Annual Meeting. Although the meeting was devoted primarily to the discussion of the rights of aliens vis-à-vis their host governments, one session was devoted to a discussion of codification generally. The Society's Committee on Codification submitted a preliminary report, which led to a discussion of the advantages and disadvantages of codification. The perceived advantages included the desirability of articulating clear norms for tribunals to apply. *Au contraire* were the risks of calcifying the law and of prematurely codifying political policies that could not reasonably be regarded as legal norms.[146]

The Committee on Codification had been divided into two subcommittees: one on the Scope and Plan of the Report, and the other on the History and Status of Codification. The preliminary report of the former subcommittee dissected the full committee's instructions as found in the 1909 resolution. It concluded that the committee's task was to declare principles of justice recognized by

---

143 Hague Convention for the Pacific Settlement of International Disputes, July 29, 1899, Art. 16, 1 Bevans 230, 187 Consol. Treaty Ser. 410, 2 Scott, *The Hague Peace Conferences*, *supra* note 8, at 81. The report of the 1909 Annual Meeting, at 263, has Scott identifying the relevant article as VI, but it is actually Article 16. The same language appears in the 1907 revision of the Hague Convention, Article 38.

144 3 *ASIL Proc.* 264 (1909).

145 See Nurnberger dissertation, *supra* note 30, at 123-25.

146 See 4 *ASIL Proc.* 27-42 (1910).

"civilized states" and identify the specific rules flowing from them "which have been sanctioned by conventional or other express assent. In addition, it would be appropriate to suggest wider application of the principles or modifications to the accepted rules that would bring them strictly into line with the declared principles."[147] This may not have been exactly what Kennedy and Scott had in mind when they interpreted the 1909 resolution, but neither was it simply an attempt to codify existing principles and rules.

The Subcommittee on Scope and Plan also identified the sources of state practice to which the committee should look, and outlined the topics to be covered. Although the subcommittee did not refer to the then-recent opinion of the U.S. Supreme Court in *The Paquete Habana*,[148] it obviously drew heavily on that case for the sources of state practice.[149] The topics to be covered read like a syllabus for a course on the public international law of peace, circa 1910.[150]

The report of the Subcommittee on the History and Status of Codification began with a justification of codification, and then briefly discussed previous codification efforts. It concluded that "[c]odification seems to be the order of the day."[151]

The Committee on Codification was unable to fulfill the Society's 1909 mandate that a draft codification be produced at the 1911 Annual Meeting. In fact, at the 1911 Meeting, no formal report of the Committee's progress was submitted. The Committee and its successors drifted on for decades after that, doing little more than reporting on the codification efforts of other bodies.[152] Scott himself became active in codification efforts outside the Society, notably the Harvard Research in International Law and the codification program of the Institute of International Law.[153]

---

147 Preliminary Report of the Committee on the Codification of the Principles of Justice in Times of Peace, 4 *ASIL Proc.* 197, 200 (1910).

148 175 U.S. 677 (1900).

149 Sources common to both the subcommittee's report and the Supreme Court opinion included treaties, diplomatic arrangements, decisions of international and municipal tribunals, state papers, municipal legislation and the writings of publicists.

150 See 4 *ASIL Proc.* 203-08 (1910).

151 Id. at 222.

152 See James Brown Scott's report to the Executive Council, May 1, 1937, in 31 *ASIL Proc.* 227 (1937). In 1921, the Committee on Codification was consolidated into the Committee on the Advancement of International Law. 15 *ASIL Proc.* 126 (1921). In 1925, the codification effort was turned over to a Special Committee on Collaboration with League of Nations Committee for the Progressive Codification of International Law. 19 *ASIL Proc.* vi, 173-75 (1925).

153 See Nurnberger dissertation, *supra* note 30, at 125.

3. The Arbitration Dream and the Real World

Arbitration as an instrument of peace – the motivating force behind the creation of the Society – was still very much on the agenda at the 1912 Annual Meeting, but the optimism of the founders was faltering. Elihu Root, still President of the Society but now a U.S. senator rather than Secretary of State, continued the practice he had begun in 1908 by opening the meeting with remarks about the principal events of the past year. When he came to arbitration, he mentioned only briefly the unratified treaties of arbitration with France and Great Britain.[154] These once-promising treaties had been so watered down by reservations in the U.S. Senate that the French and British governments backed off and Taft decided not to proceed with ratification.[155]

Root did not try to mask his disappointment that yet another blow had been dealt to the arbitration movement. He described the recently negotiated Declaration of London on the rules of blockade and neutrality in naval warfare, and noted its importance if the 1907 Hague Conference's International Prize Court were ever to become a reality. Governments – especially the all-important government of Great Britain – were reluctant to ratify the convention establishing the Prize Court if they did not know what rules it would apply. The London Declaration was designed to supply the rules and thus reassure skeptical governments, but the British House of Lords was not satisfied with the outcome and therefore had rejected the Prize Court Bill. That effectively halted the momentum in other states. Root, who viewed the Prize Court as a stepping stone to a more general permanent court of arbitration, vented his frustration.[156] The Prize Court never did come into existence.

At the 1912 Meeting, the Society for the first time as an institution urged a course of conduct on governments. The adopted resolution was non-controversial. It advocated the convening of an international conference to formulate regulations increasing the safety of travel by sea, and sought the adoption of safety-at-sea regulations by the U.S. government.[157] The motivating event was the sinking of the Titanic, which had occurred less than two weeks earlier. The Society was one voice among many around the world calling for something to

---

154 6 *ASIL Proc.* 3 (1912).

155 See Davis, *supra* note 11, at 322-25. Root had tried to amend the treaties to withhold from arbitration some essentially "American questions" that might have been arbitrable under the treaties as negotiated. Id. at 324. Senator Lodge, who had led the effort in the Senate to limit the scope of the treaties, was the principal speaker at the Society's annual banquet two days after Root made his remarks. His topic was international arbitration. Root was not present at the banquet. 6 *ASIL Proc.* 200-06 (1912).

156 Elihu Root, "The Real Significance of the Declaration of London," 6 *ASIL Proc.* 4, 6-12 (1912).

157 Id. at 191-92.

be done. The result was the first International Conference for the Safety of Life at Sea, held in London in 1914.[158]

At the 1913 Annual Meeting, Elihu Root was unavailable to lead off with his usual summary of the past year's leading international events. In his place, James Brown Scott did so. Scott duly noted the ominous war in the Balkans, and then turned to the subject he held dear – international arbitration. He was particularly enthusiastic about the decision in the *Russian Indemnity* case, decided on November 11, 1912.[159] It embodied precisely the approach to international adjudication that Scott thought would lead to a cohesive body of governing rules on the U.S. model. His words describe what he regarded as the ideal arbitral decision:

> [T]he court applied principles of law, cited decisions of courts of arbitration as precedents, and drew up its opinion in the form to which we are accustomed instead of adopting the labored and artificial system of French procedure heretofore used. The opinion in this case is a model, at once scientific and judicial. There is not a trace of compromise to be found in it.[160]

Scott also alluded to the controversy that had arisen between Great Britain and the United States over the proper interpretation of the Hay-Pauncefote Treaty of 1901, which called for equality of treatment among all nations using the Panama Canal. Great Britain had objected to an Act of Congress exempting certain American vessels from paying tolls, and had called upon the United States to arbitrate.[161] This issue, and related issues concerning the use of canals and treaty interpretation, were the principal subjects discussed at the 1913 Annual Meeting. The Panama Canal tolls issue was so sensitive that former Secretary of State Richard Olney's address to the Annual Meeting on the subject was vetted by the White House before he delivered it.[162]

The 1913 Annual Meeting, like its predecessors and successors, provided a venue for the Executive Council to meet. Even before 1913, the substantive sessions of the Annual Meeting left little time for discussion of matters on the Executive Council's agenda, and 1913 was no exception. What was noteworthy

---

158 Later conferences were held in 1918, 1948, 1960 and 1974, culminating in the International Convention for the Safety of Life at Sea, 1974 (SOLAS 1974), which – with protocols and amendments – remains in force.

159 *Russia v. Turkey*, in James Brown Scott, *The Hague Court Reports* 298 (1916), and in 7 *AJIL* 178 (1913).

160 Address by James Brown Scott, 7 *ASIL Proc.* 1, 3 (1913).

161 Id. at 5.

162 Wash. Post, Apr. 26, 1913. The address, Panama Canal Tolls Legislation and the Hay-Pauncefote Treaty, is in 7 *ASIL Proc.* 81 (1913).

in 1913 was that the Executive Council for the first time coped with this by referring most of the difficult matters to the Executive Committee for decision. Issues had been referred to the Executive Committee in earlier years as well, but not wholesale.[163] The questions referred in 1913 related to the composition of the AJIL Board of Editors and of the Committee on the Annual Meeting, a request from the publisher of the Journal for an increase in compensation, an invitation to hold the 1915 Annual Meeting in San Francisco, and "all unfinished business."[164] This was a substantial delegation of authority to the seven-member Executive Committee. Questions would arise in later years about the extent to which significant decisions on non-emergency matters should be made by the Executive Committee rather than by the larger and presumably more representative Executive Council.

4. James Brown Scott's Flair

The banquet at the 1913 Annual Meeting provided another glimpse of things to come. The Secretary of State had been scheduled to speak, but he had to back out at the last minute. Two days before the banquet, James Brown Scott contacted James L. Slayden, a member of Congress from Texas, and asked him to speak on the Interparliamentary Union for the Promotion of Arbitration. It was not to be the last time an annual dinner speaker had to be rushed into the fray at short notice.

Scott's approach to Slayden was wry, with a touch of humor, yet to the point. He assured Slayden that the members of his audience would be "patient and courteous, and they will not throw the crockery at you," whereupon Slayden agreed to speak.[165] Insofar as may be ascertained from the Society's records, Scott's assurances about the membership's behavior at annual dinners have held good through the years.

For as long as Scott served as Recording Secretary (until 1924), it fell to him to try to persuade eminent persons to speak at the annual banquets and in other sessions of the Annual Meeting. The Society's files contain several letters from

---

163 The precedent had been set at the first meeting of the Executive Council, in January 1906. See 1 *ASIL Proc.* 34-35 (1907).

164 7 *ASIL Proc.* 252-53 (1913).

165 Id. at 273. The Society's files contain evidence of other glitches from the early days regarding speakers at the Annual Meeting. For example, there is an exchange of letters in 1911 between Scott and Edward D. White, Chief Justice of the United States, showing that White accepted Scott's invitation to the annual banquet without realizing that he was being asked to be one of the speakers. Letters from Scott to White, Jan. 16, Mar. 4 and Apr. 21, 1911, and from White to Scott, Mar. 1 and Apr. 19, 1911. White did not speak at the banquet.

Scott to prospective speakers. Scott was not above flattery on such occasions, nor was he loathe to resort to tongue-in-cheek supplication.

To give just one example from the Society's first decade, in 1910 Scott tried to entice Joseph H. Choate to come down from New York to speak at the annual dinner. He asked Choate, tongue in cheek: "Do you not think that you have trifled with us long enough and that even coquetry has its limits? Will you not, provided we forgive for all that is past, be present in person as well as in spirit on Saturday evening April 30 and give the members one and all the pleasure of meeting you and hearing the perfection of after-dinner remarks?"[166] His flattery was in vain; Choate declined to speak.

Scott's letters often contained passages designed to add a little spice to the substance. To give an example from a later period, in 1924 Scott invited Charles Evans Hughes, then the Secretary of State as well as the President of the Society, to be the Toastmaster at the annual banquet. Hughes also received the same notice all other members received, stating that the cost of the banquet was USD 5 per person. When Hughes sent a USD 5 check along with his consent to be the Toastmaster, Scott returned the check and said:

> There is no provision in the Constitution of the Society, which prevents any member or non-member for that matter, from endowing the Society, but the invitation which I had the honor to extend to you on behalf of the Society, was addressed to you not as member but as guest of honor, and we like to feel that the guests of honor are ours in every sense of the word. You will, therefore, understand the spirit in which your check is returned.[167]

* * *

Scott's sense of humor was not confined to correspondence with Annual Meeting participants. An example in another context stems from 1914, when Scott, as Editor-in-Chief of the Journal, received a query from one O.M. Kelly, written on the letterhead of a New York hotel. Mr. Kelly wanted to know if there was a law prohibiting a dog fight on a ship three miles from the New York shore. He also inquired about any law prohibiting the advertising and sale of tickets in New York City to such a contest. Scott's reply was deadpan. He said that it appeared to be a question of domestic law, rather than one of international law, but he nevertheless called Mr. Kelly's attention to the case of *Wilson v. McNamee*[168] regarding the nationality of vessels at sea. In the Society's files, but presumably

[166] Letter from Scott to Choate, Feb. 1, 1910.

[167] Letter from James Brown Scott to Charles Evans Hughes, Mar. 31, 1924.

[168] Scott provided Mr. Kelly with the citation: 102 U.S. 572.

not sent to Mr. Kelly, is a supporting "memorandum" on the law of dogs. It was a howl:

> In the absence of authentic information [from Mr. Kelly about the dogs] we are thrown back upon general principles. The general term "dog" applied to the belligerents in this case has numerous variants, the best known being the Italian "doge", French "Allemand", Missouri "houn", Fifth Avenue "Sweetie" etc. To what class of belligerents the contestants in question belong is not stated, nor even their Christian names (from which sometimes the nationality can be inferred, as for instance in Fido, the petulant, or Rush, the growler). They of course might be Saint Bernhardis. In this event the German law of gnaturalization would control.[169]

A note on the "memorandum," presumably penned by Scott, says that it should have been placed in file K-9.

5. The Society's Operations During the Gathering Storm

Elihu Root's opening remarks at the 1914 Annual Meeting were surprisingly optimistic. He made only a passing reference to the gathering storm in Europe, and then proceeded to outline various plans and measures for the settlement of disputes. These included a series of arbitral proceedings and agreements to arbitrate that, he said, showed the disposition of nations to settle their differences by peaceful means.[170] He then turned to the principal topic to be discussed at the 1914 Meeting. It was the Monroe Doctrine, a topic that seems curious at a time when the forces of Europe were well on the way to their most momentous armed conflict yet. The guns of August were only three months away.

James Brown Scott reported to the 1914 Business Meeting on steps then being taken to form an American Institute of International Law. It would consist of representatives of the international law societies in North and South American countries. The meeting authorized Elihu Root to take the steps needed to enter into a relationship with the Institute.[171] Scott was the moving force in the creation of the Institute, and became its President. It held its first meeting in December 1915, attended by representatives of the national societies that had been established in all of the American Republics – including, of course, the ASIL. The Institute

169 Excerpt from an unsigned, undated memorandum attached to Mr. Kelly's letter and Scott's reply, in the Society's correspondence file for 1913-1915. Perhaps the memorandum was a team effort rather than Scott's own, but in any event Scott thought enough of it to preserve it.

170 Address by Elihu Root, 8 *ASIL Proc.* 1, 2 (1914).

171 8 *ASIL Proc.* 231-32 (1914).

at its first meeting adopted a "Declaration of the Rights and Duties of Nations" that appears to have been drafted primarily by Scott.[172]

The Institute continued to meet at irregular intervals until 1938. It adopted recommendations on international organization and 30 draft projects on international law topics.[173] The draft projects were presented to the Pan-American Union, which placed 27 of them before the International Commission of American Jurists for the Codification of International Law, in April 1927. Thirteen of the 27 drafts found their way into the Commission's codification. The subjects included statehood, the treatment of aliens, the law of treaties, diplomatic and consular agents, maritime neutrality, asylum, the duties of states in case of civil war, and pacific settlement of disputes.[174]

To return to the Society's 1914 Business Meeting, Philip Brown raised from the floor a matter going to the fundamental nature of the discussions held at the Annual Meetings. He noted that prepared papers were being read at the Meetings, with the principal presenters paying very little attention to each other's views, and with very little time for discussion from the floor. He wished that the Society in a future Annual Meeting would constitute itself into a deliberative assembly on specific questions of international law to be identified in advance of the Meeting. A committee would prepare and disseminate a report on the topics before the Annual Meeting so that members could come prepared to engage in meaningful discussions. He added, apparently without realizing how controversial it might be, that the Society would then vote some form of recommendation – presumably on the substance of the topics.[175]

James Brown Scott replied that he agreed with Philip Brown's views. He suggested that discussions of the kind Brown proposed, which Scott viewed as being too technical for non-specialists in international law, could be held in the morning and afternoon sessions when teachers and practitioners of international law would be present. "Popular" discussions or presentations could then be made in the evenings when members of the public would attend. Thus, he said, "[I]nstead of reaching one class exclusively or appealing more particularly to one class, we will be able to gather up within the confines of our sessions all elements which, working together, can advance the cause of international law and promote the establishment of international relations on the basis of law and justice."[176] The

---

172 See Finch, Biog. sketch of Scott, *supra* note 38, at 207-08, where the Declaration is quoted. It also appears in Scott's Editorial Comment, "The American Institute of International Law," 10 *AJIL* 121, 124-26 (1916).

173 The 30 draft projects appear in 20 *AJIL Special Supp.* for Oct. 1926, at 300-84.

174 See James Brown Scott, The Gradual and Progressive Codfication of International Law, 21 *AJIL* 417 (1927).

175 8 *ASIL Proc.* at 239-40 (1914).

176 Id. at 241-42.

goal of reaching both specialists and laypersons was a fundamental tenet of the Society from the beginning – though not a tenet immune from occasional challenge. The Business Meeting did not specifically endorse Scott's plan, but rather approved a vague recommendation to the annual meeting committee to include "constructive consideration of international law."[177]

The 1914 Annual Meeting ended, as did all Annual Meetings for many years, with the annual dinner. The principal speaker was then-Secretary of State William Jennings Bryan. He used the occasion to announce that the United States had that afternoon accepted a proposal from the governments of Argentina, Brazil and Chile to mediate the simmering dispute between the United States and Mexico over the treatment of Americans and American-owned property as a result of the revolution in Mexico.[178] The prospect of mediation averted what could well have been a war between the United States and Mexico. Mr. Bryan's announcement thus drew hearty applause from the diners. It was not to be the last time a speaker at an annual dinner made an important foreign policy announcement.

6. Early Society Efforts to Bolster the Teaching of International Law

In conjunction with the 1914 Annual Meeting, some 44 teachers of international law held the first of what were to be seven Conferences of Teachers of International Law and Related Subjects. The Conference was the brainchild of the ubiquitous James Brown Scott, acting in his capacity as Director of the Carnegie Endowment's Division of International Law. The Endowment's Board of Trustees had directed that a plan be carried out to strengthen the teaching in universities and law schools of "arbitration and international law and history as connected with arbitration."[179] Scott decided first to try to find out how many universities and law schools – and which ones – were teaching international law courses. Through the use of a mail survey, he identified 180 colleges and universities, and 64 law schools, that taught international law in 1911-12.[180] He then recommended that the Endowment convene a conference of international law professors, with a request that the ASIL place it on its program for the next annual meeting, to consider how the teaching of the subject might be further developed.[181] The 1914 Conference was the result.

---

177 Id. at 242.

178 William Jennings Bryan, "Address," 8 *ASIL Proc.* 336, 338-39 (1914). See also Finch, "The ASIL 1906-1956," *supra* note 16, at 305.

179 Carnegie Endowment for International Peace, *Report on the Teaching of International Law in the Educational Institutions of the United States* 1 (1913).

180 Id. at 5-10, 23-25.

181 Id. at 35-36.

The Conference met for three days. In the end it adopted 16 resolutions, all designed to enhance the teaching and study of international law. It is apparent that the teachers, like the founders of the Society, thought of the dissemination of international law rules as an important contribution to the cause of peace. At the same time they were sensitive to the need for academic integrity. For example, Resolution No. 4 said in part:

> [I]t is important that [the student] have impressed upon his mind the definiteness and positive character of the rules of international law. The teaching of international law should not be made the occasion for a universal peace propaganda. The interest of students and their enthusiasm for the subject can best be aroused by impressing upon them the evolutionary character of the rules of international law. Through such a presentation of the subject the student will not fail to see how the development of positive rules of law governing the relations between states has contributed towards the maintenance of peace.[182]

Another resolution, recognizing the power of the bar examination to sway law students' course selections, urged state bar examiners to make international law a bar subject. Yet another requested the American Bar Association to take similar action.[183] These entreaties had very little result, but the spirit behind them was not snuffed out. Efforts in the same direction continued to be made in later years.

The Conference also began what would become a sustained effort by the Society to persuade governments to make documents of state accessible and to do so in a timely fashion. This, of course, reflected the needs of the teacher/scholars who comprised the Conference, but it also served a public interest. Specifically, the Conference recommended:

> That there be published in a cheap and convenient form all documents of state, both foreign and domestic, especially Latin American, bearing upon international law, including treaties, documents relating to arbitration, announcements of state policy, and diplomatic correspondence, and that the aid of the Department of State be solicited in securing copies of such documents for publication.[184]

In fact, the American Journal of International Law had been publishing documents of state, though selectively, since 1907. The documents appeared in Supplements to the Journal. They included bilateral and multilateral treaties,

---

[182] Conference of American Teachers of International Law held at Washington, D.C., April 23-25, 1914, at 70 (1914), reprinted in 8 *ASIL Proc.* 250, 319 (1914).

[183] Id. at 322.

[184] Id. at 318.

diplomatic correspondence, national and international declarations, and some municipal legislation. Some of the documents published in the early years were quite significant in the development of international law in the twentieth century.[185]

The 1914 Conference of Teachers' recommendation induced the Society to expand its coverage. The Society undertook to publish all available documents of state in AJIL Supplements.[186] In April 1915 James Brown Scott wrote to William Jennings Bryan, then the Secretary of State, asking if the Journal could publish the official communications of the State Department concerning World War I.[187] Bryan replied that the President (Woodrow Wilson) had approved of the plan, provided that the material be assembled by the Department.[188] With financial help from the Carnegie Endowment, the Journal then published three Special Supplements containing World War I diplomatic correspondence between the United States and belligerent governments relating to neutral rights and commerce.[189] *The Nation* gave tribute to "the excellent service which that scholarly journal has rendered" in publishing the documents and called the 1915 Special Supplement "a most valuable compilation."[190]

With additional funds provided by the Carnegie Endowment, the Society established a Standing Committee on the Study and Teaching of International Law to consider some of the Conference's resolutions, including Resolution No. 4. At a meeting on April 27, 1916, the Standing Committee, chaired by Professor George Grafton Wilson, adopted a report elaborating on the resolutions. The Committee recommended:

> (a) In the teaching of international law emphasis should be laid on the positive nature of the subject and the definiteness of the rules.
>
> (b) In order to emphasize the positive character of international law, the widest possible use should be made of cases and concrete facts in international experience.

---

185 For example, the Supplement to volume 2 of the AJIL contained the Final Act and Conventions of the Second Hague Peace Conference. 2 *AJIL Supp.* 1-218 (1908). The Supplement to volume 3 contained documents relating to the 1903 Panama Canal Treaty, dating back to 1815. 3 *AJIL Supp.* 106-139 (1909).

186 See Finch, "The ASIL 1906-1956," *supra* note 16, at 301.

187 Letter from Scott to Bryan, Apr. 28, 1915.

188 Letter from Bryan to Scott, May 7, 1915.

189 9 *AJIL Special Supp.* for July 1915; 10 *AJIL Special Supp.* for Oct. 1916; 11 *AJIL Special Supp.* for Oct. 1917.

190 *The Nation* (New York), Jan. 27, 1916, at 113.

(c) In the teaching of international law care should be exercised to distinguish the accepted rules of international law from questions of international policy.

(d) In a general course in international law, the practice of no one country should be given weight out of proportion to the strictly international principles it may illustrate.[191]

Each of these recommendations reflects a point of view that most of the Society's teaching members would have shared at the time. A lesser degree of consensus would prevail in the 21st century. The need to show that international law is *law* – the motivation for recommendation (a) – would not be as widely felt in 2006, nor would all teachers wish to take a stand behind the definiteness of the rules. As for (b), not all current teachers would stress "cases," if by that is meant formal adjudications; most American teachers, though, seem to agree that real international experience should be used in the classroom, either for its intrinsic pedagogic value or to illustrate how hypothetical problems might be resolved. The Yale school would hardly concur in (c) or (d), and would have some supporters even outside New Haven.

In the year between the 1916 and 1917 Annual Meetings, the Standing Committee explored territory that (as it discovered) the Society's Executive Council did not wish to occupy. The President of Williams College, in a letter to Committee member and Williams alumnus Philip Marshall Brown, invited the Society to hold summer sessions at Williams. The Committee enthusiastically supported the idea as a needed supplement to the brief Annual Meetings. The Committee's resolution put it this way:

> A Summer Conference of say four or six weeks each year devoted to the serious presentation and discussion of the fundamental problems of International Law and international relations would be of the greatest value. Lectures could be given by the most competent man available on International Law and Related Subjects, to wit, International Private Law, Maritime Law, Diplomacy and special fields of History ...
>
> These lectures should be reserved for registered students attending the summer conference as well as members of the Society of International Law. There might also be occasional public sessions for special addresses by men of particular distinction.[192]

---

[191] Report of the Standing Committee on the Study and Teaching of International Law and Related Subjects, 10 *ASIL Proc.* 174-75 (1916).

[192] Minutes of the Meeting of the Standing Committee on the Study and Teaching of International Law and Related Subjects, Dec. 2, 1916, at 3-4. Women were not yet eligible even to join the Society, much less to be regarded as lecturers of particular distinction.

James Brown Scott, who was a member of the Standing Committee as well as Director of the Carnegie Endowment's Division of International Law, said that his recommendation for summer courses on international law had been approved by the Trustees of the Endowment. He thought the first conference, proposed for the summer of 1917, would come within the scope of the grant the Endowment had already made to the Society.

The Standing Committee also recommended that the Society establish a limited number of fellowships for graduate students and teachers to study international law at an advanced level. The Committee requested the Society to provide the funds, if possible, beginning in 1917-18.[193]

The Society's Executive Council disapproved both of the Standing Committee's recommendations. Concerns expressed about the summer conferences were that they might interfere with the regular Annual Meetings of the Society, that they would change the Society's character from an association of international lawyers to an educational institution, and that it would be better to aid and encourage universities offering summer courses in international law than to compete with them.[194] The proposed fellowships were disapproved for similar reasons.[195]

Scott thereupon resigned from the Standing Committee on the ground that his dual positions as a member of the Committee and Director of the Endowment's Division of International Law presented a conflict of interest.[196] The Carnegie Endowment, acting on Scott's recommendation, established the fellowships on its own.[197] More than 200 fellowships were awarded until the program was terminated, as having served its purpose, in the academic year 1936-37.[198]

The Standing Committee, having been rebuffed by the Executive Council, presented its report to the Society's annual Business Meeting in 1917, and – in apparent frustration – asked that the Committee be discharged.[199] After the report had been presented, Charles Fenwick asked why the summer sessions had been disapproved. Philip Brown, representing the Committee, responded curtly that perhaps someone on the Executive Council would answer. No one did.[200]

* * *

193 Id. at 5.

194 Minutes of the Meeting of the Executive Council, Mar. 10, 1917, at 1-3.

195 Id. at 3.

196 Id. at 4. Scott's letter of resignation, dated Feb. 26, 1917, is in the Society's files.

197 Id. at 2-3; ASIL Business Meeting, Apr. 28, 1917, in 11 *ASIL Proc.* 148 (1917).

198 See Finch, "The ASIL 1906-1956," *supra* note 16, at 303.

199 11 *ASIL Proc.* 146, 148 (1917).

200 Id. at 148.

A plausible explanation of this episode is that it was a microcosm of the tensions that have existed within the Society almost from the beginning between practitioners and academics. This was the first time the tension was spread upon the records of the Society, but it probably was not the first time it had been given a voice. The split between practitioners and academics, though, was not a clean one, as is shown by the fact that the motion to disapprove the summer sessions was seconded by Professor John H. Latané, of Johns Hopkins University. He then made the motion to disapprove the fellowships. Thus there may have been more to the episode than town/gown antipathy. There was some concern, even within the Standing Committee, about maintaining the Society's independence from the Carnegie Endowment, a concern acutely felt by James Brown Scott.[201] In addition, United States entry into World War I was imminent, and some Executive Council members may have thought it an inopportune time to be launching new initiatives associated with the peace movement.

The concern about the Society's independence of thought and action from its sources of funds was raised at the 1916 Annual Meeting when Charles Noble Gregory asked about the source of funds for the Standing Committee. Scott replied, with obvious discomfort, that the source was the Carnegie Endowment. He outlined the history of the Endowment's interest, in considerable detail. He acknowledged that in some quarters the Carnegie Endowment was regarded as "propagandist," and that this might taint the work of any group relying on the Endowment's funds. Thus, he said, the Endowment would withdraw into the background and would cooperate with the ASIL only insofar as it was requested to do so. Any funds from the Endowment would be placed at the disposal of the Society, for the benefit of the Standing Committee, without any strings attached. He went on to point out his own efforts to avoid conflicts of interest over money in his influential positions with both the Society and the Endowment. His explanation was accepted.[202]

The incident was a classic case of a non-profit organization, dependent on a funding source with its own agenda, trying to maintain access to the funds without sacrificing its intellectual integrity. It was a dilemma that was bound to recur as the Society increasingly relied on outside funding.

7. Members and Their Participation

The occasional stresses within the Society were evident in the Executive Council's consideration in 1916 of "the class of persons which should be sought for membership in the Society."[203] The question was whether to continue the policy

---

201 See the Report of the Standing Committee, 11 *ASIL Proc.* 146, 147 (1917).

202 See 10 *ASIL Proc.* 117-23 (1916) for the full discussion of this question.

203 10 *ASIL Proc.* 168 (1916).

of enrolling "all persons" (*i.e.* all male persons) interested in international law, or to limit membership to scholars. It was a question stemming from the Society's mixed goals of popularizing international law and of engaging in "scientific" studies of the subject. The Executive Council decided against turning the Society into a purely scholarly enterprise. Instead, the Council resolved that "the widest membership for the Society should be sought."[204]

The Executive Council in 1915 and 1916 attacked another intractable problem of the Society: long-winded speakers at Annual Meetings. In 1915, the Council resolved that the allotted time for each presentation be printed in the Annual Meeting program, and that the presiding officer be required to call the next speaker at the expiration of the allotted time – whether or not the current speaker was still holding forth.[205] This having apparently been insufficient, the Council resolved in 1916 "[t]hat a large-faced clock be placed on the wall opposite the speaker's desk."[206] Whether this was actually carried out is not recorded.

During these formative years, James Brown Scott and his assistant, George A. Finch, did almost all of the Society's administrative work. Scott, of course, was also prominent in the Carnegie Endowment, was Editor-in-Chief of the *American Journal of International Law*, and was a prolific writer/editor on international law topics – particularly those relating to peaceful dispute settlement. Elihu Root, as President of the Society, performed the more prominent public functions – giving introductory addresses at the Annual Meetings, serving as toastmaster at the annual dinners (except in 1912 and 1913, when Frederic R. Coudert filled in, often with tongue in cheek), and sometimes communicating with important people when the Society wanted something from them.

Members' participation was uneven during these years. Scott and Finch, to their credit, seem to have replied faithfully to any correspondence from members (and others). Nevertheless, there is little indication in the Society's files from these years that they actively sought to widen the inner circle of active members, other than by asking those with special expertise to participate in Annual Meetings. Scott and Finch did try to bring new members into the Society, but that was done primarily for financial reasons.

Some of the prominent scholars of the day were active members; others were less so. For example, George Grafton Wilson, first of Brown University and then of Harvard, was quite active. He chaired the Standing Committee on Selection of Honorary Members and the Standing Committee for the Study and Teaching of International Law. He later succeeded Scott as Editor-in-Chief of the Journal. On the other hand, John Bassett Moore, of Columbia, was active only occasionally. More than once he declined Scott's supplications to participate in Annual

---

[204] Id.

[205] 9 *ASIL Proc.* 143 (1915).

[206] 10 *ASIL Proc.* 169 (1916).

Meetings or on Society committees, or to attend meetings of the Journal's Board of Editors, citing the burdens of his other obligations. He asked to be relieved from his position on the Editorial Board of the Journal in 1916. The Society's Executive Council urged him to reconsider, which he did.[207]

Charles Cheney Hyde, first a practitioner in Chicago, then a professor at Northwestern and later at Columbia, became increasingly involved in the Society during this period. Others, such as Charles Noble Gregory of the University of Iowa and then of George Washington University, Amos Hershey of Indiana University, John H. Latané of Washington and Lee University and then of Johns Hopkins, and Paul S. Reinsch of the University of Wisconsin, were regular contributors to the Society's work.

8. Annual Meetings in the Years Leading to U.S. Entry into World War I

In 1915, the Annual Meeting was held in December, in coordination with the Second Pan-American Scientific Congress. Three of the five substantive sessions were held in conjunction with the Congress' Subsection on International Law. This collaboration was consistent with other efforts of the Society to spread the word about international law throughout the Americas, including James Brown Scott's active participation in the American Institute of International Law.

Elihu Root's opening address at the 1915 Annual Meeting was laden with disillusionment over the war in Europe:

> Many of the rules of law which the world has regarded as most firmly established have been completely and continuously disregarded, in the conduct of war, in dealing with the property and lives of civilian non-combatants on land and sea and in the treatment of neutrals. Alleged violations by one belligerent have been asserted to justify other violations by other belligerents. The art of war has been developed through the invention of new instruments of destruction and it is asserted that the changes of conditions thus produced make the old rules obsolete.
>
> ...
>
> It seems that if the violation of law justifies other violations, then the law is destroyed and there is no law; that if the discovery of new ways of doing a thing prohibited justifies the doing of it, then there is no law to prohibit. The basis of such assertions really is the view that if a substantial belligerent interest for the injury of the enemy come[s] in conflict with a rule of law, the rule must stand aside and the interest must prevail. If that be so it is not difficult to reach the conclusion that for the present, at

---

207 Id. at 165; letter from George A. Finch to John Bassett Moore, May 16, 1916; Moore's reply, May 22, 1916.

> all events, in all matters which affect the existing struggle, international law is greatly impaired.[208]

These passages, of course, have a modern ring. Root might just as well have been speaking in the last decade of the century or in the first decade of the next century. Be that as it may, he ended his address on a positive note, foreseeing that a stronger law might rise from the ashes of a terrible war.[209]

Two years later, leading off an Annual Meeting held just three weeks after the United States declared war on Germany, Root's disillusionment returned:

> [T]his year I have nothing to call to the attention of the Society in the field of international law, except, so far as I can recall, that every rule which has been devised by the civilization of the century just passed for confining the operations of war within the limits of humanity, so far as that may be possible, and for distinguishing war between civilized nations from the wars of the past between barbarians – every rule of that description has been systematically, flagrantly and outrageously violated during the past year by the Empire of Germany.[210]

Root went on to argue that hope for the future lay in the spread of democracy. Only "[t]he substitution of a democratic for an autocratic regime removes the chief force which in the past has led nations to break over and destroy the limitations of law; that is, the prosecution of dynastic policies."[211] That view has since become commonplace among political scientists and political leaders, though some have pointed out that it may be true only of stable, mature democracies.[212]

Except for Root's remarks, substantive discussions at the Annual Meetings in 1915 and 1916 tended either to focus on issues not directly raised by the war or, insofar as they dealt with the war, on issues of particular concern to the United States – such as neutral rights and duties. The discussions of the law and practice of neutrality, however, were far from bland. In 1916, James W. Garner of the University of Illinois addressed the arguments that had been put forth against the traditional rule allowing merchants of neutral states to sell arms to belligerents, and rejected the arguments on practical grounds.[213] Philip

---

208 Elihu Root, "The Outlook for International Law," 9 *ASIL Proc.* 2, 3 (1915).

209 Id. at 10.

210 Elihu Root, opening remarks, 11 *ASIL Proc.* 1-2 (1917).

211 Elihu Root, "The Effect of Democracy on International Law," id. at 2, 5.

212 See Edward D. Mansfield & Jack Snyder, "Democratization and War," 74 *Foreign Aff.*, No. 3, at 79 (May/June 1995).

213 James W. Garner, "Some True and False Conceptions Regarding the Duty of Neutrals in Respect to the Sale and Exportation of Arms and Munitions to Belligerents," 10 *ASIL Proc.* 18 (1916).

Marshall Brown of Princeton referred to "this weird thing called neutrality," and argued that nation states have a positive duty to intervene in the interest of order and justice.[214]

The United States declared war on Germany just three weeks before the 1917 Annual Meeting was due to begin. The meeting went ahead nevertheless, as scheduled. Much of the agenda concerned international organization. About 50 international organizations were already extant, but the one on everyone's mind had yet to be created. There still was no official draft of the Covenant of the League of Nations, but serious planning for it had begun. Influential figures from the ASIL had been involved all along – including, however, neither Elihu Root nor James Brown Scott. William Howard Taft, who was not only a former President of the United States, but also a Vice President and former Honorary President of the Society, had in 1915 become the American Branch President of the League to Enforce Peace – itself an outgrowth of the American peace movement. The League to Enforce Peace espoused three propositions for a new League of Nations: judicial settlement of justiciable disputes between signatories; conciliation for other disputes; and a commitment to use joint economic and military force against any member that resorted to war without attempting judicial settlement or conciliation of a dispute. The latter proposition, though felicitous to Taft, was much less so to Root and Scott.[215] They distrusted "internationalists" and favored the judicial settlement of disputes and the holding of periodic conferences to codify international law, rather than the creation of a world body with members ostensibly committed to using force in the name of justice.[216] Root had no faith that states would respond to the call to arms unless it seemed to be in their own interests to do so when the occasion arose.[217] Scott, in private correspondence, called the League to Enforce Peace the "League to Create War."[218]

The Society's discussion in 1917 began with some quite abstract papers on international organization, but eventually turned to the proposed "league for peace." Debate focused on the controversial issue of using joint force against a belligerent member. William C. Dennis supported the idea;[219] James Brown Scott, on the other hand, thought it naïve to assume that states not directly threatened by a member's use of force would join in using force to resist it. Instead, there

214 Philip Marshall Brown, "Munitions and Neutrality," id. at 33, 35, 42.

215 See Ruhl J. Bartlett, *The League to Enforce Peace* 43-44 (1944), for discussion of Root's importance to the League Movement and of his rejection of the invitation to join.

216 See Finch, "The ASIL 1906-1956," *supra* note 16, at 310-11; Shinohara, *supra* note 75, at 96.

217 See 2 Jessup, *Elihu Root*, *supra* note 67, at 378.

218 See Nurnberger dissertation, *supra* note 30, at 55, referring to a letter from Scott to H.C. Phillips, Apr. 25, 1916.

219 11 *ASIL Proc.* 91 (1917).

should be an appeal to reason.[220] In a lively debate, several speakers from the floor challenged Scott's approach.[221] The battle lines had been drawn between Scott, along with his generation – the defenders of the Hague Conference system – and a younger generation more amenable to some sort of concerted, sustained effort among nations to maintain and enforce peace.[222]

9. The Journal in the Pre-World War I Years

During the pre-World War I years, the *American Journal of International Law* was coming of age. In fact, it may well have come of age by 1914. At the Society's 1914 annual banquet, toastmaster Elihu Root was heard to say that the Society was blessed with "a journal which one of the greatest authorities on international law in Europe said to me last summer is the best journal of international law in the world, a journal which is self-sustaining."[223] Root the statesman took obvious pride in the encomium from Europe; Root the President of the Society no doubt took great satisfaction also in the ledger entry.

From the beginning, James Brown Scott, as Managing Editor and then Editor-in-Chief, saw to it that the Journal's lead articles, as well as its Editorial Comments, reflected the important issues of the day. Lead articles in volumes 1 and 2 dealt with such matters as the Calvo and Drago doctrines;[224] the humanitarian law of war in the aftermath of the Hague Conferences of 1899 and 1907;[225]

---

220 Id. at 101.

221 Id. at 118, 119, 121, 122, 123.

222 See Shinohara, *supra* note 75, at 107-08.

223 8 *ASIL Proc.* 325 (1914). One suspects that the source of the praise was Lassa Oppenheim, who in 1917 wrote to congratulate James Brown Scott for editing "the leading international law periodical of the world." Letter from Oppenheim to Scott, Dec. 28, 1917. See also Lassa Oppenheim, "The Science of International Law: Its Task and Method," 2 *AJIL* 313 (1908) ("Undoubtedly, this Journal has at once with its appearance taken up the position of a leading magazine of the science of international law"). Rather more colorfully, R.S. Woodward, President of the Carnegie Institution of Washington, said in 1910, "If the legal profession does not warm up to the proper pitch of enthusiasm for your journal the members thereof will prove themselves deficient in red blood corpuscles." Letter to James Brown Scott, Feb. 2, 1910.

224 See Amos S. Hershey, "The Calvo and Drago Doctrines," 1 *AJIL* 26 (1907).

225 See George B. Davis, "Doctor Francis Lieber's Instructions for the Government of Armies in the Field," 1 id. at 13 (1907); George B. Davis, "The Geneva Convention of 1906," 1 id. at 409; C.H. Stockton, "Would Immunity from Capture, During War, of Non-Offending Private Property upon the High Seas be in the Interest of Civilization?," 1 id. at 930; James Brown Scott, "The Work of the Second Peace Conference," 2 id. at 1, 15-21 (1908); Ellery C. Stowell, "Convention Relative to the Opening of Hostilities," 2 id. at 50; George B. Davis, "The Amelioration of the Rules of War on Land," 2 id. at 63; Antonio S. de Bustamante, "The Hague Convention Concerning the Rights and Duties of Neutral

international arbitration;[226] the nature of international law;[227] the evolution of international organizations;[228] and what we would call today the foreign relations law of the United States.[229]

Many of these articles are today primarily of historical significance, but some are relevant to current issues as well. For example, Oppenheim's article on the science and method of international law in the second volume of the Journal repays reading today as a demonstration of how the several sources of custom

---

Powers and Persons in Land Warfare," id. at 95; articles by James Brown Scott, George G. Wilson, C.H. Stockton, James Brown Scott (again), Louis Renault, Simeon E. Baldwin and Charles Cheney Hyde on various aspects of maritime warfare, 2 id. at 259, 271, 276, 285, 295, 307 and 507; George B. Davis, "The Launching of Projectiles from Balloons," 2 id. at 528; George B. Davis, "The Second, Third, and Fourth Voeux of the Conference," 2 id. at 811.

226 See Jackson H. Ralston, "Some Suggestions as to the Permanent Court of Arbitration," 1 id. at 321 (1907); William L. Penfield, "International Arbitration," 1 id. at 330; R. Floyd Clarke, "A Permanent Tribunal of International Arbitration: Its Necessity and Value," 1 id. at 342; David J. Hill, "The Second Peace Conference at The Hague," 1 id. at 670, 678-84; Amos S. Hershey, "Convention for the Peaceful Adjustment of International Disputes," 2 id. at 29 (1908) (dealing with good offices and mediation as well as arbitration); James Brown Scott, "The Central American Peace Conference of 1907," 2 id. at 121, 140-43 ("the crowning glory [of the Conference] is the convention for the establishment of a Central American court of justice"); Luis Anderson, "The Peace Conference of Central America," 2 id. at 144; articles by Charles Noble Gregory, Henry B. Brown and Thomas Raeburn White on the proposed International Prize Court, 2 id. at 458, 476 and 490; William I. Hull, "Obligatory Arbitration and the Hague Conferences," 2 id. at 731; James Brown Scott, "The Proposed Court of Arbitral Justice," 2 id. at 772.

227 See John Bassett Moore, "International Law: Its Present and Future," 1 id. at 11 (1907); Robert Lansing, "Notes on Sovereignty," 1 id. at 105; Richard Olney, "The Development of International Law," 1 id. at 418; James Brown Scott, "The Legal Nature of International Law," 1 id. at 831; Lassa Oppenheim, "The Science of International Law: Its Task and Method," 2 id. at 313 (1908); W.W. Willoughby, "The Legal Nature of International Law," 2 id. at 357; Elihu Root, "The Sanction of International Law," 2 id. at 451; Frederick Charles Hicks, "The Equality of States and The Hague Conferences," 2 id. at 530.

228 See Simeon E. Baldwin, "The International Congresses and Conferences of the Last Century as Forces Working Toward the Solidarity of the World," 1 id. at 565 (1907); Paul S. Reinsch, "International Unions and Their Administration," 1 id. at 579.

229 See Elihu Root," The Real Question Under the Japanese Treaty and the San Francisco School Board Resolutions," 1 id. at 273 (1907) (reprint of Root's opening address at the Society's first Annual Meeting); Albert Bushnell Hart, "American Ideals of International Relations," 1 id. at 624; Gaillard Hunt, "The History of the Department of State," Part I, 1 id. at 867, and Part II, 2 id. at 591 (1908); Wilbur J. Carr, "The American Consular Service," 1 id. at 891; W.W. Willoughby, "Citizenship and Allegiance in Constitutional and International Law," 1 id. at 914; Thomas Raeburn White, "Constitutionality of the Proposed International Prize Court – Considered from the Standpoint of the United States," 2 id. at 490 (1908).

may often be indicators of a process by which a customary rule may ultimately develop, rather than clear evidence that a custom has crystallized. As a corollary to this, he expounded on the need for, and method of, careful examination of state practice in all its forms before the existence of a customary rule is declared.[230]

Volume 2 engendered the first letter of protest from a disgruntled Journal author. It was hardly to be the last. Scott had received an unsolicited short contribution from a judge in Manila. The subject was the extraterritorial application of the Japanese Penal Code. Scott published it as an Editorial Comment rather than as a lead article, and did not give the author's name in the Journal's table of contents. That prompted a written complaint from the judge, who noted that he would be obliged to withhold other contributions he had intended to send the Journal.[231]

Book reviews, like lead articles, reflected Scott's interests, and, as we have seen, Scott wrote several of them himself. His first review in volume 1 was felicitous, in view of the stated goals of the Society and of the Journal. It was a review of John Bassett Moore's book, *American Diplomacy: Its Spirit and Achievements*. The book was a revised version of a series of articles Moore had written for *Harper's* magazine, and thus was intended for the lay public. Scott applauded "the fact that specialists and men of affairs, such as Professor Moore and John W. Foster, have found time and taken a pleasure in laying before the public the results of a lifetime in a simple, accurate and attractive form."[232] Scott penned a similar accolade a few years later for the seventh edition of T.J. Lawrence's *Handbook of Public International Law*.[233]

The April 1911 issue of the Journal carried a critical review of J.H. Ralston's by-now well known book, *International Arbitral Law and Procedure*. The review was by Edwin M. Borchardt, then of the United States Supreme Court Law Library and later, with the spelling of his last name changed slightly, of the Yale law faculty.[234] Scott had sent Ralston a copy of Borchardt's proposed review before

---

230 Lassa Oppenheim, *supra* note 223. Oppenheim, like the founders of the American Society of International Law, was interested not only in the scholarly side of international law, but also in educating the public – what he called "the popularization of international law." See id. at 323-24.

231 Scott's reply dealt with two other matters raised in the judge's letter, but did not respond to the complaint. Exchange of correspondence between Charles S. Lobingier and James Brown Scott, Jan. 5 and Mar. 11, 1909.

232 James Brown Scott, "Review of John Bassett Moore, American Diplomacy: Its Spirit and Achievements (1905)," in 1 *AJIL* 250, 252 (1907).

233 James Brown Scott, "Review of T.J. Lawrence, A Handbook of Public International Law," in 4 *AJIL* 250 (1910).

234 The review was published in 5 *AJIL* 534 (1911). According to the Library of Congress, where the Supreme Court Law Library was then housed, Borchardt changed his name to Borchard in 1911. He joined the Yale law faculty in 1917.

it was published, and Borchardt had softened some of the criticism as a result of Ralston's reply.[235] Scott must have felt that it was only fair to let the author have a chance to correct any errors or to deflect unduly harsh comments while there was still time to change the review before publication. Whether this was Scott's normal practice, or whether he simply did it as a courtesy to Ralston, does not appear.

Starting with the January 1912 issue, the Journal was published in a Spanish edition, *Revista Americana de Derecho Internacional*, as well as in the English edition. The Society had asked the Carnegie Endowment to finance the Spanish edition. James Brown Scott, putting on his other hat as the Endowment's representative, agreed to provide the funds.[236] By 1920 there were about 250 paid subscribers in Latin America plus a large free distribution list of ministries of foreign affairs and libraries,[237] bringing the total to about 500.[238] In 1922, though, the Board of Editors decided that a Spanish-language journal edited and published in Latin America would better serve the demand. The Spanish edition of the Journal was discontinued at the end of its tenth year, to be replaced by the *Revista de Derecho Internacional* edited by Antonio S. de Bustamente y Sirvén and published in Havana.[239]

The Journal's first pseudonymous article was published in 1914, on the eve of World War I. Signed "Germanicus," it was written by the then-Military Attaché of the German Embassy in Washington, one Captain Herwarth. It argued that the "Christian Teutonic world" must stick together against the rest of the world.[240]

The Journal's Board of Editors drew a distinction between pseudonymous and anonymous articles. In 1924, a British official asked George A. Finch, then the Secretary of the Board of Editors, if he could submit a reply to an Editorial Comment Finch had written on the occupation of the Ruhr Valley – a reply he said

---

235 There is a letter in the ASIL correspondence file for 1909-1912 from Ralston to Scott, dated March 2, 1911, referring to Scott's courtesy in sending Ralston a copy of the proposed review. There is also a letter from Borchardt, dated March 23, 1911, saying that Borchardt had changed several passages in response to assertions Ralston had made regarding perceived errors and exaggerations in the proposed review.

236 Letter from J.B. Scott, for the Carnegie Endowment, to the Society, Apr. 6, 1912.

237 Minutes of the Meeting of the Executive Council, Nov. 13, 1920, in 14 *ASIL Proc.* 5, 6 (1920).

238 See 10 *Y.B. Carnegie Endowment for International Peace* 138 (1921).

239 James Brown Scott, Editorial Comment: "The Revista de Derecho Internacional," 16 *AJIL* 437, 438 (1922).

240 See Germanicus (Herwarth), "The Central American Question from a European Point of View," 8 *AJIL* 213 (1914). That Herwarth was the author appears in a letter from George A. Finch to Jesse S. Reeves, Mar. 15, 1921.

would have to be anonymous because of his official position.[241] Finch answered that it was not the Journal's policy to print anonymous contributions.[242]

In 1916, the Journal began its still-standing practice of having at least two members of the Board of Editors pass on any manuscript being seriously considered for publication.[243] At the same time the Board decided that articles should be short: as a rule, no longer than about 20 printed pages.[244] It was a rule destined to be observed often in the breach.

On the eve of the United States' entry into World War I, the Journal had achieved an international reputation as a premier organ for the dissemination of international law in the English and Spanish languages. It enjoyed somewhat lesser credentials as a truly scholarly journal than it would achieve in later years, but that could be attributed to its dual – and not altogether consistent – objectives of spreading the word to non-scholars and publishing theoretical or penetrating pieces. In any case, it was well on its way to pre-eminence in its field and was thought by some leading authorities already to have achieved that pinnacle. The lion's share of the credit had to go to James Brown Scott, its Editor-in-Chief.

---

241 Letter from John Fisher Williams to Finch, Jan. 5, 1924. Finch's Editorial Comment was "The Legality of the Occupation of the Ruhr Valley," 17 *AJIL* 724 (1923).

242 Letter from Finch to Williams, Jan. 23, 1924.

243 Letter from George A. Finch to Jesse S. Reeves, Feb. 2, 1916.

244 Id.

Chapter Two

Adapting to a New World

There are those who tell us that international law is a figment of the mind; that it does not exist; that it has been destroyed. International law can never be destroyed. It may be violated, its rules may be disobeyed, but so may the rules laid down by municipal law, or by any legal system, but the law is there, and, ... so far as it is the expression of that justice toward which all law aspires, it is a reality in spite of violations.

—David Jayne Hill
Toastmaster Remarks
11 *ASIL Proceedings* 163 (1917)

A. U.S. ENTRY INTO WORLD WAR I AND THE SOCIETY'S RESPONSE

1. The Society Off Balance

On April 6, 1917, the United States declared war on Germany. The Society promptly adopted a resolution noting the need to train newly conscripted citizens in military and international law. The resolution offered the U.S. government the services of the Society's members "as instructors in such branches of law in any manner in which their services may be desired."[1] The Acting Judge Advocate General of the War Department replied with gratitude.[2] It does not appear, however, that the Society's services were ever utilized.

The Society's Annual Meeting for 1917 had already been arranged, and so it proceeded on schedule. In 1918, however, the Society's Committee on the Annual Meeting decided not to hold the regular Annual Meeting. Instead, there would be a meeting of the Executive Council to discuss the current situation and in particular to consider adopting a public statement on the status of international law.

It has been speculated that the criticism expressed at the 1917 Annual Meeting about James Brown Scott's coolness toward a "league for peace" may have been a factor in the decision to cancel the Annual Meetings for 1918 and

1 11 *ASIL Proc.* 25 (1917).

2 Letter from the Acting Judge Advocate General to James Brown Scott, July 2, 1917.

the following two years.[3] The reasons stated in 1918 by the Committee on the Annual Meeting (chaired by Scott) were that with the United States participating in a world war, "the existence of international law is at stake and ... discussions of its technical rules by the Society would probably not be commended by the members nor meet with any sympathetic response from the public."[4] Moreover, such a meeting "would divert attention from the main purpose of winning the war and ... [the meeting's] purpose might be misinterpreted should the discussion touch upon terms of peace before the war is won."[5] Scott himself said that a meeting "discussing things that seem to be so irrelevant, would really hold us up to ridicule."[6] Elihu Root concurred, and added that he had very little interest in discussing schemes to prevent future wars when no one could tell what the situation after the current war would be.[7] After the war was over, Root gave a somewhat different explanation: any discussions while the United States was at war would display so much heated feeling that they "would be without the authority which such discussions ought to have and do have when conducted impartially and without feeling."[8]

These justifications reveal a sense within the Society that what it said about international law mattered and would attract public attention; moreover, they reflect the then-prevailing view that international law was, or at least should be, a science in the sense that its rules and principles could (only) be ascertained through detached, objective examination. If detached examination was impossible under the circumstances, there was no reason to proceed.

To be sure, the justifications might have been used to mask Scott's personal discomfort either about being subjected to public criticism or about exposing

---

3 Hatsue Shinohara, "The Rise of a New International Law in America," 5 *Japanese J. Am. Studies* 85, 97 (1993-94).

4 Minutes of the Meeting of the Committee on Annual Meeting, Feb. 2, 1918, in 12 *ASIL Proc.* 65 (1918).

5 Minutes of the Meeting of the Committee on Annual Meeting, Feb. 16, 1918, in id. at 66.

6 Minutes of the Meeting of the Executive Council, Apr. 27, 1918, in id. at 5, 15-16. Scott may have been influenced by remarks like those made in a note to him in 1917 from a Minnesotan whom Scott, as Recording Secretary, had invited to join the Society. The note called the idea "absurd," and added, "There is no 'international law'. The whole thing has been scrapped." It went on to ridicule a Society that would "talk and maunder and rustle your papers over 'international law'." Letter from Ora J. Parker to Scott, Feb. 6, 1917.

7 12 *ASIL Proc.* 16 (1918).

8 Elihu Root, Opening Address, 15 *ASIL Proc.* 1 (1921). As Scott put it after the war, "we felt that it would be unwise to attempt scientific discussion when our minds and thoughts were on the war, to which we were then a party." Letter from Scott to Nicholas Murray Butler, Apr. 11, 1922.

divisions within the Society on how to keep the peace when the focus of America was on how to win a war. But they also (or instead) reflect a deep sense of disillusionment within the ASIL in 1918 about the relevance of international law as an instrument of peace anywhere in the world. Scott must have felt this disillusionment acutely, not only because of the war, but also because a judicial institution he had revered as a beacon for the attainment of justice through international law – the Central American Court of Justice – was on its last legs. The Court closed its doors on March 17, 1918, having decided only ten cases during its ten-year history.[9]

Both the disillusionment and a sense of the Society's importance can be discerned from the public statement the Executive Council issued when it met in April 1918. Gone was the Messianic urge simply to spread the word about international law, an urge that had manifested itself as recently as March 1917 when Root had heartily supported the idea of a conference for journalists in order to inculcate an appreciation of the subject in them.[10] Any such thoughts were replaced in 1918 by a somber reassessment of the place of international law in the world and in American policy. The April 1918 statement said in part:

> The Executive Council of the American Society of International Law considers that the very existence of international law is now at issue.
>
> The Committee on Annual Meeting has therefore refrained from calling the members of the Society from the active work on which most of them are engaged to meet for the discussion of questions of law. The only great question of international law today is whether that law shall continue to exist.
>
> Upon that subject the American Society of International Law reaffirms the clear and unvarying support of the United States for the rule of law, expressed in the recognition of international law in the Federal Constitution, in the decisions of its highest court and in the utterances of its Chief Magistrates and statesmen. [Quoting from Daniel Webster, Grover Cleveland and Woodrow Wilson, and noting that the diplomatic

9 See Scott's eulogy for the Court, The Closing of the Central American Court of Justice, 12 *AJIL* 380 (1918); Philippe Sands & Pierre Klein, *Bowett's Law of International Institutions* 350 (5th ed. 2001). When the Court was established a little more than ten years earlier, Scott had been euphoric: "To the powers of Europe, to the great powers of the world, who struggled with partial success, for four months at The Hague, to establish a court of arbitral justice, the young republics of Central America may recall the scriptural phrase: 'A little child shall lead them.' ... The past is indeed past, but the future is a future of hope and encouragement." James Brown Scott, "The Central American Peace Conference of 1907," in 2 *AJIL* 121, 143 (1908).

10 Letter from Root to James Brown Scott, Mar. 6, 1917. The conference was to be sponsored by the New York Academy of Political Science, which had asked the Society to participate.

> and consular services of all nations, as well as freedom of the high seas, depend on the protection of international law.]
>
> ...
>
> Therefore, those just and wise doctrines by which international relations are guided, humanized and controlled, can not be debilitated or abandoned. Therefore, they must be taught by our scholars, learned by our rising youth, declared and defined by our courts, announced by our Congress, enlarged by our treaties, and enforced by our Chief Executive.
>
> Therefore, at need, our army upon the land and our navy upon the sea, with a spirit and devotion which have never declined, must maintain and defend them, not for the good of this nation or this time alone, but for the good of all nations and all men, now and forevermore.[11]

The statement is revealing in a number of ways. It clearly reflects the view of international law that motivated the Society's founders at Lake Mohonk in 1905: international law was important primarily as a means of imposing a normative order on the interactions of nation states, and thus as a means of avoiding war. If it had failed in that mission, then of course "the very existence of international law [was] at issue." Moreover, international law was viewed not as a constantly developing normative order, but as a set of rules and dispute-settlement procedures that could be applied to peace-threatening situations, if only the rules and procedures could be inculcated in the public and in its representatives. This would serve not only American interests, but the interests of humanity worldwide.

The interests of humanity were not only consistent with American interests; they were in some sense dependent on lawful conduct by American armed forces against the forces of evil. It was American principles of proper conduct that counted. If Americans were true to their principles, others would eventually follow.

It seems to have been taken for granted that the American Society of International Law had the standing to "reaffirm" on behalf of the United States the importance of, and support for, the rule of law as the basis for international peace. This might suggest a touch of hubris. Nevertheless, with such an eminent statesman as Elihu Root placing his imprimatur on it, perhaps the identification of the Society's authority structure with that of the United States was not far from the mark.

---

11 Declaration by the Council upon the Subject of International Law, 12 *ASIL Proc.* 14-15 (1918). The full statement also appears in an Editorial Comment, 12 *AJIL* 338-40 (1918), and in George A. Finch, "The American Society of International Law 1906-1956," 50 *AJIL* 293, 306-07 (1956) (hereafter cited as Finch, "The ASIL 1906-1956").

2. The Society and the Post-War Ordering System

There was no Annual Meeting again in 1919. The Executive Council met on April 17, with Elihu Root leading a lengthy discussion on international law and the post-World War I peace settlement. Root, whom Woodrow Wilson had declined to include in the U.S. delegation to the Paris peace negotiations despite his obvious stature and expertise,[12] pointed out that the draft Covenant of the League of Nations mentioned international law only in the preamble. "Apparently," he said, "the whole Hague system [of recurring international peace conferences among nation states] was treated as scrapped."[13] Without these conferences, Root suggested, it would be difficult or impossible to know what the rules of international law were. Consequently Root had recommended to the American delegation at the Paris Peace Conference that the Covenant include a provision for a general conference of the powers to meet not less than two years or more than five years after the signing of the Covenant, "for the purpose of reviewing the condition of international law, and of agreeing upon and stating in authoritative form the principles and rules thereof."[14] After extensive discussion, the Executive Council adopted a resolution urging the Peace Conference to adopt Root's recommendation.[15]

Root had made another recommendation to the American delegation, looking toward a commitment by states to submit "justiciable" disputes to binding arbitration.[16] The definition of "justiciability" reflected a British proposal and foreshadowed the current definition in ICJ Statute Article 36(2). Professor John H. Latané proposed that the Society approve this recommendation, as well as the one on another Hague conference. Professor George Grafton Wilson demurred on the ground that there could be differences of opinion within the Society regarding justiciable disputes and binding arbitration, while there would be no such differences regarding the propriety of regular conferences for the codification and formulation of international law.[17] Professor Wilson prevailed within the Society, but the Peace Conference declined to call for a conference of the sort the Society recommended. The Peace Conference did, however, include in the League of Nations Covenant a provision calling for members to submit to arbitration or

---

12 See Mary Ellen O'Connell, "Elihu Root and Crisis Prevention," 95 *ASIL Proc.* 115, 116 (2001), and sources there cited.

13 13 *ASIL Proc.* 45 (1919).

14 Id. at 50, note 1. See also Root's exposition of his views in his letter to Will H. Hays, Mar. 29, 1919, printed in 13 *AJIL* 580 (1919).

15 13 *ASIL Proc.* 60, 63 (1919).

16 See Root's letter to Hays, *supra* note 14. See also Root's letter to Henry Cabot Lodge, June 19, 1919, printed in 13 *AJIL* 596 (1919).

17 13 *ASIL Proc.* at 57.

to enquiry by the League Council "if there should arise between them any dispute likely to lead to a rupture."[18] Thus the principal goal of the Society's founders was realized in principle, though not – as it turned out – in practice.

The contrasting approaches of Latané and Wilson provided an early example of the interplay that has occurred within the Society on several occasions when public policy issues have come up. In an organization that stands for promoting the establishment of international relations on the basis of law and justice,[19] there is inevitably an inclination to adopt positions affirming or reaffirming a need to conduct international affairs with reference to normative standards and to resolve international disputes peacefully. On the other hand, it was recognized in 1919, as it is today, that the Society represents its members, and not all members will agree on how to achieve the stated goals.

In 1919, as at some other times in the Society's history, the result was adoption of a position thought to be non-controversial by those few members participating in the decision-making body, and reticence toward positions that might spark dissent within the membership. But even the recommendation in favor of codification conferences may have been more controversial within the Society than those present at the April 1919 Executive Council meeting had thought. By 1919, some Society members, particularly academics with political science backgrounds, were less rule-oriented than were the leaders of the Society who comprised the Executive Council. These political scientists were more interested in the processes of international organization than in codifying rules of international law.[20] One of them, Albert Bushnell Hart, of Harvard, wrote to Scott in 1922 to say that "the programs might be made more human, might deal less with international law as it ought to be and more with the actual process and progress of international law as measured by international relations and agreements."[21] It is questionable whether members of such persuasion would have agreed with the resolution adopted by the Executive Council.

At first glance, it seems odd that no Annual Meeting was held in 1920. An April meeting would have occurred seventeen months after the World War I armistice

---

18 League of Nations Covenant Art. 12(1).

19 ASIL Constitution Art. II, as it existed in 1919. The current Constitution refers to the "establishment *and maintenance* of international relations on the basis of law and justice" (emphasis added).

20 See Shinohara, *supra* note 3, at 98-101, and see the remarks of Albert Bushnell Hart, Professor of Government at Harvard, 15 *ASIL Proc.* 130-31 (1921). See also 1 David Hunter Miller, *The Drafting of the Covenant* 380-81 (1928), dealing with Root's recommendation on codification. Miller was not a member of the Society in 1919, but by 1922 he was.

21 Letter from Albert Bushnell Hart to J.B. Scott, Mar. 28, 1922. Scott gave Hart an opportunity to speak at the 1922 annual banquet. Hart accepted, but was obliged to back out at the last minute for health reasons. Exchange of letters between Hart and Scott, Apr. 15, 17 and 26, 1922.

was signed. The reason given at the Executive Committee meeting of January 24, 1920, was that "the Society should not hold an annual meeting until after the Treaty of Peace with Germany had been disposed of, and it appeared doubtful to some of the members whether this event would take place by the time of the regular meeting date for the Society in April."[22] It was also mentioned that the Institute of International Law, under Root's presidency, had decided to hold its first post-war meeting in Washington in October 1920. The Executive Committee resolved that the Society should act as host for the Institute's meeting and should fix its own meeting for the same time.[23] The Institute later decided not to hold the meeting because of the failure of the United States to ratify the Versailles Treaty and the impending presidential election.[24] When the Executive Council met in November, the Society's Treasurer, Chandler Anderson, asked whether it had been settled that there would be no meeting that year. Oscar Straus, chairing the meeting, was brusque in reply: "If we settle that the next meeting is going to be in April, that will settle the question for this year, will it not?"[25]

The explanation seems clear. Root and those closely associated with him at the helm of the Society had an agenda for the next Annual Meeting, and it could not have been executed in the few remaining days of 1920. At Root's suggestion, the next meeting would focus on a recommendation of the Advisory Committee of Jurists to the effect that a new Hague Conference be held to restate the established rules of international law, to formulate new rules, to try to resolve disputes about existing rules, and to consider subjects not yet adequately regulated by international law.[26] Root himself was the author of the Advisory Committee's recommendation, which of course reflected his earlier recommendation to the American delegation at the Paris Peace Conference.[27] The ASIL had an institutional interest in the matter because it was actively engaged in the work of the American Institute of International Law and the Advisory Committee had recommended that the American Institute, among others, prepare projects for the work of the new Hague Conference.

The League of Nations Assembly had declined to adopt the Advisory Committee's recommendation. The Assembly's records suggest that the reason for rejecting the recommendation was a belief that international law was not yet

---

22 Minutes of the Meeting of the Executive Committee, Jan. 24, 1920, in 14 *ASIL Proc.* 36, 40 (1920).

23 Id.

24 11 *Y.B. Carnegie Endowment for International Peace* 158 (1922).

25 Minutes of the Meeting of the Executive Council, Nov. 13, 1920, in 14 *ASIL Proc.* 5, 24 (1920).

26 Id. at 15, 21-26.

27 See 15 *ASIL Proc.* 26 (1921); 10 *Y.B. Carnegie Endowment for International Peace* 131 (1921); and see text at note 14 *supra*.

ripe to be codified.[28] James Brown Scott was less charitable. He said that the Assembly "considered itself competent to do this work and was not willing to have a rival."[29] Root and Scott were not inclined to take "no" for an answer; hence the push to have the ASIL keep the matter alive.

The 1921 Annual Meeting went forward in April, in accordance with the Root-Scott plan. It was billed as a discussion of "the reconstruction of international law."[30] An *ad hoc* Committee for the Advancement of International Law, consisting of Root, Scott and George A. Finch, had been established to assist the Committee on the Annual Meeting in planning the program. The *ad hoc* Committee had four subcommittees, each concentrating on one of the four topics Root had brought home with him from the Advisory Committee of Jurists at The Hague.[31]

Root, as usual, gave an opening address at the 1921 Annual Meeting. He warned against the tyranny of "internationalism," by which he meant the exercise of international power or authority not based on law.[32] He stressed the need to promote the development of the law of nations through a system of conferences. His view of international law reflected the traditional view of Western statesmen of his time:

> The fundamental ideas of international law are, first, that each nation has a right to live according to its own conceptions of life; second, that each national right is subject to the equal identical right of every other nation. International law is the application of these principles through accepted rules of national action adapted to govern the conduct of nations toward each other in the contacts of modern civilization. Internationalism, by destroying the authority and responsibility of nations and the law which is designed to control their conduct toward each other, would destroy the most necessary bulwark of human liberty, the chief protection of the weak against the physical force of the strong,

---

28 Journal of the First Assembly of the League of Nations, Dec. 19, 1920, at 298-99, reprinted in 14 *ASIL Proc.* 85-86 (1920).

29 10 *Y.B. Carnegie Endowment for International Peace* 132 (1921). Scott added, "Time will again tell which body was the wiser, the jurists meeting at the Peace Palace at The Hague or the Assembly sitting at Geneva." There was little doubt about where Scott thought the wisdom lay.

30 ASIL Press Notice for release on Apr. 25, 1921.

31 Finch, "The ASIL 1906-1956," *supra* note 11, at 309; 15 *ASIL Proc.* vi-vii (1921).

32 Root was not the only prominent Society member to express such a view. See, e.g., David Jayne Hill, *Present Problems in Foreign Policy* (1919), arguing that the League of Nations represented an attempt to substitute collective power for law as the ordering mechanism in international affairs.

> and substitute the universal control which the nature of men will make an inevitable tyranny.[33]

Root did not differentiate nations from states, nor did he try to distinguish the effects of then-prevalent colonialism from the effects of "internationalism." Like others of his generation, he did not see international law as extending beyond the conduct of "nations" (states) toward each other. It is hard to fault him for failing to see that international law would eventually encompass such norms as the right of self-determination and the rights of individuals to basic protections against abuses of their own governments. That development occurred, of course, almost entirely after World War II.

James Brown Scott set the stage for the remainder of the 1921 Annual Meeting by arguing that governments would not submit to the new Permanent Court of International Justice unless they knew in advance what substantive rules the Court would apply. This required codification, and the only effective way to codify was by means of international conferences.[34] Other speakers focused on specific issues within the scope of one or another of the subcommittees' topics, and each subcommittee submitted a report. The most interesting of the reports was from Subcommittee Number 1, which was charged with restating established rules of international law, especially in fields affected by the recent war. The report – presented and apparently prepared by Charles Noble Gregory – asserted that the Regulations annexed to Hague Convention IV, on the laws and customs of war on land,[35] were (in 1921) already declaratory of existing international law. The report included the subcommittee's commentary to several of the Regulations.[36]

From November 1921 to February 1922, Elihu Root served as one of the four American delegates to the Conference on the Limitation of Armaments, held in Washington. Root presented a treaty setting forth rules of conduct for the use of submarines against merchant ships.[37] Root's statement to the Conference illustrated his regenerated faith in international law during wartime, at least to the extent that international law could reflect basic values and be clearly articulated. It also illustrated the importance that Root, Scott and other leaders

---

33 Elihu Root, Opening Address, 15 *ASIL Proc.* 1, 5 (1921).

34 James Brown Scott, "Advancement of International Law Essential to an International Court of Justice," 15 *ASIL Proc.* 21 (1921).

35 Hague Convention IV Respecting the Laws and Customs of War on Land, Annex, Oct. 18, 1907, 36 Stat. 2277, 1 Bevans 631, 2 *AJIL Supp.* 90 (1908).

36 15 *ASIL Proc.* 102, 105-15 (1921).

37 Treaty in Relation to the Use of Submarines and Noxious Gases in Warfare, Feb. 6, 1922, 16 *AJIL Supp.* 57 (1922). The treaty never entered into force.

of the ASIL placed on the role of an enlightened public as the ultimate, and perhaps only, guardians of international order in times of stress:

> We may grant that rules limiting the use of implements of warfare made between diplomatists will be violated in the stress of conflict. We may grant that the most solemn obligation assumed by governments in respect of the use of implements of war will be violated in the stress of conflict; but beyond diplomatists and beyond governments there rests the public opinion of the civilized world, and the public opinion of the world can punish. It can bring its sanction to the support of a prohibition with as terrible consequences as any criminal statute of Congress or of Parliament.
>
> We may grant that in matters which are complicated and difficult, where the facts are disputed and the argument is sophistic, public opinion may be confused and ineffective, yet when a rule of action, clear and simple, is based upon the fundamental ideas of humanity and right conduct, and the public opinion of the world has reached a decisive judgment upon it, that rule will be enforced by the greatest power known to human history, the power that is the hope of the world, will be a hope justified.[38]

About half of the 1922 Annual Meeting was devoted to consideration of reports made by the subcommittees of the Committee for the Advancement of International Law. Again, the report of Subcommittee Number 1 was particularly interesting. Among other things, it traced the customary rules of visit, search and capture at sea back to Articles 17 and 19 of the Treaty of the Pyrenees, a bilateral treaty concluded in 1659 between France and Spain.[39] Basing its conclusions on prize codes of maritime nations and instructions to naval commanders, circa 1922, the subcommittee set forth 12 propositions it considered ripe for codification.[40] The subcommittee's report went on to argue at some length that conduct during World War I, particularly attacks by German submarines on merchant vessels, did not change the traditional rules.

Within the ASIL, as the problems of the post-war world order began to replace the horrors of the conduct of the war in the minds of some members, there was some dissatisfaction with the Society's continuing focus on the law of war.

---

38 Presentation by Elihu Root, quoted in Report of the American Delegation to the Conference on the Limitation of Armament, Feb. 9, 1922, 16 *AJIL* 159, 189 (1922).

39 5 Clive Parry, *The Consolidated Treaty Series* 325 (1969).

40 16 *ASIL Proc.* 49, 53-54 (1922). The Society's files contain a long letter from Charles Burke Elliott, a member of the subcommittee, to David Jayne Hill, its Chair, setting forth Elliott's views, with citations, of the substance of the law of visit, search and capture. Letter from Elliott to Hill, Apr. 24, 1922. Elliott did not sign the subcommittee's report.

The displeasure was expressed at both the 1921 and 1922 Annual Meetings. In 1921, George W. Kirchwey, one of the Society's founders, asked the Chair of Subcommittee Number 4, Paul S. Reinsch, why no attention had been given to a league or association of nations, when public opinion would expect the Society to have some opinions on the subject. According to a news report of the meeting, this caused "an embarrassed silence."[41] Reinsch finally replied that it was too large a subject for the subcommittee.[42]

At the 1922 Annual Meeting, Charles G. Fenwick, Professor of Political Science at Bryn Mawr, questioned the subcommittees' exclusive focus on war. He raised the issue in a form that was destined to reappear in the Society's annals. Like Kirchwey in 1921, Fenwick in 1922 referred to the problem of international organization, but he did so with an eye not so much to an organization to preserve peace as to an organization to regulate both international commerce and the race to exploit raw materials.[43] The question, in other words, was whether the Society should devote its attention specifically to the law of war or whether it should move on to what Fenwick and some others, such as Jesse S. Reeves,[44] thought was a far more useful focus on the law of peace – particularly the law regulating economic affairs.

The Society responded by adopting an equivocal resolution:

> [I]t is the sense of this meeting that the Committee for the Advancement of International Law consider whether it is not within the purview of their plans to present to this Society, at some forthcoming meeting, the consideration of the feasibility of some international organization as a means of conducting the international relations of states.[45]

Another resolution was then adopted, inviting all Society members to express their views on subjects fit for consideration by the Committee for the Advancement of International Law.[46] The Committee, however, was not long for this world. Having grown to about 50 members in 1923, it was deemed too large and was disbanded. In its stead came a committee of five – the Committee on the Extension of International Law – to study and report on the existing condition, and the further extension, of the body of international law.[47]

---

41 *Wash. Post*, Apr. 30, 1921.

42 15 *ASIL Proc.* 124-25 (1921).

43 16 *ASIL Proc.* 85-87 (1922).

44 Jesse S. Reeves, "International Society and International Law," 15 *AJIL* 361, 374 (1921).

45 16 *ASIL Proc.* 92-93 (1922).

46 Id. at 96-97.

47 17 *ASIL Proc.* 136-37 (1923). The members were Jesse S. Reeves, Chair; Edwin M. Borchard, Charles G. Fenwick, Manley O. Hudson and Quincy Wright.

At the 1922 annual banquet the toastmaster was Harry Pratt Judson, the President of the University of Chicago. He made a lament that could just as well be heard in the early 21st century. He noted how few college students were studying international law. He deplored such a state of affairs:

> [I]t seems to me that intelligent young Americans ought to know the laws of nations in order to understand the relations which are coming to be so vital – the relations of one nation to another in this world. We have learned that no nation can live by itself alone; that the isolation of nations is gone. ... I do think we ought to teach in our schools and colleges of the higher grade at least, the subject of international law and international relations.[48]

Fenwick's mini-revolt against the Society's focus on the law of war had some effect. He was one of the speakers at the 1923 Annual Meeting, where he (as well as Manley O. Hudson) discussed issues relating to the international law of peace. Fenwick argued that the Society needed to study in detail such issues as how the international community could be more effectively organized in order to bring public opinion to bear on disputes before they got out of hand, and how new law-making techniques could be devised.[49] Hudson, then an Assistant Professor of Law at Harvard, argued the case for developing new international legislation.[50]

At the 1924 Annual Meeting, Fenwick was the first speaker on a topic widely regarded within the Society as one of overriding importance: the distinction between legal and political questions. The significance of the distinction was that political questions were not susceptible of decision by a tribunal, while legal questions were. The papers – by Fenwick, Edwin M. Borchard, Quincy Wright and Manley O. Hudson – presented divergent points of view about the practicality of the distinction and even about the nature of law and legal method.[51] A spirited discussion from the floor ensued. Some speakers thought the papers and the ensuing discussion were the high point of the Society's Annual Meetings to date.[52]

---

48 16 *ASIL Proc.* at 100-01 (1922).

49 Charles G. Fenwick, "An Outline of the Problems Presented in the Further Development of International Law," 17 *ASIL Proc.* 47 (1923).

50 Manley O. Hudson, "International Legislation," id. at 52.

51 Charles G. Fenwick, "The Distinction Between Legal and Political Questions," 18 *ASIL Proc.* 44 (1924); Edwin M. Borchard, "The Distinction Between Legal and Political Questions," id. at 50; Quincy Wright, "The Distinction Between Legal and Political Questions with Especial Reference to the Monroe Doctrine," id. at 57; Manley O. Hudson, "Legal and Political Questions," id. at 126.

52 Ellery Stowell, id. at 75; Philip Marshall Brown, id. at 77.

B. THE SOCIETY AND THE PERMANENT COURT

Article 14 of the League of Nations Covenant required the League Council to formulate and submit to the members plans for the establishment of a Permanent Court of International Justice. The League Council appointed Root to the Advisory Committee of Jurists that would do the preparatory work for the new Court.

Root attended the Advisory Committee's meeting at The Hague in the summer of 1920, with Scott as his technical adviser.[53] The Committee drafted a Statute for the Permanent Court – a Court sometimes known as "the Root Court," because of Root's significant role in devising and skillfully presenting a method of selecting judges by the League of Nations that would satisfy large and small states alike.[54] The method, retained in 1945 when the Statute of the International Court of Justice was prepared, gave a concurrent role to both the "elite" Council and the plenary Assembly. The two organs would vote separately; to be elected, a candidate would need a majority vote in each body. The procedure was modeled on the bicameral legislative process in the United States giving a separate but concurrent role to the Senate and the House of Representatives – a procedure also designed, of course, to satisfy large and small states alike. Scott was an important participant in the work of the Committee, and in fact edited the Committee's final draft of the Statute.[55]

The November 1920 meeting of the Society's Executive Council discussed not only the plan to revive the Hague Conferences, as mentioned earlier, but also the Statute of the new Permanent Court of Justice as proposed by the League of Nations Council to the League Assembly. The draft Statute, as proposed by the Advisory Committee of Jurists, had provided for compulsory jurisdiction for legal disputes between League members.[56] The League Council had turned that provision into one for compulsory jurisdiction between members only, pursuant to compromissory clauses in treaties to which they were parties. The Executive

---

53 Finch, "The ASIL 1906-1956," *supra* note 11, at 308.

54 The Minutes of the Executive Council Meeting of Nov. 13, 1920, include an interesting discussion by Root of the principal issues that had to be resolved in preparing the Statute of the P.C.I.J. – in particular, the method of selecting judges and the inclusion of *ad hoc* judges representing the parties. See 14 *ASIL Proc.* 5, 16-21 (1920). For a balanced examination of Root's role within the Advisory Committee, see Michael Dunne, *The United States and the World Court, 1920-1935*, Chapter 2 (1988) hereafter cited as Dunne). See also 2 Philip C. Jessup, *Elihu Root* 420-22 (1938) (hereafter cited as Jessup, *Elihu Root*); Antonio Sanchez de Bustamante, *The World Court* 126-27 (Elizabeth F. Read trans. 1925) (hereafter cited as Sanchez).

55 Manley O. Hudson, *The Permanent Court of International Justice* 107 (1934); Sanchez, *supra* note 54, at 20.

56 The Advisory Committee's draft Statute appears in 14 *AJIL Supp.* 371 (1920). The compulsory jurisdiction provision was in Article 34, id. at 378-79.

Council's discussion focused on this change.[57] Later, the League Assembly changed the jurisdictional provision to read very much along the lines now found in Article 36 (1), (2), (3) and (6) of the ICJ Statute, including – for the first time – the optional clause.

Although James Brown Scott had played an important role in drafting the compulsory jurisdiction provisions of the Advisory Committee of Jurists' proposed Statute, he ultimately regarded the adoption of the optional clause as "a happy compromise."[58] The 1920 *ASIL Proceedings* contain a useful comparative text of the Advisory Committee's draft, the League Council's changes and the version ultimately approved by the League Assembly.[59]

The November 1920 Executive Council meeting also featured a report by Elihu Root on the reason for including on the P.C.I.J. bench judges of the nationality of the parties before the Court. His report was perhaps the clearest public explanation ever given of what is now Article 31 of the ICJ Statute:

> [O]ne of the great obstacles to doing justice would be an inability to understand, an inability of the judge from one country to understand the people of another country and the origin of the litigation and the meaning and effect of what had been done. I think half the time of the meeting of the Committee was taken up by discussions which were caused solely by the fact that common law lawyers there could not understand what the continental lawyers were talking about, and that they could not understand what we were talking about. We all had different sets of ideas in our heads. So we concluded, in order that the court should understand the cases brought before it, that there ought to be one judge from each of the countries concerned. With a court of [then] eleven judges, the presence of those judges would have the effect of informing the court, not of affecting the determination of the litigation; and accordingly we provided that, if a country comes in with a case and has not a judge on the bench, and the country on the other side has a judge, the country that has not one shall name one to go on the bench, preferably from the judges of the old Court of Arbitration.[60]

---

57 Minutes of the Meeting of the Executive Council, Nov. 13, 1920, in 14 *ASIL Proc.* 5, 26-35 (1920).

58 James Brown Scott, Editorial Comment: "The Permanent Court of International Justice," 15 *AJIL* 260, 264 (1921). Scott attributed the League Assembly's rejection of obligatory jurisdiction for the Court primarily to the opposition of Great Britain and Japan. James Brown Scott, Editorial Comment: "The Institute of International Law," 16 id. 243, 247 (1922).

59 14 *ASIL Proc.* 43-76 (1920).

60 Id. at 20-21.

Once the Court's Statute had been approved and annexed to the Protocol of Signature of the Statute, the push began for U.S. participation in the Court by adherence to the Protocol. Manley O. Hudson and John Bassett Moore, the former a newly prominent member of the ASIL and the latter a member of the old guard, led the effort from outside the government. Elihu Root, no longer on the government payroll, worked quietly toward the same end until he was well into his eighties. From within the government, Charles Evans Hughes – newly a Vice President of the Society as well as the Secretary of State – sought to bring the United States into the Court.

It has been said regarding the P.C.I.J. that "[i]f indeed Elihu Root is seen as 'father of the Court', no-one has a greater claim than Manley Hudson to the title of benevolent guardian who struggled to win American recognition for the offspring."[61] Moore was working toward the same goal even while he was a member of the Court (having been nominated by the Italian members of the Permanent Court of Arbitration and elected with the first body of judges in 1921). Nevertheless, Moore was skeptical of Hudson's motives. He saw Hudson, who spent a good deal of time at the League of Nations headquarters in Geneva, as advocating U.S. participation in the Court not only on its own merits, but also as a step toward U.S. membership in the League. Moore's interest was simply in seeing that the United States participated in the Court; he feared that if participation in the Court became intertwined with entrance into the League, neither goal would be achieved.[62]

Charles Evans Hughes, speaking as the Secretary of State, used the occasion of the Society's 1923 Annual Meeting to give a major address setting forth his reasons why the United States should become a party to the Protocol of Signature.[63] Frederic R. Coudert moved that the Society approve the entrance of the United States into the Permanent Court. As had occurred on previous occasions, and as would occur again, it was pointed out that the Society's Constitution called for such policy-laden resolutions, in the discretion of the presiding officer or on the demand of three members, to be referred to a committee or to the Executive Council for a report before a vote could be taken.[64] The Meeting ultimately adopted a resolution calling on the Executive Council to ascertain the opinions of the

---

61 Dunne, *supra* note 54, at 66.

62 Id. at 70-71.

63 Charles Evans Hughes, "The Permanent Court of International Justice," 17 *ASIL Proc.* 75 (1923). James Brown Scott, in advance of Hughes' speech, called it "an historical event." Letter from Scott to Hughes, Mar. 29, 1923. The Washington press reported Hughes' speech. *Wash. Post* and *Wash. Eve. Star*, Apr. 28, 1923. The *Star* published the text of his speech.

64 17 *ASIL Proc.* 108 (1923). The relevant provision was in Article VII of the Society's Constitution as it then was. See id. at ix.

Society's members as to early entrance of the United States into the P.C.I.J., and to make a public statement as to their opinions.[65] It does not appear that a public statement was ever made.

Some indication of the Society's stature with the Washington press at that time – and of the newsworthiness of the Court issue – may be gleaned from the fact that both Washington dailies reported what had taken place at the Annual Meeting, inconclusive though it was.[66]

Manley Hudson continued to champion the Court, and began his remarkable string of annual articles on the World Court that ran in the *American Journal of International Law* from 1923 through 1959. In the early years, his enthusiasm for the Court found its way into these articles. For example, in 1925 he began:

> As the Permanent Court of International Justice completes the third year of its activities, its rôle in the international life of our time and the prospect for its cumulating contribution to international law begin to stand out more clearly. ... The year 1923 was such a busy one for the Court, and the satisfaction with its five advisory opinions and its judgment in the *Wimbledon* case was so general that lawyers began to foresee great activities in store for it, and foreign offices began to count its existence a factor in current international affairs.
>
> Its work during 1924 ... constitutes [a] new basis for the confidence of the legal profession in various countries, and builds new expectations of the court's serviceability in the peaceful settlement of international disputes.[67]

Hudson's enthusiasm and the efforts of others such as Moore and Root ultimately failed to persuade the Senate that the United States should participate unconditionally in the Court. In January 1926, the Senate voted for adherence to the Protocol of Signature to the Court's Statute, but attached five reservations. One of the reservations was intended to preclude the Court from issuing any advisory opinion "touching any dispute or question in which the United States has or claims an interest" unless the United States consented. The self-judging nature of this reservation became a point of contention with other states, as did the later Connally (domestic jurisdiction) Reservation to the U.S. declaration accepting the "compulsory jurisdiction" of the International Court of Justice[68] and the

---

65 Id. at 109.

66 *Wash. Post*, Apr. 29, 1923; *Wash. Eve. Star*, Apr. 29, 1923.

67 Manley O. Hudson, "The Third Year of the Permanent Court of International Justice," 19 *AJIL* 48 (1925).

68 61 Stat. 1218 (1946). Senator Connally argued that if the domestic jurisdiction reservation were not made self-judging, the I.C.J. might hold that questions relating to immigration,

still later U.S. decision not to become a party to the Statute of the International Criminal Court.[69]

Despite efforts by Root and others to find a compromise that would satisfy the U.S. Senate and be acceptable to states already participating in the Court, it all came to naught in the end. In January 1935 the Senate finally dealt the death blow to U.S. participation in the P.C.I.J., when the vote in favor of a somewhat modified resolution of adherence fell seven short of the requisite two-thirds.[70]

The Society's Annual Meetings dealt with this issue from time to time in the years leading up to 1935. Charles Evans Hughes, then the President of the Society, touched upon the subject in his opening addresses at the Annual Meetings in 1926 and 1927, and so did Irvine L. Lenroot, one of the speakers at the annual dinner in 1927.[71] At the 25th anniversary Annual Meeting in 1931, much of the program was devoted to the Permanent Court of International Justice. Manley Hudson was one of the speakers. He addressed the Court's independence from the League of Nations – an important issue in the debate about U.S. participation in the Court. He concluded that the Court was as independent from the League as the United States Supreme Court is from the political branches of the U.S. government. The American public, he thought, had failed to appreciate this fact, largely because it did not understand the League of Nations.[72]

At the Business Meeting in 1931, after Hudson had given his paper, John L. Harvey, a member who identified himself as interested in the Society's work but not an international lawyer, praised Hudson's paper and suggested that an effort be made through sympathetic United States Senators to have it printed in the Congressional Record.[73] James Brown Scott, then President of the Society, rather patronizingly reminded him that it was not the purpose of the Society to take positions on matters of that kind, but every effort would be made to give

---

tariffs and navigation of the Panama Canal were international rather than domestic. 92 *Cong. Rec.* 10695 (Aug. 2, 1946). Indeed it might have.

69 See Sean D. Murphy, "U.S. Notification of Intent Not to Become a Party to the Rome Statute," 96 *AJIL* 724 (2002); Curtis A. Bradley, "U.S. Announces Intent Not to Ratify International Criminal Court," *ASIL Insight*, May 2002, available at <www.asil.org>.

70 For an account of Root's efforts, see Jessup, *Elihu Root*, *supra* note 54, at 428-44. For a full account of the effort to obtain U.S. participation in the P.C.I.J., see Dunne, *supra* note 54, passim.

71 Charles Evans Hughes, "Some Observations on Recent Events," 20 *ASIL Proc.* 1, 11-12 (1926); Hughes, "Possible Gains," 21 *ASIL Proc.* 1, 14-16 (1927); Irvine L. Lenroot, Address [at the annual dinner], id. 139, 141-43.

72 Manley O. Hudson, "The Independence of the Permanent Court of International Justice," 25 *ASIL Proc.* 92, 100 (1931).

73 25 *ASIL Proc.* 189-92 (1931).

publicity to the Proceedings of the Society.[74] In light of the Society's steady interest in international adjudication – an interest long championed by Scott – one wonders why Scott shied away from publication of Hudson's paper in the Congressional Record. It could have provided a channel for informing important decision-makers and other interested persons about the Court, without having to commit the Society to any personal views Hudson expressed.

C. ADMINISTRATION OF THE SOCIETY IN THE WAKE OF WORLD WAR I

1. Male and Female

In 1920, the Executive Committee requested the Executive Council to reconsider its 1906 regulation limiting membership to men.[75] The timing, coinciding with an increase in the Journal's publication cost, suggests that pecuniary imperatives had a great deal to do with this change of heart. Nevertheless, one cannot rule out the likelihood that the leadership was beginning to recognize the non-pecuniary contributions women could make to the work of the Society. Nor can one rule out the influence of James Brown Scott, who had long been sympathetic to the women's rights movement. In a 1938 lecture Scott said, "When I was a young man, I could not understand why it was that the men were treated in a different way from women, and the passing years have not supplied me with an answer to that question. ... I could not see then and I cannot see now any reason why women should not have the rights of men."[76]

Whatever the motivation, the Executive Council unanimously amended the 1906 regulation in November 1920, changing the word "man" to "person."[77] From 1921 on, the Society's rolls have shown gradually increasing numbers of female members. A woman was first elected to the Executive Council – and to the Executive Committee as well – in 1923. She was Judge Kathryn Sellers, a judge of the Juvenile Court in the District of Columbia, who had at one time been the librarian of the State Department and then librarian of the Carnegie

74 Id. at 192.

75 14 *ASIL Proc.* 41 (1920).

76 Quoted in Ralph D. Nurnberger, "James Brown Scott: Peace Through Justice" 25 (Ph.D. dissertation, Georgetown University, 1975) (hereafter cited as Nurnberger dissertation). See also James Brown Scott, Editorial Comment: "Inter-American Commission of Women," 24 *AJIL* 757 (1930).

77 Minutes of the Meeting of the Executive Council, Nov. 13, 1920, in 14 *ASIL Proc.* 5, 13 (1920).

Endowment.[78] Even before she was eligible to be a member of the Society, she had edited two departments of the Journal: the Chronicle of International Events and the compilation of Periodical Literature of International Law.

Of course, new members during this period included men, some of whom would rise to prominence in a Society that still did not look to women for individual leadership. The Society's files contain a letter of application for membership in 1917 from a young law professor at the University of Missouri who felt that he needed to identify himself. He said, "I am professor of law here, and have done some work in both public and private International Law." It was signed, Manley O. Hudson.[79] Hudson went on to become Bemis Professor of International Law at Harvard, Director of the Harvard Research in International Law, judge of the Permanent Court of International Justice, and President of the ASIL. The Society's Hudson Medal, for distinguished contributions in international law, was established in his honor in 1956.

2. Seeking Turnover in the Executive Council's Membership

In 1921, the Executive Council thought it was time to assure some turnover in the Council's membership. As James Brown Scott described it, the Council decided on its own accord that "hereafter no member of the Executive Council shall be eligible for re-election until a year after the expiration of the term of office for which he had been elected."[80] To do it properly, though, an amendment to the Society's Constitution would be necessary.

When the Constitution was amended a year later, the amendment provided, "No *elected* member of the Executive Council shall be eligible for re-election until the next annual meeting after that at which his term of office expires."[81] The 24 elected members of the Council served three-year terms. But since the officers of the Society – the President, Honorary President, Vice Presidents, Recording Secretary, Corresponding Secretary and Treasurer – were *ex officio* rather than elected members of the Executive Council (though they were elected to their offices),[82] they were exempt from the new one-year hiatus rule. Moreover, since the Constitution required that there be nine or more Vice Presidents (there were 18 in 1922), and since the Vice Presidents were highly influential people both

---

78 17 *ASIL Proc.* v, vi, 109, 156 (1923). Her work as a librarian is mentioned in a letter from George A. Finch to I.V. Gillis, Feb. 1, 1939.

79 Handwritten letter from Manley O. Hudson, Oct. 3, 1917.

80 15 *ASIL Proc.* 129 (1921).

81 Amendment to Article IV of the ASIL Constitution, 16 *ASIL Proc.* xi (1922)(emphasis added).

82 The Recording Secretary, Corresponding Secretary and Treasurer were elected by the Executive Council. The President, Honorary President and Vice Presidents were elected by the Society. ASIL Constitution, Art. IV, 16 *ASIL Proc.* xi (1922).

within and outside of the Society, the real power structure of the Society was protected from enforced turnover.[83]

Nevertheless, the newcomers could and did wield some influence by voting together. In fact, they engineered a striking change in the composition of the Board of Editors of the Journal in 1924. More about this in due course.[84]

As we have seen, the first woman, Kathryn Sellers, was elected to the Executive Council in 1923. In every year since, except from 1926-1932 and 1964-1965, at least one woman has been a member of the Executive Council.[85]

3. Improving the Executive Council's Performance

By 1923 the Society had grown, both in numbers of members and in scope of activities, to the point at which the governing body could not adequately perform its role by meeting only in April of each year. Thus it was decided for the first time to provide for Executive Council meetings in the intervals between Annual Meetings.[86] The practice took hold, and has remained in effect.

4. Helping Out the League of Nations Treaty Series

In 1923, Manley Hudson, by then a fixture in the Society, was attempting to ensure that the League of Nations could continue to publish its Treaty Series with translations into French and English when the original treaty was in another language. He contacted James Brown Scott, who got in touch with John D. Rockefeller, Jr. on the matter. Scott said that if the Laura Spelman Rockefeller Memorial would order 403 subscriptions to the Treaty Series, and if the ASIL would undertake to place the volumes in leading libraries that did not already subscribe, it would enable the League Secretariat to continue publication.[87] The

---

83 In 1922, the list of Vice Presidents included such names as William R. Day, Charles Noble Gregory, Charles Evans Hughes, Robert Lansing, Henry Cabot Lodge, John Bassett Moore, Oscar S. Straus, William Howard Taft, George Grafton Wilson and Theodore S. Woolsey. The President was still Elihu Root.

84 See text at note 100 *infra*.

85 See Alona E. Evans and Carol Per Lee Plumb, Notes and Comments: "Women and the American Society of International Law," 68 *AJIL* 290, 294 (1974), for the experience until 1974. Women have continued to be members of the Council in each year since 1974.

86 17 *ASIL Proc.* 137 (1923).

87 Letter from Scott to Rockefeller, May 2, 1923.

Board of Trustees of the Rockefeller Memorial appropriated USD 7,500 to the Society for this purpose.[88] The grant was renewed in 1924.[89]

The project proved to be an administrative burden for George Finch, whose job was to designate the recipient libraries and to keep the list current. Misunderstandings arose between Finch and the World Peace Foundation, which served as an intermediary between the Society and the League of Nations secretariat in Geneva. Finch at one point became so frustrated that he said he wished the Society had never undertaken the "thankless task."[90] Nevertheless, the project seems to have given the League of Nations Treaty Series the boost it needed. The Series continued, with the necessary translations, and made it all the way to the demise of the League more than 20 years later.

D. THE JOURNAL AND ITS EDITORS IN THE WAKE OF WORLD WAR I

1. The Journal's Focus in the Wake of World War I

The 1919 volume of the Journal dealt extensively with issues arising from World War I, including those surrounding the Paris Peace Conference. As in earlier years, the contributions were mostly descriptive of state practice rather than theoretical. But the 1919 volume also included some work of a rather different stripe. Quincy Wright, a political scientist, wrote on the constitutionality of treaties, setting forth a taxonomy of constitutional limitations on the treaty-making power: limitations based on the division of power between national and state governments; those based on individual rights; and those based on separation of powers.[91] His article antedated by just one year the Supreme Court's decision in *Missouri v. Holland*,[92] the case that would dominate the constitutional debate on the subject for years thereafter.

A noteworthy inclusion in the 1920 volume of the Journal was the Report of the Commission on the Responsibility of the Authors of the War and on Enforcement of Penalties, presented in March 1919 to the Preliminary Peace

---

88 Letter from Beardsley Ruml, Director of the Rockefeller Memorial, to Scott, May 9, 1923.

89 Letter from Ruml to Scott, Apr. 14, 1924.

90 Letter from Finch to Allen, Jan. 23, 1924. On the same day, Finch wrote to Manley Hudson, seeking to extricate the Society from the project. At Hudson's urging, Finch relented. Letter from Hudson to Finch, Feb. 2, 1924; Finch to Hudson, Feb. 14, 1924.

91 Quincy Wright, "The Constitutionality of Treaties," 13 *AJIL* 242 (1919). Wright's work at that time was frequently concerned with aspects of treaty law.

92 252 U.S. 416 (1920).

Conference.[93] The American members of the Commission were prominent members of the ASIL: Robert Lansing, who chaired the Commission, and James Brown Scott. They dissented from some of the Commission's key recommendations. The Commission recommended, *inter alia*, that an international criminal tribunal be established to try "all enemy persons alleged to have been guilty of offences against the laws and customs of war and the laws of humanity," including even heads of state. Lansing and Scott thought that any war crimes trials should be conducted by existing national military tribunals sitting individually or jointly, rather than by taking the unprecedented step of creating an international tribunal to try offenses already committed. They also objected to inclusion of "the laws of humanity" as a standard of conduct, on the ground that the concept was too vague, and they thought that heads of state could not be subjected to external judgment without eviscerating the concept of sovereignty.[94]

Journal articles in the early 1920s ranged widely in scope and content. A few were highly speculative, such as a surprising article by Lansing, the pragmatic statesman, supporting the idea of world law administered by a world sovereign.[95] Some articles were theoretical.[96] Some addressed enduring issues of the foreign relations law of the United States.[97] But most of the lead articles then, as in other years, dealt with the legal aspects of current events or focused on legal institutions. For example, the first of Manley Hudson's long string of annual articles on the World Court appeared in the Journal in 1923.[98]

The Journal's Supplements during this period weighed in with reprints of peace treaties, documents relating to the new Permanent Court of International Justice, and League of Nations mandates. These documents, now primarily of historical interest, may be found elsewhere as well. Nevertheless, for a researcher interested in the documentary record of the new world order after the Great War, the AJIL Supplements of the period provide a convenient yet easily overlooked source.

---

93 14 *AJIL* 95 (1920), reprinted from Carnegie Endowment for International Peace, Division of International Law, Pamphlet No. 32.

94 The "Memorandum of Reservations" presented by Lansing and Scott appears in 14 *AJIL* 127 (1920).

95 Robert Lansing, "Notes on World Sovereignty," 15 *AJIL* 13 (1921). Lansing's manuscript was actually written in 1906, but was not published then because it seemed "too speculative"; by 1921 it seemed "less academic and more pertinent to present day philosophic thought." Id.

96 See, e.g., Gordon E. Sherman, "The Nature and Sources of International Law," 15 *AJIL* 349 (1921).

97 E.g., Quincy Wright, "International Law in its Relation to Constitutional Law," 17 *AJIL* 234 (1923).

98 Manley O. Hudson, "The First Year of the Permanent Court of International Justice," 17 *AJIL* 15 (1923).

2. Authors and Editors

Authors included diplomats, military officers, international officials and practitioners, as well as academics. Among the academics were an impressive number of political scientists who made their reputations in the international law arena. These included James W. Garner, of the University of Illinois, Amos S. Hershey, of Indiana University, Pitman B. Potter, then of the University of Wisconsin, Jesse S. Reeves, of the University of Michigan, and Quincy Wright, then of the University of Minnesota.[99] Perhaps the competition among these prominent midwestern state universities was not limited to the football field.

Midwesterners did not, however, corner the market in political scientists significantly involved in the work of the Journal. George Grafton Wilson, first of Brown and then of Harvard, was one of the original Board members and became Editor-in-Chief in 1924; Philip Marshall Brown, of Princeton, had been a member of the Journal's Board of Editors since 1916; Charles G. Fenwick, of Bryn Mawr, was elected to the Board in 1924.

There was unprecedented turnover in the composition of the Board of Editors in 1924, apparently as an outgrowth of the decision made in 1921 to seek turnover in the Executive Council. With the influx of new Executive Council members came dissatisfaction with the dominance of the old guard in the Board of Editors. It was the first recorded example of tension between the Executive Council and the Board of Editors. As George Finch put it in 1924 in a letter to one of the editors who had not been re-elected, "[A]t the Council meeting which took place on April 26, a large number of younger members of the Council were present and they decided to retire from the Board of Editors a number of the older members, including yourself, and replace them with younger members."[100] Clearly, the older members had not anticipated retirement just yet.

The revolution, though, was not universal. George Grafton Wilson, a member of the old guard, succeeded James Brown Scott as Editor-in-Chief in April 1924. He, too, was taken by surprise and initially asked for time to consider whether he really wanted to undertake the responsibility.[101] Ultimately, he accepted. Scott was named Honorary Editor-in-Chief.[102]

---

99 On the rising prominence of political scientists in the international law arena during this period, see Shinohara, *supra* note 3, at 98-101 (focusing on Garner and Wright).

100 Letter from Finch to Theodore S. Woolsey, May 20, 1924.

101 Letter from Wilson to Finch, May 25, 1924.

102 For other changes in Board membership during this period, see Memorandum, "ASIL History: The Journal, Its Editors and Business Practices," on file with the Society.

3. Editorial Comments and Editorial Policy

Editorial Comments in the post-World War I era covered virtually all events and issues of interest to American international lawyers. They were brief – often just two or three pages in print, though they began to expand by 1923. Because there were so many of them, they provide a useful chronicle, with brief analyses, of the issues of the time.

Some of the issues have refused to go away. For example, the 1919 volume ran an Editorial Comment by Theodore S. Woolsey on self-determination. It was a topic that would reappear in the Journal's pages over the years, transforming itself from a concern for national minorities within new or existing states (Woolsey's focus) to a principle underlying decolonization and democratization, and then full circle to the rights of national groups. Woolsey was skeptical about self-determination as a formula for peace. His rhetorical question might as well have been asked in the post-Cold War era: "Does the multiplication of small political units make for peace and stability?"[103]

An issue that had troubled the Journal's Board of Editors since at least 1915 was whether Editorial Comments should be signed or not. In 1915, they were unsigned. In November of that year John Bassett Moore wrote to James Brown Scott, the Editor-in-Chief of the Journal, complaining that a British judge in a prize case had ascribed to the Board of Editors, including Moore and Scott by name, an assertion in an Editorial Comment about the likely development of the law of conditional contraband. Scott had written the Comment in question.[104] Moore was of the opinion that expressions of opinion on legal issues should not be published in the Journal unless the author was identified.[105]

Scott wrote back to say that the policy had been to leave Editorial Comments unsigned because to do otherwise would reveal that only one author (Scott) was writing most of them. In addition, he had occasionally received editorials from persons who, he said, would have been unwilling to furnish them if they were signed.[106] Moore's riposte was that the latter point showed conclusively that opinions should be signed.[107]

---

[103] Theodore S. Woolsey, Editorial Comment: "Self-Determination," 13 *AJIL* 302, 304 (1919). Woolsey answered his own question: "On the contrary, it makes for instability and invites aggression, since defensive power is lacking." Id.

[104] For the British judge's statement and Scott's published response revealing Scott as the author of the Comment on conditional contraband, see James Brown Scott, Editorial Comment: "The Quotation from the Journal in the Decision of the British Prize Court in the Chicago Meat Packers' Cases," 9 *AJIL* 913 (1915).

[105] Letter from James Bassett Moore to James Brown Scott, Nov. 9, 1915.

[106] Letter from Scott to Moore, Nov. 10, 1915.

[107] Letter from Moore to Scott, Nov. 11, 1915.

The Board of Editors changed the policy at its December 1915 meeting. From 1916 through 1920, all Editorial Comments were signed. Scott continued to write more of them than did any other Board member, and in the October 1920 issue he contributed them all. This experience led him to complain to the Society's Executive Council in November 1920 about the difficulty of inducing other members of the Board to contribute Comments (a difficulty not confined to Scott's tenure as Editor-in-Chief, as later experience would attest). Scott told the Executive Council that it was humiliating to have to sign each Editorial Comment, thus publicly disclosing a lack of cooperation by members of the Board of Editors. He suggested modifying the rule requiring Editorial Comments to be signed. The Executive Council decided that Comments could be unsigned, provided that they were approved by two Board members other than the author.[108]

Scott's complaint seems to have galvanized the Board of Editors into sharing the burdens of writing Editorial Comments. The ratio of Comments written by Scott to those written by the rest of the Board declined noticeably in the years after 1920. In 1924, the Executive Council approved a set of regulations for the editing of the Journal, including one requiring that Editorial Comments once again be signed.[109]

Other controversies over Editorial Comments arose occasionally. For example, a Comment by Charles Noble Gregory in 1923 discussing the Permanent Court's Advisory Opinion on Nationality Decrees Issued in Tunis and Morocco[110] forecast that the Court would register essentially European views no matter whose rights or interests might be at stake, and worried that the judges might be hostile to the interests and views of the United States.[111] This prompted "a very responsible European correspondent" to write Manley O. Hudson objecting to the tone and some of the content of Gregory's Comment. Hudson, then a Harvard Professor but not yet a member of the Board of Editors, thought that the presentation of another view might be in order. He offered to submit a short note on the subject.[112] George Finch, the Secretary of the Board, replied by saying that the Journal did not enter into controversies of this sort except to correct factual errors.[113]

108 14 *ASIL Proc.* 11 (1921).

109 18 *ASIL Proc.* 190, 191 (1924).

110 P.C.I.J., Ser. B, No. 4 (1923).

111 Charles Noble Gregory, Editorial Comment: "An Important Decision by the Permanent Court of International Justice," 17 *AJIL* 298, 305-06 (1923).

112 Letter from Manley O. Hudson to James Brown Scott, June 5, 1923.

113 Letter from George A. Finch to Hudson, June 12, 1923.

Hudson had the last word. In the second of his annual essays on the World Court, he included a paragraph critical of Gregory's Editorial Comment.[114] A few months later, Hudson was elected to the Board of Editors.

Apparently there was concern in some quarters that Scott, who maintained his close ties to the State Department during his years as Editor-in-Chief, may have been too eager to preserve the Society's cordial relationship with the Department.[115] Not only was Scott close to the Department, but so were several other prominent Society members whose views Scott could not have ignored.[116] The concern is illustrated by a letter Theodore S. Woolsey wrote in 1919 to Charles Noble Gregory. The letter referred to an article Woolsey had written that was critical of the Woodrow Wilson administration.[117] Woolsey said he had always stood for freedom of speech, while Scott was leery of offending the State Department and losing its patronage.[118] Gregory replied that he had spoken with Finch, Scott's closest associate, who thought the Journal was "quite free in the matter of signed articles."[119]

Woolsey's skepticism about Scott's State Department ties may have stemmed, in part, from an earlier exchange he had with Chandler P. Anderson and Charles Gregory, who were serving as temporary Editors-in-Chief during Scott's absence at the Paris Peace Conference. Anderson and Gregory concluded in 1918 that they should not publish any articles relating to controversial questions that

---

114 Manley O. Hudson, "The Second Year of the Permanent Court of International Justice," 18 *AJIL* 1, 6 (1924).

115 Even after Scott had left his position as Solicitor of the State Department, he remained close to it both physically, from his office at 2 Jackson Place, and professionally. At the outset of World War I, Secretary of State William Jennings Bryan appointed Scott as Special Advisor to the State Department, a post he held until May 1917. Beginning in 1917 the Carnegie Endowment's Division of International Law, which Scott headed, engaged in projects for the State Department that were "of so confidential a nature that they cannot be reported upon in detail." International Conciliation No. 200, July 1924, at 223-24. In early 1918, then-Major Scott of the Judge Advocate Corps was detailed to the State Department for special research. In December 1918 he left Washington with President Wilson to serve as one of two American technical legal delegates to the Paris Peace Conference. See Nurnberger dissertation, *supra* note 76, at 239-40, 254, 255, 256-70.

116 Elihu Root, Robert Lansing and Charles Evans Hughes all served as Secretaries of State. Chandler P. Anderson, Charles Cheney Hyde, John Bassett Moore, Fred K. Nielsen and Lester H. Woolsey all served in the State Department. See 18 *ASIL Proc.* 155 (1924).

117 The article was apparently Theodore S. Woolsey, "Reconstruction and International Law," 13 *AJIL* 187 (1919), in which Woolsey described Wilson as the "apostle" of a league of nations based on the soft foundation of friendship. Id. at 199-202.

118 Letter from Woolsey to Gregory, Apr. 1, 1919.

119 Letter from Gregory to Woolsey, Apr. 8, 1919.

would come up at the Peace Conference.[120] Their reticence presumably reflected a desire shared with Scott to refrain from saying anything in print that might have to be explained by the U.S. representatives in Paris.

* * *

The Book Review department of the Journal engendered occasional controversy in the early 1920s, as it had in some earlier years. In 1924, Jackson H. Ralston, who in 1911 had complained about the Journal's review of his *International Arbitral Law and Procedure*, wrote an adverse review of Charles Fenwick's *International Law*.[121] Ralston criticized Fenwick's book for discussing the law of war without taking a strong stand against the lawfulness of war itself.[122] This elicited an anguished letter from Fenwick to George Finch, who had sent the book to Ralston for review at Ralston's request. In the letter Fenwick defended his scientific treatment of the law of war and requested space in the Journal for a reply.[123] Finch noted in response that the Journal's policy had been not to print replies of authors to adverse reviews.[124]

The Journal's Board of Editors apparently had not addressed the most significant policy question raised by this incident. The question was, and still is, whether it is appropriate to assign a book for review to someone who asks to review it. The risk is that the reviewer in such cases may have a hidden agenda, which could be either adverse or favorable to the book or its author. Whether Ralston had a hidden agenda does not appear. Fenwick thought Ralston did have an agenda, though not necessarily a hidden one. In any event, Book Review editors in more recent years have recognized the policy question. They have shied away from sending a book to be reviewed by someone who might be less than objective and who volunteers, without prodding, to write the review.

4. Referees

The Journal's practice of having two members of the Board of Editors read manuscripts to assess their publishability was made formal in the 1924 set of regulations.[125] Then as now, the rule applied only to lead articles. Under the new regulations, Editorial Comments did not have to be refereed.

The referees at that time were not necessarily anonymous to the authors. In one letter to an author, Scott revealed that Robert Lansing, of the Board of

---

[120] Letter from Anderson to Woolsey, Dec. 14, 1918.

[121] Charles G. Fenwick, *International Law* (1924).

[122] Jackson H. Ralston, Book Review, 18 *AJIL* 853 (1924).

[123] Letter from Fenwick to Finch, Nov. 12, 1924.

[124] Letter from Finch to Fenwick, Nov. 14, 1924.

[125] 18 *ASIL Proc.* 190 (1924).

Editors, had criticized the author's manuscript; Scott enclosed Lansing's letter containing the criticisms.[126] On other occasions, though, Scott withheld the names of Board critics.[127]

5. Soliciting Manuscripts

By the end of World War I, the Journal had achieved sufficient stature to attract unsolicited manuscripts. Nevertheless, Scott and his assistant, George Finch, continued the earlier practice – born of necessity when the Journal was getting off the ground – of soliciting some manuscripts from potential authors, particularly those residing abroad.[128] George Grafton Wilson, when he became Editor-in-Chief, continued the practice.[129]

Editors-in-Chief of the Journal have always solicited articles from Board members, but there has been controversy about whether they should be solicited from others – especially from scholars abroad. The concern has been that if an article were solicited, submitted and then rejected, there would be hurt feelings and misunderstandings. The misunderstandings might be acute in the case of foreign scholars who are not accustomed either to the Journal's system of peer review or to having their work turned down. Consequently, in recent years the Board of Editors has tended to tread more lightly than Scott and Finch did in soliciting manuscripts from abroad.

E. THE END OF AN ERA

Elihu Root did not attend the Annual Meeting in 1924. He was ill and was recuperating in San Francisco. James Brown Scott informed the Executive Council that Root felt he could no longer serve as President of the Society. Accordingly, Scott laid Root's resignation before the Council. It was reluctantly accepted. Root was elected Honorary President, and Charles Evans Hughes became the second President of the Society. Like his predecessor, he was the Secretary of State when he took the highest office in the Society. He seems to have been selected because – again like his predecessor – he brought both personal stature and knowledge of international affairs to the position.[130]

---

126 Letter from Scott to Baron S.A. Korff, Feb. 12, 1923.

127 E.g., letter from Scott to George A. King, Jan. 9, 1923.

128 For example, in 1919 Finch invited R.F. Roxburgh, of London, to submit an article on sanctions in international law. This appears in an exchange of letters between James W. Garner and Finch, Sept. 12 & Sept. 18, 1919.

129 Letter from Wilson to B.C.J. Loder (President of the P.C.I.J.), Aug. 6, 1924.

130 Such is the import of a letter from James Brown Scott to Charles G. Fenwick, Mar. 3, 1924.

A committee consisting of Scott, Philip Marshall Brown and Charles Henry Butler drafted a telegram, which was sent to Root in the Society's name. The telegram accepted his resignation and expressed gratitude for his 18 years of service to the Society and to the cause of international law. It had been "an inestimable privilege," the telegram said, to hear his annual presidential addresses, which had "laid the foundation of the newer and progressive Law of Nations."[131]

James Brown Scott, who knew earlier in 1924 that Root was going to resign, seized the opportunity to try to raise funds for a capital endowment in Root's name. He wrote to George W. Wickersham, senior partner in the New York law firm of Cadwalader, Wickersham & Taft and the person whom Root had successfully put forward as the first President of the American Law Institute, seeking Wickersham's support and asking him to get in touch with Root's friends. Wickersham's reply was noncommittal.[132] The project never got off the ground.

Scott took the occasion of Root's resignation as President to relinquish not only his own position as Editor-in-Chief of the Journal, but also his duties as Recording Secretary of the Society. Like Root, he had been the only occupant of the post he was relinquishing. Unlike Root, he had been actively involved in running the Society on a day-to-day basis. In fact, he had been the dominant force in the administration of the Society since its inception. As the Society's memorial to him put it:

> Dr. Scott was not merely one of the founders of the Society, but the one upon whom the chief burden fell in executing the plan and in carrying it forward to success. He brought to the Society from the beginning, and has continued to evidence throughout, a genius for organization, high scholarly ideals and an untiring industry without which the Society could not have been the force that it now is in the study of international law and in the establishment of better international relations on the basis of law and justice.[133]

Scott became Honorary Editor-in-Chief of the Journal and a Vice President of the Society. He was also elected a member of the Executive Committee, but he declined to serve in order to make room at the top for younger members.[134] He

---

131 Western Union Telegram to Honorable Elihu Root, Apr. 26, 1924. A slightly different version of the text appears in 18 *ASIL Proc.* 147 (1924). At the 1924 Annual Meeting, James Brown Scott read out a long tribute to Root, including excerpts from Root's many annual addresses. Id. at 2-41.

132 Letter from Scott to Wickersham, Mar. 31, 1924; Wickersham's one-sentence reply, Apr. 2, 1924.

133 18 *ASIL Proc.* 148 (1924).

134 Letter from Scott to George A. Finch, May 7, 1924.

was to return to the top five years later; in 1929 he would succeed Hughes as President of the Society.

Meanwhile, Scott's position as Recording Secretary was filled in 1924 by his long-standing colleague, George A. Finch. Finch was a native Washingtonian with whom Scott had worked since 1906, when Finch became Scott's assistant in the State Department Solicitor's office. When Scott moved to the Carnegie Endowment, Finch followed him and became the Assistant Secretary of the Endowment in 1912.[135]

By 1924, the Society's view of its mission had evolved from its 1906 origin. It was still concerned with educating the public about international law, but the Great War had dampened its conviction that international law and arbitral tribunals could save the world from the horrors of armed conflict. International law was now regarded as a means of achieving international justice, though the meaning of that concept was fuzzy at best.

Important as public education still was, the Society's scholarly side was by now ascendant. The Journal was solidly established as a scholarly organ, and the professoriate had begun to supply most of the ideas that fueled discussions at the Annual Meetings. Charles Evans Hughes, acting as Toastmaster at the 1924 annual dinner, could properly refer to the Society as one of the "learned societies."[136]

135 Interview with Eleanor H. Finch, May 16, 1994.

136 18 *ASIL Proc.* 157 (1924).

Chapter Three

LOOKING FORWARD IN THE TWENTIES

... I do not conceive of law in terms of definite and positive rules. There are such rules, of course, and in certain branches of the law they serve very useful ends... . But how little of public law, and particularly of the law of nations, is susceptible of such formulation! Rather it is principles and standards to which we resort, and, unless I misconceive the facts of our juristic history, which have furnished the basis of international practice in the past. For the law of nations, like municipal law, is not at any time a fixed body either of doctrines or of commands. It is always a process, a method of dealing with competitions of interest...

—Manley O. Hudson
"Contemporary Development of International Law,"
Proceedings of the Second Conference of Teachers, 85
(Carnegie Endowment for International Peace, 1926)

A. THE CHANGING SCENE IN THE SOCIETY

1. Hughes and Finch in Place of Root and Scott

Charles Fenwick, already a prominent Society member in the twenties, had opposed Charles Evans Hughes' selection as President of the Society in 1924. Fenwick thought that the Society would simply be making a political appointment. He said that if Hughes were selected, it should be for one year only.[1] After Hughes was selected, Fenwick did not relent. In 1925, he opposed Hughes' re-election. George Finch replied that Hughes had not been selected simply because he was the Secretary of State, but rather because of his accomplishments and qualifications for the office. Finch reported very strong sentiment within the Society in favor of Hughes' re-election, noting that Hughes had been an active President during his first year in office.[2]

According to Finch, the Society had been invigorated by the interest and active cooperation of Hughes. Indeed, Hughes seems to have taken his duties as President quite seriously, both during the remainder of his tenure as Secretary

1 Letter from Charles G. Fenwick to James Brown Scott, Feb. 16, 1924.

2 Letter from George A. Finch to Charles G. Fenwick, Apr. 8, 1925.

of State and thereafter. Like Root, he left the actual administration of the Society to the Recording Secretary, but he diligently performed such tasks as appointing committee members, contacting dignitaries on behalf of the Society, delivering the presidential address at Annual Meetings, and serving as toastmaster at annual dinners.

By 1927, Hughes was ready to turn the office over to someone else. He wrote to Finch just before the 1927 Annual Meeting to say that it was "time for someone else to take the chair."[3] Finch wrote back that such a suggestion would "cause consternation among the officers and members." He praised Hughes' three years in office, and stressed the need for a person with prestige to be in the Presidency. Finch's view was conservative:

> There is no one with the international standing and prestige necessary to carry on the work comparable to yourself. The Presidency of the American Society of International Law is not an office to which the system of rotation can be successfully applied. The Society is an international organization, and its head must be a person of international prominence. Rotation in office would inevitably result in a succession of presidents little known outside of their own universities or bar associations.[4]

Hughes must have been persuaded. He was renominated and re-elected.

Hughes served as President until 1929, when he resigned because of his election to succeed John Bassett Moore as a member of the Permanent Court of International Justice. He thought it necessary to resign not only because his duties as a member of the Hague Court might keep him away from Annual Meetings of the Society, but also because his judicial position would preclude him from discussing issues of international law as freely as he otherwise could.[5]

Finch, like James Brown Scott before him, devoted an enormous amount of time to the Society. He conducted its daily business, writing all the correspondence, keeping the books balanced, making arrangements for Annual Meetings, and, as Managing Editor of the Journal, performing most of the Journal's editorial duties.[6]

The documents in the Society's files reveal Finch as an efficient, highly competent successor to Scott as the person in charge of the Society's daily affairs. Unlike Scott, he did not stamp his personality or his vision of international law on the Society. Rather, he seems to have been characterized by his eye for detail and his acute sense of propriety. He was a cautious person, taking great care not to overstep the bounds of authority the Executive Council delegated to him. On

3 Letter from Charles Evans Hughes to George A. Finch, Apr. 23, 1927.

4 Letter from Finch to Hughes, Apr. 25, 1927.

5 23 *ASIL Proc.* 198 (1929).

6 Interview with Eleanor H. Finch, May 16, 1994.

more than one occasion he declined to take action suggested by some prominent member, on the stated ground that he lacked authority to do so in the absence of a decision by the Executive Council. Even if on some of these occasions he was using the ostensible lack of authority as an indirect way of declining to do what he was not inclined to do anyway, the impression remains that he interpreted quite narrowly how far his writ ran.

Finch's correspondence lacked the flair of Scott's, tending instead to be stiff and formal. He did not have the close personal relationship with members of the American foreign policy establishment that Scott had, but he nevertheless interacted with them in his own rather correct way. He was a good correspondent, replying promptly to letters from Society members and others. What he may have lacked in vision, he supplied in diligence.

Another Finch joined the Society's staff at the end of the decade. From 1929 to 1932 Eleanor H. Finch, George Finch's daughter, worked part time for the Society while she attended the George Washington University School of Law. When she graduated from law school in 1932, she took a full-time position with the Society. She took care of the membership files and addressed envelopes to prospective Society members. Before long she was assisting her father with the Journal, editing manuscripts and materials in the Supplements, and providing some translations.[7] She continued until 1940 without any formal job title, and then returned in 1948 as Executive Secretary of the Society and Secretary of the Board of Editors of the Journal.[8]

2. Amending the Society's Constitution

The 1924 Annual Meeting had resolved that a committee of seven be appointed to study the Society's Constitution and recommend any needed amendments. In February 1925 Hughes appointed the committee, consisting of Arthur K. Kuhn, Chair, George Grafton Wilson, Philip Marshall Brown, Howard Thayer Kingsbury, Thomas Raeburn White, William I. Hull, and George Finch.

The committee thought that, for the most part, the existing Constitution had served the Society well. Of the few amendments the committee recommended, the most important concerned the office of Vice President, the adoption of resolutions by the Society, and the procedure for amending the Constitution.

The Constitution at that time provided for nine or more Vice Presidents, the number to be fixed by the Executive Council. Among the eighteen Vice Presidents as of 1924 were some who added cachet to the Society, but who did

7 Interview with Eleanor H. Finch, *supra* note 6.

8 Minutes of the Executive Council, Apr. 22, 1948, in 42 *ASIL Proc.* 146, 149 (1948); id. at v, vi.

not participate actively in the Society's affairs. They included such notables as Henry Cabot Lodge and William H. Taft.

The committee thought it unseemly to list non-participants as regular Vice Presidents. Accordingly, it recommended that Article IV of the Constitution be amended to provide for only three Vice Presidents. A new category, Honorary Vice President, was recommended. The Executive Council would fix the number of Honorary Vice Presidents. The three "real" Vice Presidents would be selected from among the active members; they would be expected to attend meetings and be prepared to preside if the President could not be present. Honorary Vice Presidents would be voting members of the Executive Council, and could determine for themselves how active they would be.[9] The amendment was adopted after some debate.[10]

The amendment on adoption of resolutions had been discussed approvingly at the 1924 Annual Meeting, and was in fact the catalyst for the re-examination of the Constitution as a whole. The existing Constitution said that all resolutions offered at any meeting of the Society had to be referred to the appropriate committee or to the Council at the discretion of the presiding officer or on demand of any three members. The amendment differentiated between substantive and procedural resolutions, and limited the referral mechanism to substantive ones – defined as resolutions "relating to the principles of international law or to international relations." It was adopted without discussion.[11] The quoted language remained in the Constitution even after its overhaul in 1998.

The provision on amendment of the Society's Constitution increased the vote required for adoption from a majority of members present and voting to two-thirds. The super-majority was thought necessary "in view of the fact that only a small minority of the Society attends the Annual Meetings."[12] This proposal too was adopted, and the two-thirds voting requirement remains in force.

3. Germination of the Regional Meetings Idea

In March 1925 George Finch wrote to Arthur Kuhn, chair of the committee studying the Society's Constitution, suggesting that some provision be made:

> for branches or chapters of the Society to be organized in some of the larger American cities. ... Members at points distant often send in their regrets at their inability to attend the Society's annual meeting, and, while it may not be desirable to adopt any provision which would decrease the

---

9 Report of Arthur K. Kuhn to Charles Evans Hughes, Mar. 6, 1925; remarks by Kuhn at the Annual Meeting, 19 *ASIL Proc.* 124-28 (1925).

10 The new Article IV appears in 19 *ASIL Proc.* viii (1925).

11 Article VII, the relevant provision, appears in id. at ix.

12 Id. at 124. The amended provision, Article VIII, appears in id. at x.

> interest or attendance at the annual meeting in Washington, it may be advantageous to the work and membership of the Society if provision were made for local meetings of those members who cannot attend the general meeting.[13]

Kuhn replied that he saw no reason why Finch's suggestion should not be adopted, though he thought it would not be necessary to provide for it in the Constitution. Members in large cities could simply organize themselves for local cooperation.[14] The idea did not immediately take hold, but in it could be seen the kernel of a future regional meetings program.

4. The Passing of a Vital Charter Member

As we have seen in Chapter One, Oscar S. Straus chaired the committee in 1905 that formulated the plans for creating a Society of International Law. The committee met every week in the autumn of 1905 until December 9, when the Society's draft Constitution was unveiled at a dinner meeting at Straus' home in New York City. On January 29, 1906, Straus chaired the meeting that approved the plan for the *American Journal of International Law*. Straus died on May 3, 1926.

Remembering Straus, James Brown Scott said, "It is doubtful if the Society or the Journal would have continued to exist had it not been for Mr. Straus' enthusiasm, encouragement, and enlightened support of each during the period of their infancy."[15] Charles Evans Hughes remembered Straus as the quintessential public-spirited citizen.[16]

Because of Straus' association with the American peace movement, he caught the unsympathetic attention of at least one Nazi supporter among pre-World War II German teachers of international law. Norbert Gürke, who wrote an anti-Semitic international law treatise, singled Straus out as one of "two Jews originating in Germany" who were influential in performing "preparatory work for pacifism." Clearly, Gürke had little regard for the American Society of International Law, which he said Straus had founded.[17] It was, perhaps, a badge of honor that the Society, and one of its most important founders, should be held in such disdain by a prominent Nazi intellectual.

---

13 Letter from George A. Finch to Arthur K. Kuhn, Mar. 25, 1925.

14 Letter from Kuhn to Finch, Mar. 26, 1925.

15 James Brown Scott, Current Note: "Oscar S. Straus, December 23, 1850 – May 3, 1926," in 21 *AJIL* 147, 149 (1927).

16 Remarks of Charles Evans Hughes, 21 *ASIL Proc.* 122-23 (1927).

17 Excerpt from Norbert Gürke, *Das Einfluss Jüdischer Theoretiker auf die Deutsche Völkerrechtslehre* (The Influence of Jewish Theoreticians on German International Law Learning) (1938) (provided to the author and translated by Detlev Vagts). See also Detlev F. Vagts, "International Law in the Third Reich," 84 *AJIL* 661, 686 (1990).

B. SOME OLD MATTERS REVISITED

1. Codification Efforts

On September 22, 1924, the League of Nations Assembly adopted a resolution requesting the League Council to convene a Committee of Experts, which – "after eventually consulting the most authoritative organisations which have devoted themselves to the study of international law" – would prepare a provisional list of subjects ripe for codification by treaty.[18] The League Council did convene a Committee of Experts. It included a prominent member of the ASIL, George W. Wickersham.

The Director of the League Secretariat's Legal Section wrote to the ASIL (among other learned societies) on behalf of the committee, asking the Society to consider "what, within the meaning of the Assembly Resolution, are the problems of international law, the solution of which by international agreement would seem to be most desirable and most easily realised."[19] Before the Society could respond, the Committee of Experts prepared a provisional list of subjects to be addressed by its subcommittees: conflicts of nationality, rights in territorial seas, diplomatic privileges and immunities, immunities of state vessels in commercial service, extradition, state responsibility to aliens, rules of procedure for international conferences, suppression of piracy, acquisition of title by prescription, exploitation of ocean "riches," and possible criminal jurisdiction of states relating to infractions committed outside their territory.[20] The Committee postponed consideration of the law of war and private international law. The Director of the Legal Section transmitted the Committee's list to the Society, requesting its observations by October 15, 1925, when the subcommittees were to report.[21]

The Society treated the matter as a hot potato. First, the Executive Council, at its regular session during the 1925 Annual Meeting, voted 15 to 10 to refer the League's request to the Society's Standing Committee for the Extension of International Law for a report the next day.[22] The Standing Committee duly met and recommended that the Society cooperate with the League's Committee of Experts through a special Society committee that would prepare a draft report

---

18 League of Nations doc. A.100.1924.V, reprinted in 20 *AJIL Special Supp.* 2 (1926).

19 Letter from the Director of the Legal Section, Van Hamel, to the Society, Apr. 1, 1925, reprinted in 20 *AJIL Special Supp.* 1 (1926).

20 Committee of Experts for the Progressive Codification of International Law doc. C.P.D.I.15(1), Apr. 8, 1925, reprinted as an Annex to letter from the Chair of the Committee of Experts to the Acting President of the League Council, May 11, 1925, in 20 *AJIL Special Supp.* 13, 14-15 (1926).

21 Letter from Van Hamel to the Society, Apr. 11, 1925, reprinted in 20 *AJIL Special Supp.* 3 (1926).

22 19 *ASIL Proc.* 163 (1925).

responding to the League's request; the Society committee would circulate its draft report to each member of the Executive Council in time for a special Executive Council meeting in September.[23]

The Standing Committee's recommendation was adopted with some minor amendments, but not until an issue under the Society's constitution had been discussed and decided. Harry Pratt Judson, a member of the Executive Council, asked whether the Executive Council would have the power to commit the Society to a position on subjects ripe for codification. Charles Evans Hughes, no stranger to constitutional law, said that he had already given the matter some thought. If this matter were subject to the ASIL constitutional referral procedure, with a vote to be taken at the next Annual Meeting, the Society could not effectively respond to the League's request. That procedure was a cautionary one designed to preclude hasty adoption of unanticipated resolutions. This was not such a case. Rather, the matter could properly be considered under the Executive Council's authority to look after the general interests of the Society.[24]

The Executive Council supported Hughes, who then appointed a special committee consisting of Jesse S. Reeves, Chair, Edwin M. Borchard, Philip Marshall Brown, Charles G. Fenwick, Arthur K. Kuhn, Ellery C. Stowell and Quincy Wright. It came to be known as the Special Committee for the Progressive Codification of International Law. In 1929, it became the Standing Committee on the Codification of International Law, or simply the Codification Committee.

The Committee did not get off to a good start. Four of its seven members were outside the United States during the summer of 1925. It was unable to meet in time to submit a report to the Executive Council in September. Having missed its deadline, the Committee did not meet until its members assembled at the next Annual Meeting of the Society in April 1926. By then, the League's Committee of Experts had prepared a series of in-depth reports on the topics assigned to it, and had identified several additional topics – including some on private international law – that it considered suitable for consideration. The Society committee recommended that the Journal publish the Committee of Experts' reports, and suggested five new topics to be transmitted to the Committee of Experts: state succession, criteria for de facto recognition of new states and governments, canons of treaty interpretation, international servitudes, and the status of transient and resident aliens.[25] The Journal published the Committee

---

23 Id. at 173-74.

24 Remarks of Charles Evans Hughes, President of the Society, id. at 175 (1925).

25 Report of the Special Committee on Collaboration with the League of Nations Committee for the Progressive Codification of International Law, Apr. 24, 1926, in 20 *AJIL Special Supp.* 8-11 (1926).

of Experts' reports in a Special Supplement.[26]

The Society committee's primary reason for recommending publication is interesting, in light of the Society's stated goals at its inception in 1906. The committee had this to say:

> The Committee takes this opportunity of expressing its belief that a sound public sentiment upon the subject of the codification of international law can be developed in no better manner than by having the scientific results of these various bodies placed in the hands of the public of this country, and we believe that as an instrument for the scientific study of international law and its popularization the American Society of International Law may well avail itself of the opportunity to render this public service.[27]

Thus, twenty years after the Society's founding, and less than ten years after the end of a cataclysmic World War, the conviction remained that a significant segment of the public would take an interest in scholarly ("scientific") studies of international law, and it was up to the Society to make those studies available. Underlying these beliefs was the further conviction that if the public could be educated about international law, pressure would be brought to bear on governments to obey the rules. Moreover, democratic governments would respond positively to the pressure. Elihu Root held these convictions for a lifetime. Through him and others, they were woven deeply into the thread of the Society's existence.

The Society's 1926 Annual Meeting was devoted almost entirely to discussion of codification issues. But the Society, as an organization, was not active after 1926 in the League of Nations' codification effort, even though the mandate of its committee was expanded in 1927 to allow it not only to recommend topics ripe for further study, but also to make recommendations on the topics themselves.[28] The committee, and thus the Society, did little more at that point than maintain a watching brief until the League's effort faded out in the early 1930s.[29] In the words of George Finch:

---

26 20 *AJIL Special Supp.* 21-278 (1926). Also at the request of the Special Committee, the Journal published the texts of 30 codification projects of the American Institute of International Law (James Brown Scott, President). The projects ran the gamut from the general to the specific, including such topics as the fundamental bases of international law, responsibility of governments, navigation of international rivers and the law of treaties. 20 *AJIL Special Supp.* 300-84 (1926).

27 Report of the Special Committee, *supra* note 25, at 11.

28 21 *ASIL Proc.* 116-18 (1927).

29 For a brief summary of the demise of the League's codification effort, see Yuen-li Liang, "The Progressive Development of International Law and its Codification under the United Nations," 41 *ASIL Proc.* 24, 27-28 (1947).

> When the work of the League of Nations Committee progressed to the point where it seemed to be in order to call an international conference to consider subjects deemed "ripe for codification," the Faculty of the Harvard Law School stepped in and organized a Research in International Law with funds provided by the Rockefeller Foundation, the Commonwealth Fund, and the Bureau of International Research of Harvard University and Radcliffe College. Some fifty outstanding American scholars from all sections of the country became members of the Advisory Committee of the Research. Each subject was assigned to a particular reporter with a small corps of specialists to assist him. Progress reports were submitted every year to a full meeting of the Advisory Committee at Cambridge, Massachusetts, for discussion, criticism, and eventual approval. Substantially all members of the Harvard Research were identified in one way or another with the American Society of International Law or its Journal.[30]

The Director of the Harvard Research was Manley O. Hudson. A reporter was named for each of the three topics the League of Nations Assembly had selected for consideration at a conference planned for 1929, but actually held in 1930.[31] The reporters were Richard W. Flournoy, on nationality; George Grafton Wilson, on territorial waters; and Edwin M. Borchard, on state responsibility to foreigners. All of these men were members of the Society, and Hudson, Wilson and Borchard were prominent within it. The thirty-four members of the Advisory Committee were predominantly from the Society.

When the Harvard Research entered a second phase in 1929, a third phase in 1932 and a fourth phase in 1935, the reporters again were all Society members, most of them prominently so. The second phase reporters were Jesse S. Reeves, on diplomatic privileges and immunities; Quincy Wright, on the legal position and functions of consuls; Philip C. Jessup, on the competence of courts in regard to foreign states; and Joseph W. Bingham, on piracy. For the third phase, the reporters were Charles K. Burdick, on extradition; Edwin D. Dickinson, on jurisdiction with respect to crime; and James W. Garner, on the law of treaties. For the fourth phase: James Grafton Rogers and A.H. Feller, on judicial assistance; and Philip C. Jessup, on rights and duties of neutral states (two projects). The work

---

30 George A. Finch, "The American Society of International Law 1906-1956," 50 *AJIL* 293, 309-10 (1956) (hereafter cited as Finch, "The ASIL 1906-1956").

31 The League of Nations resolutions and reports leading to the appointment of a preparatory committee for the planned codification conference appear in 22 *AJIL Special Supp*. 1-233 (1928).

product of each phase of the Harvard Research was published in Supplements to the *American Journal of International Law*.[32]

Despite the importance of Society members to the Harvard Research, it was not a Society project.[33] In fact, the Society's Codification Committee remained firmly on the sideline, although it did meet from time to time and submitted reports to the Society.[34] In 1929, the Committee Chair, Jesse Reeves, led a round-table discussion at a plenary session of the Annual Meeting on the codification of international law. The discussion focused not on the League of Nations effort, but rather on the ongoing effort to codify international law in the Americas – especially at the Sixth International American Conference in Havana in 1928.[35]

In 1929, the Codification Committee was instructed to focus in the immediate future on the codification of private international law and on the question of whether, and to what extent, the conception of an Inter-American international law was valid.[36] The Committee never submitted a report on these matters. Instead, at the 1930 Business Meeting it offered a resolution expressing the Society's hope that the United States government would encourage the League of Nations' efforts to codify international law. Although the resolution called for the Society to take a position endorsing not only codification, but also the League of Nations' approach to it, there was no dissent. The resolution was adopted and was presented to the Secretary of State by a blue-ribbon *ad hoc* Society committee headed by James Brown Scott.[37] Such efforts were to no avail;

---

32 See 23 *AJIL Special Supp.* (1929); 26 *AJIL Supp.*, Nos. 1 & 2 (1932); 29 *AJIL Supp.*, Nos. 1 & 2 (1935); 33 *AJIL Supp.*, Nos. 1 & 2 (1939).

33 James Brown Scott was emphatic on this point. In the context of deflecting criticism of the Harvard Research at an ASIL Business Meeting, Scott said, "The Harvard Research is a private organization having nothing whatever to do with the American Society of International Law. No member of the American Society of International Law, as such, takes part in its proceedings. They take part as individuals and not as members of this Society." 28 *ASIL Proc.* 184 (1934).

34 The Executive Council, on a motion by James Brown Scott, tried to reinvigorate the Codification Committee in 1937, but to no avail. See 31 *ASIL Proc.* 227 (1937); 32 *ASIL Proc.* 167-71, 180-81 (1938). By that time, the Harvard Research had essentially occupied the field.

35 The round-table discussion is reported in 23 *ASIL Proc.* 25-54 (1929). The Conventions on public international law adopted at the Sixth International American Conference are reprinted in 22 *AJIL Supp.* 124-66 (1928). According to Manley Hudson, they were adopted without significant scholarly input from the United States. Manley O. Hudson, The Research in International Law 11-12 (address at the American Law Institute Annual Meeting, May 8, 1931). For a later summary by a member of the Codification Committee on codification efforts in the Americas, see the report by Edwin Borchard, 31 *ASIL Proc.* 187-89 (1937).

36 23 *ASIL Proc.* 43, 53-54, 201-03 (1929).

37 25 *ASIL Proc.* 180, 185, 186 n. 1 (1931).

the League of Nations' codification effort soon lost its momentum. The Harvard Research took center stage as the codifier.

Why did the Society take a back seat to the Harvard Law School, when codification of international law had been so important to James Brown Scott and other leaders of the Society in the immediate post-World War I years? Both Jesse Reeves (speaking for the Society's Codification Committee) and George Finch said that the Society could not press on with the research for its codification project because it lacked the funds to do so.[38] But that explanation does not go far enough. In the past, the Carnegie Endowment had supplied the Society with funds for projects deemed promising in the quest for peace. James Brown Scott was no longer the chief operating officer of the Society, but he remained active in the Society and was the Director of the Endowment's Division of International Law. One wonders why he did not induce the Endowment to provide ample support for the Society's participation in the League's codification effort.[39]

Scott's loosened ties to the administration of the Society might have had something to do with it. But even that would not be a full explanation. The Carnegie Endowment was not the only possible source of funds. Manley Hudson, acting on behalf of the Harvard Law School, was able to find the necessary support. Presumably, two of his sources – the Commonwealth Fund and the Bureau of International Research of Harvard and Radcliff – would not have been available to the Society, but his third source – the Rockefeller Foundation – might have been. Other sources might have been tapped as well. Whether anyone pursued them on behalf of the Society does not appear.

Perhaps non-pecuniary considerations also played a part. At the 1925 Business Meeting, when Reeves reported on the proposal by the Society's Standing Committee for the Extension of International Law for future cooperation with the League's Committee of Experts, Albert Bushnell Hart interjected a concern that bodies within the Society other than the full membership at an Annual Meeting might be committing the Society to principles and methods of codification. He thought it inappropriate for either a Society committee or the Executive Council to do so.[40]

The point Hart raised was not resolved at the Business Meeting. As soon as the Business Meeting ended, the Executive Council met; Charles Evans Hughes expressed the opinion, reported above, that the Executive Council could undertake

---

38 See the 1928 Report of the Special Committee, 22 *ASIL Proc.* 26, 27 (1928); Finch, "The ASIL 1906-1956," *supra* note 30, at 309.

39 The Carnegie Endowment did provide funds for publication of the results of the Harvard Research's very considerable efforts in supplements to the *American Journal of International Law*. See the 1936 Report of the Society's Codification Committee, 30 *ASIL Proc.* 178, 179 (1936), and see the references to these supplements in note 32 *supra*.

40 19 *ASIL Proc.* 129-31 (1925).

to cooperate with the League of Nations without further referring the matter for decision by the membership at large.[41] That seemed to satisfy the Executive Council at the time, but there may well have been a lingering unease about proceeding with anything more ambitious than a watching brief in the absence of an explicit delegation of authority from the membership at large. In 1928, Manley Hudson, the force behind the Harvard Research, expressed just such an apprehension about any preparation of draft international codes by the Society.[42] But neither he nor Hart addressed whether a Society committee might appropriately prepare draft codes without holding them out as Society positions.

2. Research Limitations

The Society's inability to conduct anything like the Harvard Research in International Law reflected the Society's lack of any ongoing research program at that time. When the American Council of Learned Societies asked the Society to respond to a survey of research in the humanistic and social sciences in 1926, George Finch replied that the Society's work was confined to the publication of the Journal, the holding of Annual Meetings and the publication of the Proceedings.[43]

The Society's finances were barely adequate to cover these activities. Disbursements related to publication of the Journal and the Proceedings exceeded subscription income. Any surplus for a given year was attributable to membership dues. Occasional outside support for specific projects came from the Carnegie Endowment, but there was no systematic effort to raise money from outside granting sources. In fact, the Society's records reveal no discussion of embarking on a research program during these years, and no thought about systematic fund-raising beyond efforts to increase membership. The one documented effort to launch a capital endowment campaign – James Brown Scott's attempt to persuade George W. Wickersham to head a drive to raise funds in Elihu Root's name – was quickly dropped when Wickersham showed little zeal for it.[44]

One reason – perhaps the major reason – for the Society's lack of any organized fund-raising scheme was the shortage of staff. As of mid-1928, the Society still had no full-time employees. Those who did work for the Society part time were regular employees of the Carnegie Endowment.[45] It would have taken staff work to maintain an ongoing fund-raising program; it may well have taken a

41 See text at note 24 *supra*.

42 Letter from Manley O. Hudson to James Brown Scott, May 19, 1928.

43 Letter from George A. Finch to Frederic A. Ogg, Apr. 19, 1926.

44 See Chapter Two, Section E, *supra*.

45 Letter from George A. Finch to United States Employees' Compensation Commission, June 11, 1928.

successful fund-raising effort to support a full-time staff. Neither could or did happen without the other.

3. The 1925 Conference of Teachers of International Law

In January 1925, Edwin D. Dickinson, the Director of the Round Table on International Affairs of the American Political Science Association, wrote to George Finch to say that the Round Table wanted to have a conference of teachers of international law in connection with the Society's 1925 Annual Meeting. He recalled the success of the 1914 conference, and suggested that Finch bring it to the attention of the appropriate ASIL officials.[46] Twenty-one political scientists joined in making the suggestion.

That the impetus for a conference of international law teachers should come from political scientists was no surprise in 1925, when international law was a thriving specialty within that discipline. Yet even then there were early indications of political scientists' disaffection with doctrinal international law – the stuff of many ASIL Annual Meeting programs and of many Journal articles. Charles Fenwick, a political scientist, may well have been speaking for more than himself when he said at the 1925 Annual Meeting that a day of the program devoted to then-current nationality issues was too limited to be of much interest to professors. Papers on such matters, he said, dealt with already familiar subjects. Professors (by which he seemed to mean especially political scientists) wished instead to discuss the development of international law.[47]

The conference was held concurrently with the 1925 ASIL Annual Meeting, as proposed. The Carnegie Endowment provided funds for the conference and for publication of its proceedings. The conference adopted fourteen resolutions and recommendations. Their tone was less didactic than in 1914. Instead of instructing others on how to teach international law, the assembled teachers pointed out the variety of offerings relating to international law and recommended that courses be tailored to the needs of the students taking them. Thus undergraduate international law courses should be less "technical" than graduate and professional school courses. Moreover, international relations courses should be separate from international law courses.[48]

The latter recommendation could be seen as the blueprint for the ensuing separation in higher education of international law from international relations, or the related separation of international law from foreign policy. Neither

---

[46] Letter from Dickinson to Finch, Jan. 5, 1925. Essentially the same letter was sent to the Carnegie Endowment.

[47] Remarks of Charles G. Fenwick, 19 *ASIL Proc.* 126-27 (1925).

[48] Recommendation II, in *Proceedings of the Second Conf. of Teachers of International Law and Related Subjects*, Apr. 23-25, 1925, at x (1926).

separation was ever complete, but both were so substantial as to breed a new school of post-World War II scholars at Yale and elsewhere, who stressed the connections between law and policy, and between law and social science. Even at the 1925 conference, Manley Hudson foreshadowed the post-World War II reaction to the compartmentalization of international studies. Hudson said that what was needed was an emphasis on the relation of international law to policy.[49] But in the years immediately following 1925, the trend was clearly in the other direction.[50]

The separations that occurred after 1925 were more substantial than the political scientists who dominated the conference intended. Indeed, in another recommendation, the conference urged universities "to recognize the indispensable character of a knowledge of the elements of international law for the proper training of any candidate for an advanced degree in political science or history."[51] The idea clearly was to retain international law as an important element of graduate work in non-law departments, even though it would be regarded as a sub-discipline distinct from international relations.

The 1925 conference, like its 1914 counterpart, recognized the importance of a basic knowledge of international law by members of the legal profession. It recommended that international law be taught in all law schools, "and that this instruction be professional in character."[52] The quoted language, of course, was consistent with the overarching theme of the conference that international law instruction should be tailored to the perceived needs of the type of student likely to enroll.

The discussions at the conference began with an emphasis on pedagogy, but then turned to substance. At that point the written proceedings read very much like the more recent Proceedings of ASIL Annual Meetings, with more emphasis on theory and process than can be found in ASIL Annual Meeting Proceedings up to about 1924.

The blurring of the distinction between the Conference of Teachers and the ASIL Annual Meetings was troublesome to some teachers. This came out in a discussion during a Saturday afternoon meeting of teachers during the 1929 ASIL Annual Meeting. The question then was how the teachers might interact with members of the Institute of International Law at a meeting of the Institute scheduled to be held in the United States in the autumn of 1929. Some thought the teachers should stick to discussing pedagogy and research programs involving

---

49 Id. at 13-14.

50 See the remarks of Ellen Deborah Ellis, of Mount Holyoke College, in *Proceedings of the Third Conf. of Teachers of International Law*, Apr. 25-26, 1928, at 54-58 (1928).

51 Recommendation IV, in *Proceedings of the Second Teachers' Conf.*, *supra* note 48, at xi.

52 Recommendation V, in id. at xi.

graduate students; others thought substantive discussions would be appropriate. No conclusion was reached.[53]

At the 1925 Conference of Teachers, Manley Hudson gave an address that could well have been given at an ASIL Annual Meeting. He directed his audience's attention away from the rule-oriented view of international law that had motivated the Society's pioneers and that had dominated much of the discussions at the early Annual Meetings. Said Hudson:

> I do not conceive of law in terms of definite and positive rules. There are such rules, of course, and in certain branches of the law they serve very useful ends. ... But how little of public law, and particularly of the law of nations, is susceptible of such formulation! Rather it is principles and standards to which we resort, and, unless I misconceive the facts of our juristic history, which have furnished the basis of international practice in the past. For the law of nations, like municipal law, is not at any time a fixed body either of doctrines or of commands. It is always a process, a method of dealing with competitions of interest ...[54]

It is difficult to imagine James Brown Scott saying such things. Clearly Scott did not concur in Hudson's view, expressed in the same address, that the League of Nations Assembly's disinclination to hold a post-World War I codification conference was a salutary development. Hudson thought that passions excited by the war had not then sufficiently subsided, nor could the self-interest of the ex-belligerents be sufficiently subdued, to produce a sound body of law even if "codification" (his quotation marks) were a goal normally to be pursued.[55] Scott, who was chairing the meeting, discreetly said that it was his duty "to preside and not take part in the proceedings, and especially on this occasion should I abstain because a host should never disagree with his guests."[56] He was not so reticent when Hudson spoke on the same subject at an ASIL Annual Meeting.[57]

Hudson's iconoclasm at the Conference of Teachers rose to new heights when he debunked the idea that non-specialists should be taught international law – an idea that had been a motivating force in the formation of the American Society of International Law and that found its way into the 1925 Conference's recommendations on the teaching of international law not only in law schools, but in graduate schools of political science and history. In Hudson's view, teaching international law to every "Tom, Dick and Harry" would vulgarize

---

[53] 23 *ASIL Proc.* 217-25 (1929).

[54] Manley O. Hudson, "Contemporary Development of International Law," in *Proceedings of the Second Teachers' Conf., supra* note 48, at 83, 85.

[55] Id. at 88-89.

[56] Id. at 94.

[57] See 18 *ASIL Proc.* 138-40 (1924).

the subject: "If a knowledge of a little law is a dangerous thing, a knowledge of a little international law is much more dangerous."[58]

4. The Quest for Access to Documents of State

One theme the Conference of Teachers carried forward from 1914 was so basic to the study of international law that unanimity could readily be achieved. Reflecting the felt need for greater access to documents of state, including treaties, diplomatic correspondence and other documents, the Conference established a standing Committee on Publications and asked it to communicate with the State Department to request that documents of state be made more easily and more immediately available to students of international law and relations.[59] In particular, the need was expressed for a regularly published collection of U.S. treaties, since no such collection was then being produced.

The Committee on Publications exercised such influence as it could on the State Department, with some success. Most importantly, the Department began to publish the United States Treaty Series in response to the Committee's supplications.[60] Still, there was no up-to-date official source of documents of state. The *Department of State Bulletin*, for example, did not appear until 1939. Manley Hudson, in a paper submitted to the Third Conference of Teachers of International Law in 1928, deplored the situation and recommended, among other things, that publications be established to make available in convenient form diplomatic correspondence, material relating to international conferences and other materials of permanent value then released only to the press.[61]

Hudson's paper, along with his forceful presentation, galvanized the 1928 Conference to put in place a mechanism that would get results. The Conference considered a draft resolution that set forth in great detail the nature of official documents the teacher-scholars wanted. It was thought to be too specific and a bit presumptuous. In its place a resolution was adopted authorizing the director of the Conference to appoint a new committee to confer with the President of the United States, the Secretary of State and others concerning the scope of State Department publications. The committee was appointed on the spot.[62]

The ASIL immediately appointed its own *ad hoc* committee to cooperate with the Conference committee. The joint committee gained access to the highest levels

---

58 *Proceedings of the Second Teachers' Conf., supra* note 48, at 142-43.

59 Recomendation IX, in id. at xii.

60 See Manley O. Hudson, "The Department of State and the Teaching of International Law and International Relations," in *Proceedings of the Third Conf. of Teachers of International Law*, Apr. 25-26, 1928, at 170, 171 (1928).

61 Id. at 176.

62 Id. at 157-62.

of government. According to George Finch, "Members of the joint committee conferred with the President of the United States, the Secretary of State, the appropriate committees of the Senate and House of Representatives and others, and urged the enlargement of the scope of publications of the Department of State."[63]

In October 1928, the chair of the Society's committee, William C. Dennis, appeared before the Director of the Budget with Finch, Scott and a few other Society members. They were joined by representatives of committees dispatched by other scholarly associations. Each representative of the Society made a presentation. As Dennis put it, the committee "has simply been asking that the State Department be given adequate funds and facilities to secure the publication of material admittedly non-confidential but practically inaccessible to most persons away from Washington in time to be useful for any except historical purposes."[64] The hearing led to a USD 50,000 increase in the State Department's appropriation for expanded publications in the 1930 fiscal year.[65]

This success led the Society in 1929 to appoint a standing Committee on State Department Publications.[66] Its chair and members began the practice of conferring with State Department officials each year and attempting to persuade Congress to provide adequate funding for the publications.[67] The standing Committee's success ebbed and flowed according to the degree of austerity in the State Department's budget.[68]

5. The 1928 Conference of Teachers of International Law

The 1928 Conference of Teachers of International Law did not devote itself entirely to questions of access to documents of state. James Brown Scott, still representing the Carnegie Endowment, opened the Conference with a vision that seems, with hindsight, to have been quite naïve:

> [T]he whole nature and conception of international law has [sic] changed. Formerly regarded as something akin to international morality, ethics, philosophy or history of the diplomatic variety, it is now the consensus

---

63 Finch, "The ASIL 1906-1956," *supra* note 30, at 304.

64 Letter from William C. Dennis to Raymond L. Buell, Research Director of the Foreign Policy Association, Nov. 9, 1928.

65 Id.

66 23 *ASIL Proc.* 263-64 (1929). The formal name of the committee at that time was the Committee on the Enlargement of the Scope of the Publications of the Department of State.

67 Letter from Dennis to Buell, *supra* note 64.

68 For the continuing efforts of the standing committee in the 1930s, see Chapter Four, *infra*.

> of opinion that international law is an integral branch of jurisprudence, which, in the course of a few years, is destined to control the actions of nations, just as, within its territory, municipal law controls the actions of the men, women and children of each member of the far-flung community of nations. We do not need to argue the matter, now that a Permanent Court of International Justice is installed at The Hague, where nation may sue nation – at present by agreement, but ultimately as State sues State in the Supreme Court of these United States ...[69]

Scott's vision, of course, was consistent with his long-standing belief that if only there were a permanent international tribunal, modeled on the U.S. Supreme Court and applying established, clear rules to resolve disputes among nation states, peaceful dispute settlement would replace armed conflict. He did not regard international rules as immutable, but at the same time he remained of the old school: law consisted primarily of rules and procedures, rather than of processes and principles shaped by convergent or conflicting policies and interests.

The remainder of the 1928 Conference dealt with pedagogy in international law at the college, graduate school and law school levels, and with problems concerning research in international law.

6. More Attention to Turnover in the Executive Council

Dissatisfaction with the slow turnover rate in the Executive Council's membership was not eliminated by the 1922 change in the Society's Constitution requiring a year's hiatus at the end of an elected member's three-year term. Charles Fenwick raised the point at the 1927 Annual Meeting. "I am sorry to see the same old names come up again," he said, "not because I have not the highest respect for the persons, but because I think it is better for our Society to have some of the so-called younger men included and given an opportunity to feel that they are active members in the work of our Society."[70] Fenwick did not mention younger (or any) women.

Fenwick's basic point about expanding the circle to make it more representative would be made again. In 1927, it had the effect of prodding Philip Marshall Brown to submit his resignation from the Council in order that a younger person might be nominated in his place. Fenwick said that would embarrass him a great deal; he hoped that his suggestion would be implemented only a year hence.[71] With that, the matter was dropped for the time being.

---

69 James Brown Scott, Opening Remarks, *Proceedings of the Third Conf. of Teachers of International Law*, Apr. 25-26, 1928, at 6, 10 (1928).

70 21 *ASIL Proc.* 119 (1927).

71 Id. at 120.

C. THE SOCIETY AND THE KELLOGG-BRIAND PACT

On April 6, 1927, the French Foreign Minister, Aristide Briand, publicly proposed a treaty between France and the United States that would renounce war between the two countries.[72] George W. Wickersham, still a prominent member of the Society, wrote to George Finch urging in rather elliptical terms that the Society do what it could to persuade the President, the Secretary of State and the Chair of the Foreign Relations Committee to pursue the matter.[73] He was, of course, asking the Society to take a position on a matter of current interest. So far as can be determined from the public record and the Society's files, the Society stuck to the principle against taking positions on such matters. It did not honor his request.

Nevertheless, the Society was hardly a disinterested spectator. The prospect of a treaty renouncing war was heartening, to say the least, to many members of a Society with its roots in the American peace movement. It was all the more interesting and attractive when U.S. Secretary of State Frank B. Kellogg countered the French proposal for a bilateral treaty with his own idea of a multilateral pact encompassing the major powers of the day.

The Society gave Kellogg a platform for his cause in the pages of the Journal, in its Supplement, and at the 1928 Annual Meeting. The Journal published the text of Kellogg's speech to the Council of Foreign Relations on the government's war prevention policy;[74] the Supplement published not only the treaty itself, but also two diplomatic notes from the State Department urging other governments to join in the treaty;[75] and the Society invited Kellogg to address the annual dinner gathering in 1928. Kellogg took advantage of the latter opportunity to outline for the first time the construction that the State Department gave to the draft treaty.[76] What he said, in response to French concerns, ironically displayed the treaty's impotence. He recognized that the treaty would not impair the right of self-defense and, tellingly, that each nation "alone is competent to decide whether circumstances require recourse to war in self-defense."[77] Moreover, he

---

72 Associated Press release, Apr. 6, 1927. The key paragraph of Briand's statement is quoted in English in a letter to the editor from Nicholas Murray Butler, *N.Y. Times*, Apr. 25, 1927.

73 Letter from George W. Wickersham, as President of the Board of the League of Nations Non-Partisan Association, Inc., to George A. Finch, May 13, 1927.

74 Frank B. Kellogg, "The War Prevention Policy of the United States," 22 *AJIL* 253 (1928).

75 22 *AJIL* Supp. 109, 171, 174 (1928).

76 22 *ASIL Proc.* 141, 143-45 (1928). The *New York Times* and the *Washington Post* gave prominent coverage to his speech. *N.Y. Times*, Apr. 29, 1928, quoting extensively from the speech; *Wash. Post*, Apr. 30, 1928.

77 22 *ASIL Proc.* 141, 143 (1928).

espoused a very broad form of the doctrine of material breach: a resort to war by any party to the "anti-war treaty" would be a breach that would release all other parties from their obligations thereunder.[78]

Despite the doubts expressed by some observers shortly after the Kellogg-Briand Pact was concluded, and despite Charles Evans Hughes' lukewarm response to the idea that war could effectively be renounced as an instrument of policy,[79] reaction in the pages of the Journal was mostly enthusiastic at first.[80] Five years later it was much less so.[81] By then, the Japanese had occupied Manchuria, Hitler had become Chancellor in Germany, and storm clouds had begun to form again over what Westerners regarded as the civilized world. A treaty to abolish war no longer provided the great hope it had in 1928.

D. ANNUAL MEETINGS

1. Substantive Discussions

As the influence of the academics within the Society began to increase significantly, the time devoted at Annual Meetings to issues other than specific current events began to expand. The 1924 Annual Meeting, for example, was dominated by a "report" of the Committee on the Extension of International Law on the distinction between legal and political questions. There was no committee report, as such. Instead, there was a series of presentations by eminent scholars who were members of the committee – Charles Fenwick, Edwin Borchard, Quincy Wright and Manley Hudson – followed by animated discussion from the floor.

---

78 Id. at 144.

79 See Charles Evans Hughes, "Institutions of Peace," 23 *ASIL Proc.* 1, 6-7 (1929); see also Betty Glad, *Charles Evans Hughes and the Illusions of Innocence* 207 (1966). Hughes was more positive toward the second article of the Pact, which was a pledge to settle all disputes or conflicts by pacific means.

80 For favorable comments, see David Jayne Hill, Editorial Comment: "The Multilateral Treaty for the Renunciation of War," 22 *AJIL* 823 (1928); C.G. Fenwick, Editorial Comment: "War as an Instrument of National Policy," id. at 826; Philip Marshall Brown, Editorial Comment: "The Interpretation of the General Pact for the Renunciation of War," 23 *AJIL* 374 (1929). Less sanguine were Edwin M. Borchard, Editorial Comment: "The Multilateral Treaty for the Renunciation of War," id. at 116; Roland S. Morris, "The Pact of Paris for the Renunciation of War: Meaning and Effect in International Law," 23 *ASIL Proc.* 88 (1929).

81 See Josef L. Kunz, "The Law of Nations, Static and Dynamic," 27 *AJIL* 630, 646 (1933); Edwin M. Borchard, Editorial Comment: "The 'Enforcement' of Peace by 'Sanctions'," id. at 518, 519.

Fenwick stressed the amorphous nature of much customary international law; only those norms that had crystallized into definite rules could properly give rise to legal questions.[82] Borchard endorsed the view that the predominance of legal over political issues, or vice versa, in any given situation depends on the extent to which the issue is deemed to threaten the power, influence or vital interests of one party or the other.[83] Wright noted that the principal condition that leads a state to disdain an appeal to law to settle a dispute arises when applicable legal rules would not give the result the state wants.[84] Hudson espoused the same view he would express a year later at the Conference of Teachers, that international law is not merely a matter of evolution of already-determined rules, but rather is largely a process "serving along with other human agencies to consciously develop a solution of current problems which will somehow serve the general peace and enlarge the satisfaction of human wants."[85] One might detect a strong hint in these words of a Harvard professor of what was to come later, not at Harvard, but rather in the hands of the post-Borchard Yale School.

In 1925, Charles Evans Hughes gave the first opening address at an Annual Meeting by anyone other than Elihu Root. Among other things, he emphasized a goal of international law that went beyond the primary motivation of the Society's founders twenty years earlier. They had been driven almost entirely by the desire to give vitality to a mechanism for peace through law. Hughes refined the idea:

> [I]t is not correct, and certainly is not adequate, to speak of peace, or the mere absence of war, as our ultimate goal. We wish to have the peace, not of the lowest forms of life, but of the highest, with its inescapable longings and strivings. Peace is but an opportunity, and our chief concern is justice. We cannot forget on this three hundredth anniversary of his epoch-making book, that it was justice that was the preoccupation of Grotius. It was selfish, aggressive war that he condemned – not war to defend the right, or to punish a guilty state. We seek justice through peace; the peace which rests on justice; the assurances afforded by the peaceable methods made possible by the instrumentalities of justice.[86]

---

82 Charles G. Fenwick, "The Distinction Between Legal and Political Questions," 18 *ASIL Proc.* 44, 47 (1924).

83 Edwin M. Borchard, "The Distinction Between Legal and Political Questions," id. at 50, 54.

84 Quincy Wright, "The Distinction Between Legal and Political Questions with Especial Reference to the Monroe Doctrine," id. at 57, 58-59.

85 Manley O. Hudson, "Legal and Political Questions," id. at 126, 127.

86 Charles Evans Hughes, "The Development of International Law," 19 *ASIL Proc.* 1, 3-4 (1925).

Hughes acknowledged that concepts of justice may differ from age to age and among diverse national communities, but he insisted that there was much common ground; it was the business of international law to find the common ground and define it.

As has already been noted, the 1926 Annual Meeting was devoted largely to discussion of codification issues. Hughes' opening address, though, covered a broader range. Among other things, he shed light on the then-recent *Eastern Carelia* case.[87] The Permanent Court in that case had declined to give an advisory opinion on the ground that it would be addressing the merits of an actual dispute, one of the parties to which (the Soviet Union) was not a member of the League of Nations and had not consented to submit the dispute to the Court. Hughes tied this outcome to the concern in the U.S. Senate – expressed in its fifth reservation to its advice and consent to U.S. adherence to the Protocol of Signature of the Court's Statute – that the Court might, without U.S. consent, give an advisory opinion relating to a dispute or question in which the United States had or claimed to have an interest.[88] Hughes noted that this concern had not been lost on the Court in the *Eastern Carelia* case. He quoted an out-of-court assertion by then-Judge John Bassett Moore, in which Moore said that the Court's opinion "should dispel the apprehensions of those who have reiterated that the Court would, as the creation or creature of the League, enforce the League's organic law, the Covenant, above all other law, without regard to the rights under international law of nations not members of the League."[89] Hughes, of course, was one of the principal proponents of U.S. adherence to the Court's Statute.

Most of the 1927 Annual Meeting was devoted to state responsibility toward aliens. It marked the debut as an Annual Meeting speaker of a young Assistant Professor from Columbia University, Philip C. Jessup. He was given five minutes to present his paper at the end of a session featuring two of his elders, Professors Edwin Borchard and Amos Hershey. Jessup made two points: a state is free under customary international law to take private property of an alien, provided that it pays adequate compensation; and not all governmental acts that adversely affect an alien's property interests are compensable, provided that the state has acted reasonably and for a public purpose.[90]

The ascendancy of the professoriate within the Society was evident in the 1927 Borchard-Hershey-Jessup panel on state responsibility, and it appeared

---

[87] 1923 PCIJ (Ser. B) No. 5.

[88] Charles Evans Hughes, "Some Observations on Recent Events," 20 *ASIL Proc.* 1, 10-12 (1926). For discussion of the Senate's reservations, see Manley O. Hudson, "The American Reservations and the Permanent Court of International Justice," 22 *AJIL* 776 (1928).

[89] The quote is from John Bassett Moore, *International Law and Some Current Illusions, and Other Essays* 129 (1924).

[90] Philip C. Jessup, Confiscation, 21 *ASIL Proc.* 38 (1927).

in some of the general discussion as well. It provoked some lighthearted but not entirely aimless comment at the annual dinner. Charles Evans Hughes, the distinguished, non-professorial President of the Society, was heard to say as Toastmaster that professors sometimes rush in where lawyers fear to tread.[91] For this he was tweaked by another prominent but non-professorial member of the Society, Frederic R. Coudert. Coudert rose to take his turn as a speaker and said that he felt obliged to take up the cudgels for the professors in order to "explain that their apparent idiosyncracies which excited the naturalistic curiosity of the learned and erudite Chairman are not confined wholly to the professorial class."[92]

The 1928 Annual Meeting was devoted to discussion of the three topics chosen by the League of Nations Assembly for possible codification: nationality, territorial waters and state responsibility for damage to aliens and their property. A single paper was presented on each topic, followed by extended discussion. Ellery Stowell, chair of the Program Committee, had proposed the single-paper format. It went over quite well. In the words of James Brown Scott, "the great success which we have had in this meeting, greater, I believe, than on any other occasion which I have had the pleasure of being in attendance, is, I believe, due to Professor Stowell's initiative … ."[93]

Carrying forward the theme of the 1927 Annual Meeting, the state responsibility topic sparked a particularly lively discussion. Professor Charles E. Hill, of George Washington University, gave the principal paper. In the ensuing discussion could be found the seeds of what would later be regarded as basic human rights law. Philip Marshall Brown, in remarks from the floor, foreshadowed what was to come – in fact, what had already begun to happen – when he expressed his own transitional thinking on state responsibility:

> [W]e are all familiar with the classic statement that international law applies only between states … . I am frank to say that I was one of those who accepted it for a long time as being true, but in later years I have come to feel it is entirely out of conformity with actual conditions, that we are beginning to discover that international law, if it has any *raison d'être* whatever, exists for the very purpose of individual rights. … [I]t seems to me we arrive at this conclusion: that in the process of time a certain body of rights has grown up, universally recognized in the practice of nations concerning the fundamental rights of aliens; that these rights exist not merely because one alien has a powerful government to present his claim, or that they do not exist because another

91 Toastmaster's remarks, 21 *ASIL Proc.* 126 (1927).

92 Address of Frederic R. Coudert, in id. at 134, 135.

93 Remarks of James Brown Scott, 22 *ASIL Proc.* 132 (1928).

> alien is entirely without a powerful government behind him to present his claim. These rights exist in themselves and there is a standard ... of international justice which we may invoke in behalf of individuals who may suffer various wrongs.[94]

Brown had in mind strictly the rights of aliens. What was yet to come was the development of the underlying principle into specific rights that could be asserted by individuals against their own governments.

At the Annual Meeting in 1929, one of the topics was the treaty-making power of the United States government in matters coming within the jurisdiction of states. Charles Henry Butler presented the principal paper. Charles Evans Hughes, still the President of the Society, presided. When Butler's paper had been delivered and discussion from the floor had run its course, Hughes added his comments on the subject. What he had to say has ever since sparked academic and, to some extent, judicial debate on the proper extent of the treaty-making power under the Constitution of the United States. The key passages from his remarks are these:

> What is the power to make a treaty? What is the object of the power? The normal scope of the power can be found in the appropriate object of the power. The power is to deal with foreign nations with regard to matters of international concern. It is not a power intended to be exercised, it may be assumed, with respect to matters that have no relation to international concerns.
>
> ...
>
> [F]rom my point of view the nation has the power to make any agreement whatever in a constitutional manner that relates to the conduct of our international relations, unless there can be found some express prohibition in the Constitution, and I am not aware of any which would in any way detract from the power as I have defined it in connection with our relations with other governments. But if we attempted to use the treaty-making power to deal with matters which did not pertain to our external relations but to control matters which normally and appropriately were within the local jurisdictions of the States, then I again say there might be ground for implying a limitation upon the treaty-making power that it is intended for the purpose of having treaties made relating to foreign affairs and not to make laws for the people of the United States in their internal concerns through the exercise of the asserted treaty-making power.[95]

---

94 Philip Marshall Brown, remarks from the floor, id. at 81-82.

95 Charles Evans Hughes, remarks from the chair, 23 *ASIL Proc.* 194, 196 (1929).

Less widely noted down through the years has been a passage in which Hughes recognized that matters once regarded as purely local could become "so related to international matters that an international regulation could not appropriately succeed without embracing the local affairs as well."[96]

The debate over the meaning and impact of what Hughes said has focused primarily on human rights. A fair reading of Hughes' remarks, including the portion just quoted, would leave room for the internationalization of at least the most fundamental human rights. The Reporters of the current edition of the *Restatement of the Foreign Relations Law of the United States* have put it more forcefully than that. They have said, "There is no principle either in international law or in United States constitutional law that some subjects are intrinsically 'domestic' and hence impermissible subjects for an international agreement."[97] After years of debate, the United States, by ratifying the Covenant on Civil and Political Rights[98] in 1992, seems to have accepted the notion that fundamental human rights are not intrinsically domestic.

2. To Take or Not to Take Positions on Current Issues?

The question has come up repeatedly as to whether or not the Society should take positions on the substantive issues of the day. As we have seen, a procedural mechanism for referral to the appropriate committee or the Executive Council has been in force, in one form or another, since the Society's earliest days. This has not dissuaded members from debating the basic issue – whether the Society should ever take a substantive position – at the Society's business meetings from time to time.

One such occasion arose at the Annual Meeting in 1923, when Frederic Coudert proposed a resolution to have the Society endorse the plan of the President of the United States for the entrance of the United States into the Permanent Court of International Justice. A debate ensued over the wisdom and propriety of adopting such a resolution. Oscar Straus, who chaired the session, is reported to have replied:

> [I]t has been the purpose of the Society, with its membership of over a thousand, to serve as a forum of discussion on international questions without passing resolutions on matters about which there may be differences of opinion among the members. ... In drafting the Constitution it was intended to leave questions brought up at the meetings to the judgment of the Council, which was assumed to be more familiar with

---

96 Id. at 195.

97 Restatement (Third), Foreign Relations Law of the United States § 302, Reporters' Note 2 (1987).

98 Dec. 16, 1966, 999 U.N.T.S. 171.

> the sentiment of the entire membership than individual members at a comparatively small meeting. The Society ... was not disinclined to take action, but it is necessary to safeguard against splitting it asunder by taking hasty action on resolutions offered at the meetings without previous notice to the membership at large.[99]

After more discussion, a resolution was adopted requesting the Executive Council to ascertain the opinions of the membership regarding the earliest practicable entrance of the United States into the Court, and to make a public statement as to the opinions.[100] The Society's files and Proceedings do not indicate whether or not the Executive Council followed this up. It is noteworthy, though, that the resolution as adopted did not contemplate that the Society would take a position if the members expressed widespread sentiment either in favor of, or against, the United States joining the Court. All that was contemplated was a public statement of the members' opinions (plural).

The question of taking an institutional position was posed again in 1926, when Hollis R. Bailey offered a motion to refer to the Executive Council the question of whether the Society should create committees to formulate legislation to be introduced in Congress after approval by the Society.[101] James Brown Scott objected, noting that the Executive Council had already considered the matter and had not approved of it.[102] Nothing came of the motion.

Bailey got further than did J.A.H. Hopkins, of New York, who in 1927 wrote a letter to the Society requesting that it sign a petition to Congress urging the United States government never to protect the properties of its citizens abroad except by amicable means. It was summarily "ordered to be filed."[103]

In 1930, Scott had occasion to explain the Society's policy against adopting substantive resolutions:

> If a resolution is moved, it is referred to the Executive Council and considered, and then left over to the subsequent meeting, and in the meantime it has already entered upon its eternal slumber; our view being that the proceedings should have the value of the various persons who have participated in the discussions; that they should have the intellectual weight which they deserve from the strength of their arguments and the

---

99 17 *ASIL Proc.* 108 (1923).

100 Id. at 109.

101 20 *ASIL Proc.* 152-53 (1926).

102 Id. at 154.

103 Minutes of the Meeting of the Executive Council, Apr. 29, 1927, in 21 *ASIL Proc.* 144, 147 (1927).

> power of their reasoning; and that no artificial value should be attributed to them by majorities or minorities.[104]

3. Meeting Divergent Goals

During his long tenure in the inner circle of the Society, James Brown Scott faithfully did what he could to enable it to meet its two not-wholly compatible goals: educating the public about international law in the interest of preserving world peace, and providing a forum for scholarly ("scientific," as he put it) discourse. By the late 1920s, the scholarly side was clearly predominant. At the Executive Council meeting on April 27, 1928, Scott proposed that an *ad hoc* committee be appointed to consider the possibility of arranging future Annual Meetings so that scientific discussions could be held in morning and afternoon sessions, with evenings devoted to "the popular exposition" of international law questions.[105] The committee was appointed, with authority also to convene the next Annual Meeting on a Wednesday rather than a Thursday.

The 1929 Annual Meeting did begin on a Wednesday, but the evening discussions were just as technical as were the daytime ones. Such evening subjects as "The Pact of Paris for the Renunciation of War: Its Meaning and Effect in International Law"[106] and "Limitations of the Treaty-Making Power of the United States in Matters Coming within the Jurisdiction of the States,"[107] presented by a professor and a former Supreme Court Justice respectively, did not seem aimed at the general public. Meeting the two goals remained elusive.

Even within the academic ambit, the Society was trying to meet more than one goal. Some academic members, especially political scientists led by Charles Fenwick, thought that the Annual Meeting programs did not sufficiently focus on the theory of international law and relations. As Fenwick put it in 1931, reverting to a theme he had espoused six years earlier, the program contained "nothing of interest from the academic point of view."[108] Such noted academics as Manley Hudson and Philip Jessup were on the program as principal presenters, but they were not ivory tower types. The gap between theorists and policy-oriented academics was beginning to appear. It was not a complete schism by any means, but it was nevertheless perceptible.

---

104 James Brown Scott, remarks as Toastmaster at the annual banquet, 24 *ASIL Proc.* 243, 244 (1930).

105 22 *ASIL Proc.* 165 (1928).

106 The paper delivered by Roland S. Morris, 23 *ASIL Proc.* 88 (1929).

107 The paper delivered by Charles Henry Butler, id. at 176.

108 25 *ASIL Proc.* 255 (1931).

4. Press Coverage of Annual Meetings

From the Society's inception until the early 1940s, the two Washington dailies, the *Post* and the *Star*, made a practice of covering the annual dinner. In 1925, George Finch raised the question of inviting some additional members of the press to be guests at the dinner. The Executive Council decided to invite a representative from each of the four leading press associations: the Associated Press, the United Press, the International News Service and the Universal Service.[109] How often they accepted the invitations does not appear.

5. Scheduling Around Meetings of Other Organizations

From time to time throughout the Society's history, questions have come up regarding coordination of the Society's Annual Meeting with meetings of other organizations. Sometimes it has been a matter of trying to schedule meetings at the same time and place, in order to allow members of the Society to mingle with members of another organization and to attend some sessions with them. At other times it has been a matter of avoiding a conflict with a meeting of another organization.

As we have seen in Chapter One, the 1915 Annual Meeting was held in conjunction with the Second Pan-American Scientific Congress, which met in Washington in December of that year. In 1926, George Finch, James Brown Scott and Ellery C. Stowell (then the chair of the Annual Meeting Committee) conceived the idea of holding the 1927 Annual Meeting in October, to coincide with the 1927 meeting of the Institut de Droit International, which was to be held in Washington. Although several other influential Society members thought it was a good idea, the Meeting ultimately was held at the end of April, as usual. The reason seems to have been the difficulty many academic members would face in getting away to attend a meeting in Washington in the autumn.[110]

At about the time Finch was exploring the possibility of moving the 1927 Annual Meeting to October, Frederic Coudert was urging him to schedule Annual Meetings to coincide with those of the American Law Institute. Then as now, the two meetings were scheduled in Washington just far enough apart in the spring to make it inconvenient and expensive for some members of both organizations to attend both meetings.[111] Finch replied that it would be very difficult for the Society to change the dates of its Annual Meetings (the last weekend in April, except in 1915) without creating a conflict for Society members who belonged to other organizations that met in the spring outside Washington. He suggested

---

[109] 19 *ASIL Proc.* 162 (1925).

[110] Letter from George A. Finch to Ellery C. Stowell, Nov. 4, 1926.

[111] Letter from Frederic R. Coudert to George A. Finch, May 10, 1926.

that the ALI reschedule its Annual Meetings for the first half of the last week in April.[112]

In 1928, the ALI scheduled its Annual Meeting in Washington to be held on the same dates as the Society's Annual Meeting. This apparently was done without any attempt to coordinate the dates with the Society, and caused problems for some members who wanted to attend sessions of both organizations.[113] Finch took the position that it was the ALI's problem, since the Society had been meeting on the last weekend of April for more than twenty years.[114] The meetings proceeded simultaneously in 1928, but the ALI undertook to avoid a conflict in the future. Coudert's effort to coordinate the meetings had failed.

In 1934, the question came up again. By then, the American Bar Association had established its Section of International and Comparative Law. That Section and the ALI met in Washington in the spring of 1934. Manley Hudson suggested that the Society coordinate its future Annual Meetings with those organizations. The response was that it would be impracticable to do so.[115]

6. The Length of an Annual Meeting

At the 1926 Business Meeting, Charles Fenwick proposed that the Society set aside two full days at each Annual Meeting for substantive discussion. The practice had been to open each Annual Meeting with the presidential address and one other address on a Thursday evening, and then to hold substantive discussions on Friday, including Friday evening, and part of Saturday morning. The Saturday morning session ended with the Business Meeting. There was no session on Saturday afternoon, but members and guests gathered on Saturday evening for the annual banquet. Fenwick wanted Saturday afternoons to be used to continue the substantive discussions of Fridays and Saturday mornings.[116]

Charles Finch, rarely an innovator, replied that the room the Society used for the discussions at the Willard Hotel was also the room used for the annual dinner. The hotel staff needed Saturday afternoon to prepare the room for the dinner. Any attempt to have a Saturday afternoon session in a different room might run into a scheduling conflict with other organizations using the hotel at the same time, and in any event would be met by objections from Society members.[117]

---

[112] Letter from Finch to Coudert, May 12, 1926.

[113] Letter from Howard Thayer Kingsbury to George A. Finch, Feb. 18, 1928.

[114] Letters from Finch to Kingsbury, Feb. 23, 1928, to Hollis R. Bailey, Feb. 20, 1928, and to Manley O. Hudson, Feb. 2, 1928.

[115] Minutes of the Executive Council, Apr. 26, 1934, 28 *ASIL Proc.* 211, 213 (1934).

[116] 20 *ASIL Proc.* 156 (1926).

[117] Id. at 157.

The Business Meeting decided to refer the question of the feasibility of having two full days of substantive discussions to the Program Committee. In that Committee, Finch's concerns about keeping Saturday afternoons free prevailed. The Society stuck with its Annual Meeting schedule until 1929. Even then, Saturday afternoon remained formally open, although the teachers of international law held a meeting at that time.[118] The biggest change in 1929 was the decision to begin a day early, with the presidential address coming on a Wednesday evening. This change allowed two full days and evenings – Thursday and Friday – for substantive discussions. In 1930, however, the Society reverted to its former practice of opening the Annual Meeting on a Thursday.

7. White House Receptions

For the Society's first twenty years the President of the United States hosted a reception for the members during the Annual Meeting. In 1926, the custom began to crack – not at the instigation of the President, but rather at hands of the chair of the Annual Program Committee. Edwin Dickinson, then serving as chair, wrote to George Finch in January 1926 that he heartily agreed with "an influential member" of the Committee that a White House reception was a waste of time and "an unnecessary trespass on the President's strength." He proposed to omit it from the program unless there was a strong desire to the contrary.[119] Finch expressed reservations, noting that members from out-of-the-way places would no doubt consider an opportunity to meet the President as a highlight of the program. In any event, he suggested that an effort be made to persuade President Coolidge to speak at the annual dinner that year.[120] Charles Evans Hughes made the effort. Coolidge declined, but invited Society members to the White House. Dickinson capitulated and approved the reception.[121] Thus was a break in tradition averted for the time being.

No further attempts to stay clear of the White House are on record from the twenties. When Herbert Hoover took up residence there in 1929, he agreed to receive the Society's members on Friday afternoon of that year's Annual Meeting.[122] Nevertheless, the practice faded out soon thereafter. The Society's records do not show exactly when that occurred.

---

118 23 *ASIL Proc.* 210 (1929).

119 Letter from Edwin D. Dickinson to George A. Finch, Jan. 7, 1926.

120 Letter from Finch to Dickinson, Jan. 18, 1926.

121 Letter from Hughes to Finch, Feb. 1, 1926; telegram from Dickinson to Finch, Feb. 2, 1926.

122 Letter from Charles Evans Hughes to James Brown Scott, Apr. 3, 1929.

E. THE JOURNAL IN THE LATE TWENTIES

1. Some Policy Changes

In 1925, the Journal's Board of Editors made some minor additions to the 1924 set of editorial regulations. The most significant was a firmly stated policy to be conveyed as "suggestions" to book reviewers that "reviews will hereafter not exceed 1,000 words in length, and be descriptive of the contents of the volume, so that the review will show the point of view of the author of the book, rather than the point of view of the reviewer."[123] The suggestions were not always followed.

In 1928, the Board of Editors tried to solve a problem that has plagued Editors-in-Chief down through the years: how to induce Board members to meet their commitment to contribute regularly to the Journal. The Board adopted a rule laying down the expectation that each Editor would contribute the equivalent of at least two Editorial Comments a year to the Journal. Any Editor who failed to comply would be subject to replacement.[124] As an enforcement device, the Managing Editor began in 1929 to prepare a written report on the contributions to the Journal (as well as the performance of other editorial duties, such as reading manuscripts) of each Editor in the previous year.

Not all Board members needed to be prodded to contribute. One of them, the indefatigable Manley Hudson, submitted so many lead articles and editorial comments that George Finch and George Grafton Wilson at one point postponed publishing one of Hudson's submissions for fear that the Journal would appear to be excessively promoting a single point of view.[125] The decision to postpone was a delicate one, since Hudson's prolific scholarship added substance and stature to the Journal. Finch and Wilson could not afford to lose his interest. They succeeded in retaining it.

---

[123] 19 *ASIL Proc.* 162 (1925). During this period, the Executive Council's regulations on the editing of the Journal appeared in the introductory pages of each year's *ASIL Proceedings*.

[124] Report of the Editor-in-Chief, George Grafton Wilson, in 22 *ASIL Proc.* 163 (1928). It was only a year later that the Society's Executive Council approved a change in its Regulations delegating to the Board of Editors the authority to determine the minimum number of contributions each Editor would be called upon to contribute. 23 *ASIL Proc.* 262 (1929).

[125] Letter from Finch to Wilson, June 3, 1932; letter from Wilson to Finch, June 6, 1932.

2. Substantive Coverage

Volume 19 of the Journal, in 1925, celebrated the 300th anniversary of the publication of *De Jure Belli ac Pacis* with five lead articles on Grotius.[126] Other themes running through the volumes of the mid- to late-1920s centered on various dispute-settlement mechanisms,[127] cases decided by international tribunals,[128] diplomatic and consular rights,[129] issues involving the Americas,[130] and the time-honored favorite of the ASIL in its early years: codification of international law.[131]

---

126 C. Van Vollenhoven, "Grotius and the Study of Law," 19 *AJIL* 1 (1925); Jesse S. Reeves, "The First Edition of Grotius' *de Jure Belli ac Pacis*," 1625, id. at 12; Jesse S. Reeves, "Grotius' *de Jure Belli ac Pacis*: A Bibliographical Account," id. at 251; James Brown Scott, "Grotius' *de Jure Belli ac Pacis*: The Work of a Lawyer, Statesman and Theologian," id. at 461; Roscoe Pound, "Grotius in the Science of Law," id. at 685.

127 In addition to Manley Hudson's annual articles on the PCIJ, there were Jasper Y. Brinton, "The Mixed Courts of Egypt," 20 *AJIL* 670 (1926); Manley O. Hudson, "The International Mixed Court of Tangier," 21 *AJIL* 231 (1927); Manley O. Hudson, "The Rendition of the International Mixed Court at Shanghai," 21 *AJIL* 451 (1927); Arthur Burchard, "The Mixed Claims Commission and German Property in the United States of America," 21 *AJIL* 472 (1927); Robert A. MacKay, "The International Joint Commission Between the United States and Canada," 22 *AJIL* 292 (1928); Sir John Fischer Williams, "The Tribunal for the Interpretation of the Dawes Plan," 22 *AJIL* 797 (1928).

128 Manley Hudson's annual pieces on the PCIJ discussed cases decided in the year under review; see also Edwin M. Borchard, "The Mavrommatis Concessions Cases," 19 *AJIL* 728 (1925); Edwin M. Borchard, "Opinions of the Mixed Claims Commission, United States and Germany," 20 *AJIL* 69 (1926); Philip C. Jessup, "The Palmas Island Arbitration," 22 *AJIL* 735 (1928).

129 Clyde Eagleton, "The Responsibility of the State for the Protection of Foreign Officials," 19 *AJIL* 293 (1925); Irvin Stewart, "American Treaty Provisions Relating to Consular Privileges and Immunities," 20 *AJIL* 81 (1926); Irvin Stewart, "Consular Privileges and Immunities under the Treaties of Friendship, Commerce and Consular Rights," 21 *AJIL* 257 (1927); Francis Deák, "Immunity of a Foreign Mission's Premises from Local Jurisdiction," 23 *AJIL* 582 (1929). Cf. C. Van Vollenhoven, "Diplomatic Prerogatives of Non-Diplomats," 19 *AJIL* 469 (1925).

130 Joseph B. Lockey, "The Meaning of Pan-Americanism," 19 *AJIL* 104 (1925); Walter Scott Penfield, "The Legal Status of the Pan American Union," 20 *AJIL* 257 (1926); John P. Bullington, "Problems of International Law in the Mexican Constitution of 1917," 21 *AJIL* 685 (1927); John P. Bullington, "The Land and Petroleum Laws of Mexico," 22 *AJIL* 50 (1928); William Manger, "The Pan American Union at the Sixth International Conference of American States," 22 *AJIL* 764 (1928); Stephen P. Ladas, "Pan American Conventions on Industrial Property," 22 *AJIL* 803 (1928); James Oliver Murdock, "Arbitration and Conciliation in Pan America," 23 *AJIL* 273 (1929).

131 Elihu Root, "The Codification of International Law," 19 *AJIL* 675 (1925); William Ledyard Rodgers, "What Parts of International Law May Be Codified?," 20 *AJIL* 437 (1926); Manley O. Hudson, "The Progressive Codification of International Law," 20 *AJIL* 655 (1926); James

3. Editorial Practices

Viewpoints among members of the Board of Editors became increasingly heterogeneous in the late twenties. With George Grafton Wilson as Editor-in-Chief, and with some new and strong-willed Board members weighing in from prestigious colleges and universities, the Board began to take on some of the flavor of a faculty in a university department or law school. The tone of correspondence by and among Board members was sometimes more critical of views expressed by others and more defensive about their own views than before.

Then, as today, the Board had some members from outside academia, but they were a distinct minority. Their approach to such Board chores as reviewing manuscripts was not always like that of the academic members.

To give an example, in 1928 the Journal published a lead article by a non-academic, Edgar Turlington, on treatment of enemy property in the United States before 1914.[132] The article had been read and approved by two non-academic members of the Board. It consisted of a review of United States treaty practice, with attention also given to relevant decisions of domestic courts. At one point, Turlington asserted that provisions on treatment of aliens in the Jay Treaty of 1794 did not reflect an *opinio juris* under the law of nations. He went on to say, "Moreover, it should be borne in mind that the branch of the government charged with the conclusion of treaties was not competent to declare the law of nations on this point. The function of declaring the law of nations on appropriate occasions devolves under our Constitution upon the courts ... ."[133]

Edwin Borchard, of Yale, said in a letter to George Finch that the doctrine, as thus expressed, "explains the misconception underlying the whole article."[134] The misconception was that the political branches of the government were not competent to interpret the law of nations. Whether this was a fair reading of what Turlington said is debatable. In any event, Borchard opined that the article should not have been approved by the editors who reviewed it. He then wrote

Brown Scott, "The Gradual and Progressive Codification of International Law," 21 *AJIL* 417 (1927); Jesse S. Reeves, "Progress of the Work of the League of Nations Codification Committee," 21 *AJIL* 659 (1927). Cf. Stephen B. Ladas, "The Efforts for International Protection of Scientific Property," 23 *AJIL* 552 (1929)(dealing with development of international legislation, rather than codification of existing state practice).

132 Edgar Turlington, "Treatment of Enemy Private Property in the United States Before the World War," 22 *AJIL* 270 (1928). Turlington was Special Counsel to the United States in the United States-Mexican Claims Commission.

133 Id. at 276.

134 Letter from Edwin M. Borchard to George A. Finch, May 12, 1928.

an Editorial Comment challenging the proposition that in the United States, the function of declaring the law of nations devolves upon the courts.[135]

The Board of Editors has always had to decide how much, and in what respect, to edit manuscripts that are accepted for publication. In 1929, the question arose in connection with a manuscript submitted by Admiral William Ledyard Rodgers on the freedom of the seas and the law of neutrality. Arthur K. Kuhn was one of the Board members to whom it was sent for review. He deemed it worthy of publication, but objected to two passages asserting that Great Britain no longer was the leading sea power in the world. Kuhn, in his letter approving publication of the piece, said that the passages were superfluous and "would cause deep offense, which should be avoided in a Journal like ours which aims to be thoroughly scientific in character."[136] The passages were expunged, presumably with Admiral Rodgers' consent, and the article was published without them.[137]

It is one thing to edit a manuscript for thoroughness, accuracy or style, and another to do so in order to avoid offending a politically important foreign government or to maintain "scientific" objectivity in a law journal. In later years, the Journal would no longer be so circumspect or so "scientific." As a later Co-Editor-in-Chief would put it, "International law, after all, is not a scientific discipline in the same sense as physics or chemistry. It is not value-free … ."[138]

F. THE SOCIETY'S DIRECTION AT THE END OF THE TWENTIES

During the 1920s the Society took on a more distinct academic hue than it had in its earlier years. The trend accelerated toward the end of the decade. Until 1924, James Brown Scott – a person with one foot in academia, but nevertheless a man of affairs – had been the Society's defining force and had guided it along a path of close attention to current events, with a mission to make international law a decisive force for peace in the world. In this, he was supported, and in many respects led, by another man of the world, Elihu Root.

When George Finch succeeded Scott at the helm of day-to-day affairs, the office became one of serving the forcefully expressed interests of the influential officers and members of the Society. Many of the influential members – such as Manley

---

135 Edwin M. Borchard, Editorial Comment: "Treatment of Enemy Private Property in the United States Before the World War," 22 *AJIL* 636 (1928).

136 Letter from Arthur K. Kuhn to Wilber S. Finch (George Finch's brother, who was temporarily filling in for the latter), Aug. 29, 1929.

137 William Ledyard Rodgers, "Political Reasons Making Undesirable an International Agreement as to Freedom of the Seas," 23 *AJIL* 739 (1929).

138 Oscar Schachter, "The Invisible College of International Lawyers," 72 *Nw. U. L. Rev.* 217, 218 (1977).

Hudson, Edwin Borchard, George Grafton Wilson, Charles Fenwick and Edwin Dickinson – were academics, as were some rising stars like Philip Jessup.

Charles Evans Hughes, of course, was not an academic. As the President of the Society, he was in a position to put his imprimatur on it. Nevertheless, even though he was an active President of the Society, he did not put the Society's business as prominently on his agenda as Root had. Unlike Root, he does not seem to have viewed the Society as one of the great hopes for the maintenance of an ordered, peaceful world. Moreover, his chief operating officer, Charles Finch, was not the prominent figure in international law that James Brown Scott was. Nor were Hughes and Finch writing on a clean slate, unlike Root and Scott. Consequently the Hughes-Finch tandem was not able to shape the Society in the way the Root-Scott team did.

By the end of the 1920s, then, the Society had taken on many of the largely academic features that would characterize it in more recent years. It was less messianic than before in its view of its role as the purveyor of international law to those who could influence governmental decision makers. As it slipped away from that principal function, it was becoming more a forum for the expression of diverse views at its Annual Meetings and in its Journal, and less an instrument for promoting peace in the world than its founders intended.

Some of the older, non-academic members became disenchanted by the shift in emphasis.[139] But not all. Frederic Coudert, not an academic, wrote to James Brown Scott in 1931, "The objectives of the Society have been realized and the ideas advocated by you and the group of lawyers and scholars who undertook the work twenty-five years ago have been carried into an ever-ripening fruition."[140]

Perhaps some disenchantment was inevitable. From the outset there had been tension between peace activism through promotion of international law, on one hand, and providing a forum for serious scholarly discussion, on the other. Full equilibrium between the two goals could not have been expected to last indefinitely. Moreover, those who saw the Society primarily as an instrument for peace had been jolted severely by the events of 1914-1918. Some optimism had returned by the late 1920s, but it could not match that of the founders in 1906. Discussions at Annual Meetings and in the Journal still were focused often on the maintenance of peace, but they generally were more detached than

---

139 In January 1930 Francis M. Anderson, a long-standing member of the Society then serving in the State Department, resigned from the Society because, he said, "the Society is more and more becoming an arena for the expounding of certain pet theories of theorists in international law, and ... a 'back scratching and self-glorification' group for the purpose of advancing younger teachers of international law to positions which they desire." Letter from Francis M. Anderson to George A. Finch, Jan. 8, 1930.

140 Letter from Coudert to Scott, Mar. 13, 1931.

members of the Society's direct ancestor, the turn-of-the-century American peace movement, would have wished.

Chapter Four

THE YEARS LEADING TO WORLD WAR II

Twenty-five years ago you could almost count on your fingers the people in the United States who knew or cared anything about international law. The formation of the American Society of International Law gave one of the great initial impulses towards laying the foundation of knowledge and understanding necessary for a democracy which is to take an active part in the affairs of the community of nations. During the twenty-five years which have passed the increase of popular interest in international law and in the study of it has been extraordinary and most gratifying.

– Elihu Root
Letter to James Brown Scott, March 6, 1931,
reprinted in 25 *ASIL Proceedings* 1 (1931)

A. ADMINISTERING THE SOCIETY IN THE THIRTIES

1. James Brown Scott, President of the Society

When James Brown Scott was elected President of the Society at the 1929 Business Meeting, several members offered encomiums. He seemed not only the logical choice to succeed Charles Evans Hughes, but the only choice. After the tributes had concluded, Scott took the chair and gave a genuinely modest response to what had just been done and said:

> I have never considered myself as possessing the attainments which a President of this Society should have and should hold. I have not held high political positions. I have from time to time held positions of trust. My belief is that the traditions of the Society should be continued in the future as they have in the past. I accept this post for the coming year as an expression of your affection, with the understanding that in the meantime you will have the opportunity of considering for the office as my immediate successor one who possesses the qualities and the titles of what may be considered the traditions of the Society. Although I shall be happy indeed to contribute as far as is humanly possible to the success of the Society during the coming year, I withdraw at this moment and in

> advance to my successor who shall be elected, as I hope and believe, at the forthcoming session of the American Society of International Law.[1]

The members of the Society did not permit Scott's withdrawal to take effect until ten years later. He served as President from 1929 until 1939.

Scott continued the tradition of delivering a presidential address at the outset of each Annual Meeting.[2] His address in 1932 characterized his beliefs, at least during his later years. The theme was that a single moral standard applies both to the individual and to the group of individuals who make up the state:

> The world, notwithstanding the artificial personality called the state, is made up of human beings. Their laws must be consistent with their nature; the laws of human kind are not and can not be the dictates of the artificial entities which we call states, since these entities in fact have no existence separate and distinct from their incorporators – the people who have made them what they are.
>
> ...
>
> There can not be two standards. There must be a single standard for the human being applying to all of his activities, whether they be isolated or communal: a house divided against itself falls. There can be but one standard for the groups of individuals which, taken together, form humanity, and the groups which, as such, compose the international community. Humanity needs and the world must have the moral interpretation of history.[3]

Scott did not identify the standard he had in mind. Clearly, though, he believed that international law needs to reflect moral principles rather than simply being controlled by state practice and *opinio juris*. Moreover, he believed he could demonstrate that modern international law had its origins in "universal justice – whether called natural law, divine law, human law, or all three."[4] Accordingly, he regarded Francisco de Vitoria, rather than Hugo Grotius, as the founder of

---

1 23 *ASIL Proc.* 201 (1929).

2 Scott's presidential address at the 25th anniversary Annual Meeting, in 1931, is discussed in Section B, *infra*.

3 James Brown Scott, "A Single Standard of Morality for the Individual and the State," 26 *ASIL Proc.* 10, 20-21 (1932).

4 James Brown Scott, *The Spanish Origin of International Law: Francisco de Vitoria and His Law of Nations* 195 (1934).

the law of nations.[5] That view has been challenged.[6] Today, Scott's view could be accepted as an explanation of the relatively few norms that are regarded as *jus cogens*, but not as an explanation of international legal norms generally.

Scott's 1937 presidential address was an appreciation of his old friend and mentor, Elihu Root, who died on February 7, 1937, just eight days shy of his 92nd birthday. Scott's opening sentence summarized what he admired in Root the statesman:

> We are meeting tonight to pay tribute to the memory of one who was our "first American citizen" throughout a long period of years, American in ancestry, American in every fiber of his being, an American, too, who recognized that there were nations other than his own which should be considered by every American statesman in forming the foreign, and indeed internal, policies of his country.[7]

No higher tribute could be paid to an American so prominently identified with a Society devoted to "the establishment and maintenance of international relations on the basis of law and justice."[8]

2. The Transition to a New President

In 1937, Scott began actively to seek a replacement for himself as President of the Society. He approached Henry L. Stimson, the former Secretary of State, but Stimson turned him down because he had just accepted the presidency of the Bar of the City of New York.

In 1938, Scott became ill and was confined to bed for several weeks. He missed the Annual Meeting because of his ill health, but he did – as he put it – sit up for a few moments in order to write to Stimson again, urging him to accept the presidency of the Society.[9] Stimson wrote a gracious reply, again declining to serve because of his duties as President of the New York City Bar.[10]

The Society then turned to the sitting Secretary of State, Cordell Hull. Charles Fenwick, who had worked with Hull in attempts to develop better relations with

---

5 Id. at 196.

6 See Arthur Nussbaum, *A Concise History of the Law of Nations* 296-306 (Rev. ed. 1954); see also Christopher R. Rossi, *Broken Chain of Being: James Brown Scott and the Origins of Modern International Law, passim* (1998).

7 James Brown Scott, "An Appreciation," 31 *ASIL Proc.* 1 (1937).

8 Constitution of the American Society of International Law, Art. II.

9 Letter from James Brown Scott to Henry L. Stimson, Apr. 22, 1938.

10 Letter from Henry L. Stimson to James Brown Scott, Apr. 26, 1938.

Latin America, was enlisted to persuade Hull to accept.[11] Fenwick succeeded. Hull became President of the Society in 1939.

Scott enthused: "It is the greatest thing that could be done. It is the salvation of our Society."[12] Hyperbole aside, the applause that greeted the announcement at the Business Meeting showed how relieved the members were to have a respected public figure accept the presidency at a time when the Society's membership was declining and the world was sliding into another conflagration. Hull served as President of the Society until 1942.

3. The Executive Council and the Body of Officers: Diversity, Turnover and Structure

Diversity in the 1930s did not mean what it does in 2006. Only a few women and no persons of color, so far as can be determined, were sought out for membership in the inner circles of the Society. Efforts at diversity focused on different professional experiences and, to some extent, geographic distribution. For example, in 1933, the Nominating Committee proposed, and the Business Meeting elected, a slate for the Executive Council that consisted of a historian from within the State Department, an Assistant Legal Adviser of the Department, two practicing attorneys (one in the District of Columbia, the other in Philadelphia), a prominent arbitrator/writer, a political scientist at an undergraduate college, and two political scientists at research universities (one at Cornell and the other at the University of Washington in Seattle).[13]

In 1935, the chair of the Nominating Committee ticked off these criteria for nomination to positions on the Executive Council: individual activity, attendance at Annual Meetings, distribution throughout the country, variation of point of view, "and such matters."[14] In 1936, the criteria mentioned were "a distribution of representation from the Department of State, from the legal profession, and from the universities, and also a certain geographical distribution as well."[15]

Charles Fenwick proposed at the 1933 Business Meeting that no more than four of the eight annual nominees for membership on the Executive Council be persons who had already served on the Council. No resolution to that effect was adopted, but a member of the Nominating Committee said that Fenwick's proposal would be taken into account.[16]

---

11 Letter from George A. Finch to Charles G. Fenwick, May 3, 1939.

12 33 *ASIL Proc.* 144 (1939).

13 27 *ASIL Proc.* 178-79 (1933).

14 29 *ASIL Proc.* 156 (1935).

15 30 *ASIL Proc.* 183 (1936).

16 27 *ASIL Proc.* 179 (1933).

In 1938, Ellery C. Stowell, chair of the Society's Nominating Committee, proposed on behalf of the Committee that in the future a Nominating Committee be appointed several months in advance of the Annual Meeting "so as to allow for the fullest expression of opinion among the members of the Society." That would require an amendment to the Society's Constitution, which then provided that the five-member Nominating Committee was to be elected at the first session of the Annual Meeting.[17] It would then submit its nominations later in the same week.

Stowell also reported that the Committee favored a much greater representation of younger members of the Society, presumably in the Society's committees and Executive Council. Further, there should be more turnover and less duplication in the membership of Society committees than had been the case.[18]

The Executive Council decided to appoint an *ad hoc* committee to consider these recommendations and any other changes to the Constitution that might be necessary or desirable.[19] Philip Jessup chaired the committee. A year later he reported that there had been more rotation in office than some had supposed.[20] His committee found that in the years 1920-1938 there had been 152 places to fill on the Executive Council; 107 different persons had filled them, of whom 58 served not more than one term. Fourteen had served more than two terms.[21]

As it turned out, the principal issue the committee confronted did not concern the participation of younger members in Society bodies or the composition of committees, although the committee did recommend a procedural change designed to broaden representation in the Executive Council, particularly to include younger members. The procedural recommendation was that the Executive Council instruct the Secretary to prepare annually a list of all persons who had served on the Executive Committee and Executive Council, with the years served, and that this list be given to the chair of the Nominating Committee.[22] The Nominating Committee thus could avoid nominating those who had already served or who had served too often. The recommendation was carried out.[23]

---

17 Constitution of the Society (Revision of Apr. 25, 1925), Art. IV, 32 *ASIL Proc.* vii, viii (1938).

18 32 *ASIL Proc.* 176 (1938).

19 32 *ASIL Proc.* 212 (1938).

20 33 *ASIL Proc.* 146 (1939).

21 Report of the Special Committee of the American Society of International Law, 33 *ASIL Proc.* 218, 219 (1939).

22 Id.

23 For example, on March 10, 1942, George Finch wrote to Edgar Turlington, chair of the Nominating Committee, enclosing a record of those who had served on the Executive Council since 1928.

The committee proposed a constitutional amendment, which was adopted without controversy in 1940, providing for election of the Nominating Committee at the last session of the Annual Meeting preceding the Meeting at which the nominations would be submitted.[24] There was some controversy over the preferred composition of the Nominating Committee. The Business Meeting finally elected five Executive Council members to the 1940-1941 Nominating Committee who would be retiring from the Council in 1941.[25]

The principal constitutional issue involved the term of office and eligibility for re-election of the President of the Society. The committee feared that there would be no more persons with the stature of Elihu Root, Charles Evans Hughes or James Brown Scott who would be willing for an indefinite term to put in the time and effort needed to energize the Society. Cordell Hull took the presidency in 1939 on the understanding that a term limit was being considered, so he did not think of his acceptance as an open-ended commitment to the Society.[26] The committee deemed it desirable to have the Secretary of State, or someone with similar stature, at the helm of the Society. It was thought that a term limit would help to entice such persons; furthermore, it would be good in any event to have turnover at the top.[27] Consequently the committee initially proposed an amendment to the Constitution that would retain the existing one-year presidential term, with re-election permitted only for an additional one-year term; then the person in office would be ineligible for re-election for five years.[28]

The Executive Council rejected the committee's recommendation.[29] A year later, the committee reached an accommodation with the Council. The compromise was that the President would not be eligible for more than three consecutive one-year terms. This, Jessup said, would put the Society in step with other learned societies in such fields as political science, history and economics.[30]

Some of the older Society members opposed any limitation on the President's term of office. Their spokesperson, William C. Dennis, pointed to the Society's success in its thirty-four years under just four Presidents. He wondered if the success would have been as great had there been frequent turnover at the top. He referred to Cordell Hull's presidential address two nights earlier, and took pride in the fact that it had made news worldwide. He thought it unlikely that

---

24 Constitution of the Society (Revision of May 15, 1940), Art. IV, 34 *ASIL Proc.* vii, viii (1940).

25 34 *ASIL Proc.* 182-85 (1940).

26 Remarks of Philip Jessup, 33 *ASIL Proc.* 146 (1939), & 34 *ASIL Proc.* 168 (1940).

27 33 *ASIL Proc.* 146 (1939).

28 Supplementary Report of the Special Committee, 33 *ASIL Proc.* 220 (1939).

29 Minutes of the Executive Council, Apr. 29, 1939, in 33 *ASIL Proc.* 201, 203 (1939).

30 34 *ASIL Proc.* 168 (1940).

lesser-known Society Presidents, intellectually capable though they would be, could make themselves heard as advocates for the rule of law in international affairs.[31] George Finch was more guarded in his opposition to a rotating presidency, but he clearly thought such a policy would diminish the Society's impact as a force for the rule of law in international affairs.[32]

Bessie C. Randolph led the defense of the proposal. She stressed that it was a compromise, but it was the best compromise attainable. What was needed was a President who not only gave luster to the Society, but who could devote time to it. Times had changed since the Society was founded; leaders of distinction would not make the long-term commitment that Root and Scott had.[33]

A motion to strike the term limit from the proposed constitutional amendments was defeated by a vote of 34 to 19.[34] The revised Constitution was then adopted by a vote of 43 to none.[35] Aside from the amendment previously mentioned, on election of the Nominating Committee, the only other significant changes were removal of elected Executive Council members from designation as officers of the organization, the elimination of the Executive Committee and a related reduction in the quorum for meetings of the Executive Council from the previous nine to seven.[36] With only seven Council members, it was thought that there was no need for an Executive Committee.[37]

Less significant structural changes were made at other times in the thirties. Until 1930 the Society had both a Recording Secretary and a Corresponding Secretary. The Recording Secretary – first James Brown Scott, and then George A. Finch – essentially ran the Society. The Corresponding Secretary did very little. By 1930 it was apparent that there was no need to have a separate office of Corresponding Secretary. Accordingly, the Constitution was amended to consolidate the two offices into a single Secretary of the Society.[38] George Finch,

---

31 34 *ASIL Proc.* 168-70 (1940). Hull's address dealt with order under law in international relations. Id. at 12-16.

32 Letter from George A. Finch to Charles G. Fenwick, May 3, 1939.

33 34 *ASIL Proc.* 172-74, 175 (1940).

34 Id. at 175-76. For the term-limit provision as adopted, see Constitution of the Society (Revision of May 15, 1940), Art. IV, 34 *ASIL Proc.* vii, viii (1940).

35 34 *ASIL Proc.* 181 (1940).

36 Constitution of the Society (Revision of May 15, 1940), Arts. IV & VI, 34 *ASIL Proc.* vii, viii-ix (1940). Charles Fenwick had proposed in 1925 that the Executive Committee be abolished, on the ground that it was not representative of the Society as a whole. 19 *ASIL Proc.* 126 (1925).

37 Report of the Special Committee, 33 *ASIL Proc.* 218, 219 (1939) (submitted before the reduction in the quorum had been proposed).

38 24 *ASIL Proc.* 241 (1930).

now the possessor of a slightly amended title, continued to do what he had been doing all along.

In 1936, the Executive Council, acting under its authority in the Society's Constitution to fix the number of Honorary Vice Presidents, increased the number by one, to fourteen.[39]

4. Opening Doors in the Society for Young Members

Since at least the 1920s it has been relatively easy for ambitious young stars in the galaxy of international law to become active, and even prominent, in the Society. Such luminous figures as Manley O. Hudson and Philip Jessup shone and were recognized early in their careers. But other capable young members, whose talents may not have been so obvious or whose personalities may not have been so strong, have not always risen rapidly to the top.

Since at least 1922 some measures have been taken to ease the way for young members to have some influence in the Society. In that year, as we have seen in Chapter Two, the Society's Constitution was amended to require a one-year hiatus before an elected Executive Council member could be re-elected when his or her three-year term ended. The goal was to ensure turnover, and it resulted in the election of some young members who undoubtedly would not otherwise have gained early entry into the inner circle. As we have also seen, attention was given in the late 1930s to procedures that would make it easier for young members to be elected to the Executive Council.[40] Moreover, as early as 1936, the Society's Annual Meeting Committee endeavored to include some young members on the program for the Annual Meeting.

Established authors have been predominant in the pages of the Journal since its inception. Nevertheless, long before the inception of the Francis Deák Award (designed to stimulate and reward contributions to the Journal by young authors), some young members of the Society had their work published. For example, in 1937, James Brown Scott received an unsolicited manuscript on changes in the Soviet approach to international law. It was submitted by a 28-year-old author who had not yet achieved faculty status at any university. The Journal published it in 1938.[41] The author, John Newbold Hazard, went on to become a renowned expert on Soviet law and a fixture on the Columbia University law faculty.

---

39 Minutes of the Executive Council, Apr. 23, 1936, in 30 *ASIL Proc.* 218, 222 (1936).

40 See text at note 23 *supra*.

41 John N. Hazard, "Cleansing Soviet International Law of Anti-Marxist Theories," 32 *AJIL* 244 (1938).

5. Selection of Honorary Members

During the 1930s there were efforts to get away from some of the rather informal ways the Society had gone about its official business. For example, until 1933 the Committee on Selection of Honorary Members each year simply made an oral report to the Executive Council, recommending the person the Committee had selected, if indeed the Committee had a person to recommend. The Executive Council would invariably go along with the Committee.

At the Executive Council meeting on April 27, 1933, there was some dissatisfaction with this informal procedure. Several possible honorees other than the one recommended were discussed. The recommended honoree, W.J.N. van Eysinga, of The Netherlands, was ultimately selected, but a motion was adopted requiring future Committees on Selection of Honorary Members to submit their recommendations in writing with full statements of the qualifications of the person recommended.[42]

This attempt to formalize the procedure was only partially successful. In 1937, the Committee decided not to recommend anyone as an honorary member. Its chair, James W. Garner, reported this to the Executive Council. James Brown Scott moved that the report of the Committee be amended by recommending the nomination of Gilbert Gidel, of France. The motion was seconded and, "after a lengthy discussion," was adopted.[43]

The Business Meeting then elected Gidel, but only after Garner – who had chaired the Committee since 1933 – questioned whether the Society had any real criteria for honorary membership.[44] One member had deplored the fact that only one of the nine honorary members was from Latin America. Garner disparagingly referred to that position as "promoting a friendly good neighbor policy."[45] George Finch suggested that in the future the Committee present several names, with a statement of the qualifications of each person considered, along with the Committee's recommendation.[46]

Garner remained the Committee's chair in 1938. Despite his suggestion a year earlier that the Society needed to come up with some criteria, he did not submit a report on policies or procedures. Instead, he reported on several persons who had been considered. He then conveyed the Committee's recommendation

42 In addition, Executive Council members could thenceforth propose their own candidates by sending names to the chair of the Committee before the meeting. Minutes of the Executive Council, Apr. 27, 1933, in 27 *ASIL Proc.* 235, 237 (1933).

43 Minutes of the Executive Council, Apr. 29, 1937, in 31 *ASIL Proc.* 220, 222 (1937).

44 31 *ASIL Proc.* 195 (1937).

45 Id.

46 Id. at 196.

that Hans Kelsen be made an honorary member.[47] The Business Meeting elected Kelsen with no discussion of policy.[48]

6. Continuing the Effort to Get Access to Documents of State

In the 1930s the Society kept up its effort, begun in the twenties, to improve public access to U.S. documents of state. In April 1931 the Society's Executive Council adopted a resolution urging the State Department to bring the Foreign Relations of the United States series "as near to date as the public interest will permit" and publish a series of proceedings of international conferences and arbitrations in which the United States had participated.[49] Although some effort was made to turn the resolution into reality, there was little if anything to show for it. By 1933, the Depression had forced retrenchments in the State Department's publications budget, leaving the joint Society-Teachers' Conference Publications Committee little choice but to place on record the history of its efforts and its desires for the future, and to propose a modest appropriation for 1934.[50]

In 1934, the Society reconstituted its own standing committee, which dated back to 1929. It was now called the Committee on Publications of the Department of State, with Herbert Wright as its chair.[51] In 1935, the standing Committee published a report containing a comprehensive description of the State Department's publications on foreign affairs, including the gratefully acknowledged treaty series then being prepared by Hunter Miller.[52] This marked the beginning of the Society's Publications Committee's practice of issuing detailed reports on State Department publications that might be of interest to international lawyers. The reports were published in the annual Proceedings. They were particularly informative in the 1930s, under Herbert Wright's tutelage.[53]

On July 1, 1939, volume 1, number 1 of the *Department of State Bulletin* appeared. It replaced the State Department's weekly pamphlet, *Press Releases*, and its monthly bulletin, *Treaty Information*, both of which had been of considerable interest to the Society's committee. The Society's archives do not reveal just

---

47 Minutes of the Executive Council, Apr. 28, 1938, in 32 *ASIL Proc.* 205, 207 (1938).

48 Id. at 165-66.

49 25 *ASIL Proc.* 260, 261 (1931).

50 Memoranda from Philip C. Jessup, Chair of the Joint Committee, to its members, Sept. 20, 1933, & Nov. 16, 1933.

51 28 *ASIL Proc.* vi, 187-88 (1934).

52 Report of the Committee on Publications of the Department of State, 29 *ASIL Proc.* 199 (1935).

53 See Reports of the Committee on Publications of the Department of State, 30 *ASIL Proc.* 234 (1936); 31 *ASIL Proc.* 233 (1937); 32 *ASIL Proc.* 218 (1938); 33 *ASIL Proc.* 222 (1939).

what influence the Society or its committee had on the decision to publish the *Department of State Bulletin*, but George Finch later said there was reason to believe that the Society's efforts during these years was a substantial contribution to the enlargement of the State Department's publication programs.[54] That presumably would include the *Bulletin*.

7. A Newcomer on the Block: the American Bar Association's International Law Section

In 1933, the American Bar Association formed its Section on International and Comparative Law. Right away, there was tension between the Society and the new Section. For one thing, the Section scheduled a special meeting for the following May in Washington, a prospect that threatened to siphon off some attendance from the Society's late April Annual Meeting. Lester H. Woolsey immediately wrote George Finch a note saying that this was evidently an attack on the Society on its home grounds, "raising a serious problem for the Society's existence."[55] That may have overstated the case a little. Nevertheless, a challenge had been laid down and the Society was forced to pay attention to it.

The tension was exacerbated when John H. Wigmore, the first Chair of the ABA Section, was quoted in the *American Bar Association Journal* as saying, "The Society of International Law in Washington consists of about eighty per cent professors of law and ten per cent members of the diplomatic service or practitioners in Washington, and as somebody has just suggested to me, about five per cent retired ministers, and they produce very valuable papers."[56] Dean Wigmore later said that it was just a passing remark, not intended to be printed, the purpose of which was to suggest that international law was of real interest to practitioners and not just to professors and diplomats.[57] In any event, George Finch immediately wrote a letter to the Editor of the *American Bar Association Journal*, pointing out that the ASIL had a total membership of about 1100, of whom only 235 were connected to colleges and universities; 400 belonged to the ABA. Nor were they concentrated in Washington: 237 were from New York, while 176 were from Washington, and the rest were scattered throughout the United States and abroad.[58]

54 See George A. Finch, The American Society of International Law 1906-1956, 50 *AJIL* 293, 304-05 (1956).

55 Handwritten note from Lester H. Woolsey to George A. Finch, Nov. 23, 1933.

56 Statement by John H. Wigmore, 19 *ABA J.* 594, 595 (1933).

57 Undated letter from John H. Wigmore to the Editor of the *American Bar Association Journal*, published in 20 *ABA J.* 186, 187 (1934).

58 Letter from George A. Finch to Joseph R. Taylor, Nov. 3, 1933, published in 20 *ABA J.* 59-60 (1934).

At about the same time Finch received a communication from the Ex-President of the ABA, who said he wanted to talk to James Brown Scott "about incorporating his Society of International Law into the Section on International and Comparative Law of the American Bar Association." Throwing diplomacy to the winds, he added, "I know that both of you will approach the subject in an antagonistic spirit, yet I would like for you to think it over from all sides. We will then discuss the subject later."[59] It is safe to assume that neither Scott nor Finch gave it more than a moment's thought.

The air cleared a bit in the spring and summer of 1934. First, Wigmore apologized for his offhand remarks and arranged to have his apology published in the *American Bar Association Journal*.[60] Then Wigmore offered to help make the Society known to Section members by giving out information on the Society at the Section meeting in August.[61] Wigmore's gesture caught Finch off-guard. He had no leaflet on the Society to send to Wigmore. Instead, he sent copies of the Society's application form, the program of the last Annual Meeting and the table of contents of the last volume of the Journal.[62] Marketing was not his strength.

The air cleared a little more in the autumn of 1934 when Nathan W. MacChesney, the newly elected Chair of the ABA Section, wrote Scott a conciliatory letter offering close cooperation between the Section and the Society.[63] By then two prominent members of the Society, Frederic R. Coudert and Edwin D. Dickinson, were members of the Council of the ABA Section.

8. The Struggle to Maintain the Society's Membership During the Depression

The Society's membership declined during the 1930s. Undoubtedly, the effects of the Depression account for a great deal of the decline. One wonders, though, whether the Depression is the complete explanation. Membership in the American Bar Association's Section on International and Comparative Law rose from a few hundred at the Section's inception in 1933 to 1,535 in 1939.[64] The Section, of course, appealed primarily to practicing lawyers, while the Society

---

59 Letter from Clarence E. Martin to George A. Finch, Oct. 10, 1933.

60 See note 57, *supra*.

61 Letter from John H. Wigmore to George A. Finch, June 14, 1934.

62 Letter from Finch to Wigmore, June 18, 1934.

63 Letter from Nathan William MacChesney to James Brown Scott, Sept. 4, 1934. MacChesney even accepted the invitation to join the Society that Scott had sent him four years earlier.

64 "Report of the [ASIL] Committee on Increase of Membership," 33 *ASIL Proc.* 208 (1939).

was increasingly – but not exclusively – the preserve of academics. It may well be that the Society was seen as too theoretical, too scholarly in its outlook to be able to attract a significant section of the internationally oriented practicing bar, which turned instead in a time of financial austerity to the body that most closely reflected its concerns.

It cannot be said whether public figures of the stature of Elihu Root or Charles Evans Hughes at the helm of the Society could have brought significantly larger numbers of the practicing bar into the fold. The Society had simply run out of larger-than-life figures.

9. Student Membership

The seeds of the student membership idea were planted in 1933, but they did not immediately take root.[65] By 1938, they had found more fertile ground. The Society's Business Meeting authorized the Executive Council "to establish a student membership upon such terms and with such dues as it shall determine."[66] The Council adopted the student membership program in 1939. Membership would be open, with reduced dues, to any "properly qualified" graduate or undergraduate student who filed appropriate evidence of student status. Student members would receive the Journal and could participate in Annual Meetings, but could not vote or hold office. They could become regular members at any time by paying the regular dues.[67]

10. To Incorporate or Not to Incorporate?

From the early years until 1950, the question came up sporadically of whether the Society should incorporate. The Society had been organized as an unincorporated association, but as early as 1917 a member proposed that it should become a corporation. The member, A.H. Snow, said that the Society had begun to receive and administer subventions from outside agencies like the Carnegie Endowment, and he thought it was unbusinesslike, as well as risky, for the Society and individuals acting for it to administer the funds on an *ad hoc* basis. He thought it would be easier to adopt articles of incorporation and by-laws to take care of this matter than to amend the Society's existing Constitution to do so. Accordingly,

---

65 For details of the process leading to student memberships, see Memorandum, "ASIL History: Details Relating to Budget, Finances and Membership" (2006), on file with the Society.

66 Minutes of the Business Meeting, Apr. 30, 1938, in 32 *ASIL Proc.* 162, 180 (1938).

67 Regulations Regarding Student Membership in the American Society of International Law, Apr. 27, 1939, in 33 *ASIL Proc.* x, 199 (1939).

he submitted a certificate of incorporation and a set of by-laws.[68] Nothing was done at that time, and the issue faded away until the 1930s.

In 1934, the issue came up again. Howard T. Kingsbury, a member of the Executive Council who was experienced in the incorporation of not-for-profit associations, made a presentation to the Executive Committee. He recommended against incorporation, since his experience suggested that associations like the Society could conduct their affairs more easily by remaining unincorporated than by incorporating. He was supported by two members of the Executive Committee. The consensus was that the Society should remain unincorporated.[69] So it did, for the time being.

11. Membership in the American Council of Learned Societies

In April 1934, the Society's Executive Council reversed an earlier decision and authorized an application for membership in the American Council of Learned Societies. Membership would entitle the Society to send two delegates and alternates to ACLS meetings, and was deemed sufficiently attractive to justify payment of the USD 35 annual ACLS dues.[70] The Society duly applied, and was informed on February 6, 1935, that it had been admitted to ACLS membership by unanimous vote.[71] The Society remained a member until 1950, when the Executive Council decided for budgetary reasons that the Society should not belong to other organizations, including the ACLS.[72] The Society would rejoin the ACLS in 1970.[73]

B. THE TWENTY-FIFTH ANNIVERSARY

Elihu Root, the President of the Society for its first seventeen years, was unable to attend the 25th anniversary Annual Meeting in 1931, but he sent a letter to be read to the membership. He was upbeat:

> Twenty-five years ago you could almost count on your fingers the people in the United States who knew or cared anything about international

---

68 Letter from A.H. Snow to George Grafton Wilson, Mar. 3, 1917. Snow was apparently motivated by his experience as chair of the Executive Committee of the Trustees of George Washington University during the U.S. government's investigation of the university's affairs in 1910. Id. at 6.

69 Minutes of the Executive Committee, Apr. 26, 1934, in 28 *ASIL Proc.* 220 (1934).

70 Minutes of the Executive Council, Apr. 26, 1934, in 28 *ASIL Proc.* 210, 215 (1934).

71 Minutes of the Executive Council, Apr. 25, 1935, in 29 *ASIL Proc.* 189, 190 (1935).

72 Minutes of the Executive Council, Apr. 29, 1950, in 44 *ASIL Proc.* 245, 247 (1950).

73 See Chapter Nine, Section A.14, *infra*.

> law. The formation of the American Society of International Law gave one of the great initial impulses towards laying the foundation of knowledge and understanding necessary for a democracy which is to take an active part in the affairs of the community of nations. During the twenty-five years which have passed the increase of popular interest in international law and in the study of it has been extraordinary and most gratifying.[74]

Appropriately, James Brown Scott was the President of the Society in 1931. Before the Annual Meeting began, he presided over a luncheon at the Carlton Hotel. In attendance were twenty-nine men who comprised the inner circle of the Society. Some of them had been present at the creation. Informal remarks were made and later published in the Society's Proceedings.[75] In the main, they consisted of tributes to the Society as a force for justice in the world, to the Journal for its stature in its field, and to Scott as the guiding light of the Society.

The Annual Meeting was held at its usual venue in the Willard Hotel. Scott took as the topic of his presidential address, "The Progress of International Law During the Last Twenty-five Years." He touched on several themes he had long emphasized: codification of international law, the need for permanent international tribunals to apply the codified law, the renunciation of war as a means of settling disputes, the common destiny of the states in the Americas, and the usefulness of U.S. experience as a model for the international system. He ended with a plea for equal rights of men and women, particularly in respect of the acquisition and loss of nationality, but across the board as well – a subject he said was fit for international regulation by means of simple, straightforward treaty provisions.[76]

Such assertions were not revolutionary in 1931, but neither were they much in vogue in the United States. Nevertheless, those who knew Scott would not have been much surprised to hear them from him. He had been a proponent of women's rights throughout his adult life.[77] He was the President of the Institute of International Law in 1929 when it adopted its *Déclaration des droits internatiounaux de l'Homme* – a declaration designed to protect individuals from discrimination on the basis of sex, race, language or religion.[78]

---

74 Letter from Elihu Root to James Brown Scott, Mar. 6, 1931, reprinted in 25 *ASIL Proc.* 1 (1931) & in 25 *AJIL* 525 (1931).

75 25 *ASIL Proc.* 242 (1931).

76 James Brown Scott, "The Progress of International Law During the Last Twenty-five Years," 25 *ASIL Proc.* 2, 28-33 (1931).

77 See George A. Finch, James Brown Scott, 1866-1943, in 38 *AJIL* 183, 209-11 (1944).

78 For the original French text of the Declaration, see [1929] 2 *Annuaire de l'Institut de Droit International* 298-300. English translations appear in George A. Finch, Editorial Comment:

A substantial part of the 1931 Annual Meeting was devoted to discussion of the Permanent Court of International Justice. An entire session had also been devoted to the Court in the previous year.[79] United States participation in the Court was very much a live issue. The Senate had given its advice and consent to U.S. participation, but had attached five reservations. The League of Nations Assembly had adopted a Protocol of [U.S.] Accession to the Statute of the Court. It was based on the "Root Formula," which amounted to a rather elastic acceptance of the U.S. reservations subject to some none-too-clear terms and conditions relating to the second part of the fifth U.S. reservation (the attempt to preclude the Court from issuing an advisory opinion without U.S. consent if the request for an opinion touched on any dispute or question in which the United States had or claimed an interest).[80]

Arthur K. Kuhn, a charter member of the Society, had suggested that a woman be invited to lead the discussion of the Root Formula, in recognition of the important role women's groups had played in keeping the Court issue alive in the United States.[81] As it turned out, a woman was asked (at the last minute) to give a short paper on the Court, but not on the Root Formula. Eleanor Wyllys Allen, of the Bureau of International Research at Harvard, discussed the obligatory jurisdiction of the Court after the main paper on the subject had been delivered by Amos J. Peaslee, of the New York Bar.[82]

The P.C.I.J. was not the only topic of discussion. Green Hackworth, the Solicitor (Legal Adviser) of the Department of State, presented a paper on U.S. policy in recognizing new governments over the preceding twenty-five years[83] – a timely topic in light of the growing belief that continued U.S. non-recognition

---

"The International Rights of Man," 35 *AJIL* 662, 663-64 (1941), and in Louis B. Sohn, "How American International Lawyers Prepared for the San Francisco Bill of Rights," 89 *AJIL* 540, 545-46 (1995). See also James Brown Scott, "The Seventh International Conference of American States," 28 *AJIL* 219 (1934), where Scott praised the work of the Inter-American Commission of Women on equal rights for men and women.

79 See the series of papers on "Contributions of the Permanent Court of Justice to the Development of International Law," 24 *ASIL Proc.* 34 (1930).

80 For discussion of the Root Formula, see Philip C. Jessup, "The Root Formula for the Accession of the United States to the Permanent Court of International Justice," 25 *ASIL Proc.* 61 (1931). The Senate Resolution, the Protocol of Accession and several other documents relating to prospective U.S. participation in the PCIJ may be found in an Appendix to the 1931 Proceedings, id. at 262-354.

81 Letter from Arthur K. Kuhn to George A. Finch, Jan. 23, 1931.

82 See Eleanor Wyllys Allen's remarks, 25 *ASIL Proc.* 57 (1931), following the paper by Amos J. Peaslee, "Obligatory Jurisdiction of the Permanent Court of International Justice," id. at 48.

83 Green H. Hackworth, "The Policy of the United States in Recognizing New Governments During the Past Twenty-five Years," id. at 120.

of the Soviet Union was counterproductive. Charles E. Martin, of the University of Washington, gave a paper on the law of neutrality during the preceding twenty-five years.[84]

Charles Evans Hughes, by then the Chief Justice of the United States Supreme Court, agreed to speak at the 25th Anniversary annual dinner. It was a gala event, attended not only by members of the Society and their guests, but also by twenty-six heads of diplomatic missions in Washington.[85] Hughes' address focused on what he perceived as increasing interest in international law and in international dispute-settlement institutions. It made the front page of the Sunday *New York Times*.[86] Both the *Times* and the *New York Herald Tribune* published the speech in full. The *Washington Herald*, though, took a dim view. Hughes had included a sentence in his speech asserting that "the best hope of the world today, so far as the development of international law is concerned, lies in the establishment of a permanent court of international justice."[87] The *Herald* took this as advocating U.S. participation in the World Court, and called for Hughes to resign as Chief Justice.[88]

C. OTHER ANNUAL MEETINGS AND SOME ISSUES THEY RAISED

1. Divergent Goals Revisited

As we have seen, throughout the Society's early years there was a certain tension between its scholarly goals and its desire to educate the public for quite practical purposes. After the Society's first few years, the scholarly side gradually ascended. Nevertheless, scholars within the membership were not always satisfied with the pace of change or with the forms it took.

The issue came into focus again in 1933. Edwin Borchard, of the Yale Law School, took exception to a proposal that the Annual Meeting of that year deal with controversial current events such as the Manchurian question and the Chaco War. Borchard posed the issue as he saw it:

> The Society is primarily a learned society, or should aim to be one, rather than a forum for the popular discussion of current political controversies. On some of the problems mentioned, the facts are still too uncertain to

---

84 Charles E. Martin, "The Legal Position of War and Neutrality During the Last Twenty-five Years," id. at 137.

85 For several years thereafter, members of the diplomatic corps were invited to the annual dinners, and quite a few attended. Those who did attend were listed in the Proceedings.

86 *N.Y. Times*, Apr. 26, 1931, p. 1.

87 Charles Evans Hughes, Remarks, 25 *ASIL Proc.* 231, 234 (1931).

88 *Wash. Herald*, May 2, 1931, p. 10.

> admit of clear opinions, particularly legal opinions. ... The danger of having the Society become a popular forum for the expression of heated political views of the moment tends to keep more thoughtful members away from the meetings and does but very little to promote the science of international law, which, I think, the Society should keep primarily in mind. ... [The Society's major function should be] to improve the science of international law after reflection and calm deliberation, which, in turn, presupposes a more thorough knowledge and digestion of the facts than current political controversies usually allow.[89]

One Society member, at least, expressed qualified agreement. Charles E. Martin agreed that the Society is a learned society and not a forum for public discussion of popular issues, but its discussions should "pertain to subjects which matter in this generation." It would thus be appropriate to "discuss and perhaps explain the legal implications of some of our contemporary international problems."[90] Borchard's reply, if any, is not a matter of record.

Borchard did not exhaust his arsenal in 1933. In 1936, the theme of the Annual Meeting was peaceful change, and the principal papers were focused accordingly. Shortly before the meeting, Borchard wrote to George Grafton Wilson complaining that the program looked more like an announcement of a foreign policy association, or of an association for the propulsion of the United States into the League of Nations, than of an international law society.[91] The program proceeded as scheduled, and Borchard was promptly appointed to head the Annual Meeting Committee for the next year. He duly noted that revenge had been taken upon him.[92]

* * *

Throughout the decade, as throughout most of the Society's history, the Annual Meetings were more topical than Borchard would have liked. That was so even when academics were heavily involved in the preparations and presentations. It was true even in 1937, the year for which Borchard served as chair of the Annual Meeting Committee. The topics that year were international agreements, the laws of war and neutrality, and civil wars.

Neutrality, in particular, was a subject of great interest in the 1930s. The storm clouds were gathering again over Europe, raising questions about whether it would be legally permissible for any country to remain neutral in the face of such instruments as the Kellogg-Briand Pact and Article 16 of the League of

89 Letter from Edwin M. Borchard to Lester H. Woolsey, Jan. 19, 1933.

90 Letter from Charles E. Martin to Edwin M. Borchard, Feb. 13, 1933.

91 Letter from Edwin M. Borchard to George Grafton Wilson, Apr. 8, 1936.

92 Letter from Edwin M. Borchard to George A. Finch, Apr. 29, 1936.

Nations Covenant (which required League members to apply sanctions against any member that went to war in disregard of its peaceful dispute-settlement obligations under the Covenant).[93] Neutrality was the theme of the entire 1935 Annual Meeting; it occupied one session at the 1936 Annual Meeting,[94] and it was the subject of one paper at the 1937 and 1938 Annual Meetings.[95]

There was some attention paid to international economic law at the Annual Meetings in the 1930s, particularly in 1934. In that year there were expositions on such topics as the international regulation of tariffs and the protection of foreign bondholders.[96] In 1937, there were three presentations on executive trade agreements.[97] In other years there were some presentations that could be considered hybrids between classical public international law and international economic law, such as the two presentations in 1933 on treatment of aliens' private property.[98]

Perhaps the 1939 Annual Meeting came closer to Borchard's preferred model than any other during the decade. Except for a presentation on collective security by Allen Dulles,[99] the program remained largely aloof from the cataclysmic events that had started to unfold in Europe. Presentations were made on the American and Soviet conceptions of international law, the idea of

---

93 The United States, of course, was not a League member.

94 The two papers presented at the session were Amry Vandenbosch, "Neutrality and Problems of Peaceful Change," 30 *ASIL Proc.* 129 (1936), and Allen T. Klots, "Neutrality Laws and Exceptions to Commercial Treaties," id. at 138.

95 In 1937, the paper was by Lawrence Preuss, "The Effect of Governmental Controls on Neutral Duties," 31 *ASIL Proc.* 108 (1937). In 1938, the paper was on neutrality in connection with international air law, and was by the Society's leading authority on the law of neutrality, Philip C. Jessup, "Neutral Rights and Duties," 32 *ASIL Proc.* 86 (1938). Jessup was the Reporter for the Harvard Research project on neutrality, and in the mid-1930s he published a book on the subject. Philip C. Jessup, *Today and Tomorrow* (1936) (volume 4 of a series, *Neutrality: Its History, Economics and Law*).

96 Charles E. Martin, "The International Regulation of Tariffs," 28 *ASIL Proc.* 44 (1934); Huston Thompson, "The Security Law for the Protection of Foreign Bondholders," id. at 136; Martin T. Manton, "Reorganization and Rehabilitation of Government Bond Issues," id. at 155. See also Edwin M. Borchard, "International Loans and International Law," 26 *ASIL Proc.* 135 (1932).

97 Henry S. Fraser, "The Executive Trade Agreements: Constitutionality," 31 *ASIL Proc.* 55 (1937); Phoebe Morrison, "The Executive Trade Agreements: Embargo Clause," id. at 67; William S. Culbertson, "The Executive Trade Agreements: Most-Favored-Nation Treatment," id. at 73.

98 John P. Bullington, "Treatment of Private Property of Aliens on Land in Time of Peace," 27 *ASIL Proc.* 103 (1933); E. Russell Lutz, "Treatment of Private Property of Aliens on Land in Time of War," id. at 110.

99 Allen W. Dulles, "Collective Security," 33 *ASIL Proc.* 118 (1939).

law in international relations, private international law, and the role of labor in international relations.

The Society's records do not reveal any conscious decision to play down what was happening in Europe in 1939. In fact, they contain a letter from Philip Marshall Brown, chair of the Annual Meeting Committee, to the rest of the committee in which he said:

> I find a consensus of opinion that the occasion should be used not merely to reaffirm our faith in international law but to make as positive a contribution as possible to a clear understanding of prevailing conditions and of the vital role of international law in meeting those conditions. The *leit motiv* of this Session would seem to be something along this line, "The Maintenance of International Law and Order," though we do not have to state it explicitly.[100]

2. The Ongoing Pursuit of Prominent Annual Dinner Speakers

Throughout the decade, James Brown Scott made valiant efforts to persuade prominent persons, from the President of the United States on down, to speak at the annual dinners. He was particularly tenacious in his pursuit of Cordell Hull, who became Secretary of State in 1933. Scott wanted Hull to use the Society's platform for major foreign policy addresses, much as Frank Kellogg had used it in 1928 to interpret the Kellogg-Briand Pact. Hull did speak at the 1933 annual dinner, but made no foreign policy pronouncement of any consequence.[101] For the remainder of Scott's ASIL presidency he tried to persuade Hull to return, promising him an audience that included significant representation from the diplomatic corps in Washington. Hull cordially but steadfastly declined, on the ground that the pressure of work did not give him time to do justice to the occasion.

The most prominent speakers at annual dinners in the 1930s were Charles Evans Hughes at the 25th anniversary Annual Meeting in 1931 and Alexander A. Troyanovsky, the Soviet Ambassador to the United States, in 1934. Troyanovsky voiced the opinion that the League of Nations experience tended to show that "at the present time at least supernational bodies are not effective in binding the nations to cooperate under established rules of international law."[102] The *Washington Evening Star* covered the speech, noting that Troyanovsky spoke to "a brilliant audience of international jurists, Federal leaders and members of the diplomatic corps."[103]

---

100 Letter from Philip M. Brown to Annual Meeting Committee, Jan. 9, 1939.

101 Address by the Honorable Cordell Hull, 27 *ASIL Proc.* 217 (1933).

102 Address of Alexander A. Troyanovsky, 28 *ASIL Proc.* 195, 196 (1934).

103 *Wash. Evening Star*, Apr. 29, 1934.

3. The Format of Annual Meetings

During the 1930s, as had been the case previously, all of the substantive sessions at the Annual Meetings were plenary. Only later would more than one substantive session be held simultaneously. Each session would typically last from two to three hours and would involve the delivery of two or three papers, followed by floor discussion usually led by someone designated in advance to do so.

The perennial problem of inducing those who were delivering papers to stay within the established time limit came up at a meeting of the Executive Council in 1934. The Council responded:

> *Resolved*, That in future annual meetings of the Society, the resolutions of the Executive Council regulating the time allowed for papers, addresses and discussions be rigidly enforced and that the chairman of the meeting read such resolutions to the Society at the opening of each session.[104]

This attempt at the mobilization of shame appears to have been no more successful than such earlier devices as placing a large clock directly opposite the speaker's lectern.

There was no problem in getting floor discussion started. The discussions, however, tended to be dominated by many of the same people from year to year, at least when they dealt with such classical public international law matters as neutrality or the law of the sea.

The Annual Meeting always ended on a Saturday evening with the annual dinner. There would be a toastmaster (the President of the Society if he was available) and more than one speaker – usually three or four. The speakers normally held forth for only a few minutes, and tried to maintain a fairly light tone.

4. The Venue of Annual Meetings

From the Society's first Annual Meeting in 1907 through to 1935, the venue was the Willard Hotel in Washington. There were frequent complaints that the meeting room (only one, in those days) allocated to the Society at the Willard was too noisy. Nevertheless, over the years both Scott and Finch were resolute in favor of the Willard, largely because the Society was given free use of the room in return for holding the revenue-producing (for the Willard) banquet there.

In 1936, the Society made the break. It held its Annual Meeting at the Carlton, where it stayed until 1942.

---

[104] Minutes of the Executive Council, Apr. 28, 1934, 28 *ASIL Proc.* 222, 225 (1934).

D. THE EXPANDING ROLE OF WOMEN

During the 1930s, female members of the Society slowly broadened the toehold Judge Kathryn Sellers had established in 1923 as the first female member of the Executive Council. As we have seen, Eleanor Wyllys Allen was asked to give a short paper at the 1931 Annual Meeting. She and other women participated in the floor discussion at that meeting, and set the stage for women's participation in the Annual Meetings in later years. In 1934, for example, Judge Florence E. Allen of the Sixth Circuit Court of Appeals gave one of the addresses at the annual banquet. She affirmed the importance of the Montevideo Convention on Rights and Duties of States, with its prohibitions of armed intervention and of the acquisition of territory by force.[105] She also urged the teaching of international law not only as it is, but as it should be.[106]

In 1932, Bessie Carter Randolph, then a professor of political science at Florida State College for Women, was elected to the Executive Council. She had been a member of the Society since 1922 and had published a lead article in the Journal in 1931.[107] In 1934, she was installed as President of Hollins College, in Virginia.[108] She continued to be active in the Society. She was the principal drafter of the amendments to the Society's Constitution that were adopted in 1940.[109]

Bessie Carter Randolph was not the only woman to publish a lead article in the Journal in the thirties. Female authors published eleven lead articles, on a variety of subjects, during the decade.[110] For some reason, though, the

---

105 Convention on the Rights and Duties of States, Dec. 26, 1933, 3 *Bevans* 145, 165 *LNTS* 19.

106 Florence E. Allen, The Objective of International Law, 28 *ASIL Proc.* 198 (1934).

107 Bessie C. Randolph, "Foreign Bondholders and Repudiated Debts of Southern States," 25 *AJIL* 63 (1931).

108 The Society was represented at her installation ceremony, but it took a last-minute appeal from a member of the Hollins Board of Trustees, as well as a formal invitation, to spur the Society into designating a representative. The appeal was in a letter from Marguerite Hearsey to George A. Finch, Feb. 14, 1934. The Society designated Professor James F. Peake, of Randolph-Macon Woman's College, as its representative.

109 34 *ASIL Proc.* 167 (1940).

110 Margaret Lambie, "Presumption of Cessation of Citizenship: Its Effect on International Claims," 24 *AJIL* 264 (1930); Bessie C. Randolph, *supra* note 107; Ernestine Fitz-Maurice, "Convention for the Suppression of Counterfeiting Currency," 26 *AJIL* 533 (1932); Anna A. O'Neill, "United States–Sweden Arbitration Relating to Motorships Kronprins Gustaf Adolf and Pacific," 26 *AJIL* 720 (1932); Lora L. Deere, "Political Offenses in the Law and Practice of Extradition," 27 *AJIL* 247 (1933); Ethel C. Phillips, "American Participation in Belligerent Commercial Controls 1914-1917," 27 *AJIL* 675 (1933); Josephine Joan Burns, "Conditions of Withdrawal from the League of Nations," 29 *AJIL* 40 (1935); Alice M. Morrissey, "The United States and the Rights of Neutrals, 1917-1918," 31

number of female-authored lead articles dropped off in the following three decades.[111]

E. THE JOURNAL AND ITS SUPPLEMENTS

1. The Board of Editors and its Functions

In 1930, Manley Hudson proposed to the Journal's Board of Editors that each member study each issue and comment on it, with the comments to be circulated to all members of the Board.[112] He typed detailed comments on the July 1930 issue and sent them to George Finch with the request that they be circulated.[113] His comments criticized several Editorial Comments, including one written by Finch, and questioned whether some of them should have been published. Finch wrote back rather defensively, urging that the comments not be circulated until a time closer to the next Board meeting so any differences of opinion could be aired face to face rather than by correspondence.[114] Hudson acquiesced.[115]

Hudson's proposal was not adopted. Nevertheless, it and some of the comments Hudson prepared on the July 1930 issue are indicative of the steady movement in the Society in general, and on the Journal in particular, toward rigorous standards of scholarship. Hudson was a very influential member of both the Society and the Board of Editors. He was a prodigious scholar and an extremely conscientious member of the Board of Editors.[116] His ideas were not always adopted, but the force of his intellect and personality had a significant impact on the Society and the Board. He was a stickler for detail.[117] He criticized any article or editorial

---

AJIL 17 (1937); Ruth E. Bacon, "Representation in the International Commission of the Danube, "31 *AJIL* 414 (1937); Louise W. Holborn, "The Legal Status of Political Refugees, 1920-1938," 32 *AJIL* 680 (1938); Virginia L. Gott, "The National Socialist Theory of International Law," 32 *AJIL* 704 (1938).

111 Alona E. Evans & Carol Per Lee Plumb, Notes and Comments: "Women and the American Society of International Law," 68 *AJIL* 290, 295 n. 29 (1974), noting that there were eight such articles in the 1940s, three in the 1950s and five in the 1960s.

112 Letters from Manley O. Hudson to George A. Finch, Sept. 8, 1930, & Oct. 10, 1930.

113 Manley O. Hudson, "Comment on the July number of the American Journal of International Law" (typescript, Sept. 9, 1930).

114 Letter from George A. Finch to Manley O. Hudson, Oct. 9, 1930.

115 Letter from Hudson to Finch, Oct. 10, 1930.

116 For example, in the year from April 1932 to April 1933, Hudson contributed to the Journal two lead articles, ten Editorial Comments and five book reviews. In addition, he reviewed six manuscripts for publication in the Journal.

117 See, e.g., his review of the *Annual Digest of Public International Law Cases* for 1927 and 1928, in 26 *AJIL* 437 (1932).

comment that did not provide full and accurate documentation, and he had little tolerance for the publication in the Journal of anything not of interest to scholars, unless the item was placed in the Current Notes section.

During the 1930s (and ever since) two members of the Board of Editors, in addition to the Editor-in-Chief, continued to read each manuscript that was seriously considered for publication. Authors, then as now, could become impatient if the review was not done expeditiously. It is difficult to determine from written records how long it normally took for that process to be completed. On one recorded occasion, however, rejection of a manuscript on neutral rights in wartime took 181 days.[118] When the disgruntled author complained, George Finch replied, "The time it took to return your manuscript was not unduly long for a manuscript of this character."[119] If indeed that was normal, one can see why authors might be disgruntled.

Editors who reviewed manuscripts were not restricted to yes or no votes on publishability. As has continued to be the case, they could and did make suggestions, sometimes extensive ones, for the improvement of pieces they deemed publishable.

2. Relations Between the Board of Editors and the Society as a Whole

At the 1934 Business Meeting of the Society, William I. Hull, a professor at Swarthmore, moved that the Editorial Board of the Journal "be requested to take into consideration the desirability of the further exploration of the best means of promoting the codification of international law."[120] The motion was a reaction to a ruling by James Brown Scott, the presiding officer, that criticism offered by another Society member of the codification effort by Harvard Research in International Law was out of order on the ground that the Harvard Research was wholly unconnected with the Society. The immediate response of Quincy Wright, a member of the Board of Editors, was, "Are we to understand, if the motion prevails, that the Editorial Board is directed by the Society as a whole to undertake the editorial discussion of this subject?"[121] Hull assured him that it was merely a recommendation. After further discussion, Scott posed the question in his own terms: "The question before the house, as has been stated by Mr. Jessup, is that the Editorial Board will invite discussion as to the codification of international law."[122] The motion carried.

---

[118] Letter from H.A. Gosnell to George A. Finch, Jan. 19, 1931.

[119] Letter from Finch to Gosnell, Jan. 21, 1931.

[120] 28 *ASIL Proc.* 188 (1934).

[121] Id.

[122] Id. at 189.

Scott had managed to water down the resolution considerably. The incident is emblematic of the strained relations that have sometimes existed between the Board of Editors and the Society at large, ever since the Executive Council demonstrated its independence from the Board in 1924.[123] The Board has been very sensitive about its prerogatives, including its editorial independence. It is not surprising that Board members present at the 1934 Business Meeting, including James Brown Scott, then the Honorary Editor-in-Chief, bridled at any suggestion that the Council or the Society's membership might significantly influence the content of the Journal – even when codification, the topic the Board was being asked to explore, was close to Scott's heart.[124]

3. Editorial Policies

In 1932, George Finch clarified the Journal's policy against publishing articles that had already appeared elsewhere. John Bassett Moore received the English text of an article by Max Schröder that had been published in German in the *Zeitschrift für Völkerrecht* and in French in the *Revue de Droit International de Sciences Diplomatiques et Politiques*. He inquired whether the Journal would ever publish in English an article that had appeared in another language.[125] The answer was no.[126]

The policy, however, did not extend to individual opinions of members of the Permanent Court of International Justice – at least if the author was the American judge who was also an Honorary Vice President of the Society. In 1931, the Journal published as a lead article the individual opinion of Frank B. Kellogg in the case of the *Free Zones of Upper Savoy and the District of Gex*.[127] The opinion had previously been published in the Court's judgments series.[128]

---

123 See Chapter Two, Section D.2.

124 The Journal did publish some pieces on codification in the ensuing years, including a lead article by Philip Marshall Brown, "The Codification of International Law," 29 *AJIL* 25 (1935), and devoted the entire volume 29 of its Supplement to three projects of the Harvard Research in International Law, but it does not appear that the Journal's Board was influenced by Professor Hull's recommendation. For example, the Journal had already published Harvard Research projects *in toto* in its 1929 and 1932 Supplements.

125 Letter from John Bassett Moore to J. Edwin Young, Chief Clerk of the Carnegie Endowment, June 30, 1932.

126 Letter from George A. Finch to John Bassett Moore, Aug. 8, 1932.

127 Frank B. Kellogg, "Limits of the Jurisdiction of the Permanent Court of International Justice," 25 *AJIL* 203 (1931).

128 *Free Zones of Upper Savoy and the District of Gex*, Order of Dec. 6, 1930, PCIJ Ser. A, No. 24, at 29 (separate opinion of Judge Kellogg).

4. Some Matters of Substance

The Journal led off the decade with an article by Charles Cheney Hyde on the Permanent Court's interpretation of treaties.[129] It was traditional legal scholarship in the best sense. Hyde discussed the plain meaning rule, observing that it had not been put to the test in the Court's jurisprudence inasmuch as there had been no case where extrinsic evidence tended to cast doubt on the meaning the Court extracted from a treaty's text. He ran through other now-familiar treaty interpretation issues, such as the use of historical context, the problem of reconciling variations between the official languages of treaties, and the examination of preparatory work. It was an insightful, perhaps even seminal, piece for its time. It was translated into French and published in the *Revue de Droit International.*

In 1932, the Journal published an article by Julius Stone on the League of Nations petitioning procedure under the post-World War I minorities treaties.[130] That procedure was a precursor of later United Nations human rights petitioning procedures. Stone's perceptions of the League procedure for minorities help to explain some of the characteristics of the later United Nations petitioning procedure under ECOSOC Resolution 1503.[131] For example, he pointed out the problem of politically motivated and possibly ill-founded petitions alleging infractions of the minorities treaties – a concern reflected also in Resolution 1503, where the focus is on petitions asserting consistent patterns of "gross and reliably attested violations of human rights and fundamental freedoms."

The 1932 volume of the Journal contained a couple of noteworthy Editorial Comments. One, by L.H. Woolsey, outlined the history until then of the office of the State Department Legal Adviser,[132] setting the stage for later and fuller studies by other authors.[133] The other was an early salvo in what would grow into Quincy Wright's monumental treatise on war.[134]

---

[129] Charles Cheney Hyde, "The Interpretation of Treaties by the Permanent Court of International Justice," 24 *AJIL* 1 (1930).

[130] Julius Stone, "Procedure under the Minorities Treaties," 26 *AJIL* 502 (1932).

[131] ECOSOC Res. 1503, 48 UN ESOR Supp. 1A (E/4832/Add.1), at 8 (1970).

[132] L.H. Woolsey, Editorial Comment: "Legal Adviser of the Department of State," 26 *AJIL* 124 (1932).

[133] See Richard B. Bilder, "The Office of the Legal Adviser: The State Department Lawyer and Foreign Affairs," 56 *AJIL* 633 (1962); Ellery C. Stowell, *The Legal Adviser of the Department of State* (1936), published by The Digest Press, of which Stowell was the Director.

[134] Quincy Wright, Editorial Comment: "When Does War Exist?", 26 *AJIL* 362 (1932). See also Quincy Wright, "The Concept of Aggression in International Law," 29 *AJIL* 373 (1935). The full study is Quincy Wright, *A Study of War* (1942), and second edition in 1965.

The Journal, and the ASIL itself, tried throughout John Bassett Moore's adult life to persuade him to be an active participant. His typical response was that he would like to do more for the Journal or the Society, but he did not have the time. George Finch thus was delighted when Moore submitted a lead article for the October 1933 number of the Journal. In the article, Moore attacked what he saw as a narrow spirit of isolationism in the United States – a spirit that manifested itself in what Moore regarded as an arrogant assumption of authority to distinguish a *de jure* from a *de facto* foreign government on the basis of its constitutionality; a disregard for the traditional law of neutrality; and an approval of the use of "boycotts" (mainly arms embargos) in the name of protecting world order.[135] In part, the article was an elaboration of a theme Moore had introduced in a Foreign Affairs article, where he had decried the notion that the threat or imposition of collective sanctions under the League Covenant was more likely to preserve peace than was the traditional principle of neutrality.[136] Edwin Borchard leapt to Moore's side with an Editorial Comment in the Journal.[137]

The 1933 volume of the Journal also included an Editorial Comment by Manley Hudson on Iraq's admission to the League of Nations, pointing out that it was the first admission of a former mandated community. Hudson supplied some history and described the process by which Iraq was admitted to the League.[138] Hudson could hardly have foreseen Iraq's future prominence in international affairs.

Toward the end of the decade Hudson wrote another Editorial Comment on a subject that was to rise again much later. The Comment dealt with the international criminal court that had been proposed in connection with the Terrorism Convention of 1937. Hudson summarized the history of efforts to establish an international criminal court and the relationship the proposed court would have with the P.C.I.J.[139]

Throughout the thirties, Hudson published his annual lead articles on the Permanent Court. Like his earlier and later articles on the Court, they contained a wealth of information and analysis, not only of the Court's judgments and advisory opinions, but also of its personnel and procedure. No detail was overlooked. These articles are a mine of information for anyone doing serious research on the output or operation of the World Court.

135 John Bassett Moore, "The New Isolation," 27 *AJIL* 607 (1933).

136 See John Bassett Moore, "An Appeal to Reason," 11 *Foreign Affairs* 566 (1933).

137 Edwin M. Borchard, Editorial Comment: "Realism v. Evangelism," 28 *AJIL* 108 (1934).

138 Manley O. Hudson, Editorial Comment: "The Admission of Iraq to Membership in the League of Nations," 27 *AJIL* 133 (1933). See also Quincy Wright, "Proposed Termination of the Iraq Mandate," 25 *AJIL* 436 (1931).

139 Manley O. Hudson, Editorial Comment: "The Proposed International Criminal Court," 32 *AJIL* 549 (1938).

It must be said, though, that Hudson's great zeal for the Court could cause him occasionally to abandon the critical eye he often focused on other institutions and persons. For example, he applauded the Court's desire to minimize the distinction between judgments in contentious cases and advisory opinions, without focusing on how the blurring of that distinction would stoke fears in the United States Senate that judgments in the guise of advisory opinions might be rendered against the United States if it were a party to the Court's Statute.[140]

The Journal paid considerable attention to the Permanent Court in the 1930s, publishing several articles on it in addition to Hudson's annual reviews.[141] Other topics featured during the decade were the law of treaties, including municipal law relating to treaties,[142] and various aspects of the law of

---

[140] See Manley O. Hudson, "The Twelfth Year of the Permanent Court of International Justice," 28 *AJIL* 1, 17 (1934). Hudson was expressing his approval of the combination of the Court's Series A (judgments) and B (advisory opinions) into a single Series A/B, begun in 1931.

[141] Charles Cheney Hyde, *supra* note 129; Manley O. Hudson, "The Election of Members of the Permanent Court of International Justice," 24 *AJIL* 718 (1930); Frank B. Kellogg, *supra* note 127; Manley O. Hudson, "The Amended Rules of the Permanent Court of International Justice," 25 *AJIL* 427 (1931); A.H. Feller, "Conclusions of the Parties in the Procedure of the Permanent Court of International Justice," 25 *AJIL* 490 (1931); Norman L. Hill, "National Judges in the Permanent Court of International Justice," 25 *AJIL* 670 (1931); Manley O. Hudson, "Two Problems of Approach to the Permanent Court of International Justice," 29 *AJIL* 636 (1935); Sidney B. Jacoby, "Some Aspects of the Jurisdiction of the Permanent Court of International Justice," 30 *AJIL* 233 (1936); H. Arthur Steiner, "Fundamental Conceptions of International Law in the Jurisprudence of the Permanent Court of International Justice," 30 *AJIL* 414 (1936); Manley O. Hudson, "The 1936 Rules of the Permanent Court of International Justice," 30 *AJIL* 463 (1936); Leland M. Goodrich, "The Nature of the Advisory Opinions of the Permanent Court of International Justice," 32 *AJIL* 738 (1938).

[142] See Charles Cheney Hyde, *supra* note 129; Kenneth W. Colegrove, "The Treaty-Making Power in Japan," 25 *AJIL* 270 (1931); R. Earl McClendon, "The Two-Thirds Rule in Senate Action upon Treaties," 1789-1901, 26 *AJIL* 37 (1932); Payson W. Wild, Jr., "Treaty Sanctions," 26 *AJIL* 488 (1932); Pitman B. Potter, "Inhibitions upon the Treaty-Making Power of the United States," 28 *AJIL* 456 (1934); Harold J. Tobin, "The Role of the Great Powers in Treaty Revision," 28 *AJIL* 487 (1934); J. Mervyn Jones, "The Retroactive Effect of the Ratification of Treaties," 29 *AJIL* 51 (1935); Charles Fairman, "Implied Resolutive Conditions in Treaties," 29 *AJIL* 219 (1935); James W. Garner & Valentine Jobst III, "The Unilateral Denunciation of Treaties by One Party Because of Alleged Non-Performance by Another Party or Parties," 29 *AJIL* 569 (1935); Henry Reiff, "The Proclaiming of Treaties in the United States," 30 *AJIL* 63 (1936); Walter Schiffer & Francis O. Wilcox, "Treaty-Making in Post-War Germany," 30 *AJIL* 216 (1936); Charles Fairman, "Competence to Bind the State to an International Engagement," 30 *AJIL* 439 (1936); Robert R. Wilson, "International Law in Treaties of the United States," 31 *AJIL* 271 (1937); Alfred von Verdross, "Forbidden Treaties in International Law, "31 *AJIL* 571 (1937); Robert B. Stewart, "Treaty-Making Procedure in the British Dominions," 32 *AJIL*

war.[143] As fascist aggression became increasingly ominous in Europe, the Journal began to focus on such timely aspects of the law of war as the law of neutrality and issues raised by the Spanish Civil War and by Italy's invasion of Ethiopia.[144]

During this period the Journal was able to attract lead articles from several foreign authors who were or soon would be prominent scholars of international law.[145] It was a sign, if one were still needed, of the Journal's pre-eminence in its field.

5. The Journal's Impact

In the October 1930 issue, the Journal published an article entitled "Rights over the Arctic."[146] It dealt in part with the 1924 treaty between Norway and

---

467 (1938); William Sanders, "Reservations to Multilateral Treaties Made in the Act of Ratification or Adherence," 33 *AJIL* 488 (1939).

[143] See Edwin D. Dickinson, "The Closure of Ports in Control of Insurgents," 24 *AJIL* 69 (1930); E.G. Trimble, "Violations of Maritime Law by the Allied Powers During the World War," 24 *AJIL* 79 (1930), and reply by James W. Garner, 25 *AJIL* 26 (1931); Charles X. Hyneman, "Neutrality During the European Wars of 1792-1815," 24 *AJIL* 279 (1930); Charles Warren, "Belligerent Aircraft, Neutral Trade, and Unpreparedness," 29 *AJIL* 197 (1935); Quincy Wright, "The Concept of Aggression in International Law," 29 *AJIL* 373 (1935); Carl J. Kulsrud, "Armed Neutralities to 1780," 29 *AJIL* 423 (1935); Alice M. Morrissey, *supra* note 111; L. Kopelmanas, "The Problem of Aggression and the Prevention of War," 31 *AJIL* 244 (1937); William J. Ronan, "English and American Courts and the Definition of War," 31 *AJIL* 642 (1937); Clyde Eagleton, "The Form and Function of the Declaration of War," 32 *AJIL* 19 (1938); Robert Y. Jennings, "The Caroline and McLeod Cases," 32 *AJIL* 82 (1938); W.L. Rodgers, "Future International Laws of War," 33 *AJIL* 441 (1939); Joachim von Elbe, "The Evolution of the Concept of the Just War in International Law," 33 *AJIL* 665 (1939).

[144] See Norman J. Padelford, "International Law and the Spanish Civil War," 31 *AJIL* 226 (1937); Edward Dumbauld, "Neutrality Laws of the United States," 31 *AJIL* 258 (1937); James Wilford Garner, "The United States Neutrality Act of 1937," 31 *AJIL* 385 (1937); Vernon A. O'Rourke, "Recognition of Belligerency and the Spanish War," 31 *AJIL* 398 (1937); Norman J. Padelford, "The International Non-Intervention Agreement and the Spanish Civil War," 31 *AJIL* 578 (1937); John H. Spencer, "The Italian-Ethiopian Dispute and the League of Nations," 31 *AJIL* 614 (1937); Raoul Genet, "The Charge of Piracy in the Spanish Civil War," 32 *AJIL* 253 (1938); Norman J. Padelford, "Foreign Shipping During the Spanish Civil War," 32 *AJIL* 264 (1938).

[145] See Julius Stone, *supra* note 130; Josef L. Kunz, "The Law of Nations, Static and Dynamic," 27 *AJIL* 630 (1933) (Kunz had not yet been to the United States); Hersch Lauterpacht, "'Resort to War' and the Interpretation of the Covenant During the Manchurian Dispute," 28 *AJIL* 43 (1934); J.G. Starke, "The Convention of 1936 for the Suppression of the Illicit Traffic in Dangerous Drugs," 31 *AJIL* 31 (1937); Alfred von Verdross, *supra* note 142; Robert Y. Jennings, *supra* note 143; Georg Schwarzenberger, "The Rule of Law and the Disintegration of the International Society," 33 *AJIL* 56 (1939).

[146] W. Lakhtine, "Rights over the Arctic," 24 *AJIL* 703 (1930).

Denmark, "according to the terms of which [as described in the Journal article] Norway recognized Greenland as Danish territory."[147] In February 1931 the Norwegian Consul General in New York wrote to George Finch, taking exception to that assertion and asking Finch to publish a short reply which the Consul General enclosed.[148] At first Finch was non-committal.[149] Then he told the Consul General that the Board of Editors had decided, before publishing his reply, to see if the original author would concur in the Norwegian position.[150] Later, he told the Consul General that the Journal would prefer to publish a comprehensive treatment of the subject, but could not do so until the issue of October 1931.[151]

The Consul General was annoyed. He said that he had waited long enough. Clearly, the Norwegian government regarded the matter as serious. In the words of the Consul General, "I have stated the official and well-known position of the Norwegian Government, who have seen and approved my article after it was sent to you. ... It seems to me a matter of no small importance that the numerous and distinguished readers of the American Journal of International Law should not longer than absolutely necessary remain misinformed about the facts of an important international issue of the present day."[152] After checking with the Secretary of the Norwegian Legation in Washington, Finch published Morgenstierne's short reply (labeled a "Correction") to the original article. It appeared in the July 1931 issue.[153]

The Journal had an impact not only on foreign legations, but on American embassies abroad as well. In the mid-1930s, the State Department continued its practice of buying copies of the Journal for the use of the Foreign Service, though apparently it was no longer sending a copy to every embassy and consulate abroad. In 1934, the American Ambassador to Japan wrote to James Brown Scott with a testimonial to the utility of the Journal:

> The JOURNAL is to me invaluable, and always has been since it started in 1907. ... Very often, when some particular official document or expert

---

147 Id. at 705. The treaty appears in 27 *LNTS* 203.

148 Letter from W. Morgenstierne, Norwegian Consul General, to George A. Finch, Feb. 19, 1931.

149 Letter from Finch to Morgenstierne, Feb. 26, 1931.

150 Letter from Finch to Morgenstierne, Mar. 13, 1931.

151 Letter from Finch to Morgenstierne, July 8, 1931.

152 Letter from Morgenstierne to Finch, July 9, 1931.

153 Wilhelm Morgenstierne, The Status of East Greenland, 25 *AJIL* 526 (1931). The contact with the Norwegian Legation is mentioned in a letter from Finch to Morgenstierne, July 13, 1931. The PCIJ settled the status of Greenland in favor of Denmark in 1933. Legal Status of Eastern Greenland (*Denmark v. Norway*), PCIJ Ser. A/B, No. 53 (Judgment of Apr. 5, 1933).

> comment on some international issue has been sought, the desired material was there, ready at hand. I remember an incident at the time of the outbreak of one of the Balkan Wars when my colleagues in the British Embassy in Vienna were uninformed concerning the Treaty of Paris and the Declaration of London, and the pride with which I produced both documents from the Journal.[154]

The Journal has often received requests for permission to reprint some of its articles. A request to reprint an article would normally indicate that the piece is thought to have some particular merit, but it is not itself much of a gauge as to how much impact the piece might have on scholarship or practice. Occasionally, though, a request for permission to reprint carries some assurance of impact. Thus, when the Naval War College in 1936 and 1937 requested permission to reprint several pieces from the AJIL in instructional pamphlets for naval officers enrolled in the War College's international law courses, the pieces would be read with some care by persons whose professional duties could be affected by them.[155]

With the outbreak of war in Europe in 1939, the Society sought to have an impact on the United States Congress' consideration of U.S. neutrality. The Harvard Research in International Law's draft convention on the rules of neutrality, with Philip C. Jessup as the Reporter, had been published in the July Supplement of the Journal.[156] A copy was sent to each member of the Senate Foreign Relations Committee and the House Foreign Affairs Committee.[157] Several committee members sent letters of acknowledgment affirming that the Supplement would be useful to them, but just how much impact the Supplement had does not appear.

6. The Plan to Publish Municipal Decisions in Supplements to the Journal

In April 1930, the Board of Editors requested the Carnegie Endowment to support publication of the texts of municipal decisions involving international law from as many countries as possible, to be published in special supplements of the Journal.[158] James Brown Scott, in his capacity as Secretary of the Carnegie

---

[154] Letter from Joseph C. Grew to James Brown Scott, July 27, 1934.

[155] Requests for permission to reprint the pieces were received in letters from H.D. Cooke, Chief of Staff of the Naval War College, and C.P. Snyder, President of the Naval War College, to George A. Finch, Dec. 30, 1936, & Oct. 23, 1937, respectively.

[156] Harvard Research in International Law, Draft Convention on Rights and Duties of Neutral States in Naval and Aerial War, with Comment, 33 *AJIL Supp.* 167 (1939).

[157] Letter from George A. Finch to Henry S. Fraser, Sept. 23, 1939.

[158] Resolution adopted by the Board of Editors of the *AJIL*, Apr. 24, 1930.

Endowment, wrote to the State Department asking for help in carrying out the plan. He wanted the State Department to instruct its diplomatic or consular agents around the world to collect these decisions in the countries to which they were posted, and to translate them into English.[159] The response was favorable, provided that the State Department did not have to incur any expense for translations.[160]

Scott, who of course wore important hats at both the Carnegie Endowment and the Society, may have been motivated by the recent inauguration in Great Britain of the *Annual Digest of Public International Law Cases*, which summarized the decisions of international and national tribunals. The first volume of that series (later designated as volume 3) was published in 1929, containing decisions from 1925 and 1926.[161] It was welcomed in the ASIL as a sorely needed contribution to the documentation of international law, and the better part of a session at the 1930 Annual Meeting was devoted to it.[162]

No special supplements to the Journal containing municipal court decisions ever appeared. Instead, the Carnegie Endowment supported the publication of what are now volumes 1 and 2 of the *Annual Digest*, covering international and municipal decisions in 1919-1922 and 1923-1924, respectively.[163] The Journal's Judicial Decisions section continued its practice of publishing full texts of selected judicial and arbitral decisions, with headnotes summarizing the decisions.[164]

7. Ensuring Accuracy of Documents Published in the Supplement

In April 1931, a question was raised about the accuracy of the version the Journal published of the Protocol of Signature of the Statute of the P.C.I.J. and the Protocol of Accession of the United States to the Statute of the P.C.I.J. Hope Thompson pointed out that the Supplements had published only the English-language versions, and had taken them from British documents rather than from the slightly different documents the President transmitted to the U.S. Senate. She

---

159 Letter from James Brown Scott to Wilbur J. Carr, Apr. 25, 1930.

160 Letter from Carr to Scott, May 1, 1930.

161 3 Arnold D. McNair & Hersch Lauterpacht, *Ann. Dig. of Pub. Int'l L. Cases*, 1925-1926 (1929).

162 24 *ASIL Proc.* 151-67 (1930).

163 See 1 John Fischer Williams & Hersch Lauterpacht, Ann. Dig. Of Pub. Int'l L. Cases, 1919-1922, at ix (1932); 2 id. at ix (1933). The series gradually expanded its coverage to include verbatim quotations from judgments and awards. To reflect the expanded coverage, the title was changed to *Annual Digest and Reports of Public International Law Cases* with volume 7, published in 1940, and to *International Law Reports* with volume 17, published in 1956.

164 The practice of adding headnotes began with volume 19, in 1925.

suggested that the documents be published as transmitted, including both the French and English versions, which she said were not precisely the same.[165]

George Finch called her criticism superficial. He said that it had never been the Journal's policy to publish documents in any language other than English, and furthermore the Journal could not afford to do so. He added that he had nevertheless obtained special authority from the Society to print the Protocol of Accession in both languages.[166] This was done in an Appendix to the 1931 *ASIL Proceedings*, rather than in a Supplement to the Journal.[167]

The questions Ms. Thompson raised – what English-language version of documents should be used, and when to include an official version in a language other than English – were and still are important so long as the Society undertakes to publish official documents, as it currently does in International Legal Materials. To take one example, Article 62 of the Vienna Convention on the Law of Treaties provides in the English language version that a fundamental change of circumstances may permit a party to terminate a treaty if, *inter alia*, the effect of the change is radically to transform the "effect of obligations" still to be performed.[168] The French version is "*portée des obligations*," which may be translated as "impact of obligations" – a phrase with a rather more precise meaning than the official English version. It would be helpful to scholars and decision-makers to have both versions easily at hand.

8. The Journal's Tribute to German International Law Professors Dismissed from Their Academic Positions

In 1939, the Journal published an Editorial Comment by James W. Garner on Nazi treatment of eminent German professors of public and private international law.[169] Garner identified twenty-four such professors who had been dismissed or compulsorily retired since the Nazis came to power in January 1933. He summarized their many accomplishments and tried to identify the reasons

---

[165] Letter from Lester H. Woolsey to George A. Finch, Apr. 21, 1931. See also Ms. Thompson's remarks at the 1931 Annual Meeting, 25 *ASIL Proc.* 79-80 (1931). She appears to have been incorrect regarding the source of the Protocol of Signature as published in the Supplement. See Official Documents, 17 *AJIL Supp.* 55 (1923), noting that it was the official text issued by the League of Nations. The Protocol of proposed U.S. Accession, 25 *AJIL Supp.* 58 (1931), was taken from the British Parliamentary Papers.

[166] Letter from George A. Finch to Lester H. Woolsey, Apr. 28, 1931.

[167] 25 *ASIL Proc.* 349 (1931).

[168] Vienna Convention on the Law of Treaties Art. 62(1)(b), 1155 UNTS 331, 8 ILM 679 (1969).

[169] James W. Garner, Editorial Comment: "The Nazi Proscription of German Professors of International Law," 33 *AJIL* 112 (1939).

why each was purged. The list included some names that were or became quite familiar in international law circles in the United States, including Jellinek, Kelsen, Nussbaum, Schücking and Verdross.

F. THE SOCIETY'S DEVELOPMENT DURING HARD TIMES

The Society steadily lost membership during the Depression. Yet the core membership remained solid. It consisted primarily of political scientists and law professors, with the political scientists continuing – as they had in the twenties – to make their presence very much felt. Nevertheless, the dominant individuals in the Society in the thirties were two law professors and the indomitable James Brown Scott. The law professors, of course, were Manley Hudson and Philip Jessup. Jessup chaired important committees, including the Committee on Organization that recommended the constitutional limit on the number of years a President of the Society could serve. Jessup was a member of other committees as well as a member of the Executive Council and Board of Editors of the Journal. He was more diplomatic in his approach than was Hudson, and thus was consulted more than was Hudson as a helpful advisor on the administration of the Society. George Finch was in touch with him frequently.

The predominantly academic character of the Society may have contributed to the decline in membership. The American Bar Association's Section on International and Comparative Law was formed in the thirties, and appealed to practicing lawyers who were or might have been Society members. In a time of financial stringency, many of them cast their lot with their own, eschewing the luxury of comporting with the more scholarly arm of the discipline.

Women began to make their mark in the Society in the thirties. Having belatedly discovered what women could contribute, the Society began to listen to them. It did not elevate any woman to a high individual position, but it did make room for women on its Executive Council, on committees, and in the pages of the Journal. One woman, Bessie Carter Randolph, was particularly influential as the principal drafter of the constitutional changes that were adopted in 1940.

In the late thirties, as storm clouds descended over Europe for the second time in the twentieth century, the Society was rather more detached than it had been in the run-up to World War I. There was little of the hand-wringing over the inability of international law and legal mechanisms to prevent war that the Society had engaged in the first time around. The Society's apparent detachment may simply have been the result of a Munich syndrome within the Society – a failure to see what the German Reich was actually doing, at least until Germany invaded Poland on September 1, 1939, causing Great Britain and France to declare war on Germany two days later. But it may also have reflected a weakening of the faith the Society's founders had in peace through law. A waning faith could have been caused by a combination of factors: the rude awakening caused by

World War I; the failure of the United States to join the League of Nations and especially its failure to become a party to the Statute of the Permanent Court; disillusionment with the League as a mechanism to keep peace; the tendency of scholars, including those in the Society, to be skeptical about the institutions or policies they examine; and a loss of steam the Society shared with other institutions in the thirties as a result of the Depression.

The Journal solidified its place as the leading international law periodical in the world. It published articles by a wide variety of scholars, many of them quite prominent, but it also found room in its pages for manuscripts from thoughtful practicing lawyers and government officials. Virtually every significant event in international affairs was covered, descriptively if not always analytically, in lead articles or Editorial Comments. These materials still provide a valuable, but often overlooked, source of information and analysis for the historical development of international law and institutions.

The Society's progress in the thirties should not be judged simply or primarily by reference to its decline in membership. It was steadily solidifying its position as a scholarly organization, and it was beginning to take account of the interests and ideas of some groups not theretofore significantly represented in its inner councils – women and young members, though not yet persons of color. It was on a course that it would follow, for the most part, into the post-World War II years.

Chapter Five

WAR YEARS AGAIN

Upon those of us who devote their lives to the improvement and application of international law there devolves today a special duty. It is our task to help our fellow-citizens to a better realization of the crucial importance which preservation of international law and of order based on law has for them and for their country. It is our task to make the immense significance of international law a living reality in the mind and heart of every American.

—Cordell Hull
Presidential Address,
34 *ASIL Proceedings* 16 (1940)

A. STAYING ON TRACK IN WARTIME

1. Cordell Hull, Secretary of State and President of the Society

Cordell Hull, the U.S. Secretary of State from 1933 to 1944 and the Society's President from 1939 to 1942, was destined to become a Nobel Peace Prize laureate in 1945 for his leadership in establishing the United Nations. He had integrity,[1] but not much flair. Abba Eban described Hull as "a Tennessean of austere mien."[2] Whether or not that description fully captured his personality, he was nevertheless an active President of the Society, even though his responsibilities as Secretary of State in those troubled years might be expected to have left no time at all for the Society. George Finch, speaking in 1941, said that Hull had taken as much interest in the Society's work as any other President in the Society's history, and had taken time to discuss Society affairs with him whenever the need had arisen.[3] Hull corresponded with another prominent Society member,

1 Charles Fenwick, referring to Hull's performance as head of a U.S. delegation to an Inter-American conference, said that he "stood as a symbol of the good faith and integrity of the United States. His word was his bond." Charles G. Fenwick, "The Inter-American Conference for the Maintenance of Peace," 31 *AJIL* 201, 225 (1937).

2 Abba Eban, "The U.N. Idea Revisited," 74 *Foreign Affairs*, No. 5, at 39 (1995).

3 35 *ASIL Proc.* 151 (1941).

Quincy Wright, on international law issues.[4] To a greater extent than some of his successors, Hull thought that international law mattered.

Hull's first presidential address to the Society, in 1940, came just three days after Germany invaded Belgium, The Netherlands and Luxembourg. The address was broadcast nationwide on radio. The NBC announcer who introduced him invoked the memory of two of his distinguished predecessors, Elihu Root and Charles Evans Hughes.[5] The address was printed in full in the *New York Times*, the *Washington Post* and the *Washington Evening Star*. It was also the subject of a long editorial in the *Post*.[6]

Hull used the occasion to warn the American people of the risks of isolationism. But in the main, he emphasized the urgent need for the preservation and development of order under law. Part of his address harkened back to the goals – idealistic, but with a practical purpose – of those who originally conceived, organized and led the Society. The words might just as well have been spoken by Elihu Root:

> Upon those of us who devote their lives to the improvement and application of international law there devolves today a special duty. It is our task to help our fellow-citizens to a better realization of the crucial importance which preservation of international law and of order based on law has for them and for their country. It is our task to make the immense significance of international law a living reality in the mind and heart of every American.
>
> While doing this, we should constantly and persistently search for ways and means of strengthening the structure of international law and of making more effective the translation of its principles into firmly established international practice. We should spare no effort to demonstrate that the spirit which has made possible, over the centuries, immense forward strides in the development of international law, still lives.[7]

Hull's second presidential address, in April 1941, was again broadcast nationally and given extensive newspaper coverage. It bore little resemblance to his address a year earlier. Instead of a call to develop and respect international law, it was a call to arms and an urgent appeal to the American public to recognize

---

4 See Robert P. Hillmann, "Quincy Wright and the Commission to Study the Organization of Peace," 4 *Global Governance* 485, 487 (1998).

5 34 *ASIL Proc.* 12 (1940).

6 *Wash. Post*, May 14, 1940. The text of his speech was printed in all three newspapers on that same date.

7 Cordell Hull, Presidential Address, 34 *ASIL Proc.* 12, 16 (1940). See also Cordell Hull, 1 *The Memoirs of Cordell Hull* 764-65 (1948).

the threat to the United States posed by the situation in Europe.[8] The die had been cast. Neutrality was out of the question. Aid to Great Britain and military preparedness in anticipation of self-defense were the orders of the day. In fact, he went further and used language that (if taken out of the context of assisting in the defense of Great Britain) could be seen as a basis for an asserted right of pre-emptive self-defense:

> Some among us, doubtless with the best of intentions, still contend that our country need not resist until armed forces of an invader shall have crossed the boundary line of this hemisphere. But this merely means that there would be no resistance by the hemisphere, including the United States, until the invading countries had acquired complete control of the other four continents and of the high seas, and thus had obtained every possible strategic advantage, reducing us to the corresponding disadvantage of a severely handicapped defense. This is an utterly short-sighted and extremely dangerous view.[9]

2. A Practicing Lawyer Takes Over

Inescapably, the time Cordell Hull was able to devote to the Society diminished after Pearl Harbor. Change in the presidency would have been in order even if it had not been constitutionally required when Hull's three-term limit ran out in 1942. As it turned out, Hull was the last Secretary of State to serve as the Society's President.

The Society selected a new type of President: a practicing lawyer with no record of high government service and no formal connection with the Society's patron, the Carnegie Endowment. He was Frederic R. Coudert, a long-standing, quite active member of the Society and a leader of the New York Bar.

Coudert was a man of great energy and ability, and highly respected as an international lawyer; moreover, he had contacts in high places. Nevertheless, since he was not a prominent public figure, his election marked a significant change in the Society's conception of its presidency. All of the previous Presidents except James Brown Scott had been Secretaries of State. Scott's election did not reflect any change in concept; rather, it was a tribute to the person who had been the Society's dominant figure from its inception. Coudert's election did represent a change in concept: no longer would the Society consider it essential, in the absence of special circumstances, to seek out a prominent public figure for the presidency. On the other hand, the break from tradition was not complete.

---

8 Cordell Hull, "The United States and the World Situation," 35 *ASIL Proc.* 9 (1941).

9 Id. at 10. Hull quoted this passage in his memoirs. See Cordell Hull, 2 *The Memoirs of Cordell Hull* 941-42 (1948).

Coudert was sufficiently well connected to assure some degree of access to those in charge of American foreign policy.

Coudert's nomination in 1942 may also have reflected a perceived need within the Society to respond to the interests of the practicing bar. The Society had suffered declining membership in the 1930s while the fledgling American Bar Association's Section on International and Comparative Law, with its appeal to practicing lawyers, was bursting with members. The Society's image was that of a scholarly association largely catering to the interests of academia and, to some extent, of government. It may well have needed a boost with the practicing bar if it was to make a mark in the real world.

Coudert was a broad-gauged lawyer who was comfortable with representatives of academia as well as with government officials. Nevertheless, as might have been expected, he was eager to solidify the Society's standing with other professional groups. He gave his support to a motion by James O. Murdock at the 1942 Business Meeting to create a Committee on Cooperation with Other Societies, in an effort to ally the Society with lawyers who could be influential in solidifying peace after a military victory had been won. The motion was adopted, and Coudert appointed the Committee.[10]

Coudert also appointed a committee to cooperate with the Inter-American Bar Association and the Pan American Union in a study of similarities and differences between the juridical systems of the Latin American countries and the United States.[11] At the same time, he suggested that the Journal broaden its scope by publishing more articles written by lawyers, judges and ex-diplomats: in other words, by persons who might be expected to deal in a practical way with current issues.[12]

3. Administrative Turnover

In the spring of 1943, George Finch, who had become Director of the Division of International Law at the Carnegie Endowment, notified the Society's Executive Council that his duties at the Endowment would require him to retire as Secretary of the Society as well as Managing Editor of the Journal. As the chair of a special search committee, he asked James Oliver Murdock, of Washington, D.C., to accept the position of Secretary. Murdock agreed, on condition that

---

[10] 36 *ASIL Proc.* 26-31 (1942); letter from Frederic R. Coudert to George A. Finch, May 13, 1942.

[11] See, e.g., letter from George A. Finch to Arthur K. Kuhn, Oct. 20, 1942, notifying Kuhn of his appointment to the committee.

[12] Letter from Coudert to Finch, *supra* note 10.

he be provided with an assistant. The Executive Council duly elected him to the position.[13]

Murdock served only one year. It was soon decided that the positions of Secretary of the Society and Managing Editor of the Journal should be held by a single person, as they had been in the person of George Finch. In 1944, Finch nominated Pitman Potter, who had become the Managing Editor of the Journal, to be Secretary of the Society. Murdock seconded the nomination. Potter was unanimously elected.[14] For the first time, the Society had a full-time Secretary/Managing Editor. Potter's USD 5,000 annual salary for the combined positions was supplied by a grant from the Carnegie Endowment.[15]

4. James Brown Scott, in Memoriam

On June 25, 1943, at the age of 77, James Brown Scott died. George Finch wrote a long encomium to him in the Journal, in which he outlined Scott's career and emphasized the core principles Scott stood for – international law as the basic ordering system for peace, with the consequent need to define (codify) it so that it could be applied fairly and objectively by a permanent international court, and equal rights for women, supported by treaty.[16]

Finch also gave a brief eulogy at the Society's 1944 Business Meeting:

> [James Brown Scott's] steadfast faith in the purposes of the Society and his organizing and administrative abilities during the early years of the Society's existence enabled it to pass successfully through the critical period of trial and doubt. Active Secretary from the organization of the Society in 1906 until 1924, Honorary Vice-President from 1924 until 1929, President from 1929 until 1939, and Honorary President from that date until his death, Editor-in-Chief of the *Journal* from its establishment in 1907 until 1924, and Honorary Editor-in-Chief from that year until his death, Dr. Scott's participation in the annual meetings of the Society and his contributions to the columns of its *Journal* have enriched the contents and added to the high quality of the Society's publications.[17]

---

13 Minutes of the Executive Council, July 21, 1943, in 37 *ASIL Proc.* 138, 139 (1943).

14 Minutes of the Executive Council, Apr. 29, 1944, in 38 *ASIL Proc.* 150 (1944).

15 Business Meeting, 38 *ASIL Proc.* 100-101 (1944).

16 George A. Finch, "James Brown Scott, 1866-1943," in 38 *AJIL* 183 (1944). Finch had intended this piece to be a sketch for a full biography Scott had requested him to write. Finch never was able to write it. For a book-length biography of Scott, see Ralph D. Nurnberger, *James Brown Scott: Peace Through Justice* (Ph.D. dissertation, Georgetown University, 1975).

17 George A. Finch, eulogy for James Brown Scott, 38 *ASIL Proc.* 98-99 (1944).

Frederic Coudert, the President of the Society, added his own tribute to Scott's personality and characteristics:

> [H]e possessed one of those attractive personalities which, as the magnet attracts iron filings, brought about him life-long friends. I was with him in the Institut de Droit International and other organizations all about Europe, and everywhere he compelled respect not only by his learning, his integrity, and his spotless character, but by his great loyalty to his friends, by that spontaneous affection for his fellow men, which is such a rare and a most admirable quality.[18]

Scott's death produced an awkward situation for the Society when it was discovered that he had left two wills. One, dated November 21, 1939, named Finch the executor and contained a USD 10,000 bequest to the Society to be applied toward the expense of editing and publishing the Journal. The second, dated June 4, 1942, left all his property to his physician, his real estate agent and his chauffeur/valet as trustees to maintain a memorial hospital, with the physician to be its superintendent and the chauffeur/valet to be its business manager. A codicil to the second will bequeathed USD 10,000 to the chauffeur/valet and his wife.[19]

The Executive Council decided to contest the second will and codicil. The District Court in Maryland admitted them to probate, and the Society appealed.[20] After what was described as "extended litigation," the bequest to the Society was established. When legal and other expenses were deducted, the Society received USD 7,862.50 from Scott's estate.[21]

5. Criteria for Election to the Executive Council

In 1941, the Nominating Committee, chaired by Norman J. Padelford, addressed the criteria that should be used in selecting members of the Executive Council. The exercise was similar to those conducted by nominating committees in the mid-1930s, but was more systematic. Padelford announced that the 1941 Committee had followed these principles:

- Nominees should be members of the Society.
- They should be active in the Society, for example by contributing to the Journal, participating in Annual Meetings, and demonstrating concern for the advancement of the aims of the organization.

---

[18] Frederic R. Coudert, eulogy for James Brown Scott, 38 *ASIL Proc.* 98, 99 (1944).

[19] Minutes of the Executive Council, July 21, 1943, in 37 *ASIL Proc.* 138, 141 (1943).

[20] Minutes of the Executive Council, Apr. 28, 1944, in 38 *ASIL Proc.* 145, 149 (1944).

[21] Minutes of Joint Meeting of the Executive Council and the Board of Editors, Oct. 4, 1947, 42 *ASIL Proc.* 142, 145 (1948).

- The Council should reflect the membership of the Society, taking into account geographical distribution, the professional occupations of the membership – government service, academia and practicing lawyers – and, as Padelford grudgingly put it, "I suppose, as well, age and sex."
- The Council should include members with experience in affairs of state involving questions of international law, and persons who would give it distinction.[22]

Interestingly, the slate Padelford's Committee produced included no law professors, no females and no one, so far as appears, whose principal work was practicing law.[23]

6. The Society Recommends a Framework for an International Ordering System

Amos J. Peaslee, who chaired the ASIL Committee on Cooperation with Other Societies, became an active participant in meetings of representatives of several bar and professional groups to set the stage for a post-war international ordering system. Frederic Coudert chaired a series of these meetings. Ultimately the representatives, acting in their individual capacities, adopted a draft resolution to be submitted to their various organizations for possible approval. The resolution included these two provisions:

> [T]he administration of international justice requires the organization of a judicial system of interrelated permanent international courts with obligatory jurisdiction; and
>
> [I]nstrumentalities, agencies and procedures should be instituted and developed to declare and make effective the considered will of the Community of Nations.[24]

---

22 Business Meeting, 35 *ASIL Proc.* 150-51 (1941).

23 The slate was: Herbert W. Briggs, of Cornell; Frederick S. Dunn, of Yale; Albert E. Hindmarsh, of the District of Columbia; Arthur K. Kuhn, of New York City; Llewellyn Pfankuchen, of the University of Wisconsin; Charles W. Pipkin, of Louisiana State University; Harold S. Quigley, of the University of Minnesota; and G. Howland Shaw, of the District of Columbia. Id. at 151.

24 "Declaration on Draft Resolutions Proposed by Officials and Members of Certain Legal Associations and Societies," 37 *AJIL* 295, 296 (1943), also found in the Report of Committee on Cooperation with Other Societies, 37 *ASIL Proc.* 146, 147 (1943). Representatives of the following organizations, or of the organizations' relevant committees, endorsed the draft resolution on March 29, 1943: the ASIL, the ABA, the American Branch of the International Law Association, the Federal Bar Association, the Inter-American Bar Association, the New York State Bar Association, the Association of the Bar of the City

Peaslee presented the draft resolution to the Society's Executive Council on April 30, 1943. After "considerable discussion," the Executive Council authorized Peaslee to present his report to the Business Meeting the next day and to move the adoption of the resolution, with the understanding that amendments could be made to it.[25]

When Peaslee moved the adoption of the resolution at the Business Meeting, Manley Hudson said that he did not understand the provision on international courts; he feared that some of his friends in various parts of the world would consider it to be an attack on the Permanent Court of International Justice since it referred to "interrelated" permanent international courts.[26] A rather heated debate ensued, not only about what the language meant, but also about whether the Society should adopt a position on the matter. Ultimately Percy E. Corbett, a member of the Committee on Cooperation, proposed an amendment that rephrased the international courts provision: "[T]he administration of international justice requires a permanent international judicial system with obligatory jurisdiction."[27]

After more debate, Corbett's amendment was adopted and the full resolution, as amended, was also adopted.[28] Hudson's forceful intervention in behalf of the Permanent Court of International Justice had deflected the meeting's attention away from the second provision quoted above. There was no discussion of that provision, even though it had been the only source of concern for George Finch at an earlier stage in the drafting process. Finch had said that the provision was not clearly drawn: "If it means that there should be an international legislature with power over and above national governments, I am completely opposed to it. If, on the other hand, it means that there should be international cooperation for the suppression of breaches of the international peace ... , I am in favor of it."[29] Although the provision was changed slightly after Finch expressed his concern, the redraft did not clear up the ambiguity. Thus the Society was on record, without debate at the meeting that made the commitment, in favor of a recommendation that could have been interpreted to favor the creation of an international legislature.

The Society went no further, remaining aloof from efforts by other organizations to shape the actual structure of a post-war ordering system. On at least four occasions in 1944 and 1945 Clark M. Eichelberger, then serving as the Director

---

of New York, the Carnegie Endowment, the Association of American Law Schools, and the Law Library of Congress.

25 Minutes of the Executive Council, Apr. 30, 1943, in 37 *ASIL Proc.* 130, 135 (1943).

26 37 *ASIL Proc.* 89-91 (1943).

27 Id. at 95.

28 Id. at 101.

29 Letter from George A. Finch to Amos J. Peaslee, Mar. 16, 1943.

of the New York-based Commission to Study the Organization of Peace (later the American Association for the United Nations and then the United Nations Association of the USA), invited the Society to participate in efforts to muster support for the Dumbarton Oaks proposals of late summer 1944. The Dumbarton Oaks proposals, of course, became the working documents for the United Nations Conference on International Organization, held in 1945 in San Francisco. Frederic Coudert and Pitman Potter declined to allow the Society to become involved, although Potter did represent the Society at an informational meeting on the Dumbarton Oaks proposals organized by the chair of the Americans United For World Organization and held in October 1944 at the State Department.[30] According to Potter, "[W]e must maintain an independent position on specific items of a temporary character particularly if there is any considerable division of opinion among our members concerning their merits."[31]

7. Annual Meetings in a Time of World Crisis

The format for Annual Meetings in 1940 and 1941 remained essentially the same as it had been: a series of plenary sessions, with everyone gathered to hear each speaker deliver a prepared paper. There would be discussion after each paper, with a designated person leading it off. A very loose theme underlay the series of presentations at each Annual Meeting, but speakers felt entirely free to follow their own predilections. Efforts were made, as always, to restrict the length of presentations; as always, success was elusive.

The 1940 Annual Meeting was a mixture of old and new topics. A session was devoted to the doctrine of neutrality.[32] There was a timely discussion of title by conquest.[33] Theories of international law were mingled with visions of the post-war future of international organization.[34] But the most interesting, non-traditional presentation was by Joseph Walter Bingham, of Stanford, ostensibly on maritime jurisdiction, but actually on international law as a process reflecting

---

30 Telegram of Oct. 17, 1944, from Clark M. Eichelberger to Pitman B. Potter; letters of Oct. 25, 1944, and Nov. 3, 1944, from Eichelberger to representatives of organizations; and letters of Oct. 18, 1944, and Nov. 18, 1944, from Potter to Eichelberger. On the October 1944 meeting at the State Department, see Dorothy B. Robins, *Experiment in Democracy: The Story of U.S. Citizen Organizations in Forging the Charter of the United Nations* 44, 182-83 (1971).

31 Letter from Potter to Eichelberger, Feb. 27, 1945.

32 Charles E. Martin, "Regionalism and Neutrality as the Bases of Peace in the Americas," 34 *ASIL Proc.* 18 (1940); Lester H. Woolsey, "Problems of American Neutrality," id. at 21.

33 Herbert W. Briggs, "Non-Recognition of Title by Conquest," id. at 72.

34 Percy E. Corbett, "Conflicting Theories of International Law," id. at 101; J. Eugene Harley, "Post-War International Organization," id. at 104.

interaction between and among actors crucially influenced by the self-interest of the public and of groups within the body politic.

Bingham criticized one of the basic articles of faith held by many founders of the ASIL, including Elihu Root and James Brown Scott, and expressed by Cordell Hull as recently as the preceding evening: the belief "that there are definitive principles of justice established in tradition, existing independently of particular contending forces, economic, political and social, and that by a resort to these principles, impartial arbiters may resolve all legal controversies without prejudice."[35] He disavowed any desire to abandon efforts toward a stable world order, arguing instead that the efforts should be made with a keen eye for "the interplay of national interests, prejudices and pressures."[36] Philip Jessup led the ensuing discussion, expressing a more traditional view.[37]

The 1941 Annual Meeting was organized around the theme of international justice. Aside from Cordell Hull's presidential address, it was remarkably detached from the widening armed conflict that had already consumed a large part of Europe and was spreading in Asia. The discussions ranged from the status of non-state entities in international law,[38] to theories of international justice,[39] to international organization.[40]

When the United States entered World War II in December 1941, George Finch asked members of the Executive Council whether the Society should hold an Annual Meeting in 1942. As we have seen in Chapter Two, the Society had decided not to hold Annual Meetings in the years immediately following the United States' entry into World War I. This time, the members of the Executive Council overwhelmingly supported the holding of the Annual Meeting, though they thought it should be shortened somewhat and there should be no formal banquet.[41]

It was no easy task to arrange for a meeting in Washington in the spring of 1942. In March 1942, the chair of the Annual Meeting Committee, James O. Murdock, wrote to George Finch to say that so many difficulties had been

---

35 Joseph Walter Bingham, "Changing Concepts of International Law: Maritime Jurisdiction in Time of Peace," id. at 54, 56.

36 Id. at 57-58.

37 Id. at 63-66.

38 Frederick S. Dunn, "The International Rights of Individuals," 35 *ASIL Proc.* 14 (1941); Edward I. Hambro, "Individuals Before International Tribunals," id. at 22; Quincy Wright, "International Law and Commercial Relations," id. at 30.

39 Herbert Wright, "The Moral Bases of International Law," id. at 52; Hans Kelsen, "Essential Conditions of International Justice," id. at 70.

40 Amos J. Peaslee, "International Constitutional Law," id. at 100; Egon Ranshofen-Wertheimer, "International Reorganization," id. at 106.

41 Minutes of the Executive Council, Dec. 22, 1941, in 36 *ASIL Proc.* 59, 60 (1942).

encountered that it seemed unwise to try to hold the usual type of meeting. Many speakers had declined to appear because they felt that public discussion was not useful under the circumstances. On a practical level, it had become extremely difficult to obtain transportation to Washington or hotel accommodation there. Consequently Murdock suggested simply holding a Business Meeting on Saturday morning, April 25, followed by a luncheon with two or three speakers.[42]

Finch polled the Executive Council and got agreement to hold the truncated meeting Murdock had proposed. The luncheon was held jointly with the American Bar Association's Section on International and Comparative Law. Four speakers, including Francis Biddle, the Attorney General, gave brief addresses. Biddle spoke of the post-war role he envisioned for lawyers, whose ingenuity would be essential for solving "the great problem of government": the tension between liberty for the individual and the authority required for effective government. He spoke also of the lawyer of the future, who would need to have a world view.[43]

In 1943, the Annual Meeting lasted from a Friday evening through to Saturday evening. Frederic Coudert, the President of the Society, began by reading a message from Franklin D. Roosevelt, the President of the United States. Roosevelt offered guarded encouragement: "There has scarcely been a time when there was greater need than now for constructive thinking looking to the supremacy of law, justice and common decency in the relations between nations and their peoples. Learned organizations, such as your Society, are in a position to play a helpful part."[44] Residents of the White House had long since abandoned the practice of receiving the Society during the Annual Meeting; the 1943 message was the first formal contact in several years from those quarters. It was the first of many White House messages to the Society on the occasion of its Annual Meetings.

The speakers at the Friday evening session in 1943 focused on the international ordering system that they thought must come at the end of the war: an organization of states capable of preventing aggression; a permanent international judicial system with obligatory jurisdiction; the legal equality of states coupled with special rights and powers for states with special responsibilities; the need for international arrangements to regulate and coordinate tariffs, trade, investment, food and agriculture, shipping and aviation.[45] These, of course, were nascent ingredients of a post-war system featuring a central organization designed to keep the peace, supplemented by specialized agencies.

---

42 Letter from Murdock to Finch, Mar. 11, 1942.

43 Francis Biddle, Address, 36 *ASIL Proc.* 43, 44-45 (1942).

44 Message from Franklin D. Roosevelt, Apr. 10, 1943, in 37 *ASIL Proc.* 1-2 (1943).

45 Frederic R. Coudert, presidential address, 37 *ASIL Proc.* 1, 10-11 (1943); Francis B. Sayre, America the Hope of the World, id. at 12, 16-17.

The Saturday sessions featured a presentation by Charles Cheney Hyde on the punishment of war criminals. Hyde identified the issues that had to be resolved. Similar issues would surface half a century later, when new war crimes tribunals were established. They included:

> (a) the obtaining and preservation of convincing evidence of guilt of all alleged wrongdoers; (b) agreement, if possible, as to tests of wrongfulness or criminality that are to be applied by such court or courts as are to be utilized; (c) the treatment of individual actors (especially of minor rank or rating) who did what they did under orders from superior authority; (d) the personnel, character and place of sitting of tribunals; (e) the imposition of penalties on guilty persons; (f) the scope of the categories of persons to be subjected to trial; and, finally, (g) the mode of actually getting control of persons in the hands of an enemy who are wanted for prosecution.[46]

At the 1943 annual dinner, Supreme Court Justice Owen J. Roberts envisioned a world government with a representative assembly having delegated powers; an executive with a police force; and a judiciary with jurisdiction not only between states, but between individuals on one side and states or the supranational government on the other. He recognized that not everyone would agree with his vision, but he encouraged Society members to take a stand and help shape public opinion.[47]

The 1944 Annual Meeting was again a truncated one, beginning on a Friday evening and ending the next evening. Frederic Coudert's presidential address brought home the contrast between the idealism of the Society's founders and the realism that two World Wars had imposed on their successors. Said Coudert:

> In 1907 the founders of this Society – many of whom I had the honor to know well – envisaged a future for the maintenance and development of international law, to which they dedicated our Society – but how different a future from that which came to pass! That two utterly devastating world wars should occur within twenty-five years of each other – the first within a few years after the founding of our Society – would have seemed to them a grotesque and an impossible happening, a mad dream, "a tale told by an idiot"! To them war seemed, indeed, a great calamity, but one which in the future could be localized and much of its rigor alleviated by rules of law to be observed by belligerent and neutral alike. They believed that war would in time tend to disappear as something too contrary to human reason and elemental morality. Rather it seemed

[46] Charles Cheney Hyde, "Punishment of War Criminals," 37 *ASIL Proc.* 39, 41 (1943).

[47] Owen J. Roberts, after-dinner speech, May 1, 1943, in 37 *ASIL Proc.* 111, 113-15 (1943).

> that progress was a steady and an inevitable concomitant of history, and that the world must ever tend in increasing degree to extend the reign of law among the nations. ... The apparent progress of law, its substitution through the methods of diplomacy, arbitration and judicial settlement for war appeared to be the natural, nay, the inevitable tendency which could not be long or seriously checked or reversed.
>
> ...
>
> [Experience had shown by 1944 that] peace and the rule of law can only be obtained through the efforts of nations who not only will it, but who are resolute enough to use their might against the aggressor who would return the world to chaos. ... In this Society, devoted as it is to the maintenance of international law, we must utilize our training as lawyers to analyze the bases on which it may be possible to establish a real peace. If, however, anything like this objective is to be attained, it must be through the creation and organization of institutions which will make international law effective as the normal system for the solution of international controversies. ... [It is necessary] to find a way in which power may be so organized that it will be combined with right and with law, and thus meet with general acceptance among the nations.[48]

Frederick S. Dunn sought to explain the circumstances that induce states to use armed force rather than resorting to mechanisms for peaceful dispute settlement. In the process he, like Coudert, showed how thinking within the Society had evolved since the early days. He pointed out that where one side's gain is entirely the other side's loss – a zero-sum game, as it would later be called – there was little hope of achieving effective methods of peaceful change. "Only where there is the assurance of mutual benefits from proposed changes is there much chance that voluntary procedures would be acceptable."[49] This, he said, should give pause to those who assume that all wars result primarily from the ineffectiveness of mechanisms of peaceful change, such as dispute-settlement procedures.[50] Thus did he challenge the basic assumption of the Society's founders.

The Society planned to return to a full Annual Meeting in 1945. On January 5, however, the Director of War Mobilization and Reconversion requested the cancellation of all conventions requiring the attendance of more than 50 persons unless they were necessary for the prosecution of the war, in order to avoid overtaxing rail and hotel facilities.[51] The Society applied for approval of

---

48 Frederic R. Coudert, presidential address, 38 *ASIL Proc.* 1, 2-4, 7 (1944).

49 Frederick S. Dunn, "Law and Peaceful Change," 38 *ASIL Proc.* 60, 62 (1944).

50 Id. at 63.

51 Minutes of the Executive Council, Feb. 10, 1945, in *Proc. of the Washington Meeting of the ASIL* (39 *ASIL Proc.*) 97 (1945).

the Annual Meeting, indicating that fewer than 50 persons would be likely to attend from outside the Washington area, and arguing that if the meeting were not held, the Society's efforts to contribute to public understanding of the issues involved in the conduct of the war and in post-war settlements would be seriously handicapped. The authorities were not impressed. The Society was told that a meeting would be approved only if it were confined to persons from the Washington area, and a permit to hold the regular Annual Meeting was denied.[52]

A meeting was nevertheless held in Washington on April 13 and 14, 1945. It was not formally designated an Annual Meeting. Instead, it was "a meeting of the members of the Society resident in the Washington area."[53] "Washington area" was defined rather broadly. Frederic Coudert, of New York City, presided at the meeting.

Supreme Court Justice Robert H. Jackson did not have to stretch the Washington area boundaries in order to be present. He gave an address that dealt in part with the prosecution of war crimes – a matter with which he was to become intimately involved. He warned against trials with pre-determined outcomes – "farcical judicial trials" that would destroy confidence in the judicial process. But good faith war crimes trials were another matter. He was not particularly troubled by problems of jurisdiction or of finding existing law by which to judge the accused. His concern was that respondents might be convicted without adequate proof, and that they might not be allowed to obtain evidence in their own defense. They should not be prosecuted if the authorities were not prepared to countenance any acquittals.[54]

George Finch made a presentation at the 1945 meeting that harkened back to the faith in international third-party dispute-settlement held by most of the Society's founders.[55] He rejected the idea, espoused by the Inter-Allied Committee on the Future of the P.C.I.J., that some disputes were political and therefore non-justiciable in the World Court. He had an ally, Hans Kelsen, who in a Journal article advocated compulsory jurisdiction for all disputes.[56]

---

52 Id. at 97-98.

53 Id. at 1.

54 Address by Robert H. Jackson, 39 *ASIL Proc.* 10, 15-16 (1945).

55 George A. Finch, "International Law in the United Nations Organization," 39 *ASIL Proc.* 28, 37-39 (1945).

56 Hans Kelsen, "Compulsory Adjudication of International Disputes," 37 *AJIL* 397 (1943).

8. Spreading the Word Through Regional Meetings

In deference to the restrictions the government had placed on travel to meetings in Washington in 1945, the Society's meeting there was a regional one. That led to the idea of holding local meetings elsewhere. The motivation was a latter-day version of one of the Society's original goals: to enhance awareness of, and support for, international law in the United States. The idea was to increase the Society's effectiveness, as James Murdock put it: "[W]e could not only furnish a great sounding board for the development of public opinion, but the Society could become a much more vital factor in the life of the nation and in the growth of international law."[57]

The Executive Council authorized the President to appoint chairs of special Society meetings in cities where "a sufficient number of members reside." Coudert subsequently designated Executive Council members in Boston, New York, Philadelphia, Chicago and San Francisco as local meeting chairs.[58]

9. Maintaining the Flow of State Department Publications

In 1942, the Senate Appropriations Committee reported a bill containing a substantial cut in the State Department's publications appropriation. George Finch personally lobbied at least three Senators to get the funds restored.[59] Eventually a House-Senate conference committee restored most of the funds, prompting the Chief of the State Department's Division of Research and Publication to write Finch a letter of gratitude for his efforts and those of other Society members.[60]

Efforts were made in the 1940s by the Society's Committee on Publications of the Department of State, and by Pitman B. Potter when he was the Secretary of the Society, to persuade the State Department to bring up to date its list of treaties in force. The Committee on Publications made a modest recommendation, that the Department publish such a list biennially.[61]

In 1944, Potter attended a meeting at the State Department that focused on how the Foreign Relations of the United States series could be improved. The Society's records do not indicate what impact, if any, Potter's presence had on publication of the Foreign Relations series, but they do show that he urged publication periodically of a list of ratifications of international instruments

57 39 *ASIL Proc.* 95, 96 (1945).

58 Minutes of the Executive Council, Apr. 13, 1945, in 39 *ASIL Proc.* 99, 102 & n. 3 (1945).

59 Letter from George A. Finch to E. Wilder Spaulding, Chief of the Division of Research and Publication, Department of State, May 20, 1942.

60 Letter from E. Wilder Spaulding to George A. Finch, June 16, 1942.

61 Report of the Committee on Publications of the Department of State, 37 *ASIL Proc.* 149, 157 (1943).

to which the United States was a party.[62] The Chief of the Division of Research and Publication at the State Department acknowledged that the situation was far from satisfactory (the last issue of *Treaties in Force* was current only as of December 31, 1941), but he doubted that much could be done about it given the Department's available resources.[63] The problem ultimately was lessened, but not eliminated.

10. Membership, Plain and Fancy

As the Depression faded, the Society's membership numbers began to rebound. But with the onset of World War II, a decline set in again. With the decrease in revenue from dues, the Society, not for the first time, was in a precarious financial position. Aiming to increase revenue, the Business Meeting in 1943 added a new paragraph to Article III of the Constitution: "The Executive Council may establish additional classes of membership upon such terms and with such dues as it shall determine."[64] The new categories were contributing members (paying twice the regular amount), supporting members (five times the regular amount) and Patrons (a one-time payment of USD 5,000 or more). Between April 1943 and April 1944, 97 Society members upgraded from annual members to contributing members and 17 became supporting members.[65]

In early 1945, Pitman Potter, the Secretary of the Society, estimated that between ten and fifteen per cent of the Society's members were political scientists.[66] On the Society's Executive Council and on the Journal's Board of Editors, political scientists held more than fifteen per cent of the seats.[67]

B. "THE INTERNATIONAL LAW OF THE FUTURE" AND PREPARATIONS FOR THE UNITED NATIONS

In the World War II years, Manley Hudson was heavily involved in a project to draft a set of postulates, principles and proposals for "The International Law of the Future."[68] In 1942 and 1943, a group of American and Canadian judges,

---

62 Letter from Pitman B. Potter to E. Wilder Spaulding, Oct. 23, 1944.

63 Letter from Spaulding to Potter, Nov. 14, 1944.

64 37 *ASIL Proc.* vii & 79 (1943).

65 38 *ASIL Proc.* 145 (1944). For more details, see "Memorandum, ASIL History: Details Relating to Budget, Finances and Membership" (2006), on file with the Society.

66 Letter from Pitman B. Potter to John E. Briggs, Jan. 2, 1945.

67 See 39 *ASIL Proc.* v-vi (1945).

68 See Manley O. Hudson's trilogy, all with the same name, "The International Law of the Future," 38 *ASIL Proc.* 9 (1944); 38 *AJIL* 278 (1944); & 30 *ABA J.* 560 (1944).

lawyers, professors and officials – several of them prominent ASIL members – met to draft a statement that they hoped would become a basis for the post-war world order.[69] About two hundred persons took part at one time or another. The postulates and principles were intended to be *de lege ferenda* rather than an attempt to express the *lex lata*. One of the postulates said that "any" failure by a state to carry out its obligations under international law was a matter of concern to the world community of states – a very broad conception of the *erga omnes* principle, then or now.[70] One of the principles contemplated a very narrow right of self-defense, conditioning it on approval by the competent agency of the community of states.[71]

The heart of the statement was its set of proposals for an "Organization of the Community of States." It bore a resemblance to drafts then being developed within the United States government for what became the Dumbarton Oaks proposals, which in turn led to the United Nations Charter. The statement and the official proposals all contained, for example, provisions for what was then called an Executive Council and a permanent court, giving the Executive Council primary responsibility for keeping the peace. The statement, however, made no provision for permanent members of the Executive Council, and provided that the court would have compulsory jurisdiction. There were also other discrepancies between the statement and the official drafts.[72]

The statement on "The International Law of the Future" has been called "[b]y far the most important private contribution" to the preparation of the U.N. Charter.[73] Nevertheless, it cannot be determined how much the statement influenced the preparation of the official drafts. Standing alone, probably not a great deal. The first official draft plan was virtually contemporaneous with the statement, but it had gone through various previous stages – as had the

---

69 For the text of the statement, see "The International Law of the Future: Postulates, Principles and Proposals," 38 *AJIL Supp.* 41 (1944), also printed in *International Conciliation* No. 399 (1944), in 22 *Canadian Bar Rev.* 277 (1944), and in an ABA booklet distributed in 1944 to all its members.

70 Postulate 4, in 38 *AJIL Supp.* at 54 (1944).

71 Principle 7, in id. at 55.

72 On Executive Council membership, see Proposal 4, in id. at 57; on jurisdiction of the court, see Proposal 17, in id. at 60. The State Department's December 1943 Plan for the Establishment of an International Organization for the Maintenance of International Peace and Security appears in Appendix F to Ruth B. Russell & Jeannette E. Muther, A History of the United Nations Charter, at 991 (1958); the United States Tentative Proposals for a General International Organization (July 1944) appear in Appendix G, id. at 995; and the Dumbarton Oaks Proposals for the Establishment of a General International Organization appear in Appendix I, id. at 1019.

73 Wilhelm G. Grewe & Daniel-Erasmus Khan, "Drafting History," in 1 *The Charter of the United Nations: A Commentary* 1, 3 (Bruno Simma ed., 2nd ed., 2002).

statement. This might suggest that there was an interaction between the drafts of the statement and the State Department's drafts, but the Department at about the same time was receiving proposals from many private sources (not including the ASIL as such, since its practice did not permit the taking of a position on a post-war organization). The Department synthesized the proposals and came up with its own drafts without trying to trace the sources.[74] The authoritative commentaries on the preparation of the Dumbarton Oaks proposals and the U.N. Charter do not mention the statement.[75]

In April 1945, the Executive Council of the Society decided to apply to the State Department for representation as a consultant to the United States delegation to the San Francisco Conference.[76] The Society had been represented (by Pitman Potter) at a meeting of non-governmental organizations with State Department officials in October 1944 at which the Dumbarton Oaks proposals were discussed, but it had declined to participate in an effort by several non-governmental organizations to persuade the American public to support the proposals.[77]

Immediately after the April 1945 Executive Council meeting, Frederic Coudert wrote to Edward Stettinius, the Secretary of State, requesting permission for the Society to be represented in San Francisco.[78] The Department turned him down. It was not willing to add to the list of forty-two organizations already authorized to appoint consultants at San Francisco. The Society nevertheless designated Edwin D. Dickinson and Amos J. Peaslee to represent it in San Francisco.[79] They, along with representatives from other organizations not among the invited group, dealt with the Department's General Office of Liaison during the San Francisco Conference, but they were not included in consultations with members of the invited group.[80]

The Society had been simply too slow to get around to applying for consultative status. Other organizations had been writing to the State Department and members of Congress since February, asking to be attached in some way to the

---

74 Russell & Muther, *supra* note 72, at 216-17.

75 See Robert C. Hilderbrand, *Dumbarton Oaks: The Origins of the United Nations and the Search for Postwar Security* (1990); Russell & Muther, *supra* note 72; Dept. of State Pub. 3580, Postwar Foreign Policy Preparation 1939-1945 (1949); 2 Cordell Hull, *The Memoirs of Cordell Hull* (1948).

76 Minutes of the Executive Council, Apr. 13, 1945, in 39 *ASIL Proc.* 99, 101 (1945).

77 See text at note 30 *supra*. For a list of the many organizations represented at the meeting, see 11 *Dept. State Bull.* 450 (1944); Dorothy B. Robins, *Experiment in Democracy*, *supra* note 30, at 182-88.

78 Letter from Frederic R. Coudert to Edward R. Stettinius, Apr. 14, 1945.

79 Informal addendum to Minutes of the Executive Council, Apr. 13, 1945, in 39 *ASIL Proc.* 99, 102, n. 2 (1945).

80 Russell & Muther, *supra* note 72, at 595-96, n. 9.

United States delegation. Although the delegation was cool to the idea of having any of them on board, President Roosevelt decided in late March "that some system of consultation with leading national organizations was necessary to ensure their support for the results of the Conference. ... A 'fair cross-section of citizen groups' – some forty-two – was [then] carefully selected and formally invited to send representatives to San Francisco to serve as consultants to the delegation."[81]

Even though the Society had no formal consultative status, some of its members were in a position to make their views known. Amos Peaslee was in San Francisco on behalf of the Society during at least the early weeks of the Conference. Edwin Dickinson was spending every afternoon as secretary to the Committee on Legal Problems (a committee of Commission IV on Judicial Organization), though Dickinson was not appointed to that position as a Society representative. Other Society members were in the Secretariat and among the technical advisers to the U.S. delegation.[82] Philip Jessup, for one, participated actively in discussions with the U.S. delegation on World Court issues.[83] So did Manley Hudson, though he did so as a member of the American Bar Association. He persuaded the A.B.A. to adopt a formal statement favoring retention of the old P.C.I.J., and he lobbied the U.S. delegation to the same effect.[84]

Perhaps the Society's late start occurred because Coudert and Potter did not feel that they could commit the Society to seeking consultative status without formal action by the Executive Council, particularly in light of their earlier disinclination to allow the Society to become involved with the Commission to Study the Organization of Peace.[85] Whatever the explanation may be, the Society's absence from the group of formal consultants can only be recorded as a missed opportunity.

The ASIL Executive Council held a special meeting on February 10 to consider whether to hold an Annual Meeting that year.[86] The question about consultative status could have been raised then, but it was not on the agenda for the meeting, and the San Francisco Conference was not a certainty until the Roosevelt-Churchill-Stalin meeting in Yalta, which ended on February

---

81 Id. at 595.

82 Letter from Edwin D. Dickinson to Pitman B. Potter, June 25, 1945.

83 See [1945] 1 Foreign Relations of the United States 495 (compulsory jurisdiction of the Court) & 513 (question whether P.C.I.J. should be retained or new Court established).

84 See [1945] 1 Foreign Relations of the United States 840-41. Hudson was still formally a P.C.I.J. judge. The A.B.A. Statement appears in 31 *ABA J.* 224 (1945).

85 See text at note 30 *supra*.

86 See Minutes of the Executive Council, Feb. 10, 1945, in 39 *ASIL Proc.* 97 (1945), and see text at note 51 *supra*.

11.[87] Moreover, Coudert, who might have been expected to raise the question at the February 10 Executive Council meeting, was unable to attend.[88] When the Executive Council next met, on April 13, the opening of the San Francisco Conference was only 12 days away. By then, it was too late.

The Society did respond in a timely fashion to a form letter from the State Department in the autumn of 1945 inviting members of interested organizations to comment on the Draft Constitution for what became UNESCO. The Department undertook to make any advice thus received available to the American delegation to the November 1945 conference that would complete the preparation of the UNESCO Constitution.[89] Pitman Potter sent the Draft Constitution to each member of the Executive Council and Board of Editors, with a letter telling them that their advice had been solicited and should be sent to the Secretary of State.[90] Neither the Society's files nor published sources reveal what became of this effort.

C. THE JOURNAL IN WARTIME

1. Patriotism Versus Critical Expression

As we have seen in Chapter Two, the Journal's Editors have had to decide how far they should go in allowing criticism of U.S. policy to be published during times of crisis, when there has been strong sentiment in favor of pulling the country together. The question came up again in 1940, before the United States had entered the war. The official U.S. policy was neutrality. Charles Fenwick submitted an Editorial Comment entitled, "Such Aid as Shall Not Be in Violation of International Law." Fenwick was critical of the announced policy of neutrality, which he thought was being honored in the breach. In any event, George Finch wrote to George Grafton Wilson, the Editor-in-Chief of the Journal, questioning whether the Editorial Comment should be printed.[91] Wilson thought that the political situation was "too delicate" to permit its publication, but suggested nevertheless that Lester H. Woolsey, another member of the Board of Editors, be consulted.[92] In the meantime the deadline for the July 1940 issue of the Journal passed, and no Editorial Comment by Fenwick appeared in that issue.

Woolsey took the position that "the Journal should speak out its independent views as to what is going on in the world about us and ... it should be a fairly

---

87 See Russell & Muther, *supra* note 72, at 590.

88 Minutes of the Executive Council, *supra* note 86.

89 Department of State circular letter of Sept. 24, 1945.

90 Circular letter from Pitman B. Potter, Oct. 3, 1945.

91 Letter from Finch to Wilson, July 8, 1940.

92 Letter from Wilson to Finch, July 10, 1940.

complete record of the times in respect of international law, not only from the technical point of view, but from the philosophical as well."[93] In the October 1940 issue of the Journal, an Editorial Comment by Charles Fenwick appeared under the title, "Neutrality on the Defensive."[94] It criticized the United States for supposedly being neutral while engaging in conduct clearly favoring one side in the still-European conflict. It argued that the United States had no duty to remain neutral; rather, it could exercise a right of collective self-defense with its allies, and it should do so without feigning neutrality. Presumably this was the Editorial Comment, perhaps with some modifications in addition to the title change, that Finch and Wilson had been reluctant to publish. The policy of open expression had prevailed.

2. A Focus on Neutrality, War and Beyond

As might be expected, the Journal's content in 1940 was heavy with the law of neutrality. To a lesser extent, neutrality occupied pages in 1941 and 1942 as well. The central concern was whether developments since the end of World War I – the League of Nations Covenant, the Kellogg-Briand Pact, the International Law Association's 1934 Budapest Articles of Interpretation,[95] and the Harvard Research Draft Convention on Rights and Duties of States in Case of Aggression[96] – had released states not formally belligerents from neutral duties of non-discrimination among the belligerent states when one or a group of the belligerent states could legitimately be branded the aggressor.

The neutrality issue came to a head in March 1941 when the United States Congress enacted the Lend-Lease Act,[97] which enabled President Roosevelt to supply munitions and equipment to Great Britain and other allied states. In the Journal, Edwin Borchard attacked the departure from the traditional rules of neutrality;[98] Frederic Coudert and Quincy Wright defended it.[99] Wright presciently concluded that "neutrality, instead of dominating international law, may

---

93 Letter from Lester H. Woolsey to George Grafton Wilson, Nov. 15, 1940.

94 34 *AJIL* 697 (1940).

95 Articles of Interpretation of the Kellogg-Briand Pact, International Law Association, Rep. of 38th Conf., 1934, at 66 (1935).

96 Harvard Research in International Law, Rights and Duties of States in Case of Aggression, 33 *AJIL Supp.* 819 (1939).

97 P.L. 11, 77th Cong., 1st Sess., 35 *AJIL Supp.* 76 (1941).

98 Edwin Borchard, "War, Neutrality and Non-Belligerency," 35 *AJIL* 618 (1941). See also Charles G. Fenwick, Editorial Comment: "Neutrality on the Defensive," 34 *AJIL* 697 (1940); compare Fenwick's later Editorial Comment, "The Fundamental Principles of International Law," 36 *AJIL* 446 (1942).

99 Frederic R. Coudert, "International Law and American Policy During the Last Thirty-five Years," 35 *AJIL* 429 (1941); Quincy Wright, Editorial Comment: "The Lend-Lease Bill and

be reduced to the inconspicuous position which champerty, maintenance, and interference with the course of criminal justice (cited as analogies to neutrality) occupy in the common law."[100]

Philip Jessup wrote a noteworthy Editorial Comment in the 1940 volume. He felt compelled to defend the very existence of international law in a time of despair about any semblance of an international order. He pointed out the plethora of international rules and practices, apart from those having to do with war-peace issues, that remained operative. His rhetorical questions made a point that has frequently been lost on lawyers and others who have expected more than law can deliver:

> International lawyers are under an obligation to their profession to keep asking the simple questions which one might put to a beginners' class: Is there to be no more extradition of criminals, say, between Cuba and the United States? Are the foreign ambassadors in Washington to be hailed into court as defendants in petty lawsuits? Should the United States relieve Mexico from her continuing obligation to pay by installments the claims of the United States under the agreements of April 24, 1934, and November 9/12, 1938, upon the theory that the obligation flows from an international law which is non-existent?[101]

The 1941 volume led off with Manley Hudson's annual review of the previous year's work of the World Court. It was a dispiriting exercise, as it would continue to be during the rest of the war years. Hudson noted in 1941 that the only output in 1940 was a pair of insignificant orders. The Court had not convened since February 26, 1940, and the Peace Palace in The Hague had become inaccessible after the German invasion on May 10. Nevertheless, Hudson's 1941 article contained interesting information on revisions by some states of their Article 36(2) declarations to take account of wartime conditions, and the responses of other states to the revisions.[102]

As early as 1942 and 1943, the Journal began to publish some articles looking ahead to a post-war world order.[103] By 1945, articles and Editorial Comments

---

International Law," id. at 305. See also Quincy Wright, "The Present State of Neutrality," 34 *AJIL* 391 (1940).

100 Quincy Wright, "Repeal of the Neutrality Act," 36 *AJIL* 8, 23 (1942).

101 Philip C. Jessup, Editorial Comment: "In Support of International Law," 34 *AJIL* 505, 506-07 (1940).

102 Manley O. Hudson, "The Nineteenth Year of the Permanent Court of International Justice," 35 *AJIL* 1 (1941).

103 See Clyde Eagleton, "Organization of the Community of Nations," 36 *AJIL* 229 (1942); D. Goedhuis, "Civil Aviation After the War," id. at 596; Percy E. Corbett, "World Order – An Agenda for Lawyers," 37 *AJIL* 207 (1943); Hans Kelsen, "Compulsory Adjudication of

on the new world order had proliferated.[104] But on the whole, the wartime Journal was eclectic in its topical approach. As has been true through most of the Journal's history, though, there was not much pure theory.[105]

War-related subjects were given considerable attention. Beginning in 1943, for example, attention was paid to war crimes and their punishment.[106] But war-related subjects did not dominate the Journal. There were articles on such varied subjects as the jurisprudence of national claims commissions,[107] international arbitration,[108] copyright,[109] fisheries,[110] economic sanctions,[111] international monetary arrangements,[112] control of narcotics,[113] demarcation of international boundaries in a historical perspective,[114] and even a piece on arbitration in the Union of International Transport by Rail written by Manley Hudson and a young research associate at the Carnegie Endowment for International Peace, Louis

---

International Disputes," id. at 397; Clyde Eagleton, "Some Questions as to the Place of the Individual in the International Law of the Future," id. at 642.

104 See Mitchell B. Carroll, "Postwar International Organization and the Work of the Section of International and Comparative Law of the American Bar Association," 39 *AJIL* 20 (1945); Hans Kelsen, "The Old and the New League: The Covenant and the Dumbarton Oaks Proposals," id. at 45; C. Wilfred Jenks, "The Need for an International Legislative Drafting Bureau," id. at 163; Manuel S. Canyes, "The Inter-American System and the Conference of Chapultepec," id. at 504; Herbert W. Briggs, "Power Politics and International Organization," id. at 664; and a host of Editorial Comments in volume 39, too numerous to mention.

105 But see Georg Shwarzenberger, "*Jus Pacis Ac Belli?* Prolegomena to a Sociology of International Law," 37 *AJIL* 460 (1943); John P. Humphrey, "On the Foundations of International Law," 39 *AJIL* 231 (1945).

106 See George Manner, "The Legal Nature and Punishment of Criminal Acts of Violence Contrary to the Laws of War," 37 *AJIL* 407 (1943); George A. Finch, Editorial Comment: "Retribution for War Crimes," id. at 81; Clyde Eagleton, Editorial Comment: "Punishment of War Criminals by the United Nations," id. at 495; Quincy Wright, "War Criminals," 39 *AJIL* 257 (1945); M.E. Bathurst, Current Note: "The United Nations War Crimes Commission," id. at 565.

107 Robert R. Wilson, "Jurisprudence of National Claims Commissions," 36 *AJIL* 56 (1942).

108 Kenneth S. Carlston, "Procedural Problems in International Arbitration," 39 *AJIL* 426 (1945).

109 Wallace McClure, "Copyright in War and Peace," 36 *AJIL* 383 (1942).

110 Gordon Ireland, "The North Pacific Fisheries," 36 *AJIL* 400 (1942).

111 Benjamin H. Williams, "The Coming of Economic Sanctions into American Practice," 37 *AJIL* 386 (1943).

112 Arthur Nussbaum, "International Monetary Agreements," 38 *AJIL* 242 (1944).

113 Bertil A. Renborg, "Principles of International Control of Narcotic Drugs," 37 *AJIL* 436 (1943).

114 Jesse S. Reeves, "International Boundaries," 38 *AJIL* 533 (1944).

Sohn.[115] There was also a Current Note co-authored by a student member of the Society who would go on to become the first female member of the Board of Editors and the first female President of the Society: Alona Evans wrote in 1944 on the international aspects of legal aid.[116]

3. The Managing Editor and the Editor-in-Chief

As we have seen, in the spring of 1943, George Finch notified the Society's Executive Council that his duties at the Endowment would not permit him to continue as Secretary of the Society and Managing Editor of the Journal. Shortly thereafter George Grafton Wilson, who had reached the age of 80, resigned as Editor-in-Chief of the Journal, a position he had held for 19 years. Finch led a search to fill all three positions. In addition to persuading James Murdock to become the new Secretary, he prevailed upon Pitman Potter, who had returned from Geneva to teach at Oberlin College, to take over the duties of Managing Editor.

Finch's correspondence with Potter reveals the dimensions of the Managing Editor's job as it then existed. The Managing Editor read all the submitted manuscripts and sent the promising ones out for review by two other Editors. Finch went on to describe the position:

> It requires a high skill in reading manuscripts, sorting out the good from the bad, and editing those which have been accepted for publication. It also requires continuous correspondence with the other members of the Board of Editors in regard to articles, editorials, book reviews and other contents of the Journal. The Managing Editor also receives and assigns the books for review, which sometimes number about two hundred per year. He also finds the judicial decisions and supplies appropriate headnotes for them. In addition, he is responsible for selecting the documentary material to be printed in the Supplement. After the Journal is in type, he is responsible for the proof-reading and seeing it through the press on time every three months. ... [He] also supplies the annual indexes which are printed in the October issue of the Journal and Supplement.[117]

In other words, the Managing Editor performed roughly the same duties later performed by the Editor-in-Chief, the Book Review Editor, the Current Decisions Editor, the Assistant Editor and the Editor of International Legal Materials. Finch

[115] Manley O. Hudson & Louis B. Sohn, "Fifty Years of Arbitration in the Union of International Transport by Rail," 37 *AJIL* 597 (1943).

[116] John S. Bradway & Alona E. Evans, Current Note: "International Aspects of Legal Aid," 38 *AJIL* 462 (1944).

[117] Letter from George A. Finch to Pitman B. Potter, May 20, 1943.

performed these duties with the assistance of his daughter, Eleanor H. Finch, while he held responsible positions with the Carnegie Endowment.

Finch tried to persuade Charles Cheney Hyde to become the new Editor-in-Chief. In his letter to Hyde, he described the duties of the Editor-in-Chief:

> [The duties,] although responsible, are not onerous. The principal duty is to act as arbitrator when two other members of the Board disagree as to the publication of articles submitted. He also determines matters of policy which may arise regarding the contents of the Journal, and to perform this duty he may veto the publication of any contribution or other material. ... Aside from a few minor matters of terminology, Professor Wilson has never been called upon to exercise this power.[118]

Despite Finch's blandishments, Hyde declined to take the position, citing the demands of editing the second edition of his book[119] and of teaching at Columbia.[120]

Apparently, Edwin D. Dickinson was also approached as a possible Editor-in-Chief, but he too turned it down.[121] Hyde and others had urged Finch himself to take the position.[122] Ultimately Finch was persuaded to do so, for a limited time.[123] The time turned out to be longer than he had anticipated. He served as Editor-in-Chief from 1943 until 1953.

4. Governing the Pre-Eminent International Law Journal

Not everyone on the Executive Council was pleased with the slow rate of turnover on the Editorial Board. In 1943, the Executive Council began to stir, as it had in 1924 when it "retired" seven incumbent Board members.[124] The Council discussed suggestions that more opportunity be given to younger Society members, and with that in mind, the possibility of adopting some form of rotating membership on the Board. The Council adopted a resolution directing the President to appoint a committee of three to consult with the Editor-in-Chief, the Managing Editor and as many other Board members as possible to come up with possible

---

118 Letter from George A. Finch to Charles Cheney Hyde, June 14, 1943.

119 Charles Cheney Hyde, *International Law Chiefly as Interpreted and Applied by the United States* (2nd rev. ed. 1945).

120 Letter from Hyde to Finch, June 18, 1943.

121 Letter from George A. Finch and L.H. Woolsey to Charles Warren, George Grafton Wilson and Arthur K. Kuhn, July 6, 1943.

122 Id.; letter from Hyde to Finch, May 26, 1943.

123 See Minutes of the Executive Council, July 21, 1943, in 37 *ASIL Proc.* 138-39 (1943).

124 See Chapter Two, Section D.2.

candidates, and to report on the practicability and desirability of a rotation system for the Board of Editors.[125]

The President, Frederic Coudert, appointed the committee. After much deliberation and consultation with Board members and others, the committee in 1944 made several recommendations designed to satisfy the Council's concerns.[126] The Board of Editors considered the committee's report before the Executive Council did. The Board was less than enthusiastic about several of the committee's recommendations. It did agree that there should be an increase in the size of the Board to fifteen and that there should be some way to bring new blood in. To this end, the Board recommended that a new status, Honorary Editor, be established for Editors who had given long service and who had reached the age of sixty-five, thus freeing their seats for the election of new regular members. The Board also agreed on three criteria that should be used in electing Editors: U.S. citizenship; capacity for scientific production; and availability and probability of activity as a Board member. The Board said that it was prepared to recommend seven names from the committee's list for the six new positions that would be created in 1944 if its views were adopted.[127]

At its meeting on April 28, 1944, The Executive Council approved the Board's recommendations.[128] The next day it adopted formal amendments to the Journal's Regulations. The amended Regulations provided for a Board of seventeen members (including the Editor-in-Chief and Managing Editor) to be elected annually by the Executive Council using the three criteria the Board had recommended. No term limits were adopted. Provision was made for an Honorary Editor-in-Chief (George Grafton Wilson was already serving as such) and Honorary Editors, to be elected annually from Board members "of long service who have reached the age of sixty-five." Honorary Editors would "continue to exercise such editorial functions as they may wish to perform."[129]

The Executive Council immediately put the new Regulations to work. It retained George Grafton Wilson as Honorary Editor-in-Chief, and elected five long-serving Editors to the new status of Honorary Editor, replacing them on the regular Board with five new members.[130]

---

125 Minutes of the Executive Council, July 21, 1943, in 37 *ASIL Proc.* 138, 139 (1943).

126 For details, see "Memorandum, ASIL History: The Journal, Its Editors and Business Practices," on file with the Society. The Report of the Committee on the Board of Editors appears in 38 *ASIL Proc.* 171 (1944).

127 Minutes of the Executive Council, Apr. 28, 1944, in 38 *ASIL Proc.* 145, 148 (1944).

128 Id.

129 Minutes of the Executive Council, Apr. 29, 1944, in 38 *ASIL Proc.* 150-51 (1944).

130 For details, see "Memorandum, ASIL History: The Journal, Its Editors and Business Practices," on file with the Society.

The Board of Editors had staved off major reform by consenting to an immediate infusion of new blood through an increase in the size of the Board – nominally an increase of one, but in effect an increase of six, since the five new Honorary Editors could continue to do exactly what they had been doing as regular Board members. Among other things, the Honorary Editors would continue to vote on matters that came before the Board, thus diluting the voting strength the new, younger members would have on a Board of seventeen members. The Board had not put to rest the concern within the Society that the Board was self-perpetuating.

5. Pseudonyms and Anonymity

As we have seen in Chapter One, the Journal in 1914 published an article by the Military Attaché of the German Embassy under the pseudonym "Germanicus." It declined, however, to publish anonymous articles. These questions arose again at the outset of World War II, when two German authors submitted separate manuscripts and asked that they be published under pseudonyms or anonymously.

George Finch wrote to George Grafton Wilson for advice, pointing out that the Journal had a policy against publishing anonymous articles; Finch added, mistakenly, that the Journal had never been asked to publish an article under a pseudonym.[131] Wilson's response was that as a general principle the Journal should not publish unsigned or anonymous articles, "and particularly not during war."[132] Accordingly, the articles were rejected even though one of them had been approved for publication by both of the Editors to whom it had been submitted for review.

6. Fluctuations in State Department Interest

As we have also seen in Chapter One, during Elihu Root's time as Secretary of State, the Department became a heavy subscriber to the Journal. In those early years, it subscribed to about 450 copies of each issue, sending one to each diplomatic mission, legation and consulate abroad. The number of copies gradually declined over the years, to 53 in 1943.[133]

Ellery C. Stowell, a member of a Society *ad hoc* committee formed in 1943 to urge an increase in the State Department's subscription, wrote a letter to an Assistant Secretary of State stressing the importance of the Journal to the conduct of America's foreign relations and the consequent desirability of having

---

131 Letter from Finch to Wilson, May 29, 1942.

132 Letter from Wilson to Finch, June 3, 1942.

133 Minutes of the Executive Council, Apr. 30, 1943, in 37 *ASIL Proc.* 130, 131-32 (1943).

it distributed to State Department missions throughout the world.[134] The response was that the matter had been carefully considered over the years, leading to the gradual reduction in subscriptions. As of 1943, the subscriptions were adequate to provide a copy for each U.S. diplomatic mission and a few consular offices where there were no missions.[135] In other words, the State Department had been unable to justify the expense of the Journal beyond a copy for each primary mission abroad.

The decline in State Department interest coincided with the decline in faith that international law and institutions could preserve peace. But at the same time, international law and institutions were expanding in a variety of areas concerning day-to-day international diplomatic and commercial relations. Perhaps the Journal did not move adroitly enough into those areas to fill whatever needs the State Department had.

Effective with the July 1944 issue of the Journal, the State Department discontinued its bulk subscription. The Society established an *ad hoc* committee to make representations to the Department for their renewal.[136] The committee succeeded. The Department subscribed to 88 copies of the Journal during the year 1945-1946.[137] The subscriptions increased slightly, to 95, by 1950.[138] Yet there would be no return to the halcyon days of 450 State Department subscriptions.

7. An Encomium for the Journal

John H. Wigmore, better known today as an authority on the law of evidence than as a disciple of international law, embarked on a self-styled crusade at the outset of World War II to persuade his fellow members of the ABA to learn something about international law. There were two important reasons to do so, he said: the need to provide intelligent representation of clients on the rules then in force for wartime, and the need for members of the bar to provide leadership in shaping a post-war new world order. Among other things, he prepared a list of basic international law materials a bar library should have. The list, of course, included the Journal. Wigmore appended a note:

> In the above list, the American Journal of International Law must be deemed indispensable. Each "volume" consists of two books – Part I, Articles, Book Reviews, Chronicle of Events, etc., and Part II, Official

---

[134] Letter from Ellery C. Stowell to Howland G. Shaw, Oct. 15, 1943.

[135] Letter from Shaw to Stowell, Nov. 9, 1943.

[136] Minutes of the Executive Council, Apr. 13, 1945, in 39 *ASIL Proc.* 99, 101 (1945).

[137] Id., n. 1; Minutes of the Executive Council, Apr. 25, 1946, in 40 *ASIL Proc.* 157, 158 (1946).

[138] Minutes of the Executive Council, Jan. 14, 1950, in 44 *ASIL Proc.* 234, 235 (1950).

> Documents: Part I is the equivalent of scores of treatises; and Part II contains the text of hundreds of the most important official documents. A set of that Journal will alone *almost* suffice to orientate the practitioner in the subject.[139]

Wigmore also sent an "announcement" of the Journal to 520 law libraries and 180 law schools in the United States, and apparently persuaded the chair of the ABA Section of International Law to send similar announcements to the members of the Section.[140] Perhaps he was atoning for his unguarded remarks about the Society on the occasion of the ABA Section's birth.[141]

D. THE SOCIETY AT WAR'S END

By 1945, World War II had taken some of the wind out of the Society's sails. So had the loss of James Brown Scott and the resignation of George Finch from his position in charge of the day-to-day affairs of the Society. Because of the war, the Society had been unable to hold a normal Annual Meeting since 1941. For the most part, its committees had been inactive.

To Finch's discomfort, the Society turned to relatively short-term Presidents during the war years. Cordell Hull fit the mold of Elihu Root and Charles Evans Hughes, but he was limited to three years. His short stint was dictated not only by the Society's Constitution, but also by his responsibilities as Secretary of State and his declining health. Frederic Coudert, though an eminent member of the New York Bar, was a new kind of President: a practicing lawyer with good connections, but with no record in either high public office or in such a powerful institution as Scott's old haunt, the Carnegie Endowment.

Some modest efforts were made during the war years to reform the structure of the Society and the Journal. New categories of membership were created in the Society, and a new status on the Board of Editors – Honorary Editor – made room for some new Board members. The changes were hardly breathtaking.

The Society's goals and methods of operation were not much different in 1945 from the 1930s. It continued to publish the pre-eminent Journal on international law – in fact, during the war, the only Journal of any standing in the field. But its activities remained limited.

---

139 John H. Wigmore, "The Importance of American International Law Today for American Practitioners," published in the *Missouri Bar Journal* and sent as an attachment to a letter dated May 20, 1942, that Wigmore sent to all teachers of international law. (Emphasis in the original.)

140 Letter from John H. Wigmore to George A. Finch, Mar. 5, 1942.

141 See Chapter Four, Section A.7.

An exchange of correspondence in January 1945 captures the limits of the Society's vision at that time. Florence B. Widutis, representing Postwar Information Exchange, Inc., sent out a "Dear Friend" letter to the Society and other organizations. It asked for information to be included in a pamphlet that would be published with the assistance of the Carnegie Endowment. The pamphlet would inform the public about the agencies engaging in "education on national and international affairs." Enclosed was a one-page questionnaire asking what public information techniques were used by local groups affiliated with each organization, requesting an illustration of each technique, seeking information about any periodical each organization published, and asking if the organization published any popular educational materials.[142]

Pitman Potter replied on behalf of the Society. In a "Dear Madam" letter, he said:

> This Society, as you may or may not know already, carries on a relatively limited program of activity. We publish the American Journal of International Law and hold an annual meeting at the end of April. At this meeting papers are read and discussed and the Proceedings are subsequently published. At times committees make reports which are incorporated in the Proceedings.[143]

Potter expressed no interest in participating further in the program the Postwar Information Exchange contemplated. The Society that had established the first English-language journal of international law primarily to "increase the general public knowledge of international rights and duties and to promote a popular habit of reading and thinking about international affairs"[144] had seemingly abandoned, or at least greatly subordinated, the goal of educating the public about international law. It was the same Society that had been unable to act quickly enough to obtain consultative status at the San Francisco Conference on International Organization. As a scholarly institution, it was without peer in its field; as an institution on a mission to foster a peaceful world order, it left something to be desired.

---

142 Letter and questionnaire from Florence B. Widutis, Editor, *Postwar Information Bulletin*, Jan. 8, 1945.

143 Letter from Pitman B. Potter to Florence B. Widutis, Jan. 16, 1945.

144 Elihu Root, "The Need of Popular Understanding of International Law," 1 *AJIL* 1, 2 (1907). See Chapter One, Section A.2.

Chapter Six

THE IMMEDIATE POST-WAR YEARS

The Society is entitled to great credit for keeping alive – I might almost say arousing – [on] the part of the members of the Bar and others, an interest in international law at a time when appreciation of its importance was at very low ebb. As things are today, people have a greater awareness – and particularly members of the profession – that it is not enough to have good solid domestic institutions unless the international situation permits you to enjoy those institutions and to develop them in peace and in cooperation with other peoples. But I think that appreciation of international law as a means to a better international society was kept alive by this Society at a time when almost no other group in our country, outside of the schools, was doing so.

—Robert H. Jackson
Remarks,
43 *ASIL Proceedings* 141 (1949)

A. DEFINING THE POST-WAR ASIL

1. A "Scientific" Society of International Law

Since the early years of the Society's existence, its leaders had regarded it as a scientific body and its Journal as an organ of scientific expression. They assumed that there was a general understanding of what this meant. Perhaps there was, in the first two decades of the century. By the late 1940s it was not at all clear that any common understanding of the concept remained, even though references to the "science" of international law continued to be made.

In the early years, the concept seems to have connoted the use of research-based methods, applied by learned persons acting dispassionately, to ascertain the content of international law (*lex lata*) or to fashion the mechanisms by which international law could most efficiently and fairly be used to settle inter-state disputes. The concept seems then to have expanded to include a dispassionate effort, again by learned persons, to ascertain what the law should be (*de lege ferenda*), at least if the standards used to make the normative judgment were generally accepted among those who were respected in the discipline. To use the words of James Brown Scott, scientific discourse in international law excluded "the language of prejudice and bias."[1] Nor was it infected by the politics of the day or by parochial, short-term interests.[2]

By the end of World War II, there was controversy over how much bias an author could display without relinquishing a claim to the mantle of science. The loss of common understanding is illustrated by an exchange of correspondence between two of the Society's prominent political scientists, Charles E. Martin, of the University of Washington, and Pitman B. Potter, of American University. Potter at the time was Managing Editor of the Journal. Martin complained that Editorial Comments in the Journal had come to "express mere personal opinion and frequently biased opinion without contributing to the advancement of international law or extending the frontiers of knowledge of the subject."[3] Potter agreed that some Editorial Comments expressed biased personal opinions, and that such Comments did not "advance the science of international law." On the other hand, he said, "the fact that a person has some bias does not necessarily condemn him, unless he is no longer open to information and reason."[4]

Potter seemed to be saying that moderate bias would not remove a written contribution from the realm of worthwhile scholarship. This could be interpreted as a concession to the view forcefully expressed by others, such as those in the post-war Yale school, that values, and the interplay of competing and complementary values in an ongoing process of give and take, are at the heart of international law. Seen through that prism, international law – indeed, all law – might seem inherently (and unapologetically) unscientific. But if such a view were to be widely acknowledged, international law, as a normative discipline, might well lose its attraction to many political scientists – as it did in ensuing years. In 1946, it was still "scientific" enough to be a vital part of political science.[5]

2. Worldly Scholars as Presidents

Frederic Coudert served as President of the Society for four years instead of the constitutionally mandated three, because the "Washington meeting" in 1945 was not an official Annual Meeting and therefore no official business could be

1 James Brown Scott, Editorial Comment, 1 *AJIL* 129, 135 (1907). See Chapter One, Section B.3, *supra*.

2 See Elihu Root, Opening Address, 15 *ASIL Proc.* 1 (1921), and see Chapter Two, Section D.3, *supra*.

3 Letter from Charles E. Martin to Pitman B. Potter, June 7, 1946.

4 Letter from Potter to Martin, June 25, 1946.

5 For an amalgam of normative analysis and *realpolitik* by a political scientist at about this time, see Herbert W. Briggs, "Power Politics and International Organization," 39 *AJIL* 664 (1945). For a later view by a law professor, see Oscar Schachter, "The Invisible College of International Lawyers," 72 *Nw. U. L. Rev.* 217 (1977).

conducted. In 1946, a new President had to be elected. It was Charles Cheney Hyde, the highly regarded scholar and professor at Columbia.

Hyde had many of the accoutrements of his predecessors, but he lacked high public visibility. Like James Brown Scott, he had been Solicitor (Legal Adviser) of the State Department (in Hyde's case, for a little over two years in the 1920s). Moreover, he and Scott had teaching experience in common. Like Coudert, he had practiced law extensively. But unlike any of the previous Society Presidents, Hyde was known primarily as an academic. Yet he was hardly in an ivory tower. His work had practical significance, rather than being primarily theoretical. His focus was on the United States and its role in shaping international law.[6] These characteristics made him an attractive candidate for the presidency, even though his name would not attract wide attention to the Society nor would he have easy access to the highest government officials.

Hyde demonstrated his practical bent with his first presidential statement to the Society:

> I think that this Society has vast work before it. We are not here as genial observers of what happens. We must not be academic; we must be realistic. I believe that as never before, in view of the pressing problems upon the United States, we have an opportunity to render a great public service.[7]

He went on to express the hope that the Society could affirmatively work for the cause of international law, as it had never worked before.[8] It was a theme he maintained consistently throughout his presidency.

When Hyde had served his three years as President, Manley Hudson was elected to succeed him. Hudson, of course, was also an academic, having held the Bemis chair in international law at Harvard since 1923. But like Hyde, he was not in an ivory tower. He was a former P.C.I.J. judge, and he knew something about lobbying: he had actively promoted the Permanent Court's cause, and other international law causes as well, in the American Bar Association and in other fora. He was not a public figure in the Root-Hughes sense, but no one in the specialized circle of international lawyers was better known, nor more highly respected for intellectual power, than he.

Hudson ran a tight ship. When he chaired meetings of the Society, he could be quite brusque with those whose remarks or suggestions he thought were

---

6 In particular, see Charles Cheney Hyde, *International Law, Chiefly as Interpreted and Applied by the United States* (1st ed. 1922 and 2nd rev. ed. 1945).

7 40 *ASIL Proc.* 137 (1946).

8 Id. See also Hyde's "call to arms" in his statement to the Joint Meeting of the Executive Council and Board of Editors, Oct. 4, 1947, in 42 *ASIL Proc.* 142-43 (1948), and his statement to the Joint Meeting, Oct. 2, 1948, in 43 *ASIL Proc.* 152, 153 (1949).

off-target. In the words of Myres McDougal, a younger man who had the greatest respect for him, "Hudson's motto was excellence."[9] It was a motto he tried to impart to the Society.

As recently as 1942, a serving Secretary of State, Cordell Hull, had been President of the Society. By 1950 it had become a "custom" that the incumbent Secretary of State be elected as Honorary President.[10] Post-war demands on a Secretary of State simply precluded active participation as a President of the Society, no matter how interested the individual might be.

The Secretary of State in 1950 was Dean Acheson, a lawyer, but not one given to visions of world peace through law. There was no apparent thought given to asking him to undertake anything more demanding within the Society than the negligible duties of Honorary President.

3. Membership, Finances and Public Relations

World War II ended with the Society in reasonably good health. Membership had begun to build again after the wartime decline, reaching 1,201 in April 1946. There was a prospect of further increases as members whose dues had lapsed during the war came back into the fold.

A membership survey was taken in 1946. Of the 750 members who responded, almost half were non-academic lawyers; almost 25 per cent were teachers; almost 20 per cent public officials; and about eight per cent writers and others.[11] The ratio of lawyers to academics had held roughly constant since 1933, when George Finch estimated that 400 ASIL members belonged to the ABA and 235 were connected to colleges and universities.[12]

About a tenth of the Society's members lived outside the United States. As of May 1947 slightly more than 130 members lived in 34 foreign countries. Canada led the list with nineteen, followed by the United Kingdom with seventeen and pre-Castro Cuba with eleven.[13]

Even though membership was on the upswing in the immediate post-war years, the Society's finances remained in their usual precarious state. Aside from annual grants by the Carnegie Endowment in the USD 5,000 to 9,000 range,

---

9 Interview with Myres McDougal, May 18, 1994 (transcript on file with the Society).

10 44 *ASIL Proc.* 69 (1950).

11 Minutes of the Executive Council, Apr. 25, 1946, in 40 *ASIL Proc.* 157-58 (1946).

12 See Chapter Four, Section A.7. The 1933 and 1946 figures are not directly comparable. Presumably, some of the 400 ABA members in 1933 were law professors and some of the ASIL members who were practicing lawyers may not have belonged to the ABA. Those who identified themselves as teachers in 1946 may not all have been college or university teachers.

13 Letter with enclosure from Pitman B. Potter to Lyman C. White, May 28, 1947.

income continued to be almost entirely from membership dues and subscriptions to the Journal.[14]

Arthur Kuhn, a founding member who was still active in the Society, thought that public interest in the Society could be boosted if more were done to publicize the Society's Annual Meetings. Kuhn suggested that the Society intensify its efforts to inform the press about Annual Meetings before they convened.[15] Pitman Potter, the Society's Secretary, pointed out that he had already been sending out press releases on forthcoming Journal issues and Annual Meetings. "The fact is," he said, "that the newspapers are not too easily sold on questions of international law or meetings of the American Society of International Law."[16] The *Washington Star* did cover the 1946 Annual Meeting,[17] but apparently the two newspapers the Society coveted most – the *New York Times* and *Washington Post* – did not.

The Society's efforts to publicize the Annual Meetings were not up to Madison Avenue standards. In the Society's files there is a draft press release announcing the 41st Annual Meeting in 1947. It started out by giving the theme of the meeting and the place and dates. Then came some dry prose describing such topics as "the rebirth of international law coincident with the termination of war and the reestablishment of international order," and "a discussion of the teaching and practice of international law, with particular emphasis upon the codification of post-war law by practicing lawyers."[18] The press, understandably, failed to respond.

If the Society's public relations campaign lacked some of the panache of Madison Avenue, it was nevertheless an attempt to recapture the spirit of the founders who wished to spread the word about international law. On the surface, it appears to have been successful. Membership increased by 50 per cent from April 1946 to April 1947.[19] But it is doubtful that the increase was primarily attributable to the publicity campaign. For one thing, the campaign was augmented by 9,000 letters sent to prospective members, some of them

---

14 The annual grant from the Carnegie Endowment began to decrease in the late 1940s. By 1950 it was USD 3,250. Treasurer's Report for the Year Ended Dec. 31, 1950, in 45 *ASIL Proc.* 250, 254 (1951). There were no more grants after June 30, 1951. Minutes of the Executive Council, Apr. 27, 1950, in 44 *ASIL Proc.* 238, 240 (1950).

15 40 *ASIL Proc.* 118 (1946).

16 Id. at 124.

17 *Wash. Sunday Star*, Apr. 21, 1946, & Apr. 28, 1946; *Wash. Eve. Star*, Apr. 27, 1946.

18 Undated, typewritten press release in the Society's files for 1946-1947.

19 By April 1947 there were 1,824 members. Minutes of the Executive Council, Apr. 24, 1947, in 41 *ASIL Proc.* 185, 186 (1947).

individually typed and sent to persons recommended by Society members.[20] The letters may well have awakened the interest of internationally minded people who had returned to civilian lives after their studies or careers had been disrupted by the war. Membership broke the 2,000 barrier in 1950.[21]

4. Taking a Position on an Article 36(2) Declaration

Secretary of State James Byrnes' letter on the occasion of the 1946 Annual Meeting advocated that the United States make an Article 36(2) declaration under the new I.C.J. Statute. Article 36(2), of course, is the "optional clause," allowing states parties to the Statute to declare that they recognize the Court's compulsory jurisdiction over broadly defined categories of legal disputes, in relation to any other state accepting the same obligation. The Society's Executive Council followed through, voting to recommend that the Society adopt a motion favoring a U.S. declaration:[22]

> Resolved, That the American Society of International Law strongly favors a declaration by the United States Government of its acceptance of the jurisdiction of the International Court of Justice in the types of legal disputes enumerated in Article 36 of the statute of the Court.[23]

At the Business Meeting, several speakers pointed out that the Society would be departing from tradition if it were to adopt a resolution on a matter of such political importance. Still, they favored doing so as an exceptional case. It was said that the Society should have some mechanism to permit the membership to consider such resolutions as this.[24] George Finch replied that the Society did have a mechanism: the Society's Constitution provided that substantive resolutions should be passed upon by the Executive Council before any vote could be taken;[25] that, he said, was just what had happened in this case.[26] Ultimately, the Business Meeting adopted both the resolution favoring a U.S. Article 36(2) declaration

---

[20] Id. at 189; Report of the Committee on Increase of Membership, 41 *ASIL Proc.* 199 (1947).

[21] There were 2,175 members as of April 21, 1950. Minutes of the Executive Council, Apr. 27, 1950, in 44 *ASIL Proc.* 238, 239 (1950). For further details regarding finances and membership during this period, see "Memorandum, ASIL History: Details Relating to Budget, Finances and Membership" (2006), on file with the Society.

[22] Minutes of the Executive Council, Apr. 25, 1946, in 40 *ASIL Proc.* 157, 160 (1946).

[23] 40 *ASIL Proc.* 125 (1946).

[24] Id. at 125-28.

[25] ASIL Constitution Art. VIII, id. at viii, x-xi.

[26] 40 *ASIL Proc.* 128-29 (1946).

and one calling for the Executive Council to consider further machinery for the consideration of resolutions.[27]

The Society's resolution on Article 36(2) was mentioned in United States Senate floor debate and in Senate committee hearings.[28] George Finch, Lester Woolsey and Pitman Potter appeared in the hearings on behalf of the Society, and several other Society members also appeared without purporting to represent the Society.[29] In the words of one seasoned observer, "The field was left to the pro-Court lobby, composed mainly of members of the American Bar Association and the American Society of International Law."[30]

The Senate consented to an Article 36(2) declaration, albeit with significant reservations. One was the Connally Reservation, which exempted from compulsory jurisdiction disputes essentially within the domestic jurisdiction of the United States as determined by the United States.[31] Several years later, the Society would come very close to taking a position urging repeal of the self-judging Connally Reservation.[32]

The resolution on Article 36(2) was not the first substantive resolution the Society had adopted. In fact, it had embraced a substantive resolution just three years earlier. As we have seen in Chapter Five, the Society adopted a resolution in 1943 calling for a permanent international judicial system with obligatory jurisdiction and for instrumentalities, agencies and procedures to declare and make effective the will of the community of nations.[33]

5. More Attempts to Have the Society Take a Position

At the 1948 Annual Meeting, during a discussion of the development of international law, Charles E. Martin moved from the floor that an *ad hoc* committee be formed to report a resolution at the Business Meeting the next day urging the government of the United States to define aggression and to pledge its support

---

27 Id. at 128 & 130. The resolution on a U.S. Article 36(2) declaration was adopted unanimously. The other resolution was adopted on a close vote.

28 Minutes of the Executive Council, Sept. 28, 1946, in 41 *ASIL Proc.* 182, 183 (1947). See 92 Cong. Rec., Pt. 8, at 10617 (1946).

29 Francis O. Wilcox, "The United States Accepts Compulsory Jurisdiction," 40 *AJIL* 699, 704, n. 9 (1946).

30 Michla Pomerance, *The United States and the World Court as a "Supreme Court of the Nations": Dreams, Illusions and Disillusion* 207 (1996).

31 The U.S. Declaration, dated Aug. 26, 1946, appeared in ICJ Yearbooks until the United States terminated it in April 1986. See, e.g., *ICJ Yearbook, 1984-1985*, at 99-100.

32 See Chapter Seven, Section A.4, *infra*.

33 See Chapter Five, Section A.6, *supra*.

for the resistance of aggression.[34] When the advisability of proceeding with such haste was questioned, the matter was referred to the Executive Council.[35] At a meeting in October 1948, the Executive Council passed the matter over to its next meeting. This had the effect of permanently postponing it. Another resolution that would have put the Society on record in favor of a conference to draft a convention calling for total disarmament was expressly shelved.[36]

An attempt to put the Society on record in 1949 suffered a similar fate. A proposed resolution called upon the Society to advise the Secretary of State that the time had arrived for an international conference to revise the rules of war. It too was shelved.[37]

A resolution was offered from the floor at the 1949 Business Meeting, to the effect that the President of the Society appoint a committee to study and report on the attitude and action of the United Nations when one or more Member States tried to have a question of competence under the Charter referred to the I.C.J. The resolution could readily have been regarded as procedural, but George Finch, the presiding officer, said that it was a resolution relating to the principles of international law or to international relations that would have to be referred to a committee or to the Executive Council if three members asked for referral. No one asked, so the resolution was put to a vote and was adopted.[38]

Louis Sohn was appointed to chair the three-member U.N. study committee. It submitted a detailed report discussing the practice of U.N. organs when some Member States had challenged their competence to act in a particular way – usually a challenge under the domestic jurisdiction provision in U.N. Charter Article 2(7). The committee also submitted a draft resolution. It dealt with the circumstances under which a U.N. organ should seek an I.C.J. advisory opinion when a challenging state makes a *prima facie* case that the organ is incompetent to do what it proposes to do.[39] But the committee's report was not unanimous. The Executive Council declined to recommend that the Society adopt the proposed resolution.[40]

The Business Meeting was held the next day, a Friday. The panel scheduled for that evening was on "Strengthening the United Nations," with Louis Sohn

---

34 42 *ASIL Proc.* 35 (1948).

35 Id. at 40-41.

36 Minutes of Joint Meeting of the Executive Council and the Board of Editors, Oct. 2, 1948, in 43 *ASIL Proc.* 152, 154 (1949).

37 Minutes of the Executive Council, Apr. 28, 1949, in 43 *ASIL Proc.* 156, 159-60 (1949).

38 43 *ASIL Proc.* 134 (1949).

39 See Report of Special Committee on Reference to the International Court of Justice of Questions of United Nations Competence, 44 *ASIL Proc.* 256, 268-69 (1950).

40 Minutes of the Executive Council, Apr. 27, 1950, in 44 *ASIL Proc.* 238, 242 (1950).

as one of the panelists. At the Business Meeting Manley Hudson deflected consideration of the committee's recommended resolution in deference to the impending discussion that evening. There was no objection to his proposal that the report should be held over "for some future consideration."[41] That was the report's death knell.

John Hazard told the Business Meeting in 1950 that many practitioners in New York were frustrated by the difficulty they were experiencing in obtaining evidence and testimony abroad for use in U.S. courts. He offered a draft resolution putting the Society on record in favor of the negotiation of international agreements of judicial assistance. Manley Hudson referred it to the Executive Council.[42] This one survived. The Executive Council approved it for presentation to the Society,[43] and the Business Meeting adopted it unanimously in 1951.[44]

Another resolution offered from the floor in 1950 was regarded as non-substantive and thus was adopted on the spot. Quincy Wright, dismayed by the Carnegie Endowment's apparent withdrawal from support of international law, asked the Society to express its conviction that international law is important to world peace and to express the hope that the Endowment would not lose interest in international law. The motion was adopted unanimously.[45]

In 1951, the Business Meeting adopted a detailed resolution on State Department publications, welcoming the inauguration of *United States Treaties and Other International Agreements*, expressing great concern over what was perceived as an imbalance between increasing funds for adult education publications and decreasing funds for official documentation, calling for a supplement to Hackworth's *Digest of International Law*, and urging use of the *Department of State Bulletin* for publication of as much current documentation as possible.[46] The resolution was consistent with the Society's efforts since 1928 to persuade both Congress and the State Department to put funds into the publication of foreign policy documents. Nevertheless, it was noteworthy for its emphasis on publication of official documentation over materials intended for public consumption. The emphasis reflected the dominance of the Society's scholarly and higher education aims over its long-standing, but fading, goal of engaging the public in the normative aspects of foreign policy-making.

---

41 44 *ASIL Proc.* 77 (1950).

42 Id. at 78.

43 Minutes of the Executive Council, Apr. 29, 1950, 44 *ASIL Proc.* 245, 248 (1950).

44 45 *ASIL Proc.* 188-90 (1951).

45 44 *ASIL Proc.* 78-80 (1950).

46 45 *ASIL Proc.* 191-92 (1951).

6. Post-War Annual Meetings

Outgoing President Frederic R. Coudert led off the first post-war Annual Meeting with a presidential address on international law under the new U.N. Charter. His remarks were insightful. He noted that the two World Wars had "destroyed the belief in the absolute sovereignty of the state as the ultimate factor in history and politics."[47] His crystal ball, however, was cloudy. "I do not believe it Utopian," he said, "to think that in less than another half century we may so complete the organization of this world community that it may function efficiently, regularly and justly for the maintenance of peace through law among men."[48] He would not be the only prominent Society member in the post-World War II years to have what later seemed a Utopian dream.[49]

Coudert closed his 1946 address with a reminiscence, at once personal and institutional:

> I am one who was present at the birth of this Society. We have witnessed a world drama unfolding with stupifying rapidity, catastrophic events on a scale that no tragedian, had he the power and vision of an Euripides or a Shakespeare, could have divined and portrayed. Yet, we have pursued our primary purpose, ever intent upon discussing freely and fully all matters and problems relating to international law and history. In that time we have built up by our "Journal" and "Proceedings" an unequalled record of all the thinking and developments affecting international law in our time. In this work, practicing lawyers, professors of law and publicists have cooperated. There has been a harmonious striving for the truth amidst a wide and healthy diversity of opinion.[50]

Manley Hudson followed Coudert to the podium and continued the theme. He asked his audience to turn its collective mind back to the world situation at the time of the Society's birth. "We were interested in international organization. What did we conceive to be the desirable end of our efforts? Why, it was the continuation of the series of peace conferences inaugurated at The Hague in 1899 ... [and establishment of] a framework for the conduct of arbitrations, which went under the very misleading name of 'The Permanent Court of Arbitration.'"[51] Both the

---

47 Frederic R. Coudert, "National Policies and International Law under the Charter," 40 *ASIL Proc.* 5, 10 (1946).

48 Id. at 11.

49 See Grenville Clark & Louis B. Sohn, *World Peace Through World Law* (1958, & rev. ed. 1960).

50 40 *ASIL Proc.* at 11-12 (1946).

51 Manley O. Hudson, "Compulsory Jurisdiction of the International Court of Justice," 40 *ASIL Proc.* 12, 13 (1946).

Society and the mechanisms of international organization, he pointed out, had come a long way, though the San Francisco Conference had fallen short of the ideal when it failed to adopt compulsory jurisdiction for the World Court. Hudson endorsed the resolutions then pending before the United States Congress for a U.S. declaration under the optional clause.[52] Both of those resolutions contained exceptions for disputes on matters essentially within the domestic jurisdiction of the United States, but they did not yet add "as determined by the United States" (the self-judging Connally Reservation).

At the 1947 Annual Meeting, President Charles Cheney Hyde led off by urging governments, particularly the U.S. government, to assess in advance probable foreign reactions to the pursuit of a desired policy. He recommended that the President or Secretary of State appoint a small body of non-governmental persons to advise on the probable effect of proposed foreign policy initiatives.[53] In the end his proposal did not come to anything, but it was a far-sighted attempt by the Society's President to influence the government to look beyond its immediate, narrow self-interest as the United States moved from adolescence toward maturity as a power in world affairs.

After Hyde had finished, he introduced V.K. Wellington Koo, then the Chinese ambassador to the United States. The ambassador dutifully addressed the topic he had been assigned: the role of diplomacy in the strengthening of international law. He distinguished the day-to-day conduct of diplomacy, where direct appeal to international law was seldom made (even then), from diplomacy by international conference, where much international law was made. He found it difficult to explain why international law was such a stranger to bilateral diplomacy. The optimistic view was that diplomats had become so familiar with principles of international law that they need not refer to them; the more cynical view was that diplomats and foreign offices merely used international law when it strengthened the position they wished to take; the middle view, which the ambassador seemed to espouse, was that stressing legal points might make the other party defensive and thus could hinder attempts to settle difficulties between governments.[54]

In 1948, the substantive program was marked by the designation of two principal speakers on each topic, followed by discussion from the floor. The discussion of one topic – the development of international law – culminated in an effort to put the Society on record as calling on the U.S. government to define aggression and to pledge itself to resist it. The effort failed.[55]

---

52 Id. at 19-20.

53 Charles Cheney Hyde, "Looking Ahead," 41 *ASIL Proc.* 1, 4-5 (1947).

54 V.K. Wellington Koo, Address, 41 *ASIL Proc.* 7, 8-9 (1947).

55 See 42 *ASIL Proc.* 35-41 (1948), and see text at note 34 *supra*.

Charles Cheney Hyde opened the 1949 Annual Meeting with a presidential address that contained an appeal for rededication to the Society's objectives:

> [I]n the long interval since the birth of our Society, in which we witnessed two world wars, one must confess that the chief role of the Society has been that of an acute but inactive observer of passing events, notwithstanding the fact that some of the most distinguished members have been and remain active participants in the official labors of our Government dealing with foreign affairs. We have an instance tonight.[56] Still, during the forty or more years since its birth our Society has taken few affirmative steps to foster the study of international law and to promote the establishment and maintenance of international relations on the basis of law and justice.[57]

Hyde went on to call for "concentrated and united thought on ways through which to strengthen the cause of international law both without and within the United States."[58] He did not suggest how the Society might best achieve that goal.

The first speaker at the annual dinner that year was U.S. Supreme Court Justice Robert H. Jackson. He offered something of an antidote to Hyde's remarks. As we have seen at the beginning of this chapter, Jackson said:

> The Society is entitled to great credit for keeping alive – I might almost say arousing – [on] the part of the members of the Bar and others, an interest in international law at a time when appreciation of its importance was at very low ebb. As things are today, people have a greater awareness – and particularly members of the profession – that it is not enough to have good solid domestic institutions unless the international situation permits you to enjoy those institutions and to develop them in peace and in cooperation with other peoples. But I think that appreciation of international law as a means to a better international society was kept alive by this Society at a time when almost no other group in our country, outside of the schools, was doing so.[59]

Justice Jackson then pointed out the parochialism of Western international lawyers and the need to become more inclusive:

---

56 Philip C. Jessup, then a United States Ambassador-at-Large, followed Hyde to the podium. See Philip C. Jessup, "International Cooperation in the Political Field," 43 *ASIL Proc.* 6 (1949).

57 Charles Cheney Hyde, "Pursuing the Objectives of the American Society of International Law," 43 *ASIL Proc.* 1, 2-3 (1949).

58 Id. at 3.

59 Robert H. Jackson, Address, 43 *ASIL Proc.* 140, 141 (1949).

> For a long time any principle could be regarded as international law if it was accepted as such by a consensus of the Western world. Not very much account was taken of opinion outside the circle of nations that made up Western culture. [Others] had their ancient cultures and views and interests, but frankly they were not counted for much by us. It was our circle of what we might call the Atlantic nations which made what we referred to as international law. Now we face a different situation. The balance of power has so shifted that certainly we must take into account, if there is to be progress in the next few years, views of people who have heretofore not counted so much.[60]

The 1950 Annual Meeting introduced several innovations. Manley Hudson broke from tradition by refraining from giving a presidential address to open the meeting. Instead, Hudson – the Harvard Professor – turned over the chair for the opening session to his young Yale friend and protégé, Myres McDougal, who led a panel discussion on world security and regional arrangements.[61] The entire meeting was organized around the theme, "World Security and International Law at Mid-Century." Aside from addresses by Hudson and John Foster Dulles at the second session, each session consisted of a panel discussion on international security issues.[62]

Dulles, the grandson of one of the Society's founders, John W. Foster, and himself an international lawyer who was destined to become Secretary of State, paid no attention to international law in his address.[63] Perhaps that came as no surprise. In 1943, Dulles had written to Henry Luce, "I confess to being one of those lawyers who do not regard 'international law as law at all' because, among other things, no nation is, or feels bound to conform to any course of action other than its own interest and, as Mr. Jessup says, international law 'can be twisted to suit any national interest.'"[64] Cynicism (or realism?) of that

60 Id. at 141-42.

61 44 *ASIL Proc.* 2 (1950). McDougal remembered that he first gained Hudson's respect when he challenged Hudson's interpretation of some cases in U.S. courts dealing with executive agreements, and Hudson acknowledged that McDougal was probably right. Interview with Myres McDougal, May 18, 1994 (on file with the Society).

62 Myres McDougal, who was in charge of the first panel on the program, arranged to have his colleague and eventual scholarly collaborator, Harold D. Lasswell, lead off the panel discussion. McDougal proudly claimed responsiblity for bringing Lasswell to Yale after having met him on a visit to the University of Chicago. Interview with Myres McDougal, May 18, 1994 (on file with the Society).

63 John Foster Dulles, "New Aspects of American Foreign Policy," 44 *ASIL Proc.* 48 (1950). Dulles was then a consultant to the Secretary of State.

64 Quoted in Ronald W. Pruessen, *John Foster Dulles: The Road to Power* 273 (1982); see also Mark G. Toulouse, *The Transformation of John Foster Dulles* 160 (1985).

sort did not bode well for the future role of international law in the conduct of American diplomacy.

7. The Regional Meeting Idea Realized

Although the regional meeting idea had its roots in travel restrictions during World War II, it soon took on a life of its own. The Society's first regional meeting was held in New York City on November 9, 1946. Philip Jessup organized the program and invited the speakers. The meeting began with a luncheon attended by approximately eighty Society members. George Finch and Pitman Potter spoke at the luncheon about Society matters, including the need for more members. After lunch, five speakers dealt with relations between the Society and other organizations.[65]

The Executive Council had authorized not only the New York regional meeting, but also meetings in Chicago, San Francisco and any other locality where Society members wished to meet. The President was authorized to invite particular members of the Society to organize the meetings.[66]

For the Chicago meeting, he called upon Quincy Wright. About fifty members attended the meeting, held on November 30. After "vigorous discussion," several resolutions were adopted. Among them were recommendations that the Society emphasize the progressive development of international law, and that it study the circumstances in which individuals should have access to international tribunals, the formulation of an international criminal code, and the extent to which national courts should treat international issues as legal rather than political questions.[67]

Hyde asked Professor Joseph Walter Bingham, of Stanford, to organize a meeting in San Francisco. The meeting was planned for December 14, 1946, and was held then. Unfortunately, notice of the meeting went out from the Society's headquarters in Washington too late to generate much attendance.[68] To make matters worse, none of the named speakers appeared, leaving it to Edwin Dickinson, who presided at the meeting, and Charles Fairman, who served as its secretary, to fill in for them.[69] The discussion focused on how the United

---

[65] Minutes of the New York Regional Meeting of the Society, Nov. 9, 1946 (unpublished, in the Society's files); Pitman B. Potter, Current Note: "Regional Meetings of Society Members," 41 *AJIL* 133, 135-36 (1947).

[66] Minutes of the Executive Council, Sept. 28, 1946, in 41 *ASIL Proc.* 182, 183 (1947).

[67] Pitman B. Potter, Current Note, *supra* note 65, at 136-37.

[68] Letter from Pitman B. Potter to West Coast members, Dec. 3, 1946.

[69] Letter from Charles E. Martin, of the University of Washington, to Joseph Walter Bingham, Dec. 26, 1946; letter from Bingham to Charles Cheney Hyde, Jan. 7, 1947.

States, and particularly the ASIL, could promote the cause of international law and organization.[70]

In April 1947, the Executive Council agreed with Hyde that the experiment of holding regional meetings should be repeated. A single topic, "The United Nations and International Law," was approved for the next series of meetings. It was contemplated that they would again be held in New York, Chicago and San Francisco, without necessarily excluding other cities.[71] As it happened, they were held only in New York and Chicago that year, but plans were made to expand the venues in the future.[72] In August 1948, a regional meeting was held in Seattle, the first such meeting outside the initial three cities.[73]

In 1947, Charles Martin had sent a telegram requesting permission to treat a weekend meeting of a Northwestern Seminar of International Law, to be held at the University of Washington, as a regional meeting of the Society. After extended discussion, the Executive Council unanimously decided that regional meetings should not be held as part of the activities of any particular university.[74] It was thought that the 1947 meetings at Columbia University and the University of Chicago were different, since no connection had been made between the meetings and any programs of the universities.[75]

The policy of dissociating ASIL regional meetings from university programs was not destined to endure. Its demise began with the Seattle meeting that Martin organized in 1948. The University of Washington underwrote part of the expense of the meeting, even though the University was not formally designated as a co-sponsor.[76]

The first regional meeting with an acknowledged co-sponsor was a Midwest meeting on United States–Soviet relations, held in Chicago on January 29, 1949. The co-sponsor was the Committee on International and Comparative Law of the Chicago Bar Association.[77]

---

70 Minutes of the San Francisco Regional Meeting of the Society, Dec. 14, 1946 (unpublished, in the Society's files).

71 Minutes of the Executive Council, Apr. 26, 1947, in 41 *ASIL Proc.* 190, 192 (1947).

72 Minutes of the Executive Council, Apr. 22, 1948, in 42 *ASIL Proc.* 146, 148 (1948).

73 Minutes of 1948 Joint Meeting, *supra* note 36, at 153.

74 Minutes of the Executive Council, Apr. 26, 1947, in 41 *ASIL Proc.* 190, 192 (1947).

75 Letter from Pitman B. Potter to Charles E. Martin, Apr. 28, 1947.

76 Minutes of the Executive Council, Sept. 17, 1949, in 44 *ASIL Proc.* 231, 232 (1950).

77 Anonymous report on Midwest Regional Meeting of American Society of International Law, 43 *AJIL* 344 (1949).

8. The Society and the State Department

Herbert Wright, the chair of the Society's Committee on Publications of the Department of State, died in 1945. Willard B. Cowles, of New York City, took his place. At the 1946 Annual Meeting, Cowles and his Committee proposed an ambitious treaty service: the government should issue a looseleaf publication on the model of tax looseleaf services, collecting data for particular articles of specific treaties so a researcher could find in one place the text of the article, any administrative regulations implementing it, court and arbitral decisions interpreting it, and so forth.[78] The Society adopted the Committee's proposal.

Several conferences took place with State Department officials. In February 1947, the Department undertook to publish the looseleaf service, and asked for the Committee's advice on content and form. Members of the Committee did give advice, and the first installment appeared in September 1947.[79] The looseleaf service lasted only until December 1950.

In 1946, the Society also adopted a resolution urging publication of a consolidated index to the *Department of State Bulletin*.[80] The effort came to naught.

In 1948, Charles Fenwick suggested establishing a Society committee to consult with the State Department on foreign policy issues.[81] An *ad hoc* committee was appointed to consider the feasibility of such an arrangement. The idea was actually an outgrowth of the suggestion Charles Cheney Hyde had made in his presidential address at the 1947 Annual Meeting. As we have seen, he had suggested that a small body of "highly competent and trustworthy persons not connected with the Government" be established to advise the government as to the probable effect of the pursuit of any foreign policy on which its advice was sought.[82] The Hoover Commission on Organization of the Executive Branch of the Government had concurred, and an *ad hoc* Society committee had offered its cooperation to the State Department.

In April 1949, it began to look as though the idea would take hold. The Under Secretary of State wrote to George Finch to say that the Department was considering the creation of a panel of outside advisers competent in the field of foreign affairs. He asked for suggestions regarding persons who might be

---

78 40 *ASIL Proc.* 132-33 (1946).

79 Report of the Committee on Department of State Publications, 41 *ASIL Proc.* 203-04 (1947). The looseleaf service was issued under the title "United States Treaty Developments."

80 40 *ASIL Proc.* 133 (1946).

81 Minutes of 1948 Joint Meeting, *supra* note 36, at 153.

82 Charles Cheney Hyde, Looking Ahead, 41 *ASIL Proc.* 1, 5 (1947).

included.[83] The Business Meeting of the Society responded with a list of eleven Society members who could serve on the panel.[84] But the State Department let the matter drop, and nothing further was done.[85]

In 1949-1950 the Society had an *ad hoc* Committee on International Law in Foreign Service Examinations. The Committee wrote to the State Department recommending that international law be made a required subject on the examination. The Foreign Service Board of Examiners turned down the proposal.[86]

9. The Society as Career Counselor

The August 1946 issue of *Glamour* magazine ran a chart on choosing college majors. One of the majors listed was International Relations. Under "Associations to Contact" for further information, it listed the American Society of International Law. When inquiries came in, Pitman Potter prepared a form letter on career opportunities in international relations, and sent it to the inquirers. He dealt briefly with careers in international business, journalism, the Foreign Service or an international institution, and teaching.[87] So far as can be determined, it was the Society's first effort at career counseling.

10. New Administrative Arrangements

In 1947, Pitman Potter was appointed Graduate Dean of the School of Social Sciences and Public Affairs at the American University. He asked the Society's Executive Council to relieve him of his duties as Secretary of the Society, though he would continue as Managing Editor of the Journal. The Council gave the President power to appoint a new Secretary, subject to Council ratification.[88] At the next Council meeting, George Finch was named interim Secretary.[89]

In 1948, Potter requested to be relieved of his duties as Managing Editor as well. The Executive Council adopted George Finch's recommendation that the

---

[83] Letter from James E. Webb to George A. Finch, Apr. 7, 1949, published in 43 *ASIL Proc.* 130 (1949).

[84] They were Frederick S. Dunn, Clyde Eagleton, Charles G. Fenwick, George A. Finch, Richard W. Flournoy, John N. Hazard, Charles Cheney Hyde, Charles E. Martin, Charles Warren, John B. Whitton and Lester H. Woolsey. 43 *ASIL Proc.* 131 (1949).

[85] Lester H. Woolsey, Editorial Comment: "Charles Cheney Hyde," 46 *AJIL* 283, 288 (1952).

[86] Minutes of the Executive Council, Apr. 27, 1950, in 44 *ASIL Proc.* 238, 244 (1950).

[87] Form letter from Pitman B. Potter, Aug. 31, 1946.

[88] Minutes of the Executive Council, Apr. 24 & 26, 1947, in 41 *ASIL Proc.* 185, 189 & 190, 191 (1947).

[89] Minutes of Joint Meeting of the Executive Council and the Board of Editors, Oct. 4, 1947, in 42 *ASIL Proc.* 142, 144 (1948).

Society have a full-time person perform the non-policy-making administrative work of the Society and editorial work of the Journal, under the direction of the officers of the Society and the Journal. The Council created the full-time office of Executive Secretary of the Society and Secretary of the Board of Editors, with an annual salary of USD 5,000.[90] George Finch's daughter, Eleanor H. Finch, was appointed to the position, effective July 6, 1948.[91] She served as Executive Secretary until the Society's first full-time Executive Director, H.C.L. Merillat, took office in November 1960. She then worked full-time for the Journal until she retired in 1972.

The position of Secretary of the Society was retained in 1948, but was redefined to encompass little more than taking care of formalities and record-keeping. Edward Dumbauld was elected as the new Secretary,[92] a position he held until 1978.

11. A Glimmering of a Full-time Executive Director

In 1947, James Oliver Murdock, who chaired the Society's Committee on Increase of Membership, prepared a memorandum recommending, among other things, that the Society have a "paid Executive Secretary, with business ability and experience." In effect, he was saying that the Society should have a full-time, professional administrator. The duties would include increasing membership in the Society and expanding library subscriptions to the Journal.[93] It would be another thirteen years until the Society hired its first full-time Executive Director, but the seed had been planted.

12. An Annual Award for International Law Scholarship

In 1948, John N. Hazard chaired an *ad hoc* Committee on Annual Awards for Outstanding Contributions in the Field of International Law. He submitted a report recommending that the Society offer an annual award or awards for the best works in international law appearing in any country and in any language. It was tentatively decided that the award should be confined to members of the Society, a decision that was later rescinded.[94]

---

90 Minutes of the Executive Council, Apr. 22, 1948, in 42 *ASIL Proc.* 146, 149-50 (1948).

91 43 *ASIL Proc.* v, vi (1949); Minutes of the 1948 Joint Meeting, *supra* note 36, at 156.

92 Minutes of the Executive Council, Apr. 24, 1948, in 42 *ASIL Proc.* 152, 154 (1948).

93 James Oliver Murdock, "Memorandum on the American Journal of International Law," Apr. 24, 1947, p. 4.

94 Minutes of 1948 Joint Meeting, *supra* note 36, at 153-54; Minutes of the Executive Council, Sept. 17, 1949, in 44 *ASIL Proc.* 231, 233 (1950).

In January 1950, the Committee submitted proposed rules for an annual award of a Certificate of Merit. After making a few amendments, the Council approved the rules. They provided for the appointment each year of a Committee on Annual Awards, comprised of three members. The Committee was instructed to recommend to the Executive Council the name of an author of a work (book, monograph or article) on international law to be awarded the Certificate of Merit. No nationality or language restriction would apply. Works to be considered would have to be published within a 24-month period before February 1 of the year of the award, but if a majority of the Committee could not agree on a single work for the award, the Committee could extend the period to 36 months.[95]

The Committee on Annual Awards, chaired by John Hazard, made its first recommendation in April 1951. The Executive Council rejected it.[96] The records do not reveal either the name of the recommended author or the reasons for the rejection.

13. More Constitutional Amendments

In April 1949, the Executive Council approved two constitutional amendments for submission to the Business Meeting a year hence. The first dealt with the Society's continuing financial woes. Since 1947, the Society's income had increased by 47 per cent with the increase in membership, but its expenditures had gone up by 82 per cent. The obvious solution was an increase in dues, but the Society's Constitution still specified, as it had since 1906, that dues for regular members would be five dollars. The Executive Council recommended deletion of the amount, leaving future dues to be determined by the Council.[97]

The second amendment dealt with the recurring question of resolutions that members from time to time wished the Society to adopt. Under the existing constitutional provision, resolutions proposed at an Annual Meeting would normally be referred to the Council, which could not report back until the next Annual Meeting. In practice, these resolutions simply disappeared from view and were never brought back to the membership. An *ad hoc* committee headed by George Finch recommended that the Constitution permit a second way to submit resolutions: they could be submitted for consideration by the Executive Council "in advance of any meeting of the Society by depositing them with the Secretary in due time."[98]

---

95 Rules Approved by the Executive Council on January 14, 1950, for an Award of Certificate for Meritorious Work in International Law, 44 *AJIL* 153 (1950).

96 Minutes of the Executive Council, Apr. 26, 1951, in 45 *ASIL Proc.* 237, 239 (1951).

97 Minutes of the Executive Council, Apr. 28, 1949, in 43 *ASIL Proc.* 156, 158 (1949).

98 Id. at 159; see also 44 *ASIL Proc.* 58 (1950).

In September 1949, the Executive Council proposed another amendment to the Constitution. The Treasurer of the Society, Howard S. LeRoy, had died in office. That left no one with authority to act as Treasurer until the Executive Council could meet to appoint someone. This was unsatisfactory, so a constitutional amendment was drafted to provide for an Assistant Treasurer with authority to act if the Treasurer was absent or became incapacitated.[99]

All three amendments were adopted at the Business Meeting in 1950.[100] The next day the Executive Council raised the annual dues rates.[101]

14. Downsizing

The Society had used the facilities of the Carnegie Endowment on Jackson Place as its headquarters, rent free, since 1911.[102] In 1950, when the Endowment decided to move its headquarters from the District of Columbia to New York City, the Society had to look for a place of its own. The venerable George Finch headed a committee to secure new quarters. The committee recommended that offices be leased in the Kellogg Building at 1422 F Street, N.W. The Society rented three rooms in the building for USD 90 a month.[103] In 1951, the Society acquired another room in the building.[104]

The move to the Kellogg Building meant a reduction in space. There would be no room for even the modest Society library that had occupied some of the space in the Endowment's building.[105] Faced with the need to downsize, the Council authorized the Editor-in-Chief of the Journal and the Treasurer of the Society to dispose of the books in the library and back numbers of the Journal. The Council also authorized the Executive Secretary to dispose of "useless correspondence and records of the Society" from time to time.[106] These authorizations were carried out. The Society later re-established a library in Tillar House and greatly expanded it, but the Society's correspondence files from 1948 to the mid-1990s are meager indeed.

In April 1951, the Executive Council decided to economize by eliminating the minutes of Executive Council meetings and some other reports from future

---

99 Minutes of the Executive Council, Sept. 17, 1949, in 44 *ASIL Proc.* 231, 232 (1950).

100 44 *ASIL Proc.* 56-59 (1950).

101 For details, see "Memorandum, ASIL History: Details Relating to Budget, Finances and Membership" (2006), on file with the Society.

102 The Society's address changed during that time from 2 Jackson Place to 700 Jackson Place, although both addresses were in the same building. 44 *ASIL Proc.* 65 (1950).

103 44 *ASIL Proc.* 66 (1950).

104 Minutes of the Executive Council, Apr. 28, 1951, in 45 *ASIL Proc.* 242, 243 (1951).

105 44 *ASIL Proc.* 67.

106 Id. at 240.

published annual Proceedings.[107] Thus ended a consistent practice, begun in 1907, of providing a reasonably complete published record of the Society's activities, concerns and decisions.

15. The Society Becomes a Corporation

In 1949, the Society began to have tax troubles with the District of Columbia. At first, its application for exemption from the Sales Tax Act of 1949 was rejected. It also received a letter to the effect that it would have to apply for an unincorporated business license under the Income and Franchise Act of 1947. The Society organized a committee of Washington lawyers to claim an exemption on the basis of the Society's nonprofit, scientific character.[108] The committee succeeded in obtaining an exemption from both the sales tax and the requirement for a business license.[109]

It appears that the imbroglio with the District of Columbia authorities was one of the reasons the Society's Committee on Finance and Incorporation, under Edgar Turlington, began to investigate the desirability of incorporating. Moreover, reorganization as a nonprofit corporation would encourage tax-deductible gifts and bequests.[110] In the same Executive Council meeting at which Turlington reported success on the tax exemption front, he and his committee recommended that the Society incorporate by Act of Congress.[111] The Council concurred.

The Society could have incorporated under the law of the District of Columbia, but D.C. corporation law required a quorum of a majority of the governing board members in order to conduct business at any board meeting. Since a quorum of that size had hardly ever been achieved in the annals of the Society's Executive

---

107 Minutes of the Executive Council, Apr. 26, 1951, in 45 *ASIL Proc.* 237, 238-39 (1951).

108 Minutes of the Executive Council, Sept. 17, 1949, in 44 *ASIL Proc.* 231, 234 (1950).

109 Minutes of the Executive Council, Jan. 14, 1950, in 44 *ASIL Proc.* 234, 236-37 (1950).

110 Notes prepared by Eleanor H. Finch for interview with Frederic L. Kirgis, May 16, 1994. In 1948, George Finch corresponded with a Maryland woman who was considering a bequest to the Society, but who was concerned about Maryland inheritance tax implications if the Society remained unincorporated. He said that the Society was considering possible incorporation, and suggested that her bequest be conditioned on the Society's incorporation within 12 months from probate of her will. Letter from George A. Finch to Sara de Ford, Dec. 22, 1948. When she died 48 years later, her will contained a bequest to that effect, worth about USD 500,000 in 1996 dollars. Letter from Sara W. De Ford's trustee to the Society, Oct. 7, 1997.

111 44 *ASIL Proc.* 236 (1950).

Council meetings, it was thought expedient to seek an Act of Congress containing no such requirement.[112]

George Finch later said that at first he had no hope the effort would succeed.[113] But it did. To steer the bill through, the Society enlisted the aid of a few key members of Congress. In addition, one of the Society's most prominent members whose views carried weight with Congress, United States Supreme Court Justice Robert H. Jackson, endorsed the bill. That lifted some of the opposition in the House of Representatives.[114] In the end, Congress duly enacted An Act to Incorporate the American Society of International Law, and for Other Purposes, effective September 20, 1950.[115]

The Act set forth the purposes of the Society as they appear in the Society's Constitution, required that it be operated as a nonprofit corporation, and prohibited the corporation, its officers and other Executive Council members, as such, from contributing to or otherwise supporting or assisting any political party or candidate for elective public office.[116] It also called for a governing board in the form of an Executive Council, consisting of a President, Honorary President, a number of Vice Presidents and Honorary Vice Presidents determined by the Constitution of the Society, a Secretary, a Treasurer, and not fewer than twenty-four additional persons. The officers and one-third of the other Executive Council members were to be elected at each Annual Meeting, except that the Executive Council could be authorized by the Constitution of the Society to elect the Secretary and Treasurer for specified terms, and to fill vacancies until the next Annual Meeting.[117] The corporation could not issue stock, declare dividends, or make loans or advances to its officers or members of its Executive Council.[118]

At a Business Meeting on Saturday, April 28, 1951, the Society formally accepted incorporation as set forth in the Act of Congress.[119] The transfer of assets from the unincorporated association to the new corporation took place

---

112 Id. at 61.

113 Business Meeting of the American Society of International Law, a Corporation, Apr. 28, 1951, in 45 *ASIL Proc.* 204, 207 (1951).

114 Id. at 208.

115 P.L. 794, 81st Cong., 2d Sess., 64 Stat. 869 (1950), 45 *AJIL* 158 (1951).

116 Id. § 2.

117 Id. § 3.

118 Id. § 7.

119 Business Meeting, *supra* note 113, at 205-08.

on May 18, 1951.[120] The Constitution and Regulations of the unincorporated Society were adopted as those of the corporation.[121]

B. THE SOCIETY AND THE UNITED NATIONS

1. Representation at the Inaugural General Assembly Session

After being disappointed that the Society was left off the consultative organizations list at the San Francisco Conference, Pitman Potter was eager to see that the Society was represented at the inaugural session of the United Nations General Assembly in London in January 1946. He chose Francis O. Wilcox, of the Library of Congress Legislative Reference Service, as the Society's representative. The representation would be a limited one. The Society, Potter said guardedly, "desires to be represented in London mainly for purposes of information and to indicate its hearty sympathy with the general objectives of the effort back of the United Nations Organization."[122]

2. Finding the Society's Role with Respect to the U.N.

As we have seen, in 1946, the Society took a position on the relationship between the United States and the International Court of Justice. The Society went on record in favor of an Article 36(2) declaration by the United States.[123]

The Society applied for consultative status with ECOSOC in the autumn of 1946.[124] So did more than 1,000 other non-governmental organizations, national and international. The ECOSOC Committee on Arrangements for Consultation with Non-Governmental Organizations was overwhelmed. Consequently it adopted a policy limiting direct access by national organizations. They were "normally" to present their views through their governments or through international NGOs to which they belonged.[125] In the United States, the State Department's Office of Public Affairs established procedures for American NGOs, including

---

[120] Instrument of Transfer, May 18, 1951, in 45 *ASIL Proc.* 210-11 (1951).

[121] Minutes of the First Meeting of the Executive Council of the American Society of International Law, a Corporation, in 45 *ASIL Proc.* 244, 246 (1951). The resolution adopting the Constitution and Regulations also referred to by-laws, but there were none.

[122] Letter from Pitman B. Potter to Francis O. Wilcox, Jan. 2, 1946.

[123] See text at note 23 *supra*.

[124] Form letter to applicants from Lyman C. White, of the U.N. Non-Governmental Organizations Section, Oct. 30, 1946; U.N. Doc. E/CT.2/12, at 3 (1946).

[125] Letter from Francis H. Russell to Charles Cheney Hyde, Sept. 30, 1946.

the Society, to obtain information on the work of ECOSOC and to make their views known.[126]

Potter demurred. He observed that channeling communications through governmental delegates "would tend to screen the views of detached scientific students and persons of broad social interest through the requirements of national politics."[127] The State Department's response was that it would be impractical, and perhaps counterproductive, for thousands of national NGOs to be in constant touch with ECOSOC. They would get much more attention by channeling their views through the U.S. delegation to the United Nations.[128]

The Society nevertheless persisted with its application for direct consultative status. In August 1947, ECOSOC notified the Society that its application had been rejected. Only four national organizations, including the Carnegie Endowment, had been approved.[129] So it was that the Society and many other national organizations remained outside ECOSOC's direct consultative ambit. The Society remained outside for nearly fifty years.[130]

Potter continued to search for an ongoing relationship with the U.N. He met with Dr. Ivan Kerno, the Assistant Secretary-General in charge of the U.N. Legal Department, and followed up with a letter in the autumn of 1946 offering such assistance as the Society might be able to render on any occasion.[131] He mentioned particularly the Society's Codification Committee, which stood ready to provide advice in connection with the forthcoming U.N. codification effort.[132]

In December 1946, the U.N. General Assembly adopted a resolution requesting the Secretary-General to seek the observations of "national and international bodies concerned with international law" on a Panamanian-sponsored Draft

---

126 Id.

127 Letter from Pitman B. Potter to Walter Kotschnig, Acting Chief, Division of International Organization Affairs, Department of State, Oct. 21, 1946.

128 Letter from Kotschnig to Potter, Nov. 12, 1946.

129 Letter from Lyman C. White, of the U.N. Non-Governmental Organizations Section, to Pitman B. Potter, Aug. 27, 1947.

130 In August 1993, after ECOSOC had changed its criteria for consultative arrangements, the Society attained Category II consultative status. *ASIL Newsletter*, Sept.–Oct. 1993, at 21.

131 Potter also offered assistance to John P. Humphrey, the newly appointed Director of the U.N. Division of Human Rights. He received a cordial reply welcoming the offer. Letter from Pitman B. Potter to John P. Humphrey, Nov. 13, 1946; letter from Humphrey to Potter, Nov. 27, 1946. How much Humphrey actually relied on Society members over the course of his long tenure as the leading U.N. human rights official does not appear.

132 Letter from Pitman B. Potter to Ivan Kerno, Oct. 16, 1946. On the codification matter, Potter was carrying out the wishes of the Executive Council. See Minutes of the Executive Council, Sept. 28, 1946, in 41 *ASIL Proc.* 182, 184-85 (1947).

Declaration on the Rights and Duties of States.[133] The U.N. Legal Department followed through in a letter from Yuen-li Liang.[134] Potter declined to provide comments on behalf of the Society, but said perhaps its Codification Committee could be enlarged for this occasion and could provide its own comments.[135] Liang welcomed any observations an enlarged ASIL Codification Committee cared to make.[136] Whether the Codification Committee made any observations does not appear.

Members of the Society had an opportunity to provide comments on codification in general, and on the rights and duties of states in particular, at its Annual Meeting in 1947. Liang was the Friday morning speaker. His topic was "Development and Codification of International Law." He presented a clear and succinct history of 20th-century codification efforts, up to and including Article 13(1)(a) of the U.N. Charter (on progressive development of international law and its codification).[137] He went on to discuss difficulties inherent in codification and made some suggestions on overcoming them. He finished with a general invitation to the Society to provide assistance to the U.N. in its embryonic efforts to codify and develop international law. In response, the Society published memoranda prepared by the U.N. Division of the Development and Codification of International Law, in a Supplement to the Journal.[138] The Journal also published an article by Liang in 1948 on progressive development and codification of international law.[139]

The extensive discussion that followed Liang's address at the 1947 Annual Meeting gave him a sample of Society members' views. The discussion concentrated on the distinction between progressive development and codification, as reflected in the Charter. That is, it did until a self-described newcomer to the organization asked for the floor. When the chair recognized him, Myres McDougal

---

133 G.A. Res. 38(I), of Dec. 11, 1946.

134 Letter from Yuen-li Liang, Director of the U.N. Division of the Development and Codification of International Law, to the Secretary of the ASIL, Apr. 2, 1947. See Minutes of the Executive Council, Apr. 24, 1947, in 41 *ASIL Proc.* 185, 189 (1947).

135 Letter from Potter to Liang, Apr. 8, 1947.

136 Letter from Liang to Potter, Apr. 10, 1947.

137 Yuen-li Liang, "The Progressive Development of International Law and its Codification under the United Nations," 41 *ASIL Proc.* 24 (1947). For an exhaustive historical survey of codification efforts, apparently also prepared by Liang, see U.N. Doc. A/AC.10/5 (1947), reprinted in 41 *AJIL Supp.* 29 (1947).

138 41 *AJIL Supp.* 29-147 (1947). These memoranda provide an excellent survey of codification efforts until then.

139 Yuen-li Liang, "The General Assembly and the Progressive Development and Codification of International Law," 42 *AJIL* 66 (1948), incorporating part of Liang's address at the New York regional meeting of the Society on November 8, 1947.

said that he intended no offense to the previous speakers, but he thought the stated premises had proved themselves unworkable. The attempted distinctions between the scientific approach and the philosophical approach to international law, and between codification of existing law and the progressive development of law, he thought, are:

> founded on a tissue of confusions about how people use words, about how the human mind works, about the variables that affect official behavior. The suggestion that we must have more *pacta sunt servanda* at all costs, that we must keep nations from breaking agreements whatever the circumstances, is, I think, just to ignore the kind of world in which we live and what we are trying to do. The fact is that agreements must change as values and conditions change.[140]

The first of many McDouglian salvos had been fired. He concluded with a prescription for a contextual, value-oriented approach to codification:

> If in the codification of international law the people who are charged with that high responsibility can get away from this mysterious notion that one simply launches words out into the void and that they have some unerring effect on the distribution of values, irrespective of context, and attempt rather to locate themselves and their words in the total social process of the world community, if they can suggest something more than the purification of doctrine and bring a creative insight to the devising of better institutions, if they consider all of these basic values like safety, the production and sharing of wealth, respect, well-being, comfort, health, and so on, and go systematically through all their traditional doctrines in terms of their relevance to these values, noting to what extent they promote or retard the goals of a world community, even with respect to such traditionally national problems as the diplomatic protection of citizens or the laws with respect to aliens and immigration – I think that we and they can share the realistic expectation that their work will bear inestimable fruit in promoting what we all want.[141]

Several subsequent speakers expressed general agreement with McDougal. It was a far cry from the codification ideas of Elihu Root and James Brown Scott, and even from the approach of the distinguished Society members, led by Manley Hudson, who had labored to produce the Harvard Research in International Law. McDougal's salvo heralded a new era in the Society in which international law would increasingly be regarded as a process reflecting the shared or conflicting values of the actors – not just states – participating in it at any given time. The

---

[140] 41 *ASIL Proc.* 42, 47-48 (1947).

[141] Id. at 49-50.

relative power of each actor became a variable to be considered explicitly in any description or analysis of the process. The rather more lofty – and more static – approach of the Harvard Research, if not put to rest, was at least faced with a formidable challenge.

When the International Law Commission was established in 1947, Manley Hudson – nearly as ubiquitous a Society member in his time as James Brown Scott had been in his – became the first United States member. The Commission's first work product, the Draft Declaration of Rights and Duties of States, was based on Panama's 1946 initiative in the General Assembly. Hudson voted against the Draft Declaration because the provisions of Article 6, on the duty of every state to respect the human rights and fundamental freedoms of all persons within its jurisdiction, went beyond the U.N. Charter and "beyond international law at its present stage of development."[142] The General Assembly never adopted the Draft Declaration.

While the document that became the Universal Declaration of Human Rights was being drafted, the State Department contacted the Society asking for its comments or suggestions.[143] Pitman Potter initially referred the matter to the Society's Codification Committee. It does not appear that the committee provided any advice, but two prominent Society members – Potter and George Finch – attended a meeting at the State Department that had been called for the purpose of consulting with several organizations on the draft of what was then called the International Bill of Human Rights.[144] Among those who made presentations at the meeting were Society members Dean Rusk, then the Director of the State Department's Office of Special Political Affairs, and Ernest A. Gross, then the Legal Adviser.

In 1950, the Executive Council established a Committee to Study Legal Problems of the United Nations.[145] The Committee's chair, Clyde Eagleton, presented its first report at the 1951 Annual Meeting. It dealt with the registration of treaties

---

[142] Report of the International Law Commission Covering its First Session, UN GAOR, 4th Sess., Supp. No. 10 (A/925), 1949 *YB Int'l L. Comm'n*, Part II, at 287, n. 21, 44 *AJIL Supp.* 1, 15 (1950). Hans Kelsen agreed with Hudson. See Hans Kelsen, "The Draft Declaration on Rights and Duties of States," 44 *AJIL* 259, 269-70 (1950).

[143] Letter from Francis H. Russell, Director of the State Department's Office of Public Affairs, to Pitman B. Potter, July 28, 1947.

[144] Letter from Russell to Potter, Oct. 11, 1947; letter from Potter to Russell, Oct. 20, 1947.

[145] Minutes of the Executive Council, Nov. 11, 1950, in 45 *ASIL Proc.* 233, 236-37 (1951).

under Article 102 and the role of the U.N. Secretariat as the depositary.[146] It was a bit dry.

3. A Brief Period as a Depository of U.N. Documents

In the autumn of 1946, before the United Nations had established its network of Information Centers and depository libraries, its Department of Public Information arranged for a limited number of institutions in various countries to receive U.N. documents and publications, free of charge, for reference purposes. The Society was one of the designated recipients.[147] It began receiving U.N. documents regularly in September 1946.[148]

At that time, the Society was still using space in the Carnegie Endowment building. As we have seen, when the Society had to move out of the Endowment's quarters in 1950, it had to dispose of its library. The U.N. documents must have departed along with other materials, thus ending the Society's stint as a U.N. depository.

C. THE JOURNAL AFTER THE WAR

1. Some Changes in Personnel

There was quite some turnover in the Journal's Board of Editors in the immediate post-war years.[149] Among the new members were William W. Bishop, Jr., then a Visiting Professor at the University of Pennsylvania Law School and future Editor-in-Chief of the Journal, and Myres S. McDougal, of the Yale Law School. McDougal was elected in 1949 as a substitute for Edwin Dickinson, a former Editor who had been re-elected but had declined to serve because of other commitments.[150] McDougal remained on the Board, as an Editor or Honorary Editor, until his death in 1998.

As has been noted above, Pitman Potter relinquished his position as Managing Editor in 1948.[151] The Executive Council revised the Journal's Regulations to

---

[146] Clyde Eagleton, "Report of Committee to Study Legal Problems of the United Nations: Handling of Treaties by the United Nations," 45 *ASIL Proc.* 139 (1951).

[147] Letter from J.B. Orrick, Chief, U.N. Section for Voluntary Organizations, to George A. Finch, Sept. 17, 1946.

[148] Letter from Pitman B. Potter to J.B. Orrick, Sept. 19, 1946.

[149] For details, see "Memorandum, ASIL History: The Journal, Its Editors and Business Practices," on file with the Society.

[150] Minutes of the Executive Council, Apr. 30, 1949, in 43 *ASIL Proc.* 160-61 (1949); Minutes of the Executive Council, Sept. 17, 1949, in 44 *ASIL Proc.* 231, 233 (1950).

[151] See text at note 90 *supra*.

eliminate the position of Managing Editor, substituting for it a Secretary of the Board of Editors. The Secretary would not have to be a member of the Board, and would serve during the Executive Council's pleasure. The duties would be the same as those of the former Managing Editor, except that the Secretary could not fill in for the Editor-in-Chief should the latter be temporarily unable to act. A Board member designated by the Editor-in-Chief or by the other members of the Board would do so.[152] Eleanor H. Finch became the Secretary of the Board in 1948.

In 1950, George Finch, at the age of 64, asked the Council to replace him as Editor-in-Chief. "I have passed the age," he said, "when I am entitled to go on the shelf."[153] The Executive Council persuaded him to stay on, but not for long.

2. Principal Topics

Manley Hudson's consecutive string of annual articles on the World Court continued unbroken after the war. His 1946 piece remains a valuable source of information about the drafting of the I.C.J. Statute, with an article-by-article commentary. Interestingly, Hudson lumped Nicaragua in with several other states that had submitted Article 36(2) declarations under the old Statute and that had ratified the U.N. Charter. Unlike the other states, Nicaragua had not formally ratified the Protocol of Signature of the old Statute. Hudson nevertheless treated the Nicaraguan declaration as remaining in force under Article 36(5).[154] Much later, the United States government would take a diametrically opposed view when Nicaragua invoked Article 36(2) against it.[155]

Among the other lead articles in 1946 was one by Francis O. Wilcox outlining the process by which the Senate consented to the United States' acceptance of the Court's jurisdiction under Article 36(2). Wilcox presented an uncritical analysis of the self-judging Connally Reservation.[156] Lawrence Preuss, writing in the same issue, was not as charitable.[157]

---

152 Regulations Regarding the Editing and Publication of the American Journal of International Law, adopted Apr. 22, 1948, in 42 *ASIL Proc.* xi, xii (1948); see also Minutes of the Executive Council, Apr. 22, 1948, in id. at 146, 149-50.

153 44 *ASIL Proc.* 72 (1950).

154 Manley O. Hudson, "The Twenty-Fourth Year of the World Court," 40 *AJIL* 1, 34 (1946).

155 See Case Concerning Military and Paramilitary Activities in and Against Nicaragua (*Nicaragua v. U.S.*), 1984 ICJ Rep. 392, 24 ILM 59 (1985).

156 Wilcox, *supra* note 29, at 710-14.

157 Lawrence Preuss, "The International Court of Justice, the Senate, and Matters of Domestic Jurisdiction," 40 *AJIL* 720 (1946). Editorial Comments by Charles Cheney Hyde and Pitman Potter came out between Wilcox and Preuss, but closer to Wilcox than to Preuss. See Charles Cheney Hyde, Editorial Comment: "The United States Accepts the Optional

From 1946 through to 1951, the United Nations was a prime topic for coverage in the Journal. But it was not a case of early euphoria slipping into later criticism. As early as 1946, the Journal published a lead article by Clyde Eagleton critical on legal grounds of Security Council practice under Chapter VI of the Charter.[158]

Other international organizations were covered as well, including the budding Organization of American States – an institution of particular interest to a venerable Society member, Charles Fenwick, who then was the Director of the Department of International Law and Organization of the Pan-American Union.[159] War crimes and the Nuremberg trial received a good deal of attention. With the advent of the four Geneva Conventions on the Law of War in 1949, the broad subject of rules of warfare came into focus. In fact, the Journal scored a coup by obtaining an article on the Geneva Conventions by Jean Pictet, the Director of the International Committee of the Red Cross.[160] As usual, purely theoretical articles were scarce, but the Journal did publish a short theoretical piece by Alfred von Verdross.[161]

3. Book Reviews

Kenneth Carlston published his book, *The Process of International Arbitration*, in 1946. He wrote to Pitman Potter, suggesting the names of potential reviewers for the Journal, including Potter himself.[162] Potter wrote back, declining to write the review himself and naming some possible reviewers.[163] There seems to have been no thought given to possible compromise of the review by allowing the author of the book to participate in the selection of a reviewer.

Even more problematic was the selection of Edwin Borchard to review a book by Charles A. Beard, *American Foreign Policy in the Making: A Study in Responsibilities*. The review appeared in the January 1947 issue of the Journal. Thomas A. Bailey, a Professor of History at Stanford, was mentioned unfavorably in the

---

Clause," id. at 778; Pitman B. Potter, Editorial Comment: "As Determined by the United States," id. at 792.

158 Clyde Eagleton, "The Jurisdiction of the Security Council over Disputes," 40 *AJIL* 513 (1946).

159 See Charles G. Fenwick, "The Ninth International Conference of American States," 42 *AJIL* 553 (1948); Josef L. Kunz, "The Bogota Charter of the Organization of American States," id. at 568.

160 Jean S. Pictet, "The New Geneva Conventions for the Protection of War Victims," 45 *AJIL* 462 (1951).

161 Alfred von Verdross, "On the Concept of International Law," 43 *AJIL* 435 (1949).

162 Letter from Kenneth S. Carlston to Pitman B. Potter, May 27, 1946.

163 Letter from Potter to Carlston, June 5, 1946. In the end, Carlston's book was given a short, lukewarm review by Manley O. Hudson in 41 *AJIL* 485 (1947).

review. Bailey pointed out in a letter to Pitman Potter that Beard in his preface had given credit to Borchard for helping him to assemble materials, for reading the entire manuscript and for providing critical counsel. Beard's acknowledgment to Borchard concluded, "No mere line in this preface can discharge my indebtedness to him."[164]

Borchard's review began, "This volume represents a study in American history by the greatest historian of our time."[165] His review ended, "The author has made a contribution of the first importance to the establishment of the truth."[166] The review did not mention Borchard's own role in the preparation of the book.

Potter's reply to Bailey offered a justification that in later years, if not then, would have raised some eyebrows:

> Beard's book was sent to Borchard for review as a result of the normal operation of arrangements in force for the distribution of books for review in the Journal. Even if the case had been any different, however, I doubt whether the fact that Borchard had collaborated in the production of the book would have operated to bar a review on his part; while there are obviously some considerations which might be invoked against the practice, it is not, as I am sure you are aware, very unusual to have books reviewed by persons who have had some connection with their preparation, if not by the authors themselves. In all such cases the position of the reviewer is fairly clear and no one is deceived, and the more the reviewer abuses his position the clearer is the revelation and the more unfavorable is the impression made.[167]

The Journal's policy did not remain as Potter described it, if indeed the policy had ever been such.

4. The Supplements

The Journal's policy in this period, and apparently earlier as well, was to refrain from publishing in its Supplement the text of any international agreement until it was actually in force.[168] This considerably delayed publication of agreements that were subject to ratification, particularly multilateral treaties. International Legal Materials later changed the policy.

---

164 Charles A. Beard, *American Foreign Policy in the Making, 1932-1940: A Study in Responsibilities*, Preface (1946); letter from Thomas A. Bailey to Pitman B. Potter, May 10, 1947.

165 Book Review, 41 *AJIL* 344 (1947).

166 Id. at 346.

167 Letter from Potter to Bailey, May 19, 1947.

168 Letter from Pitman B. Potter to Raymond Dennett, Director of the World Peace Foundation, Mar. 3, 1947.

Not surprisingly, the documents published in the Supplement during this period dealt largely with the United Nations, including the International Law Commission, as well as peace treaties and (toward the end of the period) instruments relating to the Cold War.

5. A Recommendation for Changes in the Journal

In 1947, James Oliver Murdock was the chair of the Society's Committee on Increase of Membership. He took an interest in devising ways to expand the Journal's appeal, and thus to attract new members (particularly practicing lawyers) into the Society. Murdock recommended that articles on foreign trade and finance be published in order to complement his Committee's solicitation of foreign trade executives and their legal counsel to join the Society.[169] Not much came of this. The Journal in 1947 and 1948 carried only a smattering of articles and Editorial Comments on international economic law.

Murdock then submitted a rather elaborate memorandum suggesting several changes in the Journal's style and format. First, he recommended that at the beginning of each article there should be a brief summary of its contents "in readable print," with a thumbnail sketch of the author's background. This, he said, would serve as "a teaser and [would] help induce reading of the full article."[170] The Journal did not exactly respond with alacrity. It began running abstracts of lead articles (in the Table of Contents) in 1995, long after Murdock's 1947 memorandum had been forgotten.

Murdock continued: "Long, wordy, clumsy articles are depressing to the reader. ... Such long articles should be re-written to increase readability. Effective condensation should be done by a special editor ... [who] need not be a specialist in the field, but a specialist in short concise English."[171] By 1948, Eleanor H. Finch was doing some editing for basic style, as have her successors, but she did not attempt any extensive re-writing of long articles.

Murdock went on to say that each issue should have two or three pages of short notes reporting current international activities, giving an address to which further inquiries could be directed.[172] The Journal was already running several pages of Current Notes in each issue. Some of them covered just the type of activity Murdock seemed to have in mind, and some of those contained footnotes that could lead readers to fuller information. In addition, it was still running its Chronicle of International Events, a regular department of the

---

169 Memorandum from James Oliver Murdock to Pitman B. Potter, Jan. 23, 1947.

170 James Oliver Murdock, "Memorandum on the American Journal of International Law," Apr. 24, 1947, p. 1.

171 Id.

172 Id., p. 2.

Journal from volume one in 1907 until 1950. The Chronicle cited its sources. Neither department – Current Notes or the Chronicle – appears to have changed as a result of Murdock's suggestions.

Murdock's most radical suggestions were that the Journal should be transformed from a quarterly to a monthly publication in order to keep up with world events, and should be about the size of the *Reader's Digest* in order to fit in a person's side pocket for reading on the train and at odd moments.[173] These suggestions made no impression on the Board of Editors. Even less promising was Murdock's proposal that the Journal reproduce some of the leading cartoons of the period on international affairs.[174]

According to the Minutes of the Board of Editors' meeting in October 1947, "The list of suggestions for improvement of the *Journal* submitted by Mr. James O. Murdock was ... presented and each one was considered. No further action was taken by the Board."[175]

6. Changes Adopted

In October 1947 the Executive Council and Board of Editors met together. They decided to revamp the Journal's Judicial Decisions department and to establish a new department on United Nations activities of a legal character.[176] For the first time, a member of the Board, William W. Bishop, Jr., was given specific responsibility for the Judicial Decisions department, with a mandate to expand the coverage. Theretofore the department had reprinted verbatim a few significant decisions in each issue, sometimes with brief editorial headnotes. The newly designed department contained summaries of several decisions in each issue, with selected quotations from the case reports.

The department on U.N. activities was inaugurated in 1949. Written by Yuen-li Liang, the department in that year supplied useful background information on some of the important legal issues of the day in the U.N., including the use of the double veto, the I.C.J. Advisory Opinions in the first *Admissions* case and the *Reparations* case, and possible creation of an international criminal tribunal.[177] Liang remained in charge of the department through to 1954, but then it disappeared from the Journal's pages.

---

173 Id.

174 Id., p. 3.

175 Minutes of 1947 Joint Meeting, *supra* note 89, at 146.

176 Pitman B. Potter, Current Note, 41 *AJIL* 904, 905 (1947); Minutes of 1947 Joint Meeting, *supra* note 89, at 145-46.

177 See Yuen-li Liang, "Notes on Legal Questions Concerning the United Nations," 43 *AJIL* 134, 288, 303, 460, 478, 705 (1949).

The joint meeting in 1947 decided to increase the size of the Journal for 1948 to 1200 pages, and to seek articles on international relations by distinguished public figures who would not necessarily be in the legal field.[178] It might not be a coincidence that the quarterly *International Organization* – specializing in scholarly articles on international relations – began publication a few months earlier.[179]

7. Evidence of the Journal's Impact

It is difficult to gauge the Journal's impact on the actual conduct of international relations during this or any period of its existence. It does appear, though, that the Journal played some role in preparations for the prosecution of the Nuremberg war crimes trials. The War Department requested copies of three Journal articles for use by the prosecutors.[180] Particularly prominent was Quincy Wright's article entitled simply "War Criminals."[181] In it he assessed four "systems of law" – national law, the law of war, the law of peace and universal law – that might be used to punish war criminals. Universal law, he argued, could be used to punish individuals for committing acts otherwise criminal in pursuance of aggression against the world community.

The Journal's impact on the teaching of international law is relatively clear. During the immediate post-war period, the Journal received quite a few requests from teachers, from publishers of academic texts and from adult education programs for permission to reprint a wide variety of articles that had appeared in its pages.[182] Presumably the articles became assigned or recommended reading.

D. MOVING TENTATIVELY INTO THE COLD WAR WORLD

The Cold War, and its effect on the United Nations, raised a new awareness in the Society of its own strengths and limitations. As Charles Cheney Hyde

---

[178] See, e.g., E.N. van Kleffens, "Regionalism and Political Pacts," 43 *AJIL* 666 (1949).

[179] For Pitman Potter's reaction to the new quarterly, see his Current Note: "New Quarterly on International Organization," 41 *AJIL* 456 (1947). On the surface, at least, he welcomed it.

[180] Letters from G.L. Eberle to Pitman B. Potter, Apr. 23, 1947, and from James M. Horan to George A. Finch, May 26, 1947.

[181] Quincy Wright, "War Criminals," 39 *AJIL* 257 (1945).

[182] E.g., letters from Norman J. Padelford to Pitman B. Potter, Oct. 3, 1946, Dec. 4, 1946, Dec. 20, 1946 & Nov. 14, 1947; letters from W.W. Wilson Company, Apr. 29, 1946 & Dec. 17, 1946; letter from American Foundation for Political Education, Dec. 2, 1947; letter from L.H. Chamberlain, May 5, 1947; from George H. Dession, June 13, 1947; and from Russell H. Fitzgibbon, Sept. 22, 1947.

pointed out in his 1949 presidential address, the Society had been passive when it came to accomplishing its stated objective of promoting the establishment and maintenance of international relations on the basis of law and justice. After two World Wars, and with the Cold War gaining in intensity, the need to focus on the stated objective seemed imperative. But there were many detours on the road to consensus among the membership as to positions the Society might take in order to achieve its goal. Agreement could be reached on the desirability of a U.S. declaration under the optional clause in the I.C.J. Statute, but it was difficult to find accord on other issues.

It could be argued that during these years, as indeed at other times, the Society's publication in the Journal of thoughtful, thoroughly researched articles on important issues, and its publication of timely addresses and lively discussions in the Proceedings, contributed to the achievement of its objectives by influencing policy-making in ways that could not be measured objectively. Hyde, in his 1949 address, acknowledged this argument, and Justice Jackson at the same Annual Meeting gave it some emphasis. But for Hyde, and for some others in the Society, the evidence of success was a bit thin. The trick was to determine how to buttress the Society's effectiveness without rending the Society asunder or damaging its intellectual integrity, or both.

The late 1940s saw the Society take a few tentative steps toward breaking out of its limited tradition of holding Annual Meetings, publishing the Journal and engendering committee reports. With a strong push from Hyde, the regional meetings program began. The regional meetings enabled the Society to reach persons, including some members, who otherwise were not in a position to participate much in discussions of international law.

Dues were increased for the first time since the Society's inception. This step was significant not just because of the immediate infusion of cash, but also because it established a precedent. No longer would it be considered taboo to raise dues when the Society's finances required it.

The Journal's Board of Editors benefitted from an infusion of energy supplied by young scholars like William Bishop, Herbert Briggs and Myres McDougal. Bishop, in particular, made his presence felt right away by taking over a revamped Judicial Decisions department.

In the latter years of this period, with Manley Hudson as President of the Society, the focus shifted away from Charles Cheney Hyde's vision of the Society as a force for law and justice in the world, and toward the Society as an intellectual bulwark where intelligent, vigorous scholars could make their mark. It was a drive for excellence with room for original thinkers like McDougal and Lasswell, but without Hyde's sense of urgency in injecting rules of international law directly into the shaping of foreign policy. The Hudson legacy would endure for a good many years.

Chapter Seven

THE SOCIETY IN THE FIFTIES

What we have [are] a variety of 'international' laws and an anarchy of diverse, contending orders – orders proclaiming and embodying the values of human dignity in very different degree, and aspiring to application and completion on many different scales of international, regional, and global compass.

—Myres S. McDougal
"Perspectives for an International Law of Human Dignity,"
53 *ASIL Proceedings* 107-08 (1959)

A. THE OLD MODEL AND GRADUAL CHANGE

1. The Model as it Then Was

As the previous chapters have recounted, there was plenty of tinkering with the Society's mode of operations from shortly after its inception through the two World Wars, and beyond. But the framework remained essentially the same. There was a President who performed ceremonial functions and in some cases became at least moderately involved in the Society's affairs, but the day-to-day administration was in the hands of a single person who also had other responsibilities: James Brown Scott, then George A. Finch, followed by Pitman B. Potter. Even Eleanor H. Finch, who became Executive Secretary in 1948 and who was from then on a full-time employee of the Society, had to split her time between the Society, as such, and the Journal. There was little opportunity for reflective thinking about new programs or other changes that might energize the Society, or about how any new programs might be financed if the Society's traditional patron, the Carnegie Endowment, was not willing to dole out the funds.

In this setting, the Society could do little more than present an Annual Meeting, publish its Journal, and engender committee reports. These endeavors were hardly insignificant. The Annual Meeting and the Journal were especially important fora for the serious development of ideas about what was commonly called the law of nations. But the absence of any other regular means of developing ideas or of Society expression was becoming increasingly stultifying during the

1950s, at least in the minds of some of the more policy-oriented members. The traditional model changed, but only gradually, throughout the decade.

2. Opportunities to Provide Expertise

In 1951, the U.N. Committee on International Criminal Jurisdiction prepared a report containing the committee's Draft Statute for an International Criminal Court.[1] The United States government, like the governments of other U.N. Member States, was asked to comment on the report. The Acting Legal Adviser of the State Department sent the Society the U.N. Committee's report. He requested that the report be studied by appropriate groups within the Society so the Department could have the benefit of any comments the Society might wish to make. The Executive Council considered the request at its meeting on December 1, 1951. Its only response was to refer the report and Draft Statute to the Society's Committee on the Annual Meeting, apparently in deference to the Society's practice of declining to take positions on controversial subjects.[2]

The Committee on the Annual Meeting did not include the report or Draft Statute in the agenda of the 1952 Annual Meeting, though it did arrange for a paper to be given on the impact of international law on the individual. The paper did not deal with an international criminal court, but Vespasian V. Pella, a long-standing advocate of such a court, spoke from the floor on the subject.[3] That was the sum total of the Society's response to the State Department's request for the Society's expertise, unless one counts individual contributions on the subject in the Journal.[4]

It was another missed opportunity for the Society, stemming from its chronic lack of adequate funds or staff – one might even say, its lack of vision. An *ad hoc* committee, selected with an eye to the known diversity of views of its members,

---

1 UN GAOR, 7th Sess., Supp. (No. 11), UN Doc. A/2136, & Annex I (1952), reproduced in 2 Benjamin Ferencz, *An International Criminal Court* 337 (1980). The Draft Statute also appears in 46 *AJIL Supp.* 1 (1952).

2 Minutes of the Executive Council, Dec. 1, 1951, in the Society's Minute Book for April 1951 to November 1958, at 38, 39 (hereafter cited as ASIL Minute Book, 1951-1958); George A. Finch, Editorial Comment: "Draft Statute for an International Criminal Court," 46 *AJIL* 89, 91 (1952).

Under the practice of the Society up to that time, the minutes of the Executive Council would have been published in the Proceedings of the ensuing Annual Meeting. Beginning with the 1952 Annual Meeting, however, the Society discontinued the practice of publishing Executive Council minutes. Thus, from the Executive Council meeting of December 1, 1951, to the present, the Council's minutes are available only in the Society's files.

3 The paper was by Willard B. Cowles, "The Impact of International Law on the Individual," 46 *ASIL Proc.* 71 (1952). Mr. Pella's remarks appear in id. at 156-59.

4 See Quincy Wright, "Proposal for an International Criminal Court," 46 *AJIL* 60 (1952); Finch, *supra* note 2.

might well have provided useful insights without committing the Society as a whole to any position. Whether the insights would have influenced the State Department cannot, of course, be determined. In the event, the Department took a neutral stance regarding establishment of an international criminal court.[5] It would be another forty-seven years before the Rome Statute of the International Criminal Court[6] was adopted.

3. Projects and the Need for Funds to Undertake Them

In the early 1950s the Society's Committee on Study of Legal Problems of the United Nations tackled the question whether the laws of war should be applied to U.N. enforcement action. It had been unable to reach any definitive conclusion beyond stating that the use of force by the United Nations under Chapter VII of the Charter "is of a different nature from war-making by a state." Thus it was debatable whether, or to what extent, the humanitarian law of war would apply.[7] The committee recommended that the Society seek funds to conduct a further, detailed study. The 1952 Business Meeting referred the matter to the Executive Council, with authority to take appropriate action.[8] The Council did not immediately act, but it did adopt a resolution proposed by Manley Hudson that "it is not contrary to the Society's policy to seek funds from outside sources, if approval of the Council is first had."[9]

Adopting the policy and taking effective steps to seek outside funding were two different things. The Council at its next meeting, in November 1952, postponed consideration of any search for funds.[10] In April 1953, Quincy Wright, on behalf of the Journal's Board of Editors, presented a resolution recommending that the Council appoint a special committee to seek financing from foundations for projects to promote the study and development of international law, particularly through reviving the teachers' conferences that had been held periodically from 1914 through to 1946. Those eight conferences had been held in conjunction with ASIL Annual Meetings, and had been dominated by influential Society

5 See U.N. GAOR 6th Comm., 7th Sess., 328th mtg., UN Doc. A/C.6/SR.328 (1952), reproduced in Ferencz, *supra* note 1, at 418, 421.

6 U.N. Doc. A/CONF.183/9, 37 *ILM* 999 (1998).

7 Report of Committee on Study of Legal Problems of the United Nations, "Should the Laws of War Apply to United Nations Enforcement Action?," 46 *ASIL Proc.* 216, 220 (1952).

8 46 *ASIL Proc.* 181-82 (1952).

9 Minutes of the Executive Council, Apr. 26, 1952, in ASIL Minute Book, 1951-1958, at 51, 53.

10 Minutes of the Executive Council, Nov. 22, 1952, in ASIL Minute Book, 1951-1958, at 54, 55.

members.[11] They had been financed by the Carnegie Endowment, but with that source now out of the picture, Wright and others wanted the Society to seek other foundation sources.

The resolution was amended to request the committee to seek financing not only for teachers' conferences, but also for assistance to the Journal and for the revival of the Research in International Law. The Council adopted it as amended.[12] It was further amended at the 1953 Business Meeting to accommodate a persistent Society member, W.J. Bivens, who had been trying to convince the Executive Council to seek funds for a study of the law governing the use of modern weapons and armed forces. That topic was added to those the Council had already approved.[13]

Meanwhile, the Society's Committee on an Endowment Fund had been sounding out foundations to see if they might be willing to help endow the Society. The committee discovered that foundations were not interested in supplying general endowment funds. They expected the Society to present a specific program showing the purpose for which the funds would be spent and the period during which they would be spent.[14]

The Executive Council decided in 1954 to direct all of the fund-raising effort into a single Committee on Financing and Endowment. The new Committee was authorized to decide on the priority of projects in consultation with the officers of the Society, and to present requests to foundations for the funding of the projects.[15]

In October 1954, the Committee reported that it did not then recommend seeking funds for research, but rather thought that fund-raising should be directed toward promoting understanding of international law. The Executive Council, ever cautious in those days, resolved "That it is the sense of the Council that the Society should not initiate, sponsor or manage research projects."[16]

---

11 See George A. Finch, "The American Society of International Law 1906-1956," 50 *AJIL* 293, 300-02 (1956). See also the Proceedings of each *Conference of Teachers of International Law and Related Subjects*, published by the Carnegie Endowment for International Peace.

12 Minutes of the Executive Council, Apr. 23, 1953, in ASIL Minute Book, 1951-1958, at 59, 61.

13 47 *ASIL Proc.* 145-49 (1953).

14 Minutes of the Executive Council, Apr. 23, 1953, in ASIL Minute Book, 1951-1958, at 62.

15 Minutes of the Executive Council, Apr. 24, 1954, in ASIL Minute Book, 1951-1958, at 82, 83, 84.

16 Minutes of the Executive Council, Oct. 16, 1954, in ASIL Minute Book, 1951-1958, at 85, 87-88.

In 1955, the committee submitted a draft proposal to be submitted to foundations in search of a three-year grant totaling USD 100,000 to USD 135,000. The money would be used for various purposes, none of them involving substantive research. One of the purposes, approved by the Executive Council, was to bring distinguished foreign international law scholars to the United States for regional meetings of the Society in 1956 and for the Society's fiftieth anniversary Annual Meeting. A Fiftieth Anniversary Management Committee was established.[17]

The Fiftieth Anniversary Committee submitted a proposal to the Ford Foundation requesting USD 157,900 to support projects in four categories. In addition to the proposal to bring foreign scholars to regional meetings and to the 1956 Annual Meeting, the proposals involved a study, to be conducted with other learned societies, of the actual role of international legal factors in American history; the development of instructional materials; and support for teachers' conferences. The Foundation approved a grant of only USD 22,000, for the foreign scholars proposal.[18]

Plans were made to take advantage of the availability of foreign scholars by holding fifteen regional meetings during the first part of 1956, before the Annual Meeting. The regional meetings would be tied in with the Annual Meeting by having some of the foreign scholars do double duty and by discussing topics that would later be considered at the Annual Meeting.[19]

In February 1956, the Society branched out in another way as well. For the first time, it sponsored a conference on international economic law. With USD 2,000 provided by the Rockefeller Foundation, it put on a two-day conference at the Statler Hotel in Washington, on International Investment Law. Davidson Sommers, Counsel at the World Bank, chaired the conference. Topics included problems of entry and management, tax problems, antitrust considerations, and legal incentives to foreign investment. Members of the Society and their friends were invited, free of charge.[20]

---

17 Minutes of the Executive Council, Apr. 28, 1955, in ASIL Minute Book, 1951-1958, at 106, 110-11.

18 Report of the Committee on Regional Meetings, 50 *ASIL Proc.* 265-67 (1956); Minutes of the Executive Council, Oct. 29, 1955, in ASIL Minute Book, 1951-1958, at 119, 121.

19 Id. at 122-23. For more on the 1956 regional meetings, see text at note 93 *infra*.

20 Eleanor H. Finch, Notes and Comments: "International Investment Law Conference," 50 *AJIL* 132 (1956); Minutes of the Executive Council, Apr. 25, 1956, in ASIL Minute Book, 1951-1958, at 125, 131. The amount of the grant from the Rockefeller Foundation appears in Minutes of the Executive Council, Oct. 29, 1955, in ASIL Minute Book, 1951-1958, at 119, 123.

Later in the year the Executive Council approved a second International Investment Law Conference.[21] The Ford Foundation supplied a grant of USD 3,000 for the Conference, to be held in Washington in September 1958.[22] Later in 1958 the Council decided to establish a Standing Committee on Legal Aspects of Foreign Investment.[23]

The Executive Council did an about-face in 1956. Only two years earlier it had resolved that the Society should not initiate, sponsor or manage research projects. It now amended the regulations on standing committees to provide, among other things, that the Committee on Financing and Endowment would solicit and accept grants in support not only of the general activities of the Society, but also of those intended to realize specific activities. In this connection, it would "select topics in the field of international law and related subjects for investigation or for consideration by individuals, committees or in regional or special conferences or meetings."[24] It was the first step toward a research program for the Society.

4. The Continuing Focus on the U.N. and the I.C.J.

Even without external funds, the Society's Committee on Study of Legal Problems of the United Nations continued to produce substantive reports. In 1956, its report focused principally on cases before the International Court of Justice and the work of the International Law Commission.[25] When the Committee's report was brought up at the Annual Meeting, Herman Phleger, the Legal Adviser of the State Department, took the occasion to comment on the *Aerial Incident* cases filed in the I.C.J. by the United States against Czechoslovakia and the Soviet Union to challenge the shooting down of U.S. military planes. Neither of the respondent states had consented to the Court's jurisdiction, and there was no prospect that they would do so. Phleger asserted that by filing the proceedings the United States was trying to extend the rule of law, and for that purpose a

---

21 Minutes of the Executive Council, Nov. 3, 1956, in ASIL Minute Book, 1951-1958, at 143, 145.

22 Minutes of the Executive Council, Apr. 24, 1958, in ASIL Minute Book, 1951-1958, at 172, 174. There appears to be no written record showing that the Conference was actually held, but the receipt of the Ford grant and the evidence of substantial planning strongly suggest that it was.

23 Minutes of the Executive Council, Nov. 22, 1958, in ASIL Minute Book, 1951-1958, at 192, 193.

24 Minutes of the Executive Council, Apr. 25, 1956, in ASIL Minute Book, 1951-1958, at 125, 129.

25 See Report of Committee on Study of Legal Problems of the United Nations, 50 *ASIL Proc.* 248 (1956).

habit had to be acquired of submitting controversies to adjudication.[26] When the shoe was on the other foot in 1984, the then-Legal Adviser took a rather different view in response to Nicaragua's initiation of proceedings against the United States.[27]

In 1957, the Committee on Study of Legal Problems of the United Nations produced a comprehensive study, written by Louis Sohn, on the legal issues surrounding the establishment of the U.N. Emergency Force in the Sinai Desert after Egypt's 1956 nationalization of the Suez Canal and the resulting military action by Israeli, British and French forces. Among other things, the study showed that the idea of having national military personnel available for quick peacekeeping deployment (not under Article 43 of the Charter) dated back to U.N. Secretariat proposals in 1948.[28]

In 1958 and 1959, the Committee, now chaired by Sohn, focused on the reservations the United States had attached to its declaration consenting to I.C.J. jurisdiction under Article 36(2) of the Statute. The Committee's 1958 report suggested several alternatives to the Connally Reservation, by which the United States excepted from the Court's jurisdiction disputes essentially within its domestic jurisdiction "as determined by the United States of America."[29]

In 1959, the Committee took a bolder stance. It was particularly critical of the Connally Reservation, but it went further and recommended a sweeping abolition of all the U.S. reservations. The report went on to recommend that if the reservations could not be withdrawn, other steps should be taken to broaden the Court's jurisdiction.[30] The report was controversial, both in the Executive Council and at the Society's Business Meeting. Finally the Business Meeting adopted a motion that said (after drafting changes by the Executive Council):

> After hearing the Report of the Committee and having given special consideration to the resolution of 1946 incorporated in that Report, it was voted to record as the sense of the meeting that the members warmly

---

26 50 *ASIL Proc.* 218 (1956).

27 Nicaragua initiated proceedings against the United States on April 9, 1984. Three days earlier, the United States had filed an instrument with the Court providing that its Article 36(2) Declaration would not apply during the next two years to disputes with any Central American state or arising out of events in Central America. 23 *ILM* 670 (1984). The Court held that it nevertheless had jurisdiction. Case Concerning Military and Paramilitary Activities in and Against Nicaragua, 1984 ICJ Rep. 392, 24 *ILM* 59 (1985).

28 Report of Committee on Study of Legal Problems of the United Nations, 51 *ASIL Proc.* 205, 207 (1957). These ideas were revived in Secretary-General Boutros Boutros-Ghali's *An Agenda for Peace*, U.N. Doc. A/47/277-S/24111 (1992).

29 Report of Committee on Study of Legal Problems of the United Nations, 52 *ASIL Proc.* 285, 287-88 (1958).

30 Report of Committee on Study of Legal Problems of the United Nations, 53 *ASIL Proc.* 354 (1959).

> associated themselves with the Committee's recommendation that the United States withdraw its reservations to the acceptance of the Optional Clause of the Statute of the International Court of Justice.[31]

The wording was ingenious. It came about as close to a Society position on withdrawal of the reservations as could be taken without actually adopting the Committee's position as the position of the Society as a whole.[32]

Although the Senate Foreign Relations Committee held hearings in 1960 on possible repeal of the Connally Reservation (and received statements supporting repeal from such prominent ASIL members as Herbert Briggs, Quincy Wright and Philip Jessup),[33] all of the reservations – including Connally – remained in force.

Before the fifties were out, the Society had one more piece of advice to give the United States government regarding its dealings with the I.C.J. and other U.N.-related legal bodies. In 1958, Richard Baxter wrote a confidential letter to Myres McDougal, then the President of the Society, expressing concern about the qualifications of U.S. representatives to international bodies. With Baxter's consent, the letter was circulated confidentially to the members of the Executive Council. In 1959, the Council adopted a resolution authorizing the President of the Society to form a group of eminent American jurists to present to the President of the United States, or another high U.S. official, a memorial expressing concern about "the maintenance of high standards for appointments to tribunals and other international bodies charged with the codification, creation, and application of international law" and expressing the hope that in the appointment process, consultations would be held with learned institutions and with national societies skilled in international law.[34] The Council also decided that the Journal should carry a department listing vacancies in the membership of such bodies as the International Court of Justice, the Permanent Court of Arbitration and the International Law Commission.[35]

---

31 53 *ASIL Proc.* 330 (1959). See also Minutes of the Executive Council, Apr. 30 & May 2, 1959, in ASIL Minute Book, 1959-1966, at 1, 6 & 8, 9. The 1960 Business Meeting also noted, with approval, a similar recommendation of the Committee. See 54 *ASIL Proc.* 227 (1960).

32 The Business Meeting authorized the President of the Society to testify "in the sense of the Society's action," at a hearing before the Senate Foreign Relations Committee on a pending bill to withdraw the Connally Reservation. 53 *ASIL Proc.* 330 (1959). See text at note 70 *infra*.

33 Compulsory Jurisdiction, International Court of Justice: Hearings on S. Res. 94 Before the Senate Comm. on Foreign Relations, 86th Cong., 2d Sess. 40, 110 & 409 (1960).

34 Minutes of the Executive Council, Nov. 14, 1959, in ASIL Minute Book, 1959-1966, at 20, 23-24.

35 Id. at 24.

The next U.S. nominees to the International Court of Justice and the International Law Commission, respectively, were Philip C. Jessup (elected to the I.C.J. in 1960) and Herbert W. Briggs (elected to the I.L.C. in 1961).[36] Nobody raised any question about their qualifications.

5. Membership and Finances, Continued

After modest decreases in membership in the first two years of the decade, membership in the Society rose gradually through the fifties.[37] The Society made a special effort to bring in more student members through letters to faculty members at colleges and universities. The result was a modest net increase in student memberships. In an effort to increase the Society's appeal to young persons, the Committee on Increase of Membership recommended in 1953 that a new class of membership be created in order to appeal to young professionals just beginning their careers. Persons under 30 years of age would be given a special membership fee for their first three consecutive years of membership.[38] The Executive Council amended the Society's membership regulations accordingly.[39]

In view of the Society's protracted efforts to increase membership, it is odd that the provision in the Constitution requiring nomination of new members by two existing members was retained well into the fifties. For many years it had been observed in form only. Finally, in 1955 the Society's Constitution was amended to provide simply, "New members may be elected by the Executive Council acting under such rules and regulations as it may prescribe."[40] But old habits die hard, and the resulting regulation still required that each applicant be endorsed by one member of the Society.[41]

The desire to obtain and retain members was not strong enough during the McCarthy era to keep the Society from considering whether a member might be expelled for publishing an article in a Soviet magazine. An Austrian member had done just that, publishing a piece in *Soviet State and Law*. That triggered the appointment of an *ad hoc* committee in 1955 to consider the expulsion ques-

---

36 They replaced, respectively, Green Hackworth and Douglas L. Edmonds.

37 For details, see "Memorandum, ASIL History: Details Relating to Budget, Finances and Membership" (2006), on file with the Society.

38 Minutes of the Executive Council, Apr. 23, 1953, in ASIL Minute Book, 1951-1958, at 59, 62.

39 Minutes of the Executive Council, Apr. 25, 1953, in ASIL Minute Book, 1951-1958, at 64, 66.

40 49 *ASIL Proc.* 122 (1955).

41 The endorsement provision was finally deleted in 1968. Minutes of the Executive Council, Apr. 25, 1968, in ASIL Minute Book, Dec. 1966-Oct. 1973, at 42, 46.

tion.[42] The committee concluded that "no restudy or revision of the relevant law and practice of the Society is needed at this time."[43] Apparently that was a controversial conclusion. A motion that a new committee be appointed to consider the admission and expulsion of members was made and seconded, but the Executive Council voted it down.[44]

6. Officers and Their Terms of Office

In 1952, the Nominating Committee proposed a "sense of the Society" resolution stating that "in electing a president it is the normal expectation that tenure is to be for one year only."[45] The Executive Council approved it for submission to the Society. Manley Hudson, the outgoing President, explained that "our Society is now becoming composed of so many eminent people that we would like to elect eight or ten people to one office from time to time."[46] He also stressed that the resolution did not propose a mandatory rule. The Society adopted it at the 1952 Business Meeting, with only one vote opposed.[47] Edwin D. Dickinson was then elected President. He duly noted that his vote was not the one opposed.[48]

One suspects that there may have been a reason in addition to the one Hudson gave for the new one-year expectation. By 1952, potential candidates for President of the Society were no longer among the group who were present at the creation in 1906. The Society was important to its prominent members in 1952, but it was not necessarily as central to their vision of an ordered world as it had been to the founders. The new leaders had other things to do, and may not have been willing to commit themselves to three years of intensive service to the Society. Intensive service would have been expected of them, since the Society no longer had a day-to-day administrator with the stature of a James Brown Scott, a George Finch or a Pitman Potter. One year may well have been all the presidential prospects of the fifties thought they could spare.

In addition, since the Society was no longer committed to seeking eminent public figures as its Presidents, there would be little occasion to cling as long as possible to any particular President as the Society's symbol of excellence.

---

42 Minutes of the Executive Council, Oct. 29, 1955, in ASIL Minute Book, 1951-1958, at 119, 123.

43 Minutes of the Executive Council, Apr. 25, 1956, in ASIL Minute Book, 1951-1958, at 125, 128.

44 Id.

45 Minutes of the Executive Council, Apr. 24, 1952, in ASIL Minute Book, 1951-1958, at 45, 49.

46 46 *ASIL Proc.* 178-79 (1952).

47 Id. at 179.

48 Id. at 180.

Eminent scholars – the Society Presidents of the fifties[49] – were more fungible as public representatives than were eminent public figures.

Adoption of the informal one-year term had the obvious disadvantage of imposing discontinuity on the office. In an effort to alleviate the problem somewhat, William G. Rice, a member of the Executive Council in 1952, raised the question of providing for election of a president-elect a year in advance. He did not get far. He was asked to submit a report, and when he did, it was "ordered to be filed" with no action taken.[50] In 1959, the question came up again. A committee was established to examine it and other matters.[51] Nothing happened until 1961, when the Nominating Committee reported that it had considered the question, but did not recommend any change. No change was made.[52]

With the quickened turnover in the presidency, the Society needed to find a way to keep the growing stable of ex-Presidents involved. It became the practice to elect them as Honorary Vice Presidents. This rapidly depleted the number of available honorary positions, leading the Executive Council in 1954 to increase the number of Honorary Vice Presidents from fourteen to sixteen.[53] For 1954-55, five former Presidents were listed among the Honorary Vice Presidents.[54] By 1959-60, the number had risen to seven.[55] In 1959, the Executive Council discussed creating a special office for ex-Presidents and even appointed a committee to consider the matter, but nothing came of it.[56]

In 1956, the Nominating Committee made several suggestions as to the policy it thought should be followed in selecting officers. Neither the Executive Council nor the Business Meeting took any action on them, but they are noteworthy because they dealt with recurring issues. In summary form, they were:

- The Secretary of State should not be nominated as Honorary President, as had been the practice, unless that person is willing to contribute to the

49 In chronological order, they were Manley Hudson, Edwin Dickinson, Charles Fenwick, Philip Jessup, Quincy Wright, Lester Woolsey, Robert Wilson, Myres McDougal and Herbert Briggs. Of these, only Woolsey was not an academic.

50 Minutes of the Executive Council, Apr. 26, 1952, in ASIL Minute Book, 1951-1958, at 51, 52; Minutes of the Executive Council, Nov. 22, 1952, in id. at 54, 57.

51 Minutes of the Executive Council, May 2, 1959, in ASIL Minute Book, 1959-1966, at 8, 9.

52 55 *ASIL Proc.* 196 (1961).

53 Minutes of the Executive Council, Apr. 22, 1954, in ASIL Minute Book, 1951-1958, at 77, 80.

54 48 *ASIL Proc.* v (1954).

55 53 *ASIL Proc.* vii (1959).

56 Minutes of the Executive Council, May 2, 1959, in ASIL Minute Book, 1959-1966, at 8, 9.

work of the Society. Normally, the retiring President should be nominated as Honorary President for one year.

- Honorary Vice Presidents should not automatically be renominated. Their term of office under the Constitution was one year. A retiring President, or retiring Honorary President if the suggestion above were to be adopted, should be named as an Honorary Vice President.
- The non-binding policy set only four years earlier, limiting Presidents to one year in office, should no longer be followed. Nominating Committees should consider whether a President in office should be renominated.
- A Vice President need not be continued in office, and election to that office should not imply a probability of moving up to President.
- The desire for turnover on the Executive Council should not preclude a former Council member from being nominated. It would be adequate simply to continue the practice of avoiding immediate renomination of outgoing Council members.[57]

Despite its first suggestion, the Nominating Committee in 1956 nominated none other than John Foster Dulles, the Secretary of State, to be the Honorary President. He was elected, along with the rest of the slate proposed by the committee.[58]

Myres McDougal was elected President of the Society in 1958. It came as a surprise to him. He had come to Washington for the Annual Meeting, and was awakened in his hotel room by his friend Hardy Dillard, the chair of the Nominating Committee. Dillard told him he had been nominated for President and he would have to rent a tuxedo – the wearing of which was then customary for officers at the annual banquet. According to Gertrude Leighton, who was then McDougal's assistant and a member of the Nominating Committee, Dillard had held a committee meeting in his hotel room earlier that evening. He had locked the door and told the committee members they could leave any time they wanted after they nominated McDougal for the presidency. Leighton's response was that rather than spend the night with Hardy Dillard, she would vote for McDougal.[59] She might have been so inclined anyway.

Dillard insisted that the story was apocryphal. Here is his version: "I did not lock the door. After [the committee members] were all seated and I was still standing, I said at 5:05 p.m. 'Can any of you think of anyone more deserving and better qualified to be President than Myres McDougal?' There was no immediate answer.

---

57 Minutes of the Executive Council, Apr. 25, 1956, in ASIL Minute Book, 1951-1958, at 125, 128-29; 50 *ASIL Proc.* 222 (1956).

58 Id. at 222-23.

59 Interview with Myres S. McDougal, May 18, 1994 (transcript on file with the Society).

So at 5:07 p.m. I said: 'Good, then Mac is nominated by acclamation. Meeting adjourned.' Everyone complimented me on both the choice and the harmonious manner in which it was made."[60] Leighton's version makes better reading.

At the 1958 Business Meeting, Homer Angelo rocked the boat. After the Nominating Committee's slate of officers and Council members had been adopted, he nominated Edgar Turlington as a Vice President in place of William Bishop, who had been elected by voice vote with the rest of the slate. Angelo expressed regret because all of those on the slate were well qualified to be Vice Presidents, but he thought that because of Turlington's excellent work for the Society and his long record of achievement in the profession, he should be made a Vice President. Despite a parliamentary objection, the chair (Robert Wilson) ruled that Angelo's motion was proper. A standing vote was taken, and Wilson declared the motion adopted.[61]

Turlington served as a Vice President until his death on September 27, 1959. He was eulogized as a selfless servant of the Society who brought virtue and peace wherever he went.[62]

7. Composition of the Executive Council

Myres McDougal chaired the Nominating Committee in 1952-53. His committee tried, he said, to make a balanced selection between old and new faces, as well as among the various segments represented in the Society. Eight names were proposed in 1953 for new three-year terms on the Executive Council. None of the eight had served before.[63] The slate included one woman, Ruth C. Lawson. Two others, James Nevins Hyde and Covey T. Oliver, would become future Presidents of the Society.

At the 1954 Annual Meeting, there was a discussion about the procedure for nominating candidates for office. At that time the Nominating Committee would simply present its slate orally at the Business Meeting. Several members proposed that the list of candidates be made available to all members prior to or during the Annual Meeting.[64] Despite support for the idea, advance dissemination of the names on the slate of nominees was not done in any systematic way until the advent of the Society's newsletter in the 1960s.[65]

---

60 Letter from Hardy C. Dillard to Myres S. McDougal, Dec. 11, 1974, in Daniel J. Meador (ed.), *Hardy Cross Dillard: Writings and Speeches* 341, 343 (1995).

61 52 *ASIL Proc.* 263 (1958).

62 54 *ASIL Proc.* 224 (1960).

63 47 *ASIL Proc.* 150-51 (1953).

64 48 *ASIL Proc.* 188 (1954).

65 For details, see "Memorandum, ASIL History: Details Relating to Budget, Finances and Membership" (2006), on file with the Society.

8. The President of the Society and Positions on Substantive Issues

When Edwin Dickinson was President of the Society in 1952-53, he took a strict view of the Society's practice against taking positions on matters of substance. Those were the days of the Bricker Amendment, a controversial initiative by Senator Bricker and others to amend the United States Constitution. The Bricker Amendment took several forms as it was considered and reconsidered in the Senate Judiciary Committee, but the heart of it was an attempt to provide that a treaty would be effective in U.S. domestic law only through legislation which would be valid in the absence of a treaty. Much of the impetus behind the Bricker Amendment stemmed from concern that U.N. human rights conventions would attempt to regulate treatment by the U.S. government of its own citizens – a matter many thought to be wholly within the domestic jurisdiction of the United States. The concern was buttressed by an adverse reaction to *Missouri v. Holland*,[66] a case in which the Supreme Court seemed to give wider constitutional scope to a treaty than it would to an act of Congress.[67]

Dickinson had been asked to testify before Congressional committees and to make statements on the Bricker Amendment and perhaps on other controversial matters. He told the 1953 Annual Meeting that he could not do so and have it taken simply as a statement of a professor of international law at the University of Pennsylvania, as he then was. He said, "They were interested in getting me into the record because I am President of the Society for the time being, and I decline to commit my colleagues of this Society in any such left-handed way."[68] Applause greeted him. The southpaw slur apparently went unnoticed.

Individual Society members testified or submitted statements during the Congressional hearings, but only in their personal capacities. In most instances they did not mention their affiliation with the Society. George Finch, one of the most outspoken supporters of the Bricker Amendment, identified himself by his American Bar Association affiliation, rather than by his long-standing association with the ASIL.[69]

The Bricker Amendment was not adopted. The Society had deliberately avoided any institutional attempt to influence the outcome. It had even gone so far as to keep its President on the sideline.

---

66 252 U.S. 416 (1920).

67 See, e.g., George A. Finch, "The Need to Restrain the Treaty-making Power of the United States Within Constitutional Limits," 48 *AJIL* 57 (1954). For a bibliography of the leading literature for and against the Bricker Amendment, see William W. Bishop, Jr., *International Law Cases and Materials* 112, n. 39 (3rd ed. 1971).

68 47 *ASIL Proc.* 149 (1953).

69 See Natalie Hevener Kaufman, *Human Rights Treaties and the Senate: A History of Opposition* 110, 112, 114 (1990).

By 1959, attitudes had changed somewhat. The Business Meeting authorized the President to testify before the Senate Foreign Relations Committee on the pending bill that would have withdrawn the Connally Reservation to the United States' declaration under Article 36(2) of the I.C.J. Statute. The President was not authorized to present a position of the Society, but rather was supposed to give the "sense" of the Business Meeting's "warm association" with the recommendation of the Committee on Study of Legal Problems of the United Nations that the reservations to the United States' Article 36(2) declaration be withdrawn.[70]

Herbert Briggs was the President of the Society in 1959-60. He testified in the Senate Foreign Relations Committee hearings, taking a stand in favor of withdrawal of all reservations to the declaration. In his oral presentation, he said that he was expressing his own personal views, "although I am president of the American Society of International Law."[71] In his written statement he identified himself as professor of international law at Cornell, Editor-in-Chief of the *American Journal of International Law* and President of the American Society of International Law. He wrote that although the Society has a policy against adopting substantive resolutions, it had "authorized me to testify before this committee in the sense of its recommendation 'that the United States withdraw its reservations to the acceptance of the optional clause of the statute of the International Court of Justice.' In the statement which follows I am expressing my own personal views, although they are in accord with the Society's recommendations."[72]

Briggs was not as circumspect as Dickinson had been. In fact, the Society as such had not made a recommendation on withdrawal of the Connally Reservation. The Business Meeting had simply expressed its sense that the members "warmly associated themselves with the Committee's recommendation."[73]

Although Briggs argued for withdrawal of the Connally Reservation, Eleanor Finch submitted a memorandum to the Foreign Relations Committee opposing withdrawal. She identified herself as a member of the D.C. Bar and the A.B.A. Section of International and Comparative Law, and as the Executive Secretary of the Society, but she was careful to say that the memorandum reflected solely her own views as an individual American citizen.[74]

---

70 53 *ASIL Proc.* 330 (1959).

71 Compulsory Jurisdiction, *supra* note 33 (1960).

72 Id. at 54.

73 See text at note 31 *supra*.

74 Compulsory Jurisdiction, *supra* note 33, at 426.

9. Growing Pains in the Effort to Recognize Exemplary Scholarship

As has been noted in Chapter Six, the Certificate of Merit was not awarded in 1951, when the Executive Council rejected the Annual Awards Committee's recommendation. In 1952, the Committee recommended that the Certificate be awarded to Hans Kelsen's book, *The Law of the United Nations*. Some members of the Executive Council had reservations about Kelsen's highly theoretical approach and about his conclusions, though they recognized that he had made a substantial scholarly contribution. Discussion centered on whether the granting of the award would constitute the Society's approval of the author's viewpoints or methodology. The Council adopted a policy to the effect that the award of a Certificate of Merit did not mean that the Society was adopting the views of the author as its own. On that basis, the Business Meeting approved the award to Kelsen, making him the first recipient of the Society's Certificate of Merit.[75]

In 1953, the Annual Awards Committee made no recommendation to the Executive Council.[76] At the Business Meeting, John Hazard, who had conceived the annual award idea in the first place, rose to say that the Committee was applying too demanding a standard. The award, he suggested, need not be reserved for a second Hugo Grotius.[77] Discussion then turned to whether the award could be made to Manley Hudson for his series of articles on the World Court in the Journal, despite the lack of a Committee recommendation. When it appeared that such an initiative was not contemplated by the regulations, the nimble legal minds at the meeting came up with an alternative. The Society adopted a "sense of the meeting" resolution opining that "had the committee through appropriate constitutional procedures laid before this meeting a recommendation that the award be given [to] the articles of Judge Manley O. Hudson on the International Court, this meeting would have greeted that suggestion, and greeted it gladly."[78]

Thus did Judge Hudson receive an honor in 1953, but not an award. The award came a year later, when the Committee recommended, and the Council and Business Meeting approved, awarding the Certificate of Merit to Hudson for the 31st of his series of articles on the World Court.[79]

---

75 Minutes of the Executive Council, Apr. 24, 1952, in ASIL Minute Book, 1951-1958, at 45, 47 (1952); Business Meeting, 46 *ASIL Proc.* 174 (1952).

76 Minutes of the Executive Council, Apr. 23, 1953, in ASIL Minute Book, 1951-1958, at 59, 61.

77 47 *ASIL Proc.* 137 (1953).

78 Id. at 139. The "sense of the meeting" was expressed by Philip Jessup.

79 Minutes of the Executive Council, Apr. 22, 1954, in ASIL Minute Book, 1951-1958, at 77, 79; 48 *ASIL Proc.* 185 (1954).

In 1955, the award for the first time was made to a publication not written in the English language. It went to Charles de Visscher for the first edition of his book, *Théories et Réalités en Droit International Public*, before the book had been translated into English.[80]

In 1958, the Executive Council voted to make the award to Alfred Verdross for the third edition of his *Völkerrecht*, but there were second thoughts later in the meeting about awarding the Certificate of Merit to a later edition of a work when earlier editions were available. The Council voted not to make such an award.[81] It reversed itself again the following April, permitting future awards to be made to authors for later editions of their earlier works.[82] In 1961, Verdross received the award for the fourth edition of *Völkerrecht*, published in 1959.[83]

10. The Hudson Medal

In 1955, Ralph G. Albrecht, of New York City, endowed the Society with securities valued at USD 5,350 to establish the Manley O. Hudson Medal – a gold medal bearing the likeness of Judge Hudson.[84] It was to be awarded for "pre-eminent contributions, comparable in distinction to those of Judge Hudson himself and evidenced by distinguished scholarship and achievement in international law and in the promotion of the establishment and maintenance of international relations on the basis of law and justice."[85]

Albrecht stipulated that the first award be made in 1956 to Hudson himself on the occasion of the Society's fiftieth anniversary. He proposed that the award not be made at any fixed intervals and that it not be restricted to United States nationals. In order to give the Society some (limited) flexibility, he gave it the right "to vary the conditions for making awards to the extent only that changed circumstances may render it impossible to comply with these conditions."[86]

The Society followed the donor's instructions and presented the medal to Judge Hudson at the 1956 Annual Meeting.

---

80 49 *ASIL Proc.* 120 (1955).

81 Minutes of the Executive Council, Apr. 24, 1958, & Nov. 22, 1958, in ASIL Minute Book, 1951-1958, at 172, 175 & 192.

82 Minutes of the Executive Council, Apr. 30, 1959, in ASIL Minute Book, 1959-1966, at 1.

83 55 *ASIL Proc.* 194 (1961).

84 Both sides of the medal are reproduced in 50 *AJIL*, facing page 667 (1956).

85 49 *ASIL Proc.* 111, 112 (1955). The amount of the endowment appears in Minutes of the Executive Council, Apr. 28, 1955, in ASIL Minute Book, 1951-1958, at 106, 113.

86 49 *ASIL Proc.* 111, 112 (1955).

11. The Regional Meetings Program Comes of Age

In 1952, the Executive Council adopted a policy for an ongoing regional meetings program. Each meeting would have to be approved by the Regional Meetings Committee. The Society would assume no financial responsibility for regional meetings, and organizers would have to make it clear that no expression of views at a regional meeting could be taken as action of the Society. Membership efforts would be undertaken at regional meetings. Finally, reports on regional meetings would be filed with the Executive Council, and the Regional Meetings Committee should from time to time re-examine the entire matter.[87] It was an initiative whose time had come.

William Bishop, chair of the Regional Meetings Committee, duly published in the Journal an appeal to local groups of members to organize regional meetings, preferably on a Saturday, in order to increase the Society's impact on citizens concerned with public affairs and to "fulfill [the Society's] proper role of leadership in the field of a wider public understanding of international law." The program should be limited to one or two topics of particular interest in the region. He suggested several topics.[88]

The first regional meeting under the new policy was held in an old venue, Chicago, on Saturday, March 21, 1953.[89] It was followed in November 1953 by a Friday-Saturday regional meeting in Seattle and a Saturday meeting in San Francisco.[90] Another one was held in Washington, D.C., in February 1954.[91]

As has been noted above, in 1955, the regional meetings program got a significant boost when the Ford Foundation granted the Society USD 22,000 to help it bring foreign scholars to the United States. This enabled the Society to plan fifteen regional meetings to be held in the first few months of 1956. A major objective was to interest practitioners in joining the Society.[92]

87 Minutes of the Executive Council, Nov. 22, 1952, in ASIL Minute Book, 1951-1958, at 54-55.

88 William W. Bishop, Jr., Current Note: "Regional Meetings of the Society," 47 *AJIL* 289 (1953).

89 Quincy Wright, Notes and Comments: "Regional Meeting of the American Society of International Law," 47 *AJIL* 476 (1953).

90 Richard C. Solibakke, Notes and Comments: "Northwest Regional Meeting of the Society," 48 *AJIL* 130 (1954); Myron E. Etienne, Jr., "San Francisco Regional Meeting of the Society," id. at 135.

91 Minutes of the Executive Council, Apr. 22, 1954, in ASIL Minute Book, 1951-1958, at 77, 80.

92 See Minutes of the Executive Council, Oct. 29, 1955, in ASIL Minute Book, 1951-1958, at 119, 122-23; see also text at note 19 *supra*.

As it turned out, fourteen regional meetings were held throughout the country in March and April 1956.[93] New venues included Baton Rouge, Charlottesville, Columbus, Dallas, Denver, Miami, Ithaca, Los Angeles, Philadelphia and St. Louis. Each meeting was administered by a regional committee chaired by someone on the local scene – usually a faculty member of a university providing facilities for the meeting. There was an overarching topic for all of the regional meetings: "The Role of International Law in National Courts and Agencies – 50 Years of Development."[94]

Covey Oliver, chairing the Regional Meetings Committee, recognized that this ambitious undertaking could make international law more meaningful for practicing lawyers, by bringing the law to them. He was well aware that the legal profession exercised great social power in the United States, yet he thought the Society had been gradually isolating itself from the profession. At the end of the series of regional meetings he thought that some progress had been made toward increasing the practicing bar's awareness of the role of law in international life.[95]

Without externally supplied funds, the Society returned to a more modest regional meetings program in 1957. It arranged for six meetings, in Chicago, Columbus, Detroit, New Orleans, San Francisco and Seattle.[96]

12. Advising the United Nations and the State Department on Their Publications

The Society had long had a Committee on Publications of the Department of State to give advice on improving the flow of information to the interested public. In 1953, the Society branched out and gave advice, through its Committee on Research in International Law, to the United Nations as well.[97]

---

93 Minutes of the Executive Council, Apr. 25, 1956, in ASIL Minute Book, 1951-1958, at 125, 126.

94 Eleanor H. Finch, Notes and Comments: "Regional Meetings of the Society," 50 *AJIL* 130 (1956); for a full report, including the names of speakers and their topics at each regional meeting, see Report of the Committee on Regional Meetings, 50 *ASIL Proc.* 265, 268-75 (1956). Leonard C. Meeker, of the Office of the State Department Legal Adviser, and Wolfgang Friedmann, of Columbia University, appeared on several of the programs.

95 Report of the Committee on Regional Meetings, 50 *ASIL Proc.* 265, 278-79 (1956).

96 Minutes of the Executive Council, Apr. 25, 1957, in ASIL Minute Book, 1951-1958, at 149, 151. Six regional meetings were held from April 1958 to April 1959, in Evanston, Madison, Columbus, New Orleans, Miami and New York City. Minutes of the Executive Council, Apr. 30, 1959, in ASIL Minute Book, 1959-1966, at 1, 4.

97 In 1955, the responsibility of the Committee on State Department publications was enlarged to include U.N. publications as well. Minutes of the Executive Council, Oct. 29, 1955, in ASIL Minute Book, 1951-1958, at 119, 123.

The U.N. Secretary-General, Trygve Lie, contacted the Society and several other learned organizations in 1952, requesting advice on the content of the then-proposed *U.N. Juridical Yearbook*. The yearbook had originally been recommended by the International Law Commission, on a proposal from Manley Hudson, as a means of making the evidence of customary international law readily available. As thus conceived, the yearbook would have contained significant legislative developments in various countries, arbitral awards, and significant international law decisions of domestic courts.[98]

The Society's Committee on Research in International Law, chaired by Herbert Briggs, took a different approach. Rather than focusing on instruments that would supply evidence of custom, it emphasized the desirability of publishing instruments by and about the United Nations itself. First on its list was the need to do something about the limited availability and impermanent (mimeographed) form of many U.N. materials bearing on international law.[99]

Ultimately the *U.N. Juridical Yearbook* was established, though it took several more years and some prodding from the Society before it appeared in print.[100] When it did, it bore a closer resemblance to the Society's model than to that of the International Law Commission.

Much of the Society's concern regarding State Department publications remained as it had been in previous years, urging the timely publication of treaties and their indexing. In addition, there was the perennial expression of the need to reduce the backlog in the *Foreign Relations* series. The Society's effort had become an exercise in futility.

In 1956, the State Department's Historical Division proposed to establish an advisory committee regarding the publication of *Foreign Relations* volumes. Three organizations – the American Historical Association, the American Political Science Association and the ASIL – were invited to be represented. The Executive Council accepted the invitation, stipulating that the Society's representatives would act in their personal capacities only.[101] Two members represented the Society on the advisory committee.[102]

---

98 Report of the International Law Commission Covering its Second Session, UN GAOR, 5th Sess., Supp. No. 12 (A/1316), 1950 *YB Int'l L. Comm'n*, Vol. II, at 373, 44 *AJIL Supp.* 105, 124 (1950).

99 Report of the ASIL Committee on Research in International Law, "Publication by the United Nations of a United Nations Juridical Yearbook," 47 *ASIL Proc.* 188, 192-93 (1953).

100 See, e.g., the Society's resolution on Publications of the United Nations, 50 *ASIL Proc.* 221 (1956).

101 Minutes of the Executive Council, Nov. 3, 1956, in ASIL Minute Book, 1951-1958, at 143, 146.

102 55 *ASIL Proc.* 195 (1961).

13. Another Temporary Home

The Society's lease in the Kellogg Building expired in the spring of 1953. Since another tenant was waiting, the Society had to find a new home. The Treasurer of the Society, James Murdock, found suitable offices consisting of three rooms on the top floor of a remodeled residence at 1826 Jefferson Place, N.W., in the District of Columbia.[103] The Society occupied those offices from August 1, 1953, through the remainder of the decade.[104]

14. Coordination with Other Non-governmental Bodies

In 1955, the Society established a committee to explore the idea of cooperating or merging with the American Branch of the International Law Association. The committee did not recommend a merger, but did recommend closer cooperation. The Executive Council established a new committee on cooperation with the ILA and its American Branch, with directions to explore such things as granting reciprocal privileges of attendance at meetings and reciprocal reductions in subscription rates.[105] Nothing came of the idea.

By 1958 the committee's mandate had been broadened and Hardy Dillard was now its chair. He proposed that cooperative arrangements be entered into between the Society and the American Law Institute committee then working on what became the *Restatement Second, Foreign Relations Law of the United States* (there having been no Restatement First on the subject). He also recommended cooperation with the World Peace Through Law Committee of the American Bar Association. The Executive Council approved the recommendations.[106] Dillard's committee performed an oversight role, with individual Society members participating in the work of the A.L.I. and the A.B.A.[107]

15. The Passing of George Finch and Manley Hudson

George A. Finch died on July 17, 1957, at the age of 72. He had devoted more than fifty years of his life to the study and development of international law,

---

103 47 *ASIL Proc.* 149 (1953).

104 Minutes of the Executive Council, Apr. 23, 1953, in ASIL Minute Book, 1951-1958, at 59, 60; Minutes of the Executive Council, Apr. 25, 1953, in id. at 64, 67; Notes and Comments: Society's New Headquarters, 47 *AJIL* 467 (1953); The American Society of International Law: The Sixtieth Year, 18th (unnumbered) page (1966).

105 Minutes of the Executive Council, Apr. 25, 1956, in ASIL Minute Book, 1951-1958, at 125, 127-28.

106 Minutes of the Executive Council, Nov. 22, 1958, in ASIL Minute Book, 1951-1958, at 192, 198-99.

107 See Minutes of the Executive Council, Apr. 30, 1959, in ASIL Minute Book, 1959-1966, at 1, 6.

starting as a law clerk in the State Department. He had held the top managerial positions for many years in the Society and on the Journal, at the same time serving with the Carnegie Endowment for International Peace.

The Society's memorial to him mentioned these things, but it stressed his personal qualities. It was a sign not only of the respect his colleagues had for him, but also of a Society still intimate enough, at least in its inner circle, to know about and appreciate the family life of one of its leaders. The memorial said, "George Finch had in a high degree ability, industry, loyalty, kindness, and courage. Most of all he had character. He was a truly good man in every relation of life, not only in his profession, but as husband, father and citizen."[108]

Lester Woolsey, writing in the Journal, noted that George Finch was a conservative in his attitude toward international questions. Woolsey concluded his remembrance with these words: "As I look back on the years of close association with George Finch, I carry away deeply engraved impressions of unbounded energy, dogged determination, unbiased sense of justice, deep sincerity relieved with a vein of benign humor – all inspiring respect and affection in the hearts of those fortunate enough to know and work with him."[109]

As the fifties drew to a close, Manley Hudson – for many years the leading intellectual force within the Society – fell into declining health and was no longer the towering figure he once was. He died on April 13, 1960. He had been a member of the Journal's Board of Editors since 1924, and had served as President of the Society from 1949 to 1952. He served for ten years as the United States judge on the Permanent Court of International Justice, and for thirty-seven years his annual articles on the World Court appeared in the Journal.[110]

Hudson's defining achievement, however, was his work on the Harvard Research in International Law. In the words of Philip Jessup, "This notable enterprise, which made contributions of enduring value, was Manley Hudson's in conception, in creation, in management and in results. ... Manley Hudson secured the financial support, organized the Advisory Committee, enlisted the reporters, chaired the meetings, and from beginning to end inspired and drove his colleagues to the production of the best that was in them."[111]

Hudson gave no quarter in intellectual combat – a characteristic that may not have endeared him to "sensitive souls" (Jessup's words), but one that clearly established him as an intellectual powerhouse. He was not so arrogant that he could not acknowledge, with good humor, a weakness in his own position as

---

108 52 *ASIL Proc.* 253 (1958).

109 Lester H. Woolsey, Editorial Comment: "George A. Finch," 51 *AJIL* 754, 757 (1957). Woolsey's Comment provides a summary of Finch's career, as well.

110 See Ruth E. Bacon's memorial to Hudson in 54 *ASIL Proc.* 223 (1960). Hudson's last annual article on the World Court appeared in 53 *AJIL* 319 (1959).

111 Philip C. Jessup, Editorial Comment: "Manley Hudson," 54 *AJIL* 603 (1960).

pointed out by those with the fortitude to parry with him.[112] Like his younger friend and sometime adversary, Myres McDougal, he applied a standard of excellence to his own endeavors and to the efforts of those with whom he was associated.

B. ANNUAL MEETINGS IN THE FIFTIES

1. Broadening the Program

At the 1953 Annual Meeting, Clyde Eagleton, chair of the Society's Committee on Study of Legal Problems of the United Nations, recommended that the Committee be dissolved. It did not seem possible, he said, to carry out the purpose for which the Committee was formed: to inform members of the Society and spark discussions at the Annual Meetings. Because of the Society's rules for vetting Committee reports through the Executive Council, and because the Program Committee controlled the content of the Annual Meeting, there was virtually no chance that the Committee's substantive report could be discussed at the Annual Meeting for which it was prepared.[113]

Kenneth S. Carlston suggested that the problem might be solved by having round-table discussions at Annual Meetings, so that small, interested groups could meet and discuss topics of particular interest to them. He conceded that this would be a departure from the Society's long-standing practice of having only plenary meetings that would presumably be of interest to all members.[114] He made no motion, but the seed had been planted.

Eagleton agreed to keep his Committee going. There were no round tables at the next Annual Meeting, but the report of his Committee found a place on the program.[115] The seed Carlston had planted in 1953 sprouted five years later. On an experimental basis, each of the Friday daytime sessions at the 1958 Annual Meeting consisted of three panels.[116] All three of the panels at each session dealt with an aspect of an overarching theme having to do with the relationship between national policy and international law, ranging from the problems of foreign public entities in U.S. courts to an examination of the *Interhandel* case.

---

112 Id. This point also came out in an interview with Myres S. McDougal, May 18, 1994 (transcript on file with the Society).

113 47 *ASIL Proc.* 131 (1953).

114 Id. at 133-34.

115 48 *ASIL Proc.* 164 (1954).

116 See Minutes of the Executive Council, Nov. 2, 1957, in ASIL Minute Book, 1951-1958, at 167, 168; 52 *ASIL Proc.* iii-v (1958).

At each session, one of the three panels was designed to be of particular interest to practicing lawyers.[117]

Myres McDougal, the President of the Society in 1958-59, put his unmistakable stamp on the 1959 Annual Meeting. The multiple-panels experiment was continued, but all of the panels dealt with world public order issues, including examinations of world public order systems, coercion, jurisdiction, allocation of resources, human rights, trade and investment, and the law of treaties.[118]

The experiment became the practice. Daytime substantive sessions thereafter were devoted to at least two panels each. Evening sessions remained plenary.

2. The Fiftieth Anniversary Meeting

As we have seen, the fiftieth Anniversary Meeting in 1956 was conceived as the culmination of an outpouring of meetings – fourteen regional meetings in all – across the United States. The daytime sessions of the first day, a Thursday, were devoted to reports on the regional meetings. The morning session examined the overarching theme of the regional meetings, "International Law in National Courts and Agencies – 50 Years of Development," from the standpoint of American law and practice. The afternoon session did so from the standpoint of foreign law and practice, taking advantage of the expertise of foreign visitors whose travel to the regional and Annual Meetings had been supported by the Ford Foundation grant. They came from Pakistan, Taiwan, Japan and Cuba.[119]

The keynote speaker was John Foster Dulles, who was the Secretary of State, the Honorary President of the Society and the grandson of John W. Foster, another Secretary of State and one of the original Vice Presidents of the Society. Dulles' topic was "The Institutionalizing of Peace." It led him to recall, among other things, that he had accompanied his grandfather to the 1907 Hague Peace Conference as a junior secretary. He summarized the results of that conference – which aimed not to institutionalize peace, but rather to make war more tolerable – and outlined efforts since then to create and sustain institutions devoted to maintaining peace. Even if the goal of maintaining effective institutions for peace could not be immediately realized, he said, the peoples of the world had the capacity to move steadily toward it.[120]

---

117 52 *ASIL Proc.* 48-134, 135-228 (1958).

118 53 *ASIL Proc.* 1-80, 81-136, 137-185, 186-254 (1959).

119 50 *ASIL Proc.* 26 & 58 (1956); Eleanor H. Finch, Notes and Comments: "50th Annual Meeting of the American Society of International Law," 50 *AJIL* 668, 669 (1956).

120 John Foster Dulles, "The Institutionalizing of Peace," 50 *ASIL Proc.* 11, 24 (1956).

Another feature of the Meeting, as already noted, was the first award of the Manley O. Hudson Medal to the person whose achievements it commemorates. Quincy Wright, the President of the Society, made the presentation.[121]

Fittingly, in light of the emphasis on foreign scholars at the regional and 50th Anniversary Meetings, the Society's Certificate of Merit in 1956 went to Professor Julius Stone, of the University of Sydney, for his book, *Legal Controls of International Conflict*.[122]

At the 50th Anniversary annual dinner, the rostrum was turned over to the diplomatic corps. The speakers were the Ambassador of Mexico to the Organization of American States, the Ambassador of Austria to the United States, a former Ambassador of Egypt to the United States, and U.S. Ambassador Amos J. Peaslee, Deputy Special Assistant to the President. The toastmaster and incoming President of the Society, Lester H. Woolsey, was not a professional diplomat, but he had a fitting credential for the occasion: he had been a member of the Society for the entire 50 years of its existence.

3. Some Highlights

In the first three years of the decade, the Korean War dominated the international scene. The Society was not nearly as traumatized as it had been during the two World Wars. It devoted a few sessions at its Annual Meetings to issues connected with the war, examining them with scholarly dispassion. In a 1951 session on sanctions under the U.N. Charter, Quincy Wright saw no legal objection to the United Nations "police force" under U.S. command in Korea. He dismissed with the back of his hand any legal objection to the General Assembly's Uniting for Peace Resolution.[123] That Resolution had been adopted in November 1950 when the Soviet Union – after absenting itself from the Security Council when that body originally authorized the United States to lead an armed effort to repel North Korea's attack across the 38th parallel into South Korea – returned to the Council and blocked any further Security Council action. In the Uniting for Peace Resolution, the General Assembly gave itself the authority to make recommendations to Member States for collective measures, including acts of force, when the Security Council is prevented by a veto from acting to preserve international peace and security. Wright found adequate authority in General Assembly practice and in reasonable interpretation of U.N. Charter Articles 10, 11 and 14, taking account of the purposes of the United Nations.[124]

---

121 For Wright's tribute to Hudson, see 50 *ASIL Proc.* 24-25 (1956).

122 50 *ASIL Proc.* 219 & 225 (1956).

123 G.A. Res. 377, UNGAOR, 5th Sess., Supp. No. 20, at 10, U.N. Doc. A/1775 (1950).

124 Quincy Wright, "Collective Security in the Light of the Korean Experience," 45 *ASIL Proc.* 165, 169 (1951).

The Korean War engendered another noteworthy Annual Meeting session, in 1953. The Society's Committee on Study of Legal Problems of the United Nations had addressed the question of whether the humanitarian law of war should apply to U.N. enforcement action. Said the committee, "[T]he proper answer would seem to be, for the time being, that the United Nations should not feel bound by all the laws of war, but should select such of [them] as may seem to fit its purposes (*e.g.*, prisoners of war, belligerent occupation), adding such others as may be needed, and rejecting those which seem incompatible with its purposes."[125] Richard Baxter, then a major in the Army Judge Advocate General's Corps, took issue. With a touch of sarcasm, he observed:

> How can the view that the law of war is not applicable to a United Nations action be reconciled with the humanitarian inspiration of the law of war? The committee's conclusion would seem to suggest that the laws relating to prisoners of war, to the wounded and sick, to belligerent occupation, are not of their own force applicable to the United Nations forces. If these bodies of law are set aside, one can only conclude that the United Nations forces are not to be influenced by humanitarian considerations in the conduct of hostilities. It must be that the United Nations will be guided by some new standard of humanity, yet unknown to us, when it starts the selective process of deciding what principles will guide its conduct.[126]

Baxter went on to point out that the U.N. Command in Korea and the United States acting as the Unified Command had declared that they would comply with the humanitarian principles of the law of war, and had even assumed an obligation to apply Hague Convention No. IV and the 1949 Geneva Conventions.[127]

In examining the relevance of humanitarian law to United Nations-authorized use of force, the Society dealt with an issue that was not only timely then, but that would reappear years later in the Persian Gulf War of 1991 and in the several instances of U.N. peacekeeping operations in the latter part of the century. The United Nations eventually acknowledged that the operations of its forces would be conducted with full respect for the principles and spirit of the conventions on humanitarian law.[128]

---

125 Report of Committee on Study of Legal Problems of the United Nations, *supra* note 7, at 220.

126 Richard R. Baxter, "The Role of Law in Modern War," 47 *ASIL Proc.* 90, 95 (1953).

127 Id. at 96.

128 See 1992 *UN Juridical YB* 430, and see the U.N. Secretary-General's Bulletin on the Observance by United Nations Forces of International Humanitarian Law, 38 *ILM* 1656 (1999).

Dean Acheson, the Secretary of State in 1952, was one of the featured speakers at the opening session of the 1952 Annual Meeting. He spoke about international legislation, broadly defined, but his real emphasis was on the importance to international law of what he called the companion concepts of the unity of society and the worth of the individual. He added:

> It seems sometimes to be assumed that the only thing which is lacking in a search for Utopia is the perfection of organization. Sometimes this has led to the theory that all we need is a code of international rules carefully drawn up and written down and applied by an international court to effect the solution of every international conflict.
>
> We know that this is not true. Organization, whether national or international, is merely an instrument and must be used by skillful craftsmen.[129]

Perhaps he did not realize that he was challenging the very articles of faith that had led to the creation of the Society nearly fifty years earlier. Or perhaps he did. Two World Wars, the Korean War and the Cold War may well have made Acheson sadder but wiser to the ways of the world than his State Department predecessor several times removed, Elihu Root, had been.

Percy Spender, then the Ambassador of Australia to the United States, struck much the same chord in his speech at the 1952 annual dinner. He said that a strong case could be made that the failure of the League of Nations was due to a belief that war could be prevented simply by reducing legal concepts to a codified system that would then be observed by all nations. Before that would work, he said, there must be accepted moral approaches to the conduct of foreign policy.[130]

Another speaker at the 1952 Annual Meeting was an assistant professor at the Harvard Law School. Louis Sohn spoke of a developing world law through the practice of the United Nations.[131] With hindsight, his model seems utopian or, to some, even anathema. Nevertheless, he was able to point out ways in which U.N. organs had already begun to shape new concepts and practices having legal significance. It was a glimpse of a veritable flood of insights about the United Nations yet to come from the same scholar.

In 1953, Philip Jessup took on the daunting task of discussing the current state of international law. Along the way he addressed the relationship

---

129 Dean G. Acheson, "The Development of the International Community," 46 *ASIL Proc.* 18, 24 (1952).

130 Percy Spender, "Law, Morality, and the Communist Challenge," 46 *ASIL Proc.* 190, 192 (1952).

131 Louis B. Sohn, "The Impact of the United Nations on International Law," 46 *ASIL Proc.* 104 (1952).

between international lawyers and political scientists – a relationship that had changed since the Society's inception. The fifties were a time in the Society of rising influence of the lawyers and diminishing influence of "pure" political scientists. To be sure, some of the lawyers – notably those of the Yale school – were heavily influenced by the social sciences and worked closely with social scientists, but aside from Harold Lasswell and a few others, the up and coming social scientists were moving their intellectual bases to scholarly associations not primarily "legal."

Jessup acknowledged that he was a member of both the Faculty of Political Science and the Faculty of Law at Columbia. "When I meet myself crossing the Columbia campus . . . I do not find difficulty in recognizing myself. ... As a political scientist I know that lawyers are just as much interested in the architecture of society. As a lawyer, acknowledging that law is not 'a brooding omnipresence in the skies,' I know that all of the various departments of political science as well as other disciplines have much to contribute. The problem is not law or politics but human society."[132] The gulf between political scientists and international lawyers nevertheless continued to widen.

In 1954, the Bricker Amendment was on the agenda. As has been noted above, it would have amended the United States Constitution to provide that a treaty would be effective in U.S. domestic law only through legislation which would be valid in the absence of a treaty.[133] George Finch presented a paper reflecting his firm support for the Amendment.[134] He raised the specter of treaties otherwise encroaching on states' rights by regulating such things as the relations between U.S. nationals and their own government, including the imposition of socialistic norms akin to those found in Communist countries. This prompted a spirited rebuttal from William Bishop and a rather lighthearted, though genuinely felt, one from Edwin Dickinson.[135] One needs only to read this part of the 1954 Proceedings to comprehend the heat of the controversy over the Bricker Amendment at that time.

The 1957 Annual Meeting was held in the wake of the Israeli-Anglo-French military intervention in Egypt after the nationalization of the Suez Canal.[136] Quincy Wright addressed the legality of armed intervention under the U.N. Charter, concluding that it was restricted to cases of self-defense against armed

132 Philip C. Jessup, "International Law in 1953 A.D.," 47 *ASIL Proc.* 8, 13-14 (1953).

133 See text at note 66 *supra*.

134 George A. Finch, "Observations on Proposed Amendments to United States Constitution," 48 *ASIL Proc.* 128 (1954). See also George A. Finch, "The Need to Restrain the Treaty-Making Power of the United States Within Constitutional Limits," 48 *AJIL* 57 (1954).

135 Remarks of William W. Bishop, Jr., 48 *ASIL Proc.* 141, and of Edwin D. Dickinson, id. at 147.

136 For discussion of the 1956 (50th anniversary) Annual Meeting, see Section B.2 *supra*.

attack, Security Council authorization under Chapter VII of the Charter, or explicit treaty permission from the state in which the intervention occurs. He regarded the intervention in Egypt as unlawful – in the case of Britain and France, because they did not meet any of the tests for intervention; in the case of Israel because it acted disproportionately even though it may have had cause for exercising its right of self-defense.[137]

At the 1958 annual dinner, the first speaker was the State Department Legal Adviser, Loftus E. Becker. The first Geneva Conference on the Law of the Sea was just drawing to a close. Becker had returned from it with a rather jaded view of the bloc-voting tactics of third-world and Communist countries. The segment of his speech dealing with the Conference would not qualify as an exemplar of diplomacy. It was, however, informative for those interested in the State Department's view of what had kept the Conference from reaching agreement on the key issue: the breadth of the territorial sea. Becker castigated the newly independent states for (in his view) opposing the traditional three-mile limit solely because the major maritime powers had adopted it before those states had come into existence.[138]

In 1959, the theme for the Annual Meeting was "Representative Systems of World Order Today." The panels were liberally sprinkled with associates and protégés of Myres McDougal. The program represented an endeavor to move away from discussions that were largely doctrinal and into ones that were policy-oriented. It was an important example of what McDougal regarded as one of his major contributions to the Society: focusing it on policy.[139]

C. THE JOURNAL IN THE FIFTIES

1. More Changes in the Board of Editors

In the span between the 1951 and 1952 Annual Meetings, three long-standing members of the Board of Editors died. The length of their service on the Board testifies not only to their eminence as scholars, but also to what some Society members, then and later, regarded as an encrusted old boy system within the Board of Editors. The three were Edwin Borchard, George Grafton Wilson and

[137] Quincy Wright, "The Legality of Intervention under the United Nations Charter," 51 *ASIL Proc.* 79 (1957).

[138] Loftus E. Becker, "Some Political Problems of the Legal Adviser," 52 *ASIL Proc.* 266, 269-72 (1958).

[139] Interview with Myres S. McDougal, May 18, 1994 (transcript on file with the Society). McDougal's other major contribution, he said, was getting Harold Lasswell involved in the Society.

Charles Cheney Hyde.[140] Borchard had served as an Editor or Honorary Editor for twenty-seven years, Wilson for forty-four, and Hyde for forty-two.

In 1952, George Finch reinstated his request to be relieved of his duties of Editor-in Chief.[141] The Executive Council was as reluctant to let him go as it had been in 1950. Manley Hudson apparently persuaded him to serve another year. He was duly re-elected.[142] His wish was finally granted in 1953, when William W. Bishop, Jr., became the Editor-in-Chief.

The Society adopted a resolution expressing its appreciation of Finch's many years of service,[143] but a more meaningful encomium arrived in the form of a letter to Finch from William C. Dennis, one of the Society's founding members. Dennis wrote:

> I have had the great pleasure and advantage of knowing you for nearly fifty years. When I first knew you, you were a newly appointed clerk in the State Department paid, I think, out of the emergency fund until Secretary Root got your position regularized. But you did your duties every one, and you were always equal to any duty you were called upon to do. You have continued from that day to this to do your whole duty and to measure up to constantly growing responsibilities from that day to this. I do not know anything better I could say about any man, or any man about whom this could more truly be said.
>
> You have been a splendid Editor-in-Chief of the *Journal*, absolutely worthy in your way, to be bracketed with our two other editors, remarkable as they were in their respective ways.[144]

In November 1953 the Executive Council elected Oliver J. Lissitzyn, of Columbia University, to the Board of Editors. He was immediately put in charge of the Judicial Decisions department, thus relieving Bishop, the new Editor-in-Chief, of sole responsibility for that department. At the same meeting, Edwin Dickinson was elected as an Honorary Editor.

Although the record is not entirely clear, it appears that neither Lissitzyn as a regular Editor nor Dickinson as an Honorary Editor were nominated by action of the Board of Editors. Further elections to the Board were postponed until the

140 Tributes to them may be found in 46 *ASIL Proc.* 172-73 (1952). For a fuller tribute to Hyde, see Lester H. Woolsey, Editorial Comment: "Charles Cheney Hyde," 46 *AJIL* 283 (1952).

141 Minutes of the Executive Council, Apr. 24, 1952, in ASIL Minute Book, 1951-1958, at 45, 46.

142 Minutes of the Executive Council, Apr. 26, 1952, in ASIL Minute Book, 1951-1958, at 51.

143 47 *ASIL Proc.* 128-29 (1953).

144 Id. at 129.

Council's April 1954 meeting, "when recommendations from the Board might be available."[145] It thus appears that election without a recommendation from the Board was regarded as out of the ordinary, but not improper.

Bishop resigned as Editor-in-Chief in 1954, citing the press of other business. On the recommendation of the Board of Editors, the Executive Council elected Herbert Briggs to replace him.[146] Bishop later returned to the position.[147]

As will appear below, the Turlington Committee in 1958 made several recommendations for the future direction of the Society. One of the recommendations was that there be rotation of the Journal's Board of Editors. Myres McDougal, who had just become President of the Society, demurred.[148] McDougal had been a member of the Board of Editors since 1950. He was committed to the principle of excellence, as he has put it, and he was not interested in what he has called democratization at the leadership level of the Society or of the Journal.[149] A mild rotation system was in the Board's future, but not just yet.

2. Soliciting Manuscripts

In 1954, the Board of Editors revisited a question that has arisen from time to time since the Journal's inception. The question was whether, and to what extent, to solicit manuscripts from persons not on the Board. The answer in 1954 was that some articles should be solicited from "outstanding persons in the field."[150]

3. Noteworthy Articles and Comments

In 1955, the Journal carried two particularly noteworthy contributions, one by Hersch Lauterpacht and one by Myres McDougal. The Lauterpacht article dealt with codification, a subject long held dear by the Society, but did so in the specific context of the work of the International Law Commission.[151] He did not espouse codification in the traditional sense (the transformation into written rules of

---

145 Minutes of the Executive Council, Nov. 28, 1953, in ASIL Minute Book, 1951-1958, at 75.

146 Minutes of the Executive Council, Apr. 29, 1955, in ASIL Minute Book, 1951-1958, at 106, 108.

147 For other changes in Board membership during this period, see "Memorandum, ASIL History: The Journal, Its Editors and Business Practices," on file with the Society.

148 Minutes of the Executive Council, Apr. 26, 1958, in ASIL Minute Book, 1951-1958, at 177, 178.

149 Interview with Myres S. McDougal, May 18, 1994 (transcript on file with the Society).

150 Minutes of the Executive Council, Oct. 16, 1954, in ASIL Minute Book, 1951-1958, at 85, 88.

151 Hersch Lauterpacht, "Codification and Development of International Law," 49 *AJIL* 16 (1955).

norms reflected in consistent state practice supported by an *opinio juris*), since there was a dearth of ascertainable unwritten norms even for such basic subjects as the law of treaties. With few agreed legal standards, there could hardly be an ordered international society. Thus the International Law Commission could and should inject clarity and certainty into the law, even though it would be engaged almost entirely in "progressive development" rather than traditional "codification," to use the terms of the U.N. Charter.[152]

The McDougal contribution was in the form of an Editorial Comment on the lawfulness of U.S. hydrogen bomb tests at sea. It contained one of the most widely cited passages ever to appear in the Journal, a passage that captured the ongoing process of developing and adapting international law by means other than codification:

> From the perspective of realistic description, the international law of the sea is not a mere static body of rules but is rather a whole decision-making process, a public order which includes a structure of authorized decision-makers as well as a body of highly flexible, inherited prescriptions. It is, in other words, a process of continuous interaction, of continuous demand and response, in which the decision-makers of particular nation states unilaterally put forward claims of the most diverse and conflicting character to the use of the world's seas, and in which other decision-makers, external to the demanding state and including both national and international officials, weigh and appraise these competing claims in terms of the interests of the world community and of the rival claimants, and ultimately accept or reject them. As such a process, it is a living, growing law, grounded in the practices and sanctioning expectations of nation-state officials, and changing as their demands and expectations are changed by the exigencies of new interests and technology and by other continually evolving conditions in the world arena.[153]

The passage, of course, could be and has been used to describe the development of legal norms in many branches of international relations, not just the use of the oceans.

During the late fifties, the pages of the Journal served as one of the vehicles by which McDougal and his Yale associates further developed their policy-

---

[152] See U.N. Charter Art. 13(1)(a).

[153] Myres S. McDougal, "The Hydrogen Bomb Tests and the International Law of the Sea," 49 *AJIL* 356-57 (1955), citing the more comprehensive treatment of the subject in Myres S. McDougal & Norbert A. Schlei, "The Hydrogen Bomb Tests in Perspective: Lawful Measures for Security," 64 *Yale L.J.* 648 (1955).

oriented jurisprudence of world public order.[154] It was an innovative approach to international law, one that brought to the center of discourse an examination of the values that underlay decisions having international dimensions. Paradoxically, perhaps, it incorporated some of the thinking of social scientists while it disavowed what many of the older generation of political scientists in the Society would have called the scientific ("objective") approach to international law. For McDougal and his associates, law was seen as a process reflecting the sometimes-conflicting, sometimes-converging values of those who participated in it and reflecting also world power structures, rather than as a set of rules that could be objectively ascertained and applied by neutral tribunals.[155]

A different "school" also found a place in the Journal's pages. In 1956, Wolfgang Friedmann addressed one of the crucial post-World War II influences on international legal relations. His article investigated the extent to which changes in internal social organization – in particular, government conduct of or control over a widening range of activities – were affecting international legal responsibilities.[156] In this article and elsewhere, Friedmann contributed significantly to the transformation of international legal thought from its focus on the law of nations *inter sese* to a new concept of transnational law encompassing a multiplicity of actors, institutions and transactions. It may be no coincidence that Philip Jessup's Storrs Lectures leading to the publication of his book, *Transnational Law*, were delivered in February 1956.[157] Friedmann and Jessup, colleagues at Columbia, no doubt influenced each other. Nevertheless, Friedmann in his Journal article did not call his expanded horizon "transnational law."

* * *

Back in the era when James Brown Scott was in charge of the Journal, it was sometimes thought that his close contacts with the State Department tempered or even quashed any criticism of U.S. foreign policy in the pages of the Journal.[158] In later years that accusation was not made about the Journal,

---

154 See Myres S. McDougal & Florentino P. Feliciano, "The Initiation of Coercion: A Multi-Temporal Analysis," 52 *AJIL* 241 (1958); Myres S. McDougal & Leon Lipson, "Perspectives for a Law of Outer Space," id. at 407; Myres S. McDougal & Harold D. Lasswell, "The Identification and Appraisal of Diverse Systems of Public Order," 53 *AJIL* 1 (1959).

155 On the McDougal-Lasswell approach, see Frederick S. Tipson, *Consolidating World Public Order: The American Study of International Law and the Work of Harold D. Lasswell and Myres S. McDougal, 1906-1976* (Ph.D. dissertation, University of Virginia, 1977).

156 Wolfgang Friedmann, "Some Impacts of Social Organization on International Law," 50 *AJIL* 475 (1956).

157 See Philip C. Jessup, *Transnational Law* (1956). Friedmann further developed his approach in his book, *The Changing Structure of International Law* (1964).

158 See Chapter Two, Section D.3 *supra*.

at least not publicly, but the Journal and the Society remained dependent on the State Department for documents and other information. Moreover, for many years after World War II the Society made the Secretary of State its Honorary President. Thus there were incentives to support the Department's foreign policy decisions. But the successors to Scott and Finch as Editors-in-Chief of the Journal were not as closely tied to the State Department as those two men had been. By 1957 one finds the Editor-in-Chief, Herbert Briggs, writing a lead article criticizing the State Department for its refusal to submit to arbitration or conciliation with the Swiss government regarding the *Interhandel* case.[159] His characterization of the State Department's position was unflattering to the Department, to say the least.

Another 1957 article is noteworthy in three respects: first, it was one of the relatively rare Journal articles dealing with legal theory; secondly, it was written by a leading continental European legal scholar – not a first for the Journal, but not commonplace either; and thirdly, it was a re-publication (in translation) of an article that had previously been published elsewhere. The article, by Roberto Ago, argued that international legal science needed to free itself from its reliance on positivism in order to accept the proposition that law may be created spontaneously.[160]

The October 1958 issue featured two lead articles, one by Arthur Dean and the other by Marjorie Whiteman, and an Editorial Comment by Philip Jessup, on the recently concluded Geneva Conference on the Law of the Sea.[161] They provide an extremely useful summary and analysis of the issues raised at the Conference.

In 1959, the Journal published a significant article on the law of international watercourses. Written by William Griffin, of the State Department Legal Adviser's Office, it was based on a memorandum he had prepared for submission to a Congressional committee.[162] It was a refutation of the 19th-century Harmon Doctrine, which had asserted that an upper riparian could do as it wished with waters in its territory, regardless of harm to lower riparian states. Griffin's

---

159 Herbert W. Briggs, "Towards the Rule of Law?," 51 *AJIL* 517 (1957).

160 Roberto Ago, "Positive Law and International Law," 51 *AJIL* 691 (1957), previously published in both Italian and German. Not everyone accepted Ago's theory. See Josef L. Kunz, Editorial Comment: "Roberto Ago's Theory of a 'Spontaneous' International Law," 52 *AJIL* 85 (1958).

161 Arthur H. Dean, "The Geneva Conference on the Law of the Sea: What Was Accomplished?," 52 *AJIL* 607 (1958); Marjorie M. Whiteman, "Conference on the Law of the Sea: Convention on the Continental Shelf," id. at 629; Philip C. Jessup, Editorial Comment: "The Geneva Conference on the Law of the Sea: A Study in International Law-Making," id. at 730.

162 William L. Griffin, "The Use of Waters of International Drainage Basins under Customary International Law," 53 *AJIL* 50 (1959).

assertion of a duty to notify and consult the lower riparian before undertaking potentially damaging activities provided a basis for some aspects of the modern development of international watercourse law.[163]

The 1959 volume also contained the leading pre-*Sabbatino* scholarly analysis of the act of state doctrine. Michael Zander took the position that "Where the judge is directed by the rules of his own conflict of laws to a foreign law which he deems to be contrary to international law, he should be able to disregard such foreign law."[164] In the *Sabbatino* case, the U.S. Supreme Court severely limited that proposition in the United States, though it did not do away with it entirely.[165]

4. Official Documents

In October 1955, the Executive Council approved a plan of the Board of Editors to publish official documents in the main body of the Journal, rather than in a separate Supplement.[166] This was done, apparently as a cost containment measure, beginning with volume 50 in 1956.

The official documents published in the Journal's Supplements, or in the Journal itself from the mid-fifties, included some items of little interest today and many items more conveniently found today in other sources, such as official treaty collections. But some significant materials from the fifties are most conveniently found in the Journal's Official Documents. These include the annual reports of the International Law Commission, the 1951 Draft Statute for an International Criminal Court, prepared by the U.N. General Assembly's Committee on International Criminal Jurisdiction,[167] and Department of State

---

163 For an authoritative set of current norms, see the United Nations Convention on the Law of the Non-Navigational Uses of International Watercourses, UN Doc. A/51/869 (1997), 36 *ILM* 700 (1997), based on the International Law Commission's Draft Articles on the same subject, in Report of the ILC on the Work of its 46th Sess., 49 UN GAOR Supp. No. 10 (A/49/10) at 197 (1994).

164 Michael Zander, "The Act of State Doctrine," 53 *AJIL* 826, 841 (1959).

165 *Banco Nacional de Cuba v. Sabbatino*, 376 US 398, 427-428 (1964). The Court left open the possibility of using international law to review the validity of an official act of a foreign state within its territory if there is a high degree of consensus as to the particular area of international law, or if the implications of the issue are not especially important for the foreign relations of the United States, or if the government that perpetrated the act is no longer in existence. See also *W.S. Kirkpatrick v. Environmental Tectonics Corp.*, 493 US 400 (1990), limiting the act of state doctrine to cases in which the validity, rather than just the motivation, of the foreign state's act is at issue.

166 Minutes of the Executive Council, Oct. 29, 1955, in ASIL Minute Book, 1951-1958, at 119, 124.

167 46 *AJIL Supp.* 1 (1952).

Circular Number 175 – the State Department's answer to the proposed Bricker Amendment to the U.S. Constitution.[168]

D. SETTING THE STAGE FOR NEW IDEAS AND PROGRAMS

1. The Turlington Committee Report

In November 1958, Edgar Turlington, in his capacity as chair of the Society's Committee on Administration, presented a report to the Executive Council. The report included two landmark recommendations, both of them contingent on obtaining the necessary funds:

- The Society's offices should be moved to quarters adequate to accommodate an enlarged staff and a working international law library; and
- The Executive Council should employ an Executive Director and such assistants as might be required for the effective stimulation and coordination of the Society's present and proposed undertakings.[169]

In a major step that set the stage for revitalizing the Society, the Executive Council approved the recommendations.[170] It also decided to establish Standing Committees on Special Studies and on Legal Aspects of Foreign Investment,[171] thus taking another step toward a full-fledged studies program.

It was said of Edgar Turlington after he died in September 1959 that "he galvanized members into a reassessment of the somewhat modest role of the Society and indicated the way to greater usefulness, to more co-ordinated effort."[172] One could say that he was the catalyst for the revitalized American Society of International Law.

---

[168] 50 *AJIL* 784 (1956).

[169] Covey Oliver recalled that Walter Surrey and Seymour Rubin were the ones who originally decided, in 1957 or 1958, that the Society needed an Executive Director. Interview with Covey T. Oliver, Aug. 13, 1995 (transcript on file with the Society).

[170] Minutes of the Executive Council, Nov. 22, 1958, in ASIL Minute Book, 1951-1958, at 192-93.

[171] Id. at 193.

[172] Herbert W. Briggs, Editorial Comment: "Edgar Turlington," 53 *AJIL* 876 (1959). For a summary of Turlington's professional career, see Robert R. Wilson, Editorial Comment: "Edgar Turlington," 54 *AJIL* 117 (1960).

2. Looking Toward a Relationship with Student International Law Groups

At the Executive Council meeting in November 1958, Richard Baxter submitted a proposal looking toward establishing a relationship with student international law clubs. The Council appointed Baxter and Alona Evans to an *ad hoc* committee, and authorized them to invite representatives of student international law clubs to an organizational meeting during the Society's Annual Meeting in April 1959.[173]

The committee conducted an extensive survey of colleges and universities to ascertain how many student international law clubs there were, and where they were. It found only two – one at Harvard and the other at the University of Virginia. A third was in the nascent stage at Columbia. The committee reported to the Executive Council that it planned to explore the possibility of establishing some sort of affiliation between the clubs and the Society, and recommended that "any program for the development of student interest should to a considerable extent be administered by the students themselves with the advice and assistance of the Committee and of the Society."[174] The Executive Council took no action either on the report or on Baxter's suggestion that a student international law moot court competition be held during the 1960 Annual Meeting.[175]

Baxter had an idea whose time had not quite come. The sixties would be different.

3. Tillar House and Plans for the Future

Henry F. Butler, chair of the Society's Finance Committee from 1953 through the remainder of the decade, had a friend of the family who mentioned to him in 1958 that Genevieve E. Tillar owned a house on Sheridan Circle in the District of Columbia that she wished to give to a charitable organization. She was the widow of Benjamin J. Tillar, a Texas lawyer and businessman who died in 1923 and left her very well off.[176] She had lived in the Sheridan Circle house with her second husband, Allen A. Zoll. At Butler's suggestion, she sent her accountant

---

173 Minutes of the Executive Council, Nov. 22, 1958, in ASIL Minute Book, 1951-1958, at 192, 199.

174 Report of the Committee on Student International Law Clubs, Apr. 28, 1959, at 3 (in file designated Student Societies (Supplementary) from Professor Baxter's files, 1958-1964); see also Minutes of the Executive Council, Apr. 30, 1959, in ASIL Minute Book, 1959-1966, at 1, 5.

175 Baxter's moot court suggestion is apparent from a letter he wrote to the Executive Secretary of the Columbia Society of International Law, Dec. 2, 1959, in the file identified in note 174 *supra*.

176 "The Petroleum Club of Forth Worth Celebrates 50 Years of Excellence 1953-2003" (leaflet issued by the Club).

to see Eleanor Finch about the possibility of giving the house to the Society. He must have been impressed. Mrs. Tillar agreed to give the house to the Society, but tax considerations led her to do it in a roundabout way.[177]

Mrs. Tillar agreed to give the Society USD 144,000 in securities in four annual installments, beginning in 1958. It was a staggering gift, at the 1958 value of the dollar. The Society agreed to purchase the Sheridan Circle house from her for USD 133,000 (its appraised value) payable in four installments, each timed to follow the receipt of one of her four installments. The Society also agreed to name the premises the Benjamin Johnston Tillar Memorial Building, in honor of Mrs. Tillar's first husband. In addition, the Society agreed not to dispose of the house for thirty-five years from the date of the agreement (November 21, 1958). The reason for the thirty-five-year restriction on disposal was to prevent one Allen A. Zoll from acquiring any interest in it.[178] Mrs. Tillar had married him many years after her first husband's death, but their marriage apparently had been annulled.[179] The Society took title to the premises on February 27, 1959.[180]

The house is in an area of the District of Columbia zoned for residential use, with an overlay permitting diplomatic use. Since the Society would not be using the house for residential or diplomatic purposes, an exemption from the zoning classification would be necessary. The Society requested an exemption from the D.C. Zoning Board, but was turned down.[181] Undeterred, Henry Butler turned to the Congress of the United States, just as the Society had done when it wished to incorporate. In July 1959, a hearing was held before a subcommittee of the Senate Committee on the District of Columbia, at which no one appeared in opposition to the Society's proposed use of the premises.[182] Congress then enacted Public Law 86-208, authorizing the Society to use the premises as its headquarters.[183]

---

177 Interview with Eleanor H. Finch, May 16, 1994 (transcript on file with the Society).

178 The two agreements with Mrs. Tillar (one for the gift of securities and the other for the sale of the house) and the Executive Council's resolution appear verbatim in Minutes of the Executive Council, Nov. 22, 1958, in ASIL Minute Book, 1951-1958, at 192, 194-97.

179 Application for Probate of the Will of Genevieve Eagon Tillar, in the County Court of Tarrant County, Texas, filed on Jan. 10, 1962. According to an article in *Parade* magazine in 1967, a court in Reno, Nevada, granted Mrs. Tillar an annulment in January 1955. Thanks go to J.P. Barentine, III, of Dallas, Texas, for supplying this information.

180 Sen. Rep. No. 681, Aug. 12, 1959, 1959 [2] U.S. Code Cong. & Admin. News 2183, 2184.

181 53 *ASIL Proc.* 331 (1959).

182 Sen. Rep. No. 681, *supra* note 180.

183 P.L. 86-208, Aug. 25, 1959, 86th Cong., 1st Sess., 73 Stat. 431 (1959).

With the acquisition of Tillar House and completion of the legal arrangements, the stage was set for a dramatic expansion of the Society's programs and staff. It remained, though, for the Society to find the approximately USD 40,000 needed to remodel and maintain Tillar House. The Executive Council authorized the President and Treasurer to borrow USD 35,000 for this purpose. The Society took out a secured loan.[184]

In order to obtain an exemption from District of Columbia real estate tax, the Society would have to open its library to the general public and/or conduct educational programs involving the relationship of teacher and student. Henry Butler suggested that the Society do both, in order to ensure its eligibility for the tax exemption. No immediate decision was taken.[185]

Planning and fund-raising for new programs also remained to be done in order to take full advantage of the new quarters. The Committee on Financing and Endowment foresaw a wide variety of new programs and activities for the Society: establishing a library, preparing an analytical index for the Journal, employing an Executive Director, a librarian and other personnel, conducting regional and local meetings, investment law conferences and teachers' conferences, providing travel expenses for Society staff and officials as well as for visiting scholars and guests of the Society, and setting up scholarships and prizes for students. The Committee also suggested the possibility of issuing special studies in international law and an American yearbook of international law. The cost was estimated at USD 150,000 annually; a capital sum of at least USD 3,750,000 would be required to produce that income.[186]

A plan like this was a tall order for an organization accustomed to eking out a living on members' dues and occasional modest subventions. Nonetheless, the reinvigoration stemming from Mrs. Tillar's gift augured well for the future. The Society again had a vision, and it had gotten down to some hard-headed planning for the new directions it was to take in the sixties.

The leadership wanted to move forward without waiting for all the funds to appear. The Executive Council first attempted to find an Executive Director who would work without compensation. It turned to James O. Murdock "pending further developments,"[187] but that was not a long-term solution. Edgar Turlington reported to the 1959 Business Meeting that it had not been possible to find someone with the necessary qualifications and ability who would take

184 Minutes of the Executive Council, Nov. 14, 1959, in ASIL Minute Book, 1959-1966, at 20, 21.

185 Id.

186 Id. at 22.

187 Minutes of the Executive Council, Nov. 22, 1958, in ASIL Minute Book, 1951-1958, at 192, 199.

on the position without compensation.[188] The Society headed into the sixties, still without an Executive Director. It would not take much longer to find one who had a vision for expanding the Society's interests and who had the energy to make it happen.

[188] 53 *ASIL Proc.* 332 (1959).

Two of ASIL's founders, Secretary of War William Howard Taft and Secretary of State Elihu Root, in 1904.

Elihu Root, first ASIL president (1907-1924). In addition to serving as Secretary of State, Root was Secretary of War and a U.S. Senator. He received the Nobel Peace Prize in 1912.

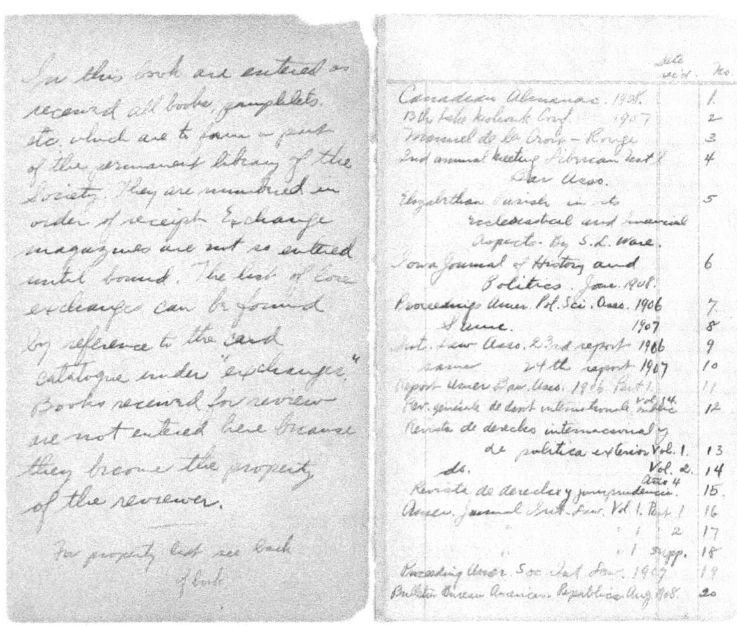

In this book are entered as received all books, pamphlets, etc. which are to form a part of the permanent library of the Society. They are numbered in order of receipt. Exchange magazines are not so entered until bound. The list of [illegible] exchanges can be found by reference to the card catalogue under "exchanges". Books received for review are not entered here because they become the property of the reviewer.

For property list see back of book

	Date rec'd.	No.
Canadian Almanac. 1908.		1.
13th Lake Mohonk Conf. 1907		2
Manuel de la Croix-Rouge		3
2nd annual meeting African Nat'l Bar Asso.		4
Elizabethan Parish in its Ecclesiastical and Financial Aspects. By S. L. Ware.		5
Iowa Journal of History and Politics. Jan. 1908.		6
Proceedings Amer. Pol. Sci. Asso. 1906		7.
Same. 1907		8
Int. Law Asso. 23rd report 1906		9
same 24th report 1907		10
Report Amer Law Asso. 1906 Part 1		11
Rev. générale de droit international public vol. 14.		12
Revista de derecho internacional y de politica exterior Vol. 1.		13
do. Vol. 2.		14
Revista de derecho y jurisprudencia. Año 4		15.
Amer. Journal Int. Law. Vol 1. Part 1		16
" 1 " 2		17
" 1 Supp.		18
Proceeding Amer. Soc. Int. Law. 1907		19
Bulletin Bureau American Republics Aug. 1908.		20

James Brown Scott's logbook of "received ... Books, pamphlets, etc. which are to form a part of the permanent library of the Society" (c. 1907).

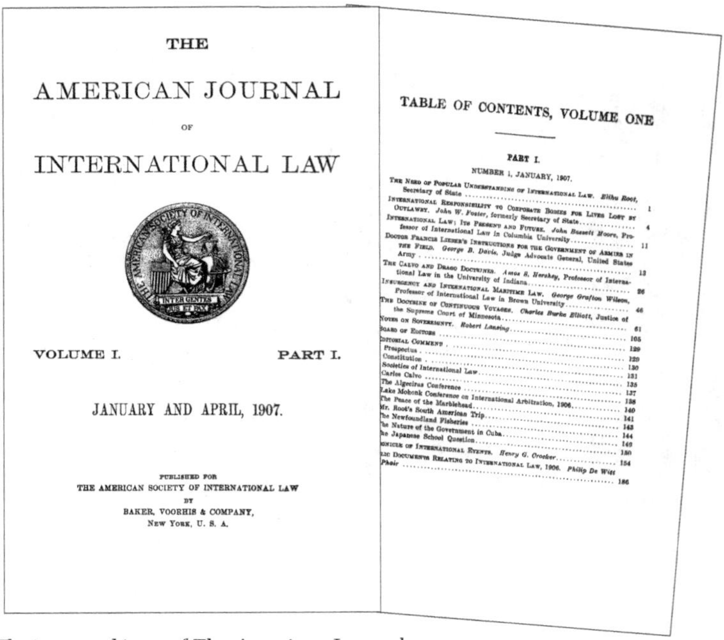

THE

AMERICAN JOURNAL

OF

INTERNATIONAL LAW

VOLUME I. PART I.

JANUARY AND APRIL, 1907.

PUBLISHED FOR
THE AMERICAN SOCIETY OF INTERNATIONAL LAW
BY
BAKER, VOORHIS & COMPANY,
NEW YORK, U. S. A.

TABLE OF CONTENTS, VOLUME ONE

PART I.

NUMBER 1, JANUARY, 1907.

The inaugural issue of The American Journal of International Law *(AJIL), 1907.*

Senator Elihu Root and Chandler P. Anderson (c. 1918). Anderson served as the Society's first treasurer.

LAW COULD END WAR

Root Declares World's Peace Lies in a World's Court.

INDORSES MR. KNOX'S PLAN

New York Senator, in Address Before American Society of International Law, Says Way Is Clear for United States to Recognize the Supreme Court of Nations.

The future reign of a "world peace" through a "world law" was the basic thought of the address of Senator Root, of New York, president of the American Society of International Law, in opening the fourth annual meeting of that organization in the New Willard last night.

He tarried in his erudite discussion of abstract principles long enough to indorse Secretary of State Knox's recent note to the powers on behalf of a court of arbitral justice, and said the way is now smoothed for the United States to subdue "the lion which has stood in its path"—the Constitution—in recognizing a tribunal superior in powers to the Supreme Court of the nation.

"We have the highest hopes of a practical fruition of the plan," he said. "Of course, there is no constitutional provision for any higher tribunal in the settlement of our affairs than our own Supreme Court. ...

Early ASIL annual meeting presidential addresses were front-page news stories.

ASIL founder John Basset Moore (c. 1913) would later become the first American judge on the Permanent Court of International Justice.

Oscar S. Straus, founding ASIL officer and founding member of the AJIL Board of Editors, 1912. He served as Theodore Roosevelt's Secretary of Commerce and Labor.

Members of the American Society of International Law at the White House with President Warren G. Harding, April 29, 1921.

U.S. Secretary of State Charles Evans Hughes (center, with watch chain), ASIL's second president (1924-1929) with representatives of the "Big Nine" nations at the World Disarmament Conference, Washington, DC, 1921.

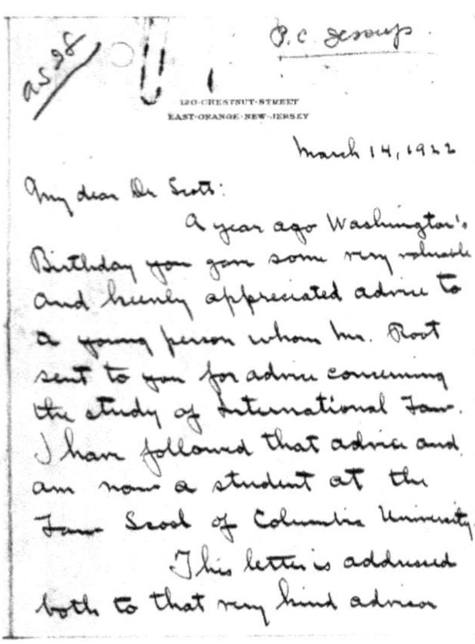

AS 98

P. C. Jessup

120 CHESTNUT STREET
EAST ORANGE NEW JERSEY

March 14, 1922

My dear Dr Scott:

A year ago Washington's Birthday you gave some very valuable and kindly appreciated advice to a young person whom Mr. Root sent to you for advice concerning the study of International Law. I have followed that advice and am now a student at the Law School of Columbia University.

This letter is addressed both to that very kind advisor

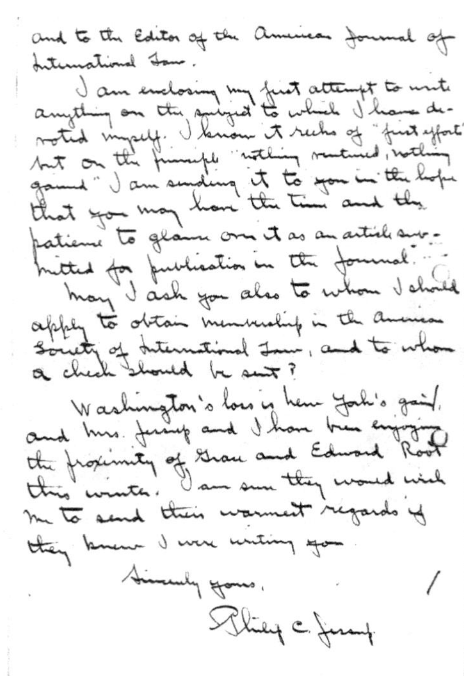

and to the Editor of the American Journal of International Law.

I am enclosing my first attempt to write anything on the subject to which I have devoted myself. I know it reeks of "first effort" but on the principle "nothing ventured, nothing gained" I am sending it to you in the hope that you may have the time and the patience to glance over it as an article submitted for publication in the Journal.

May I ask you also to whom I should apply to obtain membership in the American Society of International Law, and to whom a check should be sent?

Washington's loss is New York's gain, and Mrs. Jessup and I have been enjoying the proximity of Grace and Edward Root this winter. I am sure they would wish me to send their warmest regards if they knew I were writing you.

Sincerely yours,

Philip C. Jessup

Philip C. Jessup letter of March 14, 1922, to James Brown Scott, accompanying his first submission to the American Journal of International Law, which was rejected.

Members of the Permanent Court of International Justice, 1922.

The Permanent Court of International Justice pronounces a decision, 1922.

Frankenstein View of State Decried by Peace Advocate

James Brown Scott Tells International Lawyers Government Not Artificial But "a Thing of Men, Women and Children."

"If we continue to look upon the State as an artificial person, instead of a thing of men and women and children, we may end by being the victims of our own Frankenstein, a soulless mechanical thing which inevitably destroys itself," James Brown Scott said last night at the opening session of the twenty-sixth annual meeting of the American Society of International Law at the Willard Hotel.

The speaker is secretary of the Carnegie Endowment for International Peace and director of its division of internatinoal law. His topic was "A Single Standard of Morality for the Individual and the State."

Following the talk, a discussion of

A round table discussion will take place at the morning session today on "The Treaty Situation in the Far East." The director of the discussion will be John V. A. MacMurray of the Walter Hines Page School of International Relations, Johns Hopkins University, and former American Minister to China.

Other talks scheduled for today include "Treaties Made Under Duress," by Charles Henry Butler, and "The Doctrine of Rebus Sic Stantibus," by William C. Dennis and Joseph P. Chamberlain.

The organization's annual dinner will be held at 7:30 at the Willard Saturday with Dr. Scott presiding. The speakers will include Ambassador Tytus Filipowicz, from Poland, and

James Brown Scott's 1932 presidential address, as reported in The Washington Post.

ASIL founder, first secretary, and third president (1929-1939), and first editor-in-chief of the AJIL, James Brown Scott.

George A. Finch, close associate of James Brown Scott and secretary to the Journal's Board of Editors, became the Society's recording secretary in 1924.

Charles Evans Hughes served briefly as the second American judge on the Permanent Court of International Justice, until he was appointed Chief Justice of the U.S. Supreme Court in 1930.

Cordell Hull, U.S. Secretary of State and 4th ASIL president (1939-1941), by James Montgomery Flagg, 1941.

U.S. Secretary of State Cordell Hull delivers an address over NBC Radio (c. 1945; Walter Cronkite is to the right). Hull's presidential address to the 1941 ASIL Annual Meeting was similarly broadcast live over NBC Radio.

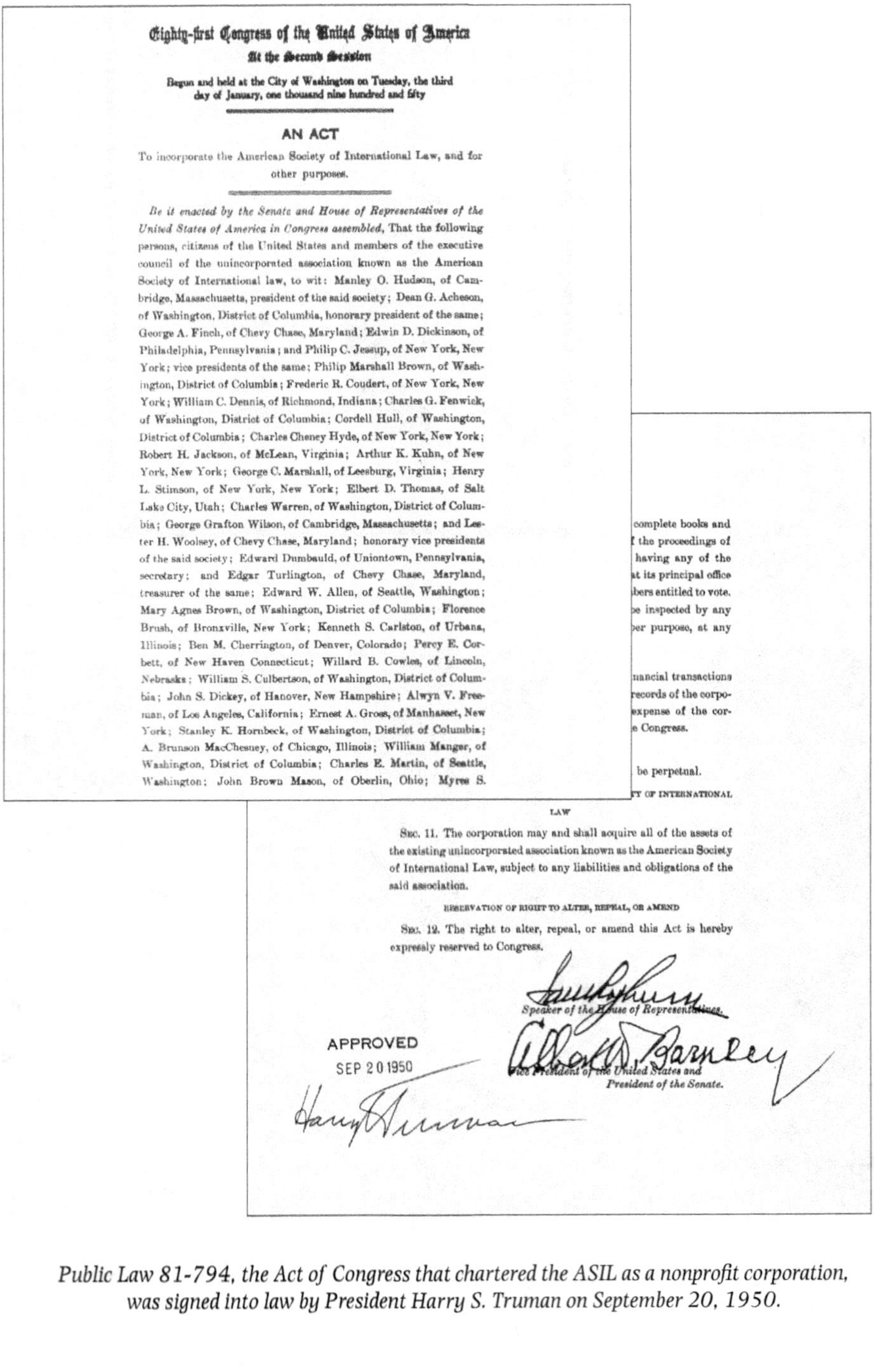

Eighty-first Congress of the United States of America
At the Second Session

Begun and held at the City of Washington on Tuesday, the third day of January, one thousand nine hundred and fifty

AN ACT

To incorporate the American Society of International Law, and for other purposes.

Be it enacted by the Senate and House of Representatives of the United States of America in Congress assembled, That the following persons, citizens of the United States and members of the executive council of the unincorporated association known as the American Society of International law, to wit: Manley O. Hudson, of Cambridge, Massachusetts, president of the said society; Dean G. Acheson, of Washington, District of Columbia, honorary president of the same; George A. Finch, of Chevy Chase, Maryland; Edwin D. Dickinson, of Philadelphia, Pennsylvania; and Philip C. Jessup, of New York, New York; vice presidents of the same; Philip Marshall Brown, of Washington, District of Columbia; Frederic R. Coudert, of New York, New York; William C. Dennis, of Richmond, Indiana; Charles G. Fenwick, of Washington, District of Columbia; Cordell Hull, of Washington, District of Columbia; Charles Cheney Hyde, of New York, New York; Robert H. Jackson, of McLean, Virginia; Arthur K. Kuhn, of New York, New York; George C. Marshall, of Leesburg, Virginia; Henry L. Stimson, of New York, New York; Elbert D. Thomas, of Salt Lake City, Utah; Charles Warren, of Washington, District of Columbia; George Grafton Wilson, of Cambridge, Massachusetts; and Lester H. Woolsey, of Chevy Chase, Maryland; honorary vice presidents of the said society; Edward Dumbauld, of Uniontown, Pennsylvania, secretary; and Edgar Turlington, of Chevy Chase, Maryland, treasurer of the same; Edward W. Allen, of Seattle, Washington; Mary Agnes Brown, of Washington, District of Columbia; Florence Brush, of Bronxville, New York; Kenneth S. Carlston, of Urbana, Illinois; Ben M. Cherrington, of Denver, Colorado; Percy E. Corbett, of New Haven Connecticut; Willard B. Cowles, of Lincoln, Nebraska; William S. Culbertson, of Washington, District of Columbia; John S. Dickey, of Hanover, New Hampshire; Alwyn V. Freeman, of Los Angeles, California; Ernest A. Gross, of Manhasset, New York; Stanley K. Hornbeck, of Washington, District of Columbia; A. Brunson MacChesney, of Chicago, Illinois; William Manger, of Washington, District of Columbia; Charles E. Martin, of Seattle, Washington; John Brown Mason, of Oberlin, Ohio; Myres S.

complete books and
the proceedings of
having any of the
t its principal office
bers entitled to vote.
e inspected by any
er purpose, at any

nancial transactions
records of the corpo-
expense of the cor-
e Congress.

be perpetual.

Y OF INTERNATIONAL
LAW

SEC. 11. The corporation may and shall acquire all of the assets of the existing unincorporated association known as the American Society of International Law, subject to any liabilities and obligations of the said association.

RESERVATION OF RIGHT TO ALTER, REPEAL, OR AMEND

SEC. 12. The right to alter, repeal, or amend this Act is hereby expressly reserved to Congress.

Speaker of the House of Representatives.

APPROVED
SEP 20 1950

Vice President of the United States and President of the Senate.

Public Law 81-794, the Act of Congress that chartered the ASIL as a nonprofit corporation, was signed into law by President Harry S. Truman on September 20, 1950.

Philip C. Jessup testifies before Congress in 1951 during the third day of his nomination hearing to become a delegate to the UN General Assembly. Jessup was ASIL president from 1954 to 1955.

Myres S. McDougal, ASIL president, 1958-1959.

Tillar House, the ASIL's new headquarters, c. 1962.

ASIL EXECUTIVE DIRECTORS 1961-2006

ASIL's first executive director, H.C.L. "Chris" Merillat, is on the left at a 1963 meeting of foreign legal advisers hosted by ASIL at Princeton.

Stephen M. Schwebel, the Society's second executive director (1967-74), became judge on the International Court of Justice in 1981 and served until 2000, the last four years as president.

Seymour J. Rubin, ASIL executive director, 1974-1985.

John Lawrence Hargrove, ASIL executive director, 1985-1992.

Barry Carter, ASIL executive director, 1992-1993.

Charlotte Ku, ASIL executive director, 1994-2006.

Manley Ottmer Hudson, ASIL president, 1949-1952, namesake and first recipient of the Hudson Medal for preeminent scholarship and achievement in the field of international law. His donation of approximately 1,000 volumes was a major factor in the ASIL library's development.

Over the years, the ASIL Annual Meetings covered many different as well as recurring issues in international law.

Oscar Schachter, ASIL president, 1968 - 1970, and co-editor-in-chief, AJIL, 1978-1984.

In 1980, Alona E. Evans became the first woman elected ASIL president. She died before completing her term.

Louis Henkin, ASIL president, 1992-1994, and co-editor-in-chief, AJIL, 1978-1984.

Thomas M. Franck, ASIL president, 1998-2000, and editor-in-chief, AJIL, 1984-1993.

Frederic L. "Rick" Kirgis, ASIL Secretary, 1994 – present, ASIL Insights editor, and author of this history.

ASIL Honorary President and Judge on the International Court of Justice, Thomas Buergenthal (c. 2003).

U.S. Supreme Court Justice Ruth Bader Ginsburg and U.S. Secretary of State Condoleezza Rice at the 99th Annual Meeting, 2005.

Plans for the Tillar House renovation in 2001 include flexible and expandable public meeting space that would become The Hauser Learning Center in honor of the generosity of Rita E. Hauser and the Hauser Foundation.

Tillar House is rededicated on November 1, 2002. Former ASIL President Charles N. Brower, who chaired the successful fundraising campaign, delivers remarks as President-Elect James H. Carter, Executive Director Charlotte Ku, and President Anne-Marie Slaughter look on.

"The Society gained more than a permanent address when it was given Tillar House. Mrs. Tillar's generosity enabled a vibrant institution truly to prosper in pursuit of the ideals that had launched the Society at the beginning of the last century."

—Charles N. Brower, 2001
Former ASIL president and Co-Chair,
Launching the Second Century Campaign.

Chapter Eight

A New Beginning

It is one of the achievements of this Society that, from its inception, it has spread the realization that the United States cannot opt out of the community of nations – that international affairs are part of our national affairs.

—Dean Rusk
Address, 59 *ASIL Proceedings* 247 (1965)

A. PUTTING A NEW PROGRAM TOGETHER

1. An Executive Director

As the sixties began, at the top of the Society's agenda were two items: fund raising in order to turn Tillar House into a useable headquarters for an ambitious new program of activities, and finding the right person to be the Society's first Executive Director.

By November 1960 an Executive Director had been found. He was H.C.L. (Chris) Merillat, a former Rhodes Scholar and Sterling post-graduate Fellow at the Yale Law School, where he had been a student of Myres McDougal. McDougal regarded him as an extraordinarily brilliant man with a strong interest in world affairs.[1]

In 1960, Merillat was finishing a six-year stint with the Ford Foundation. He had just spent two years in India on a Ford program designed to help establish an Indian Law Institute modeled roughly on the American Law Institute.[2] McDougal had visited him in India and was impressed, as he had been during Merillat's time at Yale.[3] McDougal recommended him to Hardy Dillard, chair of the Society's search committee. Merillat welcomed the idea of coming back to Washington, where he had previously held government posts. He liked the look of Tillar House, and he had ideas about the direction the Society should take – largely designed to expand its focus beyond traditional public international law, to include all

---

1 Interview with Myres McDougal, May 18, 1994 (transcript on file with the Society).

2 Letter from H.C.L. Merillat to Frederic L. Kirgis, May 23, 1994.

3 Interview with Myres McDougal, *supra* note 1.

international aspects of law.[4] Moreover, his ties with the Ford Foundation would be useful, to say the least, in enabling the Society to branch out.

At the November 1960 Executive Council meeting, Dillard reported that his committee recommended Merillat's appointment as the Society's first Executive Director. The committee proposed that the Society enter into a three-year contract with Merillat at a stated salary, with the first year's salary guaranteed by Herman Phleger and Arthur Dean. The additional two years were contingent on the raising of funds necessary for the Society to carry out its expanded program. On this basis, the Executive Council formally approved the appointment and Merillat accepted it. He began his duties on November 15, 1960, serving on a half-time basis for the first two and a half months.[5]

Merillat had a high regard for the role of lawyers in international affairs, but he was skeptical about the importance of substantive rules of public international law and formal dispute-settlement mechanisms.[6] His vision for the Society was a far cry from that of Elihu Root and James Brown Scott, but it reflected a realist's view of the mid-century strengths and limitations of international law. Much later, reflecting back on his time as Executive Director, Merillat said that when he began it was probably with a predilection, based on his previous experience, "toward helping to understand the needs of the post-colonial developing world and to open up established institutions to re-examination."[7] The Society's new program quickly reflected that predilection. In an organization long guided by leaders who were predominantly interested in the more traditional contours of public international law, Merillat's success in opening a new vista was a tribute to his set of values and his ability to work effectively with an executive body such as the Council.[8]

With an Executive Director selected, the Society needed a job description. New Regulations were adopted. They provided that the Executive Director would be appointed by the Executive Council to serve at its pleasure. It would be a full-time job, assisting the President and the committees, making recommendations as to

---

4 Interview with H.C.L. Merillat, May 17, 1994 (transcript on file with the Society); letter from H.C.L. Merillat to Frederic L. Kirgis, May 23, 1994.

5 Minutes of the Executive Council, Nov. 19, 1960, in ASIL Minute Book, 1959-1966, at 43, 44.

6 Letter from Richard W. Edwards, Jr. to Frederic L. Kirgis, Oct. 8, 1997.

7 Letter from H.C.L. Merillat to Frederic L. Kirgis, May 23, 1994.

8 Richard W. Edwards, Jr., who served directly under Merillat for almost all of Merillat's tenure with the Society, has said that Merillat "was a marvelous judge of personalities. He had a great sense of how to work with an executive board. He knew how to get things done and move forward when there were log jams." Edwards said that Merillat was the best teacher he ever had. Letter from Richard W. Edwards, Jr. to Frederic L. Kirgis, Oct. 8, 1997.

programs and budget, appointing the staff, attending meetings of the Executive Council and Executive Committee, writing an annual report, and performing other duties as assigned by the Executive Council.[9]

2. Defining the New Program and Beginning to Pay for it

The Consultative Committee on Expanded Program of the Society was charged with charting the new directions the Society would take. In November 1960, the Committee presented several proposals, which it estimated would cost about USD 155,000 in all:[10]

- Increasing the scope of the Journal by including articles on such things as private international law and comparative law; expanding the Judicial Decisions section, which at that time consisted of digests of cases with quotations from the more important opinions, to include comments on particularly significant decisions; publishing digests of current diplomatic correspondence; re-publishing selected articles appearing in foreign journals; and preparing a new cumulative index;
- Resuming the previous practice of distributing free copies of the Journal to foreign libraries, governments and educational institutions;
- Establishing an adequate international law library for the use of scholars and lawyers;[11]
- Carrying on studies and research in international law through Society committees;
- Expanding relations with related groups in other countries;
- Holding public conferences on international political or economic problems;
- Resuscitating the Conferences of Teachers of International Law.

The Society's regular dues structure had remained constant since 1954. In November 1960, the Executive Council raised the dues in all categories.[12] The Executive Council also voted to propose amendments to the Society's Constitution that would give the Council discretion to set dues for life members and for a new category, corporate non-voting members. The 1961 Business Meeting adopted

---

9 ASIL Regulations, as amended to Apr. 27, 1962, in 56 *ASIL Proc.* xv, xxiv-xxv (1962).

10 Minutes of the Executive Council, Nov. 19, 1960, in ASIL Minute Book, 1959-1966, at 43, 44-46.

11 The Library Committee estimated that about 1,500 books would be needed. Id. at 49.

12 For details, see Memorandum, "ASIL History: Details Relating to Budget, Finances and Membership" (2006), on file with the Society.

the amendments.[13] The life membership fee was set at USD 500 and corporate membership dues were pegged at USD 1,000 a year.[14]

More than 180 corporations were invited to become corporate members or annual patrons.[15] Within a few months there were eleven corporate members.[16] In April 1962, the Society's Executive Director pointed out that corporate memberships, annual patrons and contributions other than dues accounted for one-quarter of the annual receipts in the Society's general budget.[17]

The first substantial grant to the Society in its new mode came in 1961 from an offshoot of an old source. The Carnegie Corporation of New York gave the Society USD 40,000 to support its expanded program of activities.[18]

Meanwhile Chris Merillat was spending time not only getting Tillar House and its new staff organized, but also doing some planning to put into effect the new programs contemplated when he was hired.[19] In particular, he had explored possible subjects to be considered by study groups – preferably subjects that might appeal to a funding body like the Ford Foundation, which was heavily into supporting international relations projects that would have some impact on resolving the issues of the day.[20]

With this in mind, Merillat identified three promising fields: problems of foreign investment in developing countries, reflecting the predilection he had brought with him to the Society; outer space issues, reflecting a broader interest he had in science and technology; and disarmament/arms control.[21] In each of these fields, the Society could have an impact.

---

13 55 *ASIL Proc.* 194 (1961).

14 Minutes of the Executive Council, Nov. 19, 1960, in ASIL Minute Book, 1959-1966, at 43, 47-48. Corporate members became entitled to receive five copies of each issue of the Journal and the Proceedings. ASIL Regulations, as amended to Nov. 18, 1961, Section I(11), in ASIL Minute Book, 1959-1966, at 78, 81. The same provision appears in the Regulations as amended to Apr. 27, 1962, Section I(12), in 56 *ASIL Proc.* xv, xviii (1962).

15 Minutes of the Executive Council, Apr. 26, 1962, in ASIL Minute Book, 1959-1966, at 93, 99.

16 They are listed in ASIL Letter to Members No. 4 of 1961, at 3 (hereinafter cited as Letter to Members).

17 Minutes of the Executive Council, Apr. 26, 1962, in ASIL Minute Book, 1959-1966, at 93, 100; remarks at Business Meeting, 56 *ASIL Proc.* 72 (1962).

18 Id. at 54; Letter to Members No. 2 of 1961, at 1.

19 Unpublished Report of the Executive Director, Apr. 27, 1961, in which Merillat noted that in his first few months on the job, at least 75 per cent of his time had been spent on straight administration, and the rest on substantive program and planning.

20 Interview with H.C.L. Merillat, May 17, 1994 (transcript on file with the Society).

21 Minutes of the Executive Council, Apr. 27, 1961, in ASIL Minute Book, 1959-1966, at 51, 56.

Merillat made frequent trips to New York to meet with John Howard and others at the Ford Foundation. Howard was particularly instrumental in making grant money available to the Society in the Merillat years.

Some prominent members thought the Society was moving too far and too fast in new directions. Others, including Hardy Dillard, G.W. Haight, James N. Hyde, Harold Lasswell, Myres McDougal, Stanley Metzger, Stefan Riesenfeld, Eric Stein and Walter Surrey, favored the change of direction and provided support. Hardy Dillard, in particular, became a close and frequently consulted confidant of Merillat, particularly during Dillard's tenure as President of the Society in 1962-63.[22]

With the planned acceleration of activity, the Society would need a mechanism by which program and policy decisions could be made more often than at the semi-annual meetings of the Executive Council. Merillat and others conceived the idea of resuscitating the Executive Committee, which had been banished from the Society's governing structure in 1940. The revived Executive Committee could function with the powers of the Council between meetings, and would in fact become the governing body of the Society.[23] The Executive Council revised the Society's Regulations in April 1961 to re-create the Executive Committee,[24] though not everyone on the Council regarded the it as the *de facto* governing body.

In 1961, the Executive Committee consisted of the President and Treasurer of the Society, *ex officio*, two Honorary Vice Presidents and three members of the Executive Council.[25] By 1965 it consisted of the President, Executive Vice President,[26] Treasurer, and seven other Council members elected by the Council.[27]

During Merillat's time as Executive Director, the governing body gave him a loose rein over devising and carrying out programs. This was how he operated best.[28] He had his trusted confidants within the Society's power structure, but he was uncomfortable with attempts by officers or governing body members to micro-manage.

---

22 Telephone interview with Richard W. Edwards, Jr., Oct. 3, 1997.

23 Id.

24 Minutes of the Executive Council, Apr. 27, 1961, in ASIL Minute Book, 1959-1966, at 51, 57.

25 55 *ASIL Proc.* vii (1961); Letter to Members No. 5 of 1961, at 1.

26 In practice, once the office of Executive Vice President had been created, it was held by the Executive Director. See text at note 84 *infra*.

27 Minutes of the Executive Council, Apr. 22, 1965, in ASIL Minute Book, 1959-1966, at 194, 198.

28 Telephone interview with Richard W. Edwards, Jr., Oct. 3, 1997.

3. Dedicating Tillar House

The Society dedicated Tillar House as its headquarters on April 28, 1961. Mrs. Tillar was there, as was John J. McCloy, who gave the dedicatory address. John F. Kennedy, the President of the United States, sent a message:

> I understand that the American Society of International Law today dedicates its new headquarters in Tillar House to its continued search for law and justice in international relations.
>
> This brings my greetings and best wishes for success in the Society's new endeavors. I know you will effectively contribute to the cause which I urged in my inaugural address – that both great groups of nations create "not a new balance of power, but a new world of law, where the strong are just and the weak secure and peace preserved."[29]

The Society had acquired a permanent residence at last. Its fifty-five years without a home of its own, first as a long-standing tenant at will of the Carnegie Endowment and then as a tenant in the commercial real estate market of Washington, were a thing of the past. It could look forward not only to physical stability, but also to the new programs and directions that its energetic Executive Director had already begun to map out.

4. Starting to Build a Library

The Tillar House library's first books came from the libraries of the late Edgar Turlington and Manley Hudson, as well as from several other sources.[30] The gift from Manley Hudson's estate amounted to nearly 1,000 volumes.[31]

The library opened in October 1961, with Marie S. Klooz as Librarian. Its aim was to build and maintain a working collection in international law, including American and foreign periodicals in the field. It started out also with a small collection of current materials on the legal problems of foreign investment.[32] By early 1962, the library had 1,600 books, 1,800 pamphlets and the current issues of forty-seven legal periodicals from sixteen foreign countries.[33] By 1966,

---

[29] Quoted in 55 *ASIL Proc.* 162 (1961), and in *The American Society of International Law: The Sixtieth Year* (ASIL booklet, 1966).

[30] Minutes of the Executive Council, Apr. 27, 1961, in ASIL Minute Book, 1959-1966, at 51, 55.

[31] Letter to Members No. 3 of 1961, at 2.

[32] Letter to Members No. 5 of 1961, at 2; Letter to Members No. 7 of 1961, at 1.

[33] Letter to Members, Feb. 1962, at 3. The books came not only from the estates of Manley Hudson and Edgar Turlington, but also from the estates of Ivan Kerno and Lester Woolsey. Id.

the collection had grown to about 3,800 books and documents, 2,300 pamphlets and offprints, and 1,100 volumes of periodicals.[34]

5. Keeping Members Informed

One of Chris Merillat's early innovations was the creation of a Letter to Members – the forerunner of the *ASIL Newsletter*. Letter Number 1 appeared in early 1961. Merillat described the purposes of the new project:

> The letters will contain information on current activities in the field of international law and related matters. They will include brief notes on such matters as research under way in universities and other organizations; conferences, meetings, and other activities; appointments to public office or posts in other organizations concerned with international legal affairs; and other activities of groups here and abroad.[35]

The Letter to Members thus was conceived as more than simply a way to inform members of the Society's activities. It was to serve as a clearing-house of information that would be of interest to scholars, practitioners and others working in the international law field.[36]

6. The Breakthrough: A USD 500,000 Ford Foundation Grant

Using funds provided by the Carnegie Corporation grant, in the summer and autumn of 1961, Chris Merillat and the Society's new planning groups developed proposals based on the ideas he had presented to the Executive Council in April.[37] Merillat later observed, "We had to persuade the Ford Foundation in particular that we were branching out into areas of concern that went beyond public international law in the classic sense."[38] Merillat requested the Foundation to make a grant of USD 523,450.[39]

The presentation was spectacularly successful. The Ford Foundation provided a USD 500,000 grant to be used for specific projects and programs over a five-year period: USD 119,000 for studies on Foreign Investment and Economic Development; USD 48,000 for studies and discussion of Legal Aspects of Space Activities;

---

34 *The American Society of International Law: The Sixtieth Year*, 19th unnumbered page (ASIL booklet, 1966).

35 Letter to Members No. 1 of 1961, at 1.

36 From its inception until the summer of 1970, each issue consisted of four typewritten, photocopied pages.

37 Letter to Members No. 8 of 1961, at 2.

38 Interview with H.C.L. Merillat, May 17, 1994 (transcript on file with the Society).

39 ASIL, *A Proposal for Foundation Support of the Society's Expanded Program of Activities* 7 (1961).

USD 120,000 for studies of the International Legal Problems of Federations; USD 56,000 for studies of International Legal and Organizational Problems of Arms Control and Disarmament; USD 52,000 for Strengthening the Teaching of International Law; USD 15,000 to support the Society's Regional and Local Meetings; and USD 90,000 for staff expenses.[40] These amounts were later reallocated somewhat, to increase the amount for staff expenses (to USD 115,000) and to set aside USD 10,000 for a conference of foreign office legal advisers.[41]

The Ford grant enabled the Society to establish advisory groups and steering committees for the projects, pay honoraria for professional consultants, and grant research fellowships to carry out the projects.[42] Particularly important for the Society's daily operation was the ability to charge some of its staff and other expenses to the Carnegie and Ford grants. By 1966-67, USD 52,000 of the Society's budgeted USD 99,900 for personnel expenses was chargeable to Ford Foundation grants.[43] The charge was justified in order "to meet increased overhead reflecting the time expended by Society officers and employees in the discharge of their responsibilities under the Ford Foundation grants."[44]

7. The Burdens of Land Ownership

If the Society was to sustain the momentum provided by Mrs. Tillar's benefaction, the renovation of Tillar House could not wait. Consequently the refurbishing had gone forward even though the Society did not have the cash on hand to pay for it. As we have seen, the Society took out a secured loan of USD 35,000 to finance the work.[45]

In November 1961, the Society had outstanding obligations of almost USD 45,000 for the renovation, including about USD 32,400 owed on the mortgage. About USD 7,700 was owed to contractors. Using some creative financing devices, the Society was able to pay the contractors without having to dip into grant funds or increase the mortgage.[46]

---

40 Minutes of the Executive Council, Nov. 18, 1961, in ASIL Minute Book, 1959-1966, at 69, 70; Letter to Members No. 8 of 1961, at 1-2.

41 Minutes of the Executive Council, Apr. 25, 1963, in ASIL Minute Book, 1959-1966, at 129, 133.

42 Minutes of the Executive Council, Nov. 18, 1961, in ASIL Minute Book, 1959-1966, at 69, 70-71.

43 Minutes of the Executive Council, Apr. 28, 1966, in ASIL Minute Book, 1959-1966, at 227, 230.

44 Id. at 231. By then the Society had received an additional USD 600,000 grant from the Foundation. See text at note 162 *infra*.

45 See Chapter Seven, Section D.3, *supra*.

46 For details, see Memorandum, "ASIL History: Details Relating to Budget, Finances and Membership" (2006), on file with the Society.

There remained the nagging problem of the District of Columbia real estate tax. As Henry Butler had pointed out when Tillar House was acquired, if the Society wanted an exemption from the tax it would have to open its library to the public or conduct teacher-student educational programs, or both. In November 1961, just a month after the Tillar House library had opened, the Executive Council decided that it should be available to non-members.[47] This gesture was only partially successful as a tax avoidance device. The District of Columbia authorities limited the exemption to one-third of the real estate tax burden.[48]

8. Expanding Horizons Beyond "Pure" Public International Law

Until 1960, the Society had been predominantly concerned with classic international law issues – the law of war, the law of the sea, the law of public international institutions. There had been occasional presentations at Annual Meetings and articles in the Journal on issues of international economic law, but they were overshadowed – one could even say overwhelmed – by coverage of public international law in the traditional sense.

Chris Merillat's agenda, as reflected in his planning for the Ford Foundation proposal, stressed expanding the interests and influence of the Society, and reaching out to lawyers engaged in international transactions. In this endeavor he had the powerful support of John Laylin, an influential Executive Council member who practiced law with the prestigious firm of Covington and Burling in Washington. He had other supporters as well.[49]

The new focus on foreign investment and international transactions could not have been more timely. The 1960s were turbulent times for foreign investors. Communist governments had long since expropriated privately owned means of production, and disputes over compensation were rife. Newly established third-world governments joined the expropriation movement and rejected U.S. assertions that international law required prompt, adequate and effective compensation. In 1962, a compromise was reached in the U.N. General Assembly with the adoption of the Resolution on Permanent Sovereignty over Natural Resources, calling for appropriate compensation in accordance with the rules in the expropriating state and with international law.[50] But the near-consensus supporting that compromise collapsed later in the sixties and in the early seventies. The General

---

47 Minutes of the Executive Council, *supra* note 42, at 76.

48 Minutes of the Executive Council, Apr. 25, 1963, in ASIL Minute Book, 1959-1966, at 129, 132; Minutes of the Executive Council, Nov. 9, 1963, in id. at 151, 154.

49 Interview with H.C.L. Merillat, May 17, 1994 (transcript on file with the Society). See Merillat's remarks at the 1962 Business Meeting, in 56 *ASIL Proc.* 72 (1962), and see text at note 22 *supra*.

50 G.A. Res. 1803 (XVII), Dec. 14, 1962, 2 *ILM* 223 (1963).

Assembly's Charter of Economic Rights and Duties of States, adopted in 1974, genuflected toward appropriate compensation for expropriated property, but did not tie it to any duty under international law.[51] The United States and five other capital-exporting nations voted against it. The international law of foreign investment seemed to be in acute need of study and clarification.

Merillat's effort resulted not only in obtaining a substantial portion of the Ford grant for studies relating to foreign investment and economic development; it also accounted at least in part for the library's acquisition from the outset of materials on foreign investment, and it gave impetus to the desire of some Society members, particularly in New York and Washington, to hold meetings on topics of particular interest to practitioners. Thus the Society's 1961 regional meeting in New York City was on economic development and foreign investment.[52] In October 1961, a group met at Tillar House to discuss the international aspects of United States securities laws.[53] In 1962, a regional meeting in Toledo considered legal problems in international trade, and one in Newark was devoted to legal problems of foreign investment and foreign enterprise.[54]

It was not lost on Merillat or on the Committee on Financing and Endowment, headed by John Stevenson, that an emphasis on international business transactions could boost the interest of businesses in becoming corporate members and annual patrons. The Executive Council agreed with Stevenson that it would be appropriate to solicit financial support from foreign corporations as well as domestic ones.[55]

Another keystone in Merillat's edifice, as we have seen, was the law of outer space. It, too, was timely. Before the sixties were out, the U.N. General Assembly had adopted its Declaration of Legal Principles on the Exploration and Use of Outer Space,[56] and the Outer Space Treaty[57] had been concluded. Nevertheless, the Society as an institution did not do very much space exploration. There were some panel discussions on outer space issues at Annual Meetings,[58] but most of the influential institutional work was done or sponsored by such organizations

---

51 G.A. Res. 3281 (XXIX), Dec. 12, 1974, 14 *ILM* 251 (1975).

52 Letter to Members No. 2 of 1961, at 3.

53 Letter to Members No. 8 of 1961, at 2-3.

54 Letter to Members, Apr. 1962, at 2. See also text at note 184 *infra*.

55 Minutes of the Executive Council, Nov. 18, 1961, in ASIL Minute Book, 1959-1966, at 69, 76.

56 G.A. Res. 1962 (XVIII), Dec. 13, 1963, 3 *ILM* 157 (1964).

57 Treaty on Principles Governing the Activities of States in the Exploration and Use of Outer Space, Including the Moon and Other Celestial Bodies, Jan. 27, 1967, 18 U.S.T. 2410, 610 U.N.T.S. 205, 6 *ILM* 386 (1967).

58 See Panel on Current Developments in Air Space and Outer Space, 55 *ASIL Proc.* 165 (1961); Panel on The Status of Competing Claims to Outer Space, 57 id. 173 (1963);

as the American Bar Foundation,[59] the International Institute of Space Law,[60] and the Institute of Air and Space Law.[61]

9. The Birth of International Legal Materials

In April 1961, Leo Gross suggested to the Executive Council that a committee be appointed to explore the possibility of establishing an international law looseleaf service on the model of the Commerce Clearing House services in such other fields as taxes.[62] The President of the Society, Arthur Dean, appointed Myres McDougal to chair an *ad hoc* Committee on a Current Reporting Service.

Initially, there was debate over the form such a service might take. Richard Baxter expounded the view that it should consist primarily of commentary and indexing.[63] Ultimately, though, the Committee recommended that the Council authorize preparation of three experimental numbers of a collection of source materials important to international legal affairs, in mimeographed volumes of one to two hundred pages each. To gather the materials, the Society should seek out qualified persons in the Washington area, along with a small number of reporters who would serve part time and without remuneration. Space should be provided in Tillar House for the preparatory and secretarial work.

Despite concerns about the cost of such a venture, the Executive Committee approved the idea on an experimental basis.[64] The first issue of *International Legal Materials*, in mimeographed form, appeared in August 1962. The Society's Letter to Members explained the venture:

> In August 1962 the Society will make available the first experimental compilation of current official documents, designed to meet the needs for up-to-date information of scholars, practicing lawyers, legal advisers to government agencies and corporations, government officials, and others concerned with the legal aspects of public and private international

---

Panel on International Co-operation in Satellite Communications Systems, 61 *ASIL Proc.* 24 (1967).

59 See Leon Lipson & Nicholas deB. Katzenbach, *The Law of Outer Space* (1961); S. Houston Lay & Howard J. Taubenfeld, *The Law Relating to Activities of Man in Space* (1970).

60 See the annual *Proceedings of the International Institute of Space Law*, which began in the late 1950s.

61 The Institute of Air and Space Law at McGill University grew out of the Institute of International Air Law after the first Sputnik launch in 1957. It began publishing the *Annals of Air & Space Law* in 1976.

62 Minutes of the Executive Council, Apr. 29, 1961, in ASIL Minute Book, 1959-1966, at 65, 67.

63 Letter from Richard W. Edwards, Jr. to Frederic L. Kirgis, Oct. 8, 1997.

64 Minutes of the Executive Council, Nov. 18, 1961, in ASIL Minute Book, 1959-1966, at 69, 74-75.

> dealings. There is, of course, a vast amount of material to choose from – recent U.S. and foreign legislation, administrative regulations and rulings, reports of national and international agencies, national and international court decisions, treaties and agreements, and other documentary source materials. We have attempted to select a number of documents, likely to be of interest to a broad group of members, that are not readily available elsewhere or will not become available in more permanent collections until a later date.[65]

Throughout I.L.M.'s formative years, a great deal of the work was done by Richard W. Edwards, Jr., who was hired as a recent graduate of the Cornell Law School, first as a Program Assistant and soon thereafter as Assistant Editor. The original editorial advisory group – advising on selection of materials and other editorial matters – consisted of Stanley D. Metzger, Arthur S. Miller and Walter S. Surrey. They were handpicked not only because they were within convenient consulting range in the District of Columbia, but more importantly because they would be sympathetic to a broad scope of coverage.[66]

From the outset, the cost of I.L.M. was not included in members' dues, nor was it conceived as a service exclusively for members. In December 1962, after the Executive Council had decided to move beyond the experimental phase, an annual subscription price was set.[67] I.L.M. was institutionalized in the Society's Regulations in November 1965.[68] Myres McDougal, who had seen the need for a published source of current international documents, could look with pride at I.L.M.'s quick success.[69]

I.L.M. was designed to be much more than a mere continuation in a new form of the Journal's Official Documents section or of the old Supplements to

---

65 Letter to Members, July 1962, at 1.

66 Letter from Richard W. Edwards, Jr. to Frederic L. Kirgis, Oct. 8, 1997. See the Forewords to 1 *ILM* Nos. 1 & 2 (1962).

67 Minutes of the Executive Committee, Dec. 1, 1962, in ASIL Minute Book, 1959-1966, at 136A; Letter to Members, Nov.–Dec. 1962, at 1.

68 Minutes of the Executive Council, November 13, 1965, in ASIL Minute Book, 1959-1966, at 203, 211.

69 Monroe Leigh recalled that McDougal pushed for the establishment of I.L.M., in order to make current materials available to people who needed them quickly. Interview with Monroe Leigh, Oct. 26, 1995 (transcript on file with the Society). McDougal credited his Yale colleague, J.W. Moore, with the original idea for a service like the one McDougal's committee recommended. Interview with Myres S. McDougal, May 18, 1994 (transcript on file with the Society). Richard Edwards, who bore most of the day-to-day responsibility for I.L.M. in the early years, remembers that F.W. Haight and James N. Hyde were the ones who gave him the most encouragement. Letter from Richard W. Edwards, Jr. to Frederic L. Kirgis, Oct. 8, 1997.

the Journal. Reflecting Chris Merillat's predilections, I.L.M. was tailored not only for an audience interested in public international law, but also for practitioners and others whose interests would be on the private or commercial side. "The term international law," said the Statement of Editorial Policy, "is interpreted broadly for the purposes of this publication."[70]

10. Richard Baxter and Student International Law Groups

Richard Baxter could be thought of as the Society's missionary for international law during the sixties. He had a zeal for spreading the word, and apparently had the active support of his Dean at the Harvard Law School.[71] One of Baxter's campaigns was to get students actively involved in the Society, and thus in international law.

Baxter chaired – one could say willed into existence – the Society's Committee on Student International Law Clubs. In April 1961, the Committee presented a report to the Executive Council noting the growing student interest in such clubs and suggesting that a place be found in future Annual Meetings for a program of particular interest to students, such as an inter-school moot court competition. The report concluded:

> Over the years ahead, the degree of interest and attention which the Society devotes to its younger members will have a significant impact on the strength and size of the Society. To the extent that students and young members are drawn into the work of the Society and are given a sense of being an important part of the organization, they will remain active in the affairs of the Society as they grow older. At the same time, the Society can help to discharge its obligation to stimulate interest in international law by the aid and encouragement it gives to those who are just entering this field.[72]

During the 1961 Annual Meeting, Baxter and the rest of the Committee met with representatives of the four clubs then in existence – those at Columbia, Harvard, Virginia and Yale. They discussed future activities and the formation of new clubs. Meanwhile, the clubs at Columbia, Harvard and Yale participated in the first international law moot court competition, held at Columbia. They argued a case involving injury to a foreign corporation. The panel consisted of

---

[70] 2 *ILM* No. 1, Statement of Editorial Policy (1963).

[71] Interview with Monroe Leigh, Oct. 26, 1995 (transcript on file with the Society).

[72] Report of the Committee on Student International Law Clubs, Apr. 21, 1961, at 2 (in file: Student Societies (Supplementary) from Prof. Baxter's files, 1958-1964) (hereinafter referred to as Baxter files).

three distinguished Society members: Oscar Schachter, Edward D. Re and James N. Hyde.[73]

The second competition was held in conjunction with the Society's 1962 Annual Meeting, as Baxter's Committee had suggested. It was no coincidence that Baxter chaired the Annual Meeting Committee for that year.

Student teams from Osgoode Hall, Duke and Columbia argued for Belgium, the United Arab Republic and the United States, respectively, before a bench consisting of Green H. Hackworth, John G. Laylin and Maxwell Cohen at the Statler Hilton Hotel in Washington. The arguments dealt with the request for an I.C.J. Advisory Opinion, then actually pending before the Court, on whether the expenditures authorized for U.N. peacekeeping operations in the Congo and the Middle East were "expenses of the organization." The moot court panel, of course, did not decide that question. But in the best tradition of moot court judges, the panel gave each team something to take home. Osgoode Hall received the best oralist award, Duke got the award for best responses to questions from the bench, and Columbia was given the best memorial award.[74]

By mid-1962, momentum was building toward a formal relationship between the Society and the growing number of student international law clubs. The matter was raised at the November 1962 Executive Council meeting, but the minutes reflect simply that the Society was trying to assist the clubs when requested to do so.[75] Apparently, the time was not yet ripe for an institutional structure that could facilitate a continuing relationship between the student group and the Society.

11. Establishing Contacts with Other Organizations

In 1962, the Asia Foundation made a grant of USD 2,500 to the Society for two purposes: subsidies for new memberships in the Society or new subscriptions to the Journal for Asian officials, educators and institutions; and a few individual travel grants to officials and scholars from Asia who were in the United States, to enable them to participate in various meetings of the Society. The grant applied to eighteen Asian countries, not including Communist China.[76] The Foundation made another USD 2,500 grant in 1963 for the same purposes.[77]

In the early 1960s, the Society explored possible forms of collaboration with the American Branch of the International Law Association. In April 1963, the

73 Letter to Members No. 3 of 1961, at 3-4.

74 56 *ASIL Proc.* 158-59 (1962).

75 Minutes of the Executive Council, Nov. 10, 1962, in ASIL Minute Book, 1959-1966, at 118, 128.

76 Letter to Members, Aug. 1962, at 3.

77 Letter to Members, July–Aug. 1963, at 1-2.

Society's Executive Council voted to try to establish a permanent joint coordinating committee of the two organizations.[78] Rather than creating a single joint committee, the Society and the American Branch of the International Law Association created standing committees to arrange specific forms of cooperation between them. Although they considered having a single Annual Meeting in Washington in 1964,[79] they simply held a single joint session during the Society's Annual Meeting.[80]

12. Amending the Constitution and Adopting New Organizational Practices

In 1962, the Business Meeting adopted several amendments to the Society's Constitution, in part to conform it to existing practice. In light of the Society's expanding activities, some of which required oversight by groups of members, the most important of the amendments was a grant of formal authority to the President to appoint committees.[81]

In December 1962, the Executive Committee discussed the need for more continuity in the direction and management of the Society. It designated Chris Merillat and the Society's Treasurer, Monroe Leigh, as a subcommittee to prepare a statement of possible structural changes to accomplish the goal.[82]

Their proposals led to further amendments to the Constitution and to a resolution on the organization of the Society, both adopted at the 1963 Business Meeting. The first constitutional amendment increased the number of Vice Presidents from the previous three to four, with authority given to the Executive Council to elect one of the Vice Presidents to the newly created office of Executive Vice President – the full-time chief executive officer of the Society.[83] The purpose was to enable the Executive Director to be the Executive Vice President.[84] As soon as the constitutional amendment had been adopted, Merillat was nominated from

---

78 Minutes of the Executive Council, Apr. 27, 1963, in ASIL Minute Book, 1959-1966, at 147, 149.

79 Letter to Members, June 1963, at 1.

80 58 *ASIL Proc.* 33 (1964).

81 The more significant amendments allowed nominations for office to be made not only by the Nominating Committee, but also by a motion signed by not fewer than ten members of the Society; allowed the Executive Council to fill any vacancies in office until the next Annual Meeting; authorized the President to appoint committees except as the Executive Council otherwise determined; and changed the quorum requirement for Business Meetings to fifty (from twenty-five). 56 *ASIL Proc.* 72-73 (1962).

82 Minutes of the Executive Committee, Dec. 1, 1962, in ASIL Minute Book, 1959-1966, at 136A, 136B.

83 See Letter to Members, Apr. 1963, at 2.

84 57 *ASIL Proc.* 263-64 (1963).

the floor and elected to the fourth vice presidential slot.[85] The Executive Council then named him Executive Vice President.[86]

The Business Meeting also accommodated the Executive Committee's desire for some continuity in the Executive Council. It amended Article VI of the Constitution to allow elected members of the Council to serve two consecutive three-year terms, instead of only one term, before having to sit out at least a year.[87]

The Business Meeting then adopted a resolution on the organization of the Society. It set a policy of re-electing at least half of the elected Executive Council members, so they could serve for six consecutive years. The resolution also advocated re-election of a President for two or three terms, as the Constitution permitted, as another element of continuity. (In 1964, the Society began the practice of re-electing a President to a second one-year term.) Finally, the resolution called for the creation of a Board of Permanent Operations to formulate long-term plans and to keep in touch with major donors.[88]

13. The Board of Review and Development Emerges

In September 1963, the Board of Permanent Operations met with the Executive Committee to consider the future program of the Society. Foremost on the agenda was the formalization of the Society's study programs. The Society should have a mechanism to review the international legal process and to clarify thought in selected problem areas. To do this, "A continuing general committee would take under review the whole field of international legal affairs, assisted by a research director. The group might meet two or three weekends through the year and for [at] least a full week once a year."[89] The group was not then given a name.

The meeting identified four problem areas ripe for attention: law and economics, by which was meant primarily the legal aspects of international business; law and science, including outer space issues, weather control and uses of nuclear energy; control of force and peacekeeping, including but not limited to United Nations peacekeeping; and international organizations, including legal

---

85 Id. at 266.

86 Minutes of the Executive Council, Apr. 27, 1963, in ASIL Minute Book, 1959-1966, at 147, 148.

87 57 *ASIL Proc.* 264 (1963).

88 Resolution on the Organization of the Society, in id. at 264-65. The Executive Council amended the Regulations to authorize the establishment of a Board of Permanent Operations. Minutes of the Executive Council, Apr. 27, 1963, in ASIL Minute Book, 1959-1966, at 147, 148. The Board consisted of the President, the two immediate past Presidents, the Executive Vice President, and two other members appointed by the President.

89 Minutes of the Meeting of Executive Committee and Board of Permanent Operations, Sept. 7, 1963, in ASIL Minute Book, 1959-1966, at 156, 157.

problems of integration in what was then the European Common Market, as well as problems of more conventional organizations like the U.N.[90]

The Executive Council created the Board of Review and Development in November 1964. The groundwork had already been done to raise the funds it would need. Chris Merillat, working with his friend John Howard of the Ford Foundation, quickly obtained a grant from Ford for the new B.R.D.

The B.R.D. replaced the Board of Permanent Operations. Its mandate was to review current transnational developments, identify problems that required further study, organize the studies through committees or individual research, recommend the allocation of funds for these projects from grants or other sources, and recommend publication of the work products. *Ex officio* B.R.D. members would be the President of the Society, the two immediate past Presidents, the Executive Director and the Editor-in-Chief of the Journal. The fifteen other members, serving staggered five-year terms, would be selected by the B.R.D. itself. The Regulation mandated that at least three members be persons known for their contributions to disciplines other than law.[91]

The B.R.D. held its first meeting in March 1965. The discussion centered on the question: "On what kinds of problems ... can the legal specialist (and more especially the *international lawyer*) make a distinctive and valuable contribution?"[92] It was the question that would animate Chris Merillat's tenure as Executive Director of the Society.[93]

At the outset the B.R.D. had only fourteen members, all of them leaders in the international law field and all of them established or rising powers within the Society.[94] By November 1965 it had added five more members, including a couple who were not fixtures in the Society.[95]

---

90 Id. at 157-58.

91 Minutes of the Executive Council, Nov. 14, 1964, in ASIL Minute Book, 1959-1966, at 182, 188-89.

92 H.C.L. Merillat, Notes and Comments: "Board of Review and Development: A New Activity of the Society," 59 *AJIL* 574 (1965) (hereafter cited as Merillat, "A New Activity of the Society") (emphasis in the original).

93 Letter from Richard W. Edwards, Jr. to Frederic L. Kirgis, Oct. 8, 1997.

94 Including the *ex officio* members, they were Richard Baxter, William Bishop, Hardy Dillard, Richard Falk, Wolfgang Friedmann, John Hazard, James Hyde, Brunson MacChesney, Myres McDougal, H.C.L. Merillat, Stanley Metzger, Oscar Schachter, Carl Spaeth and John Stevenson. Minutes of the Executive Council, Apr. 22, 1965, in ASIL Minute Book, 1959-1966, at 194-95.

95 Those added since March were Kenneth Boulding, Joseph Goldsen, Harold Lasswell, Stefan Riesenfeld and Eric Stein. Minutes of the Executive Council, Nov. 13, 1965, in ASIL Minute Book, 1959-1966, at 203, 205.

The B.R.D. was conceived as a new and exciting venture. "Phrases like 'creative ferment' and 'the clash of creative minds' [recurred] in the planning papers."[96] In the words of Chris Merillat, the B.R.D. was to "consider, on a continuing basis, developments and research in the whole international sector of law, to identify existing and 'horizon' problem areas needing further intensive study, to stimulate work on these problems, and in some instances, where funds and other resources permit, to follow up with study groups within the Society."[97]

At the core of the planning was the proposition that the Board would be a genuinely interdisciplinary enterprise. Merillat later put it this way:

> Certainly one central aim at the outset was to draw on the talents of well-qualified people concerned with emerging problems of world order, without regard to disciplinary labels. International lawyers, appropriately enough, would form the core of the group and predominate in numbers, but in the selection of members a major consideration was to find individual international lawyers who were most alert and responsive to the contributions that could be made by those working in world affairs outside the specialized discipline of public international law.[98]

It was an ambitious undertaking. In Merillat's vision, the B.R.D. "should take a continuing overview of the whole international sector of law, while more specialized groups will take up particular problem areas. As these processes continue over a period of years there will be, it is hoped and expected, a cumulative appraisal of the role of law in the developing historical context, with fresh looks at old problems and intelligent anticipation of new ones."[99]

The B.R.D., in other words, was to be just what one might expect of a project that reflected the ideas of Myres McDougal and Harold Lasswell. Left behind were the days when codification of existing international law was regarded as the overarching goal to be achieved by international lawyers and scholars. These were the days of policy-oriented, interdisciplinary research.

The B.R.D.'s first substantive meetings focused on law and developing countries, law and war-peace problems, the law of international trade, and the law of treaties.[100] Rapporteurs were appointed for three of these topics: Richard Falk for war-peace problems, Stanley Metzger for international trade, and Egon Schwelb

---

[96] H.C.L. Merillat, "Review of the Work of the Board of Review and Development," May 28, 1969, at 4 (unpublished memorandum) (hereafter cited as Merillat, Review of the BRD).

[97] Merillat, "A New Activity of the Society," *supra* note 92, at 574.

[98] Merillat, "Review of the BRD," *supra* note 96.

[99] Merillat, "A New Activity of the Society," *supra* note 92, at 574-75.

[100] Minutes of the Executive Council, Nov. 13, 1965, in ASIL Minute Book, 1959-1966, at 203, 206.

for the law of treaties.[101] The fourth topic – law and developing countries – was the subject of a small, two-day conference sponsored by the B.R.D. in July 1965. It brought together a handpicked group of officials, professors and lawyers to discuss the roles of law and legal training in development.[102] Eventually, study panels were set up for all four topics.[103]

14. Interest Groups, a Mere Gleam in the Eye

In February 1966, Kenneth Carlston wrote to Brunson MacChesney, the President of the Society, suggesting that the Society's membership be organized into sections. There might be sections on public international law, foreign law, international economic law, international organizations, and so forth. MacChesney presented the idea to the Executive Committee, which rejected it.[104]

Carlston's idea may not have been fully enough developed; in any event, it was put forward before its time had come. Nevertheless, he was on to something that later would become a basis for establishing the Society's Interest Groups.

B. THE NEW PROGRAM IN OPERATION

1. Awarding Research Fellowships

In order to carry out the research projects the Ford Foundation had funded, the Society created research fellowships. The first to be announced were on legal aspects of space activities and on international problems of federalism. The stipends were modest, ranging from USD 2,500 to USD 10,000, designed to supplement funds from the applicants' own institutions.[105]

The Society then announced the availability of not more than five research fellowships on foreign investment and economic development. These were to be used for studies of the legal setting for foreign capital in Brazil, Colombia, India, Mexico and Nigeria, and were designed for more mature scholars than were the earlier fellowships. Each recipient was expected to put in six months to a year of full-time research.[106] As Chris Merillat put it, the studies would "help meet

---

101 Letter to Members, Dec. 1965, at 3.

102 H.C.L. Merillat, Notes and Comments: "Law and Developing Countries," 60 *AJIL* 71 (1966).

103 Report by Richard W. Edwards, Jr., Assistant to the Executive Director, 60 *ASIL Proc.* 172 (1966).

104 Minutes of the Executive Committee, Apr. 1, 1966, in ASIL Minute Book, 1959-1966, at 223, 224.

105 Letters to Members, Jan. & Feb. 1962, at 1.

106 Letter to Members, Mar. 1962, at 2.

a need for greater understanding of the legal factors that impede or facilitate foreign private investment in individual countries and of the problems facing capital-exporting and capital-importing countries in the transfer of private capital, technology, and management skills to developing countries."[107]

It was hardly an open competition for the fellowships. The Advisory Groups (for the outer space and federalism projects) and the Steering Committee (for the foreign investment project) were authorized to recommend – apparently to the Executive Committee – qualified individuals to be invited to undertake the studies.[108]

Most of the fellowships were awarded in 1962. Under the flagship foreign investment and economic development project, four were granted for book-length studies: to Dan Fenno Henderson, of the University of Washington, for a country study of Japan (not one of the countries previously designated); to Matthew J. Kust, of Washington, D.C., for India; to Paul O. Proehl, of UCLA, for Nigeria; and to Seymour W. Wurfel, of the University of North Carolina, for Colombia.[109] A fifth major foreign investment fellowship was awarded in 1963, to Harry K. Wright, of the University of Texas, for a study of Mexico.[110] Four fellowships were awarded in 1962 for studies of the legal aspects of outer space, and ten were awarded under the program on problems of federalism.[111]

2. Carrying out the Study Programs

Early on, the Society co-sponsored a two-day seminar organized by the New York University School of Law on the international problems of federations. Attended by eight American legal scholars and sixteen representatives of African and Asian states, it was designed primarily to acquaint persons having legal responsibility in African states with the experience of the United States and Canada in solving legal problems of federalism.[112]

That seminar was followed in October 1962 with a two-day conference at Tillar House attended by eighteen scholars in law, economics and political science, on the quasi-federal problems of economic integration. The conference drew on

---

[107] H.C.L. Merillat, "Annual Report of the Executive Director for 1963-64," in 58 *AJIL* 987 (1964).

[108] Minutes of the Executive Council, Apr. 26, 1962, in ASIL Minute Book, 1959-1966, at 93, 96.

[109] Letter to Members, May–June 1962, at 2; Letter to Members, Oct. 1962, at 2-3.

[110] Letter to Members, May 1963, at 2.

[111] Letter to Members, May–June 1962, at 2-4. Another federalism fellowship was awarded in 1963, to Albert H. Garretson, to study the agreements between the European Community and the associated African states. Letter to Members, July–Aug. 1963, at 2.

[112] Letter to Members, Oct. 1962, at 2.

the experience of the United States, the European Economic Community, Latin America and parts of Africa.[113]

Meanwhile, the research projects were going forward. The advisory groups and steering committees, which included social scientists as well as legal specialists, provided assistance to the research fellows.[114]

The research fellowships began to bear fruit in 1964, with the publication of the first book-length study, on foreign enterprise in India, accompanied by shorter studies on the Socialist Commonwealth of Nations, East African unity, and federations in the Middle East.[115] Publication of other studies from this first round of fellowships followed in due course, with those on foreign enterprise being particularly prominent.[116]

By November 1966, twelve study panels had been established. Chairs and rapporteurs or researchers had been designated, initial panel meetings had been held or were scheduled for the near future, and financing had been arranged.[117]

In forming the study panels, Chris Merillat and Richard Edwards, in consultation with the Presidents of the Society during these years, made an effort to identify promising young persons and include them.[118] It was an antidote to the tendency of the Journal's Board of Editors to re-elect its own members and to the increasing age of Executive Council members.

---

113 Letter to Members, Nov.–Dec. 1962, at 2-3.

114 Minutes of the Executive Council, Nov. 9, 1963, in ASIL Minute Book, 1959-1966, at 151, 153.

115 Matthew J. Kust, *Foreign Enterprise in India: Laws and Policies* (1964); Kazimierz Grzybowski, *The Socialist Commonwealth of Nations: Organizations and Institutions* (1964); Thomas M. Franck, *East African Unity Through Law* (1964); Jasper Y. Brinton, *Federations in the Middle East* (1964); Jasper Y. Brinton, *Aden and the Federation of South Arabia* (1964).

116 The other major studies on foreign enterprise were Seymour W. Wurfel, *Foreign Enterprise in Colombia* (1965); Paul O. Proehl, *Foreign Enterprise in Nigeria: Laws and Policies* (1965); Harry K. Wright, *Foreign Enterprise in Mexico: Laws and Policies* (1971); Dan Fenno Henderson, *Foreign Enterprise in Japan: Laws and Policies* (1973).

117 The panels were: The International Law Commission's Draft on the Law of Treaties; Developing Countries – Legal Training; Trade Regulation; Role of International Law in Government Decision-Making in War-Peace Crises; Relationship of Law and Force in Contemporary International Systems; Role of International Law in Civil Wars; Securities Regulation and Capital Formation; Communications and Linguistics; Nuclear Development; Peaceful Settlement of International Disputes; Developing Countries – Investment Practice; and Regional Integration. Minutes of the Executive Council, Nov. 12, 1966, in ASIL Minute Book, 1959-1966, at 249, 253-54.

118 Letter from Richard W. Edwards, Jr. to Frederic L. Kirgis, Oct. 8, 1997.

3. Conferences of Legal Advisers

The Society was able to use some of the Ford Foundation grant to organize an informal conference on the role of legal advisers in foreign affairs, held at Princeton in September 1963. There were twenty-four participants from twelve countries and two international organizations. Three broad topics were discussed: how offices of legal advisers were organized and staffed; the kinds of problems with which they were concerned; and career matters. No record of the proceedings was published, but the Society did produce a summary report that was included in a book on the conference published by Oceana.[119] Sir Gerald Fitzmaurice, reviewing the book, hailed it as "a serious, extremely interesting, and ... comprehensive and successful attempt to give the subject the consideration it deserves."[120]

A second conference, this time involving legal advisers from eleven international organizations and scholars from six countries, was held in August 1965 at the Rockefeller Foundation's Villa Serbelloni, in Bellagio, Italy. The Ford grant provided travel funds for some of the participants. The discussions focused on legal problems common to international organizations, including their place in the international legal order, their modes of operation and the roles of their legal offices. Equally important, if not more so, was the opportunity the conference gave the legal advisers of the various organizations – particularly the advisers of regional organizations who would not otherwise interact with each other – to exchange views and get to know one another. Participants included lawyers from such regional organizations as the Inter-American Development Bank, the Organization of American States, the European Communities and the Council of Europe. The Society again produced a summary report, which was published with background papers.[121]

In 1967, after Stephen M. Schwebel had succeeded Merillat as Executive Director, the Society organized a third conference of legal advisers, held again in Bellagio. This one concentrated on the effectiveness of decisions of international organizations in member states. The participants, in addition to a few prominent scholars, were legal advisers to several international organizations. John R. Stevenson, then the President of the Society, chaired the conference. The papers and proceedings were published in a much more comprehensive volume than had

---

[119] H.C.L. Merillat, *Legal Advisers and Foreign Affairs* (1964). The book also contains the background papers prepared for the conference.

[120] Sir Gerald Fitzmaurice, Review Article: "Legal Advisers and Foreign Affairs," 59 *AJIL* 72, 75 (1965).

[121] H.C.L. Merillat, *Legal Advisers and International Organizations* (1966), reviewed by Sir Gerald Fitzmaurice in 62 *AJIL* 114 (1968).

appeared after either of the first two conferences.[122] Many years later, it still served as an indispensable guide to the legal work of international organizations.

A fourth, more specialized, conference was held in 1968. It brought together legal advisers of national and international development lending and assistance agencies. Like the third conference, it generated a book of papers and proceedings.[123]

A fifth conference, in 1971, explored legal and institutional responses to global environmental problems. With the Carnegie Endowment as co-sponsor, it was held at Arden House in New York state. The National Science Foundation and the Council on Environmental Quality supplied additional funding.[124] The papers and an analysis of the proceedings were published.[125]

Years later, Chris Merillat looked back on these conferences as comprising a unique and successful initiative by the Society to develop understanding about how legal advisers in national and international agencies concerned with international affairs carry out their responsibilities.[126]

4. I.L.M. Quickly Comes of Age

The response to *International Legal Materials* was so enthusiastic that the Executive Council decided in November 1962 to continue it with six issues a year beginning in January 1963.[127] Chris Merillat served as its Editor. The press of his other duties as Executive Director, though, dictated the need for an assistant. Richard W. Edwards, Jr., became the Assistant Editor with the first issue of volume 2, in January 1963.

I.L.M. reflected Merillat's vision for the Society. As described in a booklet celebrating the Society's sixtieth year in 1966, "The larger part of the documents made available in the Society's new periodical publication *International Legal Materials* consists of the texts of documents bearing upon international economic activity – national investment codes, treaties of commerce and establishment, settlements of investment disputes, changes in the international organizations

122 Stephen M. Schwebel (ed.), *The Effectiveness of International Decisions* (1971).

123 Seymour J. Rubin (ed.), *Foreign Development Lending – Legal Aspects* (1971).

124 ASIL Newsletter, Aug./Sept. 1971, at 2.

125 Law, Institutions, and the Global Environment: Papers and Analysis of the Proceedings of the Conference on Legal and Institutional Responses to Problems of the Global Environment (1972).

126 Letter from H.C.L. Merillat to Frederic L. Kirgis, May 24, 2001.

127 Minutes of the Executive Council, Nov. 10, 1962, in ASIL Minute Book, 1959-1966, at 118, 125.

regulating trade, developments in the European Economic Community, and the like."[128]

During the 1960s, I.L.M. paid particular attention to the *Sabbatino* case, a *cause celebre* that wound its way through the federal courts. The question was whether an American court should sit in judgment on the validity of an expropriation by a foreign sovereign (the Castro government of Cuba), done in its own territory, when the expropriation allegedly violated international law. The first document published in Volume I, Number 1 was the Second Circuit's opinion in *Sabbatino*.[129] Volume II carried the U.S. government's *amicus* brief before the Supreme Court along with the parties' briefs.[130] The government's *amicus* brief called for diplomacy, not "sporadic American judicial decisions" to deal with foreign acts of state that violate international law.[131] The Supreme Court agreed.[132] Much later, the Executive Branch would change its tune on the act of state doctrine, expressing greater tolerance for the judiciary to use international law standards in cases involving acts of foreign governments within their own territories.

5. The Association of Student International Law Societies Takes Hold

In April 1962, during the Society's Annual Meeting, students from Columbia, Duke, Harvard, the University of North Carolina, the University of Virginia and Yale met to discuss student activities in the international law field. High on the agenda was an initiative to turn the international law moot court competition, then in its second year, into a continuing, annual event. There was a consensus that preliminary rounds should be held, followed by a final competition at the Society's Annual Meeting.

The student meeting adopted an organizational structure for the Association of Student International Law Societies (A.S.I.L.S.). The charter members were Columbia, Duke, Harvard, Virginia and Yale. There would be an Executive Committee consisting for the time being of one or two representatives from each school, with each school having one vote. Gabriel Wilner, then the President of

---

128 *The American Society of International Law: The Sixtieth Year* (ASIL booklet, 1966).

129 *Banco Nacional de Cuba v. Sabbatino*, 307 F.2d 845 (2d Cir. 1962), 1 *ILM* 1 (1962).

130 2 *ILM* 1009 (U.S. brief) & 1142 (parties' briefs).

131 2 *ILM* at 1018 (1963).

132 *Banco Nacional de Cuba v. Sabbatino*, 376 U.S. 398 (1964), 3 *ILM* 381 (1964), reversed on its facts by act of Congress, 22 U.S.C. § 2370(e)(2).

the Columbia International Law Society and later a law professor at the University of Georgia, was elected chair of the Executive Committee for 1962-63.[133]

The formation of A.S.I.L.S. caused Richard Baxter some anxiety. He wrote to Chris Merillat to express his concern that the student program could move away from the Society. He thought the Society should propose to A.S.I.L.S. that it affiliate with the Society.[134] Merillat's response was non-committal. Baxter persisted. He said that the student groups needed guidance, and the Society needed them lest their members graduate into the A.B.A. Section of International and Comparative Law or the American Branch of the International Law Association. He suggested that the Society hold a meeting with the A.S.I.L.S. Executive Committee in Tillar House, conduct the moot court competition again in connection with the Society's Annual Meeting, and offer to draw up facts and rules for the competition.[135] Merillat saw no problem with the first two suggestions, but he wondered who would have time to draw up facts and rules for the moot court competition.[136]

As it turned out, the Society undertook not only to designate the person (Covey Oliver) who would draft the problem for the 1963 competition, but also to provide facilities for the finals and to organize the panel of judges.[137] Essentially the same arrangement was maintained in the following year.[138]

In 1963, A.S.I.L.S. decided to honor Philip C. Jessup by naming the competition after him. As had been contemplated, the final round was held in conjunction with the Society's Annual Meeting – a practice that became a tradition. The United States had been divided into a southern and a northern region, with the winners of each region (the University of North Carolina and Columbia) pitted against each other in the national finals. Columbia was declared the winner.[139]

A.S.I.L.S. had become a functioning organization. In April 1963, it elected Ved Nanda, then a graduate student at the Yale Law School and soon to become a member of the University of Denver law faculty, as its chair. Seven international law societies were members, representing Columbia, Duke, Harvard, N.Y.U. (a new member in 1963), the University of Pennsylvania, the University of Virginia and

---

133 Minutes of the Organizational Meeting of the Association of Student International Law Societies, Apr. 27-28, 1962, in Baxter files, *supra* note 72.

134 Letter from Richard R. Baxter to H.C.L. Merillat, June 12, 1962, in Baxter files, *supra* note 72.

135 Letter from Baxter to Merillat, July 20, 1962, in Baxter files, *supra* note 72.

136 Letter from Merillat to Baxter, July 24, 1962, in Baxter files, *supra* note 72.

137 Memorandum of Conversation between H.C.L. Merillat and Stephen E. Doyle, Sept. 11, 1962, in Baxter files, *supra* note 72.

138 Letter from James C. Hickey, Assistant Secretary of ASILS, to Richard R. Baxter, Nov. 9, 1963, and reply from Baxter, Nov. 18, 1963, in Baxter files, *supra* note 72.

139 57 *ASIL Proc.* 268 (1963); Letter to Members, May 1963, at 1.

Yale.[140] They were joined later in 1963 by the student societies at Georgetown, Michigan and Texas.[141] Membership grew steadily from that point on.

Georgetown's application for membership in A.S.I.L.S. engendered a mini-incident that helps to explain why the Society sought to exercise some form of supervision over the student organization. When the Assistant Dean at Georgetown inquired about membership in A.S.I.L.S. for its student society, the Secretary of A.S.I.L.S. wrote back to say that a formal application would be necessary; it should contain information on (*inter alia*) the size and background of the Georgetown student body, the library, faculty, student program, and the accreditation of the Georgetown University Law Center.[142] He sent a copy of his letter to Richard Baxter, who was incredulous. Baxter thought it "altogether superfluous to ask whether Georgetown Law School is accredited" and he regarded questions about the student body, the library and the student program as out of place.[143] A.S.I.L.S. simplified its application form.[144]

In February 1964, the Society and A.S.I.L.S. co-sponsored a regional meeting of the Society at Duke University. The meeting dealt with the Soviet impact on international law.[145] A summary of the proceedings was produced by the State Department and sent to interested teachers in political science departments and law schools.[146] The papers were published in Duke's faculty-edited journal, *Law and Contemporary Problems*.[147]

Fifteen law schools competed in the Jessup Competition in 1964. Regional competitions were held in New York City, Ann Arbor, Austin and the District of Columbia.[148] The four regional winners went to the finals at the Society's Annual Meeting in Washington, where the Texas International Law Society emerged victorious.[149]

In 1964, A.S.I.L.S. also initiated a competition for the best student paper on an international law topic. The first winner was Ibrahim F.I. Shihata, then a student

---

140 Id. at 3. The cadet international law society at the Air Force Academy was an associate member.

141 Letter to Members, Jan. 1964, at 3.

142 Letter from David G. Warren to Richard A. Gordon, Aug. 16, 1963, in Baxter files, *supra* note 72.

143 Letter from Baxter to Warren, Aug. 23, 1963, in Baxter files, *supra* note 72.

144 Letter from Warren to Baxter, Aug. 29, 1963, in Baxter files, *supra* note 72.

145 Letter to Members, Jan. 1964, at 2.

146 Id.

147 Symposium, The Soviet Impact on International Law, 29 *Law & Contemp. Probs.* 843 (1964).

148 Minutes of the ASILS Executive Session, Feb. 28, 1964, at 4, in Baxter files, *supra* note 72.

149 Letter to Members, May 1964, at 2.

at the Harvard Law School and later the General Counsel of the World Bank, for a paper on "Treaties as Evidence of General Rules of International Law."[150]

6. Efforts to Strengthen the Teaching of International Law

A Conference of Teachers of International Law was held on Thursday morning, April 27, 1961, just before the first session of the Annual Meeting. It represented a revival of an old, discontinued event. About sixty teachers attended.

The Conference made four proposals: (a) a survey of international law courses in higher education should be considered; (b) the Society should help to establish a clearing-house of information on the teaching of international law; (c) teachers' conferences should be held more regularly; and (d) efforts should be made to get financial support for these activities.[151] The Society took no immediate action.

The Society's first effort under the Ford grant to strengthen the teaching of international law came in 1962. It was in the form of a survey, in cooperation with the American Political Science Association, of international law courses offered by political science departments at the undergraduate and graduate levels. Richard Edwards conducted the survey, with student assistants. Two questionnaires were sent out. One went to chairs of political science departments, asking them what courses were offered in international law and related subjects, and how student and faculty interest in those courses compared with interest in other political science offerings. The second questionnaire went to international law teachers in political science departments. It was designed to obtain information on course content, teaching methods and materials, and the relationship of courses in international law to other courses.[152]

Some of the survey results were quite revealing, but not always as guides to teaching. For example, while undergraduate student interest in international law appeared to be rising markedly, graduate student interest was static. Graduate students, of course, would be the political science professors of the future. A further ominous portent for the future of international law scholarship by political scientists came from a question about faculty interest in international law. Among political scientists at undergraduate colleges, interest seemed to be rising; but among political scientists at universities offering the Ph.D., where most of the scholarship would be produced, interest apparently was declining.[153]

---

[150] Letter to Members, June 1964, at 2.

[151] Minutes of the Executive Council, Apr. 29, 1961, in ASIL Minute Book, 1959-1966, at 65-66.

[152] Letters to Members, Apr. 1962, at 1, & Oct. 1962, at 1-2.

[153] American Society of International Law & American Political Science Association, *A Survey of the Teaching of International Law in Political Science Departments* 24-26 (Richard

A question on the major area of faculty members' teaching interests produced another disturbing result. Of the responding political scientists, about half of those who taught international law as a separate course said it was their major area of teaching interest. But this represented about two-thirds of the older teachers who responded and only about one-third of the youngest group of teachers.[154]

As one might have predicted from the survey, the influence of political scientists in the Society and on the Journal was destined to decline in the sixties and afterwards. Harold Lasswell and Alona Evans made their presence felt during that period, but things were not the same as in the heydays of political scientists James W. Garner, George Grafton Wilson, Philip Marshall Brown, Quincy Wright, Charles G. Fenwick, Pitman Potter and Herbert Briggs.

From 1963 through to 1965, Conferences on Teaching and Research were held in connection with the Society's Annual Meetings.[155] In addition, in June 1964, the Society sponsored a conference of teachers in American law schools. The conference, held at the Cornell Law School, considered issues related to the teaching of international law, international organization, international business and foreign law. A report of the conference was prepared, and the Society distributed it without charge to anyone who requested it.[156]

During the 1963-64 academic year, the Society conducted its second Ford Foundation-supported survey of international law courses, again under the supervision of Richard Edwards. This time it was a survey of teaching in law schools, conducted in collaboration with the Association of American Law Schools. The survey encompassed not only public international law, but also foreign and comparative law, international business transactions, and international organizations courses. It found an impressive increase in international law offerings since 1952-53, particularly in public international law.[157] Thirty-one law schools awarded post-LL.B. law degrees; each of these schools offered some work in international and foreign law.[158]

W. Edwards, Jr., Reporter, 1963).

154 Id. at 47-50.

155 57 *ASIL Proc.* 18-49 (1963); 58 *ASIL Proc.* 54-81 (1964); 59 *ASIL Proc.* 82-107 (1965).

156 *Teaching of International Law and Related Courses in American Law Schools* (ASIL Occasional Paper, 1964); see also Letters to Members, Oct.–Nov. 1964, at 2 & Dec. 1964, at 1.

157 Forty-five law schools had added it to the curriculum. In all, 91 law schools offered public international law in 1963-64; 51 offered foreign or comparative law; 45 offered international business transactions; and 22 taught international organizations (including regional organizations). Richard W. Edwards, Jr., International Legal Studies: A Survey of Teaching in American Law Schools 1963-1964, at 7 (1965).

158 Id. at 23.

7. International Law and the Social Sciences

Social science research was not one of the Society's top priorities, even in its new incarnation. Nevertheless, as we have seen, the Society had long been home to some prominent political scientists, and it demonstrated an interest in the teaching of international law by political science departments with its 1962 survey.

Early in 1964 at a panel meeting in Tillar House, the assembled international lawyers and law professors voiced their frustration about finding the relevant social science literature when they needed it. Shortly thereafter the Society decided to support the production of a bibliography of social science literature that was relevant to international law. Wesley L. Gould and Michael Barkun tackled the project. It took them appreciably longer than they had expected, in large part because they found a need for a more substantive volume on international law and the social sciences – a project, also sponsored by the Society, to which they turned before they completed what turned out to be an extensive, annotated bibliography. Both volumes were eventually published for the Society by Princeton University Press.[159]

8. More Major Foundation Grants and Other Significant Contributions

In September 1964, with the original Ford grant about to expire and with the groundwork being carried out for an ambitious research program through the creation of the Board of Review and Development, the Executive Committee decided to make a hefty new proposal to the Ford Foundation for USD 1,260,000 to be spent over ten years. The principal request was for funds to support the new B.R.D., including staff support. The Executive Committee added a separate proposal to administer a USD 75,000 fund for each of five years to support individual research by scholars who would compete to be Research Fellows of the Society.[160]

The Foundation rejected the request for the individual research fund,[161] but it granted the Society USD 600,000 primarily to finance the Board of Review and Development.[162] The grant came in even before the original Ford grant had

---

[159] Wesley L. Gould & Michael Barkun, *International Law and the Social Sciences* (1970); Wesley L. Gould & Michael Barkun, *Social Science Literature: A Bibliography for International Law* (1972).

[160] Minutes of Joint Meeting of the Executive Committee and Board of Permanent Operations, Sept. 26, 1964, in ASIL Minute Book, 1959-1966, at 190-91.

[161] Minutes of the Executive Council, Nov. 14, 1964, in ASIL Minute Book, 1959-1966, at 182, 183.

[162] Letter to Members, Jan. 1965, at 1.

expired. Moreover, like the earlier grant, it was disbursed in a lump sum, enabling the Society to enhance it by earning interest on the funds until they were used. At the same time, the Foundation gave a sign of harder times to come when it indicated that future grants would not be available to support publications or annual and regional meetings.[163]

In keeping with the Society's emphasis in the sixties on international economic transactions, the two allocations first authorized under the new Ford grant were for studies on international trade and on capital formation.[164]

Although the USD 600,000 Ford grant did not require a matching grant, the Society set out to raise another USD 600,000 in order to ensure the continuity of its programs. Walter S. Surrey, chair of the Finance Committee, outlined five uses for the funds to be raised: a Tillar House Fund, a Library Fund, a General Research Fund (to provide research awards to individual scholars or to support Society research projects), an Overseas Subscription Fund (to provide memberships and subscriptions to persons in "appropriate countries"), and enhancement of the Reserve Fund. The Executive Council approved Surrey's plan,[165] but it does not appear that anything significant came of it.

In June 1966 the Carnegie Corporation awarded the Society a grant of USD 54,500, payable over three years, for studies of the role of international law in regulating civil wars. Richard A. Falk became the general director of the studies.[166] Case studies were planned, focusing on the Algerian war of independence, the American and Spanish Civil Wars, and the war in the Congo following independence. In addition, studies were commissioned concerning United States involvement in civil strife in Latin America, and on United States involvement in civil wars since World War II.[167] The commissions were duly carried out under the auspices of the Board of Review and Development, and books were published.[168]

---

163 Minutes of the Executive Council, Apr. 22, 1965, in ASIL Minute Book, 1959-1966, at 194, 195.

164 Minutes of the Executive Council, Nov. 13, 1965, in ASIL Minute Book, 1959-1966, at 203, 204-05.

165 Minutes of the Executive Council, Nov. 13, 1965, in ASIL Minute Book, 1959-1966, at 203, 206-07.

166 Minutes of the Executive Committee, June 20, 1966, in ASIL Minute Book, 1959-1966, at 246, 247-48; Letter to Members, July–Aug. 1966, at 1.

167 Letter to Members, Oct. 1966, at 3-4.

168 See Chapter Nine, Section B.1, *infra*.

C. OLD WINE, SOMETIMES IN NEW BOTTLES

1. The Role of International Law in Shaping Foreign Policy

The Society was founded on the conviction that international law, and international dispute-settlement mechanisms, should be central to the shaping of foreign policy in the United States and elsewhere. If policy-makers did not always seem to share that belief, neither could they shake off international law entirely. It was always lurking somewhere; the questions that never seemed to be fully resolved were (and still are) when, how and how much it would play a role in the making of foreign policy decisions.

These questions were put to the test in the 1960s, especially during the Cuban missile crisis in October 1962 and the Vietnam War later in the decade. At the Society's Annual Meeting in 1963, Dean Acheson, a former Secretary of State, participated in a panel on the U.S. quarantine against Soviet missile-bearing ships bound for Cuba. The quarantine effectively ended the crisis caused by the emplacement of Soviet missiles and launchers in Cuba. Acheson concluded that the propriety of the quarantine was not a legal issue: "The power, position and prestige of the United States had been challenged by another state; and law simply does not deal with such questions of ultimate power – power that comes close to the sources of sovereignty."[169] He conceded, though, that there were useful legal principles imposing certain procedural hurdles before unilateral action could legitimately be taken. Not surprisingly, his view of the law's relationship to ultimate power was challenged in the ensuing discussion.[170]

Dean Rusk, another Secretary of State who was active in the Society, gave law and legal principles a more prominent place in the formulation of policy than Acheson had. Rusk was the Society's Honorary President from 1961 until 1969, in keeping with the tradition (as it then was) for sitting Secretaries of State to occupy that undemanding position. In September 1965 he delivered an address to the American Political Science Association. In it he described the role of the Legal Adviser in shaping foreign policy. This part of his address was regarded as of such interest to ASIL members that it was reproduced in the Society's Letter to Members. Rusk said, in part:

> If [the policy-maker] ... has fixed the question he must answer, defined his objective, considered our interests and past commitments, and ascertained the relevant views and interests of other countries ... he is not yet ready to propose an answer. There are other factors to be weighed.
>
> The office of the Legal Adviser in the State Department will be quick to bring some of these to his attention. Strengthening the United Nations

[169] Remarks by the Honorable Dean Acheson, 57 *ASIL Proc.* 13, 14 (1963).

[170] Id. at 15.

> and building international law are important parts of our effort to build a decent world order. The policy framer, in addressing a problem, will thus want to know what principles of international law are involved. Are the accepted norms of international law relevant? He will also want to know whether the UN Charter and UN resolutions are involved. And whether any treaties or agreements are applicable. ...
>
> The test of policy by reference to law goes beyond the technical issues of law or even the broader objective of the rule of law. Law is the custodian of the standard of generalized conduct. Our Legal Adviser is responsible for putting to us the questions: What happens if everyone else acts as we are proposing to do? How are we prepared to act if a similar situation arises elsewhere?
>
> The law liberates by making it possible to predict, with reasonable assurance, what the other fellow is going to do. ... The gravitational pull of law in policy is and must be a powerful factor in policy decision.[171]

The Vietnam War had already begun to put Rusk's paradigm to a test. Nevertheless, the paradigm appears to have been sincerely set forth, not simply as an ideal but as a working model. Rusk in fact believed, in the words of his biographer, that "international law should determine the behavior of nation-states and set the criteria for making judgments about international conflict."[172]

When he defended the increasing U.S. involvement in the Vietnam War, Rusk took comfort in the Gulf of Tonkin Resolution. The Congress adopted it in August 1964, in response to an alleged North Vietnamese attack on U.S. destroyers in the Gulf. The Resolution approved the President's determination "to take all necessary measures to repel armed attack against the forces of the United States and to prevent further aggression" and "to take all necessary steps, including the use of armed force, to assist any member or protocol state of the Southeast Asia Collective Defense Treaty requesting assistance in defense of its freedom."[173] With the Resolution in hand, Rusk believed that the United States' conduct of the Vietnam War was lawful under both domestic and international law.[174] He expounded that position as the Society's annual banquet speaker in 1965.[175]

If international law was to have an impact on the behavior of nation states, there would have to be a renewed effort to achieve what Elihu Root had advocated in the first issue of the Journal: the education of a significant segment of the public

---

171 Quoted in Letter to Members, Sept.–Oct. 1965, at 1-2.

172 Thomas J. Schoenbaum, *Waging Peace and War: Dean Rusk in the Truman, Kennedy, and Johnson Years* 134 (1988).

173 51 *Dept. State Bull.* 268 (1964).

174 Id. at 431.

175 59 *ASIL Proc.* 247, 249-53 (1965). See text at note 196 *infra*.

in principles of international law that could perhaps guide public opinion. At the 1961 Annual Meeting, the President of the Society, Charles Martin, urged the Society and its members to spread knowledge about international problems.[176] The Society had been doing some of this all along, and it made new efforts in the sixties with its re-discovered emphasis on the teaching of international law and with its growing support of student international law groups. The seed that Root planted had sprouted over the years, but it had not yet grown to full bloom.

2. Taking Positions on Matters of Policy

An issue that seems always to be somewhere on the Society's agenda is whether or not to take positions on matters of policy.

It surfaced again in 1965, when the Executive Council was asked to take a position favoring U.S. ratification of the Hague Convention on Service of Process Abroad. An *ad hoc* committee was appointed to study the matter and report back to the Council. The committee, consisting of Hans Smit (chair), Hardy Dillard and Stefan Riesenfeld, recommended that the Council adopt a resolution stating that it would be in the interest of orderly administration of justice for the United States to ratify the Convention. This sparked a debate in the Council about the propriety of the Council's endorsing any particular treaty or legislation. Stanley Metzger led the opposition.

On a motion by Metzger, the Council resolved that the Executive Committee should examine the implications of the Council's taking such positions. On a motion by Dillard, the Council adopted the resolution recommended by the *ad hoc* committee on the Service Abroad Convention. Brunson MacChesney, the presiding officer, tried to untangle the situation by pointing out that adoption of the *ad hoc* committee's resolution did not prejudice the Council's later consideration of the issue Metzger's resolution had put into play.[177]

After a subcommittee of the Executive Committee reported back to the Executive Council in April 1966, the Council unanimously adopted a policy statement:

> The Council in the future will recommend that the Society adopt resolutions urging action by persons outside the Society in only two types of circumstances:
>
> (i) Resolutions relating to technical matters primarily of professional interest to international lawyers and scholars.

---

[176] Charles E. Martin, The Decade Ahead: The Society's Role in the Nation's Service, 55 *ASIL Proc.* 41, 46 (1961). Martin did not offer specific proposals.

[177] Minutes of the Executive Council, Nov. 13, 1965, in ASIL Minute Book, 1959-1966, at 203, 209-10.

(ii) Resolutions relating to principles of international law or international relations, when all of the following conditions have been satisfied:

(a) The matter is one which is generally considered by members of the Council to involve a matter of truly fundamental importance in promoting the establishment and maintenance of international relations on the basis of law and justice.

(b) The matter is one in respect of which most members of the Society can reasonably be expected to be informed without the preparation of a special committee report.

(c) There is no significant disagreement within the Society as to the desirability of the proposed action.[178]

There was extended discussion of how the Council would determine whether there was "significant disagreement" within the Society. The subcommittee had suggested a mechanical test: the Council would not recommend adoption of a resolution on principles of international law or international relations unless it was favored by all Council members present and voting. When that test was not warmly received, John Stevenson, representing the subcommittee, withdrew it.[179] No other test commanded sufficient support to be included in the policy statement.

The 1966 policy statement has to be read against the backdrop of the Vietnam War. By then the United States was deeply involved in the War, having begun bombing attacks on North Vietnam in February 1965. Congress had adopted the Gulf of Tonkin Resolution supporting the President's use of armed force. The deep national controversy that was to divide American society had begun. Foreseeably, at the Society's Business Meeting two days after the Council adopted its policy statement, a resolution was offered from the floor calling on the Council to appoint an *ad hoc* committee to consider the legality of the use of force by the United States in Vietnam. It was referred to the Council under the relevant provision in the Society's Constitution.[180]

The policy statement effectively forestalled taking any position on such a controversial matter. To use the words James Brown Scott had uttered thirty-six years earlier, the resolution on Vietnam, having been referred to the Council, "entered upon its eternal slumber."[181] Nor did the Society take a position later

---

178 Minutes of the Executive Council, Apr. 28, 1966, in ASIL Minute Book, 1959-1966, at 227, 233.

179 Id. at 232-33.

180 60 *ASIL Proc.* 174 (1966).

181 24 *ASIL Proc.* 244 (1930). Formally, the resolution on Vietnam was tabled in the Executive Council. Minutes of the Executive Council, Apr. 30, 1966, in ASIL Minute Book,

in the War. For better or for worse, the Society thus did not make a significant contribution, *qua* Society, to the legal debate in the United States on a foreign relations policy that shook American society to its core and shaped a generation of American youth. Nevertheless, as we shall see, individual Society members did contribute to the debate and the Society supplied them with a rostrum.

3. Meetings, Regional and Otherwise

"The Society is pre-eminently a forum for discussion." So said the booklet issued in commemoration of the Society's sixtieth anniversary.[182] It had always been thus, but with the advent of significant sums of grant money in the 1960s, the discussions took the new forms and embraced the new subjects that we have already seen. One existing form, the regional meeting program, received only a small share of the new money, but it was enough to re-invigorate the program.

In November 1962, the Executive Council adopted revised rules for regional and local meetings. The rules gave preference for Society support to meetings in which universities in the same general locality participated with local bar groups. The Society's financial contribution was normally to be limited to USD 350 per meeting.[183]

The first regional meeting to reap the benefit of Ford money was held in Toledo in February 1962, before the revised rules were in place. The topic was International Trade and International Law, in furtherance of the Society's new emphasis on international transactions. Speakers were brought in from Washington, Newark, Chicago, Cleveland and New Haven.[184] This set the pattern for other regional meetings, which also brought in speakers from outside each region.

Several ensuing regional meetings were also devoted to legal problems raised by international business transactions. A crescendo was reached in 1966, when regional meetings in New York City, Syracuse, Denver, Austin, Stanford, Ann Arbor and Vancouver addressed international economic law issues.[185] In addition, the Annual Meeting that year was heavily trade and investment-oriented,

---

1959-1966, at 241, 243.

182 *The American Society of International Law: The Sixtieth Year*, 3d unnumbered page (1966).

183 "Rules Governing Regional or Local Activities Sponsored or Cosponsored by the A.S.I.L.," Nov. 1, 1962, in ASIL Minute Book, 1959-1966, at 128a-128b. For Council approval, see id. at 119. The Society's financial support could not be used for honoraria or entertainment (except entertainment for diplomatic and official guests).

184 Letter to Members, Jan. 1962, at 2.

185 Letters to Members, Feb. 1966, at 2, Mar. 1966, at 2, and Oct. 1966, at 2.

focusing on the developing countries.[186] And that was not all. A meeting on capital formation and securities regulation was held at Tillar House in October 1966,[187] and in December the Society co-sponsored a course of study at the University of Miami on problems of doing business with Latin America.[188]

A significant regional meeting was held at Syracuse University in March 1964. Organized by Richard B. Lillich, then a Syracuse University law professor and later a member of the University of Virginia law faculty, the title of the meeting was Procedural Aspects of International Law. The program featured a paper by Richard A. Falk on the role of domestic courts in the international legal order.[189] Falk's paper was based on a longer manuscript he had written on that subject – a manuscript that became a book, nominally the third in the Procedural Aspects of International Law series, but actually the first to be published originally under that imprint.[190] The regional meeting turned a developing program of studies at Syracuse University into a full-fledged series on procedure – an aspect of international law that had received relatively little scholarly attention until Lillich began to work in the field.

Another noteworthy regional meeting was held in December 1965. The Society co-sponsored a Canada-wide meeting in Toronto of the Canadian Branch of the International Law Association.[191] It was the first regional meeting of the Society held outside the United States.

The computer age came to the Society in 1966, at a two-day discussion meeting on the application of electronic data-processing techniques to international law materials. The discussion addressed such forward-looking matters as use of computers for indexing and searching treaties, and for doing research in U.N. documents and other primary materials.[192]

4. Annual Meetings in a Time of Increasing National Stress

In the early sixties, the Annual Meetings presented a potpourri of topics, ranging from Cold War concerns to economic issues. In 1963, under Hardy Dillard's

---

[186] 60 *ASIL Proc. passim* (1966).

[187] Minutes of the Executive Council, Nov. 12, 1966, in ASIL Minute Book, 1959-1966, at 249, 259.

[188] Letter to Members, Nov. 1966, at 3.

[189] Letter to Members, Oct. 1963, at 3.

[190] See Richard A. Falk, *The Role of Domestic Courts in the International Legal Order* (1964). The two earlier books in the series were Richard B. Lillich, *International Claims: Their Adjudication by National Commissions* (1962), and Richard B. Lillich & Gordon A. Christenson, *International Claims: Their Preparation and Presentation* (1962).

[191] Letter to Members, Dec. 1965, at 3.

[192] Richard W. Edwards, Jr., Note: "Electronic Data-Processing and International Law Documentation," 61 *AJIL* 87 (1967).

presidency, the Society adopted "Law and Conflict" as the overriding theme. Dillard spoke of the case that could be made in the Geneva disarmament negotiations for the monopolization of force in a central world body.[193] The meeting led off with a panel discussion of the future implications of the naval quarantine that had ended the Cuban missile crisis in October 1962.[194]

In 1964, the theme was "Causing Compliance with International Law." Panels addressed a variety of compliance objectives and techniques. The techniques ran the gamut from the use of domestic courts to mobilizing public opinion to applying economic sanctions.

In 1965, Dean Rusk was the featured speaker at the annual dinner.[195] He was the Secretary of State, and he seized the occasion, as the *Washington Sunday Star* put it, to deliver "the sharpest counter attack to date by an administration spokesman against domestic critics of our Vietnam policy."[196] He outlined the administration's legal basis for U.S. military involvement, based on collective self-defense with South Vietnam against aggression from North Vietnam. Then, in the segment of his address picked up by the news media, he stressed the "gullibility" of the government's academic critics who, he thought, had failed to understand the U.S. stake in Vietnam and had misread North Vietnam's intentions and actions. Media coverage was extensive. *U.S. News & World Report* printed virtually the entire speech, identifying it as an address before the American Society of International Law.[197]

Dean Rusk was not the only annual dinner speaker to make news in the mid-sixties. In 1966, the featured speaker was Under Secretary of State George W. Ball. He used the podium to denounce "the decision of the government of one European nation state to separate itself from the others and to seek a special position of primacy in Western Europe."[198] He did not name France in his address as the renegade state, but at a background session for reporters he did.[199] France, under Charles de Gaulle, had recently renounced its military obligations under NATO and had developed its own nuclear force.

---

193 Hardy C. Dillard, "Conflict and Change: The Role of Law," 57 *ASIL Proc.* 50, 58-59 (1963).

194 Panel on Cuban Quarantine: Implications for the Future, 57 *ASIL Proc.* 1 (1963). See text at note 169 *supra*.

195 59 *ASIL Proc.* 247 (1965).

196 *Washington Sunday Star*, Apr. 25, 1965.

197 *U.S. News & World Report*, May 10, 1965, p. 74. See also *Washington Post*, Apr. 24, 1965, p. A1; *Washington Evening Star*, Apr. 24, 1965, p. A1; *Time*, Apr. 30, 1965, p. 29; *Newsweek*, May 3, 1965, p. 23.

198 George W. Ball, "The Larger Meaning of the NATO Crisis," 60 *ASIL Proc.* 190, 194 (1966).

199 *Washington Post*, Apr. 30, 1966; *Washington Evening Star*, Apr. 30, 1966.

5. Continuing the Effort to Upgrade the Qualifications of U.S. Delegates to International Organizations

As indicated in Chapter Seven, the Executive Council in 1959 expressed its concern about the standards the United States government was using for appointments to such bodies as the International Court of Justice, the Permanent Court of Arbitration and the International Law Commission.[200] Richard Baxter had initiated that effort.

In 1964, Baxter took the initiative again. He drafted a resolution, adopted by the Executive Council, broadening the field of concern to include all organs of international organizations dealing primarily with legal questions. The resolution recited that there had been instances over many years of the appointment to such bodies "of principal delegates of the United States who have been neither lawyers nor qualified in international law." Thus the Council resolved that "appointments of principal delegates to organs of international organizations dealing primarily with legal questions be made only from amongst persons highly qualified in international law or in that field of law with which the organization is concerned." The President of the Society was directed to communicate this view to the Secretary of State.[201]

6. Annual Resolutions on Publications of the State Department and United Nations

In the sixties the Society continued its practice of adopting annual resolutions urging improvement in the supply of official publications that would be useful to researchers. In the early sixties, the focus was largely on getting Marjorie Whiteman's *Digest of International Law* published, reducing the time lag for publication of the *Foreign Relations* volumes, and seeking publication of the papers of the Inter-American Juridical Committee.[202] The effort to speed up the publication of *Foreign Relations* continued into the seventies and beyond.

7. Some Noteworthy Society Elections

In 1962, Marjorie Whiteman was elected as one of the three Vice Presidents for the following year. It was the first time the Society had elected a woman as a Vice President.[203]

---

200 See Chapter Seven, Section A.4, *supra*.

201 Minutes of the Executive Council, Apr. 25, 1964, in ASIL Minute Book, 1959-1966, at 179, 180-81.

202 See 56 *ASIL Proc.* 74 (1962); 57 *ASIL Proc.* 265 (1963).

203 56 *ASIL Proc.* 74-75 (1962).

A dynastic first, of sorts, occurred in 1963 when James Nevins Hyde was elected as President of the Society.[204] His father, Charles Cheney Hyde, had also been a President.

8. Balancing the Regular Budget

In the early sixties, Ford Foundation money kept the Society well in the black, but it was apparent that Ford money could not be counted on indefinitely. Trouble appeared on the horizon when it was disclosed that the Society faced a USD 12,000 operating deficit for the 1963-64 fiscal year.[205]

A significant part of the deficit was attributable to a reduction in income from corporate memberships. When Arthur Dean had been President of the Society, he had recruited new corporate members, but since then the number had decreased. The reason apparently was that the Society's programs, even with their new emphasis on business-related issues, did not have sufficient appeal to the corporate boards that had to approve outlays for things like membership dues. The remedy, it was thought, was a renewed effort to bring in corporate members and to persuade individuals to contribute funds in excess of their dues.[206] The results were modest.[207]

D. THE JOURNAL'S STEADY COURSE

1. The Board of Editors

In 1961, Philip Jessup, having been elected to the International Court of Justice, felt obliged to resign from the Board of Editors.[208] He was not immediately replaced.[209] Leo Gross, one of the two Acting Editors-in-Chief during the sabbatical abroad of Editor-in-Chief Herbert Briggs, asked the Executive Council

204 57 *ASIL Proc.* 266 (1963).

205 Minutes of the Executive Council, Nov. 9, 1963, in ASIL Minute Book, 1959-1966, at 151, 153-54.

206 Id. at 154.

207 For details, see Memorandum, "ASIL History: Details Relating to Budget, Finances and Membership" (2006), on file with the Society.

208 For other changes in Board membership during this period, see Memorandum, ASIL History: The Journal, Its Editors and Business Practices, on file with the Society.

209 Minutes of the Executive Council, Apr. 27, 1961, in ASIL Minute Book, 1959-1966, at 51, 53.

to authorize an increase in the size of the Board to twenty, without electing anyone to fill the new slots immediately. The Council concurred.[210]

In November 1966, the Executive Council increased the size of the Board to twenty-two. It filled only one of the new positions: Alona E. Evans became the first female to serve on the Board.[211]

2. Prominent Articles and Comments

In 1961, the Journal published its second pseudonymous lead article, the first having appeared in 1914.[212] This time Oscar Schachter was the author, publishing his article on United Nations action in the Congo under the pseudonym E.M. Miller. Schachter was still the Director of the General Legal Division of the U.N. He was also an editor of the Journal, and was in a position to provide insights on how the U.N. action was shaped by legal considerations.

Schachter argued that the initial Security Council resolutions after the Congo became independent could be justified under Article 40 of the Charter. He addressed the function of the law of the Charter and of customary law in providing "the framework of authority that enabled action to be taken quickly in unprecedented circumstances."[213] Such a channeling function, of course, is common in domestic law and legal institutions. Schachter showed how the same function operates in a global and very public international organization.

In 1961, the Journal also published a throwback to an earlier time – an endeavor to codify an aspect of international law of particular interest to the United States. The Harvard Law School had been asked to revise the draft Convention on Responsibility of States for Damage Done on Their Territory to the Person or Property of Foreigners, which Edwin Borchard had prepared in 1929 for the Harvard Research in International Law. Louis Sohn and Richard Baxter undertook the job. The Journal published their draft Convention and their commentary to some of the key articles.[214]

---

210 Minutes of the Executive Council, Apr. 29, 1961, in ASIL Minute Book, 1959-1966, at 65, 67. See ASIL Regulations, as amended to Apr. 27, 1962, Section V(1)(c)(2), in 56 *ASIL Proc.* xv, xxiii (1962).

211 Id. at 255; see also Alona E. Evans & Carol Per Lee Plumb, "Women and the American Society of International Law," 68 *AJIL* 290, 292 (1974).

212 The 1914 article was written by the Military Attaché of the German Embassy in Washington, on the eve of World War I. See Chapter One, Section C.9 *supra*.

213 E.M. Miller (Oscar Schachter), "Legal Aspects of the United Nations Action in the Congo," 55 *AJIL* 1, 28 (1961).

214 Louis B. Sohn & Richard R. Baxter, "Responsibility of States for Injuries to the Economic Interests of Aliens," 55 *AJIL* 545 (1961).

Richard Bilder's classic article on the Office of the State Department Legal Adviser was published in 1962.[215] It was a comprehensive treatment of the organization, functions and impact of the principal international lawyers in the United States government, written by an insider. It even contained some heartening news for those who were concerned about the government's adherence to international legal norms:

> Generally speaking, policy officers of the Department tend to regard the Office's legal opinions as controlling, particularly when the matter concerns a question of interpretation of a statute or treaty, and rarely propose that measures inconsistent with the Office's legal views be taken. ... The influence of the Office may also on occasion extend beyond strictly legal matters. It is commonplace that the distinction between "law" and "policy" is, as a practical matter, hard to draw and harder to maintain. Most of the problems in which the Office becomes involved lie in fact in a "grey area" where a variety of types of judgments have a bearing. Thus, in terms of the realities of the counseling situation, the Office is frequently drawn into questions of substantive policy. In some of these situations, the Office's views on such policy matters may have considerable influence ... .[216]

The importance of Bilder's article is apparent from the treatment the Society gave it. The Society sent complimentary copies to all embassies in Washington and made copies available to the participants at its 1963 conference on the role of legal advisers in foreign affairs.[217]

Alona Evans' article on the political offense doctrine was given place of prominence in volume 57.[218] It analyzed the problems of defining "political offense" and of applying the doctrine in a variety of contexts, supplying valuable examples of practice in the United States and elsewhere.

The Cuban missile crisis erupted in 1962. The Soviet Union had stealthily introduced strategic missiles into Cuba. The United States responded with what looked very much like a blockade of Cuban ports. A blockade, though, could be deemed an "act of war" (to use the non-technical term for a use of force not strictly in accordance with the U.N. Charter), and in fact some reporters had

---

215 Richard B. Bilder, "The Office of the Legal Adviser: The State Department Lawyer and Foreign Affairs," 56 *AJIL* 633 (1962).

216 Id. at 654-55.

217 Minutes of the Executive Council, Nov. 10, 1962, in ASIL Minute Book, 1959-1966, at 118, 124; H.C.L. Merillat, *Legal Advisers and Foreign Affairs* vi (1964). For discussion of the conference, see text at note 119 *supra*.

218 Alona E. Evans, "Reflections upon the Political Offense in International Practice," 57 *AJIL* 1 (1963).

descended on the Tillar House library to research the point.[219] The U.S. response ultimately was justified as a quarantine under authority from the Organization of American States, rather than a blockade.

The Journal's July 1963 number contained three lead articles and three Editorial Comments on the quarantine. Leonard Meeker, then the Deputy Legal Adviser in the State Department, led off by distinguishing the quarantine from a traditional blockade, which could lawfully have been undertaken only if there already was a state of war or belligerency. Meeker relied on the Rio Treaty of 1947,[220] and argued that the regional quarantine measures did not violate U.N. Charter Article 53(1) (no regional enforcement action without the authorization of the Security Council) because "enforcement action" means obligatory enforcement action. The O.A.S. resolution authorizing the quarantine under the Rio Treaty was not obligatory on O.A.S. members.[221] Quincy Wright, on the other hand, argued that whatever legitimacy the O.A.S. resolution may have given to U.S. action against Cuba, it could not legitimize the threat or use of force against the Soviet Union, a non-party to either the O.A.S. Charter or the Rio Treaty. "The episode," he concluded, "has not improved the reputation of the United States as a champion of international law ... ."[222]

In 1964, Philip Jessup – no longer an editor since his election to the I.C.J. – contributed an article on diversity and uniformity in the law of nations, based on a lecture he had given at the University of Leiden.[223] Jessup pointed out some apparent discontinuities between practice and doctrine, between civil and common law systems, and between regional and global systems. He went on to show how the discontinuities, though genuine, did not irrevocably stand in the way of developments in the law of nations toward realization of common interests and even toward uniformity in important contexts.

In 1964, the Journal also carried Richard Falk's prophetic analysis of the freshly decided *Sabbatino* case.[224] Falk applauded the textured, non-absolute

---

219 Letter from Richard W. Edwards, Jr., to Frederic L. Kirgis, Oct. 8, 1997, p. 1.

220 62 Stat. 1681, TIAS No. 1838, 43 *AJIL Supp.* 53 (1949).

221 See Leonard C. Meeker, "Defensive Quarantine and the Law," 57 *AJIL* 515 (1963).

222 Quincy Wright, "The Cuban Quarantine," id. at 546, 563. The other pieces were Carl Q. Christol and Charles R. Davis, "Maritime Quarantine: The Naval Interdiction of Offensive Weapons and Associated Matériel to Cuba, 1961," id. at 525; Charles G. Fenwick, "The Quarantine Against Cuba: Legal or Illegal?," id. at 588; Brunson MacChesney, "Some Comments on the 'Quarantine' of Cuba," id. at 592; Myres S. McDougal, "The Soviet-Cuban Quarantine and Self-Defense," id. at 597.

223 Philip C. Jessup, "Diversity and Uniformity in the Law of Nations," 58 *AJIL* 341 (1964).

224 Richard A. Falk, "The Complexity of Sabbatino," 58 *AJIL* 935 (1964). The case is *Banco Nacional de Cuba v. Sabbatino*, 376 U.S. 398 (1964). See also text at note 132 *supra*.

approach the Supreme Court majority took toward the act of state doctrine, and pointed out the weakness of the majority's emphasis on separation of powers as the principal rationale for declining to superimpose an exception to the doctrine whenever the foreign government's act could be said to violate international law. Subsequent cases have demonstrated the strength of Falk's analysis, which he rendered in the Journal before the avalanche of law review commentary on *Sabbatino* and the act of state doctrine hit the academic presses. As the later cases have shown, the issue has more to do with the proper role of the domestic judiciary, *qua* judiciary, in politically sensitive international matters than with the separation of powers among the branches of government.

Wolfgang Friedmann took to the pages of the Journal in 1965 to discuss his perception of the crisis of international law. France and the Soviet Union had repudiated the I.C.J.'s advisory opinion in the *U.N. Expenses* case. The Court had determined that peacekeeping expenses in the Middle East and the Congo were expenses of the Organization under U.N. Charter Article 17(2) and thus Member States were obligated to pay their allocated shares. By running up two years' arrears in the payment of dues, France and the Soviet Union had thrown the U.N. into its first serious financial crisis. The United States also had challenged the international order by seeking to justify its military assistance to South Vietnam on controversial legal grounds, and had invaded the Dominican Republic under a vulnerable legal justification. Friedmann was profoundly disturbed: "The real significance of the U.S. actions in Viet-Nam and the Dominican Republic ... is that the most powerful champion and defender of the existing international order against revolutionary ideologies may have come to the conclusion that it can no longer abide by international law ... ."[225] His concern was akin to that of Quincy Wright at the time of the Cuban missile crisis.[226] It was a concern that would reappear even more vividly in the twenty-first century.

Vietnam generated not only heated public debate in the mid-sixties and early seventies, but also reams of legal analysis. Quincy Wright was one of the prominent scholarly critics of the escalation of the use of force by the United States against North Vietnam in February 1965. Writing in the Journal in 1966, he methodically examined the legal issues in light of the facts as he understood them. He found little legal justification for what the United States was doing.[227]

John Norton Moore responded in 1967 with a defense of U.S. policy. He concluded that the people of South Vietnam could reasonably be thought to have a right of self-determination, including freedom to choose their own government and to decide for themselves whether to be unified with North Vietnam. Since

---

[225] Wolfgang Friedmann, United States Policy and the Crisis of International Law, 59 *AJIL* 857, 870 (1965).

[226] See text at note 222 *supra*.

[227] Quincy Wright, "Legal Aspects of the Viet-Nam Situation," 60 *AJIL* 750 (1966).

North Vietnam was trying to nullify that right by using force, opposition by defensive assistance would be lawful.[228]

Another widely debated topic among international legal scholars in the sixties and later – though a far cry from Vietnam when it came to public interest – concerned the normative effect of U.N. General Assembly resolutions. In an Editorial Comment in 1966, Richard Falk made a forceful argument for limited legislative competence on the part of the General Assembly.[229] His position accorded greater competence to the Assembly than most other scholars were ready to concede.

3. Covering International Economic Law

In 1966, William Bishop, the Editor-in-Chief of the Journal, told the Executive Council that he would like to see more articles from them, particularly on the law of international trade and investment, and on international organizations.[230] This failed to produce an outpouring of scholarship, but Stanley Metzger – a member of the Executive Council who was also an Editor of the Journal – persuaded the Board of Editors to institute a new department in the Journal devoted to the law and institutions of international economic relations.

As Metzger put it, the purpose of the new department was "to bring to our readers more frequent and systematized treatments of major developments in international economic relations, emphasizing their legal and institutional aspects."[231] Metzger wrote the first piece for the department, on UNCTAD. It was published in the July 1967 issue.[232]

The original plan was that the department would appear twice a year, but it proved difficult to stick to that prescription. The department appeared sporadically until 1976. During its lifetime it gave voice to a variety of economic issues, including two pieces in the long and impressive string of publications on international monetary law by Sir Joseph Gold, who for many years served as General Counsel to the International Monetary Fund.[233]

---

[228] John Norton Moore, "The Lawfulness of Military Assistance to the Republic of Viet-Nam," 61 *AJIL* 1, 32 (1967).

[229] Richard A. Falk, Editorial Comment: "On the Quasi-Legislative Competence of the General Assembly," 60 *AJIL* 782 (1966).

[230] Minutes of the Executive Council, Apr. 28, 1966, in ASIL Minute Book, 1959-1966, at 227, 229.

[231] Stanley D. Metzger, Editor's Note, 61 *AJIL* 756 (1967).

[232] Stanley D. Metzger, "UNCTAD," 61 *AJIL* 756 (1967).

[233] Joseph Gold, "Unauthorized Changes of Par Value and Fluctuating Exchange Rates in the Bretton Woods System," 65 *AJIL* 113 (1971); Joseph Gold, "Weighted Voting Power: Some Limits and Some Problems," 68 *AJIL* 687 (1974).

E. THE EXECUTIVE DIRECTOR RESIGNS (TWICE)

In February 1964, Chris Merillat submitted a letter of resignation to the Society's President, James N. Hyde. His resignation, he said, would be effective on September 1, 1964. He cited, in particular, the Society's need to seek new grants and the likelihood that major foundations would be reluctant to contribute unless the Society had an Executive Director committed to the job for a substantial period of time. He felt that he could not make such a commitment at that point. Hyde reluctantly accepted the resignation.[234]

A search committee for a new Executive Director was appointed, but before it could report, Merillat was persuaded to stay. Business continued as usual with Merillat as Executive Director in the autumn of 1964 and for the next two years, except when he took a leave of absence from January to March 1966. During that time, Richard Edwards, by then the Assistant to the Executive Director, took over his responsibilities.[235]

Merillat submitted his second letter of resignation in the autumn of 1966. He resigned, effective February 28, 1967, to complete a book on Indian constitutional law and to accept a visiting appointment at the University of Washington School of Law.[236] The Executive Council regretfully accepted his resignation. Merillat, the Council said, had compiled an impressive record of achievements: "the development of the Society's new programs in challenging new areas of international law and relations, the introduction of two new publications – *International Legal Materials* and the Society's newsletter, the building of an effective administrative staff, the institution of sound budgetary and forward-planning procedures, and the establishment and maintenance of close and beneficial relations with institutional and other supporters of the Society."[237]

Merillat's interest in entering the teaching world was apparently what prompted the Executive Council, immediately after it had accepted his resignation, to amend the Society's Regulations to permit an Executive Director to engage in part-time teaching activities. The amended Regulation provided that the Executive Director shall devote "the major part of his time" to the work of the Society.[238] It had formerly required full time.

---

234 Minutes of the Executive Council, Apr. 23, 1964, in ASIL Minute Book, 1959-1966, at 161, 162-64.

235 Minutes of the Executive Council, Nov. 13, 1965, in ASIL Minute Book, 1959-1966, at 203, 205.

236 Minutes of the Executive Council, Nov. 12, 1966, in ASIL Minute Book, 1959-1966, at 249, 250; Letter to Members, Feb. 1967, at 4.

237 Minutes of the Executive Council, Nov. 12, 1966, in ASIL Minute Book, 1959-1966, at 249, 251.

238 Id.

Upon accepting Merillat's resignation, the Executive Council authorized the Executive Committee to appoint a new Executive Director and to determine his compensation. Thus the Executive Committee became both the search committee and the appointing agency for the new Executive Director. John R. Stevenson, then the President of the Society, personally approached Stephen M. Schwebel,[239] who at that time was with the State Department. The Executive Committee appointed Schwebel in December 1966;[240] he took office three months later.[241]

239 Interview with Stephen M. Schwebel, Dec. 19, 1995 (transcript on file with the Society).

240 Minutes of the Executive Committee, Dec. 20, 1966, in ASIL Minute Book, Dec. 1966-Oct. 1973, at 1.

241 Letter to Members, Jan. 1967, at 1. See Chapter Nine *infra*.

Chapter Nine

BUILDING ON THE NEW FOUNDATION IN A TIME OF NATIONAL TURMOIL[1]

I think it is the special quality of this Society that our emphasis on scholarship and discussion rather than on official public positions on specific issues permits a cosmopolitan breadth of approach in bringing about greater recognition of the legal component of international affairs and in broadening the general understanding of the many ways in which law and legal techniques may and should influence international policy.

—John R. Stevenson
Remarks, 61 *ASIL Proceedings* 232 (1967)

A. THE LIFE OF THE SOCIETY IN THE VIETNAM YEARS

1. The Second Executive Director

Stephen M. Schwebel embarked on his duties as Executive Director in March 1967. It was a time of national turmoil over the Vietnam War. Both the War and the turmoil would continue throughout his term as Executive Director, and would at times tear at the fabric of a Society dedicated to the maintenance of international relations on the basis of law and justice. The burden of keeping the Society on track as a non-partisan body devoted to that goal would fall heavily on Schwebel and the other leaders of the organization. For the most part, they succeeded.

Schwebel came to the Society from his post as Special Assistant to the Assistant Secretary of State for International Organization Affairs. He had served previously as an Assistant Legal Adviser of the State Department and as Legal Adviser to the U.S. Delegation to the U.N. General Assembly. In addition, he had experience as a private practitioner with White & Case and as a member of the

[1] I am grateful to James A.R. Nafziger for his extremely helpful suggestions regarding the coverage and content of this chapter. Any errors or omissions are my own.

Harvard Law School faculty.[2] His credentials, in other words, very nicely reflected the gamut of interests and careers within the Society's membership.

From the start, Schwebel availed himself of the revised Society Regulation permitting the Executive Director to do part-time teaching. The Executive Committee authorized him to devote about one-fourth of his time to teaching international law at the Johns Hopkins School of Advanced International Studies, in Washington.[3] He did so, first as Professor of International Law and then as the school's first Edward B. Burling Professor of International Law and Organization.

Richard Edwards, who served on the Society's staff under both Chris Merillat and Steve Schwebel, remembers the two as being quite different. As we have seen, Merillat wanted to move away from a focus purely on classical international law; Schwebel had no problem with that approach, but was much more comfortable in the classical *genre*. As an administrator, Schwebel was more inclined than Merillat to seek and follow direction from the Executive Council. Schwebel was the more focused and organized of the two.[4]

James A.R. Nafziger joined the Society's staff as its first Fellow in 1969. He regarded Schwebel as the model administrator. He remembers Schwebel as "well-organized, somewhat formal but respectful of staff members, always setting a good example for us, and able to delegate authority to us so as to encourage creativity and a sense of responsibility. He had a superb internal system of communications that kept the staff routinely in close contact with each other ... . Steve would consult on a regular basis with individual staff members, sometimes over the tea and Pepperidge Farm cookies his secretary, Betty Posniak, would serve him every afternoon."[5]

2. Terms of Employment at the Top

In April 1968, the Executive Council decided to tie the Executive Director's salary to the salary of a GS-18 federal civil servant. Henceforth, if the GS-18 salary increased, so would that of the Executive Director.[6]

Neither H.C.L. Merillat nor Stephen Schwebel had been offered a contract of employment when he became Executive Director. In February 1973, the Execu-

2 For a full biography, see the entry in the Yearbook of the International Court of Justice on Stephen M. Schwebel for any year during his tenure as a judge, e.g. 1991-1992 *ICJ YB* 25-27. See also ASIL Letter to Members, Jan. 1967, at 1-2.

3 Minutes of the Executive Committee, Dec. 20, 1966, in ASIL Minute Book, Dec. 1966–Oct. 1973, at 1.

4 Telephone interview with Richard W. Edwards, Jr., Oct. 3, 1997.

5 Letter from James A.R. Nafziger to Frederic L. Kirgis, Aug. 17, 2001.

6 ASIL Minute Book, Dec. 1966–Oct. 1973, at 44.

tive Committee decided that the Executive Director should have the job security that such a contract would afford. It invited the Executive Council to amend the Regulations to provide that the Executive Director should serve for such term as the Executive Council shall from time to time prescribe, and recommended that the term be five years.[7] The Executive Council concurred.[8]

3. Staff Changes During the Schwebel Years

In early 1968, Richard W. Edwards, Jr., was appointed Assistant Director of the Society.[9] He continued also to serve as the Editor of *International Legal Materials*, a position he had held since early 1967. He resigned effective June 30, 1970, to enter academia after eight and a half years on the Society's staff.[10] James A.R. Nafziger took over his duties, though with a different title – Administrative Director.[11] He served until 1974, when he resigned to take a teaching position.

A new Assistant Editor of *International Legal Materials* was appointed in 1968. She was Marilou M. Righini, and she was destined to stay awhile. She came to the Society from four years as a Research Assistant at the Washington Center of Foreign Policy Research of Johns Hopkins University.[12] Almost immediately, she assumed principal responsibility for I.L.M.[13] In April 1970 her title caught up with her responsibility; she was appointed as Editor of I.L.M.[14]

By the late 1960s, munificent Ford Foundation support for new Society programs could no longer be taken for granted. Stephen Schwebel perceived that if the Society's studies program was to prosper, someone was needed to develop ideas for research programs and to interest foundations in supporting them. The Board of Review and Development concurred. It wanted the Society to add a senior staff person who could imaginatively counsel the Board on the direction of its research and the generation and disposition of funds. The new

---

7 Minutes of the Executive Committee, Feb. 9, 1973, in ASIL Minute Book, Dec. 1966–Oct. 1973, at 254.

8 Minutes of the Executive Council, Apr. 12, 1973, in ASIL Minute Book, Dec. 1966–Oct. 1973, at 262 & 264.

9 Letter to Members, Mar. 1968, at 2.

10 Minutes of the Executive Council, Apr. 24, 1970, in ASIL Minute Book, Dec. 1966–Oct. 1973, at 139, 141; Letter to Members, May 1970, at 2.

11 Minutes of the Executive Council, Nov. 9, 1970, in ASIL Minute Book, Dec. 1966–Oct. 1973, at 181, 182.

12 *ASIL Newsletters*, Apr. 1972, at 3; July–Aug. 1972, at 1.

13 Minutes of the Executive Council, Nov. 23, 1968, in ASIL Minute Book, Dec. 1966–Oct. 1973, at 61, 64.

14 Minutes of the Executive Council, Apr. 26. 1970, in ASIL Minute Book, Dec. 1966–Oct. 1973, at 165, 166.

person should work effectively with the Board's study panels, and should ensure publication and other dissemination of the work of panels.[15]

Accordingly, a new Director of Studies position was established. To fill the position, Schwebel recommended that the Society recruit John Lawrence Hargrove, with whom he had worked closely at the State Department and for whom he had very high regard.[16] Hargrove had been an Attorney-Adviser at State, and in 1966 had become Senior Adviser for International Law to the U.S. Mission to the United Nations.[17] He was duly recruited, and he accepted the job. Beginning in May 1970, he became the staff person in charge of administering the Society's scholarly activities other than publication of the Journal.

In 1972, Eleanor Finch retired. She had devoted practically her entire adult life to the Society, beginning as a part-time assistant to her father in 1929 while she was attending law school. In 1948, she had become Executive Secretary of the Society and Secretary of the Board of Editors. This meant that she was the chief administrative officer of the Society until Chris Merillat became its first Executive Director, while at the same time serving as Assistant Editor of the Journal – a title formally bestowed on her in 1968. Her duties included taking care of membership files, doing all the typing of correspondence, making all the administrative arrangements for the Annual Meetings, and ultimately being responsible for the essential, but thankless, jobs of detailed editing and arranging for the publication of both the Journal and the Proceedings.

Stephen Schwebel recalls that "She would edit the Proceedings and publish them effortlessly, it appeared, on time. In Miss Finch's day there was never a problem of late publication of the Proceedings of which I was aware. ... The Journal and the Proceedings of her day, as she turned them out, were impeccable, and we took her for granted, I'm afraid."[18] Richard Baxter noted that the pages of the Journal reflected her meticulous attention to detail and her sense of style. "She became," he said, "the real element of continuity in the Journal."[19]

Eleanor Finch's retirement ended sixty-two years of devoted service to the Society by the Finch family – first the father, then father and daughter together, then the daughter.

---

15 Minutes of the Executive Committee, Dec. 15, 1969, in ASIL Minute Book, Dec. 1966–Oct. 1973, at 126, 128.

16 Id.; interview with Stephen M. Schwebel, Dec. 19, 1995 (transcript on file with the Society).

17 Letter to Members, May 1970, at 2.

18 Interview with Stephen M. Schwebel, Dec. 19, 1995 (transcript on file with the Society).

19 Richard R. Baxter, Editorial Comment: The Retirement of Miss Eleanor Finch as Assistant Editor of the Journal, 66 *AJIL* 815, 816 (1972).

4. Electing Officers

In 1969, the Society's Nominating Committee evaluated the practice of nominating the President from the roster of Vice Presidents. It adopted a consensus statement:

> There is no requirement that a President of the Society be elected from among the Society's Vice Presidents. Tradition has been to draw Presidents from among Vice Presidents, though there has been one recent, notable exception. The Nominating Committee believes that this tradition should not be jeopardized, but that the President should not necessarily be drawn from among Vice Presidents who have served in the immediately preceding period.[20]

The committee proceeded to nominate a sitting Vice President, Harold Lasswell, to be the next President. The "notable exception" was Arthur H. Dean, who had been elected President for 1961-62.

In 1972, the Nominating Committee wished to re-nominate Philip Jessup as Honorary President. Jessup said that he was not able to accept the nomination. The committee then nominated him as an Honorary Vice President and recommended – in order to accommodate other candidates – that the number of Honorary Vice Presidents be increased from sixteen to eighteen.[21] The Executive Council approved the increase.[22]

When Jessup turned down the opportunity to continue as Honorary President, the Nominating Committee turned to Myres McDougal. There is a tale here, just as there was when McDougal was nominated to be President.[23] We shall let him tell it:

> [M]y telephone rang in the middle of the night ... and it was Whitney Debevoise. He was very excited. He had great news for me. I thought he was going to offer me a big part in a big case, or admit me to the International Commission of Jurists. Instead, he said, "Our Committee wants to nominate you for Honorary President of the Society."
>
> You can imagine how that hit me. I said, " ... Why don't you make Phil Jessup continue?"
>
> Whit came back, "Phil won't do it because there is too much the Honorary President has to do. He had a hard life over at The Hague and now he has retired and wants to rest."

---

20 Letter to Members, Nov. 1969, at 1-2.

21 *ASIL Newsletter*, Sept. 1972, at 1.

22 Minutes of the Executive Council, Oct. 21, 1972, in ASIL Minute Book, Dec. 1966–Oct. 1973, at 249, 252.

23 See Chapter Seven, Section A.6, *supra*.

> As my next avenue of escape, I said, "The next most venerable member of our group is Judge Hardy Dillard. Why don't you ask him to do this?"
>
> Whit replied, "Well, we consulted Judge Dillard and he finds a conflict of interest. He thinks the duties of Honorary President are so onerous that it would interfere with his work on the [International] Court."
>
> I named two or three other members of the Society who I thought were a little more venerable than I, to which the reply was that the Committee couldn't agree on them. I finally said, "If I'm the only guy who will take it, I'll do the best I can."[24]

None of the putative candidates spelled out just what the onerous duties were. Presenting awards at the annual dinner, though a duty (actually, the primary formal duty) of the Honorary President, probably was not considered onerous – at least, not for accomplished raconteurs like Dillard and McDougal or for a gracious diplomat like Jessup.

5. Governing the Society

By 1967, the Executive Committee had established itself as the usual decision-making body of the organization for matters not constitutionally required to be decided by the Business Meeting or the Executive Council, and not just in the interims between regularly scheduled Executive Council meetings. Nevertheless, the Executive Council retained the authority to overrule the Executive Committee. It exercised its authority occasionally. In November 1968 it rescinded an Executive Committee decision that would have precluded the Society from accepting any further funds from the Asia Foundation on account of the Foundation's past ties to the C.I.A.[25] The matter was sensitive because of the C.I.A.'s tarnished reputation, particularly among young people, during the Vietnam War.

The Vietnam War influenced another tussle between the Executive Committee and Executive Council in the autumn of 1968. The Executive Committee had adopted a policy statement precluding receipt of grants from the National Science Foundation and other government agencies "in areas sensitive to government policy."[26] The primary concern was that the integrity and reputation of the Society be maintained.[27] After extensive discussion, the Executive Council changed the

---

24 67 *ASIL Proc.* 292 (1973).

25 Minutes of the Executive Council, Nov. 23, 1968, in ASIL Minute Book, Dec. 1966–Oct. 1973, at 61, 62-63.

26 Minutes of the Executive Committee, Sept. 14, 1968, in ASIL Minute Book, Dec. 1966–Oct. 1973, at 57, 58.

27 Minutes of the Executive Council, Nov. 23, 1968, in ASIL Minute Book, Dec. 1966–Oct. 1973, at 61, 62.

policy to read, "The nature of the grant shall not jeopardize the integrity or credibility of the research financed."[28]

6. Money and Membership

New staff positions in the late 1960s, and the Journal's increasing difficulty in staying within its budget,[29] created budgetary problems for the Society. They were addressed over Schwebel's time in office by various dues increases and efforts to boost membership. About a thousand new members were added between April 1967 and April 1969.[30] But dues increases took their toll, and membership declined a bit from 1970 to 1972. In 1973, it began to inch back up.[31]

In 1968, the last vestige of the Society as a selective club disappeared. Of course, the Society had long since abandoned any pretense of actual selectivity in admitting new members, but it had maintained a requirement in its Regulations that an applicant be endorsed by a member. The Executive Council in April 1968 finally dropped that formality.[32]

7. Tillar House, Vietnam and the Cold War

Richard Edwards' office was on the fourth floor of Tillar House. It offered excellent views of the Embassy of Vietnam across the street, and of Sheridan Circle. He recalls that during the Vietnam era, F.B.I. agents would typically come to his office about 5 p.m. and leave sometime during the night. They did not come every night. When they did come, they had shoulder bags with radios. Edwards was told that the F.B.I. needed to use his office to observe Sheridan Circle for law

---

28 Id. The full policy statement, as adopted by the Council, said:

(1) The nature of the grant shall not jeopardize the integrity or credibility of the research financed;

(2) The research results may be published without censorship, and the research shall not be susceptible to any governmental influence as to its tone and conclusions;

(3) The Society need not be secretive about the sources of the funds or their use; and

(4) The amount of the grant shall be small in relation to the Society's total budget.

29 Minutes of the Executive Council, Apr. 27, 1967, in ASIL Minute Book, Dec. 1966–Oct. 1973, at 6, 9, 10.

30 Minutes of the Executive Council, Apr. 25, 1968, and Apr. 24, 1969, in ASIL Minute Book, Dec. 1966–Oct. 1973, at 42, 46 & 83, 85, respectively.

31 For details, see Memorandum, "ASIL History: Details Relating to Budget, Finances and Membership" (2006), on file with the Society.

32 Minutes of the Executive Council, Apr. 25, 1968, in ASIL Minute Book, Dec. 1966–Oct. 1973, at 42, 46.

enforcement purposes, but years later he learned that the agents were observing the area to assure that other agents inside the Embassy of Vietnam would not be caught there.

During this time there was concern about threatened Weathermen attacks on the Embassy. Edwards recalls one occasion when a bus load of police in riot gear occupied Tillar House to prepare to repel a threatened attack on the Embassy.

Edwards believes that the Society's telephones were tapped during this era. They were frequently out of order. When Edwards walked to work in the morning, he would often encounter a man working in the telephone manhole on R Street, ostensibly "switching wires."[33]

Jim Nafziger recalls that during this period, Schwebel received a request from the East Germans to help them meet folks in Washington as an overture that could lead to cultural exchange and eventual diplomatic relations. At Schwebel's suggestion, Nafziger met from time to time with East German cultural emissaries.[34] It does not appear that these meetings produced much of a thaw in U.S.–East German relations at the time.

8. Investing with a Conscience

The Vietnam years brought to the fore an issue that would come up again. To what extent should the Society's investment portfolio be influenced by non-financial considerations? The Executive Council considered the issue in November 1969. As the minutes of the meeting rather gingerly put it, "Following discussion, it was agreed that the minutes should show that several, though not all, members of the Council expressed the view that the purposes of the Society should be taken into account by the Treasurer in choosing investments, it being recognized, however, that persons viewing a corporation from outside may not be fully informed of the character of its operations."[35]

When the Ford Foundation made its third grant to the Society in 1970, with a three-for-one matching funds requirement, generation of the required funds prevailed over other considerations. The emphasis was placed on investments producing the maximum possible annual income.[36]

---

33 Letter under the Privacy Act and the Freedom of Information Act, from Richard W. Edwards, Jr., to Louis J. Freeh, Director of the F.B.I., July 5, 1997; letters from Richard W. Edwards, Jr., to Frederic L. Kirgis, July 13, 1997 & Oct. 8, 1997.

34 Letter from James A.R. Nafziger to Frederic L. Kirgis, Aug. 17, 2001.

35 Minutes of the Executive Council, Nov. 1, 1969, in ASIL Minute Book, Dec. 1966–Oct. 1973, at 113, 121.

36 Minutes of the Executive Council, Nov. 9, 1970, in ASIL Minute Book, Dec. 1966–Oct. 1973, at 181, 185.

9. The Library's Growth

Helen Philos became the Society's librarian in 1964. Jim Nafziger later described her as "a well-educated, highly competent and characteristically cheerful wizard of librarianship [working] in very cramped quarters."[37] She presided over a period of expansion in the use of the library and in its collection.

By the late 1960s, in excess of seven hundred readers a year were signing in as users of the Society's library. About three-quarters of the signed-in readers were students.[38]

In 1970, the Society's library was recognized in an article published by the Law Librarians' Society of Washington. The article noted that the Society's collection had grown to about 18,000 items, including books, pamphlets, documents, briefs, reprints and periodicals. More than 250 periodicals were being received, at least half of them by virtue of exchange arrangements. Substantial book donations to the library, in addition to the important initial gift from Manley Hudson's estate, had come from Henry F. Butler, Ivan S. Kerno, Philip C. Jessup, Edgar Turlington, Lester H. Woolsey, and the law firm of Covington & Burling.[39]

In the following year Denys P. Myers donated his international law collection, rich in League of Nations materials.[40] That gift and others raised the library's book count to more than 20,000 by April 1971.[41]

The library's growth was a mixed blessing. Finding space in the building became a problem, as did keeping up with cataloguing and finding an adequate niche in the Society's budget for further book acquisitions. In 1972, the Society's Committee on the Library said that if the cataloguing and space problems could not be remedied and funds raised, serious consideration should be given to abandoning the library as an integral component of Tillar House.[42] In 1973, the Society's Ad Hoc Committee on the Future of the Library recommended turning it into a joint library with the Carnegie Endowment, to be housed in new headquarters the Endowment was expected to establish near Tillar House.

---

37 Letter from James A.R. Nafziger to Frederic L. Kirgis, Aug. 17, 2001.

38 Library Report for Apr. 1, 1968–Mar. 31, 1969, prepared for the Executive Council meeting of Apr. 24, 1969.

39 *ASIL Newsletter*, Jan. 1971, at 3.

40 *ASIL Newsletter*, June–July 1971, at 3-4.

41 Minutes of the Executive Council, Apr. 29, 1971, in ASIL Minute Book, Dec. 1966–Oct. 1973, at 199, 205-06.

42 Report of the Committee on the Library for the Executive Council meeting of Apr. 27, 1972, at 1.

There was some concern in the Executive Council that moving the library would make the work of the Journal staff more difficult.[43]

In 1974, the Committee on the Library recommended emphatically against moving the library out of Tillar House "under present circumstances." The Executive Council decided, for the time being, to keep the library where it was.[44] It became a fixture in Tillar House even though it took nearly 30 more years to solve the space problems.

10. Examining the Role of Women in the Society

Alona Evans and Carol Plumb, in their study of women in the Society, found that in 1973 there were 271 women in the total membership of 5,146. Ever since 1943, women had constituted between six and seven per cent of the membership.[45]

Only two women had ever served as officers of the Society – Marjorie Whiteman and Rosalyn C. Higgins, elected as Vice Presidents in 1962 and 1972, respectively. In 1972, Rita E. Hauser became the first woman member of the Executive Committee. Since 1923, there had been at least one woman on the Executive Council, except in 1926-1932 and 1964-1965. In 1973, there were three. As of 1973, there were nine women serving on nine of the sixteen standing committees of the Society; three of them were chairs of their committees.[46] Only one woman, Rosalyn Higgins, had served as a member of the Board of Review and Development.[47]

From 1960 through to 1973, 319 addresses or papers were presented at the Society's Annual Meetings; of those, eight were by women. Of the 244 contributions by panelists or round table participants, thirteen were by women. Most women participants in Annual Meetings were rapporteurs.[48]

Alona Evans had been the first woman elected to the Journal's Board of Editors, in 1966. In 1973, she and Marjorie Whiteman were the two women editors on a Board of twenty-four regular members and nine honorary members. Lead articles by female authors published in the Journal had peaked in the thirties, then

---

43 Minutes of the Executive Council, Apr. 13, 1973, in ASIL Minute Book, Dec. 1966–Oct. 1973, at 269, 270.

44 Minutes of the Executive Council, Apr. 26, 1974, in ASIL Minute Book, Apr. 1974–Oct. 1981, at 10-11.

45 In 1973, 138 of the female members were students, 15 were teachers in political science departments, 13 were practitioners, nine were government officials and eight were teachers in law schools. Alona E. Evans & Carol Per Lee Plumb, Notes and Comments: "Women and the American Society of International Law," 68 *AJIL* 290, 293 (1974).

46 Id. at 293-94.

47 Id. at 295.

48 Id. at 294-95.

declined, and had begun to pick up again in the early seventies. Women's written contributions to the Journal were principally in the Book Review section.[49]

Although women's contributions to the Society and to the Journal had expanded in the thirties, the situation changed with the onset of World War II. It was not until the seventies that women's roles in the Society began to regain some of the prominence that seemed within reach in the thirties. Whether the dropoff in the interim was primarily a matter of men's attitudes, of women's interests or of something else does not appear.[50]

11. Attempting to Sensitize the Cosmos Club

The Cosmos Club, one of Washington's more exclusive establishments, is located on Massachusetts Avenue, one block from Tillar House. For many years, the Society and the Journal held meetings at the Cosmos Club, particularly when the meetings involved lunch or dinner. The Club admitted only men to membership. Moreover, the Club's traditional policy was to allow only men to enter the front door of the building; female guests were relegated to a side entrance. At one point, Marilou Righini and Jim Nafziger sought an explanation for the policy barring the front door to women. They were told that male residents were afraid they would be seen before lunch in their pajamas and bathrobes in the front lobby. Not being satisfied with this explanation, Righini and Nafziger entered by way of the front door the next time the Society held a lunch meeting there. They passed through unchallenged.[51]

Stephen Schwebel, with the support and urging of the Society's Executive Council, made numerous attempts to get the Club to change its policy regarding how female guests could enter the building. He got nowhere until the Society imposed an economic sanction. It ceased holding lunches of its study panels and dinners of the Journal's Board of Editors at the Club. On January 15, 1973, the Cosmos Club, on a motion by Schwebel, changed its bylaws to allow women to enter by the front door.[52]

The change in the bylaws satisfied the (male-dominated) Executive Council for a while. But in November 1974, Mary Ellen Caldwell, a member of the Executive Council, proposed that the Council adopt a resolution to the effect that the Society would no longer use the facilities of any organization that discriminated

---

49 Id. at 292, 295.

50 The full report of the Committee on the Professional Interest and Status of Women in International Law appears in the dossier for the 1974 Annual Meeting. See Minutes of the Executive Council, Apr. 25, 1974, in ASIL Minute Book, Apr. 1974–Oct. 1981, at 3, 5.

51 Letter from James A.R. Nafziger to Frederic L. Kirgis, Aug. 17, 2001.

52 Minutes of the Executive Council, Oct. 21, 1972, in ASIL Minute Book, Dec. 1966–Oct. 1973, at 249, 253; *ASIL Newsletter*, Feb. 1973, at 4.

against admission to membership solely on the basis of sex. Everyone understood that the resolution was directed at the Cosmos Club. It was adopted without opposition.[53] The Cosmos Club eventually reformed its membership policy, but whether the Society's pressure significantly influenced the decision is an unanswered question.

12. Developing the Relationship with Students and Young Professionals

By the time Stephen Schwebel took over as Executive Director, the Association of Student International Law Societies had twenty-five member societies at law schools throughout the United States. It was in the process of drafting a formal Constitution, which was adopted in 1968.[54] Under its energetic Chair, Peter Trooboff (a future President of the Society), it had undertaken to become a national clearing house for information about visits to the United States by international law scholars and practitioners.[55] Despite an encouraging initial response from abroad, the endeavor does not seem to have thrived after Trooboff's term as Chair ended.

The Jessup International Law Moot Court Competition continued to be the dominant A.S.I.L.S. activity. Another significant A.S.I.L.S. program was the organization of workshops for student international law journals, begun in 1970.[56]

By 1967, the practice of holding the finals of the Jessup Competition in conjunction with the Society's Annual Meeting was well established. The Competition was growing steadily. By 1968, there were six regional competitions, with a total of thirty-eight teams from as many schools.[57]

In 1968, the Society and A.S.I.L.S. began a joint effort to obtain foundation grants to support the Jessup Competition and for some other purposes.[58] The effort – much of it by Jack Stevenson – paid off at the end of the year, when the Henry Luce Foundation made a USD 72,000 grant to the Society and A.S.I.L.S. for three purposes: the Jessup Competition, including extending it to include teams from outside North America; establishing a central A.S.I.L.S. office in

---

53 Minutes of the Executive Council, Nov. 2, 1974, in ASIL Minute Book, Apr. 1974–Oct. 1981, at 19, 22-23.

54 ASILS Ann. Rep., 62 *ASIL Proc.* 295, 297 (1968).

55 ASILS Ann. Rep., 61 *ASIL Proc.* 265, 266 (1967).

56 ASILS Ann. Rep., 64 *ASIL Proc.* 315, 318 (1970).

57 Attachment to letter from Francis Conte to Stephen M. Schwebel, Jan. 26, 1968, in 1968 Annual Meeting First File.

58 E.g., letter from Schwebel to Conte, Feb. 5, 1968, in 1968 Annual Meeting First File.

Tillar House; and supporting regional meetings of the Society held jointly with student international law societies.[59]

With the help of the grant, the Society and A.S.I.L.S. decided to establish a position for a graduating law student who would serve both as Executive Secretary of A.S.I.L.S. and the Society's resident Fellow. It was conceived on the model of a clerkship, with a one-year term. The person selected would participate in the Society's scholarly and organizational activities (as it turned out, by assisting the Society's study panels), as well as administering A.S.I.L.S. and thus the Jessup Competition.[60] James A.R. Nafziger was appointed in the spring of 1969 as the first holder of the joint position.[61] As we have seen, after his one-year term was up he became the Administrative Director of the Society. The job of administering the Jessup Competition soon became nearly full-time, leaving the A.S.I.L.S. Executive Secretary very little time for the Society.

In 1969, for the first time, a team from outside North America participated in the Jessup Competition. Wolfgang Friedmann, of Columbia, was a visiting professor that year at the University of Paris. He took the lead in organizing a French regional competition. The winning team, from the Faculté de Droit et Sciences Economiques de Paris, came to the United States courtesy of the Luce Foundation grant, as one of eight semi-final teams.[62]

In 1970, three teams from outside North America competed in the semi-finals. They came from the University of Paris, Oxford University, and the National University of Rosario, Argentina.[63] The 1971 semi-finalists included teams from Argentina, Ethiopia and Northern Ireland.[64]

When the Luce Foundation grant expired at the end of 1971, Schwebel tried unsuccessfully to replace it with new grant money. He finally had to ask the Executive Committee for authorization to dip into the Society's operating budget for one year to cover basic A.S.I.L.S. operating expenses, including the salaries of its Executive Secretary and of a part-time secretary. The Executive Committee agreed,[65] and later in 1972 the Executive Council allocated USD 11,500 for student activities.[66]

---

59 Letter to Members, Jan. 1969, at 1.

60 Id.

61 Letter to Members, Apr. 1969, at 2.

62 Id. at 1-2.

63 Letter to Members, Mar.–Apr. 1970, at 1.

64 *ASIL Newsletter*, May 1971, at 2.

65 Minutes of the Executive Committee, Feb. 14, 1972, in ASIL Minute Book, Dec. 1966–Oct. 1973, at 222-23.

66 Minutes of the Executive Council, Apr. 27, 1972, in ASIL Minute Book, Dec. 1966–Oct. 1973, at 227, 234.

The State Department was persuaded to finance the travel to the 1972 Jessup Competition of teams from Ethiopia, Zambia and Argentina, and of observers from Nigeria.[67] In 1973, the Henry L. and Grace Doherty Charitable Foundation supplied a USD 10,000 grant. The Jessup problem in that year dealt with the law of the sea, a topic that appealed to the Doherty Foundation.[68] The grant was renewed for 1974, when another law of the sea problem was selected.[69] The State Department chipped in again with a USD 43,250 grant for the travel of teams from developing countries in 1974.[70]

The 1972 Jessup Competition, for the first time, was divided into separate domestic and foreign semi-final rounds. The winners of each semi-final division, the University of Miami and Haile Sellassie I University of Ethiopia, met during the Annual Meeting. Miami prevailed.[71]

This format was retained in the ensuing years. In 1973, more than a hundred schools took part in the competition, with teams from ten foreign countries participating in the international semi-final round.[72]

Meanwhile, A.S.I.L.S. had been growing in membership and in activity. Growth brought the need for more structure. In 1972, it established an Advisory Board consisting of six former A.S.I.L.S. officers who could advise it on matters of interest and who could provide administrative continuity.[73] Two years later the Advisory Board was expanded to include a maximum of twelve members, serving two-year terms.[74] In 1973, A.S.I.L.S. formalized its Executive Committee to consist of four students and the A.S.I.L.S. Executive Secretary.[75]

In the early seventies, Oceana Publications established a prize in memory of Francis Deák for the best student article published in a student-edited international law journal.[76] The prize was first awarded in 1973, to Allan R. Pearl for an article in the *Harvard International Law Journal* on the liberalization of capital in Japan.[77]

---

67 66 *ASIL Proc.* 303 (1972).

68 *ASIL Newsletter*, Jan. 1973, at 3.

69 *ASIL Newsletter*, Aug. 1973, at 1.

70 *ASIL Newsletter*, Nov. 1973, at 1-2.

71 *ASIL Newsletter*, May 1972, at 2.

72 *ASIL Newsletter*, Sept. 1973, at 2-3.

73 ASILS Ann. Rep., 67 *ASIL Proc.* 324 (1973).

74 ASILS Ann. Rep., 68 *ASIL Proc.* 351 (1974).

75 *ASIL Newsletter*, Sept. 1973, at 3. The Executive Secretary was then Judith R. Hall. She went on to be an ASIL staff member.

76 ASILS Ann. Rep., 67 *ASIL Proc.* 324, 327 (1973).

77 Allan R. Pearl, "Liberalization of Capital in Japan," Part I, 13 *Harv. Int'l L.J.* 59 (1972), and Part II, id. at 245.

By 1974, student international law societies at sixty-eight schools in the United States belonged to A.S.I.L.S., in just its eleventh year of existence.[78]

Meanwhile, the Society had been addressing the recurring issue of getting its younger members actively involved in the Society's programs. Edward Gordon, reporting in 1969 for the Committee on Intermediate Membership, recommended an all-out effort to broaden the participation of younger members at all levels of the Society's operation, including the Executive Council. The Committee also recommended that each new young member be personally contacted by a Society representative and encouraged to become active. The Executive Council agreed in principle that greater involvement of young members was desirable, but took no formal action.[79]

The Society also established a Committee on Student and Professional Development, chaired by Peter Trooboff. It produced a survey of international law societies and journals, and addressed issues related to teaching international law, Society membership and outreach. The committee also arranged some broadcasts of the Society's regional meetings on local National Public Radio outlets.[80]

13. Changes in the Newsletter

Under Stephen Schwebel, the Letter to Members – eventually renamed the *ASIL Newsletter* – expanded its coverage beyond purely in-house news, and began to carry brief summaries of pending cases involving international law.[81] The summaries appeared whenever there were significant judicial or arbitral proceedings that would be of interest to members. Sometimes these summaries supplied the first readily available news of pending proceedings or current decisions. Such was the case in 1973, for example, when Judge Gunnar Lagergren rendered his award in favor of British Petroleum in the arbitral proceedings arising out of Libya's expropriation of BP's oil concession.[82] Judge Lagergren's award was pathbreaking at the time. He held that Libya's action violated international law because it was done "for purely extraneous political reasons and was arbitrary and discriminatory in character."[83] He added that it was confiscatory, but the

---

78 ASILS Ann. Rep., 68 *ASIL Proc.* 351, 352 (1974).

79 Minutes of the Executive Council, Nov. 1, 1969, in ASIL Minute Book, Dec. 1966–Oct. 1973, at 113, 117-19.

80 Letter from James A.R. Nafziger to Frederic L. Kirgis, Aug. 17, 2001. Nafziger was the Rapporteur for the committee.

81 See Letter to Members, Apr. 1967, at 2-4.

82 *ASIL Newsletter*, Oct. 1973, at 2.

83 *BP Exploration Co. (Libya) Ltd. v. Libyan Arab Republic*, 53 *Int'l L. Reports* 297, 329 (1979).

clear implication was that the lack of public purpose and the discrimination were enough to constitute a violation.

When Larry Hargrove became the Acting Executive Director in 1974, he suggested further changes. He proposed that the Newsletter include greater coverage of significant events, an exchange-of-opinions department for members, and a President's column.[84] His suggestions got nowhere at the time, though one of them – the President's column – later became a newsletter fixture.

14. Rejoining the American Council of Learned Societies

The Society's on-again, off-again relationship with the American Council of Learned Societies was on again in January 1971, when the Society rejoined.[85] It had been a member of the A.C.L.S. from 1934 to 1950, when it had withdrawn for financial reasons.[86] Myres McDougal became the Society representative to the A.C.L.S. when the Society rejoined, and soon rose to prominence among his peers in the humanities.[87]

15. A Leave of Absence, Musical Chairs and the Resignation of the Executive Director

At the same time Stephen Schwebel was given formal terms of appointment, he was granted a one-year leave of absence. The purpose was to enable him to become the Counselor on International Law in the State Department. It was noted that the period of his requested leave would approximate the seventh year of his service to the Society, and thus could be considered a sabbatical. It would be without pay from the Society, but his fringe benefits would continue.

To fill the resulting gap, John Lawrence Hargrove was appointed as Acting Executive Director. Robert E. Stein accepted a temporary appointment as Acting Director of Studies.[88]

Schwebel never returned to the Executive Directorship from his sabbatical. While he was at the State Department, Carlisle Maw became the Legal Adviser under Secretary of State Henry Kissinger. Maw was close to Kissinger and thus had a great deal of clout in the Department. When Maw asked Schwebel to

---

84 Notes for the Report of the Acting Executive Director, in the dossier for the November 1974 meetings of the Executive Committee and Executive Council.

85 Minutes of the Executive Council, Apr. 26, 1970, in ASIL Minute Book, Dec. 1966–Oct. 1973, at 165, 170; *ASIL Newsletter*, Mar. 1971, at 3.

86 See Chapter Four, Section A.11, *supra*.

87 Letter from James A.R. Nafziger to Frederic L. Kirgis, Aug. 17, 2001.

88 *ASIL Newsletter*, June–July 1973, at 1.

stay on as Deputy Legal Adviser, the prospect was attractive indeed.[89] Schwebel resigned as Executive Director and Executive Vice President of the Society, effective June 30, 1974.[90]

B. DEVELOPING THE SOCIETY'S PROGRAMS

1. The Board of Review and Development in Full Swing

In its early years, the Board of Review and Development was a hotbed of creativity. Its meetings were brainstorming sessions that generated an impressive roster of projects. The projects encompassed international economic law (such as capital formation, foreign investment in developing countries and international monetary policy) as well as standard subjects of public international law (such as the law of armed conflict, the law of treaties, the law of the sea); some were familiar to the Society (such as codification and progressive development of international law) and some were new (like the international movement of art treasures); some were doctrinal (such as self-determination), and some were policy-oriented (like international telecommunications policy).[91] It was a crazy

---

89 Interview with Stephen M. Schwebel, Dec. 19, 1995 (transcript on file with the Society).

90 *ASIL Newsletter*, June 1974, at 1.

91 The active projects by the summer of 1967 were Capital Formation and Securities Regulation; China and International Law; Codification and Progressive Development of International Law; Communication and Linguistics; Conflict Control by Non-Violent Means; Developing Countries (with two components: Legal Training and Foreign Investment); International Law Commission Draft Convention on the Law of Treaties; Nuclear Energy and World Order; Regional Integration; Relationship of Law and Force in Comparative International Systems; Role of International Law in Civil Wars; Role of International Law in Government Decision-Making in War-Peace Crises; and Trade Regulation. See Richard W. Edwards, Jr., Note: The June, 1967, Meeting of the Society's Board of Review and Development: Identification of Problems for Research, 62 *AJIL* 127 (1968). By November 1968, three more projects were underway: International Telecommunications Policy; Resources of the Deep Ocean Floor (later broadened into a Law of the Sea panel); and Self-Determination. Minutes of the Executive Council, Nov. 23, 1968, in ASIL Minute Book, Dec. 1966–Oct. 1973, at 61, 64. A year later there were four more: International Movement of National Art Treasures; International Law and Humanitarian Problems; International Monetary Policy; and Inter-American Legal Questions. Letters to Members, Aug.–Sept. 1969, at 2, & Dec. 1969, at 4. In 1970, panels on International Law and the Global Environment, on International Implementation of Human Rights, and on the Future of the International Court of Justice joined the list. ASIL Newsletters, Nov. 1970, at 1, & Dec. 1970, at 1. Panels on the Protection of Diplomats, on State Responsibility and on Legal Aspects of the Control of U.S. Foreign Policy were added in 1972. ASIL Newsletters, Jan. 1972, at 3, March 1972, at 3, & Dec. 1972, at

quilt of subjects, reflecting the interests of B.R.D. members, foundations and individual Society members.

Each project had a rapporteur and a study panel. By April 1972, forty study panels had been established. Nineteen of them had finished their work or had otherwise gone out of business. Of the twenty-one functioning panels, seventeen were meeting periodically.[92]

The panel on the Role of International Law in Government Decision-Making in War-Peace Crises received a USD 50,000 grant from the Old Dominion Foundation (at that time one of the Mellon Foundations), thus relieving some of the pressure on the allocation of funds from the Ford Foundation.[93] The panel commissioned studies on the ways in which international law had affected government decision-making in four cases: Suez in 1956, Congo in 1960-1964, the Cuban Missile crisis in 1962, and Cyprus in 1958-1967.[94] All four case studies resulted in published books.[95]

More financial pressure was relieved, and new initiatives were begun, when the National Science Foundation made two grants in 1971 – one for USD 134,000 and one for USD 176,000. The Society used the USD 134,000 grant for a one-year interdisciplinary research program, largely conducted by its panels on International Law and the Global Environment, Law of the Sea, International Telecommunications Policy, and Nuclear Energy and World Order.[96] An outgrowth of this grant was a Conference on Direct Broadcasting from Satellites, held in Bellagio, Italy, in February 1974.[97] The participants included officials, lawyers and academics from a number of countries. A summary of their discussion was published in 1975 in the Society's *Studies in Transnational Legal Policy* series.[98]

---

1. A panel on International Trade Policy and Institutions made its appearance in 1973. *ASIL Newsletter*, Nov. 1973, at 1.

92 66 *ASIL Proc.* 304 (1972).

93 Letter to Members, Feb. 1968, at 3. At that time John R. Stevenson was the President of the Society; he had close ties to the Mellon Foundations. Interview with Stephen M. Schwebel, Dec. 19, 1995 (transcript on file with the Society).

94 *ASIL Newsletter*, Nov. 1971, at 3-4.

95 Robert R. Bowie, *Suez 1956* (1974); Georges Abi-Saab, *The United Nations Operation in the Congo 1960-1964* (1978); Abram Chayes, *The Cuban Missile Crisis* (1974); Thomas Ehrlich, *Cyprus 1958-1967* (1974). The panel's chair published a fifth volume in the series, not devoted to a particular case study. Roger Fisher, *Points of Choice* (1978).

96 *ASIL Newsletter*, June–July 1971, at 2-3; Minutes of the Executive Committee, Oct. 29, 1971, in ASIL Minute Book, Dec. 1966–Oct. 1973, at 212.

97 *ASIL Newsletter*, Mar. 1974, at 3-4.

98 *Direct Broadcasting from Satellites: Policies and Problems*, Part III (1975).

The second grant supported a two-year study under the direction of David M. Leive on "The International Regulation of Specialized Activities."[99] Leive was given office space and a small staff at Tillar House. It was the first major in-house research project the Society had undertaken. Leive focused on three regulatory regimes: the World Health Organization's International Health Regulations (which aim to preclude the international spread of disease without unduly interfering with international trade and travel), the FAO/WHO Codex Alimentarius Commission (which adopts hygienic standards for internationally traded foods and food additives), and the regulatory scheme of the World Meteorological Organization (such as the WHO Congress' standards under the World Weather Watch). In addition to his library research, Leive held extensive discussions with U.S. international officials.[100] The work product was a pathbreaking two-volume study of these relatively apolitical regulatory regimes.[101]

The National Science Foundation made another one-year grant, of USD 148,770, to the Society in January 1974 for a second in-house research project on "Applications of International Regulatory Techniques to Scientific-Technical Problems." David Leive having gone on to other things, David A. Kay was brought in to direct the project.[102] Under this project and one other, he produced nine case studies over a period of four years.[103] His studies focused on specific regimes such as those relating to pesticide residues in food and pharmaceutical drugs, and on more general matters such as technical assistance by specialized agencies of the United Nations.[104]

Panels unsupported by special grants made headway as well. The study panel on the Law of Treaties had an unusually good opportunity to influence the development of United States policy. It was, of course, quintessentially a lawyers' subject. The panel was conceived at the first meeting of the B.R.D. in 1965, when Chris Merillat was Executive Director. Initially the idea was to critique the work of the International Law Commission as it finished its draft articles on the law of treaties. When the draft articles were completed, the panel became the briefing and planning group for the U.S. delegation to the Vienna Conference on the Law of Treaties. At that point, panel members who had official positions with foreign

99 Minutes of the Executive Committee, Oct. 29, 1971, in ASIL Minute Book, Dec. 1966–Oct. 1973, at 212-13.

100 *ASIL Newsletter*, Dec. 1973, at 1-2.

101 David M. Leive, *International Regulatory Regimes: Case Studies in Health, Meteorology and Food* (2 vols., 1976).

102 *ASIL Newsletters*, Jan. 1974, at 1, & Mar. 1974, at 1.

103 73 *ASIL Proc.* 111 (1979).

104 See David A. Kay, *The International Regulation of Pesticide Residues in Food* (1976); David A. Kay, *The International Regulation of Pharmaceutical Drugs* (1976); David A. Kay, *Technical Assistance Through the Regular Budgets of the United Nations Specialized Agencies* (1978).

governments, such as Shabtai Rosenne, left the panel. Papers produced by panel members were made available to officials of the United States and other governments.[105] The State Department provided materials for the panel, including its tentative position papers.[106] Richard D. Kearney and other members of the U.S. delegation to the Vienna Conference were members of the study panel. Kearney was one of its most active members.[107]

The State Department sent 120 copies of the Journal's October 1967 "Law of Treaties" issue, which included lead articles by the study group's chair, Oliver J. Lissitzyn, and its Rapporteur, Egon Schwelb, to U.S. embassies abroad for presentation to the chairs of delegations to the Vienna Conference.[108]

Lissitzyn criticized the International Law Commission's 1966 draft article on changed circumstances. One of his points – the draft article should provide for suspension as well as termination of a treaty – clearly influenced the final version of the Vienna Convention. At the Vienna Conference on the Law of Treaties, the Canadian representative introduced an amendment expressly contemplating suspension on this ground, and relied on Lissitzyn's Journal article in support.[109] Finland introduced a similar amendment. The principle of suspension in the Canadian/Finnish amendments was adopted, and what became Article 62 of the Vienna Convention includes paragraph 3 on suspension of the operation of a treaty when there is a fundamental change of circumstances.[110]

Lissitzyn also criticized the requirement in the ILC Draft Articles that the change of circumstances radically transform the "scope" of obligations still to be performed. Unless "scope" meant "burden" – an interpretation he thought

105 Edwards, "The June, 1967, Meeting of the Society's Board of Review and Development," *supra* note 91, at 129, n. 3 (1968).

106 Letter from Richard W. Edwards, Jr. to Frederic L. Kirgis, Oct. 8, 1997; Minutes of the Executive Council, Nov. 23, 1968, in ASIL Minute Book, Dec. 1966–Oct. 1973, at 61, 64.

107 Report of Oliver J. Lissitzyn, chair of the panel, autumn 1968, in Report of Activities of BRD Study Panels for the Executive Council Meeting, Nov. 23, 1968, at 13. The list of panel members may be found in 62 *ASIL Proc.* x (1968).

108 Report of Oliver J. Lissitzyn, *supra* note 107. The articles were Oliver J. Lissitzyn, "Treaties and Changed Circumstances (*Rebus sic Stantibus*)," 61 *AJIL* 895 (1967); Egon Schwelb, "Some Aspects of International *Jus Cogens* as Formulated by the International Law Commission," id. at 946. See also Oliver J. Lissitzyn, "Stability and Change: Unilateral Denunciation or Suspension of Treaties by Reason of Changed Circumstances," 61 *ASIL Proc.* 186 (1967).

109 U.N. Conf. on the Law of Treaties, First Sess., Official Records 366, U.N. Doc. A/CONF.39/11 (1969); see also Richard D. Kearney & Robert E. Dalton, "The Treaty on Treaties," 64 *AJIL* 495, 544 (1970).

110 Vienna Convention on the Law of Treaties, May 23, 1969, Art. 62(3), 1155 *UNTS* 331, 8 *ILM* 679 (1969).

unnatural – it was supported neither by logic nor by state practice. This point, too, may have had some effect on delegates to the 1968-69 U.N. Conference on the Law of Treaties. The conference changed the word "scope" in the English version to "extent."[111] Lissitzyn presumably was not entirely satisfied with this change, since "extent" would not fully connote "burden." Lissitzyn's view was better expressed in the French version ("*portée des obligations*," which could be translated as *impact* of the obligations).

The treaties study panel also had an impact on the U.S. position regarding what became Vienna Convention Articles 31 and 32 on treaty interpretation. Myres McDougal, a prominent member of the panel, strongly favored using an integrated approach to treaty interpretation rather than the "plain meaning" approach. Under McDougal's method, the *travaux préparatoires* would be examined along with the treaty text and other indicators of intent, rather than being relegated to a subordinate role. The U.S. delegation adopted McDougal's approach, and he presented it on behalf of the United States at the Vienna Conference. The Conference rejected it, in part because of concern that something could always be found in the preparatory work to support almost any interpretation.[112]

McDougal may have lost the battle, but he won the war. Regardless of what tribunals may say about consulting *travaux* only to confirm a treaty's plain meaning or to clear up an ambiguity, obscurity or absurd meaning, they clearly consider whatever preparatory work the parties put before them.[113]

Joseph M. Sweeney, another member of the Society treaties panel, helped frame the definition of a peremptory norm as adopted by the Conference and as included in Vienna Convention Article 53. He successfully advocated inserting the phrase "as a whole" in the definition: "a norm accepted and recognized by the international community of States as a whole as a norm from which no derogation is permitted … ."[114]

William Rogers and Stephen Schwebel put together the study panel on International Movement of National Art Treasures in order to assist the State Department in responding to a Mexican request for help in preventing the looting and removal to the United States of valuable Mexican artifacts.[115] The panel's

---

111 Official Records, *supra* note 109, at 479.

112 Kearney & Dalton, "The Treaty on Treaties," *supra* note 109, at 519-20.

113 See, e.g., Anthony Aust, *Modern Treaty Law and Practice* 197 (2000); Stephen M. Schwebel, "May Preparatory Work be Used to Correct Rather than Confirm the 'Clear' Meaning of a Treaty Provision?," in *Theory of International Law at the Threshold of the 21st Century* 541, 545-47 (1996).

114 Id. at 537-38.

115 Letter from James A.R. Nafziger to Frederic L. Kirgis, Aug. 17, 2001. See also Paul M. Bator, "An Essay on the International Trade in Art," 34 *Stan. L. Rev.* 275, 282 n. 16 (1982). Bator was the Panel's Rapporteur.

research and consultations with the State Department helped shape the Treaty of Cooperation [with Mexico] Providing for the Recovery and Return of Stolen Archaeological, Historical and Cultural Properties.[116] It was the first treaty of its kind by the United States with any other country.[117]

A subcommittee of the panel influenced significantly, as well, the approach taken to the multilateral control of illicit traffic in cultural objects in the UNESCO Convention on that subject.[118] The subcommittee's report analyzed the UNESCO Secretariat's utopian draft convention, which would have created a seamless web of export and import controls on any item of cultural property. The report was submitted to the Secretary of State in October 1970.[119] In the words of the rapporteur of the Society panel, "The State Department, influenced by advice from the ASIL Panel, made it clear that the United States found the Secretariat Draft unacceptable."[120] A comprehensive State Department draft was never formally introduced because of UNESCO procedural rules permitting only the Secretariat draft to be the basis for discussion. The UNESCO Convention that ultimately emerged was a compromise containing a rather porous regulatory scheme.

The panel on the Role of International Law in Civil Wars was especially productive. One of its objects of study was the Vietnam War. Vietnam, of course, unleashed a torrent of publications in law journals and elsewhere arguing legal and policy issues. The Society's panel published four volumes, edited by Richard A. Falk, reproducing articles and documents about the Vietnam War, and in some cases publishing original works.[121]

In addition, the panel presented two sessions at the 1967 Annual Meeting covering a range of civil wars.[122] Greatly expanded versions of some of those case studies, along with others, were published in a volume edited by Richard Falk.[123] The panel also was responsible for a series of books on the Arab–Israeli

---

[116] July 17, 1970, 22 U.S.T. 494, 791 *UNTS* 313. See also 116 *Cong. Rec.* 20365-66 (1970), where an exchange of letters between William D. Rogers, chair of the panel, and the Secretary of State appears, along with two resolutions of the panel and a list of the panel's members.

[117] *ASIL Newsletter*, Sept. 1970, at 2.

[118] UNESCO Convention on the Means of Prohibiting and Preventing the Illicit Import, Export and Transfer of Ownership of Cultural Property, Nov. 14, 1970, 823 *UNTS* 231, 10 *ILM* 289 (1971), 65 *AJIL* 887 (1971).

[119] See Bator, *supra* note 115.

[120] Id. at 372.

[121] Richard A. Falk (ed.), *The Vietnam War and International Law*, vols. 1-4 (1968-1976).

[122] "Panels on International Law and Civil Wars – I & II," in 61 *ASIL Proc.* 1 & 50 (1967).

[123] Richard A. Falk (ed.), *The International Law of Civil War* (1971).

conflict.[124] And there was more: William Kane's book on civil strife in Latin America emanated from this panel.[125]

Other books stemming from the work of Society study panels during this period included ones on nuclear proliferation,[126] nuclear energy,[127] and international telecommunications.[128] There was also a study on international law and social science and one on foreign enterprise in Mexico, mentioned in Chapter Eight.

Despite the overall record of productivity during this period, the B.R.D. was not able to sustain its vitality as a forum for interdisciplinary discourse on international affairs.[129] It proved difficult to recruit social scientists and natural scientists to serve on the Board, and those who did agree to serve did not always faithfully attend meetings. It was somewhat easier to get the active participation of non-lawyers on individual panels and study groups, where they could mesh their interests with those of legal specialists dealing with a defined topic, but even the panels and study groups were dominated by lawyers. Moreover, there was a strain of thought within the B.R.D. from the outset that the Society should not put too much emphasis on problem areas outside the traditional law of nations. Some of the study panels on traditional topics, such as the one on the Law of Treaties, held little interest for non-lawyers.

By 1968 the B.R.D. meetings had become heavily devoted to consideration of administrative matters, review of interim panel reports, and consideration of proposals from outside the Board for new study projects. The "creative ferment" and the "clash of creative minds" envisioned for B.R.D. meetings had not disappeared altogether, but intellectual jousts did not drive the meetings as had been hoped. Nor did the outlook improve much in the ensuing years.[130]

Study projects emanating from the B.R.D. reflected more the interests of individual Board members and the availability of funds than they did any systematic review and appraisal of gaps or shortcomings in existing research.

---

[124] They are discussed in Chapter Ten, *infra*.

[125] William E. Kane, *Civil Strife in Latin America: A Legal History of U.S. Involvement* (1972).

[126] Bennett Boskey & Mason Willrich (eds.), *Nuclear Proliferation: Prospects for Control* (1970).

[127] Mason Willrich, *Global Politics of Nuclear Energy* (1971).

[128] David M. Leive, *International Telecommunications and International Law: The Regulation of the Radio Spectrum* (1970). Leive also prepared a report, published by the Carnegie Endowment, on issues facing the ITU 1971 Conference on Space Communication and 1973 Plenipotentiary Conference. *ASIL Newsletter*, Apr. 1971, at 3.

[129] The points made in this and the following paragraphs on the BRD are based principally on a study of the first four years' work of the BRD, H.C.L. Merillat, "Review of the Work of the Board of Review and Development," May 28, 1969 (unpublished memorandum).

[130] See Minutes of the Executive Committee, Apr. 11, 1973, in ASIL Minute Book, Dec. 1966–Oct. 1973, at 259, 260.

The Ford Foundation was no longer willing to make large, virtually unrestricted grants; instead, its new and less internationally minded staff expected the Society to justify individual projects for grant support.

To deal with this situation, one suggestion was to appoint a rapporteur or secretary to the Board who would monitor research in other organizations, in order to provide the Board with data that could be used as a basis for useful research. It was a small step from this idea to the creation in 1970 of the post of Director of Studies.

The execution of the studies, and to some extent the topics themselves, tended to be safe in the sense that they posed little challenge to the Establishment. The panel on the Role of International Law in Civil Wars was an exception. Its four volumes on the Vietnam War, for example, presented views across the legal and political spectrum, including views quite critical of the official American position.

2. Paying Honoraria

In the late 1960s, the Society was paying honoraria to rapporteurs of study panels and authors of monographs. Authors were being paid varied honoraria depending on their seniority (seniors got more than juniors), on the magnitude of their assigned work, and on the subject matter of the study panel. This had produced some anomalies, not to mention some queries from Ford Foundation staff members about the propriety of paying honoraria to authors or rapporteurs who would receive other forms of recognition for their work. Moreover, one commissioned book was five years overdue, despite payment of USD 18,000 to the author's university for the project.[131] That book eventually was published, but a few remunerated scholars never produced anything.[132]

3. More Grants and Their Progeny

The grants for individual projects enabled the Society to conduct research it could not otherwise have considered. But it was time-consuming and inefficient to seek an individual grant for each project. What was needed was a way to bring in regular infusions of funds not tied to specific projects. The Ford Foundation had come through before, having supplied a USD 500,000 grant in 1961 and USD

131 Minutes of the Executive Committee, Nov. 1, 1969, in ASIL Minute Book, Dec. 1966–Oct. 1973, at 108 & 111.

132 Efforts were made to get finished products or refunds. See Minutes of the Executive Committee, Mar. 31, 1970, Sept. 26, 1970 & Nov. 7, 1970, in ASIL Minute Book, Dec. 1966–Oct. 1973, at 136, 138; 172, 173-74; & 177, 179. See also Minutes of the Executive Committee, Apr. 24, 1974; Nov. 1, 1974; & Apr. 23, 1975, in ASIL Minute Book, Apr. 1974–Oct. 1981, at 1, 2; 12, 17; & 28-29.

600,000 in 1964. In 1968, the Society applied for a third Ford grant, requesting USD 620,700 for five years. The Foundation offered a USD 376,500 grant for three years, but to receive funds in the second and third years, the Society would have to raise three dollars for every grant dollar. In the end the Society was given three years to raise the matching funds.[133] With the aid of grants from other foundations, the Society was able to meet the requirement and then some.[134]

Another three-year Ford grant was received in 1973. This time the amount was only USD 300,000, and the matching requirement was raised to four to one.[135] Ford also made a special grant to the Society in 1973 to enable members of two subcommittees of the State Department's Law of the Sea Advisory Committee to attend meetings in connection with the opening of the Third U.N. Conference on the Law of the Sea.[136]

Jack Stevenson, the Society's President from 1966 to 1968, enjoyed the confidence of those in charge of the various Mellon Foundations.[137] He and Schwebel approached them for grants, with some success. A USD 50,000 grant from the Old Dominion Foundation has already been mentioned. In the summer of 1968, the Avalon Foundation (like Old Dominion, a Mellon foundation) gave a boost to the general budget by making a USD 50,000 grant.[138]

By 1971, the Old Dominion and Avalon Foundations had been folded into a single Mellon Foundation. Schwebel continued his fund raising efforts with Mellon, and succeeded in obtaining a USD 50,000 grant to the Society for general

---

133 Minutes of the Executive Committee, Sept. 26, 1970, in ASIL Minute Book, Dec. 1966–Oct. 1973, at 172.

134 See 65 *ASIL Proc.* 326-27 (1971).

135 Minutes of the Executive Committee, Apr. 11, 1973, in ASIL Minute Book, Dec. 1966–Oct. 1973, at 259-60, 261; *ASIL Newsletter*, June–July 1973, at 1.

136 Minutes of the Executive Committee, Oct. 19, 1973, in ASIL Minute Book, Dec. 1966–Oct. 1973, at 272, 273.

137 Interview with Stephen M. Schwebel, Dec. 19, 1995 (transcript on file with the Society).

138 Letter to Members, June–July 1968, at 1. The money was used not only for general operations, but also for such things as support for one of the Society's study panels, complimentary sample copies of ILM to non-subscribing Society members (a one-time effort to increase subscriptions), a membership survey and travel grants, including payment of travel expenses for students participating in the semi-finals and finals of the Jessup Competition in 1969. See Minutes of the Executive Committee, Sept. 14, 1968, in ASIL Minute Book, Dec. 1966–Oct. 1973, at 57, 59; Minutes of the Executive Council, Nov. 23, 1968, in id. at 61, 67; Minutes of the Executive Committee, Apr. 24, 1969, in id. at 77, 78.

support.[139] Mellon granted another USD 50,000 to the Society in 1972.[140] Applications to the Johnson, Agnelli and Rockefeller Foundations were initially unsuccessful,[141] though the Johnson and Rockefeller Foundations eventually provided relatively insignificant amounts for individual projects.[142]

The Rockefeller grant, supplemented by National Science Foundation funds, supported a Bellagio conference held in July 1974 under the auspices of the Society's working group on Avoidance and Adjustment of Environmental Disputes.[143] The Society published a summary of the discussion in 1975.[144]

The Ford, Mellon and other grants left the Society in a strong financial position at the end of the sixties. According to the minutes of the April 1969 Executive Council meeting, "There was in fact difficulty in spending money on worthwhile things fast enough."[145] That sounds like an enviable dilemma, and perhaps it was for a while. But the looming expiration of these grants posed a classic fund raising problem. The Society was heavily dependent on new or renewed grants, but it could not show that it had found uses for all the money awarded under the expiring grants. Schwebel spent ever-increasing amounts of time seeking replenishment of expiring grants, including those whose funds had not been fully drawn down.

He seems to have spent his time well. In the autumn of 1970, the Society received official notice of the third major Ford Foundation grant, mentioned above. It also received a USD 40,000 commitment from an old friend, the Carnegie Endowment, to be spent at a rate of USD 20,000 in each of two years.[146] The Executive Committee decided to use part of the Carnegie funds to hold two meetings between U.S. and Soviet international lawyers.[147] The first

---

139 Minutes of the Executive Committee, Apr. 28, 1971, in ASIL Minute Book, Dec. 1966–Oct. 1973, at 193, 194.

140 Minutes of the Executive Committee, Oct. 21, 1972, in ASIL Minute Book, Dec. 1966–Oct. 1973, at 245, 247.

141 Minutes of the Executive Committee, Oct. 30, 1971, in ASIL Minute Book, Dec. 1966–Oct. 1973, at 215, 217.

142 The Society received USD 6,000 from Johnson for the Society's Human Rights panel and USD 24,800 from Rockefeller for Environmental Dispute Settlement. These grants are included in the list of currently active grants in the dossier for the 1974 Annual Meeting.

143 *ASIL Newsletter*, May 1975, at 2.

144 *The Avoidance and Adjustment of Environmental Disputes* (1975).

145 Minutes of the Executive Council, Apr. 24, 1969, in ASIL Minute Book, Dec. 1966–Oct. 1973, at 83, 86.

146 Minutes of the Executive Committee, Sept. 26, 1970, in ASIL Minute Book, Dec. 1966–Oct. 1973, at 172-73.

147 Id. at 174-75; Minutes of the Executive Committee, Nov. 7, 1970, in id. at 177-78.

meeting was held in January 1974 in New York City and Washington, on legal questions related to the the U.S.–U.S.S.R. Trade Agreement of 1972. It was a Cold War breakthrough: the first meeting of its kind between American and Soviet lawyers. A second meeting was held in Moscow in June 1975, focusing on protection of the marine environment.[148]

As we have seen in Chapter Eight, the Society convened a conference on environmental problems in the autumn of 1971 at Arden House in New York state. The National Science Foundation and the Council on Environmental Quality provided funds.[149] It led to a continuing program of Society activities and studies on international environmental protection.[150]

In June 1972, the Society held a conference on Individual Rights and the State in Foreign Affairs, aimed primarily at academics, diplomats and practitioners. The agenda ranged from freedom of movement of individuals to the act of state doctrine.[151]

4. Solidifying *International Legal Materials*

Meanwhile, under the leadership of Marilou Righini, I.L.M. had quickly developed a format that served it well for many years. There were sections on treaties and other international agreements, judicial and similar proceedings, legislation and regulations, reports and a catch-all category for other items of interest. Its Editorial Advisory Committee grew from three members in 1966 to ten in 1970 and fourteen in 1971 (including two *ex officio* members, the Executive Director and the Director of Studies).

From the outset, the policy has been to include a broad range of international legal materials, not just those relating to public international law. The composition of the Editorial Advisory Committee reflected that policy. A majority of the twelve elected members as of 1971 had a significant interest in international economic law.

Circulation of I.L.M. was close to 1,700 in mid-1971, almost three times what it had been in 1967.[152]

---

148 *ASIL Newsletters*, Jan. 1974, at 2-3 & Aug. 1975, at 1.

149 Minutes of the Executive Committee, Apr. 28, 1971, and Oct. 29, 1971, in ASIL Minute Book, Dec. 1966–Oct. 1973, at 193, 194 and 212, 214. See John Lawrence Hargrove (ed.), Law, Institutions and the Global Environment (1972).

150 *ASIL Newsletter*, June 1974, at 1-3.

151 *ASIL Newsletters*, Apr. 1972, at 3, and July–Aug. 1972, at 1.

152 65 *ASIL Proc.* 326 (1971).

5. Programs on Vietnam and Cambodia

To the American public, the Vietnam War was a political bombshell. The international law community was hardly immune from the passion, but the public expressions of Society members managed to remain focused for the most part on the legal issues. The legal issues, at least in the early stages of the conflict, had to do primarily with whether it was an international or civil war, whether South Vietnam and the United States enjoyed a right of collective self-defense under U.N. Charter Article 51, and if so, whether North Vietnam had committed an armed attack on South Vietnam.

The State Department's position was that the 1954 Geneva Accords had established an international demarcation line that created North and South Vietnam as separate entities even if they were not technically separate states; moreover, North Vietnam's hostile infiltration into the South was tantamount to an armed attack, so South Vietnam was entitled to exercise a right of self-defense and could do so collectively with the United States under Article 51.[153] John Norton Moore, writing in the Journal, elaborated on these points.[154] On the other side, it was argued that the 1954 demarcation line was simply a cease-fire line in a struggle for all of Vietnam; it was drawn after Ho Chi Minh's forces had defeated the French, and was expressly contingent on an election to be held in all of Vietnam in 1956; South Vietnam reneged on holding the election, thus committing a material breach of the Geneva Accords and justifying North Vietnam in considering the cease-fire line suspended; the ensuing conflict was therefore a civil war rather than a case of an armed attack by the North against the South.[155]

Stephen Schwebel recalls that although opinion in the Society about the Vietnam War was very sharply divided, it did not tear the Society apart. As he put it, "[E]ven on an issue that led to such divisiveness, bitterness even, the Society could present the distinctive viewpoints, not take a position on any, and keep its integrity as a forum for legal analysis and expression of divergent viewpoints."[156]

---

[153] See Dept. of State, The Legality of United States Participation in the Defense of Viet-Nam, Mar. 4, 1966, in 112 *Cong. Rec.* 5274 (daily ed. Mar. 10, 1966), reprinted in 60 *AJIL* 565 (1966) and in 1 *The Vietnam War and International* Law 583 (Richard A. Falk ed. 1968). See also Leonard Meeker, "Viet-Nam and the International Law of Self-Defense," 46 *Dept. St. Bull.* 54 (1967).

[154] John Norton Moore, "The Lawfulness of Military Assistance to the Republic of Viet-Nam," 61 *AJIL* 1 (1967).

[155] See, e.g., Quincy Wright, "Legal Aspects of the Viet-Nam Situation," 60 *AJIL* 750 (1966).

[156] Interview with Stephen M. Schwebel, Dec. 19, 1995 (transcript on file with the Society).

Although the legal issues had made their way into the Journal beginning in the mid-sixties, the Annual Meetings did not devote as much attention to the war as one might have expected. Instead, the Society organized two special programs in the early seventies on Vietnam and Cambodia.

First, the Society presented a program on Law and the Cambodian Incursion: International and Domestic Legal Issues, at the Cosmos Club in Washington on the evening of June 16, 1970. On April 30, large-scale U.S. and South Vietnamese military operations had been undertaken against North Vietnamese forces in the border regions of Cambodia. The operations caused a furor in the United States. They raised domestic legal issues regarding the decision by the President, as Commander-in-Chief of U.S. armed forces, to escalate the use of force, and international law issues regarding the necessity and proportionality of the military action on ostensibly neutral Cambodian territory. The principal speakers on the international legal issues were Richard A. Falk, of Princeton, and John Norton Moore, of the University of Virginia; on the domestic legal issues, the speakers were William H. Rehnquist, then of the Office of Legal Counsel in the Department of Justice, and William D. Rogers, of Arnold & Porter. Commentators were George H. Aldrich, Deputy Legal Adviser in the State Department, Robert H. Bork, of the Yale Law School, Wolfgang Friedmann, of Columbia, and John Lawrence Hargrove, the Society's Director of Studies. Three of the principal papers (all except Rehnquist's) and the remarks of the commentators were published in the Journal.[157] Rehnquist's paper appeared in the *New York University Law Review*.[158]

Falk argued that the Cambodian incursion met neither the necessity nor proportionality requirements for individual or collective self-defense under international law. He regarded any consent by the Lon Nol government of Cambodia as a sham. Moore's differences with Falk were largely factual, with Moore arguing that the necessity and proportionality requirements had been met and that the Cambodian government had at least tacitly consented to the incursion.

On the U.S. constitutional law issues, Rogers argued that there was no precedent in American history for the Commander-in-Chief, without participation by the Congress, to order such a large-scale attack (in this case, involving more than 50,000 American troops along with bombing); nor could such a decision be

---

157 For the three principal papers, see Richard A. Falk, "The Cambodian Operation and International Law," 65 *AJIL* 1 (1971); William D. Rogers, "The Constitutionality of the Cambodian Incursion," id. at 26; John Norton Moore, "Legal Dimensions of the Decision to Intercede in Cambodia," id. at 38. For the comments by Aldrich, Friedmann, Bork and Hargrove, see id. at 76-83 (1971).

158 See William H. Rehnquist, "The Constitutional Issues – Administrative Position," 45 *NYU L. Rev.* 628 (1970).

justified, he thought, as simply a tactical maneuver to protect U.S. armed forces in South Vietnam. Rehnquist countered by saying that even under a narrow construction of the President's powers as Commander-in-Chief, he had authority over the manner in which ongoing hostilities were conducted, including authority to destroy enemy sanctuaries in Cambodia. Rogers and Rehnquist differed also on the scope of the Gulf of Tonkin Resolution, in which Congress – responding to what was reported to be a North Vietnamese attack on American naval vessels in the Gulf – supported the determination of the President to repel any armed attack against U.S. forces and to prevent further aggression.

The second Society program on Vietnam was held on October 7, 1971. The subject was "Applying the International Law of War and Individual Responsibility in the Indo-China Conflict." During the day, the sessions were open only to working group members; the evening session, featuring an impressive roster of speakers, was open to the public.[159] The evening session was broadcast on National Public Radio.[160]

The 1971 program led to publication of a book edited by Peter Trooboff, featuring contributions by twenty of the conference participants.[161] As Arthur J. Goldberg noted in his Foreword, the Vietnam War posed new challenges for the humanitarian law of war, including issues raised by such tactics as bombing in free-fire zones and defoliation-herbicide operations. Among the difficult issues:

> What is the status of the Vietnamese man who tends rice fields by day and carries food, information, or weapons to guerrilla forces by night? Or of the Vietnamese mother who hides guerrillas in her home, because they demand something under threat of force, or because her son, who was pressed into service, is among those seeking refuge, or because her sympathies are with the Viet Cong? Finally, how does a foot soldier respond to an eleven-year-old who may have a grenade?[162]

And as Peter Trooboff noted in his Introduction, the war posed a complex legal issue under the 1949 Geneva Conventions – an issue that would arise again in subsequent conflicts: was it an international conflict, to which the full scope of the Conventions would apply, or a non-international one, to which only common Article 3 would apply?[163] The participants struggled with these questions without reaching – or intending to reach – agreed conclusions.

---

159 *ASIL Newsletter*, Aug.–Sept. 1971, at 1.

160 *ASIL Newsletter*, Oct. 1971, at 1.

161 Peter D. Trooboff (ed.), *Law and Responsibility in Warfare: The Vietnam Experience* (1975). See also *ASIL Newsletter*, May 1975, at 3.

162 *Law and Responsibility in Warfare, supra* note 161, at ix-x.

163 Id. at 11-13.

When the Paris ceasefire agreements of 1973 seemed to bring about a settlement of the Vietnam conflict, the Society and the A.B.A. Section of International Law sponsored a luncheon at the Society's Annual Meeting, on "The Justness of the Peace."[164] The speakers were Richard Falk and Eugene Rostow. As might be expected, their viewpoints differed sharply. Falk criticized the Nixon administration for failing to disassociate the United States from the existing South Vietnamese government. Rostow praised the Paris agreements, which he saw as confirming the propositions that there were two Vietnams and that North Vietnam had no right to intervene in South Vietnam. Two years later, North Vietnam captured Saigon (Ho Chi Minh City) and took control of a unified Vietnam.

6. Keeping up with International Economic Law

During this period the Society renewed its emphasis on international economic law. The emphasis was partly a reflection of the interest of some prominent Society members such as Stanley Metzger and Seymour Rubin, but it was also a conscious attempt to entice new corporate members into the Society – an effort that would be intensified when Rubin later became Executive Director.

As has been noted above, I.L.M. included economic law in its coverage. The Society also organized programs and conferences around economic law issues. For example, the Society presented a program at Tillar House in 1969 on the expropriation of International Petroleum Company's properties in Peru.[165] It sponsored a conference in Bellagio, Italy, on foreign development lending, attended by senior officials of public lending institutions around the world. The papers of the Bellagio conference were published.[166] One-day panel sessions were held at Tillar House in 1972 on the Andean Foreign Investment Code and on Chilean nationalizations of foreign investments.[167] Some regional meetings dealt with aspects of international economic law.

Some of the Society's study panels focused on economic issues. There was strong private sector representation in the Panel on Capital Formation and Securities Regulation.[168] But place of prominence in the economic sphere went to the Panel on International Monetary Policy. After the monetary crisis of August 1971, when the United States suspended the convertibility of the U.S. dollar into

---

164 67 *ASIL Proc.* 258 (1973).

165 Minutes of the Executive Council, Apr. 24, 1969, in ASIL Minute Book, Dec. 1966–Oct. 1973, at 83, 90.

166 Seymour J. Rubin (ed.), *Foreign Development Lending: Legal Aspects* (1971).

167 *ASIL Newsletter*, Apr. 1972, at 3.

168 The Panel's membership appears in the report of Robert L. Knauss, its Rapporteur, in the compiled Report of Activities of Study Panels of the BRD prepared for the Executive Council meeting of Nov. 23, 1968.

gold, the Panel proposed an amendment to the International Monetary Fund's Articles of Agreement. The Panel's proposal, issued in February 1972, would have strengthened the Fund's power to enforce its international standards against uncooperative Member States, subject to strict procedural safeguards.[169] It was given prominent coverage on the first business page of the *New York Times*,[170] and several months later it influenced the substance of the U.S. government's proposals for monetary reform.[171] In the end, though, its model of a highly coordinated international monetary system with effective sanctions was too much for other governments to accept.

The Society continued to give some emphasis to economic law issues throughout Schwebel's time as Executive Director. In 1973, for example, a new study panel on International Trade Policy and Institutions was organized. It was an interdisciplinary body designed to consider improvement of the GATT and other trade institutions, with Anthony Solomon as its chair.[172] The panel produced a booklet on reform of the world trade system.[173]

7. Participation in Nominating Candidates for the International Court of Justice

Philip Jessup's term as a member of the I.C.J. expired in February 1970. In anticipation of the need to nominate a new American judge, Oscar Schachter – the President of the Society in 1969 – appointed a special committee to advise the U.S. National Group on the Permanent Court of Arbitration regarding nominees.

After consulting the Executive Council, the special committee – consisting of Richard Baxter, Hardy Dillard, James Hyde, Brunson MacChesney and Arthur Larson – proposed Myres McDougal and Oscar Schachter as the U.S. candidates. What then happened within the U.S. National Group is not a matter of record, but it may be worth noting that nomination of either McDougal or Schachter could have raised some inbreeding concerns. Schachter had appointed the special committee and McDougal had been a member of the U.S. National Group until June 26, 1969.[174] In any event, when it was over on August 1, 1969, the

---

169 The Panel was chaired by Stanley Surrey; its Rapporteur was Michael Bradfield. The Panel report, *Long Term International Monetary Reform: A Proposal for an Improved Adjustment Process* (1972), was soon out of print.

170 *N.Y. Times*, Feb. 21, 1972, p. 43.

171 *ASIL Newsletter*, Nov. 1972, at 1.

172 *ASIL Newsletter*, Nov. 1973, at 1.

173 *Re-making the System of World Trade: a Proposal for Institutional Reform* (1976).

174 See Dept. State Press Release No. 177, June 26, 1969, 61 *Dept. St. Bull.* 54 (1969), reprinted in 63 *AJIL* 815 (1969).

Group (which by then included Baxter, but not McDougal, as a member) had nominated Hardy Dillard as the next U.S. judge.[175] Since the special committee had not proposed him and he was not a member of the Group, inbreeding was not regarded a problem. The Executive Council expressed its gratification.[176]

8. Studies in Transnational Legal Policy

The report of the panel on International Monetary Policy became the first number in the Society's occasional papers series, *Studies in Transnational Legal Policy*. As Larry Hargrove, the Director of Studies, put it, the object of the series was "to provide a further publication outlet for certain materials emanating from the work of the Society's study and research panels which seem better suited to the occasional paper format than to publication either in the *Journal* or in the form of a book or part of a book."[177] Three titles were published in 1972.[178] The series was destined to endure until the end of the century.

9. The Role of Women in International Law

In 1971, Richard Baxter suggested that the Society establish an *ad hoc* committee to examine the role of women in international law. He thought that fewer women were entering the field than in earlier years. The Executive Council established the committee in May 1971.[179] Called the Committee on Professional Interest and Status of Women in International Law, it was chaired by Alona Evans.[180]

The Committee produced a study, drafted by Alona Evans and Carol Plumb, on the history of women in the ASIL and on women's interest in international law.[181] To gather data, the Committee sent a questionnaire to the 271 women members of the Society, receiving a 26 per cent response. Evans and Plumb came up with a profile:

---

175 Id.; see also William W. Bishop, Jr., "Former A.S.I.L. Presidents Named for High Offices," 63 *AJIL* 793, 794 (1969).

176 Minutes of the Executive Council, Nov. 1, 1969, in ASIL Minute Book, Dec. 1966–Oct. 1973, at 113, 114.

177 66 *ASIL Proc.* 305 (1972).

178 Minutes of the Executive Council, Oct. 21, 1972, in ASIL Minute Book, Dec. 1966–Oct. 1973, at 249, 250. The three titles were *Long-Term International Monetary Reform: A Proposal for an Improved International Adjustment Process*; *The Question of an Ocean Dumping Convention*; and *The Future of the International Telecommunication Union*.

179 Id. at 209.

180 *ASIL Newsletter*, Aug.–Sept. 1971, at 1-2.

181 Alona E. Evans & Carol Per Lee Plumb, Notes and Comments: "Women and the American Society of International Law," 68 *AJIL* 290 (1974). The portion of the study dealing with the then-recent history of women in the ASIL is discussed at note 45 *supra*.

> The typical woman member is a professional person, either a teacher of international law in a Political Science Department or, less frequently, in a law school, or she is a practitioner specializing in some phase of transnational law. She resides in one of the metropolitan areas between Boston and Washington, D.C. ... [She] became interested in international law through her academic training, particularly through undergraduate courses, or less frequently, through graduate courses, but had her interest further stimulated by employment experience and professional contacts, and in recent years, by participation in various activities sponsored by the Society, such as the Philip C. Jessup International Law Moot Court Competition, student international law societies, student international law journals, or research under the auspices of the Society.[182]

Evans and Plumb concluded that women perceived greater international law teaching opportunities in political science departments than in law schools. Women also saw opportunities in the federal government and in international organizations. To stimulate further interest in international law among women, Evans and Plumb recommended early academic training in the subject, along with counseling of women students so they are not led to conclude that international law is inherently a more masculine area of study than political theory or that some aspects of international law are more congenial to women than others.[183]

The committee thought that the Society could do its part by developing an educational program designed to interest women in international law. Moreover, women members of the Society could assist other women in finding professional openings through establishing contacts with male employers and through concerted efforts to identify emerging female talent in the international law field.[184] What became of these suggestions does not appear.

10. Co-sponsoring Programs Developed by Other Institutions

The Society has generally taken a cautious stance toward invitations to co-sponsor other institutions' programs. The Vietnam years were no exception. In 1968, an invitation was received from the Fund for Education in World Order, asking the Society to co-sponsor a national convocation on "The Challenge of Building Peace." The Executive Committee decided against it, since the Society was asked to make little or no intellectual contribution.[185]

---

182 Id. at 296.

183 Id. at 296, 298.

184 Minutes of the Executive Council, Apr. 25, 1974, in ASIL Minute Book, Apr. 1974–Oct. 1981, at 3, 5.

185 Minutes of the Executive Committee, Nov. 23, 1968, in ASIL Minute Book, Dec. 1966–Oct. 1973, at 72-73.

The Executive Committee was more receptive to Richard Kearney's proposal that the Society join in sponsoring and financing an international law seminar for government legal officers at the Harvard Law School in the summer of 1969. It was noted that the seminar would fit nicely into the Society's series of conferences of government and international organization legal advisers. From its discussion approving the proposal, two basic criteria evolved for Society participation in programs developed by other institutions:

- The Society should be involved in the planning; and
- The program should fit into the Society's overall program.[186]

The Executive Council affirmed the Executive Committee's two criteria and decided that the Society should not co-sponsor conferences in which its involvement was only formal.[187]

11. Another Effort at Outreach

As it had at various times since its inception, the Society in the early 1970s took steps to spread the gospel about international law. It applied for a grant from the National Endowment for the Humanities, to be used in part for a program to advise the media on legal aspects of current world events and to fund an interdisciplinary committee to develop television and film presentations with international legal content.[188] Despite the best efforts of Stephen Schwebel and Peter Trooboff, the application was unsuccessful.[189]

12. President Lasswell's Valedictory

Harold Lasswell served as President of the Society in 1971-72. On his last day in office, he revived an old, neglected tradition: the presidential address. It came not as the opening salvo of the Annual Meeting, as it had in the early days, but rather as an eloquent institutional assessment at the Business Meeting.

He began by noting that the Society in its infancy had relied for outside support primarily on the Carnegie Endowment for International Peace, and later had turned to the Ford Foundation. "I think it is fair to say," he said, "that while we were in principle willing to leave the arms of Uncle Andrew and Mother Ford, we

---

186 Id. at 73-75.

187 Minutes of the Executive Council, Apr. 24, 1969, in ASIL Minute Book, Dec. 1966–Oct. 1973, at 83, 84.

188 Minutes of the Executive Committee, Oct. 29, 1971, in ASIL Minute Book, Dec. 1966–Oct. 1973, at 212.

189 Minutes of the Executive Council, Apr. 12, 1973, in ASIL Minute Book, Dec. 1966–Oct. 1973, at 262, 267. Trooboff was then the chair of the Committee on Student and Professional Development.

did not promptly bestir ourselves to don our orange robes and take our chances in the highways and byways of the cold, cold world."[190] But the situation had changed in recent years. As shown by one of the eight charts he unfurled, other foundations were coming on board.[191]

Lasswell then recalled the Society's idealistic origins, anchored in the belief that peace could and would be achieved if only the world had a system of arbitral tribunals applying international law to disputes among nation states. But, he said, "The halo effect that created a climate of genteel optimism at the coupling of the rhetoric of law and peace has melted like the legendary wings of wax. ... Can the language of law contribute to peace; or is it a tattered semantic garment wrapped around the sword handles of the barbarians who sacked Rome and have been sacking one another ever since?"[192] He did not answer his own rhetorical question. Instead, in Lasswellian fashion, he set forth a taxonomy that might be used to evaluate the Society's contribution to an ongoing process of decision-making in international affairs:

> Fundamentally the Society is open to appraisal by foundations and other agencies and individuals in terms of the estimated role of international law itself in the flow of decision. If such a role is acknowledged, the next question is the Society's impact on decision.
>
> That the overriding aim of the ASIL is to activate international law as an instrument of at least minimally tolerable public order is evident. ... International law is specialized to the task of achieving and effectuating perspectives of shared interest. The inference is that to cultivate international law is to assist in evolving an *intelligence* function that clarifies specific objectives and strategies in the light of realistic information and critical estimates of the relevant context; to foster *promotional* activities that successfully mobilize effective demand for appropriate official and private action; to assist in formulating *prescriptive* norms that consolidate authoritative expectations in relevant ways; to invigorate *invoking* procedures that inaugurate the measures required to give effect to prescriptions; to execute the *application* functions necessary to accomplish tenable invocations; to *terminate* incompatible and obsolete prescriptions and deal equitably with established expectations; to *appraise* the degree to which policy goals have been optimally realized and to locate instrumental and imputed responsibility for success or failure. The Society is a professional society whose role in affecting decision is,

---

190 Harold D. Lasswell, Presidential Address: "Toward a Continuing Appraisal of the Impact of International Law and the ASIL on the Transnational Decision Process," 66 *ASIL Proc.* 281 (1972).

191 Id. at 291.

192 Id. at 281-82.

> for the most part, deliberately restricted to the intelligence and appraisal functions.[193]

Lasswell thought that the Society was performing its intelligence and appraisal functions rather effectively. He found it difficult to assess the extent to which the Society might effectively perform some of the others, such as the invoking and application functions. He noted, apparently with regret, that the Society had refrained almost completely from participating in the promotional function.

He conceded that his evaluation of the Society's activities was "rudimentary," but he nevertheless found implications in it for the future. The Society's reports could be made more comprehensive and realistic, particularly as legal scholars learned to work closely with their colleagues in complementary disciplines; a "demand for deference to the component of legal authority must be generated and mobilized during the early years of life and training" as well as during higher education; and the Society should bring into its membership the leaders of all sectors of the American polity, not just persons engaged in international law or international studies.[194]

Lasswell concluded by reminding his listeners of the tremendous gap in well-being between the developed and developing worlds. Non-governmental organizations were springing up to try to narrow the gap. "It may be that in coming days our successors will visualize the ASIL as a vanguard organization that becomes a more broadly based territorial and pluralistic instrument. They may hasten its transformation into a Society for Transnational Law and Social Justice. Do not, however, hold your breath until this happens."[195]

Lasswell may have been a little too pessimistic. In the ensuing years, the Society would indeed become a more broadly based territorial and pluralistic instrument. Not only that; it also discarded whatever antipathy it may have had toward Lasswell's "promotional function" when it conceived and implemented an ambitious outreach program. Whether it has become a Society for transnational law and justice might, however, depend on the eye of the beholder.

C. A PROFILE OF THE MEMBERSHIP

In the spring of 1969, the Society surveyed its membership. Fifty-five per cent of the members returned the questionnaires. Among the more interesting findings:

---

[193] Id. at 284-85.

[194] Id. at 299-300.

[195] Id. at 300.

- Of the total membership, slightly less than one-third were practicing lawyers; somewhat more than one-fourth were academics; one-sixth were government officials.
- One-fifth had been personally involved in the work of the Society, by serving as officers, serving on committees or study panels, speaking at the Annual Meeting, or writing for the Journal.
- In relation to their numbers in the Society, academics were considerably more involved in the Society's activities than were practitioners.
- Twenty-seven per cent of the members who had served on committees or study panels were under forty years of age.[196]

D. THE COMMITTEE ON GOVERNANCE AND ITS IMPACT ON THE SOCIETY

Richard Lillich was a force for change in the Society in the late sixties and thereafter. At the November 1969 meeting of the Executive Council, he proposed the creation of an *ad hoc* Committee on the Governance of the Society to report on the roles and procedures of the Executive Council, the Executive Committee, the Board of Review and Development and the Board of Editors of the Journal, including the procedures by which members of those bodies were appointed or elected. His primary concerns were that the Executive Council did not appear to exercise sufficient control over important decisions made by other bodies; the membership of the Executive Committee was not sufficiently representative of the full Executive Council; and the B.R.D. and Board of Editors were disturbingly self-perpetuating. The Council unanimously established the Committee.[197]

Richard Baxter chaired the Committee on Governance. On its behalf, he submitted an interim report to the Council on April 24, 1970. It recommended several changes in the way the Society conducted its business. In particular, it recommended that:

- Student members be eligible to vote and hold office.
- A procedure be established for nomination of officers and Executive Council members by petition if there is a challenge to the Nominating Committee's slate, with a mail ballot to be used if there is more than one candidate for an office.

196 Minutes of the Executive Council, Nov. 1, 1969, in ASIL Minute Book, Dec. 1966–Oct. 1973, at 113, 115-17; Letter to Members, Nov. 1969, at 1-3.

197 Minutes of the Executive Council, Nov. 1, 1969, in ASIL Minute Book, Dec. 1966–Oct. 1973, at 113, 125.

- The President, rather than the Executive Committee, should advise the Executive Council (and ultimately the Business Meeting) as to the composition of the Nominating Committee.
- The B.R.D. should continue to select its own new members, but with the consent of the Executive Council.
- The Board of Editors of the Journal should be increased to twenty-four members serving four-year terms with the terms of six members expiring each year (instead of annual terms that in effect became life-time appointments), but with no requirement that members be ineligible to succeed themselves.[198]

The Executive Council adopted the committee's first recommendation. It deleted the provision in the Regulations that precluded student members from voting or holding office.[199] The Executive Director was instructed to circulate the interim report to all Society members before any action was taken on the other recommendations.

The Committee submitted its final report to the Executive Council in April 1971. It filled in the details of the petitioning/mail ballot procedure mentioned in its interim report, giving time limits for the Nominating Committee's report and for petitions, and disallowing nominations from the floor of the Business Meeting as to any office for which no petition was received. The idea was to open up the nominating and electing procedures. The committee explained:

> As things now stand, a slate of officers for the Society could be elected by a majority of the fifty persons required for a quorum ... on the basis of nominations made from the floor .... This simply will not do for an organization of over five thousand members.[200]

At the Business Meeting, the required number of signatures on a nominating petition was reduced from fifty to twenty. With that change, the Constitution

198 Minutes of the Executive Council, Apr. 24, 1970, in ASIL Minute Book, Dec. 1966–Oct. 1973, at 139, 141-143. The interim report also recommended that the Executive Committee should normally consist of the President, the Executive Vice President, the three other Vice Presidents, the immediate past President, the Treasurer, and three at large Council members. In its final report, the committee backed off and made no recommendation on the composition of the Executive Committee.

199 Id. at 145.

200 Condensed Final Report of the Ad Hoc Committee on Governance of the American Society of International Law, Spring 1971, at 4 (as sent to ASIL members in advance of the 1971 Annual Meeting).

was amended to reflect the election procedure the Committee on Governance had proposed for officers and Council members.[201]

The Executive Council unanimously adopted the rest of the Committee's recommendations, requiring changes in the Regulations.[202] These changes confirmed the Committee's interim recommendations that the President, rather than the Executive Committee, advise the Executive Council on nominations for the Nominating Committee, and that the B.R.D. appoint its own new members subject to the consent of the Executive Council.[203]

As for the Board of Editors of the Journal, the Committee on Governance recommended, and the Council approved, amendments to the Regulations providing for twenty-four elected members whose terms of office would be four years. The Executive Council would elect six members each year. In a departure from the Committee's interim recommendations, the amendments provided that a member of the Board who had served for twelve years after the first election under the new procedure would be ineligible for re-election for one year.[204] Although this was a small step in the direction of turnover on the Board, it fell short of satisfying those in the Society who regarded the Board as rather inbred and lacking in imagination.

Under the amendments, the Executive Council would also elect an Editor-in-Chief from among the members of the Board. The Editor-in-Chief would serve for four years. It was not made clear whether the Editor-in-Chief was subject to the new twelve-year rule.

The new I.L.M. Editorial Advisory Committee was set up to consist of twelve members elected by the Executive Council for staggered three-year terms.[205]

---

201 65 *ASIL Proc.* 328-30 (1971). The full Constitution as revised appears in id. at 423-26.

202 Minutes of the Executive Council, Apr. 29, 1971, in ASIL Minute Book, Dec. 1966–Oct. 1973, at 199, 202.

203 Condensed Final Report, *supra* note 200, at 4-5.

204 Condensed Final Report, *supra* note 200, at 5.

205 Condensed Final Report, *supra* note 200, at 6. This and all the other changes to the Regulations are reflected in the revised Regulations published in 65 *ASIL Proc.* 427-39 (1971).

E. ANNUAL AND REGIONAL MEETINGS IN THE LATE SIXTIES AND EARLY SEVENTIES

1. Newsworthiness

Until 1950, the *New York Times* regularly covered the Society's Annual Meetings. The Washington papers did so until the early 1960s; thereafter, they covered addresses or panels they regarded as particularly newsworthy, but in some years they found nothing interesting to report.

From time to time, the Society's chief administrative officer has tried to induce more media coverage. Such a time was 1968, when Stephen Schwebel wrote a long letter to Max Franckel, head of the *New York Times*' Washington Bureau, describing the various topics that would be discussed at the upcoming Annual Meeting and urging the *Times* to cover it. He wrote a shorter letter to the head of the Washington Bureau of *Time* magazine.[206] The result was meager. The *Times* ran a three-paragraph story on Under Secretary of State Nicholas Katzenbach's annual dinner address on the then-draft Nuclear Nonproliferation Treaty.[207]

Several years later, Seymour Rubin – by then the Executive Director – deplored the lack of press interest in the Society's meetings:

> We have on many occasions tried to get representatives of the press, radio, TV, etc., to come to the meetings to talk with panelists and others with, I am sorry to say, very little success. We do distribute press releases as a regular matter and ordinarily I call a number of people I know in press associations, the Washington Post, the Washington office of the New York Times, etc., and despite this – perhaps because of it – there has not been a great deal of interest.[208]

The opening panel at the 1969 Annual Meeting addressed North Korea's seizure of a U.S. navy vessel, the *U.S.S. Pueblo,* about 15 nautical miles off its coast in January 1968. The incident had made the front pages. For international lawyers, it raised such issues as the immunity of warships on the high seas and the right of self-defense. At the Annual Meeting George Aldrich, of the Department of State, challenged the lawfulness of the seizure; William Butler, then a Research Associate at the Harvard Law School, presented the arguments North Korea might make in response.[209] The *New York Times* and *Washington Post* covered it in some

---

206 Letters from Stephen M. Schwebel to Max Franckel, Apr. 22, 1968, and to William Mader, Apr. 22, 1968, in the Society's 1968 Annual Meeting Second File.

207 *N.Y. Times*, Apr. 28, 1968. Katzenbach's address appears in 62 *ASIL Proc.* 274 (1968).

208 Memorandum to the Executive Council, Dec. 21, 1982, at 3, in briefing materials for Apr. 1983 Executive Council meetings.

209 63 *ASIL Proc.* 1, 2, 7 (1969).

detail. Both of them played up Butler's arguments. According to the headline in the *Times*, "Legal Society Told Pueblo's Seizure May Have Been Justified."[210] The *Post* chimed in: "Legal Position of U.S. On Pueblo Challenged."[211] International law and the Society had made the news, even if the casual reader would not have gotten the full tenor of the debate.

The featured speaker at the 1970 annual dinner was William P. Rogers, the Secretary of State. Most of his address concerned matters of little interest to the media – breathing new life into the International Court of Justice and encouraging greater use of multilateral law-making treaties. Of interest to the Society audience but not to the media, he mentioned that the day before, the United States had signed the Vienna Convention on the Law of Treaties. His third and last point, that nations should live up to their obligations under international agreements, would hardly have made headlines if he had not used it to attack North Vietnam's invasion of Laos and Cambodia, which he said violated the 1954 Geneva Accords, and to ask whether the international community should not look for ways to shoulder its responsibilities in the matter.[212] "Rogers Suggests Nations Weigh Cambodia Action," proclaimed the *Washington Post* headline;[213] "Rogers Urges World Action on Hanoi Treaty Violations," added the *Sunday Star*.[214] Perhaps such headlines were just what the administration wanted, in order to gauge the public response to the impending expansion of the war into Cambodia. Five days after Rogers' speech, President Nixon announced the U.S. incursion into Cambodia.[215]

In 1971, former Secretary of State Dean Rusk chaired the opening panel discussion on Chinese participation in the United Nations. Two papers and three sets of prepared comments were given by others, with Rusk participating simply as master of ceremonies until Stephen Schwebel asked him what he would do if he were still Secretary of State. Rusk replied that in cases of conflict such as that between mainland China and the Republic of China (Taiwan), both countries should be admitted to the U.N.[216] Rusk's brief statement was what made the Washington Post.[217]

---

210 *N.Y. Times*, Apr. 25, 1969.

211 *Wash. Post*, Apr. 25, 1969.

212 William P. Rogers, "The Rule of Law and the Settlement of International Disputes," 64 *ASIL Proc.* 285, 289-91 (1970), 62 *Dept. State Bull.* 623, 626-27 (1970).

213 *Wash. Post*, Apr. 26, 1970.

214 *Wash. Sunday Star*, Apr. 26, 1970.

215 Address by President Richard M. Nixon, "The Cambodia Strike: Defensive Action for Peace," 62 *Dept. State Bull.* 617 (1970).

216 65 *ASIL Proc.* 28 (1971).

217 *Wash. Post*, Apr. 30, 1971.

Secretary of State Rogers' appearance at the 1970 annual dinner was something of a milestone for this period. The Society regularly invited the sitting Secretary of State to address the annual dinner. Usually the Secretary waited until the last minute to commit himself. Knowing that times had changed since Secretaries of State Elihu Root and Charles Evans Hughes could be relied upon to speak, the Society would arrange for a backup speaker. The backup normally became the speaker.[218]

2. Maintaining a Balance Between Academics and Practitioners

The planners of Annual Meetings through most of this period attempted to strike a balance between the interests of academics and practitioners, and between topics of classical international law and those of international economic law. Even in 1970, when the Annual Meeting theme was "The United Nations: Appraisal at 25 Years," there were panels on such topics as the U.N. system and financing investment, extraterritorial application of law, and practical aspects of international litigation.[219] The latter was an innovative panel featuring persons who had actively participated in international litigation. There were three speakers, and others were primed in advance to enter into the discussion.[220]

3. A Theme Revisited: Taking Positions

At the 1969 Business Meeting, Michael Reisman offered a resolution stressing the importance to the world community of protecting human rights; it proposed that the Society establish a committee to consider deviations from accepted human rights standards and to recommend effective means for guaranteeing human rights. Under Reisman's proposal, the committee would begin by examining the then-current problem of Biafra, the Nigerian province that had attempted to secede from the rest of Nigeria. Biafra's attempt sparked a devastating civil war in which ethnic animosities played a major part.[221] The matter was referred to the Executive Council under Article VIII of the Society's Constitution.[222] At its November 1969 meeting, the Council referred it to the study panels being formed on humanitarian law and human rights.[223] That allowed the Society to stick to its course, declining to take a position on a matter of current public

[218] Telephone interview with Richard W. Edwards, Jr., Oct. 3, 1997.

[219] 64 *ASIL Proc.* 87, 130 & 238 (1970).

[220] Telephone interview with Richard W. Edwards, Jr., Oct. 3, 1997.

[221] The secession attempt was ultimately crushed by the central government.

[222] 63 *ASIL Proc.* 226 (1969).

[223] Minutes of the Executive Council, Nov. 1, 1969, in ASIL Minute Book, Dec. 1966–Oct. 1973, at 113, 122.

interest without simply ignoring the international legal implications of an ongoing civil war.

4. Attempting to Loosen Things Up

Some questions within the Society never seem to get resolved – how to balance the budget, whether it is ever proper to take positions on substantive matters, whether there is too much inbreeding in the Executive Council and in the Journal's Board of Editors. Joining the list, though not with quite the same sense of urgency, is whether speakers at the Annual Meeting should prepare papers in advance and read them aloud, or should speak from notes and keep it brief.

In 1967, Charles Fenwick, by then an *eminence grise* in the Society, took a stand in favor of spontaneity and brevity. Oscar Schachter agreed with him. The ensuing Executive Council discussion was inconclusive.[224]

Written instructions were sent to panel chairs, speakers and commentators before the 1968 Annual Meeting, imploring them to "speak, and not read an address."[225] Apparently the instructions were in vain. In November 1968 the Council took the position that papers should not be read.[226]

Another attempt to enliven matters was made in 1969. The commentators were asked to be interrogators instead.[227] Their role was to ask incisive questions of the speakers. In the event, some commentators interrogated, some commented and most did both.

The Executive Council also agreed with Richard Lillich, who complained that in some cases individuals who spoke at panels or commented from the floor at the 1968 Annual Meeting had revised their remarks so extensively after the fact that they were barely recognizable when published in the Proceedings. The Council advised that henceforth, reports of panel proceedings should be submitted to the chair of the panel for final editing before publication.[228]

In 1973, Thomas M. Franck was appointed to chair the Annual Meeting Committee for the following year. His fertile mind came up with a much more focused theme than usual and with a broad spectrum of speakers and viewpoints. The panels at the 1974 meeting dealt with North America, or, as the opening panel discussion was dubbed, "The Perils of Proximity." In addition, Franck proposed a

---

224 Minutes of the Executive Council, Apr. 29, 1967, in ASIL Minute Book, Dec. 1966–Oct. 1973, at 19, 20-21.

225 Memorandum from Stephen M. Schwebel to Panel Chairmen, Speakers, and Commentators at the 1968 Annual Meeting, Feb. 23, 1968, in Annual Meeting 1968 First File.

226 Minutes of the Executive Council, Nov. 23, 1968, in ASIL Minute Book, Dec. 1966–Oct. 1973, at 61, 70.

227 Minutes of the Exective Council, Apr. 24, 1969, in ASIL Minute Book, Dec. 1966–Oct. 1973, at 83, 84.

228 Id.

procedural innovation: in addition to panels, there would be workshops involving groups of persons interested in particular problems who would discuss them in an informal setting. Unlike the panels, the workshops would not be limited to United States–Canadian–Mexican relations. Kay Boals was put in charge of the workshops.[229] Society members were invited to organize workshops that would be of interest to them.[230] Out of that process came discussions of the law of war, space stations, non-elites in the international community, human survival, and women and international law.[231]

5. Publishing the Proceedings

In 1970, the Executive Council decided to publish the annual Proceedings as an issue of the Journal, in order to take advantage of the Journal's second-class postage rates.[232] The problem was that with the proliferation of panels at Annual Meetings – in 1970, for the first time, three panels were held simultaneously in some time slots – the cost of publishing and separately mailing the Proceedings was escalating. Nevertheless, the experiment of combining the Proceedings with the Journal lasted only until 1973.

6. Co-sponsoring Panels with Other Institutions

In November 1968, the Executive Committee considered whether to co-sponsor some panels with the American Bar Association's Section of International and Comparative Law at the Society's 1970 Annual Meeting. There had been some difficulties in the past when the A.B.A. Section and the Society had tried to coordinate their meetings. In particular, the A.B.A. had organized a session on the Vietnam War at the same time as the Society's Business Meeting in 1966. Nevertheless, the Executive Committee decided to cooperate with the A.B.A. Section in the planning of a single panel (on extraterritoriality) for the 1970 Annual Meeting, and said it would also be pleased to collaborate in a joint reception.[233]

---

229 Minutes of the Executive Committee, Oct. 19, 1973, in ASIL Minute Book, Dec. 1966–Oct. 1973, at 272.

230 *ASIL Newsletter*, Nov. 1973, at 1.

231 68 *ASIL Proc.* 301 (1974).

232 Minutes of the Executive Council, Apr. 26, 1970, in ASIL Minute Book, Dec. 1966–Oct. 1973, at 165, 169.

233 Minutes of the Executive Committee, Nov. 23, 1968, in ASIL Minute Book, Dec. 1966–Oct. 1973, at 72, 75. For the panel discussion, see "Extraterritorial Application of Law," 64 *ASIL Proc.* 130 (1970).

7. The Committee on Publications

The Society's Committee on Publications of the Department of State and the United Nations, carrying on a long-standing tradition, kept a close eye on official publications throughout the sixties and seventies. Its mission was not one to excite the imagination, but it was important nonetheless. Its annual reports to the Business Meeting supplied useful information for researchers about documents and other publications relating to international law of the U.S. government and of the United Nations. Its 1969 report filled almost seventeen pages of the Proceedings, identifying and summarizing a wide variety of publications in the previous year.[234]

8. Holding an Annual Meeting Outside Washington

In 1970, the Society for the first time held its Annual Meeting outside Washington. The occasion was the 25th anniversary of the United Nations. It seemed natural to celebrate the anniversary in New York City. The Meeting was held at the Waldorf-Astoria Hotel.[235] Panels focused on such U.N. endeavors as peacekeeping, law-making, searching for peace in the Middle East, reducing or eliminating racial discrimination, science and technology, disarmament, and the environment.[236]

In another departure from tradition, the New York meeting was held from Friday morning through to Sunday morning.

9. Strengthening the Regional Meetings Program

Stephen Schwebel and his staff worked hard to give the Society visibility outside the Boston–New York–Washington corridor. Sixteen regional meetings were scheduled for the academic year 1970-71. The Society's budget for them was not enough to cover the Society's normal practice (at that time) of contributing USD 500 toward the expense of a regional meeting. The nominal registration fees set by regional meeting organizers did not supply much extra revenue. Not all organizers were as resourceful as Ved Nanda, whose successful regional meetings at the University of Denver had already become fixtures in the Society's annual calendar. He was able to supplement the normal revenues by obtaining

---

[234] Report of the Committee on Publications of the Department of State and the United Nations, 63 *ASIL Proc.* 252 (1969). As usual, the Business Meeting responded by adopting a resolution urging more prompt publication of the *Foreign Relations of the United States* volumes. Id. at 225-26.

[235] At Stephen Schwebel's urging, the hotel picked up the expenses of the ASIL staff. Telephone interview with Richard W. Edwards, Jr., Oct. 3, 1997.

[236] 64 *ASIL Proc. passim* (1970), published as 64 *AJIL* No. 4 (Sept. 1970). See also text at note 220 *supra*.

the support of local bar associations, his university and the local branch of the United Nations Association.

In 1971-72, eighteen regional meetings were held. Some of them were quite successful, but some were poorly attended. Stephen Schwebel noted his concern about the disappointing attendance at some of the meetings. He observed, though, that the lunch meetings Edward Gordon and Keith Highet had organized in New York City were quite successful.[237] Efforts continued to be made to hold regional meetings beyond the eastern seaboard, and some were held abroad – in Canada, Argentina and England.[238]

F. THE JOURNAL UNDER BISHOP AND BAXTER

1. A New Editor-in-Chief and an Assistant Editor

In 1970, William Bishop resigned from his second stint as Editor-in-Chief. The Board proposed that Richard Baxter succeed him, and the Executive Council unanimously agreed.[239] Baxter's service as Editor-in-Chief was interrupted in 1971-72, when he served as the State Department's Counselor on International Law. Brunson MacChesney filled in for him.[240]

In April 1968, the Executive Council promoted Eleanor Finch from Secretary of the Board of Editors to Assistant Editor of the Journal.[241] Rosemary G. Conley was appointed Editorial Assistant.[242]

When Eleanor Finch retired in 1972, Anne P. Simons became the new Assistant Editor.[243] The Executive Council decided that she, like her predecessor, would edit the Proceedings as well.[244]

---

237 66 *ASIL Proc.* 302 (1972).

238 Letter from James A.R. Nafziger to Frederic L. Kirgis, Aug. 17, 2001.

239 For other changes in Board membership during this period, see Memorandum, "ASIL History: The Journal, Its Editors and Business Practices," on file with the Society.

240 *ASIL Newsletter*, May 1971, at 1; Minutes of the Executive Council, Apr. 29, 1971, in ASIL Minute Book, Dec. 1966–Oct. 1973, at 199, 204.

241 Minutes of the Executive Council, Apr. 27, 1968, in ASIL Minute Book, Dec. 1966–Oct. 1973, at 55. Her analytical index to the Journal was published in October 1968. See Eleanor H. Finch, *Analytical Index to the American Journal of International Law, Supplements, and Proceedings, 1941-1960* (1968).

242 Letter to Members, Apr.–May 1968, at 3.

243 Minutes of the Executive Council, Oct. 30, 1971, in ASIL Minute Book, Dec. 1966–Oct. 1973, at 215, 217.

244 Minutes of the Executive Council, Oct. 21, 1972, in ASIL Minute Book, Dec. 1966–Oct. 1973, at 249, 252-53.

2. The End of an Era

The era of indefinite, uninterrupted service on the Board ended in the 1970s. Not only did the Executive Council mandate term limits for new Board members,[245] but some of the old guard passed on. Josef Kunz and Quincy Wright died in 1970. Both were Honorary Editors. Wright had served on the Board for forty-seven years.[246] When Charles Fenwick died in 1973, he had served for forty-nine years.

3. International Law in the Twentieth Century

For the sixtieth anniversary of the Society and the Journal in 1966, the Executive Council wished to commemorate the occasion by (among other things) commissioning a volume reproducing the finest works the Journal had published in its first sixty years. The volume was duly published. To quote from Leo Gross' Preface:

> In 1966 the Executive Council of the Society requested the Board of Editors of the *Journal* to consider the suggestion to prepare a collection of papers which appeared in the first sixty volumes of the *Journal* and the *Proceedings*. The Board of Editors approved the suggestion and decided to entrust the task of selection to a Committee of its Members consisting of Richard R. Baxter, Herbert W. Briggs, Charles G. Fenwick, Leo Gross (Chairman), and Oliver J. Lissitzyn. The Editor-in-Chief of the *Journal*, Professor William W. Bishop, Jr., actively participated in the work of the Committee. The procedure was a simple one: each member of the Committee submitted a list of selected papers; these selections were circulated to the members along with a tentative master list prepared by the Chairman; on the basis of the comments received from the members, he prepared a list which was submitted to and approved by the Board of Editors and the Executive Council.[247]

The volume, *International Law in the Twentieth Century*, began with George Finch's summary of the Society's first fifty years, and went on to present articles dealing with issues generic to international law as a whole (the history, outlook, theory and sources of international law) and with specific issues such as territory, jurisdiction, state responsibility, recognition, the use of force, and international institutions. The list of authors is very nearly a Who's Who of international

---

245 See text at note 204 *supra*.

246 Minutes of the Executive Council, Nov. 9, 1970, in ASIL Minute Book, Dec. 1966–Oct. 1973, at 181, 183.

247 Leo Gross, Preface to *International Law in the Twentieth Century* vii (1969).

legal scholarship in the English-speaking world from 1906 to 1966, with an emphasis on the latter part of the period.

4. The Journal and the Vietnam War

As we have seen, the Society responded to the U.S. incursion into Cambodia in 1970 by presenting a forum on the international and domestic legal issues.[248] The papers presented by Richard A. Falk, John Norton Moore, William H. Rehnquist and William D. Rogers analyzed the international and domestic legal arguments raised by the incursion. The Journal undertook to publish the papers and the remarks of the commentators at the forum, but wound up publishing only three of the main papers, since Rehnquist had placed his in the *New York University Law Review* before the Journal's symposium issue could be published.[249]

5. Some Other Memorable Articles

In the late sixties some noteworthy issues of the Journal were devoted largely to single topics. The October 1967 issue focused on the International Law Commission's draft articles on the law of treaties. Its eminent cast of authors included Oliver Lissitzyn, Shabtai Rosenne, Egon Schwelb, Herbert Briggs, William Bishop, Myres McDougal, Quincy Wright, Pitman Potter and Stanley Metzger.[250] After the

---

248 See text at note 157 *supra*.

249 For the principal papers, see Richard A. Falk, "The Cambodian Operation and International Law," 65 *AJIL* 1 (1971); William D. Rogers, "The Constitutionality of the Cambodian Incursion," id. at 26; John Norton Moore, "Legal Dimensions of the Decision to Intercede in Cambodia," id. at 38; William H. Rehnquist, "The Constitutional Issues – Administrative Position," 45 *NYU L. Rev.* 628 (1970). For the comments by George H. Aldrich, Wolfgang Friedmann, Robert H. Bork and John Lawrence Hargrove, see 65 *AJIL* 76-83 (1971).

250 The lead articles were: Oliver J. Lissitzyn, "Treaties and Changed Circumstances (*Rebus Sic Stantibus*)," 61 *AJIL* 895 (1967); Shabtai Rosenne, "The Despositary of International Treaties," id. at 923; Egon Schwelb, "Some Aspects of International *Jus Cogens* as Formulated by the International Law Commission," id. at 946; Herbert W. Briggs, "Procedures for Establishing the Invalidity or Termination of Treaties under the International Law Commission's 1966 Draft Articles on the Law of Treaties," id. at 976. The Editorial Comments were: William W. Bishop, Jr., "Law of Treaties" Issue of the Journal, id. at 990; Myres S. McDougal, "The International Law Commission's Draft Articles upon Interpretation: Textuality *Redivivus*," id. at 992; Quincy Wright, "The Termination and Suspension of Treaties," id. at 1000; Pitman B. Potter, "Treaties and International Legislation," id. at 1005; Stanley D. Metzger, "Treaty Interpretation and the United States–Italy Air Transport Arbitration," id. at 1007. The Official Documents department of the same issue published the U.S. government's comments on Parts I, II and III of the draft articles, id. at 1123. In an earlier issue of volume 61, the Journal published the Report of the International Law Commission on the Work of the Second Part of Its Seventeenth Session, which included the draft articles and the Commission's commentary. Id. at 248.

Vienna Convention on the Law of Treaties had been adopted, the Journal published Richard Kearney and Robert Dalton's narrative guide to the Convention.[251]

Hardly less eminent was the roster for the human rights issue in October 1968: Egon Schwelb, John Humphreys, José Cabranes, Louis Sohn, Brunson MacChesney and Marjorie Whiteman.[252] They examined U.N. and regional mechanisms for implementing human rights.

In 1968, Myres McDougal and Michael Reisman published a defense of U.N. enforcement action against Rhodesia (Zimbabwe) after the Ian Smith government had unilaterally declared independence from the United Kingdom.[253] Dean Acheson, the former Secretary of State, gave a scathing response in an address before the A.B.A. Section of International and Comparative Law. He decried "the arrogance of international lawyers" and concluded by asking the Good Lord to deliver him and others "from the United Nations Charter as distorted by professors of international law."[254] McDougal and Reisman, it must be assumed, went about their business unabashed.

In 1971, the Journal published an article by Leo Gross on the International Court of Justice.[255] Years later, Covey Oliver described it as "the greatest single piece in the Journal ever written."[256] It was a thorough, insightful piece in a genre Oliver and others believe represents the Journal's great opportunity for meaningful contributions – the systematic study of international institutions. The Society's Panel on The Future of the International Court of Justice sent it to the legal advisers of U.N. Member States, along with a statement supporting the creation of a U.N. *ad hoc* committee to study how the Court's effectiveness could be enhanced.[257]

---

[251] Richard D. Kearney & Robert E. Dalton, "The Treaty on Treaties," 64 *AJIL* 495 (1970).

[252] The lead articles were: Egon Schwelb, "Civil and Political Rights: The International Measures of Implementation," 62 *AJIL* 827 (1968); John P. Humphrey, "The United Nations Sub-Commission on the Prevention of Discrimination and the Protection of Minorities," id. at 869; José A. Cabranes, "The Protection of Human Rights by the Organization of American States," id. at 889. The shorter pieces were: Louis B. Sohn, "United Nations Machinery for Implementing Human Rights," id. at 909; Brunson MacChesney, "Should the United States Ratify the Covenants? A Question of Merits, Not of Constitutional Law," id. at 912; Marjorie M. Whiteman, "Mrs. Franklin D. Roosevelt and the Human Rights Commission," id. at 918.

[253] Myres S. McDougal & W. Michael Reisman, "Rhodesia and the United Nations: The Lawfulness of International Concern," 62 *AJIL* 1 (1968).

[254] Dean Acheson, "The Arrogance of International Lawyers," 2 *Int'l Lawyer* 591, 599 (1968), reprinted in Dean Acheson, *Fragments of My Fleece* 155, 167 (1971).

[255] Leo Gross," The International Court of Justice: Consideration of Requirements for Enhancing its Role in the International Legal Order," 65 *AJIL* 253 (1971).

[256] Interview with Covey Oliver, Aug. 13, 1995 (transcript on file with the Society).

[257] See 2 *The Future of the International Court of Justice* 728 (Leo Gross ed. 1976).

Gross, agreeing with Manley Hudson before him, acknowledged that the World Court had not proven to be the great bulwark of peace that Elihu Root and James Brown Scott had envisaged. Instead, Gross saw the Court as a rather modest contributor to peace by strengthening the underpinnings of law.[258] Taking account of the wide variety of transnational actors concerned not merely with war and peace, but also with such things as stable economic relations, Gross thought it would be useful to consider whether a range of transnational actors (not just states or public international organizations) might be given access to the Court. He suggested a variety of ways in which recourse to the Court might be expanded. But that was not all. His article was an imaginative think piece on reform of the Court's procedures, composition and practices, including its advisory as well as its contentious jurisdiction, with proposals for reform that would not necessarily require amendment of the Charter or the Statute.

The 1971 volume was particularly rich in both theoretical and practical contributions to public international law. Not only did it include the symposium, already mentioned, on United States action in Cambodia;[259] it also contained Oscar Schachter's and Daniel Serwer's interdisciplinary study of marine pollution, Rupert Emerson's influential piece on self-determination, Herbert Briggs' review article on the *travaux préparatoires* of the Vienna Convention on the Law of Treaties, Robert Rosenstock's insider's explication of the U.N. Declaration of Principles of International Law concerning Friendly Relations, and Louis Henkin's reaffirmation of Article 2(4) of the Charter.[260] Henkin's piece was a response to Thomas Franck's rather less sanguine view of Article 2(4)'s fate, published in the Journal in 1970.[261]

Richard Falk's 1969 article on reprisal by the use of force created a stir among Journal readers. Falk used Israel's December 1968 raid on the Beirut International Airport as a case study. In the raid, Israeli commandos blew up thirteen commercial aircraft belonging to Arab airlines, in response to an attack two days earlier by two members of the Popular Front for the Liberation of Palestine on an El Al passenger aircraft at the Athens Airport. Falk was critical of the Israeli retaliation, but he tried to draw from the incident more than just a

---

258 Leo Gross, *supra* note 255, at 258-59. For Hudson's similar view, see Manley O. Hudson, *International Tribunals, Past and Future* 238-39 (1944).

259 See note 249 *supra*.

260 Oscar Schachter & Daniel Serwer, "Marine Pollution Problems and Remedies," 65 *AJIL* 84 (1971); Rupert Emerson, "Self-Determination," id. at 459; Herbert W. Briggs, "The *Travaux Préparatoires* of the Vienna Convention on the Law of Treaties," id. at 705; Robert Rosenstock, "The Declaration of Principles of International Law concerning Friendly Relations: A Survey," id. at 713; Louis Henkin, Editorial Comment: "The Reports of the Death of Article 2(4) Are Greatly Exaggerated," id. at 544.

261 Thomas M. Franck, "Who Killed Article 2(4)?," 64 *AJIL* 809 (1970).

censure of a specific use of force. He concluded by setting forth a twelve-element framework for assessing the legitimacy of the use of force in periods of peace.[262] The framework made it quite difficult to justify the use of force.

Falk's article generated responses in the Journal extending over the next three years. It even provided the catalyst for the occasional publication of "scholarly correspondence" to the editors.[263] Derek Bowett's 1972 article on reprisals by armed force used Falk's piece to frame the issues.[264] Bowett's article demonstrated the occasional symbiosis between the Society's study panels and the Journal's interest in publishing scholarship on important topics. The article was a revised version of his working paper for the Society's study panel on reprisals and retaliation.

6. The Deák Prize

Oceana Publications, having established an annual prize in the name of Francis Deák in 1972 for a student article in a student-edited journal, established a second Deák prize a year later for a particularly meritorious article in the Journal by a young, non-student author.[265] It was first awarded in 1974 to Frederic L. Kirgis for an article on United States practice involving the use of technology in ways that could affect the shared environment.[266]

G. AN ORGANIZATION ROOT AND SCOTT BARELY WOULD HAVE RECOGNIZED

By the mid-seventies the Society had come a very long way from its origin as a body of men, led by an elite core group personified by Elihu Root, the statesman, and James Brown Scott, the administrator/editor/scholar, meeting once a year and publishing a Journal conceived as a scholarly, yet popular, organ for conveying ideas and information. That body had been held together during the early years by an abiding faith, stemming from the legalists within the American peace movement, in arbitration based on codified rules of international law as an alternative to war.

---

262 See Richard A. Falk, "The Beirut Raid and the International Law of Retaliation," 63 *AJIL* 415, 440-42 (1969).

263 Exchange of correspondence between Julius Stone and Richard A. Falk, 64 *AJIL* 161 & 162 (1970).

264 Derek Bowett, "Reprisals Involving Recourse to Armed Force," 66 *AJIL* 1 (1972).

265 *ASIL Newsletter*, May 1974, at 2.

266 68 *ASIL Proc.* 321-22 (1974). The article is Frederic L. Kirgis, "Technological Challenge to the Shared Environment: United States Practice," 66 *AJIL* 290 (1972).

By the mid-seventies the Society was an organization of men and women (albeit with men still dominating its affairs) that was no longer closely associated with the sources of real power in government, but that had expanded its horizons beyond any limits Root and Scott could have thought possible or even wise. The Society was now directly involved not just in issues of war and peace, but in such wide-ranging matters as science and technology, foreign trade and investment, human rights, and international organizations. The faith in international adjudication and the codification of international law as primary means of averting war had faded substantially, though the interest in law and legal processes as means of effectuating widely shared values, including values emphasizing non-violent dispute-settlement, remained high.

A measure of the Society's loss of innocence in the nearly seventy years since the peace movement brought it to life was its response to the Vietnam War. World War I had brought on a sense of near-despondency within the Society. International law had failed to do the very thing that the Society's leaders had set out to show it could do: to provide a viable alternative to all-out war. The Vietnam War was not World War III, but it nevertheless tore apart American society (with a small "s"). The ASIL, though, did not sink into despondency. Rather, it plunged into debate over the legal and moral issues, particularly those raised by the conduct of the United States government. The Society's World War I patriotism (once the initial shock of war had been absorbed) was hard to find in the Vietnam years; even those who supported the government's decisions did so not because it was their government, for better or worse, but because they found legal justification for the decisions. Other Society commentators, of course, were quite critical of the government. Whether they had any significant effect on government policy or practices was debatable, but they were forthright in their analyses and in their prescriptions for change.

The Society continued to think of its Annual Meetings and its Journal as its showcases, but they were far from the only games in town. Fueled by foundation grants undreamed of in the early days, the Society supported a wide variety of study panels that in turn produced a steady stream of books and other publications. It proudly published *International Legal Materials*, a source of current documents unmatched anywhere in its scope and timeliness of coverage.

That these products were of high quality is borne out by an encomium from the Ford Foundation when it granted the Society USD 300,000 in 1973. Arthur Cyr, representing the International Division of the Foundation, wrote to Stephen Schwebel:

> [W]e have been very much impressed by the energy and quality characteristic of the Society's overall program, including the study panels and related publications. As part of our review, we have consulted with a large number of international law scholars in different parts of the

> country having varied degrees of association with ASIL. The high regard in which the Society is held is striking.[267]

Studies and related publications were not all. The Society had fostered and nurtured an international law moot court program that had become truly international, with teams coming to Washington from all over the world. It had a permanent home with a growing library, offices and a meeting room. It was staffed by an Executive Director and others who supported the myriad of activities it now pursued.

The vast expansion of activities and programs was not only fueled by the large foundation grants; it was utterly dependent on their continuance. The old revenue-raising staple, membership dues, continued to be a significant source of income, but there was no hope of maintaining the Society's research and study program on the basis of dues income alone. The consequence was that a very great deal of Stephen Schwebel's time and energy had to go into raising new grant money. The Society was well rewarded by his efforts, but each new grant brought only temporary relief. Maintaining the momentum would be a central concern for succeeding Executive Directors.

Another central concern would be broadening the membership base, especially expanding it beyond its established core within the professoriate. The Society's next Executive Director would be particularly well suited for the task, but would find it difficult to boost total membership.

267 Letter from Arthur Cyr to Stephen M. Schwebel, Mar. 2, 1973.

Chapter Ten

A CHANGE OF EMPHASIS

The demand for human rights and human dignity ... has taken on universal proportions in the years that have elapsed since the founding of the American Society of International Law. In no other period of history have more human beings been killed, tortured, arbitrarily imprisoned, and made to disappear than in the past 75 years.

—Thomas Buergenthal
Remarks, *The Demand for Freedom*,
75 *ASIL Proceedings* 94 (1981)

A. STAYING AFLOAT WITH SHIFTING HORIZONS

1. A New Executive Director

As soon as Stephen Schwebel announced his resignation as Executive Director, effective June 30, 1974, the Society's Executive Committee met in closed session to consider the appointment of his successor. It decided to solicit the views of members of the Executive Council, after which the Executive Committee would "reconvene to select a successor to Mr. Schwebel."[1] The Executive Committee pointedly did not say that it would reconvene to recommend Mr. Schwebel's successor to the Executive Council.

The Society published a notice in the Newsletter soliciting recommendations and applications.[2] What happened next is not a matter of record. The minutes of the Executive Committee meeting on November 1, 1974, say cryptically that Richard Baxter, the President of the Society, "expected that the Executive Director question would be settled that evening."[3] At the Executive Council meeting the next day, Baxter presented the report of the Executive Committee. It emphasized "the importance of choosing a seasoned scholar of recognized standing, as well as a person capable of dealing effectively with foundations, government organizations, and other donors or grantors of funds." The Executive

---

1 *ASIL Newsletter*, June 1974, at 1.

2 *ASIL Newsletter*, July–Aug. 1974, at 1.

3 Minutes of the Executive Committee, Nov. 1, 1974, in ASIL Minute Book, Apr. 1974–Oct. 1981, at 12, 16.

Committee recommended Seymour J. Rubin for the position, and the Executive Council duly appointed him.[4]

In Rubin's words, "All I know is that Dick Baxter came over to see me and asked me if I would become the Executive Director of the Society."[5] Rubin was reasonably sure that Walter Sterling Surrey, a former law partner of Rubin's and a Vice President of the Society in 1974, had something to do with his selection.

Rubin at that time was a member of the faculty at the Washington College of Law of American University, and was counsel to his former firm, Surrey, Karasik and Morse. He had recently become a member of the Inter-American Juridical Committee. Before he joined the American University law faculty, he had been the General Counsel of the Agency for International Development and had also served as the U.S. Representative to the Development Assistance Committee of the O.E.C.D. in Paris. He thus came to the Society with considerable experience in government, private practice and academia. He knew his way around Washington and had contacts abroad. His qualifications were just what Baxter and the Executive Committee had sought.

Baxter sold Rubin on the Executive Director's position. Rubin later recalled, "[T]his sounded like a place where you could do some work in the field of international law in which I was interested, and I thought particularly that there was some opportunity to do some work in the field of international economic law since I seemed to be one of the few people around here who was interested in it at the time."[6]

Rubin took office on January 1, 1975. Like his predecessor, he maintained a position in academia while he served as Executive Director. He continued to be a professor of law at American University.

2. Expiring Grants and Economy Measures

Rubin inherited a cluster of large, expiring grants from the Ford and Mellon Foundations. These relatively unrestricted grants, along with funds from some other sources such as the National Science Foundation, supplied overhead that helped the Society balance its books. The overhead allocations from research and study grants were then contributing about 36 per cent of the funds in the general account, making the Society quite reliant on the major grants.[7] Yet,

---

4 Minutes of the Executive Council, Nov. 2, 1974, in ASIL Minute Book, Apr. 1974–Oct. 1981, at 19, 23.

5 Interview with Seymour J. Rubin, May 17, 1994 (transcript on file with the Society).

6 Interview with Seymour J. Rubin, May 17, 1994.

7 Minutes of the Executive Council, Apr. 25, 1975, in ASIL Minute Book, Apr. 1974–Oct. 1981, at 41, 42.

new grant money – at least after 1976 – was likely to be restricted to specific programs without funds for general overhead.

In addition, Rubin inherited the problem of trying to collect refunds from the Society's own grantees who had failed to produce the work for which they had already been paid. His efforts to get the money back were unsuccessful.[8] To deal with the problem in the future, the Society stopped making advance payments to scholars.[9]

Very soon after Rubin took office, Larry Hargrove's previous efforts to obtain a new grant from the National Science Foundation bore fruit. The NSF made a one-year grant to study the international legal implications of ocean thermal energy conversion. Gary Knight and Daniel Nyhart were appointed to co-chair the multidisciplinary project.[10] It resulted in a two-day workshop with over 100 registrants in January 1976. Panel members presented papers on a variety of technical, legal and economic issues.[11]

Hargrove's efforts also produced a USD 56,000 grant from the State Department for a study of international terrorism. The co-chairs for this project were Alona Evans and John Murphy. In addition, a new USD 29,000 grant from the Rockefeller Foundation was received for a study of the future of the Inter-American system. Overhead from these grants helped to defray the Society's operating deficit for the fiscal year 1975-76.[12]

The Society seemed to be caught in a revolving door of seeking project grants, obtaining some of them, using some of the funds to support operations, and then starting over again. Worse, many private foundations limited their funding to direct project costs, supplying no overhead for operations.[13] Accepting such grants actually could have cost the Society money, since it could incur unreimbursed overhead expenses in administering them – unless senior staff time could be attributed as direct costs to the funded programs. The Society adopted this

8 Interview with Seymour J. Rubin, May 17, 1994.

9 Minutes of the Executive Committee, Nov. 1, 1974, in ASIL Minute Book, Apr. 1974–Oct. 1981, at 12, 17. See also Minutes of the Executive Committee, Nov. 1, 1975, in ASIL Minute Book, Apr. 1974–Oct. 1981, at 44, 47.

10 *ASIL Newsletter*, Feb. 1975, at 2.

11 The materials were made available to Society members at cost. *ASIL Newsletter*, Jan./Feb. 1976, at 1.

12 Minutes of the Executive Committee and Executive Council, Apr. 23 & 24, 1975, in ASIL Minute Book, Apr. 1974–Oct. 1981, at 28, 29 & 32, 33.

13 Minutes of the Executive Committee, Jan. 9, 1976, in ASIL Minute Book, Apr. 1974–Oct. 1981, at 59.

allocation practice despite some doubts about its propriety. Apparently it was a widespread practice among non-profit organizations.[14]

In order to keep overhead allocations coming in, the Society made special efforts to get new grants from foundations such as Ford and Mellon. In the spring of 1976 it was able to announce a new USD 180,000 grant from Mellon for four research projects on international environmental problems.[15] In 1977, the Ford Foundation supplied a USD 175,000 grant for five human rights projects and one on environmental management, with an overhead component.[16] One of the Ford-funded projects quickly produced a book examining the Helsinki process on security and cooperation in Europe.[17] The Mellon grant ultimately produced three books.[18]

In 1984, the Rockefeller Foundation awarded a grant to bring together legal and economic experts at the Foundation's study center in Bellagio, Italy, for a five-day seminar on issues relating to international trade. The idea was to contribute to the preparatory work for the next GATT negotiations, the Uruguay Round. The seminar was held in April 1985.[19]

At about the same time, Ford made a new USD 50,000 grant for human rights, enabling Louis Sohn to extend a project on the Economic, Social and Cultural Rights Covenant that Ford had included in its 1977 grant. Exxon Corporation provided a grant of USD 10,000 for activities related to international investment.[20]

---

14 Minutes of the Executive Committee, Oct. 30, 1976, in ASIL Minute Book, Apr. 1974–Oct. 1981, at 75, 76.

15 The projects dealt with coastal ocean environment, environmental protection by international organizations, the management of international rivers, and the relationship between environmental standards and international trade. *ASIL Newsletter*, Mar./Apr./May 1976, at 1.

16 Minutes of the Executive Council, Apr. 21, 1977, in ASIL Minute Book, Apr. 1974–Oct. 1981, at 89, 90.

17 Thomas Buergenthal (ed.), *Human Rights, International Law and the Helsinki Accord* (1977). For the text of the Helsinki Accord, see 14 *ILM* 1292 (1975).

18 Seymour J. Rubin & Thomas R. Graham (eds.), *Environment and Trade: The Relation of International Trade and Environmental Policy* (1982); Jonathan I. Charney (ed.), *The New Nationalism and the Use of Common Spaces: Issues in Marine Pollution and the Exploitation of Antarctica* (1982); David A. Kay & Harold K. Jacobson, *Environmental Protection: The International Dimension* (1983).

19 *ASIL Newsletter*, Sept./Oct. 1984, at 1; Memorandum from Seymour J. Rubin to Executive Council (undated, 1987), in briefing book for Apr. 1987 Executive Council meetings.

20 Summary Report of the Director of Studies, Oct. 27, 1984, in briefing book for Executive Council meeting of Oct. 27, 1984.

Rubin thought that the most promising means of exiting the revolving door with grantors was to court corporate memberships.[21] Some efforts to develop ongoing relationships with corporations had already been undertaken before he became Executive Director, but he thought much more should be done.[22] More was done, but corporate memberships never provided the sustenance that large foundation grants had.

Meanwhile, in the late seventies, the Executive Council raised dues for student, regular and overseas members. I.L.M. subscription rates were increased, as was the Journal subscription rate.

Dues increases notwithstanding, money problems persisted. Membership in the Society was essentially stagnant, a condition that lasted well into the eighties.[23] In the autumn of 1975 there was an anticipated deficit of USD 190,000 for fiscal year 1976-77 if no additional funding could be found. Various sources of funds were explored, but anxieties arose over fostering too intimate an association with such wellsprings as the government, oil companies, labor unions, multinational corporations or any special interest group.[24] A tightwire fund-raising act was needed. So were economy measures.

The Society was able to reduce the anticipated deficit to about USD 150,000 by withholding cost-of-living increases from the staff, turning the Newsletter first into a bimonthly and soon thereafter into a quarterly,[25] and eliminating the modest subventions that had been given for regional meetings.[26] In addition, the expense of publishing Annual Meeting Proceedings was reduced in 1976 by including summaries of presentations rather than full text.[27] In 1978, the Society began charging separately for the Proceedings.

The struggle to support the Tillar House library continued during this period. In December 1976, Seymour Rubin sent out letters to senior partners at virtually

---

21 Minutes of the Excutive Committee and Executive Council, Apr. 23 & 24, 1975, in ASIL Minute Book, Apr. 1974–Oct. 1981, at 28, 30 & 32, 33.

22 Interview with Seymour Rubin, May 17, 1994 (transcript on file with the Society).

23 *ASIL Newsletter*, Mar.–Apr. 1979, at 3; Report on Membership and Computers, Apr. 12, 1985, in briefing materials for Apr. 1985 Executive Council meetings.

24 Minutes of the Executive Council, Nov. 1, 1975, in ASIL Minute Book, Apr. 1974–Oct. 1981, at 44, 46-47.

25 Minutes of the Executive Committee, Jan. 9, 1976, in ASIL Minute Book, Apr. 1974–Oct. 1981, at 59; *ASIL Newsletter*, Mar./Apr./May 1976, at 2. In January 1979 the Newsletter reverted to a bimonthly, but with smaller print and smaller pages. *ASIL Newsletter*, Jan.–Feb. 1979, at 1.

26 *ASIL Newsletter*, Oct. 1975, at 3.

27 Minutes of the Executive Council, Apr. 22, 1976, in ASIL Minute Book, Apr. 1974–Oct. 1981, at 66, 71. The 1976 Proceedings ran to 228 pages, including the Index, down from 317 pages in 1975.

all the major Washington law firms, urging their support for the library. The results were modest. Ten contributions came in, totaling USD 2,975.[28]

3. The Seventy-fifth Anniversary Fund

Although the Society had some investment funds when Seymour Rubin took office, he regarded the available reserves as woefully inadequate for the Society's needs. Rubin and Hargrove also became weary of the constant struggle to pry funds out of foundations for Society projects. In his 1979 Executive Director's report, Rubin proposed that on the occasion of the Society's diamond jubilee in 1981, a major funding drive should be undertaken. "Such an endowment," he said, "would make it possible for the Society to channel its research on the basis of the merits of proposed projects, rather than (as is now the case) on the basis of their appeal to foundations and other prospective donors."[29] Thus was the Seventy-fifth Anniversary Fund born.

In April 1980, a year before the seventy-fifth anniversary, President Alona Evans appointed an Ad Hoc Committee on the Seventy-fifth Anniversary Fund, initially chaired by David Gill.[30] Gill reported to the Executive Council that the goal was to raise at least USD 1 million, with matching grants from foundations of another USD 1 million. The strategy was to start with major gifts from corporations and law firms, and then smaller contributions would be sought.[31]

Ultimately John J. McCloy chaired the committee. By the end of the seventy-fifth anniversary year, 1981, the Fund remained well short of its USD 2 million goal, with total donations and pledges of about USD 750,000.[32] Nevertheless, the boost to the Society's resources was significant, and there were some promising after-effects. In 1983, efforts begun during the campaign to entice a grant from the National Endowment for the Humanities bore fruit. The NEH offered a matching grant of up to USD 500,000, with the Endowment providing one dollar for every three the Society raised.[33] By August 1987, the Society had raised the necessary funds.[34]

---

28 Report on the Library, Nov. 1977.

29 Report of the Executive Director, 73 *ASIL Proc.* 109, 110 (1979).

30 Minutes of the Executive Council, Apr. 19, 1980, in ASIL Minute Book, Apr. 1974–Oct. 1981, unnumbered page.

31 Minutes of the Executive Council, Oct. 25, 1980, in ASIL Minute Book, Apr. 1974–Oct. 1981, unnumbered page.

32 *ASIL Newsletter*, Nov./Dec. 1981, at 3.

33 *ASIL Newsletter*, Mar./Apr. 1983, at 2.

34 Report of the Executive Director for Executive Council meeting of Oct. 24, 1987, in briefing book for that meeting.

Despite Sy Rubin's expectation that the Fund would be used primarily as endowment, persistent budget deficits in the mid- and late-eighties necessitated net expenditures from the Fund to balance the current account.[35] Worrisome though these invasions of capital were, they enabled the Society to continue its robust program of studies, workshops and reports after the initial flush of Ford Foundation grants had been relegated to distant memory.

4. The Question That Hardly Ever Disappears: Taking Positions on Substantive Issues

At the Executive Council meeting in November 1974, Richard Falk brought up the question that never seems to go away: whether the Society should take a position on a matter of current importance. President Gerald Ford had recently held a press conference at which he indicated that he did not know whether international law dealt with covert operations of the sort the United States apparently was conducting in Chile. Falk did not suggest that the Society comment on the legality of covert operations, but rather that it should comment on the apparent insensitivity of the President of the United States toward important international legal questions. Falk argued that such a comment might even be mandatory under the provision in the Society's Constitution calling on it to promote the establishment and maintenance of international relations on the basis of law and justice.

After considerable debate, the Executive Council affirmed the Society's policy of avoiding positions on public issues, but called for a procedure to be established "for the Society to take a position as an organization on matters of exceptional importance bearing on the status of law in the conduct of foreign relations." In addition, the Council asked the President of the Society to establish a procedure for developing a response to President Ford's press conference. Richard Baxter, the President of the Society, appointed a committee to look into those matters, but it was unable to agree on a response to President Ford.[36]

On the broader question of taking positions, the committee reaffirmed the Executive Council's policy statement of April 1966.[37] It limited Society statements to technical matters and truly important substantive matters as to which Society members could be expected to be knowledgeable and as to which there is no significant disagreement within the Society regarding the desirability of the proposed action.

---

35 Report of the Executive Director (Hargrove) for the Executive Council meeting of Oct. 15, 1988, in briefing book for that meeting.

36 Minutes of the Executive Council, Nov. 2, 1974, and Apr. 24, 1975, in ASIL Minute Book, Apr. 1974–Oct. 1981, at 19, 20-22 and at 32, 39.

37 Quoted in Chapter Eight, Section C.2 *supra*.

The 1974-75 committee also proposed that the President of the Society be authorized to refer to the Executive Committee any such matter that appeared to warrant prompt Executive Council action; if the Executive Committee agreed, the matter would be put on the agenda of the next Council meeting or Council members could be polled if the matter were very urgent. All members of the Society could bring such matters to the attention of the President. If the Executive Committee thought there could be substantial disagreement about the desirability of the proposed action, a public meeting to discuss it could be called. The Executive Council unanimously accepted the committee's report.[38]

Of course, the matter was not thereby laid to rest. At the Executive Council meeting in October 1976, Leonard Meeker said he thought the Society had an obligation to take a stand on important questions, and that the President of the Society should express an opinion on them. The procedure he had in mind would be informal, and would not require obtaining a consensus within the Society. The pros and cons were discussed once again, with no closure.[39]

Something akin to what Meeker had in mind occurred in December 1979, when Clyde Ferguson, then the President of the Society, initiated a message that was sent to Iranian authorities during the hostage crisis in Tehran. The crisis had arisen after the overthrow of the Shah, when Iranian militants occupied the U.S. embassy and two U.S. consulates, holding American diplomatic and consular personnel hostage. Ferguson and several other leading international law figures signed the message in their individual capacities. It urged release of the hostages on grounds of universally accepted international law, including provisions of the Vienna Convention on Diplomatic Relations. It was published in the Society's Newsletter.[40]

It was *deja vu* in October 1983, when the Executive Council considered a request from the Canadian Council on International Law to condemn the forcible abduction of a Canadian citizen from Canadian territory by two U.S. citizens acting pursuant to a Florida bench warrant. After extensive discussion, the Executive Council decided that the President should appoint an *ad hoc* committee to re-examine the practice of eschewing substantive positions on controversial issues. President Covey Oliver appointed Keith Highet to chair a Committee on the Expression of Views.[41] Its functions were later subsumed into those of the Committee on the Future of the Society, discussed later in this Chapter.

---

38 Minutes of the Executive Council, Nov. 2, 1974, and Apr. 24, 1975, in ASIL Minute Book, Apr. 1974–Oct. 1981, at 40; *ASIL Newsletter*, May 1975, at 1.

39 Minutes of the Executive Council, Oct. 30, 1976, in ASIL Minute Book, Apr. 1974–Oct. 1981, at 78, 86-88.

40 *ASIL Newsletter*, Jan./Feb. 1980, at 1.

41 *ASIL Newsletter*, Nov./Dec. 1983, at 2-3; Minutes of the Executive Council, Oct. 8, 1983, in ASIL Notebook of Executive Council Minutes, Apr. 1982–Nov. 1990.

Events stemming from U.S. support for the Nicaraguan Contras upstaged the committee. The U.S. State Department got wind of the fact that Nicaragua was about to institute proceedings against the United States in the International Court of Justice, challenging American military and paramilitary action in support of the Nicaraguan Contras against the Sandinista government. The State Department acted with uncommon alacrity and won (by three days) the race to the courthouse. It deposited an instrument on April 6, 1984, proclaiming that the U.S. Article 36(2) acceptance of the Court's jurisdiction "shall not apply to disputes with any Central American State or arising out of or related to events in Central America," effective immediately and extending through the next two years. This, despite the proviso in the U.S. Article 36(2) declaration that it would remain in force until six months after notice was given to terminate it.

The Society's Annual Meeting began a week later. In the words of Covey Oliver, the Society's President, "[The State Department's] action swept through the Annual Meeting of the ASIL at Washington and resulted in a Societal Resolution of Condemnation ..., the first and only such condemnation ever issued by the ASIL against the United States or any other state."[42] The Executive Council presented the resolution to the Business Meeting, which amended and then adopted it:

> Although the American Society of International Law ordinarily does not take positions on matters of policy, the Society has previously departed from this practice to support the acceptance by the United States of the jurisdiction of the International Court of Justice. The Society was founded "to foster the study of international law and to promote the establishment and maintenance of international relations on the basis of law and justice." It now reaffirms that international adjudication, and the application of international law, constitute appropriate procedures for resolving justiciable international disputes. The Society therefore deplores, and strongly favor[s] rescission of, the recent action of the United States Government in attempting to withdraw from the jurisdiction of the International Court of Justice "disputes with any Central American state."[43]

The resolution was made public immediately, in the form of a press release. It had no effect on the United States government, which allowed its instrument of April 6 to stand and then withdrew from participation in the proceedings after the Court held that the instrument did not defeat the Court's jurisdiction.[44]

---

42 "Covey's Notes on ASIL and his Relations Therewith," Aug. 13, 1995, prepared in conjunction with his interview with F.L. Kirgis on the same date (on file with the Society).

43 78 *ASIL Proc.* 133, 137 (1984).

44 Case Concerning Military and Paramilitary Activities in and Against Nicaragua (*Nicaragua v. United States*), 1984 *ICJ Rep.* 392, 24 *ILM* 59 (1985).

The Society's Executive Council met in special session after the United States withdrew from the proceedings. Ultimately the Council recommended, and the 1985 Business Meeting adopted, another resolution:

> The American Society of International Law, referring to its resolution of April 12, 1984, reaffirms its strongly held conviction that international adjudication and the application of international law constitute appropriate procedures for resolving justiciable international disputes. The Society expresses its concern that developments in the Nicaraguan litigation, relating to and following the decision of the International Court of Justice of November 25, 1984, present major problems for the future of international adjudication and the International Court of Justice itself.[45]

At about the same time, the Committee on the Future of the Society took up the broader question of taking positions on substantive issues. It reported to the Executive Council in April 1985. The Committee noted the Society's long-standing policy of avoiding, whenever possible, the adoption of resolutions on substantive issues. It concluded that, "while this basic policy is entirely sound, it is also true that some way should be sought for the Society to provide a means of response to what may from time to time emerge as a strong desire of a significant majority of the Society's members in attendance at an annual and other meetings of the Society to record a position or views on issues of international policy."[46] The Committee suggested that resolutions might be adopted on some matters of substance, provided that there is an opportunity to hear presentation (including by mail) on all sides of an issue, with procedural safeguards for recording votes for and against any such resolutions.[47]

Another way in which the Society might be heard, in the Committee's view, would be by forming a panel of experts who could be made available to the media and others without committing the Society in any way.[48] Keith Highet had made a similar suggestion as chair of the Committee on the Expression of

---

45 79 *ASIL Proc.* 148-49 (1985); see also *ASIL Newsletter*, Apr./May 1985, at 2.

46 Minutes of the Executive Council, Apr. 24, 1985, in ASIL Notebook of Executive Council Minutes, Apr. 1982–Nov. 1990.

47 Final Report of the Committee on the Future of the Society, Apr. 18, 1985, at 13, in briefing materials for Apr. 1985 Executive Council meetings.

48 Minutes of the Executive Council, Apr. 24, 1985, in ASIL Notebook of Executive Council Minutes, Apr. 1982–Nov. 1990; Final Report of the Committee on the Future of the Society, Apr. 18, 1985, at 12-14, in briefing materials for Apr. 1985 Executive Council meetings.

Views.[49] In the end, the Executive Council took no action on the Committee's suggestions.[50]

5. Redefining the Annual Certificate of Merit

In 1975, the Committee on Annual Awards recommended that the Society's Certificate of Merit be awarded to Arthur Rovine for *The Digest of U.S. Practice in International Law*. Myres McDougal objected. He said that the award should not be given to works that by their nature are not creative scholarship. It was pointed out, though, that the award had been given to collections of materials in the past.[51] McDougal received support from several Council members. Richard Falk suggested that a special commendation of some sort be given to the current *Digest*, but that it should not receive the award for creative scholarship. Ultimately Richard Baxter, the President of the Society, announced what he perceived to be the gist of the discussion. In the coming year consideration would be given to making two awards, only one of which would be for creative scholarship. In the meantime, something had to be done about the current year. By a margin of one vote, the Executive Council decided to make the award to Rovine's *Digest*.[52]

In November 1975, the Executive Council amended the Regulations to permit the award of more than one Certificate of Merit. Without requiring that two awards be made in any given year, it was contemplated that one would be given for individual scholarship and one for a collection.[53]

6. Redefining the Role of the Executive Committee

In the early seventies the Executive Committee was no longer the *de facto* decision-making body of the Society. Ostensibly its role then was to act as the review body for the Board of Review and Development. By the mid-seventies it was not performing that role either. It was meeting just before Executive Council meetings, as it had for several years past, but was simply discussing many of the same items that would be taken up a few hours later by the Executive Council.

---

49 Memorandum from Keith Highet to Messrs. Gill, Oliver, Hargrove and Rubin, Apr. 12, 1984, in briefing materials for Apr. 1984 Executive Council meetings.

50 Consistent with the Society's reaffirmed policy permitting adoption of resolutions on technical matters, the annual Business Meetings continued to urge prompt publication of the State Department's *Foreign Relations of the United States* series. See, e.g., 69 *ASIL Proc.* 275-76 (1975).

51 For example, it had been given to Marjorie Whiteman in 1965 for her *Digest of International Law*.

52 Minutes of the Executive Council, Apr. 24, 1975, in ASIL Minute Book, Apr. 1974–Oct. 1981, at 32, 35-37.

53 Minutes of the Executive Council, Nov. 1, 1975, in ASIL Minute Book, Apr. 1974–Oct. 1975, at 50, 55.

To try to rectify this inefficient arrangement, the Council adopted a revised Regulation making the Executive Committee the interim arm of the Council.[54] It would henceforth meet between Council meetings, to deal with matters that could not comfortably be held over until the next Council meeting.

In practice, this turned the Executive Committee into a moribund body. It was seldom convened between 1976 and 1982.[55]

7. Disquiet about Governance: Rubin v. Rubin

At the Executive Council meeting in April 1977, Seymour Rubin was put on the defensive when a couple of Council members questioned whether the Society's elected body – the Council – really exercised control over the Executive Director or the Director of Studies. A direct question was asked: Had the Council ever overruled the management of the Society? Answer: No, but "messages did get back to the staff from the Council."[56] An uneasy truce resulted.

The truce did not last long. Starting in May 1977, Alfred Rubin (no relation to Seymour) persistently raised questions about how the various positions of responsibility in the Society were being filled. In addition, he challenged what he regarded as a lack of attention to scholars as panelists at the 1977 Annual Meeting.[57]

At the November 1977 Executive Council meeting, he questioned particularly the appointment or election of persons to governing bodies who had not been active in the Society or, in the case of the Board of Editors of the Journal, who had not published in the Journal. He also questioned the nomination in that year of one member of the Nominating Committee to be a Vice President. The near-consensus (with one dissent) was that in the future, Nominating Committee members should not be nominated for office, but the other questions remained unanswered.[58]

At the 1978 Business Meeting, the heated debate continued. Alfred Rubin again raised the question of criteria for selection of members of the Board of Review and Development. Walter Surrey, the Society's President, responded that B.R.D. members who had not attended a meeting for two years were being asked

---

[54] Minutes of the Executive Council, Oct. 30, 1976, in ASIL Minute Book, Apr. 1974–Oct. 1975, at 78.

[55] Undated, unsigned memorandum for Covey T. Oliver, in briefing materials for Apr. 1982 Executive Council meetings.

[56] Minutes of the Executive Council, Apr. 22, 1977, in ASIL Minute Book, Apr. 1974–Oct. 1981, at 97, 99.

[57] Memorandum of Sept. 1, 1977, from Alfred P. Rubin to "Concerned ASIL members"; letter from Walter Sterling Surrey to Alfred P. Rubin, Sept. 26, 1977.

[58] Minutes of the Executive Council, Nov. 12, 1977, in ASIL Minute Book, Apr. 1974–Oct. 1981, at 124, 132-35.

to resign. Edward Gordon asserted that there was a deep alienation between the members of the Society on one hand and the people who governed it on the other. The membership's perception, he said, was that the Society was in the hands of people with close ties to the State Department and to the Eastern academic elite – Harvard, Yale and Columbia.

Seymour Rubin thought the dissidents were being inconsistent when they asserted that faithful service to the Society should be rewarded while they complained that newcomers were being kept out of positions of influence. He also saw an inconsistency between trying to diversify membership on the Executive Council and the B.R.D. while striving for high attendance at meetings that members away from the East Coast might not be able to attend. The exchange of views satisfied almost nobody.[59]

When the time came to vote for members of the Nominating Committee, Alfred Rubin rose again. He proposed, forcefully, that guidelines be formulated promptly for use by the Nominating Committee. Clyde Ferguson, the new President, said that he would appoint an *ad hoc* committee to draft guidelines.[60]

Alfred Rubin chaired the *ad hoc* committee. It came up with a detailed set of guidelines for use by Nominating Committees.[61] The Executive Council engaged in a spirited debate on the proposed guidelines, with several members expressing the view that they were too rigid. When no consensus could be reached, Ferguson charged the committee to come up with a new draft.[62]

The committee's new guidelines were intended to do four things: (a) assure diversity, and a breadth of personal and career experiences, among Executive Council members; (b) ensure that Council members would have personal knowledge of, and experience in, the activities of the Society; (c) reward active participation in the Society, as indicated by attendance at Annual Meetings or participation in the Jessup semi-final or final rounds; and (d) provide for turnover in Council membership. In addition, the committee recommended that the Nominating Committee be required to report to the general membership at each Business Meeting on how the guidelines had been implemented.[63]

The Executive Council adopted a resolution directed to the Business Meeting. It read simply, "The Executive Council thanks and commends the committee,

---

59 72 *ASIL Proc.* 146-51 (1978).

60 Id. at 161-64.

61 The proposed guidelines were set forth in full in *ASIL Newsletter*, Aug.–Oct. 1978, at 2-4.

62 Minutes of the Executive Council, Oct. 28, 1978, in ASIL Minute Book, Apr. 1974–Oct. 1981, at 151, 162-66.

63 Report of the Ad Hoc Committee on Nomination Guidelines, attached to letter from Alfred P. Rubin to C. Clyde Ferguson, Feb. 26, 1979, in briefing book for Executive Council meeting of Apr. 26, 1979.

takes note of its report, and commends it to future nominating committees for consideration and such use as they may wish to make of it."[64] After an extensive debate, the Business Meeting took no action.[65] Nevertheless, the Rubin committee guidelines became the non-binding standards that future Nominating Committees took into account in the nominating process.

The first Nominating Committee to operate under the Rubin Committee guidelines nominated Alona Evans to be the first woman to serve as President of the Society. She was elected, but her term was tragically cut short by her untimely death on September 23, 1980.[66]

Monroe Leigh was designated to fill out Alona Evans' term as President, and then was elected President in his own right at the next Business Meeting.

The 1979-80 Nominating Committee nominated a rather diverse slate of eight candidates for the Executive Council. Each of them had considerable experience in international law and was active in the Society. The younger members of the Society rebelled, submitting petitions nominating three young members as additional candidates. This necessitated the use of a ballot distributed to all members as an insert in the January/February 1980 Newsletter.[67] Seven of the eight persons on the Nominating Committee's slate were elected; Linda Mabry, one of the nominees by petition, was elected to the final slot.[68]

When the Executive Council recommended a 1982-83 Nominating Committee consisting only of members in and around the Washington, D.C. area, Alfred Rubin and Edward Gordon objected. Rubin moved in the Business Meeting that the guidelines be made binding on the Nominating Committee that year. After much discussion, the motion was defeated. Edith Brown Weiss moved to reaffirm the continued force of the guidelines "as morally persuasive for the Nominating Committee." Her motion was adopted.[69]

8. Discontent Regarding the Board of Review and Development

In 1980, Larry Hargrove presented to the Executive Council a slate of nominees for the Board of Review and Development that included a political scientist who

---

64 73 *ASIL Proc.* 112 (1979); Minutes of the Executive Council, Apr. 26, 1979, in ASIL Minute Book, Apr. 1974–Oct. 1981, at 168, 171.

65 73 *ASIL Proc.* 114. The next item on the agenda was election of the following year's Nominating Committee. Alfred Rubin questioned the slate presented by the President, and another contentious debate followed. Id. at 114-17.

66 In her will she left a bequest to the Society of about USD 40,000. Minutes of the Executive Council, Oct. 24, 1981, in ASIL Minute Book, Apr. 1974–Oct. 1981, unnumbered page.

67 *ASIL Newsletter*, Jan./Feb. 1980, at 1 & insert.

68 74 *ASIL Proc.* 104 (1980).

69 76 *ASIL Proc.* 105 (1982).

was not a member of the Society. The ensuing discussion led to questions about the utility of the B.R.D., which seemed no longer to be the creative, scholarly body it once was. Hargrove argued that it remained useful in generating ideas for research and sometimes in formulating the proposals themselves. By the slimmest of margins, the Council postponed a decision on the recommendations as to new members until a decision could be made on the continued existence of the B.R.D. Later in the meeting, Sy Rubin and Larry Hargrove asked that the motion to postpone be reconsidered. By that time some of the Council members had left the meeting. The remaining members rescinded the motion and decided to poll the entire Executive Council on the matter by mail ballot.[70] The B.R.D. was spared, but it was in trouble. Although it would remain alive until 1993, it never regained the vitality it once had.

9. Interest Groups Arrive on the Scene

As has been noted in Chapter Eight, Kenneth Carlston in 1966 first put forward the idea of forming interest groups, or sections. The Executive Committee rejected it.[71] When John Jackson made a similar suggestion in 1979, it fell on somewhat more sympathetic ears. As Jackson formulated it, any group of members could form a section, or committee, around a subject of mutual interest. Financial support, if any, would be the responsibility of the committee members. Each committee could have a business meeting at the Annual Meeting, and could present a panel.[72] Membership in any section or committee would be open to any ASIL member.[73]

The Executive Council discussed the idea at its October 1979 meeting. No consensus emerged.[74] But by October 1981, the Council was ready to act. It adopted a resolution encouraging "interested members to form interest groups or sections of the Society to broaden interest in and study of international law, and to encourage inquiry into particular fields of international law."[75] A Committee on Interest Groups and Sections was formed, with authority to vet proposals emanating from any two or more Society members.

70 Minutes of the Executive Council, Apr. 19, 1980, in ASIL Minute Book, Apr. 1974–Oct. 1981, unnumbered page.

71 See Chapter Eight, Section A.14, *supra*.

72 Letter from John H. Jackson to Seymour Rubin, May 30, 1979, in briefing book for Executive Council meeting, Oct. 27, 1979.

73 Letter from John H. Jackson to Seymour Rubin, July 17, 1979, in briefing book for Executive Council meeting, Oct. 27, 1979.

74 Minutes of the Executive Council, Oct. 27, 1979, in ASIL Minute Book, Apr. 1974–Oct. 1981, unnumbered page.

75 Minutes of the Executive Council, Oct. 24, 1981, in ASIL Minute Book, Apr. 1974–Oct. 1981, unnumbered page; *ASIL Newsletter*, Nov./Dec. 1981, at 3.

Based on the Committee's recommendations, the Executive Council in October 1982 approved Policy Guidelines for what became interest groups: "[M]embers of the Society who are interested in particular subjects or areas of international law [may form groups] for the purpose of following current developments, pursuing mutual interests in particular subject matters, conducting studies, exchanging views, holding seminars and [subject to higher approval] publishing occasional or regular papers thereon."[76] The process for approving formation of an interest group evolved over time. By October 1984 the Executive Director's office was given the authority to consider requests for interest groups.[77] The Society's Regulations, though, remained silent on interest groups.

Some Council members felt that the groups would be a divisive force within the Society. Their concerns were overcome primarily on the ground that the groups would make the Society more interesting and would attract new members.[78] Moreover, the interest groups would be self-sustaining through the assessment of modest dues.

The first interest group, on International Economic Law, was formed contemporaneously with the Council's approval of the Guidelines. As early as 1984, it began to sponsor panel discussions at Annual Meetings.[79] The group prospered, becoming one of the most vital forces in the Society.

Other interest groups soon followed. Among the first were those on Antarctica, Dispute Resolution in International Commercial Contracts, Indigenous Rights, International Environmental Law, Private International Law, Space Law, Human Rights Advocacy, and International Organizations.[80]

---

[76] Minutes of the Executive Council, Oct. 30, 1982, in briefing materials for April 1983 Executive Council meetings. The Policy Guidelines, as proposed by the Committee, appear in the Committee's Report of Oct. 19, 1982, in briefing book for Oct. 30, 1982, Executive Council meeting.

[77] Minutes of the Executive Council, Oct. 27, 1984, in ASIL Minute Book, Apr. 1982–Nov. 1990.

[78] Id.; Minutes of the Executive Council, Oct. 30, 1982, in ASIL Notebook of Executive Council Minutes, Apr. 1982–Nov. 1990.

[79] Panel on Domestic Economic Adjustments and International Trade, 78 *ASIL Proc.* 187 (1984). Apparently the group also sponsored the Panel on Exchange Controls and External Indebtedness: Are the Bretton Woods Concepts Still Workable?, id. at 240. See *ASIL Newsletter*, Nov./Dec. 1983, at 4.

[80] Unattributed, undated memorandum in the Society's files (circa 1984), "The American Society of International Law: A History," at 8; *ASIL Newsletters*, Mar./Apr. 1984, at 4, May/June 1984, at 2; July/Aug. 1984, at 2; Minutes of the Executive Council, Apr. 11, 1984, in ASIL Notebook of Executive Council Minutes, Apr. 1982–Nov. 1990.

10. The Ad Hoc Committee on the Structure of the Society

In mid-1980, President Alona Evans appointed an Ad Hoc Committee to Review the Organization and Activities of the Society, chaired by Alfred Rubin.[81] One of the Ad Hoc Committee's key recommendations, that interest groups and sections be established, was essentially an endorsement of the movement toward interest groups that was already under way.

Another key recommendation was that regional activity in the Society be increased. In 1981, the Executive Council adopted a new Regulation that provided for Regional Directors throughout the country who would encourage and coordinate meetings in their localities.[82] Under a Regulation adopted in 1982, the Society could co-sponsor regional meetings organized by other groups, if the Executive Director or the Chair of the new Committee on Regional and Local Activities approved.[83]

The Ad Hoc Committee also examined the Society's publications. The report, prepared by Paul Szasz, found little need for change in the Journal except for the possible elimination of the Official Documents section, which overlapped with *International Legal Materials*. As for I.L.M., the report noted the rather eclectic collection of documents in each issue, and suggested that some sort of digest by topic be considered. The report urged prompt publication of the Proceedings of Annual Meetings.

The report noted also that the Society had no vehicle for prompt comment on breaking events on the international scene. It thus suggested the launching of an informal publication to be distributed to policy- and opinion-makers, as well as to the media, giving Society members an organ for short contributions on current events. The suggestion was ahead of its time. Not until 1994 did the Society take a meaningful step in that direction, with the advent of its *ASIL Insight* series.

On the administrative side, the Ad Hoc Committee suggested that the Society publish an annual report of its activities, and a pamphlet notifying members how they could participate actively in the Society's programs and projects.[84]

Another report of the Ad Hoc Committee dealt with communications to the public or media. As the report put it, "The basic message of this short paper is to urge the Society's leadership to devote more attention to making the Society

---

81 *ASIL Newsletter*, July/Aug. 1980, at 1.

82 75 *ASIL Proc.* 290 (1981). See also *ASIL Newsletter*, Nov./Dec. 1981, at 4.

83 76 *ASIL Proc.* 384 (1982).

84 Report of the Ad Hoc Committee to Review the Organization and Activities of the American Society of International Law (hereinafter Report of Ad Hoc Committee), Part III, 1982, in briefing materials for Apr. 1983 Executive Council meetings. The Report is summarized, with the Committee's recommendations, in 77 *ASIL Proc.* 448 (1983).

more visible to the public." Suggestions included providing non-technical summaries of Journal articles to the media; drawing the attention of the media to the Annual Meeting; making members of interest groups available to the media for questions in their specialties; issuing background papers on current international law problems; and a "state of international law" address at the Annual Meeting by the President of the Society.[85]

Edith Brown Weiss, a member of the Ad Hoc Committee, prepared a report suggesting that the Society establish collaborative efforts with other countries, arrange bilateral or regional meetings, and enter into more formal relations with other national societies of international law. She also thought that the Journal could be more international in its approach. Interdisciplinary links should be developed not only with political science and economics, but also with anthropology, sociology, the humanities and the physical sciences.[86] Several years later, when she became President of the Society, she would pursue these ideas vigorously.

11. The Committee on the Future of the Society

David Gill appointed the Committee on the Future of the Society in June 1984. Its mandate was to prepare a report on steps the Society could undertake to improve its overall image and functioning in view of its rather shaky financial situation. Keith Highet chaired the Committee.[87]

The Committee rendered its final report on April 18, 1985.[88] Part of it dealt with the Society's policy on taking positions regarding substantive issues, as we have already seen.[89] Another part dealt with Tillar House and the staff, recommending (among other things) that a new committee should examine Tillar House itself, including such questions as whether the Society should move elsewhere, or if not, what steps could be taken to make Tillar House more functional. In the event, it took until the beginning of the next century for such questions to be resolved in favor of staying in Tillar House and making it more serviceable.

On research programs and publications, the Committee proposed that the Board of Review and Development consider how the role then being played by

---

85 Report of Ad Hoc Committee, *supra* note 84, Part IV.

86 Report of Ad Hoc Committee, *supra* note 84, Part I. A separate report on International Dimensions of the American Society of International Law was prepared by Gerard J. Mangone. Id., Annex I.

87 *ASIL Newsletter*, Sept./Oct. 1984, at 1.

88 Final Report of the Committee on the Future of the Society, Apr. 18, 1985, in briefing materials for Apr. 1985 Executive Council meetings.

89 See text at note 46 *supra*.

the Director of Studies should be filled. A single person should supervise the Society's publications, except for the Journal. The Newsletter should be made more useful to members, with a member designated as its Editor-in-Chief. The Proceedings should continue to be the responsibility of members outside Tillar House, and the long lags between Annual Meetings and publication of the Proceedings should be eliminated.

The Committee thought that membership activities should be strengthened. A special category should be established, giving recognition to members who make contributions above their regular dues, and other components of an annual giving program should be put in place. There should be law firm members, as well as corporate members of the Society. Emphasis should be placed on drawing students into membership and providing students with programs of interest to them. A special effort should be made to diversify the membership. Every effort should be made to increase the already substantial non-U.S. membership, including having programs and meetings that would be accessible to such members.

The committee's report was presented to the Executive Council at its meeting on April 24, 1985. No immediate action was taken, but some of the recommendations – particularly on membership – eventually crept into the Society's practice.

12. Tensions between the Society and A.S.I.L.S.

By 1977, it was obvious that the Society's "Fellow" could not perform both of the tasks contemplated for him/her: administering the Jessup Competition and doing research under the Society's auspices. Moreover, A.S.I.L.S. had evolved into an association with its own agenda, including the publication of a journal. Yet the Society had taken effective control over A.S.I.L.S. finances. As Ellen Behravesh, the Fellow in 1977-78, put it:

> [T]he executive director of ASIL effectively has the power to dictate Jessup fees, ASILS dues, ASILS International Law Journal prices, etc., as well as to approve or refuse ASILS expenditures. In the past the ASIL has heavily subsidized ASILS activities and, in an effort to balance ASILS receipts and debits, the ASILS' separate checking account was closed several years ago, with all ASILS assets put into the ASIL account. The auditors view ASILS as a sub-division of ASIL, and ... the ASIL executive director must approve and sign all payments made on behalf of ASILS. Nevertheless, the exact relationship between the two organizations has never been formally set out, and therefore ... the increased activity of ASILS has led to the necessity of defining the ASIL/ASILS relationship.[90]

[90] Ellen Behravesh, Memorandum to the Executive Committee, Nov. 10, 1977.

The Society's response was to form a special committee to look into the relationship.[91]

Michael Cardozo, chair of the special committee, reported to the Executive Council in April 1978. He pointed out the lack of clear guidelines to regulate the relationship. The Society indeed had financial control. Still, there was a question of the extent to which A.S.I.L.S. officers could make decisions that the Society would have to honor. It was not clear who could make final decisions regarding the Jessup Competition. The committee, however, had been unable to reach agreement on what the ASIL should do. Thus Cardozo looked to the Executive Council for advice. About all he got was a request from the President that the committee continue its work.[92]

The committee next proposed to the Council a formal agreement between the Society and A.S.I.L.S. in order to deal with the increasing tensions between the Society staff and A.S.I.L.S. representatives. Seymour Rubin was so dissatisfied with the committee's approach that he threatened to resign as Executive Director if the proposed agreement were adopted.[93] Ultimately Clyde Ferguson, the President of the Society, dissolved the committee and offered his good offices in resolving the dispute between the two organizations.[94]

About the only tangible result of all this was the Business Meeting's adoption in 1979 of an amendment to the Society's Constitution providing that the current President of A.S.I.L.S., if a member of the ASIL, would be an *ex officio* member of the Society's Executive Council.[95]

Tensions appeared again in December 1979. The ASIL, apparently without consulting anyone representing A.S.I.L.S., proposed that A.S.I.L.S. pay 100% of the salary of the Fellow's administrative assistant plus "overhead" to cover indirect costs ASIL incurred for A.S.I.L.S.'s use of office space, heat and light in Tillar House. Cynthia Huber, the Fellow in 1979-80, complained about the Society's "apparent lack of clean hands or fairness."[96] Seymour Rubin was offended; he

---

91 Minutes of the Executive Council, Apr. 27, 1978, in ASIL Minute Book, Apr. 1974–Oct. 1981, at 138, 146.

92 Minutes of the Executive Council, Apr. 28, 1978, in ASIL Minute Book, Apr. 1974–Oct. 1981, at 147-49.

93 Letter from Seymour J. Rubin to Bill Braswell, Apr. 17, 1979, in briefing book for the Apr. 26, 1979, Executive Council Meeting.

94 Minutes of the Executive Council, Oct. 28, 1978, in ASIL Minute Book, Apr. 1974–Oct. 1981, at 151, 156-59. See also 1979 *ASILS Ann. Rep.*, in 73 *ASIL Proc.* 334, 340 (1979).

95 73 *ASIL Proc.* 344 (1979).

96 Memorandum from Cynthia S. Huber to Seymour J. Rubin, Dec. 18, 1979, in Executive Committee Meetings notebook, 9-30-83 (sic) to 11-16-90.

pointed out how much time he and Larry Hargrove had spent trying to obtain funding for the Jessup Competition.[97]

In April 1980, the Society's Budget Committee proposed that the Society charge A.S.I.L.S. overhead of USD 5,000. A.S.I.L.S. objected on the grounds that this would take money away from worthwhile student projects, and that the services and facilities actually provided by the Society amounted to less than $5,000.[98] A.S.I.L.S. proposed that it pay only for that portion of rent, utilities and time of the Society Executive Director that could be attributed to non-Jessup student-related activities.[99] The Executive Council failed to resolve the matter. It remained on the table, and became entwined with issues relating to the Society's commitment, or lack thereof, to younger members.

13. A New Treasurer and a New Secretary

After twelve years as Treasurer, Franz M. Oppenheimer resigned from his post in 1976. The Executive Council appointed James Patton in his place. James Connor continued to serve as Assistant Treasurer.[100]

Edward Dumbauld's thirty years as Secretary ended with his resignation in 1978. Michael H. Cardozo was named the new Secretary.[101]

B. PROGRAMS AND PUBLICATIONS

1. Significant Regional Meetings

On February 1-2, 1975, a regional meeting in Boston provided an opportunity for many of the participants in the Caracas session of the Third United Nations Conference on the Law of the Sea to meet in advance of the next session.[102] This occurred at an early stage of the long-running Conference, giving participants from a variety of countries with a variety of interests in the law of the sea a

---

97 Memorandum from Seymour J. Rubin to recipients of Huber memorandum, Dec. 20, 1979, in id.

98 Minutes of the Executive Council, Apr. 17, 1980, in ASIL Minute Book, Apr. 1974–Oct. 1981, at 175, 182.

99 Memorandum from Cynthia S. Huber, Executive Secretary of ASILS, to ASIL Executive Council, Apr. 15, 1980, in briefing packet for ASIL Executive Council meeting, Apr. 17, 1980.

100 Minutes of the Executive Council, Apr. 23, 1976, in ASIL Minute Book, Apr. 1974–Oct. 1975, at 73. Edward Dumbauld was elected to another term as Secretary. Id.

101 Minutes of the Executive Council, Apr. 28, 1978, in ASIL Minute Book, Apr. 1974–Oct. 1981, at 147; *ASIL Newsletter*, Apr.–July 1978, at 1.

102 *ASIL Newsletter*, Dec. 1974, at 3.

chance to exchange views before their governments' positions became written in stone.

On February 14-15, 1975, Seymour Rubin's plan to strengthen the Society's international economic law program got started with a regional meeting at his law school, the Washington College of Law, on the trade and investment implications of the scarcity of primary resources. Several panels were held, featuring eminent speakers from academic and government backgrounds.[103]

These meetings illustrate how the Society was able to adapt its role as a participant in the shaping of international relations after World War II, when the conduct of American foreign policy had become infinitely more complex than during the Society's youth. Society leaders were no longer the American foreign policy decision-makers, or even the top advisers to the decision-makers. Direct input was thus rare. Nevertheless, the Society could, and, in the instances just mentioned, did provide a forum for decision-makers to meet not only with each other, but also with experts from academia and the private sector. The Society, in other words, became (on occasion) a catalyst for the development of policy, even though it was not the progenitor of official policy. It may not have been a conspicuous role, but it could nevertheless be a useful one.

2. Corporate Consultations

Corporate consultations were an important part of Seymour Rubin's emphasis on international economic law and were a means of enticing corporations to become corporate members of the Society. The first of his corporate consultations, in the autumn of 1975, brought corporate members together with government officials, academics and public interest lawyers to talk about the impact of measures adopted by the U.N., the O.A.S. and the U.S. Senate on corporate activities abroad.[104] The second, in March 1976, dealt with codes of conduct for transnational enterprises – a topic that remained on the corporate consultation agenda in ensuing years.[105] Other topics addressed over the next five years included technology transfer, foreign corrupt practices, bilateral investment treaties, and legal aspects of recognizing the People's Republic of China, as well as further attention to codes of conduct.[106] By 1979, some corporate consultations were being held in Paris.[107]

Rubin was pleased with the corporate consultations. In his words:

---

103 *ASIL Newsletters*, Dec. 1974, at 3, and Jan. 1975, at 3.

104 *ASIL Newsletter*, Nov./Dec. 1975, at 2-3.

105 *ASIL Newsletters*, Mar./Apr./May 1976, at 2, & Mar.–Apr. 1979, at 3.

106 List of corporate consultations in briefing book for Apr. 22, 1981 Executive Council meeting.

107 *ASIL Newsletter*, Jan.–Feb. 1979, at 3.

> [W]e would have some sessions here in Tillar House mainly with people from the government, and they would be able to explore issues which were of considerable interest to those corporations. That program worked very well because we had a relatively small number of people. We couldn't contain more than thirty people at the most [in the board room] … . I chaired all of those things and I was pretty good at saying let's stick to the issue. That meant that you had a [meaningful] briefing session with some people in the government … .[108]

As in the case of the regional meetings discussed earlier, the Society had managed to get a foot in the door of the decision-making inner sanctum, even if the Society's President and Executive Director were not major players themselves.

3. Innovations in the Annual Meetings

At the 1975 Annual Meeting, Friday was designated as Practitioners' Day. All panels except the evening one were devoted to topics of particular interest to practicing lawyers: trade policy, international securities transactions, international commercial arbitration, and control of international restrictive business practices.[109] The experiment was repeated in 1976, when the opening day was set aside.[110] Later years did not see formally designated Practitioner's Days, but they did include panels tailored to the interests of practitioners. To give an example, in 1985, a block of time was devoted to a Practitioner's Workshop on the practical aspects of international and foreign law litigation.[111]

The 1977 Annual Meeting was held in San Francisco. The decision was made at a time when the Society faced a large budget deficit, and the obvious question was whether it made sense to incur the extra cost of a West Coast meeting. Richard Baxter, the Society's President, carried the day by saying that the meeting "should be regarded as an outing; it should also make the Society more widely known and emphasize that it is a national organization, not localized in the northeast megalopolis only."[112] Arthur Albrecht, a leading Society member in San Francisco, persuaded West Coast organizations and corporations to support the meeting, and he provided financial support himself, as did Herman Phleger, a

---

108 Interview with Seymour J. Rubin, May 17, 1994 (transcript on file with the Society). See also Rubin's report to the 1976 Business Meeting, 70 *ASIL Proc.* 190, 192 (1976).

109 69 *ASIL Proc.* 128-92 (1975). See also *ASIL Newsletter*, Jan. 1975, at 1.

110 *ASIL Newsletter*, Jan./Feb. 1976, at 3.

111 79 *ASIL Proc.* 328-36 (1985).

112 Minutes of the Executive Council, Apr. 22, 1976, in ASIL Minute Book, Apr. 1974–Oct. 1975, at 66, 67.

prominent San Francisco lawyer and former State Department Legal Adviser.[113] When the meeting convened, there were 474 registrants, of whom 210 were from the West Coast.[114]

The Annual Meeting was again held outside Washington in 1985, when the venue was the Roosevelt Hotel in New York City. It was more a matter of necessity than of choice; all suitable Washington hotels had been booked before the Society came calling, so the Tillar House staff had to look elsewhere.[115]

In 1979, an open forum was included in the Annual Meeting program. It provided an opportunity for persons not formally on the program to present papers on topics that might not otherwise be covered. The open forum was repeated in 1980, omitted at the Seventy-Fifth Anniversary Convocation in 1981, and resuscitated in 1982.[116] It remained in the Annual Meeting program through to 1987.[117]

A recurring tension surrounding Annual Meetings has existed between a desire for scholarly presentations and a preference for some spontaneity. Over the years, many formal papers have been read aloud in the name of scholarship. The format for the 1985 Annual Meeting instead stressed spontaneity and audience participation. The Executive Council, as usual, was divided on the matter.[118]

4. The Seventy-fifth Anniversary Convocation

The 1981 Annual Meeting was no ordinary affair. Called the Seventy-fifth Anniversary Convocation, its theme was Order, Freedom, Justice, Power: The Challenges for International Law. It looked backward over the Society's seventy-five years, and forward toward the developing international legal order. In addition to three luncheon speeches and the banquet address, eight plenary sessions were scheduled. Workshops were squeezed into available time slots.

William Bishop opened the Convocation by looking at the development of international law during the preceding seventy-five years:

> In 1906 the states principally concerned with international affairs were European, of European descent, or with European-derived cultures.

113 *ASIL Newsletter*, Apr./May/June 1977, at 2; Rep. of the Budget Comm., Oct. 26, 1977, at 2.

114 Id. at 1.

115 *ASIL Newsletter*, Mar./Apr. 1984, at 3.

116 *ASIL Newsletter*, Jan./Feb. 1982, at 1.

117 A student open forum was initiated in 1985. 79 *ASIL Proc.* 208 (1985). See also ASILS Executive Secretary's Report, id. at 395, 398. The idea was continued in 1986 and 1987.

118 Minutes of the Executive Council, Oct. 27, 1984, in ASIL Notebook of Executive Council Minutes, Apr. 1982–Nov. 1990.

> International law focused on the Hague Peace Conferences of 1899 and 1907, with far greater interest than today in the law of war and neutrality. The Permanent Court of Arbitration dates from that period. The comparatively recent memory of the success of the Alabama Claims Arbitration after our Civil War, the Fur Seals Arbitration, and the ten tribunals of 1903 between Venezuela and other nations – all these contributed to the hope that international arbitration would gradually become a substitute for war in settling international disputes. One much-discussed aspect of international law then was belligerent interference with neutral commerce in time of war; that now almost-forgotten "prize law" of blockade, contraband and the like ... has become archaic, if not obsolete ... .
>
> How different the scene became as these 75 years have rolled on! Two world wars, the founding of the League of Nations after the first, and of the United Nations and its family of specialized organizations after the second; the economic and ideological split between the West and the Communist (or "Socialist") group of nations; above all, decolonization and the great influx of a hundred new nations onto the international scene since World War II; the "Cold War" and the "nuclear balance of terror"; all of these factors, and others, have changed the world of international relations in which international law must grow and function![119]

Bishop went on to note the great growth in the number of states; the increasing predominance of treaties as a source of international law; the controversies over the normative significance of U.N. General Assembly resolutions; the proliferation of international organizations; the reluctance of governments to refer disputes to international adjudication or arbitration; the rise of the individual as a subject of international law; the generation of norms against the offensive use of armed force; and developments in such fields as the law of the sea, state responsibility, sovereign immunity, the law of nationality, aviation and space law, the law of telecommunication, and environmental law.

It was, as Richard Falk observed, a masterful presentation, encapsulating seventy-five years of international law in a little more than seven printed pages.[120] Falk went on to lament "a very important decline in significant law-oriented leadership in the powerful countries of the world." He continued:

> [T]here is a discernable loss of access to the central domains of national power by those who place their hopes for the future on the growth of world law in some form. Let us reflect upon the absence of any functional equivalent to Elihu Root at the present time. Indeed, there is no way to

---

[119] William W. Bishop, Jr., International Law, 1906-1981, in 75 *ASIL Proc.* 1, 2 (1981).

[120] See Richard Falk, The Future of International Law, 75 *ASIL Proc.* 8 (1981).

> discredit oneself more quickly in the corridors of serious politics than to be at all pious about the prospect for law in world affairs.[121]

Falk's pessimism did not carry the day. The Convocation went forward with spirited plenary sessions on a wide variety of issues including the global heritage of humankind, order and security, the demands for freedom and for economic justice, the relationship between theory and reality in international law, and the tasks of education in international law.

The Society had hoped to publish the Convocation papers as a book, but that proved not to be feasible. They came out, instead, in the form of normal Society Proceedings.

5. A Newsworthy Annual Meeting

The 1984 Annual Meeting was held at the height of public debate about U.S. support for the Nicaraguan *Contras* in their attempt to overthrow the Nicaraguan (Sandinista) government. Not only that, it was held just a few days after the State Department had filed an instrument with the International Court of Justice purporting to suspend U.S. consent to the Court's jurisdiction for two years in cases related to events in Central America.[122]

A featured event was a luncheon co-sponsored by the A.B.A. Section of International Law and Practice. The speaker was Jeane J. Kirkpatrick, then the U.S. Permanent Representative to the United Nations. She outlined the Sandinistas' support for the left-wing insurgency in El Salvador, which she characterized as an armed attack on El Salvador. For international law to have relevance in the modern world, she said, "it must be protected against those who would subvert its fundamental purposes by using it as an instrument to legitimate aggressive violence and to deligitimate the use of force in self-defense." As for the U.S. decision to modify its Article 36(2) declaration, she said that "it is not the United States which has abused adherence to the compulsory jurisdiction of the Court. The vast majority of nations, some two-thirds of them, do not even submit to the voluntary jurisdiction of the Court. And even in cases where others have agreed to the Court's jurisdiction, many states have attached reservations and others have not complied with the decisions of the Court."[123]

The President of the Society (and a good many members of the audience) did not think highly of Kirkpatrick's views. In Covey Oliver's words, "The President [Oliver] did, however, have to sit at luncheon with the distinguished guest of the

121 Id. at 11.

122 See text at note 42 *supra*.

123 Address by Dr. Jeane J. Kirkpatrick, 78 *ASIL Proc.* 59, 64-65, 66 (1984).

opposite persuasion, Ambassador Jeane Kirkpatrick! The issue of the day was not discussed at table, but the atmosphere and the soup were chilly."[124]

At the annual dinner, the Society offered an antidote to Kirkpatrick in the form of an address by Donald McHenry, the former U.S. Permanent Representative to the United Nations. He deplored the Reagan administration's apparent insensitivity to international law and institutions. McHenry cited chapter and verse, including the mining of Nicaragua's harbors and the attempt to avoid the World Court's jurisdiction.[125]

Kirkpatrick's speech was videotaped by ABC, CBS and NBC news, as well as by a Washington, D.C. public broadcasting station. The PBS station also videotaped several panels, including one on World Court Jurisdiction and U.S. Foreign Policy in Latin America. It later televised all of the tapes in the Washington area.[126]

6. Problems with the Proceedings

Throughout the early eighties, the publication of the Proceedings lagged far behind the close of the Annual Meetings.[127] It began with vacillation in 1981 over whether to publish the Seventy-fifth Anniversary Convocation as a book. When it was finally decided that the book was not feasible, the Proceedings were already six months behind. In 1982, several presenters did not get their written versions in until late summer. The 1982 Proceedings were not published until July 1984, and so it went for several years.[128]

7. The Jessup Competition, A.S.I.L.S. and the A.S.I.L.

In 1975, for the first time, a team from outside the United States won the Jessup Competition. The winner was the team from Cambridge University, which

---

[124] Interview with Covey T. Oliver, Aug. 13, 1995 (transcript on file with the Society).

[125] 78 *ASIL Proc.* 318, 319 (1984).

[126] *ASIL Newsletter*, May/June 1984, at 1.

[127] Delay was not the only problem connected with the Proceedings. Their cost impacted the Society's budget. The Executive Council decided in 1977 to charge separately for the Proceedings, and amended the Regulations accordingly in 1978. Minutes of the Executive Council, Nov. 12, 1977 & Apr. 27, 1978, in ASIL Minute Book, Apr. 1974–Oct. 1981, at 124-25 & 138, 144. In 1984, the Executive Council decided to limit or eliminate footnotes from the Proceedings "except in special situations." Minutes of the Executive Council, Oct. 27, 1984, in ASIL Notebook of Executive Council Minutes, Apr. 1982–Nov. 1990.

[128] For the situation up to autumn 1984, see the memorandum from Judith R. Hall, *Proceedings Publication*, in briefing book for Executive Council meeting of Oct. 27, 1984.

defeated Georgetown in the final argument.[129] Not to be outdone, the University of Toronto took home the Jessup Cup in 1976.[130]

On the domestic side, disputes arose between A.S.I.L.S. and several law schools over whether A.S.I.L.S. could give right of first refusal to student international law societies, rather than moot court boards, as representatives of the schools in the Jessup Competition. Some Deans resented what they saw as an effort by A.S.I.L.S. to dictate which student organization would represent their schools. A.S.I.L.S. stuck to its guns.[131]

Another Jessup controversy arose in 1983. The University of Kansas had been declared the winner of the National Division Runoff, defeating Tulane. The faculty advisor of the Tulane team contended that the Jessup rules had been misinterpreted, and asked the ASIL Executive Council to overturn the designation of Kansas as the winner. The Executive Council declined to accept jurisdiction over the matter.[132]

In November 1975, the Executive Council created the Philip C. Jessup International Law Moot Court Competition Endowment. The idea stemmed largely from frustration with the unwillingness of potential donors, such as the American Bar Foundation, to support the Competition, despite considerable efforts by Society officials. The designated trustees were the President, Executive Vice President and Treasurer of the Society, acting in consultation with the Fellow of the Society.[133] In 1976, the Endowment's Regulations were amended to allow its funds to be used for student-related activities and not just for Jessup expenses.[134]

To tide the Jessup program over while the Endowment was built, the Rockefeller Brothers Fund granted USD 7,500 for each of the years 1977 and 1978.[135] The Dana Foundation followed with a USD 15,000 grant that was used in the

---

[129] 69 *ASIL Proc.* 288 (1975); *ASIL Newsletter*, June 1975, at 4.

[130] 70 *ASIL Proc.* 212 (1976); *ASIL Newsletter*, Mar./Apr./May 1976, at 1.

[131] *ASILS Ann. Rep.*, 72 *ASIL Proc.* 352, 354-55 (1978).

[132] In the Executive Council discussion, it was pointed out that the Jessup regulations provided that disputes were to be decided by the Executive Secretary of the student association. Minutes of the Executive Council, Apr. 15, 1983, in ASIL Notebook of Executive Council Minutes, Apr. 1982- Nov. 1990.

[133] Income was to be used to defray expenses of the Competition, and up to 25 per cent of principal could be invaded with the consent of two trustees. Minutes of the Executive Council, Nov. 1, 1975, in ASIL Minute Book, Apr. 1974–Oct. 1981, at 50, 52-53.

[134] Minutes of the Executive Council, Oct. 30, 1976, in ASIL Minute Book, Apr. 1974–Oct. 1981, at 78, 83. The Endowment's principal balance in October 1980 was USD 30,655. Memorandum from Louis E. Emery, ASILS Executive Secretary, to ASIL Executive Council, Oct. 25, 1980, in briefing book for Oct. 25, 1980 Executive Council meeting.

[135] *ASIL Newsletter*, Aug./Sept. 1976, at 3.

following two years.[136] Dana increased its grant to USD 20,000 a year through to 1985, and then discontinued it.[137] The Dana grants were used for the salary of the A.S.I.L.S. Executive Secretary, who became known as the Dana Fellow. When the Dana grants disappeared, the ASIL had to pick up the salary in 1986.[138]

Funding for the participation of teams from developing countries came at first from the State Department and then from the International Communication Agency. The ICA contributed USD 70,000 for 1980, but that was the last year it provided funds.[139]

Meanwhile, the Association of Student International Law Societies continued to grow. By April 1979 it had 111 member societies, including foreign participants.[140]

Volume one of the A.S.I.L.S. *International Law Journal* was published in October 1977, serving as a vehicle for student-authored articles. It enjoyed only a modest reception. The A.S.I.L.S. Executive Committee questioned the viability of the project, but decided to continue.[141] Volume two also received only a "moderate welcome by the international legal community," but the project was kept on the boards. It was thought that publication of the Jessup Competition Best Memorials made the new Journal a unique resource.[142]

By 1981, it had become apparent that the new Journal could not continue unless editorial responsibilities were undertaken by individual international law societies. Thus was born the idea of having each volume parceled out to a student society at a particular school. Willamette, where James Nafziger was the faculty advisor, was the first school to undertake the full responsibility (for volume 6).[143]

---

136 Notes to the Budget for the General Account for the Fiscal Year 1979-1980, at 5.

137 Draft Report of the Budget Committee, Oct. 17, 1985, at 3, in briefing book for Oct. 26, 1985, Executive Council meeting.

138 For details, see Report of the ASILS Executive Secretary to the ASIL Executive Council, Oct. 1986, in briefing book for Oct. 25, 1986, Executive Council meeting; Report of the Budget Committee, Mar. 19, 1987, in briefing book for Apr. 1987 Executive Council meetings; Minutes of the Executive Council, Apr. 8, 1987, in ASIL Notebook of Executive Council Minutes, Apr. 1982–Nov. 1990.

139 Memorandum from Louis E. Emery, ASILS Executive Secretary, to ASIL Executive Council, Oct. 25, 1980, in briefing book for Oct. 25, 1980 Executive Council meeting.

140 *1979 ASILS Ann. Rep.*, in 73 *ASIL Proc.* 334, 335 (1979).

141 *1978 ASILS Ann. Rep.*, in 72 *ASIL Proc.* 352, 355 (1978).

142 *1979 ASILS Ann. Rep.*, in 73 *ASIL Proc.* 334, 337 (1979).

143 Memorandum from Richard W. Nelson, ASILS Executive Secretary, to ASIL Executive Council, Oct. 24, 1981, in briefing materials for Oct. 24, 1981 Executive Council meeting.

8. Accelerating the Publications Program

Under Sy Rubin and Larry Hargrove, the Society's publications program moved into high gear. The output included *Studies in Transnational Legal Policy* (short books published for the Society by West Publishing Company) and full book-length studies. The roster of authors comprised virtually an all-star cast of international law scholars.[144] Because of the great interest in the law of the sea during these years of lengthy negotiations in the Third U.N. Conference on the Law of the Sea, several of the studies dealt with the oceans, particularly addressing conservation and environmental issues.[145]

In 1976, the Society came out with the two-volume set, *The Future of the International Court of Justice*.[146] Edited by Leo Gross, the study was the outgrowth of the Society's Panel on the Future of the International Court of Justice. It

---

[144] In the three-year period, 1975 through 1977, the Society published twenty-three books and pamphlets on a variety of international law topics. See *The Avoidance and Adjustment of Environmental Disputes* (summary of a conference at Bellagio, Italy; 1975); *Direct Broadcasting from Satellites: Policies and Problems* (1975); Mason Willrich, *Energy and World Politics* (1975); Lee G. Anderson *et al.*, *The Future of International Fisheries Management* (1975); Valerie Hood, Mary E. Kimball & David A. Kay, *A Global Satellite Observation System for Earth Resources* (1975); David A. Kay, *International Regulation of Pesticide Residues in Food* (1975); Peter D. Trooboff (ed.), *Law and Responsibility in Warfare: The Vietnam Experience* (1975); *Policy Issues in Ocean Law* (1975); W. Michael Reisman, *Puerto Rico and the International Process: New Roles in Association* (1975); Nathaniel L. Nathanson & Egon Schwelb, *The United States and the United Nations Treaty on Racial Discrimination* (1975); John Lawrence Hargrove (ed.), *Who Protects the Ocean? Environment and the Development of the Law of the Sea* (1975); H. Gary Knight, *Consequences of Non-Agreement at the Third U.N. Law of the Sea Conference* (1976); Francis O. Wilcox & Richard A. Frank (eds.), *The Constitution and Conduct of Foreign Policy* (1976); Richard A. Frank, *Deepsea Mining and the Environment* (1976); Leo Gross (ed.), *The Future of the International Court of Justice* (2 vols., 1976); David A. Kay, *The International Regulation of Pesticide Residues in Food* (1976); David A. Kay, *The International Regulation of Pharmaceutical Drugs* (1976); David M. Leive, *International Regulatory Regimes: Case Studies in Health, Meteorology and Food* (2 vols., 1976); ASIL Panel on International Trade Policy, *Re-making the System of World Trade: A Proposal for Institutional Reform* (1976); John Norton Moore (ed.), *The Arab–Israeli Conflict: Readings and Documents* (1977); Thomas Buergenthal (ed.), *Human Rights, International Law and the Helsinki Accord* (1977); Elihu Lauterpacht (ed.), *Individual Rights and the State in Foreign Affairs* (1977); Michael H. Cardozo, *The Practical State of Teaching and Research in International Law* (1977).

[145] See, e.g., *Policy Issues in Ocean Law* (Studies in Transnational Legal Policy No. 8, 1975); H. Gary Knight (ed.), *Who Protects the Ocean?* (1975); J.L. Hargrove (ed.), *The Future of International Fisheries Management* (1975); H. Gary Knight, *Consequences of Non-Agreement at the Third U.N. Law of the Sea Conference* (1976); Richard A. Frank, *Deepsea Mining and the Marine Environment* (1976); H. Gary Knight, J.D. Nyhart & Robert E. Stein (eds.), *Ocean Thermal Energy Conversion: Legal, Political and Institutional Aspects* (1977).

[146] Leo Gross (ed.), The Future of the International Court of Justice (1976).

included the Panel's recommendations for enhancing the role of the Court, some of which had to do with the Court's functioning under its current Statute, while others would have required amendments to the Statute. The latter included recommendations for eliminating the President's casting vote in the event of a tie among the Court's members; widening access to the Court's contentious jurisdiction to comprehend international organizations; and amending Article 38 of the Statute "to find an appropriate place for declarations and resolutions of the General Assembly of a lawmaking character."[147]

Overall, the study was less than sanguine about the Court's role as a significant international dispute-settlement body. For example, the study noted how "over the years more emphasis has come to be placed in the election process [of judges] on the geographic representation than on the personal-professional competence factor."[148] But in the view of Leo Gross, the ultimate problem was the "total opposition [by many governments] to the normative character of international law itself."[149] It was a pessimistic conclusion to an important study.

The Society's Panel on International Trade Policy and Institutions produced a report on reforming the world trade system, including a recommendation for the creation of a new International Trade Organization. The German Marshall Fund supported a meeting of experts in London to discuss the issues raised in the report. The meeting called for further work on mechanisms for settling international trade disputes.[150]

A great many other studies and reports came forth during this period. Some were the outgrowth of conferences; others were simply the work product of individual scholars. Some were funded by the Society's traditional donor, the Ford Foundation, but not in the munificent amounts of the early Ford grants. Among the Ford-supported projects were studies of the Covenants on Civil and Political Rights and on Economic, Social and Cultural Rights, as well as a project on the New International Economic Order.[151] Other studies, like the Society's pioneering book on the cross-cutting relationship between the environment and international trade, were funded by foundations other than Ford.[152]

---

[147] Leo Gross, "Conclusions," in 2 id. at 727, 733.

[148] Id. at 743.

[149] Id. at 764.

[150] Minutes of the Executive Council, Nov. 12, 1977, in ASIL Minute Book, Apr. 1974–Oct. 1981, at 124, 128.

[151] Minutes of the Executive Council, Oct. 25, 1980, in ASIL Minute Book, Apr. 1974–Oct. 1981, unnumbered page.

[152] Seymour J. Rubin & Thomas R. Graham (eds.), *Environment and Trade: The Relation of International Trade and Environment Policy* (1982), the product of a study panel supported by a grant from the Andrew Mellon Foundation. Details of the Society's publications appear in the annual reports by John Lawrence Hargrove, the Society's Director of Studies,

9. Government Grants for Projects with Political Overtones

In 1976, the Society undertook to perform a study of the legal issues surrounding the proposed Maqarin Dam on the Yarmuk River, a major tributary of the Jordan River. The State Department had approached Larry Hargrove to do the study personally, but he had declined. The Agency for International Development then approached the Society. Although the Society went ahead with the project, the consensus in the Executive Council was that the Society should not get heavily into government contracting.[153]

Nevertheless, the Society did not shun Agency for International Development funding for other projects. One such project was the Role of Law in Social Change, to study law reform, legal aid and public interest law in Latin America and the Caribbean.[154] It arose out of a cooperative effort with the Inter-American Juridical Committee, of which Sy Rubin was a member.[155] The Society also submitted a report to the Agency for International Development on human rights and the Helsinki Accords.[156] A project on the legal aspects of international terrorism was prepared for the State Department and funded by it. The study was published in 1978,[157] and became a resource for a conference sponsored in that year by the State Department, the Law Enforcement Administration and the Society.[158] This, of course, was long before terrorism became a daily media topic in the United States.

10. I.L.M.'s Steady Progress

International Legal Materials is one of the Society's success stories, despite its lack of pomp and circumstance. It ploughs quietly ahead, supplying print versions of important documents long before they appear in official publications. To take just one year during Sy Rubin's tenure as an example:

> During 1982, [I.L.M.] was first to publish the OAU Charter on Human Rights, the Convention on the Law of the Sea, the seabed mining legislation of France, the Federal Republic of Germany, the Soviet Union and

---

in each issue of the Proceedings, and in the Executive Director's reports printed in the Newsletter.

153 Minutes of the Executive Council, Oct. 30, 1976, in ASIL Minute Book, Apr. 1974–Oct. 1981, at 78, 79-80.

154 Minutes of the Executive Council, Apr. 21, 1977, in ASIL Minute Book, Apr. 1974–Oct. 1981, at 89, 91.

155 71 *ASIL Proc.* 103-04 (1977).

156 Buergenthal, *supra* note 17.

157 John F. Murphy & Alona E. Evans (eds.), *Legal Aspects of International Terrorism* (1978).

158 See John F. Murphy, *Legal Aspects of International Terrorism: Summary Report of an International Conference* (Studies in Transnational Legal Policy No. 19, 1980).

> the United States. The U.S. bilateral investment treaties with Egypt and Panama first appeared in ILM. The AMINOIL arbitration and the ICSID arbitrations were also reproduced in English in ILM before appearing elsewhere.[159]

During the late seventies and early eighties the subscriber base continued to grow. Subscriptions increased from 2,217 in November 1976[160] to 2,430 in April 1983.[161]

In 1981, Marilou Righini undertook to ensure better geographic coverage of materials for I.L.M. She invited persons from around the world to become corresponding editors.[162] Their efforts supplemented those of the regular I.L.M. Advisory Committee, which continued to function. By mid-1983, there were eighteen corresponding editors.[163] The number was up to twenty-five by 1985. At that point, the network was expanded to include persons with responsibility for substantive areas (e.g. environment, human rights, international trade, etc.) as well as persons responsible for geographic zones.[164]

In the early eighties, a grant from the Dana Fund for International and Comparative Law enabled the Society to explore the possibility of expanding I.L.M. toward "a more comprehensive reporting, reproduction, indexing, and digesting system for the raw materials of international law, and concurrently the possibility of developing an encyclopedia of international law."[165] The resources were never found to make these ideas a reality.

C. THE JOURNAL IN THE LATE SEVENTIES AND EARLY EIGHTIES

1. Editors-in-Chief

When Richard Baxter resigned as Editor-in-Chief of the Journal in 1978, Louis Henkin and Oscar Schachter were elected to replace him. The Society's Regulations

---

159 *Report [to the Executive Council] on International Legal Materials*, Apr. 13, 1983.

160 *Report on International Legal Materials*, Nov. 12, 1977.

161 *Report on International Legal Materials*, Apr. 13, 1983. The largest subscriber group was ASIL members, followed by libraries.

162 *Report on International Legal Materials*, Oct. 24, 1981.

163 *Report on International Legal Materials*, Oct. 8, 1983.

164 *ASIL Newsletter*, Apr./May 1985, at 2.

165 John Lawrence Hargrove, "Report of the Director of Studies," 76 *ASIL Proc.* 101, 102 (1982).

were amended to authorize election of Co-Editors-in-Chief.[166] It was the Journal's first experience with a tandem at the top, but it would not be the last.

Henkin and Schachter served for six years, working closely together out of their offices at Columbia University. Leadership of the Journal passed from Morningside Heights to Washington Square when the Executive Council appointed Thomas M. Franck, of N.Y.U., to succeed them. He took over the reins with the October 1984 issue.[167]

2. More Ferment About Inbreeding in the Board

When the Board nominated five current editors and only one new one (Peter Trooboff) in 1980, there was a mini-revolt in the Executive Council. Edward Gordon objected to the practice of members of the Board re-selecting themselves. John Barton offered a motion that would have directed the Board to nominate no more than one third of its members from those who were already serving. Barton's motion was shelved.[168] To shelve the motion, however, was not to shelve the issue forever. It would reappear.

There was a little more turnover in the ensuing years.[169] Nevertheless, at the Executive Council meeting of April 13, 1984, Alfred Rubin proposed that the Society's regulations be amended to require Board members to step down for at least a year after four years of service. He accepted an amendment that would have allowed eight consecutive years of service, but in the end his motion was shelved. The President was instructed to appoint a committee to consider the matter.[170] He did so, naming Richard Lillich as its chair. We will turn to the results of the Lillich committee's deliberations in Chapter Eleven.[171]

---

166 Minutes of the Executive Council, Apr. 27, 1978, in ASIL Minute Book, Apr. 1974–Oct. 1981, at 138, 144-45.

167 *ASIL Newsletter*, May/June 1984, at 1. Because his third four-year term on the Board expired in 1984 and he thus would not normally be eligible for re-election, the Executive Council had to waive the requirement in the Regulations that the Editor-in-Chief be selected "from among the members of the Board." Inaccurately, this was described as an amendment to the Regulations "to the extent necessary to permit" his election as Editor-in-Chief. 78 *ASIL Proc.* 364 (1984).

168 Minutes of the Executive Council, Apr. 19, 1980, in ASIL Minute Book, Apr. 1974–Oct. 1981, unnumbered page.

169 For details regarding changes in Board membership during this period, see Memorandum, "ASIL History: The Journal, Its Editors and Business Practices," on file with the Society.

170 Minutes of the Executive Council, Apr. 13, 1984, in ASIL Notebook of Executive Council Minutes, Apr. 1982–Nov. 1990.

171 See Chapter Eleven, Sections D.1 & 2, *infra*.

3. A New Assistant Editor

In the summer of 1978, Anne Simons resigned as Assistant Editor, a post she had held since 1972.[172] Anna Ascher became the new Assistant Editor. She was destined to serve under not only the co-editorship of Henkin and Schachter, but also under Thomas Franck and the ensuing co-editing teams of Theodor Meron and Detlev Vagts, Jonathan Charney and Michael Reisman, and Lori Damrosch and Bernard Oxman. Her title was changed to Associate Editor in 1989 and to Senior Associate Editor in 2001.

4. A New Department

With the July 1979 issue, the Journal inaugurated a new department, Current Developments. It featured – and still did years later – short, descriptive pieces on current developments in international law and institutions, with an emphasis on the work of institutions. For example, regular reports on the sessions of the International Law Commission have appeared in this department.

5. An Old Department

In 1982, the Board of Editors addressed the overlap in coverage between the Official Documents department and *International Legal Materials*. Although there was initially some confusion about whether the Board wished to drop the department entirely (as had been suggested by the Ad Hoc Committee on the Structure of the Society), ultimately the decision was simply to cut it back considerably.[173] Official Documents continued to appear, sporadically, in the Journal long after 1982.

6. Noteworthy Articles and Comments

While the Third U.N. Conference on the Law of the Sea was playing itself out, the Journal – first through John R. Stevenson and Bernard H. Oxman, and then through Oxman alone – provided its readers with a running commentary and analysis.[174] These articles provide a contemporary history of the negotiations

---

172 *ASIL Newsletter*, Apr.–July 1978, at 3.

173 Letter from Oscar Schachter to Seymour Rubin, Mar. 3, 1983, in briefing materials for Apr. 1983 Executive Council meetings.

174 John R. Stevenson & Bernard H. Oxman, "The Preparations for the Law of the Sea Conference," 68 *AJIL* 1 (1974); Stevenson & Oxman, "The Third United Nations Conference on the Law of the Sea: The 1974 Caracas Session," 69 *AJIL* 1 (1975); Stevenson & Oxman, "The 1975 Geneva Session," id. at 763; Oxman, "The 1976 New York Sessions," 71 *AJIL* 247 (1977); Oxman, "The 1977 New York Sessions," 72 *AJIL* 57 (1978); Oxman, "The Seventh Session," 73 *AJIL* 1 (1979); Oxman, "The Eighth Session," 74 *AJIL* 1 (1980); Oxman, "The Ninth Session," 75 *AJIL* 211 (1981); Oxman, "The Tenth Session," 76

leading to the comprehensive new order of the oceans embodied in the 1982 Convention on the Law of the Sea.

Oscar Schachter's widely cited Editorial Comment on nonbinding international agreements appeared in 1977.[175] Stefan Riesenfeld's trenchant analysis of the Fifth Circuit's misapplication of the doctrine of self-executing treaties was published in 1980.[176] Thomas Buergenthal introduced readers to the procedure and practice of the Inter-American Court of Human Rights in 1982 and 1985.[177] Michael Glennon's argument for use of traditional treaty-making domestic processes found its way into the Journal in 1983, as did Editorial Comments by Leo Gross deploring constitutional excesses in the United Nations and Anthony D'Amato raising prescient questions about the widespread denunciation of Israel's raid on the Iraqi nuclear reactor in June 1981.[178]

In 1981, the Journal published an important trilogy of articles on the international law of expropriation, including one offering the insights of two of TOPCO's counsel in the TOPCO/CALASIATIC arbitration with Libya.[179] The arbitration was particularly significant because of its acceptance of General Assembly Resolution 1803 as representing an *opinio juris* requiring nationalization to be for a public purpose and calling for "appropriate compensation" in conformity with international law, and because of the arbitrator's award of specific performance as the appropriate remedy for Libya's violation of "inter-

---

AJIL 1 (1982). As soon as the negotiations were completed, the Journal published three more articles: Philip Allott, "Power Sharing in the Law of the Sea," 77 *AJIL* 1 (1983); Luke T. Lee, "The Law of the Sea Convention and Third States," id. at 541; Shigeru Oda, "Fisheries under the United Nations Convention on the Law of the Sea," id. at 739.

175 Oscar Schachter, Editorial Comment: "The Twilight Existence of Nonbinding International Agreements," 71 *AJIL* 296 (1977).

176 Stefan A. Riesenfeld, "The Doctrine of Self-Executing Treaties and U.S. v. Postal: Win at Any Price?," 74 *AJIL* 892 (1980).

177 Thomas Buergenthal, "The Inter-American Court of Human Rights," 76 *AJIL* 231 (1982); Buergenthal, "The Advisory Practice of the Inter-American Human Rights Court," 79 *AJIL* 1 (1985).

178 Michael J. Glennon, "The Senate Role in Treaty Ratification," 77 *AJIL* 257 (1983); Leo Gross, Editorial Comment: "On the Degradation of the Constitutional Environment of the United Nations," id. at 569; Anthony D'Amato, Editorial Comment: "Israel's Air Strike upon the Iraqi Nuclear Reactor," id. at 584.

179 Robert B. von Mehren & P. Nicholas Kourides, "International Arbitrations Between States and Foreign Private Parties: The Libyan Nationalization Cases," 75 *AJIL* 476 (1981); the others were Burns H. Weston, "The Charter of Economic Rights and Duties of States and the Deprivation of Foreign-Owned Wealth," id. at 437; Rudolf Dolzer, "New Foundations of the Law of Expropriation of Alien Property," id. at 553.

nationalized" concession contracts.[180] The expropriation theme was revisited in the Journal in the mid-eighties.[181]

When the United States invaded Grenada in 1983, ostensibly to protect a thousand U.S. nationals endangered by a revolution, the Journal ran a mini-symposium featuring arguments for and against the legality of the invasion.[182]

The I.C.J.'s determination that it had jurisdiction in *Nicaragua v. United States*, and the consequent U.S. withdrawal from participation in the proceedings, attracted a barrage of comment in the Journal in 1985.[183] The U.S. government's unwillingness to subject itself to adjudication drew considerable criticism.

D. CHANGING THE GUARD IN TILLAR HOUSE

1. Selecting the Fourth Executive Director

Seymour Rubin moved toward stepping down as Executive Director in September 1983, when he wrote to members of the Executive Committee to say that he would reach the age of seventy in 1984. An extant Executive Council resolution called for retirement at that age. Rubin proposed that he remain as Executive Director for another year, during which Larry Hargrove would gradually take over most of the functions of the office. At the Annual Meeting in April 1985,

---

180 See *Texaco Overseas Petroleum Co. (TOPCO)/California Asiatic Oil Co. (CALASIATIC) v. Libyan Arab Republic*, 17 *ILM* 1 (1978).

181 Oscar Schachter, Editorial Comment: "Compensation for Expropriation," 78 *AJIL* 121 (1984); "Agora: What Price Expropriation?," including M.H. Mendelson, "Compensation for Expropriation: The Case Law," 79 *AJIL* 414 (1985), and Oscar Schachter, "Compensation Cases – Leading and Misleading," id. at 420.

182 Christopher C. Joyner, "Reflections on the Lawfulness of Invasion," 78 *AJIL* 131 (1984); John Norton Moore, "Grenada and the International Double Standard," id. at 145; Detlev F. Vagts, "International Law under Time Pressure: Grading the Grenada Take-Home Examination," id. at 169; Francis A. Boyle *et al.*, "Letter on International Lawlessness in Grenada," id. at 172.

183 Editorial Comments: Herbert W. Briggs, "*Nicaragua v. United States*: Jurisdiction and Admissibility," 79 *AJIL* 373 (1985); Thomas M. Franck, "Icy Day at the ICJ," id. at 379; Anthony D'Amato, "Modifying U.S. Acceptance of the Compulsory Jurisdiction of the World Court," id. at 385; Frederic L. Kirgis, "*Nicaragua v. United States* as a Precedent," id. at 652; Anthony D'Amato, "Nicaragua and International Law: The 'Academic' and the 'Real,'" id. at 657. See also Notes and Comments: Michael J. Glennon, "*Nicaragua v. United States*: Constitutionality of U.S. Modification of ICJ Jurisdiction," id. at 682; Keith Highet, "Litigation Implications of the U.S. Withdrawal from the Nicaragua Case," id. at 992; and Correspondence: "Observations by the U.S. Department of State on the ICJ's November 26, 1984 Judgment," id. at 423.

Hargrove would be named Executive Director.[184] To enable Rubin to remain as Executive Director until April 1985, the Executive Council waived for one year the requirement that staff members retire at age seventy.[185]

President Covey Oliver appointed Stephen M. Schwebel to chair an advisory committee on the selection of a new Executive Director.[186] The committee considered four candidates, recommending only Hargrove for the position. The Executive Council accepted the committee's recommendation. On April 11, 1984, the Council appointed Hargrove as the next Executive Director, effective on May 1, 1985.[187]

2. A Job Description

Schwebel's committee came up with a description of the ideal Executive Director. It should be a person competent in international law, with administrative ability and experience, comfortable working with academics, practitioners and government officials. The person should have breadth of outlook, and be capable of dealing with various nationalities and viewpoints. Moreover, the Executive Director should be likely to increase the Society's membership and encourage diversity; he or she should be vigorous, outgoing, resourceful, energetic and patient, with the talent not only to lead a small staff, but also to lead a distinguished, scholarly society. An aptitude for fund-raising would be an indispensable part of the job.[188]

No one on the Executive Council challenged the description. Several years later, another committee would come up with its own description.[189]

---

184 Memorandum of Sept. 23, 1983, from Seymour J. Rubin to Members of the Executive Committee, in Executive Committee Meetings notebook, 9-30-83 to 11-16-90.

185 Minutes of the Executive Council, Oct. 8, 1983, in ASIL Notebook of Executive Council Minutes, Apr. 1982–Nov. 1990. At the same time, the Council adopted a waiver for Helen Philos, the Society's librarian. Id.

186 In addition to Stephen Schwebel, the advisory committee consisted of Christopher Joyner, Monroe Leigh, Ved Nanda, John R. Stevenson, Edith Brown Weiss and Stephen Zamora.

187 78 *ASIL Proc.* 142 (1984); *ASIL Newsletter*, May/June 1984, at 1.

188 Report to the Executive Council on the Appointment of an Executive Director of the Society, Mar. 10, 1984, in briefing materials for Apr. 1984 Executive Council meetings.

189 See Chapter Fourteen, Section C.1, *infra*.

E. THE SOCIETY'S IMPACT ON EVENTS, POLICIES AND THE ACCESSIBILITY OF INFORMATION

It is no easier to measure the Society's impact on events in the seventies and eighties than at other times in its history. By adhering rather closely to its general policy against taking positions on substantive matters (except in relation to U.S. participation in the I.C.J.), the Society has consciously refrained from acting as an organization aspiring to influence national or international decision-makers on specific issues. Nevertheless, the Society's Annual Meetings with their published Proceedings, and the Journal, have consistently addressed the international legal issues of the day. Participants in the Meetings and authors in the Journal have not been reticent about offering their prescriptions for change. Sometimes their prescriptions have attracted media attention, albeit more often when well-known speakers have addressed Annual Meetings than when scholars have published in the Journal. With or without the publicity, one must assume that at least those who have responsibility for giving legal advice in the United States government and in some international organizations take account of pertinent prescriptions emanating from the Annual Meetings and the Journal.

This assumption is strengthened when active members of the Society are or become officials at policy-making levels or in positions that have access to the policy-makers. In the early days, Elihu Root and Charles Evans Hughes were classic examples. By the mid-seventies, Secretaries of State and other top-level foreign policy officials were no longer drawn from the ranks of active ASIL members. But the pipeline to Washington policy-making was not completely closed. For example, in January 1975, Monroe Leigh was appointed Legal Adviser to the Department of State. At the time he was an Honorary Vice President of the Society, a member of the Journal's Board of Editors and an active participant in the Society's affairs. Other active Society members at other times have served as Legal Advisers, including – to name a few – Jack Stevenson, Charles Brower and Leonard Meeker. None of them turned to the Society, as such, for advice while he was serving, but they all brought to the office the values that attracted them to the Society and the experience they gained within it.

The Legal Adviser's office did not have a monopoly on the services of prominent Society members during this period. Seymour Rubin, while he was the Society's Executive Director, headed the United States delegation to the first session of the U.N. Commission on Transnational Corporations in March 1975.[190] Rubin also served as a member of the Inter-American Juridical Committee for many

---

[190] *ASIL Newsletter*, Apr. 1975, at 1.

years. Other Society members served as experts on advisory panels at the State Department and other federal agencies.[191]

The Society's corporate consultation program during Seymour Rubin's time as Executive Director had some impact on the content of bilateral investment treaties then being negotiated by the United States government.[192] The impact seems to have been greatest in the area of expropriation, as corporate counsel and practitioners within the Society took advantage of contacts with government officials in these consultations to press for inclusion of a strong standard of protection for American investors abroad.

Other consultations and meetings have supplied fora for attempts to influence governmental policy-making. The regional meeting in 1975 on the law of the sea has already been mentioned.[193] To take another example, when the International Court of Justice held that it had jurisdiction in *Nicaragua v. United States*, the Society convened an informal session involving the then-current Legal Adviser of the State Department, several former Legal Advisers and some other experts. They discussed what the United States' response ought to be.[194] But whether they had any impact on the development of U.S. policy does not appear.

Demand for the Society's work product provides some measure of the influence of its projects. Unfortunately, the demand (beyond normal subscriptions) for a given published product is often not recorded. An exception during this period was the Jacob Kaplan study on coordination of foreign aid policies. The World Bank ordered three hundred copies.[195]

The Society's continuing effort to pry published materials out of the State Department – particularly the *Foreign Relations* series – may have had some impact. Dean Rusk, who had been in a position to know, said in 1976 that the Society's annual resolution on publications served "some useful purpose at budget time at the State Department."[196] In any event, the annual reports of the Society's Committee on Publications provided an invaluable, but under-appreciated, guide to State Department and U.N. publications of interest to international lawyers and scholars.

The Society's role during this period, then, was not significantly different in kind from the role it had been playing since World War II. It was a catalyst for

---

[191] See the Report of the Executive Director in *ASIL Newsletter*, Jan./Feb./Mar. 1978, at 2, 4.

[192] Interview with Monroe Leigh, Oct. 26, 1995 (transcript on file with the Society).

[193] See text at note 102 *supra*.

[194] *ASIL Newsletter*, Jan./Feb./Mar. 1985, at 2.

[195] Postscript to letter of Feb. 16, 1982, from Seymour J. Rubin to Alfred P. Rubin, in materials for Executive Council meetings, Apr. 1982.

[196] Minutes of the Executive Council, Apr. 22, 1976, in ASIL Minute Book, Apr. 1974–Oct. 1981, at 66, 69.

ideas and prescriptions relating to the legal norms that arguably did, or ought to, influence the conduct of official decision-makers on the international scene. It was a forum for information and the exchange of views on normative issues that transcended national boundaries, including issues of particular interest to businesses. Its expanded publication program and the widening scope of its interests made it a player on a broader field than ever before. Its impact on decisions actually made at official levels was indirect at best, but it offered no apologies for that. It had no aspiration to be a power broker.

Chapter Eleven

PERSEVERING DURING LEAN YEARS

Democracies exist under the rule of law; they cannot function without it; and in a constantly shrinking world, that applies just as much for international law as it does for national law. I think it applies to the United States, the democratic superpower, especially, because it can only continue to lead and defend democracy around the world if it does so in ways that pay respect to a principled view of international law.

—Lloyd N. Cutler
"The Right to Intervene,"
80 *ASIL Proceedings* 7 (1986)

A. CONTINUITY AND STAYING ON COURSE

1. Larry Hargrove's Initial Goals

The selection of John Lawrence Hargrove as Executive Director represented a choice for continuity rather than for change. When Hargrove took office on May 1, 1985, he had in mind two primary goals. Both of them emanated from the Society's existing interests and programs. One was to strengthen the Society's concern with the interfaces between law and policy. The other was to sustain the position of the Journal and of *International Legal Materials* as the pre-eminent publications in their fields.

On a day-to-day level, he gave attention to improving the quality of the Newsletter, which had become little more than a medium for announcements and internal Society news. He also had to complete the challenge grant from the National Endowment for the Humanities, left over from the Seventy-fifth Anniversary campaign. In addition, he continued the efforts he and Seymour Rubin had already undertaken to wean the Society away from its dependence on overhead components of study grants that had become increasingly difficult to obtain. He continued to seek grants, but he tried at the same time to boost income by establishing a realistic pricing structure for the goods (publications) and services the Society provided its members and others.[1]

2. Money Matters

Larry Hargrove inherited a history of chronic budget deficits. Foundations had become increasingly selective in doling out grants for international law at a time when many other worthy causes beckoned. At the same time, grant applications in the international law/international relations field were proliferating. In the 1980s, international law was not seen in Washington power circles as a significant force in maintaining a world order of the sort the U.S. government sought. The government's disillusionment with the World Court over the adverse jurisdictional and substantive rulings in *Nicaragua v. United States* seemed to carry over to international law generally. In such an atmosphere, making ends meet in an international law society committed to an ambitious publications and meetings program was a problem indeed.

To some extent, the budget deficits were the result of conservative accounting practices. But there were also concerns about lax management practices and about unrealistically low rates for membership dues, annual meeting fees, and subscriptions to the Journal and I.L.M. All of these rates were increased during this period.[2]

There was a temporary return to the good old days of Ford Foundation institutional support in 1991 and 1992. Ford supplied a grant of about USD 77,000 in each of those years, without tying it to any specific projects. The intent was to enable the Society to hire a new professional staff member.[3] Together with increased receipts from dues and subscriptions, plus some reduced expenditures, the Ford grants helped generate modest surpluses in those years. Nevertheless, the Society's President, Peter Trooboff, continued to have qualms about chronic budget deficits and problems of management within Tillar House. He pressed for tightened management practices.[4]

---

1 Interview with John Lawrence Hargrove, Aug. 3, 1994 (transcript on file with the Society).

2 For details, see Memorandum, "ASIL History: Details Relating to Budget, Finances and Membership" (2006), on file with the Society.

3 Minutes of the Executive Council, Nov. 17, 1990, in ASIL Notebook of Executive Council Minutes, Apr. 1982–Nov. 1990. The intent of the Ford Foundation appears in Anna D. Tapay, Richard Frank & Crauford Goodwin (Ford Foundation evaluation team), *The American Society of International Law: A Report and an Evaluation* (Jan. 1992) (hereinafter *Ford Foundation Evaluation*).

4 For example, under Trooboff's direction the Executive Committee decided that the budget for the allocation of all significant Society grants would henceforth be presented to the Executive Committee as well as the Budget Committee for review and approval. *ASIL*

James Conner bowed out as Treasurer in April 1992. During his eight and a half years in office, the stock portfolio had increased in market value from about USD 624,000 in April 1983 to about USD 1,563,000 despite substantial withdrawals from principal to cover the Society's annual deficits during the late eighties.[5] The growth in principal was attributable to capital contributions, largely from the Seventy-fifth Anniversary campaign, and to generally favorable stock market trends.[6]

3. A New Professional Staff Member

When Larry Hargrove succeded Sy Rubin as Executive Director, nobody was appointed to succeed Hargrove as Director of Studies. Rubin remained on the payroll as a half-time employee, but with a more circumscribed mandate than even a half-time Director of Studies would have had. The Executive Council and Hargrove were determined to proceed apace with the existing research and study program, but it put a severe strain on Hargrove and the staff. In effect, Hargrove became both the Executive Director and the *de facto* Director of Studies.[7]

Throughout the extensive consideration of financial issues in 1988 and 1989, the Executive and Budget Committees recognized the need for another professional on the Society's staff who could help particularly in the grant-seeking process. With the help of the Ford Foundation grants mentioned above, the Society hired Dr. Charlotte Ku, a political scientist with teaching and administrative experience. Ku took office in January 1990 as the Society's Adminstrative and Programs Director.[8] In effect, she became the Deputy Executive Director, a formal title later bestowed on her before she became the Executive Director.

4. Continuing Efforts to Increase Membership

During the eighties the Society continued its perennial efforts to entice new members and to retain current ones. The efforts have consistently been driven by revenue needs, though they have had secondary goals as well, such as diversifying the Society's intellectual resource base.

Newsletter, Jan.–Feb.–Mar. 1991, at 1, 2; see also Peter Trooboff, Notes on ASIL Financial Position, Nov. 15, 1990, in ASIL Notebook of Executive Committee Meetings, Sept. 30, 1983 to Nov. 16, 1990.

5 The withdrawals from principal totaled about USD 418,000.

6 Report of the Treasurer for Year Ended Dec. 31, 1991, in briefing book for Apr. 1992 Executive Council meetings.

7 Report of the Executive Director, in *ASIL Newsletter*, Mar./Apr. 1987, at 1, 2, and in 81 *ASIL Proc.* 200, 202, 205 (1987).

8 *ASIL Newsletter*, Jan./Feb. 1990, at 1.

Despite promotional efforts, membership remained static at about 4,000 for most of this period, though it increased to 4,320 in 1991.[9]

5. Improving the Newsletter

Early in Hargrove's tenure as Executive Director, he persuaded John Murphy to work with Judy Hall and others to produce a more interesting Newsletter. By 1986 the Newsletter began to publish in-depth reports of such developments as the U.S. unilateral reduction in its payment of U.N. dues,[10] the World Court's judgment on the merits in *Nicaragua v. United States*,[11] and the Inter-American Commission on Human Rights' finding admissible an application brought against the United States alleging that the U.S. had bombed a non-military target during the 1983 invasion of Grenada.[12]

In mid-1988, the Newsletter slipped back into its old format, focusing almost entirely on information about the Society and about programs that might be of interest to Society members. It re-emerged as a purveyor of substantive information with the July–September 1989 issue.

When Peter Trooboff became President of the Society in March 1990, he began the practice of writing a Newsletter column, "Notes from the President."[13] In it he reported on his goals and policies, and on a variety of Society activities.

6. The Passing of Philip Jessup

Philip Jessup died on January 31, 1986, at the age of eighty-nine. The *New York Times* obituary described him as "a rangy 6-footer with bushy eyebrows, a wide brow and a scholarly mien." The *Times* noted that he had served on the I.C.J. from 1960 until 1969, and that he had played a crucial role in ending the Berlin Blockade in 1949.[14]

Later in 1986, the Journal ran a special section in tribute to Jessup. Oscar Schachter wrote the lead article.[15] "Philip Jessup's life," he began, "was richly

---

9 Report of the Membership Dept. for the Executive Council meeting of Oct. 26, 1991, in briefing book for that meeting. For details regarding membership promotional efforts and results during this period, see Memorandum, ASIL History: Details Relating to Budget, Finances and Membership (2006), on file with the Society.

10 *ASIL Newsletters*, May–July 1986, at 1-3, Jan./Feb. 1987, at 1-2, & July–Sept. 1989, at 1, 3-6.

11 *ASIL Newsletter*, May–July 1986, at 1, 3-5.

12 *ASIL Newsletter*, Nov./Dec. 1986, at 1-2.

13 The first such column appeared in *ASIL Newsletter*, Mar.–May 1990, at 1.

14 *N.Y. Times*, Feb. 1, 1986, p. 13.

15 The other contributors were Manfred Lachs, Stephen M. Schwebel, James N. Hyde and Philip C. Jessup, Jr.

varied. Scholar, practitioner, teacher, administrator, diplomat, judge, prolific writer – he moved from role to role, displaying in each his abundant gifts of character and intellect."[16] Early on, Jessup sat at the knee of Elihu Root, who was a scholar in residence at his alma mater, Hamilton College, when Jessup was a senior there. Through Root, Jessup met James Brown Scott. He began teaching at Columbia in 1925, and began his foray into diplomacy in 1930 as legal adviser to the American Ambassador to Cuba. He went on to serve in various diplomatic positions, becoming involved after World War II in a variety of behind-the-scenes negotiations with the Russians – not just concerning the Berlin blockade. All the while, he remained a scholar. As Schachter put it, Jessup's 1947 book, *The Modern Law of Nations*, "was widely acclaimed, probably receiving more attention in the public media than any other book on international law ever had."[17] Jessup served on the A.J.I.L. Board of Editors from 1929 until his election to the I.C.J. in 1960, and as an Honorary Editor from 1970, when his term on the Court had ended, until his death.

Jessup incurred the wrath of Senator Joseph R. McCarthy in the 1950s. According to Schachter, "Next to General George Marshall, he was the most prominent target of McCarthy."[18] McCarthy asserted in particular (and without any basis) that Jessup had favored recognition of the People's Republic of China, an unthinkable transgression in McCarthy's eyes.

Jessup's nine-year term on the then-quiescent I.C.J. placed him on the margin of international affairs, an experience not entirely to his liking. The Court marginalized itself during his tenure, when in 1966 it reversed its 1962 judgment on the standing of Ethiopia and Liberia to challenge South Africa's administration of the League of Nations Mandate for South West Africa (Namibia). Jessup dissented, and was deeply hurt by the reversal.[19] Nevertheless, he remained a supporter of the Court even after he left it, and he took great pride in having the international law moot court competition – set each year as though the proceedings were being argued in the I.C.J. – named the Jessup Competition.[20]

Throughout his life, Jessup espoused the ideals that animated the founders of the American Society of International Law, to which he was devoted. Like Root, Scott and the other founders, "he had the abiding conviction that the United States would have to take the lead, in keeping with its traditions and principles,

---

16 Oscar Schachter, Philip Jessup's Life and Ideas, 80 *AJIL* 878 (1986).

17 Id. at 882.

18 Id. at 885.

19 *South West Africa* Case (*Ethiopia & Liberia v. So. Afr.*), Second Phase, 1966 ICJ Rep. 6, 323 (dissenting opinion); see Manfred Lachs, Jessup: Memorials and Reminiscences, 80 *AJIL* 896, 898 (1986).

20 Schachter, *supra* note 16, at 890.

to achieve an international society governed by law."[21] That the United States government did not seem to be doing so toward the end of Jessup's life was a matter of keen disappointment to him.

B. PROGRAMS AND POLICIES IN OPERATION

1. Responses to U.S. Unilateralism

Reacting to the United States' decision to withdraw from the proceedings in *Nicaragua v. United States*, the Executive Council in 1985 decided to establish a study panel.[22] A Panel on International Adjudication and the Jurisdiction of the International Court of Justice was duly formed with John R. Stevenson as its Chair and Lori Fisler Damrosch as its Rapporteur. The idea was not so much to arrive at recommendations of its own, but rather to provide research and analysis as a basis for judgments by policy-makers about the future U.S. relationship with the Court. The Panel consisted of a long list of experts on the I.C.J. and on international adjudication.[23] The Ford Foundation supported it with a grant of almost USD 50,000.[24]

The project resulted in a widely acclaimed book edited by Damrosch, *The International Court of Justice at a Crossroads*.[25] Its contributors produced a mosaic of essays on the Court, broken down into four main parts: The System of Compulsory Jurisdiction; The Suitability of Certain Kinds of Disputes for Resolution by the International Court; Special Problems of International Adjudication; and The United States and the International Court. Seven annexes provided source materials needed to assess the U.S. withdrawal from the *Nicaragua* proceedings and the U.S. termination of its Article 36(2) declaration. Included were the voting records of World Court judges from 1946 to 1986.

Among the many interesting contributions to the *Crossroads* book was one by Richard Bilder pointing out (*inter alia*) some possible advantages of adjudication by a permanent court rather than by *ad hoc* arbitration. He stressed a court's ready availability; its independence; its opportunity to develop a consistent body of law; its importance as a symbol of peaceful dispute settlement; and the

---

21 The quote is in id. at 895.

22 79 *ASIL Proc.* 148 (1985).

23 *ASIL Newsletter*, June/July 1985, at 2.

24 Report of the Executive Director, Oct. 26, 1985, in briefing book for Oct. 26, 1985, Executive Council meeting.

25 Lori Fisler Damrosch (ed.), *The International Court of Justice at a Crossroads* (1987).

message it can send about the rule of law in the international system.[26] A decade later, Georges Abi-Saab argued that the Court was showing a tendency toward *ad hoc* "transactional justice" as part of a trend toward arbitralization, rather than developing and applying the consistent body of law that – as Bilder had noted – should be one of the positive results of resorting to the I.C.J.[27]

In 1985, the U.S. Congress enacted legislation reducing U.S. contributions to the United Nations. Among other things, the so-called Kassebaum Amendment mandated a reduction in the U.S. share of U.N. dues from the established 25 per cent to 20 per cent if the United States were not given voting power on budgetary matters proportionate to its contribution to the U.N. budget.

Because this unilateral reduction in dues payment seemed to fly in the face of the requirement in Article 17(2) of the U.N. Charter that Member States bear the expenses of the Organization as apportioned by the General Assembly, the Society took an interest in the matter from the outset. The Newsletter reported on the bill before and after it was enacted.[28] The Society then convened a series of meetings: first, a private meeting in Tillar House with representatives from the U.N., the U.S. government, foreign missions to the U.N., congressional offices, non-governmental organizations and the Society's Interest Group on International Organizations; next, a public panel discussion on Capitol Hill, on International Law and United States Withholding of Payments to International Organizations, with a range of speakers including U.S. government representatives, the Legal Counsel of the United Nations and the Chair of the United Nations Association of the United States; and then a co-sponsored briefing session in the chambers of the House Foreign Affairs Committee.[29] A Committee on U.N. Relations, chaired by Ernest A. Gross, was appointed to delve further into the issues raised by the U.S. withholding of U.N. dues.

The Society organized a few other U.N.-related briefing sessions during this period. In November 1991, it convened a meeting of Senate Foreign Relations Committee staff members, State Department officials, N.G.O. representatives and scholars to discuss issues relating to U.S. ratification of the U.N. Covenants on human rights.[30] In February 1992, a briefing was held on legal issues before the

---

[26] Richard B. Bilder, "International Dispute Settlement and the Role of International Adjudication," in *The International Court of Justice at a Crossroads*, *supra* note 25, at 155, 173-74.

[27] Georges Abi-Saab, "The International Court as a World Court," in Vaughan Lowe & Malgosia Fitzmaurice (eds.), *Fifty Years of the International Court of Justice: Essays in Honour of Sir Robert Jennings* 3, 11 (1996). This book was not an ASIL project.

[28] *ASIL Newsletters*, June/July 1985, at 1, & Aug. 1985, at 1.

[29] *ASIL Newsletters*, Mar./Apr. 1986, at 1, & May/June 1986, at 1-3.

[30] Report of the Executive Director on Current Research and Study Activities, 86 *ASIL Proc.* 652, 656 (1992).

Preparatory Committee for the U.N. Conference on Environment and Development. It was aimed principally at members of the U.S. delegation and the media, although others attended as well.[31]

When Keith Highet became President of the Society in 1986, he appointed several study committees. In addition to the Committee on U.N. Relations, he formed a Committee on Maritime Claims, chaired by Bernard H. Oxman, to examine a clash that had occurred between the United States and Libya over the Gulf of Sidra and to consider how similar conflicts might be avoided; a Committee on the *Nicaragua* Decision, chaired by Oscar Schachter, to consider the implications for the United States of the World Court's judgment on the merits in *Nicaragua v. United States*; a Committee on Responses to State-Sponsored Terrorism, chaired by John F. Murphy, to consider issues arising from attempts to combat state-sponsored terrorism; and a Committee on the Optional Clause, under Monroe Leigh, to consider what new acceptance, if any, of the Optional Clause of the I.C.J. Statute should be undertaken by the United States.[32]

Eventually, all of these committees received external funding support. The Committees on Maritime Claims and on Terrorism received support from the United States Institute for Peace; the others, from the Ford Foundation.[33] Later, yet another study committee was appointed: the Committee on Legal Aspects of Arms Control and Disarmament, chaired by Paul Warnke.

The Committee on Maritime Claims was the first to finish its work, in early 1988. The Newsletter published the text of its report, which criticized theories of international law that require a state to take action that risks armed conflict (as the United States did in the Gulf of Sidra incident) simply to preserve its contested claim of a right to conduct activities in a maritime area. The report went on to urge negotiation and observance of the principle of compulsory arbitration of navigation disputes set forth in the U.N. Convention on the Law of the Sea.[34]

Later in 1988, the Committees on State-Sponsored Terrorism and on Arms Control produced their reports.[35] In the autumn of 1989 the reports of the committees on Maritime Claims and on State-Sponsored Terrorism were discussed by two small conferences on successive days at Tillar House.[36] The conferences

31 Id. at 658.

32 *ASIL Newsletter*, Aug./Sept./Oct. 1986, at 2. Memoranda containing the terms of reference of these working committees are in the briefing book for the Oct. 25, 1986, Executive Council meeting.

33 *ASIL Newsletter*, Jan./Feb. 1988, at 1.

34 *ASIL Newsletter*, Mar.–May 1988, at 1, 5-6.

35 Minutes of the Executive Council, Oct. 15, 1988, in ASIL Notebook of Executive Council Minutes, Apr. 1982–Nov. 1990.

36 *ASIL Newsletter*, Mar.–May 1990, at 4.

led to revisions in the reports, which were eventually published together as an offering in the Society's *Studies in Transnational Legal Policy*.[37]

In 1989 the Committee on U.N. Relations adopted a resolution asserting that all U.N. Member States, including the United States, are subject to an international obligation to pay their assessed contributions, irrespective of any provision of their domestic law. The resolution, and the report on which it was based, were published in the Newsletter. The resolution was sent to key Executive Branch officials and members of Congress.[38] The committee thus did what the Society, *qua* Society, would not do: it took a position on a contested issue of international law, and endeavored to have an impact on the relevant decision-makers.

The Committee on the Optional Clause completed its work in 1990. Its report recommended that the United States submit a new Article 36(2) declaration, with designated exclusions and conditions. The report recommended against resurrecting the Connally Reservation, by which the United States in its original Article 36(2) declaration had excepted disputes essentially within the jurisdiction of the United States, as determined by the United States. The Committee regarded the Connally Reservation as politically and legally damaging. Nor did the Committee favor a new Vandenburg Reservation, which had excepted disputes under a multilateral treaty unless all treaty parties affected by the decision were parties to the case or the United States specially agreed to the Court's jurisdiction. The Committee recommended, though, that a new reservation should be attached, excluding disputes with respect to the alleged threat or use of force between states in violation of international law. Excluded, too, would be disputes the parties had entrusted to other tribunals (re-enacting an exclusion in the original U.S. declaration).[39]

One commentator characterized some of the language in the report as the work of those "who continue to adhere to the idealist judicialist credo and for whom the Court remains the embodiment of the U.S. 'Supreme Court of the Nations' ideal."[40]

---

37 Report of the Executive Director for the Executive Council Meeting of Nov. 17, 1990, in briefing book for that meeting; *ASIL Newsletter*, June–July–Aug. 1991, at 8. See Nonviolent Responses to Violence-Prone Problems: The Cases of Disputed Maritime Claims and State-Sponsored Terrorism (ASIL Studies in Transnational Legal Policy No. 22, 1991).

38 *ASIL Newsletter*, July–Sept. 1989, at 1, 3-6.

39 Report of the ASIL Special Working Committee on the Optional Clause 13-19 (Oct. 1990).

40 Michla Pomerance, *The United States and the World Court as a "Supreme Court of the Nations": Dreams, Illusions and Disillusion* 413 (1996).

2. A Potpourri of Projects

In December 1984 and 1985, the Society held conferences in New York on International Economic Cooperation: Strategies for the Eighties. In both years a co-sponsor was the Asian-African Legal Consultative Committee; in 1985 the Inter-American Juridical Committee co-sponsored as well. Financial support was received from Exxon Corporation, which also provided its conference center for the meetings. The focus was on legal aspects of foreign investment. The conferences brought together for informal exchanges lawyers and development experts from developing country governments, representatives of multinational enterprises, international organization officials, and lawyers and scholars from the United States.[41]

In the autumn of 1986, a project on improvement of the administration of justice in Latin America and the Caribbean got under way, with Seymour Rubin directing it. The co-sponsor was the Inter-American Juridical Committee, of which Rubin was the senior member. The Agency for International Development provided USD 30,000 for an initial conference, which was held in August 1987 in Rio de Janeiro.[42] A second Rio meeting was held in August 1988 under the auspices of the Juridical Committee, but with leadership provided by the Society. The project sought to encourage Latin American institutions to identify problems in the administration of justice and to find remedies for them.[43] Eventually it proposed a private Inter-American Association for the Administration of Justice.[44]

At about the same time, the Ford Foundation made a grant of USD 37,700 for a project on the participation of women and minorities in international law. The Society conducted the project in collaboration with the Procedural Aspects of International Law Institute.[45] The project sponsored a workshop on women and minorities in international law at the 1987 Annual Meeting[46] and a two-day conference in Washington in September of that year.[47] In 1990 the project produced a study of existing programs in the United States designed to facilitiate the participation of minorities in law, international affairs and public

---

41 *ASIL Newsletter*, Dec. 1985, at 1.

42 Report of the Executive Director, Oct. 25, 1986, in briefing book for Oct. 25, 1986, Executive Council meeting; *ASIL Newsletter*, July/Aug./Sept. 1987, at 1.

43 Report on the Project on Improvement in Administration of Justice in the Americas, Sept. 8, 1988, in briefing book for Oct. 15, 1988, Executive Council meeting.

44 *ASIL Newsletter*, Mar.–May 1990, at 5.

45 Id.

46 81 *ASIL Proc.* 519 (1987).

47 Report of ASIL/PAIL Project on Women and Minorities in International Law, prepared for Oct. 24, 1987 Executive Council meeting, in briefing book for that meeting.

policy.[48] It also came up with a computerized résumé bank for women interested in international law and formed a working group on the Convention on the Elimination of All Forms of Discrimination Against Women.[49]

A project with an unusual twist concerned the protection of democratic institutions in multi-ethnic societies, with a particular focus on South Africa. Co-directors were Rita and Howard Taubenfeld. What was unusual was that Rita Taubenfeld, a senior Foreign Service Officer, was seconded to the Society for an extensive "sabbatical" to conduct the project. The External Research Office of the State Department provided a small grant for administrative and travel costs and the costs of an advisory committee.[50]

In the winter of 1987-88, the Ford Foundation approved a USD 81,000 grant for a Society project on resolution of ocean boundary disputes. Later, the Andrew W. Mellon Foundation provided an additional USD 50,000, and the Amoco Foundation, the Mobil Foundation and the Exxon Corporation supplied smaller grants. Jonathan Charney chaired the project with the assistance of Lewis Alexander.[51] The Society provided staff support and hosted a meeting of the project participants in Tillar House. The project became a massive undertaking involving twenty-four authors in its first phase, which resulted in a two-volume set analyzing more than 130 maritime boundaries settled since 1940, along with the relevant agreements, awards or judgments and illustrative maps.[52] Its publication in 1993 was celebrated with a public briefing at Tillar House.[53]

One might have expected such an exhaustive review of state practice to produce evidence of existing or emerging customary rules on delimitation of maritime boundaries. It was not to be. Charney concluded that "no normative principle of international law has developed that would mandate the specific location of any maritime boundary line. The state practice varies substantially."[54] He did, however, identify some relevant factors that should be considered in future delimitations. Primary attention, he said, would be placed on the geography of the coastline. Moreover, the equidistance line will usually be relevant and sometimes determinative. He mentioned other factors as well.[55]

---

48 *ASIL Newsletter*, Mar.–May 1990, at 4.

49 *ASIL Newsletter*, Sept./Oct. 1990, at 4.

50 *ASIL Newsletter*, Mar./Apr. 1987, at 1, 2.

51 *ASIL Newsletters*, Jan./Feb. 1988, at 1, Jan.–Feb.–Mar. 1991, at 8, & Apr./May 1991, at 3.

52 Jonathan I. Charney & Lewis M. Alexander (eds.), *International Maritime Boundaries*, vols. 1 & 2 (1993).

53 *ASIL Newsletter*, Mar.–May 1993, at 10.

54 Jonathan I. Charney, "Introduction," in Charney & Alexander, *supra* note 52, at xxiii, xlii.

55 Id. at xliv-xlv.

A second phase of the maritime boundary project, supported by royalties received by the Society from sales of the first two volumes, produced a third volume in 1998. It took account of the new ocean boundary issues emanating from the breakup of existing states in Europe, the merger of the two Germanies, the entry into force of the U.N. Convention on the Law of the Sea, and other developments around the globe.[56]

It is hard to imagine that any participant in a maritime boundary delimitation conducted after the publication of these volumes would proceed without consulting them. As a reviewer said, writing after the third volume was published:

> As they stand, this set is an invaluable source of State practice and analysis. ... It is inconceivable that any practitioner or scholar active in this field should not wish to have access to so major a resource in one form or another. The editors express the hope that "the delimitations reported in the three volumes of this book will continue to provide a foundation of history, practices and trends that will guide diplomats and tribunals in the future and provide a resource for scholars seeking to make new contributions to the field." These aspirations are already achieved.[57]

Separately from the maritime boundary project, the Society convened a two-day workshop that amounted to a post mortem on the decision in the *Gulf of Maine* maritime boundary case between the United States and Canada. The workshop brought together principal participants in the preparation and presentation of the case for the two governments, along with well-informed scholars and practitioners. The proceedings were published as one of the Society's Studies in Transnational Legal Policy.[58]

A major study of the United Nations system began in 1989, financed by a grant from the Ford Foundation. It brought together twenty-three scholars and practitioners under the leadership of Oscar Schachter and Christopher Joyner. As Schachter put it:

> The main objectives were two-fold. One was to present a scholarly analytical study of developments that would throw light on gaps and deficiencies as well as on accomplishments of the United Nations. It was hoped that this would be valuable in looking ahead to future possibilities. A second aim was to provide accessible and useful material to the many

56 Jonathan I. Charney & Lewis M. Alexander (eds.), *International Maritime Boundaries*, vol. 3 (1998).

57 Malcolm D. Evans, Book Review, [1999] *Lloyd's Mar. & Com. L.Q.* 447, 448.

58 *ASIL Newsletter*, June–Aug. 1988, at 1; Lewis M. Alexander (ed.), *The Gulf of Maine Case: An International Discussion* (Studies in Transnat'l Legal Policy No. 21, 1988).

> non-specialists in and outside of the international law community who have relevant professional interests.[59]

The result was a two-volume work published in 1995, analyzing the U.N. legal system, including the specialized and related agencies.[60] Schachter, in an overview of the work, suggested an architectural metaphor to describe the U.N. legal order:

> On its ground floor, I place the actions of states – including the demands and goals of the governments and other organized groups in furtherance of their needs, wishes and expectations.
>
> On the second level are the activities of a legal character – the formation and invoking of legal norms, and their application to particular situations.
>
> On the third level, I would place the broad policy goals, aspirations and ideals that influence governments and other actors.[61]

Schachter noted that there is movement from level to level. The legal processes on the second level are influenced by what happens on the first and third levels, and in turn influences what goes on there.[62]

Thomas Franck, the reviewer for the Journal, described the two-volume work as a "magisterial [but] pricey set that turns out to be a true bargain once price is weighed against value."[63] He continued:

> The subject of these volumes is by no means limited to the United Nations' political, economic and social activities, but encompasses the vast array of legal activities – lawmaking, administering, compliance monitoring and enforcement – that are to be found in both the most highly visible and the obscurest corners of the UN system. ... Perhaps only Schachter and Joyner could have marshaled such a panoply of experts on such a multitude of subjects and, *mirabile dictu*, made them pull together to a richly satisfying, even historic, purpose.[64]

The Ford Foundation supplied a USD 50,000 grant in 1989 for the planning and initial phase of a joint program of U.S.–Soviet research in international law. The

---

59 Oscar Schachter, "The UN Legal Order: An Overview," in 1 Oscar Schachter & Christopher C. Joyner (eds.), *United Nations Legal Order* 1 (1995) (hereinafter Schachter, "An Overview").

60 Schachter & Joyner, *supra* note 59.

61 Schachter, "An Overview", *supra* note 59, at 31.

62 Id.

63 Thomas M. Franck, "Review of United Nations Legal Order," in 90 *AJIL* 519 (1996).

64 Id.

idea was to produce a joint study on international law and politics dealing with peaceful settlement of disputes, and a joint textbook on international law. Lori Damrosch was named coordinator of the project for the Society.[65] The project began with a conference in Washington in October 1990 on international law and the non-use of force, attended by about 100 international lawyers, scholars, government officials and practitioners.[66]

An outgrowth of the conference was the publication of a book, *Law and Force in the New International Order*. It was "the first published result of a collaborative effort by U.S. and Soviet experts to rethink international law in light of new political conditions."[67] The book focused on five sets of issues: self-defense, collective security, intervention, arms control and judicial procedures. Ford then supplied an additional USD 183,000 for a second (two-year) phase, which included sessions in Moscow and Minsk in 1992 after the breakup of the Soviet Union.[68]

Meanwhile, working sessions on the joint textbook took place. Ultimately a book was produced, representing the collaborative efforts of paired authors from the United States and the former Soviet Union. The book covered such topics as use of force, terrorism, human rights, law of the sea, environmental law, space law, and peaceful dispute settlement.[69]

The MacArthur Foundation approved a USD 200,000 grant in the spring of 1989, enabling the Society to explore the possibility of producing a comprehensive "restatement" of public international law. It was an echo of the Society's past. As we have seen, a preoccupation of Elihu Root, James Brown Scott and other early Society leaders was the codification of international law as a means of providing arbitrators with an objective source of rules to apply in the peaceful settlement of international disputes.

Much the same animating spirit was at work in 1989, though not with quite the same missionary zeal. Called the "Governing Rules of International Law" project, the exploratory effort was directed by Louis Sohn and a small steering

---

65 Report of the Executive Director for the Executive Council Meeting of Nov. 18, 1989, in briefing book for that meeting.

66 Report of the Executive Director for the Executive Council Meeting of Nov. 17, 1990, in briefing book for that meeting; *ASIL Newsletter*, Nov./Dec. 1990, at 7-8; Lori Fisler Damrosch & David J. Scheffer (eds.), *Law and Force in the New International Order*, Preface (1991).

67 Id.

68 *ASIL Newsletters*, Jan.–Feb.–Mar. 1991, at 6, Apr./May 1991, at 7, & Jan./Feb. 1993, at 18.

69 Lori Fisler Damrosch, Gennady Danilenko & Rein Mullerson (eds.), *Beyond Confrontation: International Law for the Post-Cold War Era* (1995).

group.[70] A meeting of twenty-three judges, scholars and practitioners from around the world was held in France in the summer of 1990 to discuss not only the scope and possible methodology of the project, but also such fundamental issues as the desirability or need for it.[71]

As a trial run, a study of the law of movement of persons across borders was undertaken. Proposed rules and commentary were drafted on that topic in 1991,[72] a session at the 1991 Annual Meeting was devoted to it,[73] and an abridged version was published as one of the Society's Studies in Transnational Legal Policy.[74] Funding ran out before any further body of rules could be drafted. The "restatement" project came to naught.

The Society's efforts to bring international law to regions outside Washington, New York and Boston received a boost in 1990, when the Ford Foundation funded a project directed by Alfred Rubin on Regional Conferences in International Law and Organization. The project was designed to complement the Society's regional meetings program. Funds were made available for ten regional conferences during 1990-91.[75] Venues ranged from Georgia to the Pacific Northwest.

Yet another project, completed in October 1990, was a joint effort with the American Branch of the International Law Association to examine the role of the Legal Adviser of the State Department. Under the direction of Oscar Schachter, the project report examined possible conflicts of interest a Legal Adviser could face, analyzed the relationship between the Legal Adviser and counsel for other government departments, and concluded with recommendations for improving the ability of the Legal Adviser to serve effectively.[76]

Meanwhile the Society's long-standing Panel on State Responsibility worked on a variety of projects. One of them culminated in a conference at the University of Colorado in October 1991 on the International Law Commission's draft articles on the non-navigational uses of international watercourses. Edited versions of the papers were published in 1992.[77]

---

70 Summary Description of Project on Governing Rules of International Law, in briefing book for Nov. 18, 1989, Executive Council meeting.

71 *ASIL Newsletter*, June–Aug. 1990, at 5.

72 *ASIL Newsletter*, Sept./Oct. 1991, at 2.

73 "Governing Rules Project: Review and Discussion on the Movement of Persons Across Borders," 85 *ASIL Proc.* 51 (1991).

74 Louis B. Sohn & Thomas Buergenthal (eds.), *The Movement of Persons Across Borders* (ASIL Studies in Transnational Legal Policy No. 23, 1992).

75 *ASIL Newsletter*, Mar.–May 1990, at 3-4.

76 The joint committee's report appears in 85 *AJIL* 358 (1991).

77 "Doman Colloquium on the Law of International Watercourses," 3 *Colo. J. Int'l Envmt'l L.* & Policy 1 (1992).

An endeavor of a different kind involved co-sponsoring summer workshops devoted to international organizations studies. The co-sponsor was (and is) the Academic Council on the United Nations System (A.C.U.N.S.), a body composed largely of political scientists and international relations specialists. The workshops, supported by the Ford and MacArthur Foundations, have brought together small groups of young scholars and public servants, some with primarily legal backgrounds and others hailing from international relations. The goal has been to stimulate interest in research on international organizations, with a distinctly interdisciplinary flavor. The first A.S.I.L./A.C.U.N.S. workshop was held at Dartmouth College in the summer of 1991.[78] After two summers at Dartmouth, the venue was shifted to Brown University, later to Yale and then to Wilfrid Laurier University in Ontario, Canada.

3. Still on the Agenda in a Time of U.S. Unilateralism: Whether to Take Substantive Positions

In October 1985, the Executive Council took up the question it had left hanging in April: whether to adopt a position on the United States' withdrawal of its declaration accepting the International Court's jurisdiction under Article 36(2) of the I.C.J. Statute. The question was referred to the Panel on International Adjudication.

Meanwhile, a group convened by Anthony D'Amato, and identifying itself as composed of Society members, had formulated a statement expressing their concern about the U.S. decision to revoke its Article 36(2) declaration. The statement also advocated a new U.S. declaration. The Executive Council frowned on identifying the signers as Society members. It was agreed that the statement would be submitted to Society members for signature, merely identifying them as international lawyers, scholars and practitioners.[79] It appeared as a letter to the editor of the New York Times over the signatures of D'Amato and Keith Highet, who said they spoke for 40 of their colleagues. They mentioned that the compulsory jurisdiction of the I.C.J. had been approved by an A.S.I.L. resolution in 1946. They concluded that the United States should re-establish its long-standing commitment to international law and peaceful dispute resolution by carefully considering the adoption of a new or amended instrument of general adherence to the Court's compulsory jurisdiction.[80]

In March 1988, the Attorney General of the United States, acting pursuant to the Anti-Terrorism Act of 1987, ordered the U.N. observer mission of the

---

78 *ASIL Newsletter*, June/July/Aug. 1991, at 2.

79 Minutes of the Executive Council, Oct. 26, 1985, in ASIL Notebook of Executive Council Minutes, Apr. 1982–Nov. 1990.

80 *N.Y. Times*, Feb. 1, 1986, p. 26.

Palestine Liberation Organization to close. The U.N. General Assembly viewed it as a violation of the Headquarters Agreement between the United States and the United Nations. The State Department conceded as much. When the United States declined to submit the matter to arbitration under the arbitration clause of the Headquarters Agreement, the Society's Business Meeting considered whether to adopt a resolution calling on the United States to arbitrate. After debate, the matter was referred to the Executive Council in accordance with the Society's Constitution. Nevertheless, the A.S.I.L. Committee on U.N. Relations sent a letter to the Secretary of State and the Attorney General asserting that U.S. refusal to appoint an arbitrator would violate the Headquarters Agreement.[81] Ultimately, arbitration became moot when a U.S. District Court held that under the *Charming Betsy* canon, it would interpret the statute not to require closing the P.L.O. mission because any other interpretation would cause the United States to violate the Headquarters Agreement (and Congress, said the Court, had not sufficiently expressed an intention to force the P.L.O. mission to close if that would violate the Agreement).[82] The mission remained open.

In November 1989 the Executive Council discussed whether to adopt, as its own, the resolution of the Society's Committee on U.N. Relations asserting that all U.N. members, including the United States, have an international obligation to pay their assessed contributions. Most Council members felt that the Society should stand by its policy of eschewing the taking of positions on such matters. Thus the Council simply accepted the Committee's report and directed that it be disseminated as widely as possible.[83] As we have seen, the Committee's resolution was sent to key Executive Branch officials and members of Congress.[84]

* * *

For many years the Business Meeting of the Society routinely adopted resolutions calling on the State Department and the United Nations to hasten the dissemination of documents and other official publications. Normally, these resolutions were non-controversial. In 1987, though, the resolution contained two new criticisms of U.S. government policy. The first attributed the lag in publication

---

81 82 *ASIL Proc.* 231-32 (1988); Minutes of the Executive Council, Apr. 22, 1988, in ASIL Notebook of Executive Council Minutes, Apr. 1982–Nov. 1990. The text of the letter to the Attorney General appears in *ASIL Newsletter*, Mar.–May 1988, at 4-5.

82 *United States v. Palestine Liberation Organization*, 695 F.Supp. 1456 (S.D.N.Y. 1988). The *Charming Betsy* canon says that "an act of Congress ought never to be construed to violate the law of nations if any other possible construction remains." *Murray v. The Charming Betsy*, 6 U.S. (2 Cranch) 64, 118 (1804).

83 Minutes of the Executive Council (prepared by Sandra Liebel), Nov. 18, 1989, in ASIL Notebook of Executive Council Minutes, Apr. 1982–Nov. 1990.

84 See text at note 38 *supra*.

of U.N. documents to the withholding of assessed contributions by the United States; the second called on the United States to live up to its obligation under Article 102 of the Charter to register its treaties as soon as possible with the U.N. Secretariat.[85] There was some controversy as to whether these criticisms departed from the usual Society policy against taking substantive positions.[86]

The annual resolution was again more assertive than usual in 1990, when it protested the failure of the State Department to grant its own external advisory committee the chance to review material to be excised from *Foreign Relations of the United States*, and opposed the discontinuance of the *Department of State Bulletin*.[87]

The Society's incoming President, Peter Trooboff, transmitted the resolution to the Secretary of State, urging a meeting to discuss reinstating the *Bulletin*.[88] In May 1990, he led a delegation of interested persons in a meeting with the State Department's Director of Public Communication. He also wrote to every member of the Senate Foreign Relations Committee urging reinstatement of the *Bulletin*. Ultimately the State Department decided to publish a scaled-down version called the *Department of State Dispatch*.[89] Its first issue appeared in September 1990. It lasted only until December 1999.

4. Disinvestment in South Africa

In the mid-eighties, public and private non-profit bodies across the country faced the question of whether to retain investments in companies that did business in apartheid South Africa. Within the Society, an Ad Hoc Committee on Investment Policy recommended in April 1986 that "[I]nvestments shall be made in companies that have employees in South Africa or equity in a South African subsidiary only if the company is a signatory to the Sullivan Principles [setting forth unofficial fair employment standards for companies in South Africa] and has a [favorable] rating under those Principles."[90] A substitute motion was offered in the Executive Council that would have precluded any Society investments in companies with employees in South Africa or an equity stake in a South

85 81 *ASIL Proc.* 209, 210 (1987).

86 Id. at 208-09.

87 Minutes of the Executive Council, Mar. 30, 1990, in ASIL Notebook of Executive Council Minutes, Apr. 1982–Nov. 1990.

88 *ASIL Newsletter*, Mar.–May 1990, at 1, 3.

89 *ASIL Newsletter*, June–Aug. 1990, at 3-4.

90 Report of Ad Hoc Committee on Investment Policy, Apr. 9, 1986, in briefing book for Oct. 25, 1986, Executive Council meeting (where other materials on this issue may also be found).

African subsidiary. After considerable debate, the Executive Council adopted the Committee's recommendation, subject to later review.[91]

At the next Executive Council meeting, in October 1986, the Council narrowly adopted a motion made by Henry Richardson:

> That the Society divest itself of stock of all corporations with direct investments in South Africa because of the best interest of the Society;
>
> Divestiture should be conducted as quickly as possible, in phases consistent with the continuing integrity of the overall portfolio.[92]

During the debate the argument was made that apartheid was such a clear violation of basic international law that the Society could not in good conscience continue to profit from investments there.[93] The other side argued that disinvestment would hurt the very segment of the population the Society was trying to help, and that it might cause corporate members of the Society to cancel their memberships.

By early 1989 the Society's eight holdings of tainted stock had been liquidated. James Conner, the Society's Treasurer, had done his duty, but he did not like it. He felt strongly that the Society, by what he called its "South Africa free" policy, had foregone attractive investment opportunities.[94]

When apartheid ended in South Africa, the Executive Council removed the restriction on investing in companies doing business there.[95]

5. Annual Meetings in Washington and Elsewhere

The 1985 Annual Meeting was held in New York City, to commemorate the fortieth anniversary of the United Nations. An innovation was an off-the-record session with U.N. officials, including Carl-August Fleischhauer, the Legal Counsel, and Brian Urquhart, the Under Secretary for Special Political (Peacekeeping) Affairs. More than three hundred Society members and guests attended the session.[96]

The United States' termination of its acceptance of the compulsory jurisdiction of the International Court of Justice became effective on April 6, 1986,

---

91 Minutes of the Executive Council, Apr. 11, 1986, in ASIL Notebook of Executive Council Minutes, Apr. 1982–Nov. 1990.

92 Minutes of the Executive Council, Oct. 25, 1986, in ASIL Notebook of Executive Council Minutes, Apr. 1982–Nov. 1990.

93 The argument for divestment also appeared in Henry J. Richardson III, "Current Developments: Divestment of the Stock Portfolio of the Society," 81 *AJIL* 744 (1987).

94 Report of the Treasurer for Year Ended Dec. 31, 1988, in briefing book for Apr. 1989 Executive Council meetings.

95 Minutes of the Executive Council, Apr. 7, 1994, in briefing materials for Nov. 5, 1994, Executive Council meeting.

96 79 *ASIL Proc.* 1 (1985).

just three days before the Society's 1986 Annual Meeting began. A panel was convened on the World Court, featuring a presentation by Abraham D. Sofaer, the State Department's Legal Adviser. It had become clear, he said, "that our acceptance [of compulsory jurisdiction] failed to advance our interests in any tangible manner."[97] Not everyone agreed.

In 1987, the Annual Meeting was held in Boston because of a lack of suitable hotel space in Washington.[98] It offered a rich variety of panels and discussion groups, resulting in a 697-page volume of Proceedings.

Abraham Sofaer was again on the program in 1988. He gave a luncheon address discussing the role of law and legal advice relating to several U.S. threats or uses of armed force since World War II. He approved of Abram Chayes' conception at the time of the Cuban missile crisis, "in which international law is left open to a broad range of interpretation and emphasis, with terms that do not dictate conduct so much as orient deliberation, order priorities, and guide within broad limits."[99] He went on to criticize – even ridicule – the decision on the merits in *Nicaragua v. United States*. The decision, he said, "ignored actual custom and practice, and relied on rules that were seemingly derived for the purpose of depriving the United States and El Salvador of inherent rights."[100]

The 1988 Annual Meeting also featured a session on Capitol Hill examining the War Powers Resolution.[101] Chaired by Louis Henkin, it included a lively exchange on Congressional and Executive powers among Professor Henkin and Professors Philip Trimble (a former Assistant to the Legal Adviser of the State Department) and Michael Glennon (a consultant to the Senate Foreign Relations Committee).

An innovation at the 1988 Meeting was a series of unstructured "seminars" led by prominent Society members.[102]

Washington hotels were again fully booked for the spring of 1989. This time the staff selected the Palmer House in Chicago as the venue for the Annual Meeting. The theme was Respect for International Law in the 1990s. Thomas

---

97 Abraham D. Sofaer, "The United States and the World Court," 80 *ASIL Proc.* 204, 210 (1986).

98 Annual Meeting Report, Oct. 26, 1985, in briefing book for Oct. 26, 1985, Executive Council meeting.

99 Abraham D. Sofaer, address to the Joint Luncheon with the Section of International Law and Practice of the A.B.A., 82 *ASIL Proc.* 420, 422 (1988).

100 Id. at 426.

101 Panel on War Powers and the Responsibility of Congress, 82 *ASIL Proc.* 1 (1988).

102 Anthony D'Amato, moderator, "The Theory of Customary International Law," 82 *ASIL Proc.* 242 (1988); W. Michael Reisman, "Straight Baselines in International Law: A Call for Reconsideration," id. at 260; Louis B. Sohn, "Equity in International Law," id. at 277.

R. Pickering, the newly appointed U.S. Permanent Representative to the United Nations, was the speaker at the annual dinner. He gave an upbeat assessment of the U.N.'s role as a force for a better world order, and he heralded a new era of U.S. support for the United Nations. United States foreign policy, he said, would be much less effective without the U.N.[103] The invasion and occupation of Iraq 14 years later would corroborate his viewpoint.

During this period the Society, together with the Oceana Publishing Group, organized an annual symposium on international economic law and policy, held during the two days immediately preceding the Annual Meeting.[104] At the Annual Meeting in 1989, the Oceana symposium made way for a special session at the Chicago Mercantile Exchange on global trading in financial instruments. Co-sponsors were the Society's Interest Group on International Economic Law and the IIT Chicago-Kent College of Law Graduate Program in Financial Services Law.[105]

In 1990, back in Washington, the Annual Meeting featured several panels on major events of the day, such as the end of the Cold War and the U.S. intervention in Panama.[106] Environmental and economic issues were prominent as well.[107]

In 1991, three panels, including a special session on Capitol Hill, addressed the first Persian Gulf War.[108] A plenary session looked at foreign affairs and the United States Constitution in its third century.[109] And the Society's Governing

---

103 83 *ASIL Proc.* 1, 7 (1989).

104 Letter from John Lawrence Hargrove to Karel E. Vosskuhler (of the Ford Foundation), Aug. 23, 1990, at 3, in briefing book for Nov. 17, 1990, Executive Council meeting; *ASIL Newsletter*, Nov./Dec. 1990, at 10. A separate registration fee was charged.

105 "Global Trading in Financial Instruments: Market Developments and Regulatory Challenges," 83 *ASIL Proc.* 19 (1989).

106 "International Law After the Cold War," 84 *ASIL Proc.* 156 (1990); "The Panamanian Revolution: Diplomacy, War and Self-Determination in Panama," Parts I & II, id. at 182 & 236.

107 "Transfrontier Environmental Damage," 84 *ASIL Proc.* 12 (1990); "Self-Help in International Trade Disputes," id. at 32; "Attribution Issues in State Responsbility," id. at 51; "Present at the Creation: A New Development Bank for Europe in the Age of Environmental Awareness," id. at 77; "Effects and Effectiveness of Economic Sanctions," id. at 203; "What's Going On in Intellectual Property Law?," id. at 256; "World Climate Change – Greenhouse Effect," id. at 344.

108 "Special Capitol Hill Session on The Gulf War: Collective Security, War Powers and Laws of War," 85 *ASIL Proc.* 1 (1991); "The Gulf War: The Law of International Sanctions," id. at 169; "The Gulf War: Environment as a Weapon," id. at 214.

109 "The U.S. Constitution in its Third Century: Foreign Affairs," 85 *ASIL Proc.* 191 (1991).

Rules Project received an airing in the form of discussion of the pilot "restatement" of the law of persons moving across borders.[110]

An innovation in 1992 was an interactive panel consisting of a member of Congress, judges, academics and government officials who were asked to respond to a hypothetical problem Thomas Franck posed. The problem was based on the break-up of the Soviet Union and Yugoslavia, and the imaginary reaction of the U.S. Congress. It spawned a free-flowing discussion with Franck as the orchestrator.[111] Of related interest was a Capitol Hill session on state succession.[112] Two of the 1992 panels featured relatively rare Annual Meeting excursions into the world of pure jurisprudence.[113]

6. Interest Groups and Annual Meetings

As interest groups proliferated in the late eighties, they clamored for time and space at the Annual Meetings. The typical arrangement was a breakfast meeting for any interest group that wanted one. But some of the larger, more active interest groups wanted more than that. In particular, they sought to present panels that would be virtually indistinguishable from panels organized by the Program Committee. Sometimes this was done, but not always without friction.

For example, the Human Rights Advocacy Interest Group organized a panel at the 1989 Annual Meeting in Chicago. Anthony D'Amato, the interest group Chair, complained when it was over that the panel had been left off the preliminary program for the Annual Meeting; it had no Rapporteur; its session was not tape recorded; the papers were not included in the Proceedings; and the panelists were not given the reduced registration fee that regular panelists received.[114]

Matters improved at the 1992 Annual Meeting. With the blessing of the Program Committee, the interest groups on Women in International Law, International Economic Law, Southern Africa, International Organizations, and

---

110 "Governing Rules Project: Review and Discussion on the Movement of Persons Across Borders," 85 *ASIL Proc.* 51 (1991).

111 "Panel, The Role of the Judiciary in Foreign Policy Litigation," 86 *ASIL Proc.* 211 (1992).

112 "Special Capitol Hill Session on State Succession and Relations with Federal States," 86 *ASIL Proc.* 1 (1992).

113 "The Jurisprudence of International Law: Classic and Modern Views," 86 *ASIL Proc.* 108 (1992); "International Law and International Relations Theory: Building Bridges," id. at 167.

114 Letter from Anthony D'Amato to Sandra Liebel, Feb. 8, 1990, in briefing book for Mar. 1990 Executive Council meetings.

Human Rights sponsored panels during the early time slot on Friday morning. They had the same status as other panels.[115]

7. An Interest Group Work Product: Basic Documents of International Economic Law

In 1986, the Society's Interest Group on International Economic Law began the process of selecting documents to include in a compendium of core international economic law instruments. Surveys were sent out to all members of the interest group and to all teachers of international transactions courses in U.S. law schools. Ultimately Ronald Brand and Stephen Zamora compiled and edited a two-volume set of documents, with introductory notes and a select bibliography for each document.[116] The compilation quickly became the standard reference work in its field.

Not only was the compilation published in traditional book form, but the database from which it came was put online in Westlaw. In fact, the online version appeared in the spring of 1989, before the two-volume set did.[117] The advantages of going online, of course, were that the material could be searched easily and updated quickly.

8. A New Journal on International Economic Law?

In November 1989, Stephen Zamora asked the Executive Council to consider establishing a new journal on international economic law. He argued that the Journal did not have sufficient space to deal with important economic law subjects while maintaining its position as the premier public international law journal.[118] Nothing came of Zamora's proposal at that point, but the idea would resurface in the mid-nineties.

9. Biennial Meetings with the Netherlands Society of International Law

In the late 1980s, the Society staff investigated the possibility of holding an Annual Meeting in The Hague. The Dutch government was receptive, even

[115] Report from Co-Chairs of 1992 Annual Meeting Committee to Executive Council, Oct. 15, 1991, in briefing book for Oct. 26, 1991, Executive Council meeting; Final Program for the 86th Annual Meeting, Apr. 1-4, 1992.

[116] Stephen Zamora & Ronald A. Brand, *Basic Documents of International Economic Law* (2 vols., 1990).

[117] *ASIL Newsletter*, Mar.–June 1989, at 5. The database went online on April 4, 1989.

[118] Letter from Stephen Zamora to J. Lawrence Hargrove, Nov. 2, 1989, in briefing book for Nov. 18, 1989, Executive Council meeting.

offering a subsidy for every paid registrant.[119] The Executive Council, however, discarded the idea as too risky.[120]

Peter Trooboff, the Society's President in 1990, refused to let the idea disappear. At the March 1990 Executive Council meeting it re-emerged as a proposal for a joint conference in The Hague that would be similar in format to the Annual Meeting, but entirely separate from it. The conference would be held in the summer, when academics and others could attend. The ASIL and the Netherlands Society of International Law would be equal partners in the endeavor.[121]

The proposal became reality. The first joint conference was held in July 1991 under the theme, "Contemporary International Law Issues: Sharing Pan-European and American Perspectives." The Society pronounced it a success, with nearly three hundred registrants from more than twenty-six countries attending lively sessions. The proceedings were published.[122] Plans were immediately made for a second joint conference in 1993.[123]

10. Fading Emphasis on Corporate Consultations

When Seymour Rubin stepped down as Executive Director, some of the Society's emphasis on the business side of international law stepped down with him. Rubin was still in and around Tillar House as a consultant, but he no longer ordered the priorities of the Society. A manifestation of this was the reduced emphasis on corporate consultations in the late eighties. The consultations did not disappear altogether, but they were few and sporadic.

The Society did not get back in close touch with the business community until the mid-1990s, under Edith Brown Weiss and Charlotte Ku.[124]

11. A Survey of International Law Teaching

In the winter of 1989-90, the Society received a grant from the Ford Foundation to design and conduct a survey of international law teaching in the United States and Canada, and in selected institutions outside North America. It was the third such Ford-supported survey, the earlier ones having been conducted

---

119 Report of the Annual Meeting Coordinator for Executive Council meeting of Apr. 5, 1989, in briefing book for Apr. 1989 Executive Council meetings.

120 Minutes of the Executive Council (prepared by Sandra Liebel), Nov. 18, 1989, in ASIL Notebook of Executive Council Minutes, Apr. 1982–Nov. 1990.

121 *ASIL Newsletter*, June–Aug. 1990, at 3.

122 Contemporary International Law Issues: Sharing Pan-European and American Perspectives (Proc. of Jt. Conf., The Hague, July 4-6, 1991).

123 *ASIL Newsletter*, June/July/Aug. 1991, at 1-2.

124 See Chapter Twelve, *infra*.

in 1963-64 under Richard Edwards and in 1973-74 under Michael Cardozo. This time John King Gamble was selected as the project director.[125]

Beginning in the autumn of 1990, Gamble sent out questionnaires to administrators and international law teachers in law schools and political science departments in the United States and Canada. The results were published in 1993, as a number in the Society's Studies in Transnational Legal Policy.[126] Among his interesting findings was the perception among law school Deans and faculty that student and faculty interest in international law was increasing. The basic course in public international law had become a fixture in almost all law schools.[127]

About 66 per cent of the political science departments responding to Gamble's questionnaires reported offering an undergraduate course in international law.[128] But in these political science departments, chairs and faculty members alike perceived interest in international law as static at best.[129] Perhaps even more disturbing, political scientists with an interest in teaching international law were an aging breed.[130]

As Gamble put it in the summary at the end of his report:

> To oversimplify, international law is prospering in law schools and limping along, at best, in departments of political science. ... [I]nternational law is seen as an important element of the stature of a law school, virtually essential, surely one necessary component to a school's claim to excellence. The same is not true for political science where some of the most distinguished departments offer no courses in international law and do not feel that their status is diminished.[131]

The disparity between law schools and political science departments was predictable from Richard Edwards' survey of international law teaching in the 1960s. His survey found static interest in international law among graduate political science students and an already aging cadre of those political science teachers who regarded international law as their primary teaching interest.[132]

---

125 *ASIL Newsletter*, Jan./Feb. 1990, at 1.

126 The questionnaires are reproduced in appendices to Gamble's final report, *Teaching International Law in the 1990s* (ASIL Studies in Transnational Legal Policy No. 24, 1993).

127 Id. at 34-35.

128 Id. at 64.

129 Id. at 60.

130 The average age of the sample group was fifty-three; only twenty-five per cent of the sample had received their baccalaureate degree within the preceding twenty years. Id. at 41.

131 Id. at 118.

132 See Chapter Eight, Section B.6, *supra*.

Gamble, a political scientist, recommended that the Society welcome political scientists as valued members – something he perceived not to have been the case at that time – and that the Society make a long-term commitment to emphasize international law teaching.[133]

12. Judge Schwebel on Campus

The Ford Foundation gave the Society a grant for 1991 and 1992 to enable Stephen Schwebel, the U.S. judge on the International Court of Justice (and, of course, a former Executive Director of the Society), to spend a few days in residence at selected U.S. universities. A major criterion for selecting the schools was the presence of significant numbers of Hispanic, Native American, Asian-American and African-American students whose interest in international law might be stimulated.[134] Schwebel's campus visits involved lectures on the Court and other topics, as well as informal meetings with faculty, students and others.[135]

13. Changes in *International Legal Materials*

At the beginning of 1987, I.L.M. added extensive headnotes ("Content Summaries") to the documents it published, giving readers an opportunity to check quickly what was covered, and where, in the documents.[136] For some of the documents, it also added Introductory Notes – short narratives by knowledgeable individuals, placing the documents in historical and contemporary context.

In 1989, the Society concluded arrangements with Mead Data Central to place I.L.M. (and the Journal) on Lexis, Mead's online legal research service. I.L.M. made its appearance on Lexis in late September 1990.[137] In 1995 it appeared on Westlaw.[138]

14. A Change in the Annual Awards

Since 1976 the Society's annual awards had been bifurcated into two categories: one for a pre-eminent contribution to creative scholarship, and one for high technical craftsmanship and high utility to practicing lawyers and scholars. In 1991 Paul Szasz, a member of the Committee on Annual Awards, proposed that a third category be added, for the best casebook or other publication designed for

---

133 *Teaching International Law in the 1990s, supra* note 126, at 135.

134 *Ford Foundation Evaluation, supra* note 3, at 11-12.

135 *ASIL Newsletter*, Jan.–Feb.–Mar. 1991, at 7.

136 Report on International Legal Materials, Oct. 25, 1986, in briefing book for Oct. 25, 1986, Executive Council meeting.

137 *ASIL Newsletter*, Sept.–Oct. 1990, at 7.

138 *ASIL Newsletter*, Mar.–May 1995, at 13.

use in classroom teaching. He argued that neither of the two existing categories was well suited for teaching materials.[139]

The Executive Council decided not to establish the third category. It regarded teaching materials as works of technical craftsmanship and utility, falling within the existing second category.[140]

The issue, however, would rise again. In March 1996, the Committee on Annual Awards suggested that six categories be considered so that books in different genres would not compete against each other. No action was taken on that suggestion, but in 1997 the Council established a category for a work in a specialized area of international law, such as business transactions, economic law, environmental law, human rights or private international law.[141]

15. A Change at the Helm of the Library

On June 30, 1987, Helen Philos retired. She had been the Society's librarian since 1964, having previously served (since September 1962) as a cataloguer. She oversaw the growth of the Society's collection to about 22,000 volumes and almost 300 periodical titles. That growth supplied her with more than a few challenges, as overflow books had to go somewhere. They wound up in the Tillar House wine cellar, in bathrooms and anywhere else that could accommodate a bookshelf or two.

Upon her retirement, her successor, Jill McC. Watson, wrote:

> The qualities that make Helen a great librarian – her intelligence, her encyclopedic memory, her patience, her thrill in the reference chase, her tenacity in stalking the elusive fact, and above all her cordiality and generosity to her patrons and colleagues who quickly become her friends – will be sorely missed.[142]

It was the Society's good fortune that Jill Watson turned out to have essentially the same characteristics.

16. A Change at the Helm of the Society

In an open letter to members of the Society in April 1991, Peter Trooboff announced that Larry Hargrove wished to reduce the heavy administrative burden

---

139 Memorandum from Peter D. Trooboff to Executive Council, Apr. 9, 1991, in briefing book for Apr. 1991 Executive Council meetings.

140 Minutes of the Executive Council, Apr. 17, 1991, in briefing book for Oct. 26, 1991, Executive Council meeting.

141 Minutes of the Executive Council, Apr. 9, 1997, at 9.

142 Report of the Library for Apr. 8, 1987 Executive Council meeting, in briefing book for that meeting; *ASIL Newsletter*, Mar./Apr. 1987, at 3, 4.

he had been carrying for many years, and would resign as Executive Director not later than April 1992. At that point he would become Senior Director of Studies for a transitional two-year period.[143] Hargrove retired from full-time service to the Society in April 1994.[144]

In consultation with the Executive Council, Trooboff appointed a search committee in the spring of 1991 and gave it a mandate to seek someone with a strong background in international law, administrative experience and talent, ability to work effectively with diverse constituencies, and a commitment to broadening opportunities for involvement of Society members in the programs of the Society. The search committee was asked to recommend a new Executive Director to the Executive Committee and Executive Council by November 1991. Applications and nominations were encouraged, under assurance of confidentiality.[145]

The committee solicited applications, pared them down to a group of finalists, held an interview with each finalist, and ultimately submitted a single name to the Executive Committee, which – under then-current working arrangements – exercised *de facto* responsibility for making decisions about professional staff. Although there was some controversy about being asked to vote "yes" or "no" on a single candidate, the Executive Committee ultimately confirmed the search committee's choice: Professor Barry E. Carter, of the Georgetown Law Center. The result was reported the next day to the Executive Council.[146] Carter's formal appointment as Executive Director and his election as Executive Vice President occurred at the Executive Council and Business meetings in April 1992.

17. Larry Hargrove's Valedictory

When Larry Hargrove stepped down in April 1992, he wrote about his seven years as Executive Director. He took pride in the continuing pre-eminence of the Journal and I.L.M., in the growth of the Annual Meeting and Proceedings, in the stability of the Jessup Competition, and in new ventures such as the joint meeting with the Dutch Society of International Law.

Hargrove then turned to a more jurisprudential theme. The central mission of the Society, he said, "is to understand the role of law in international public

---

143 Open letter from Peter D. Trooboff, President of the Society, to Society members, Apr. 2, 1991, in *ASIL Newsletter*, Apr./May 1991, at 1-2.

144 Minutes of the Executive Committee, Feb. 18, 1994, in briefing materials for Apr. 1994 Executive Council meetings.

145 *ASIL Newsletter*, Apr./May 1991, at 2-3.

146 *ASIL Newsletter*, Nov./Dec. 1991, at 1-2.

life, and to promote its sound and humane development."[147] It was a neoclassical view of international law and of the Society's place in the world. It reflected Hargrove's real strength – an appreciation of, and devotion to, serious research into the international legal issues of his day.

Unlike Elihu Root and James Brown Scott, who thought of international law and of the Society largely in utilitarian terms, Hargrove thought of the Society primarily as a center for intellectual activity. Scholarly endeavor would produce insights that could then be used to develop the body of law of interest to the Society. There would be practical benefits for international relations, but they would often be the indirect products of excellent scholarship.

Hargrove's approach may have been partly a bow to reality in an era when U.S. decision-makers had little faith in international law as a desirable ordering mechanism. When direct impact on decision-making is likely to be slight, it would make sense to concentrate on more scholarly, less worldly, activities. But it would be too harsh to suggest that Hargrove merely took refuge in scholarship during a time of governmental apostasy. He had shown, before he became Executive Director, a commitment to scholarship and to the life of the mind. There is no indication that his commitment to intellectual excellence was born of expediency.

C. A REORGANIZED STUDENT ASSOCIATION

1. The New Structure

On November 6, 1987, the Association of Student International Law Societies (A.S.I.L.S.) formally became the International Law Students Association (I.L.S.A.), with the adoption of a new constitution. A.S.I.L.S. had been an association of student associations; I.L.S.A., on the other hand, established parallel memberships for individual students and for student associations. The benefit to I.L.S.A. from individual memberships was direct contact with the students it was designed to serve.[148] The benefit to the Society was perceived to be the identification of a pool of potential student members.[149] Like A.S.I.L.S., I.L.S.A. was an unincorporated association with its own officers and Executive Director. Later, it would incorporate.

---

[147] Report of the Executive Director, 86 *ASIL Proc.* 648, 649 (1992), reprinted in *ASIL Newsletter*, Apr.–June 1992, at 5, 6.

[148] Annual Report of the ILSA Executive Director, 82 *ASIL Proc.* 627 (1988).

[149] Report of the [ASIL] Executive Director for Executive Council meeting of Apr. 20, 1988, in ASIL Notebook of Executive Council Minutes, Apr. 1982–Nov. 1990.

I.L.S.A. reorganized the Jessup Competition. It eliminated the separate national and international divisions that had existed since 1972. In place of the two divisions was a single international competition featuring teams from around the world, including the United States.

I.L.S.A. soon began to formalize what had theretofore been a strictly informal support group, the Friends of the Jessup.[150] The Friends, composed largely of former Jessup Competition participants, would raise funds for the competition and would serve in an advisory capacity. The first meeting of the Friends took place on April 21, 1988.[151]

2. New Programs and Products

In 1987-88, the Benjamin N. Cardozo School of Law of Yeshiva University was in its fourth year of editing and producing what was by then called the *ILSA Journal of International Law*, a continuation of the A.S.I.L.S. *International Law Journal*. Cardozo wanted to take it on permanently, but representatives of other schools objected. I.L.S.A. decided to have individual schools host the Journal for five years at a time, with Cardozo continuing for the time being.[152] In the event, Cardozo edited and produced the Journal through to Volume XIV (1990). After a year's hiatus, the City University of New York School of Law took it over with Volume XV in 1992.

I.L.S.A. developed a video lecture series in 1987-88. One of the videotapes was of the 1987 Jessup World Championship Round. Another was a lecture by Alfred Rubin, "Introduction to the Theory of Public International Law." A third was on I.L.S.A. and its programs.[153]

During this period I.L.S.A. also published *The ILSA Guide to Education and Career Development in International Law*, organized regional conferences, and inaugurated an exchange program with the European Law Students Association. Under the exchange program, American law students could work in a European law firm for part of a summer in exchange for placing a European law student with a firm in the United States.[154]

150 Annual Report, *supra* note 148, at 631.

151 The Friends' first fund-raising effort netted approximately USD 1,900 for the ILSA/Jessup 1988 fiscal year. Report of the [ILSA] Executive Director to the [ASIL] Executive Council for the meeting of Oct. 15, 1988, in briefing book for that meeting.

152 Annual Report, *supra* note 148, at 633.

153 Id. at 634.

154 *Ford Foundation Evaluation, supra* note 3, at 30.

3. The A.S.I.L.–I.L.S.A. Relationship

In the mid-eighties the Executive Directorship of the student association became a two-year post – an arrangement that became formalized when I.L.S.A. was created in 1987. I.L.S.A.'s quarters in Tillar House were consolidated on the top floor, where I.L.S.A. shared space with a great many Society files. Pamela Young, the assistant to the I.L.S.A. Executive Director, began giving full time to I.L.S.A. rather than sharing her time with the Society.

In 1989 the United States Information Agency, which had been supplying an annual grant to defray travel expenses of Jessup Competition teams from developing countries, decided at the last minute to discontinue the practice. This put I.L.S.A. in a bind and posed a dilemma for the Society, which had been an unofficial guarantor of the Competition in the sense that it absorbed any I.L.S.A. deficit at the end of its fiscal year. The Society was having severe budget problems of its own, and could not afford to "guarantee" the travel expenses of Jessup teams from developing countries.[155] Nor were the relatively modest funds raised by the Friends of the Jessup adequate for this purpose. The difficulty continued until 1991, when the Ford Foundation provided a USD 50,000 grant for travel of developing-country teams.[156] Ford declined to renew the grant in 1992, but the competition received contributions of USD 20,000 from Mead Data Central and USD 10,000 from the American Bar Association Section of Litigation.[157]

Throughout the life of A.S.I.L.S./I.L.S.A., there have been intermittent tensions with the Society. In the late 1980s and early 1990s, friction grew out of the Society's accounting practice of charging overhead to I.L.S.A. for its use of space and services in Tillar House.[158] This practice was not well documented, and gave rise to misunderstandings on both sides. Ultimately, as will appear in Chapter Twelve below, a Memorandum of Understanding was concluded, but even that did not resolve the tensions.

---

155 Report of the [ASIL] Executive Director, *ASIL Newsletter*, Mar.–May 1990, at 1, 6.

156 Report of the [ASIL] Executive Director, *ASIL Newsletter*, Apr./May 1991, at 1, 6, and in 85 *ASIL Proc.* 585, 588 (1991).

157 Report of the [ILSA] Executive Director for the ASIL Executive Council meeting of Apr. 1, 1992, in briefing book for Apr. 1992 Executive Council meetings.

158 If ILSA wound up with a deficit for an accounting year, the Society would absorb the overhead. Report of Ad Hoc Committee on ASIL/ILSA Relationship, Oct. 22, 1993, at 2.

D. THE JOURNAL UNDER TOM FRANCK

1. Eligibility for Election to the Board of Editors

In 1985, the Committee on Tenure of the Board of Editors, chaired by Richard Lillich, articulated a set of principles to be followed by Board nominating committees in proposing slates of candidates. Known as the Lillich Principles, they provided:

> [T]he single most important [criterion] for initial election to the Board should be the scholarship of the candidate, as demonstrated in his or her books, articles and other written work appearing over a reasonable period of years. The Committee believes that the Board should adhere to this approach rigorously, although scholarship being equal it might wish to consider other factors such as a candidate's area of expertise or his or her professional perspective (i.e. academic, practitioner, government official or international civil servant) or discipline (i.e. law, political science, international relations). When a member of the Board is up for reconsideration, however, his or her record of past performance of editorial duties – including prompt and thorough evaluation of assigned manuscripts, submission of scholarly contributions to the Journal and other Journal-related activities – also becomes an important factor to be taken into account.[159]

The Lillich Principles have consistently been used by Board nominating committees, albeit loosely at times.

In 1985, the Society's Regulations were amended to add the Executive Director of the Society, *ex officio*, as a twenty-fifth member of the Board of Editors.[160] In 1990, the Regulations were amended to exempt the Editor-in-Chief, the Book Review Editor and the Cases Editor from term limits on the Board.[161]

2. Honorary Editor Status

Before 1985, the Society's Regulations permitted the Executive Council to elect as Honorary Editors any present or former Board members of long service who had reached the age of sixty-five. They were voting members, but were not obligated to perform all the normal editorial functions.

---

159 Report of the Committee on the Tenure of the Board of Editors, Sept. 23, 1985, prepared for the Board of Editors meeting, Oct. 25, 1985.

160 Minutes of the Executive Council, Oct. 26, 1985, in ASIL Notebook of Executive Council Minutes, Apr. 1982–Nov. 1990.

161 Minutes of the Executive Council, Nov. 17, 1990, in ASIL Notebook of Executive Council Minutes, Apr. 1982–Nov. 1990.

Lillich's committee proposed a new Regulation making Honorary Editors non-voting members. Eligibility still began at age sixty-five, but the candidate was required to be off the board for at least a year unless he or she was then serving as the head of a department of the Journal. Honorary Editors would henceforth serve five-year terms, except that those already serving would continue to serve without term. The Council adopted the new Regulation.[162]

3. The Executive Council's Role in Electing Board Members

At the Executive Council meeting on April 7, 1989, there was a protracted discussion of the process by which candidates for the Board of Editors were nominated. According to the minutes of the meeting, "There was strong sentiment for earlier reporting of the nominees, with indication of the basis of their eligibility or qualifications, such as publication of writings in the Journal and elsewhere."[163] The Council took no action, but it had served notice – as it occasionally had before – that the Board was in some sense accountable to it.[164]

4. Corresponding Editors

In April 1987, the Board of Editors decided, after a long debate, to propose a new category of Board membership. As adopted by the Executive Council, the new Regulation provided for as many as eight non-voting Corresponding Editors who would identify important international legal developments outside the United States and who would recommend manuscripts for publication and authors for prospective articles and reviews. A Corresponding Editor would be eligible for only two consecutive four-year terms, and then would have to sit out a year.[165]

The Board's 1987-88 Nominating Committee was charged with making recommendations on the role and functions of the Corresponding Editors. Having found that deep divisions existed among regular Board members as to what the role and functions should be, the Nominating Committee recommended against electing Corresponding Editors at that time.[166] There the matter rested.

---

[162] 79 *ASIL Proc.* 404 (1985); Minutes of the Executive Council, Apr. 24, 1985, in ASIL Notebook of Executive Council Minutes, Apr. 1982–Nov. 1990.

[163] Minutes of the Executive Council, Apr. 7, 1989, in ASIL Notebook of Executive Council Minutes, Apr. 1982–Nov. 1990.

[164] For changes in Board membership during this period, see Memorandum, "ASIL History: The Journal, Its Editors and Business Practices," on file with the Society.

[165] Minutes of the Executive Council, Apr. 10, 1987, in ASIL Notebook of Executive Council Minutes, Apr. 1982–Nov. 1990; Regulations of the Society, Sec. V.1(d)(7), 81 *ASIL Proc.* 632, 638-39 (1987).

[166] Report to the Board of Editors by the Nominating Committee, Mar. 16, 1988, in briefing book for Apr. 1988 Executive Council meetings.

No Corresponding Editors were ever elected, and the category was ultimately abolished.

5. Agora

Soon after Tom Franck took over as Editor-in-Chief, he brought a new department to the Journal. The first Agora – a marketplace of ideas – appeared in the January 1985 issue. It focused on the *Tel-Oren* case, in which a panel of the District of Columbia Circuit held that federal subject matter jurisdiction was lacking in an action brought by Israeli survivors and representatives of persons murdered in an attack on a bus in Israel.[167] The plaintiffs had asserted jurisdiction under (*inter alia*) the Alien Tort Claims Act, which gives federal courts jurisdiction over actions by aliens alleging torts committed in violation of the law of nations.[168] All three judges wrote opinions, agreeing as to the result but disagreeing as to the reasons for it. In the Agora, Anthony D'Amato criticized Judge Robert Bork's narrow reading of the Act as a misunderstanding of the law of nations as of 1789, when the Alien Tort Claims Act was enacted.[169] Alfred Rubin criticized D'Amato's grasp of history, and D'Amato replied.[170]

For the remainder of Franck's tenure as Editor-in-Chief (and beyond), Agora appeared whenever a current topic seemed to warrant the succinct presentation of divergent scholarly views.

6. Foreign Affairs and the Constitution

To commemorate the bicentennial of the United States Constitution, the Journal published a special issue in October 1989 on *The United States Constitution in its Third Century: Foreign Affairs*. Edited by Louis Henkin, Michael Glennon and William D. Rogers, it featured articles by twenty-one authors on such topics as constitutional history, separation of powers, judicial deference in the foreign affairs field, federalism, substantive human rights and U.S. law enforcement

---

[167] *Tel-Oren v. Libyan Arab Republic*, 726 F.2d 774 (D.C. Cir. 1984). The Agora, "What Does Tel-Oren Tell Lawyers?," appeared in 79 *AJIL* 92 (1985).

[168] 28 U.S.C. §1350.

[169] Anthony D'Amato, "Judge Bork's Concept of the Law of Nations Is Seriously Mistaken," 79 *AJIL* 92 (1985).

[170] Alfred P. Rubin, "Professor D'Amato's Concept of American Jurisdiction Is Seriously Mistaken," 79 *AJIL* 105 (1985); Anthony D'Amato, "Professor Rubin's Reply Does Not Live up to Its Title," id. at 112.

abroad.[171] It was, as Henkin remarked, "a fresh look at old dogma."[172] Unlike some non-Society collective efforts on the same theme at about the same time, it presented a variety of viewpoints on the issues.[173] In 1990 the special issue was republished, with the addition of several appendices, as a book, *Foreign Affairs and the U.S. Constitution*.[174]

7. Analyzing the Legal Issues of the Day

The World Court's denial of El Salvador's request to intervene in *Nicaragua v. United States* sparked a particularly perceptive lead article by Christine Chinkin in 1986. Chinkin used that case as a springboard to examine the whole range of issues surrounding intervention in I.C.J. proceedings.[175]

The Court's judgment on the merits in *Nicaragua* generated an outpouring of views in the Journal on topics ranging from evidentiary questions to general appraisals of the judgment, including appraisals of the Court's use of customary international law.[176] The rekindled interest in the I.C.J. spawned other articles as well.[177]

---

171 Symposium, "The United States Constitution in its Third Century: Foreign Affairs," 83 *AJIL* 713-900 (1989).

172 Louis Henkin, "The Constitution for Its Third Century: Foreign Affairs," in id. at 713, 716.

173 Compare the Introduction to David Gray Adler & Larry N. George (eds.), *The Constitution and the Conduct of American Foreign Policy* 1, 6 (1996): "The thesis of the [Adler & George] book is simple: unilateral presidential control of U.S. foreign relations poses a grave threat to our democratic society and is without constitutional warrant."

174 Louis Henkin, Michael J. Glennon & William D. Rogers (eds.), *Foreign Affairs and the U.S. Constitution* (1990).

175 Christine M. Chinkin, "Third-Party Intervention before the International Court of Justice," 80 *AJIL* 495 (1986).

176 Keith Highet, "Evidence, the Court, and the *Nicaragua* Case," 81 *AJIL* 1 (1987); Appraisals [by 16 scholars] of the ICJ's Decision: *Nicaragua v. United States* (Merits), id. at 77.

177 Lead articles: Gary L. Scott & Craig L. Carr, "The ICJ and Compulsory Jurisdiction: The Case for Closing the Clause," 81 *AJIL* 57 (1987); Stephen M. Schwebel, "Ad Hoc Chambers of the International Court of Justice," id. at 831; Jonathan I. Charney, "Compromissory Clauses and the Jurisdiction of the International Court of Justice," id. at 855; Roberto Ago, "'Binding' Advisory Opinions of the International Court of Justice," 85 *AJIL* 439 (1991). Editorial Comments: W. Michael Reisman, "Has the International Court Exceeded its Jurisdiction?," 80 *AJIL* 128 (1986); Anthony D'Amato, "The United States Should Accept, by a New Declaration, the General Compulsory Jurisdiction of the World Court," id. at 331; W. Michael Reisman, "Respecting One's Own Jurisprudence: A Plea to the International Court of Justice," 83 *AJIL* 312 (1989); Keith Highet, "The Peace Palace Heats Up: The World Court in Business Again?," 85 *AJIL* 646 (1991); Thomas M. Franck, "The 'Powers of Appreciation': Who Is the Ultimate Guardian of UN Legality?," 86 *AJIL* 519 (1992).

Legal issues raised by current events were frequently vetted in Agora. During this period, Agora appeared on the downing of Iran Air Flight 655 by a missile from the U.S.S. *Vincennes* in the Persian Gulf,[178] the U.S. incursion into Panama and the capture of General Manuel Noriega,[179] the crisis that led to the 1991 Persian Gulf War,[180] and international kidnaping of the sort that produced the *Alvarez-Machain* case in the U.S. Supreme Court.[181] But a catastrophic terrorist attack – the planting of a bomb on Pan American flight 103 that brought the aircraft down over Lockerbie, Scotland in December 1988 – did not lead to an Agora.[182]

Writings on the Persian Gulf crisis and on kidnaping were not confined to Agora. Oscar Schachter provided a U.N. Charter analysis of the Persian Gulf crisis,[183] and Andreas Lowenfeld wrote a series of pieces on kidnaping.[184]

Other pathbreaking articles in the Journal included one on feminist approaches to international law,[185] one on the emerging right to democratic governance,[186] and one ready-made for international lawyers with a Shakespearean bent, on *Henry the Fifth* and the law of war.[187]

---

178 Agora: "The Downing of Iran Air Flight 655," 83 *AJIL* 318-41 (1989).

179 Agora: "U.S. Forces in Panama: Defenders, Aggressors or Human Rights Activists?," 84 *AJIL* 494-524 (1990).

180 Agora: "The Gulf Crisis in International and Foreign Relations Law," 85 *AJIL* 63-109 (1991), and id. at 506-35.

181 Agora: "International Kidnaping," 86 *AJIL* 736-56 (1992). See *United States v. Alvarez-Machain*, 504 U.S. 655 (1992).

182 Journal discussions stemming from the Lockerbie incident dealt with the ICJ's decision not to grant interim measures of protection in the proceedings brought by Libya against the United States and United Kingdom, and focused on the relationship between the ICJ and the UN. See Thomas W. Franck, "The 'Powers of Appreciation': Who Is the Ultimate Guardian of UN Legality?," 86 *AJIL* 519 (1992); W. Michael Reisman, "The Constitutional Crisis in the United Nations," 87 *AJIL* 83, 86-96 (1993).

183 Oscar Schachter, "United Nations Law in the Gulf Conflict," 85 *AJIL* 452 (1991).

184 Andreas F. Lowenfeld, "U.S. Law Enforcement Abroad: The Constitution and International Law," 83 *AJIL* 880 (1989); Lowenfeld, "U.S. Law Enforcement Abroad: The Constitution and International Law, Continued," 84 *AJIL* 444 (1990); Lowenfeld, "Kidnaping by Government Order: A Follow-Up," id. at 712; Lowenfeld, "Still More on Kidnaping," 85 *AJIL* 655 (1991).

185 Hilary Charlesworth, Christine Chinkin & Shelley Wright, "Feminist Approaches to International Law," 85 *AJIL* 613 (1991).

186 Thomas M. Franck, "The Emerging Right to Democratic Governance," 86 *AJIL* 46 (1992).

187 Theodor Meron, "Shakespeare's Henry the Fifth and the Law of War," 86 *AJIL* 1 (1992).

8. Unsolicited Book Reviews

On at least two occasions in 1991, the Journal received unsolicited book reviews. Detlev Vagts, then the Book Review Editor, notified the reviewers that the Journal did not accept reviews it did not solicit.[188] This was a continuation of a policy dating back to Leo Gross' tenure as Book Review Editor.

Three reasons were given for the policy. First, an unsolicited review was likely to come from someone linked to the author. Secondly, such a review would lack any input from the Book Review department about content and style. Finally, when space in the Journal for reviews was scarce (as it has been in recent times), it would be unfair to solicited reviewers to crowd out their work in favor of unsolicited contributions.[189]

9. The Journal Goes Online

In the spring of 1990, the Journal went online in Lexis.[190] Coverage began with 1980.[191] Westlaw followed suit in December 1991, with coverage made retroactive to 1982.[192]

E. AN EXTERNAL EVALUATION OF THE SOCIETY

In 1991-92 the Ford Foundation conducted a comprehensive evaluation of the Society and its various programs. The Foundation, of course, was the primary vehicle for the Society's emergence in the Merillat years into a multifaceted operation featuring a wide range of research, publications, consultations and public programs in addition to its traditional emphasis on the Annual Meeting and the Journal. The Society hoped to continue the relationship with the Foundation, so there was good reason to cooperate fully with its evaluation effort – the more so, since the Foundation was comparing the Society with other providers of international law research and programs, including other non-governmental organizations, universities and individuals.[193]

The Foundation's three-member evaluation team had high praise for the Society's traditional programs and activities, particularly the Annual Meeting, I.L.M. and

188 Letters from Detlev Vagts to reviewers, May 6, 1991, & June 4, 1991.

189 Letter from Detlev Vagts, June 4, 1991.

190 *ASIL Newsletter*, Sept.–Oct. 1990, at 7.

191 Lexis/Nexis Library Contents, at 9 (1994).

192 *ASIL Newsletter*, Jan./Feb. 1992, at 1.

193 Memorandum from Peter D. Trooboff to ASIL Executive Council, Apr. 8, 1991, in brfiefing book for Apr. 1991 Executive Council meetings.

the Journal.[194] "ILM," it said, "is the sole effective and timely dissemination of relevant international law documents; it is used by academics, practitioners, government officials and non-U.S. nationals alike. The AJIL is the best periodic, concentrated compilation of articles and views of international law."[195]

The team was less enthusiastic about the Society's effectiveness in influencing public policy. For example, it cited with approval the reports of the Society's Committee on United Nations Relations on the obligatory character of assessments under the U.N. Charter and on the U.S. threat to withhold dues if Palestine were admitted to membership in specialized agencies, but "there is little evidence in this instance that the Committee's work had any impact on policy. The initial attempt at dissemination of its work was paralyzed by the lack of follow-up to determine if either report had been read and considered by Congressional staff or Executive Branch personnel or if the appropriate NGOs (e.g., the Washington office of the UNA-USA) had received and used the report in their public education efforts."[196]

The team complimented the Society on its role in promoting and supporting the Jessup Competition, which it said "is a renowned international law moot court that gives students from many places the opportunity to interact, compete, and excel."[197] The Society, though, had "almost totally ignored all other student activities." Student leaders were not integrated into any aspects of the Society's activities other than the Jessup.[198]

The Society received low marks for interdisciplinary activities, though the team understood the difficulties of mounting effective interdisciplinary programs in a scholarly world of ever-narrowing specialties. The team observed that until about twenty years earlier, legal scholars could be found in most major political science departments; not so any more. Persons in such disciplines as political science "felt little involvement with international law, or indeed that they were welcomed as peers within that discipline."[199]

The team played down the criticism often heard from some practitioners that the Society is too theoretical to be of much use to them. The Society was praised for making a special effort to keep its agenda relevant to the practicing bar, in particular through the creation of interest groups that focused on private

194 *Ford Foundation Evaluation*, *supra* note 3, at 11-12, 27-28, 49.

195 Id. at 49.

196 Id. at 26.

197 Id. at 49.

198 Id. at 31-32.

199 Id. at 34.

international law issues. The team pointed out that the private bar represented a real membership opportunity for the Society.[200]

Government employees were seen both as a constituency the Society serves and as a resource for the Society. As a resource, they sometimes provide "inside" information not otherwise readily available to Society members. The team urged the Society to reach out more to officials – not necessarily lawyers – at high levels of government, to ensure that the Society's work could affect policy making.[201]

The team took the Society to task for failing to put its message about the importance of international law across to the general public. To disseminate complex ideas to the public, effective interpreters or popular publications would be needed, yet the Society had chosen not to pursue these avenues. It had no ready and willing media-friendly expositors on call, nor was there any periodical aimed at general readers. A more pro-active role in courting the media could well be taken, if not by the Society, then by some organization like it.[202] These, of course, were trenchant criticisms of a Society that had once displayed an almost-messianic zeal for educating the public about the role of international law in peaceful dispute settlement.

The Society was praised for serving its foreign members, primarily through the Journal and I.L.M. Team members thought, though, that the Society could do more for and with third world constituencies. More third world scholars could be represented in the pages of the Journal or could be panelists at Annual Meetings; joint meetings could be held in third world countries, and steps could be taken to ensure more third world participation in the Jessup Competition. Raising funds for these steps was recognized as a problem.[203]

The team's principal recommendation was that the Society undertake a serious outreach program, directed at such groups as policy-makers and media, in order to make international law more relevant to decision makers and the public. Several steps were suggested:

- The A.S.I.L. could focus on and interact more often with policy makers, whether in study groups, visits, testimony, or written communication.
- Media could be targeted with a view to having international law discussed more often when foreign affairs is a media topic. Such an effort would involve far more than the passive role of having a list of experts available if the media should ask.

---

200 Id. at 36.

201 Id. at 37-38.

202 Id. at 38-41.

203 Id. at 42-43.

- A.S.I.L. consideration of subject matter would have to be timely. A.S.I.L. staff would need to forecast tomorrow's important issues.
- A.S.I.L. output would need to be re-packaged. Thirty-page pamphlets on relevant and discrete issues addressed to non-international lawyers would supplement larger tomes on more general subjects. The output would not merely be published or distributed; the A.S.I.L. rather would be active in inducing its serious consideration.
- Society members and participants would be far more interdisciplinary and non-lawyers would play a greater role. For example, media/public affairs members could help with content but play the primary role in packaging. To attract non-lawyers as members, the Society would need to provide a reason to join, for example by a real sharing of the agenda.
- The Society would devote efforts to teaching persons who are not international law scholars or students. Suggestions included conducting a course at the Foreign Service Institute for foreign service officers or at the National Center for judges.
- The Society would devote more efforts to building and maintaining capacity, both among younger scholars and students in the United States, and among scholars, practitioners, and legal advisors abroad, particularly in the third world.[204]

As will be seen in the next chapter, the Society's officers and staff took many of these recommendations to heart. In fact, the incoming President, Louis Henkin, and Executive Director, Barry Carter, made outreach their first priority.[205] They came up with a wide-ranging program designed to bring international law home to policy makers, judges and the public. The timing was propitious, given such prominent international events of the day as the dissolution of the Soviet Union, the end of the Cold War, the emergence of new states, the 1991 Persian Gulf War, and the re-emergence of a host of humanitarian law issues extending well beyond the Gulf War.

---

204 Id. at 50-51.

205 *ASIL Newsletters*, Jan./Feb. 1992, at 1, & Apr.–June 1992, at 1, 2, 4.

Chapter Twelve

AN EXTERNAL FOCUS AT THE END OF THE COLD WAR

"International law is no longer, if it ever was, a peripheral body of law, practiced by an exclusive group of lawyers and visually personified by the International Court of Justice and the Untied Nations. International law is now pervasive and central to what happens internationally, nationally and even locally."

—Edith Brown Weiss
Address, 88 *ASIL Proceedings* 382 (1994)

A. AN ENERGETIC TANDEM IN CHARGE

1. An Outspoken President

In his first column for the Newsletter as President in 1992, Louis Henkin asserted that "The principal challenge and the principal opportunity for the Society lie in a major new program to help *make international law more relevant, more material – to help to assure that governments and peoples take international law seriously.*"[1] Echoes of Elihu Root could be heard in that statement. It was not quite the way Root would have put it, but the message was essentially the same. The Society should be true to one of the purposes its constitution proclaimed: "to promote the establishment and maintenance of international relations on the basis of law and justice."[2]

In his second column for the Newsletter, Henkin took on the U.S. Supreme Court. In the *Alvarez-Machain* case,[3] Henkin said, "the U.S. Supreme Court had one of its infrequent opportunities to take international law seriously and to assure that the Executive Branch takes international law seriously. The Supreme

---

1 Notes from Incoming President Louis Henkin, *ASIL Newsletter*, Apr.–June 1992, at 1, 2 (emphasis in the original).

2 Constitution of The American Society of International Law, Art. II, in 87 *ASIL Proc.* 622 (1993).

3 *United States v. Alvarez-Machain*, 504 U.S. 655 (1992).

Court failed."[4] In *Alvarez-Machain*, the Supreme Court found no violation of the U.S.–Mexican extradition treaty when U.S. agents kidnaped a Mexican citizen in Mexico and brought him to the United States for trial on criminal charges. Nor did the Supreme Court take note of any relevant customary international law – not even the well-known passage from the World Court's judgment in the *Lotus* case: "[T]he first and foremost restriction imposed by international law upon a State is that – failing the existence of a permissive rule to the contrary – it may not exercise its power in any form in the territory of another State."[5]

Henkin went beyond criticizing the Supreme Court. "The larger, longer question," he said, "is whether the Government of the United States – all branches – is prepared to commit itself to taking international law seriously."[6] That became the recurring theme of his two-year tenure as President of the Society. It was a theme destined to endure into later presidencies as well.

Henkin had some personal opportunities in this regard. He testified before the Senate Foreign Relations Committee in 1992 on international and constitutional law issues arising out of Chapter VII of the U.N. Charter, asserting (*inter alia*) that because Security Council decisions – as distinguished from recommendations or authorizations – under Chapter VII are binding on the United States, the U.S. President has a constitutional duty and authority to carry them out.[7] Henkin also wrote an open letter to incoming President Clinton urging him to dedicate his administration to the rule of law in relations between nations.[8] His hopes were dealt a blow when U.S. forces fired missiles at Iraqi intelligence headquarters in Baghdad in June 1993, claiming a right of self-defense arising out of an apparent Iraqi attempt to assassinate former President George Bush. Henkin wrote disapprovingly of reliance on flabby definitions of self-defense.[9]

In a 1993 column, Henkin took on the Supreme Court again. This time the case was *Sale v. Haitian Centers Council, Inc.*,[10] in which the Court held that the *nonrefoulement* rule in the Refugee Convention did not prohibit a state from

---

4 *ASIL Newsletter*, Aug./Sept. 1992, at 1. The Newsletter later published a rebuttal by John M. Rogers and a surrebuttal by Henkin. *ASIL Newsletter*, Jan./Feb. 1993, at 5 & 6.

5 S.S. Lotus (*Fr. v. Turk.*), 1927 *PCIJ* (ser. A) No. 10, at 18.

6 *ASIL Newsletter*, Aug./Sept. 1992, at 1, 2.

7 Arming the United Nations Security Council: Hearing on The Collective Security Participation Resolution, S.J. Res. 325 Before the Senate Comm. on Foreign Relations, 102d Cong., 2d Sess. 19 et seq. (1992). For a summary of Henkin's remarks, see *ASIL Newsletter*, Nov./Dec. 1992, at 1-2.

8 *ASIL Newsletter*, Jan./Feb. 1993, at 1-2.

9 *ASIL Newsletter*, June–Aug. 1993, at 3-4.

10 509 U.S. 155 (1993).

intercepting a refugee en route and returning him/her to the home state. Henkin called it "an eccentric, highly implausible interpretation of a treaty."[11]

2. A Vigorous Executive Director

Barry Carter, in his first meeting with the Executive Council as Executive Director, described some of his plans. He had in mind setting up a conference in collaboration with the Federal Judicial Center, on the role of international law in U.S. courts; convening a similar conference with Congressional staff members; maintaining active relations with the State Department Legal Adviser's office; and establishing vigorous contact with the news media.[12]

Henkin and Carter set out immediately to do what they could to induce Congress to take international law seriously. They met with the chair of the Senate Foreign Relations Committee and with the person likely to be the next chair of the House Foreign Affairs Committee, along with Capitol Hill staff members, to indicate the readiness of ASIL members to provide testimony, prepare briefing papers or hold oral briefings on international law issues for members of Congress and staff.[13]

Henkin and Carter did not hold out much hope that many members of Congress or their staffs would take the initiative to seek out ASIL members' views on international law. Instead, it fell to the Society to act.

3. An Ambitious Outreach Program

At the October 1992 Executive Council meeting, Carter submitted a Strategic Plan for the Society. He called it a "high energy" program, with two major components – a new study program and a comprehensive outreach program. The results of the studies were to be widely disseminated to government officials and others. Thus even the study program was conceived as a form of outreach.[14] An example was the Ford Foundation-supported interdisciplinary project examining the impact on the international trading system of differences in the regulatory

---

11 *ASIL Newsletter*, Sept./Oct. 1993, at 1, 7.

12 Minutes of the Executive Council, Apr. 1, 1992, in briefing book for Oct. 24, 1992, Executive Council meeting.

13 *ASIL Newsletter*, Aug./Sept. 1992, at 2-3.

14 A Strategic Plan for the American Society of International Law, Oct. 1992, at 4, in briefing book for Oct. 24, 1992, Executive Council meeting. See also *ASIL Newsletter*, Nov./Dec. 1992, at 8.

laws and policies of national governments.[15] It resulted in a two-volume set on fair trade and harmonization,[16] designed to be useful to policy-makers.

Another Ford Foundation-supported project formulated a human rights agenda for the post-Cold War world. The twenty-five-member working group made recommendations for the 1993 World Conference on Human Rights in Vienna.[17] The recommendations advocated strengthening the protection of a host of substantive rights, promoting national enforcement of human rights, and enhancing international enforcement mechanisms. One noteworthy recommendation called for the establishment of a special commissioner for human rights "as an independent high-level authority with a sole and specific human rights mandate."[18] It was a timely proposal. In December 1993, the United Nations General Assembly established the post of United Nations High Commissioner for Human Rights.

The explicit outreach component of the Strategic Plan elaborated on the ideas Carter had outlined at the previous Executive Council meeting. In addition to informing the three branches of government and the media, the Society would reach out to non-governmental organizations concerned with foreign relations, as well as to bar associations, the business community, the general public, schools, and constituencies in other countries.[19]

After Bill Clinton had been elected President of the United States, but before he took office, the Society held a Town Meeting attended by over 130 Society members, students and media representatives. Louis Henkin opened the meeting and Barry Carter presided. The discussion dealt with issues of concern to the incoming administration, including extraterritoriality, the U.S. role in the U.N., the desirability of a new U.S. Article 36(2) declaration accepting the World Court's jurisdiction, and the effect of customary international law on the President.[20]

On December 3, 1992, the Society held its first Tillar House briefing for the Washington area press and for embassy, government and non-governmental organization representatives. It focused on the recently published monograph, *The Movement of Persons Across Borders*, an outgrowth of the Society's Governing Rules project. Twenty-seven guests attended.[21] More briefings at various venues

---

15 *ASIL Newsletter*, Jan./Feb. 1993, at 16-17.

16 Jagdish N. Bhagwati & Robert E. Hudec (eds.), *Fair Trade and Harmonization: Prerequisites for Free Trade?* (1996).

17 *ASIL Newsletter*, Mar.–May 1993, at 12-13.

18 Id. at 13.

19 Strategic Plan, *supra* note 14, at 10-14.

20 *ASIL Newsletter*, Jan./Feb. 1993, at 10.

21 *ASIL Newsletter*, Jan./Feb.f 1993, at 12. The monograph was Louis B. Sohn & Thomas Buergenthal (eds.), *The Movement of Persons Across Borders* (ASIL Studies in Transnational Legal Order No. 23, 1992).

in Washington were held, including some on a monthly basis in 1993-1994 under the Society's Outreach Project funded by the Ford Foundation.[22]

4. A Regional Network

Part of the outreach plan contemplated a reinvigorated regional activities program. Henkin asked Burns Weston to chair the Committee on Regional Activities. Weston, working with Charlotte Ku, who was at that time the Deputy Executive Director, put together a regional outreach committee with members allocated to regions in which they resided. The regional mandate was to lead others to take international law seriously, by doing everything possible to participate in radio and television programs, writing op-ed pieces for local and regional newspapers, staging conferences that would attract the general public, and organizing regional workshops for the judiciary, secondary school administrators and instructors, politicians and media personnel.[23]

The country was initially divided into seven regions, with each to have its own network of participating Society members. The New York Regional Subcommittee was particularly active under Ruth Wedgwood's leadership. In May and June 1993, it cosponsored with the Mexican Mission to the U.N. a series of luncheon meetings for members of the General Assembly's Sixth Committee and various academics. In October of that year it co-sponsored a reception for Legal Advisers of Foreign Ministries, members of the Sixth Committee and members of the U.N. Office of Legal Affairs.[24]

The regional network was not so active outside the New York region. In the autumn of 1994 it was restructured. There were now ten regions, each with a regional center and a regional coordinator responsible for initiating communication and activity within the regional center.[25]

A noteworthy effort by a regional coordinator was a symposium in San Francisco in 1995 to commemorate the fiftieth anniversary of the U.N. Charter. Homer Angelo, the coordinator for the Northwestern Region, organized the program in cooperation with Richard Buxbaum of Boalt Hall. The Bar Association of San Francisco and the Commonwealth Club served as co-sponsors. Speakers included Senator Daniel Patrick Moynihan, David J. Scheffer, Paul C. Szasz and Oscar Schachter. Among all the fiftieth anniversary commemorative meetings in San Francisco, it was the only one devoted specifically to the rule of law.[26]

---

22 See text at note 40 *infra*.

23 Letter from Burns H. Weston to Louis Henkin, Oct. 6, 1992, in briefing book for Oct. 24, 1992, Executive Council meeting; *ASIL Newsletter*, Jan./Feb. 1993, at 9-10.

24 Tillar House Report for Executive Council meeting of Nov. 6, 1993, at 15.

25 *ASIL Newsletter*, Nov./Dec. 1994, at 11-12.

26 *ASIL Newsletter*, June–Aug. 1995, at 1, 3, 6.

Despite the efforts of the Tillar House staff and of regional coordinators, some problems remained. As the Northeast Regional Coordinator, Valerie Epps, put it, the lack of funding, staff, premises and support limited the likelihood of success for the regional network. She recommended that the network be brought into the governing structure of the Society and be given access to funds.[27] It did not happen, and the regional network lost much of its energy.

5. ECOSOC Consultative Status

In 1992 the Society applied for consultative status with the U.N. Economic and Social Council. Approval, in Category II, came in 1993.[28] Thus the Society became eligible to submit statements to the Council on international law and to nominate observers to ECOSOC-sponsored conferences, beginning with the Rio de Janeiro Conference on Environment and Development in 1992. A.S.I.L. observers were enjoined to respect the Society's practice of refraining from taking positions on policy matters, but could make remarks in their personal capacities.[29]

In 1995, the Society designated five members as its N.G.O. observers to the Fourth World Conference on Women, in Beijing. In addition, three Society-sponsored workshops were planned for the parallel N.G.O. Forum. Because of the weather and bureaucratic interference, only one of the workshops went off as planned. It played to more than fifty people in a small classroom, on the topic of human rights, nationality and the girl child.[30]

B. EDITH BROWN WEISS, CHARLOTTE KU AND THE NEW PROGRAM

1. The First Female Executive Director

Barry Carter resigned as Executive Director in July 1993, to accept a position as the Deputy Under-Secretary of Commerce for Export Administration in the new Clinton Administration. The Executive Committee approved Charlotte Ku as Acting Executive Director while a new search committee did its job.[31]

Frederic (Rick) Kirgis, who had chaired the previous search committee, was appointed to chair this one as well. The committee culled its list down to a few finalists, and ultimately recommended Charlotte Ku for the position. Her

---

27 Minutes of the ASIL North East Regional Outreach Executive Committee, Mar. 15, 1995, in briefing materials for Apr. 1995 ASIL Executive Council meetings.

28 *ASIL Newsletter*, Sept./Oct. 1993, at 21-22.

29 *ASIL Newsletter*, Mar.–May 1993, at 15-16.

30 *ASIL Newsletter*, Nov./Dec. 1995, at 18-21.

31 *ASIL Newsletter*, June–Aug. 1993, at 1.

résumé included a Ph.D. from the Fletcher School of Law and Diplomacy, where she studied under prominent Society member Leo Gross, followed by teaching stints in China and at the University of Virginia before she joined the ASIL staff. The Executive Council appointed her as the new Executive Director – the sixth overall and the first woman to hold the position – effective on January 1, 1994.[32] She was given a three-year renewable term.[33] In 1996 the Executive Council appointed her to a new four-year term (effective in 1997),[34] which was renewed for another four years in 2001.[35] Her term was later extended through the end of the Society's centennial year, 2006.[36]

2. The Second Female President

By 1993, it had become the practice to alternate academics and practitioners as successive Presidents of the Society. The 1993 Nominating Committee considered whether this practice had become a mandatory policy. It thought not, but suggested that the idea of alternation be kept alive as a guideline aimed at achieving diversity.[37]

The Nominating Committee put forward Edith Brown Weiss, of the Georgetown University Law Center, to succeed Louis Henkin as President, even though that meant succeeding one academic with another. The committee noted, though, that she had very recently served for two years in a non-academic post in the U.S. Environmental Protection Agency.[38] Her nomination was unopposed, and in 1994 she became the second woman (Alona Evans having been the first) to be elected as the President of the Society.

Among her top priorities were continuing the Society's outreach program, developing new collaborations with foreign organizations, and ensuring that the Society's research efforts were sustained and strengthened.[39] She achieved a considerable measure of success in all three areas. In the process, she nudged the Society toward participation in the electronic age by stressing the use of e-mail as a mainstream means of communication.

---

32 *ASIL Newsletter*, Nov./Dec. 1993, at 1.

33 Minutes of the Executive Committee, Feb. 18, 1994, in briefing materials for Apr. 1994 Executive Council meetings.

34 Minutes of the Executive Council, Oct. 26, 1996, at 11.

35 Minutes of the Executive Council, Apr. 4, 2001, at 1. See Chapter Thirteen, *infra*.

36 Minutes of the Executive Council, Nov. 2, 2002, at 14.

37 Memorandum from Keith Highet to Louis Henkin, Oct. 7, 1993, in briefing book for Nov. 6, 1993, Executive Council meeting.

38 Report of the Nominating Committee for the Executive Council meeting of Nov. 6, 1993, in briefing book for that meeting.

39 See, e.g., Message from the President, *ASIL Newsletter*, June–Aug. 1994, at 1, 4-5.

3. A New Ford Grant and a Structured Outreach Program

In July 1993 the Ford Foundation made a USD 150,000 grant to the Society to fund a more structured outreach program than the Society had been able to mount theretofore.[40] Its four parts were:

- A.S.I.L. Briefings, headed by Lee Kimball and held monthly in Washington, beginning in November 1993. The briefings were geared to late-breaking events or the appearance of Society-sponsored works. The aim was to educate not only the public, but also the media. The topics ranged from the World Court to trade and environment to intervention in Haiti. Although the briefings were relatively well attended by the public, usually only one or two media representatives showed up. The exception was a timely briefing on the upcoming Asia-Pacific Economic Conference in November 1993, when forty-two media representatives came to the National Press Club to hear the Deputy U.S. Trade Representative speak.[41]
- A.S.I.L. Insights, headed by Rick Kirgis. The initial Ford grant supported twelve information bulletins on the international law dimensions of current events. Four-page A.S.I.L. Insight pieces appeared as centerfolds in the Newsletter and were distributed to Capitol Hill staffers, media representatives, embassies, U.N. missions and others. In addition, shorter Flash Insights were prepared on the legal implications of late-breaking headline events. The Flash Insights were faxed to news media and others, usually within two or three days of the events.[42] Later, they were simply called Insights and were e-mailed to the designated audience and posted on the Society's web site.
- A.S.I.L. World Conference Issues Papers, headed by Michael Schechter. These papers were policy analyses prepared in advance of selected world conferences. The conferences included those on population and development, extension of the Nuclear Non-Proliferation Treaty, social development, Habitat II, and the Fourth World Conference on Women.[43]
- A Judges Seminar, headed by Barry Carter and Charles Gustafson. In March 1994, the Society joined with the Georgetown University Law Center and the Federal Judicial Center to sponsor a seminar for twenty-four federal

---

40 Tillar House Report for Executive Council meeting of Nov. 6, 1993, at 41.

41 ASIL Interim Report to Ford Foundation on its Outreach Grant, July 20, 1994, Tab D.

42 Id., Tab E. On at least one occasion, a Flash Insight was published verbatim in a Washington newspaper. *Washington Times*, June 9, 1995 (Flash Insight on punitive import duties on Japanese luxury cars).

43 ASIL Interim Report, *supra* note 41, at 2.

judges on the role of international law in U.S. courts.[44] An outgrowth was publication (with the Federal Judicial Center) of the International Judicial Observer, an insert in the *State-Federal Judicial Observer* containing information for judges on international law, on conferences relating to courts and judges around the world, and on judicial reform in various countries. Four issues were ultimately published, beginning in September 1995 and ending in June 1997. Susan Karamanian served as the Society's representative in this venture.

4. More Outreach: Publications, Radio Programs, the World Wide Web and a Video Course

The *ASIL Bulletin: Educational Resources on International Law* was inaugurated in 1994. Intended primarily for college and secondary school classroom use, the *ASIL Bulletin* included reprints of important material from the *ASIL Newsletter* (such as Presidential Notes and guides to what is online in international law) and proceedings or summaries of significant workshops (such as the roundtables on the relevance of law in international relations and on the legal framework for multilateral action, held at the 1993 and 1994 annual meetings of the American Political Science Association).[45]

In 1995, the Society received a USD 140,000 Ford Foundation grant to extend the outreach program. Using some of those funds, the Society, in conjunction with the Dean Rusk Center for International and Comparative Law at the University of Georgia and WUGA-FM, undertook to produce radio programs on international law and its effects on the individual.[46] Dorinda Dallmeyer, the project director, completed it in 1998 with the production of "The Individual in a Global Society," comprising four programs on two audio cassettes.[47] The programs were broadcast on National Public Radio stations across the country. They received awards from the State Bar of Georgia and the Society of Professional Journalists.[48]

Also included in the 1995 Ford grant was money to continue the ASIL Insight series and to extend its distribution – along with other information – by way of

---

44 Id. at 1; Report of the Executive Director, in Tillar House Report for Executive Council meeting of Nov. 5, 1994, at 4.

45 *Publications of The American Society of International Law* 13 (1995).

46 *ASIL Newsletter*, Mar.–May 1995, at 2; ASIL Proposal [to the Ford Foundation] for an International Law Communications Network (1995); Tillar House Operations Report for the Executive Council meeting of Oct. 28, 1995, at 57-58.

47 The four programs were "The Emerging System of Global Governance," "The Individual in a Global Economy: Interdependence and Power," "Responding to Individual Needs: Human Rights," and "Facilitating a Sustainable Future."

48 *ASIL Newsletter*, May–June 1999, at 10.

a new ASIL home page on the worldwide web.[49] The web site was unveiled in 1996 at the ninetieth Annual Meeting.[50] An important feature of the new home page for researchers was the ASIL Guide to Electronic Resources for International Law, inaugurated in 1997, with links to useful home pages and other electronic information in a variety of international law-related fields. The web site would soon expand and become a key element in the Society's outreach efforts.

In December 1995, the Society released a ten-part video course of instruction on international law, produced by Elizabeth Defeis, of Seton Hall University School of Law. Each program was about 30 minutes long, dealing with an aspect of basic international law.[51]

It is next to impossible to determine whether efforts such as the radio and video projects have had a significant impact, since the Society has never had the resources to do systematic follow-up work.

5. Internationalizing the Society

In 1982, when Edith Brown Weiss was a member of the Ad Hoc Committee on the Structure of the Society, she urged that the Society collaborate with comparable bodies in other countries, including arranging bilateral or regional meetings.[52] It took several years for her initiative to become reality, but in the nineties it did – even before she became President in 1994.

The second biennial joint conference with the Dutch Society of International Law was held at The Hague in July 1993. The theme was Contemporary International Law Issues: Opportunities at a Time of Momentous Change. The conference attracted 390 participants from twenty-four countries, and featured a keynote address by Sir Robert Jennings, President of the International Court of Justice.[53] Like the first joint conference, this one resulted in published proceedings.[54]

The third conference in The Hague was held in July 1995. This time the theme was Contemporary International Law Issues: Conflicts and Convergence. Clusters of panels focused on European integration, trade, investment and environment,

---

49 The Ford grant also included funds to establish an international law experts database from which to draw authors and resource persons. Tillar House Operations Report for the Executive Council meeting of Oct. 28, 1995, at 58.

50 See *ASIL Newsletter*, Mar.–May 1996, at 1. The web site address is <http://www.asil.org>. From the outset it has included information about the Society as well as outreach items.

51 *Publications of The American Society of International Law* 17 (1995).

52 See Chapter Ten, Section A.10, *supra*.

53 *ASIL Newsletters*, Mar.–May 1993, at 20, & Sept.–Oct. 1993, at 17.

54 *Contemporary International Law Issues: Opportunities at a Time of Momentous Change* (Proc. of 2d Jt. Conf., The Hague, July 22-24, 1993).

peacekeeping, human rights, dispute resolution and a fifty-year review of the U.N.[55] Again, the proceedings were published.[56]

Peter Trooboff was particularly interested in setting up a program in Japan. His idea came to fruition in July 1994 when the first trilateral symposium was held in Tokyo. In cooperation with the Japanese Society of International Law and the Canadian Council on International Law, the Society brought together scholars from Japan, Canada and the United States to discuss international law-making, with emphasis on the law of the sea and environmental law, extraterritorial application of domestic law, Japan–North American economic frictions, settlement of international disputes, and international peacekeeping.[57] The papers were published.[58]

With support from the Japan Foundation, a second trilateral symposium was held in March 1996. It began with four panels in Atlanta, Georgia, organized by Thomas Schoenbaum. The panels covered international trade and development, theoretical perspectives on compliance with international law, arms control and nonproliferation, and human rights. A final session, on non-binding norms and compliance, was held in conjunction with the ASIL Annual Meeting in Washington, D.C.[59]

In May 1995, the Society co-sponsored, with the Graduate Institute of International Studies, a one-day forum in Geneva on the implications for dispute resolution of the proliferation of international adjudicatory bodies.[60] The forum was attended by members of the International Law Commission, resident legal advisers in Geneva, and Society members in the area. The proceedings were published as an *ASIL Bulletin*.[61]

The internationalization effort extended to China and Mexico, as well. In June 1995 the Society co-sponsored a conference in Guangzhou (Canton) for young international law teachers from all parts of China. The conference focused on the fiftieth anniversary of the U.N. Charter.[62] In Mexico City, the Society co-spon-

---

55 *ASIL Newsletter*, Nov./Dec. 1995, at 16.

56 *Contemporary International Law Issues: Conflicts and Convergence* (Proc. of 3d Jt. Conf., The Hague, July 13-15, 1995).

57 *ASIL Newsletters*, Mar.–May 1994, at 13, & Sept./Oct. 1994, at 1, 6.

58 Michael K. Young & Yuji Iwasawa (eds.), *Trilateral Perspectives on International Legal Issues: Relevance of Domestic Law and Policy* (1996).

59 *ASIL Newsletter*, Jan./Feb. 1996, at 9.

60 *ASIL Newsletter*, Mar.–May 1995, at 2.

61 "Implications of the Proliferation of International Adjudicatory Bodies for Dispute Resolution" (*ASIL Bulletin* No. 9, 1995).

62 *ASIL Newsletter*, June–Aug. 1995, at 16-17.

sored a conference in June 1996 with an institute of the National Autonomous University of Mexico, on the role of international law in the Americas.[63]

6. The Goler T. Butcher Medal

Goler T. Butcher died on June 9, 1993. She was a prominent scholar, practitioner and public official in the human rights field, as well as a long-standing member of the Society. On the initiative of Henry J. Richardson, III, the Executive Council decided to honor her by striking the Goler Teal Butcher Medal for Excellence in Human Rights Law.[64] The award was funded through earmarked contributions.[65]

Henry Richardson chaired a Committee on the Butcher Medal, charged with establishing a procedure for awarding the medal and to begin raising funds for it. On the Committee's recommendation, in 1996 the Executive Council adopted an amendment to the Society's Regulations authorizing the Committee to recommend to the Council from time to time as a recipient of the medal "a distinguished person of American or other nationality as identified under the Guidelines of the Committee, for excellence in international human rights law."[66]

The Guidelines created a presumption that the medal would be awarded on the basis of a life's work or the work of a defined career or sustained period of time. In exceptional cases, though, the medal could be awarded for intense, excellent and notable work during a shorter period. It need not be awarded every year.[67]

The medal was first awarded to Thomas Buergenthal, in 1997.[68] He was cited for his life-long work in the human rights field, including his scholarship and his service as a member, Vice President and President of the Inter-American Court of Human Rights and as a member of the U.N. Human Rights Committee.

7. New Fund-raising Efforts

When Edith Brown Weiss became President in 1994, she appointed Charles N. Brower, who was then one of the Vice Presidents, to chair a Committee on Development. Brower began to devise a development plan,[69] but it did not jell

---

63 See Chapter 13, *infra*.

64 *ASIL Newsletter*, Jan./Feb. 1994, at 16.

65 Memorandum from Tillar House Staff to the Executive Committee, Nov. 5, 1993, in briefing book for Nov. 6, 1993, Executive Council meeting.

66 Minutes of the Executive Council, Mar. 27, 1996, at 3.

67 Guidelines for Awarding the Butcher Medal, Mar. 1996.

68 Minutes of the Executive Council, Apr. 9, 1997, at 9.

69 Statement from the Chair of the Committee on Development, in Report on ASIL Committees for Executive Council meeting of Nov. 5, 1994, in briefing materials for that meeting.

into a concentrated capital fund raising effort until he became President of the Society in 1996.[70]

In the meantime, the Society, in the autumn of 1995, mounted a ninetieth Anniversary Annual Giving Campaign. The funds would be used for a variety of purposes, including outreach, research, intensified membership efforts, and use of new technologies.[71] From 1996 through to 1998, annual contributions ran more than USD 25,000 above contributions recorded in 1994.[72]

8. A New Deputy Executive Director

In the spring of 1995, Jennifer L. Krieger became the Society's new Deputy Executive Director. She came to the Society from American Express, where she had been an advisor on tax and financial matters.[73] She quickly became heavily involved in budgetary and other financial aspects of the Society's work.

C. ONGOING PROGRAMS, POLICIES AND FACILITIES

1. Honorary Vice Presidents and Counsellors

In 1992 the Nominating Committee was asked to clarify the hazy role and selection criteria for Honorary Vice Presidents. The committee responded:

> [Honorary Vice Presidents] can be thought of principally in two categories. First, there are senior members who are not likely to occupy a major active post again although they are still closely connected to the Society. Second, there are those who are prospects for election to one of the higher offices at a later date, in which event they would be more useful to the Society if they had kept in touch with the Society's processes in the interim.[74]

There were twenty-seven Honorary Vice Presidents at that time. True to the Nominating Committee's word, they fit into both categories. Some were well along in years (John Hazard, Myres McDougal and Dean Rusk, for example) and others were indeed prospects for future high office (including Edith Brown

---

70 See text at note 164 *infra*.

71 *ASIL Newsletter*, Sept./Oct. 1995, at 7.

72 Summary of Operating Revenue and Expense, attached to the Report of the Budget Committee for the Executive Council meeting of Mar. 24, 1999.

73 *ASIL Newsletter*, Mar.–May 1995, at 11.

74 Minutes of the Executive Council, Apr. 1, 1992, in briefing book for Oct. 24, 1992, Executive Council meeting.

Weiss, who was to become Louis Henkin's successor as President). By tradition, they were almost always re-elected to new terms unless they were nominated for other posts.

In November 1994, the Executive Council set the number of Honorary Vice Presidents at twenty-five. It also established a new category of officers, Past Presidents of the Society.[75]

In 1997, a new Committee on Governance recommended that there be only three Honorary Vice Presidents – the three most recent past Presidents of the Society. The recommendation was incorporated into the Society's revised Constitution, and a new non-voting category, Counsellors, was created. The twenty-four elected Counsellors serve three-year, renewable terms.[76]

2. The Executive Committee and President-Elect

When Louis Henkin became President, he appointed a larger Executive Committee than had theretofore existed. In addition to seven members of the Executive Council plus the President, Treasurer and Executive Vice President, he appointed as new *ex officio* members the three Vice Presidents.[77] When Charles N. Brower became the President in 1996, he reconstituted the Executive Committee. He made the three Vice Presidents regular members, along with the President, Executive Vice President, Treasurer, Secretary and three members of the Executive Council. Under his administration, the Executive Committee met once a month and became the governing body of the Society between the semi-annual Executive Council meetings.[78]

In 1997, the Committee on Governance and the Executive Committee recommended that the Society establish the office of President-Elect. The occupant would become a member of the Executive Committee as well as the Executive Council. The Executive Council and the members at the Annual Business Meeting agreed. Because the Society's Act of Incorporation did not provide for such an office, the President-Elect formally became a "Special Vice President designated the President-Elect."[79]

---

75 Minutes of the Executive Council, Nov. 5, 1994, in briefing materials for April 1995 Executive Council meetings.

76 Constitution of the ASIL, as amended to Apr. 2, 1998, Art. VII.

77 Minutes of the Executive Council, Apr. 1, 1992, in briefing book for Oct. 24, 1992, Executive Council meeting.

78 Minutes of the Executive Council, Mar. 29, 1996, in briefing materials for Oct. 26, 1996, Executive Council meeting.

79 Constitution of the ASIL, as amended to Apr. 2, 1998, Art. IV.

3. Turnover in the Offices of Treasurer and Secretary

In 1992, James C. Conner stepped down as Treasurer, a post he had held since 1983. Stephen L. Gibson was elected as the new Treasurer, with Patricia A. Sherman as Assistant Treasurer.[80] Gibson stepped down in 1996 to devote his energies to the other major position he held as Chair of the Society's Budget Committee. Joseph Guttentag took his place as Treasurer. Nancy Perkins became the Assistant Treasurer.[81]

In 1994 Frederic L. Kirgis succeeded Michael H. Cardozo as Secretary.[82] Cardozo had served since 1978.

4. Tight Budgets, as Usual

The two-year Ford Foundation general support grant (at USD 77,000 a year) expired at the end of 1992. The Society ended that year with a small surplus. But by 1994, the Society recorded a substantial deficit, and it grew larger in 1995. Reforms were instituted, including the hiring of new auditors, Raffa and Associates, who initiated new controls and reporting procedures.[83]

5. The Omnipresent Membership Question

At the end of 1993, total membership in all categories stood at 4,429, a continuation of the gradual upward trend in the early 1990s. A membership profile based on a questionnaire indicated that law faculty continued to be the largest group of Society members, with law firm members not far behind. The Society's departure from the strong political science base it enjoyed in earlier times was implicit in the numbers: law faculty members outnumbered "other faculty" by about nine to one.[84] In an attempt to draw political scientists into the Society, an agreement was made with the American Political Science Association to offer an interdisciplinary membership in both organizations with reduced dues owed to each of them.[85]

---

80 Minutes of the Executive Council, Apr. 3, 1992, in briefing book for Oct. 24, 1992, Executive Council meeting.

81 Minutes of the Executive Council, Mar. 27 & 29, 1996, in briefing book for Oct. 26, 1996, Executive Council meeting.

82 Minutes of the Executive Council, Apr. 8, 1994, in briefing materials for Nov. 5, 1994, Executive Council meeting.

83 For details, see Memorandum, "ASIL History: Details Relating to Budget, Finances and Membership" (2006), on file with the Society.

84 "Demographic Breakdown of ASIL Members," in Tillar House Report for Executive Council meeting of Apr. 7, 1994.

85 Membership report, in Tillar House Report for Exective Council meeting of Apr. 5, 1995, at 6.

In March 1996, the Society's total membership remained roughly where it had been in 1993, at about 4,400.[86] Intermediate members (those under thirty years of age) had increased by approximately sixty-nine per cent since 1994, suggesting both the prospect of a dynamic future and the importance of measures to retain existing members.[87]

6. Reviving an Interest in the Business Community

Edith Brown Weiss and Charlotte Ku undertook to revive the Society's contacts with the corporate world. A Corporate Counsel Committee was appointed with a view to increasing corporate counsel membership and participation in the Society, and to coordinate programs of interest to corporate practitioners.

As a first step, the committee presented a panel at the 1994 Annual Meeting on International Enforcement in the Clinton Administration. The committee also collaborated with its counterpart committee of the A.B.A. Section of International Law and Practice, to present a Midwest International Law Forum in Chicago in October 1994.[88] A second Chicago forum was held in October 1995.[89]

In June 1995, the Society held its first Corporate Counsel briefing. Ellen L. Frost, Counselor to the U.S. Trade Representative, came to Tillar House to discuss current trade issues.[90] The Corporate Counsel briefings became regular events, held in Tillar House every other month for about two years.[91]

7. Re-examining the Society's Contributions to International Economic Law

In 1995 an *ad hoc* Committee on International Economic Law, chaired by Ronald A. Brand, recommended that the Society should:

- regularly seek funding for international economic law projects designed, *inter alia*, to apply interdisciplinary research and analysis to current problems in the field;

---

86 Report of the Executive Director, March 1996, in briefing materials for Mar. 1996 Executive Council meetings.

87 For further details, including a summary of the report of an ad hoc Committee on Membership in 1995, see Memorandum, "ASIL History: Details Relating to Budget, Finances and Membership" (2006), on file with the Society.

88 *ASIL Newsletter*, Sept./Oct. 1994, at 21. The Annual Meeting panel appears at 88 *ASIL Proc.* 89 (1994).

89 *ASIL Newsletter*, Sept./Oct. 1995, at 12.

90 *ASIL Newsletter*, June–Aug. 1995, at 14-15.

91 Minutes of the Executive Council, Oct. 28, 1995, at 2, in briefing materials for Mar. 1996 Executive Council meetings. The last one appears to have been in May 1997, on the Multilateral Agreement on Investment.

- seek out opportunities to cooperate with other organizations on issues of international economic law;
- present annually a program designed to influence the development of policy and practice in international economic law;
- systematically encourage submission of articles on international economic law to the Journal and other Society publications;
- establish a *Yearbook of International Economic Law*, which could be coordinated with the annual program mentioned above;
- use new technologies to disseminate information on international economic law.[92]

The committee recognized that its recommendation for a Yearbook would be controversial, and so it was. Concern was expressed that it would draw economic law submissions away from the Journal. Moreover, there were obvious budgetary implications. The recommendation went the way of many other proposals disfavored by the Society's leadership: never adopted, never defeated, and ultimately abandoned.

The specter of a Society publication on international economic law galvanized the Journal editors. They let it be known that they would welcome economic law submissions, and they accepted several for publication in 1996.[93]

8. Published Studies

Several human rights study projects came to fruition during this period. The study on U.S. ratification of the Covenants on Civil and Political Rights and on Economic, Social and Cultural Rights was published in 1993.[94] It was the result of an initial Ford Foundation grant, supplemented by a grant from the Jacob Blaustein Institute for the Advancement of Human Rights. The project had been put to one side during the Reagan administration, when U.S. ratification of the Covenants was not on the political agenda. It was revived as a multi-author effort, featuring article-by-article commentaries relating substantive rights in each Covenant to individual rights and governmental obligations already prescribed by United States law. The final product also analyzed the U.S. reserva-

92 Final Report of the Ad Hoc Committee on International Economic Law, Jan. 17, 1995, in briefing materials for Apr. 1995 Executive Council meetings.

93 See note 159 *infra*.

94 Hurst Hannum & Dana D. Fischer (eds.), *U.S. Ratification of the International Covenants on Human Rights* (1993).

tions, understandings and declarations relating to the Covenant on Civil and Political Rights.[95]

In 1994, the Society published a major human rights study on substantive rights and enforcement mechanisms, looking ahead to the next century. Supported by a Ford Foundation grant, it emanated from an ASIL conference at Airlie House in Virginia in March 1993. The conclusions and recommendations of the conference, outlining the rights that should be protected and the recommended national and international enforcement mechanisms, became part of the official preparatory documents for the 1993 World Conference on Human Rights in Vienna.[96] The papers presented at the ASIL conference provided a basis for recommendations to the U.S. delegation and to others involved in the World Conference.[97]

In 1994, the Special Representative of the U.N. Secretary General on Internally Displaced Persons, Dr. Francis Deng, requested the Society and the International Human Rights Law Group to analyze the legal standards applicable to internally displaced persons. Robert Goldman supervised the study.

In March 1995, Dr. Deng presented the draft legal analysis as part of his report to the U.N. Commission on Human Rights.[98] Eventually, with the help of Goldman and others, he submitted to the Commission a two-part "Compilation and Analysis of Legal Norms" relating to internally displaced persons.[99] The Compilation became the basis of a reference manual for the field staff of the U.N. High Commissioner for Refugees on international legal standards concerning the protection of internally displaced persons[100] – a group that did not qualify for refugee protection under then-existing law. It also became the supporting document for the non-binding, but influential, Guiding Principles on Internal Displacement – a set of thirty legal principles adopted by the U.N. system's Inter-Agency Standing Committee and designed not only to clarify existing international law, but also to fill in gaps in existing law.[101] With the approval of

---

95 Part V, by Dinah Shelton, in id. at 269. The Covenant, 999 UNTS 171, entered into force for the United States on Sept. 8, 1992.

96 See *ASIL Newsletter*, Mar.–May 1993, at 12-13, where a summary of the conclusions and recommendations is set forth.

97 Louis Henkin & John Lawrence Hargrove (eds.), *Human Rights: An Agenda for the Next Century, Foreword* (1994).

98 See U.N. Docs. E/CN.4/1995/CRP.1 & E/CN.4/1995/50/Add.3.

99 U.N. Docs. E/CN.4/1996/52/Add.2 & E/CN.4/1998/53/Add.1.

100 See Dr. Deng's 1998 report to the Commission on Human Rights, U.N. Doc. E/CN.4/1998/53, at 6-7.

101 See David A. Korn, *Exodus Within Borders: An Introduction to the Crisis of Internal Displacement* 89-91 (1999); Roberta Cohen, "A New Tool to Protect Internally Displaced Persons: 'The Guiding Principles on Internal Displacement,'" 6 *Human Rights Tribune*, No. 1, at

the Commission on Human Rights, Dr. Deng began to use the Guiding Principles in his dialogs with governments and international organizations.[102] What began as rather modest ASIL participation in an externally initiated project had led to a significant contribution to the development of articulated principles in a relatively underdeveloped area of international law.

A Society project on national treaty law and procedure was designed to produce brief comparative reports on the law and practice of fifteen countries, from ratification of treaties to their execution and termination. It grew out of conferences held in 1977 and 1979 at the Rockefeller Foundation's Villa Serbelloni in Bellagio, Italy. Representatives of fourteen countries attended the conferences, which were designed to promote greater understanding of the treaty-making processes in each other's legal and political systems. Directed by Monroe Leigh, the project produced its first series of reports in 1994, examining the law and practice of France, Germany, India, Switzerland, Thailand and the United Kingdom. Attention was given to the roles of the executive, the legislature and sub-national governmental entities in each country, and to the domestic legal status of treaties in each. The Society published the papers in its Studies in Transnational Legal Policy series.[103]

The Andrew W. Mellon Foundation awarded the Society a grant in 1993 to explore how to improve the use of specialized information and analysis for decision-making under environment/development conventions. The project, conducted by Lee A. Kimball, examined scientific and technical input into the development of international environmental conventions and the use made by those conventions of scientific and technical advice in monitoring and protecting

---

16 (1999). The Guiding Principles appear in U.N. Doc. E/CN.4/1998/53/Add.2, annex, in the Appendix to Korn's book, *supra*, and in U.N. Doc. E/CN.4/2000/53/Add.2, annex. They also appear in Roberta Cohen & Francis M. Deng, *Masses in Flight: The Global Crisis of Internal Displacement* 305 (1998), a book emanating from the project to which Goldman and the Society contributed. See also the "International Law Association's Declaration of International Law Principles on Internally Displaced Persons," 69 ILA, *Conference Report* 39-40, 794-821 (2000).

[102] See Commission on Human Rights Res. 2000/53, ¶ 6, in the Commission's Report on its 56th Sess., U.N. ECOSOC OR, 2000, Supp. No. 3, U.N. Docs. E/2000/23 & E/CN.4/2000/167, at 235, 237.

[103] Monroe Leigh & Merritt R. Blakeslee (eds.), *National Treaty Law and Practice: France, Germany, India, Switzerland, Thailand, United Kingdom* (ASIL Studies in Transnational Legal Policy No. 27, 1995). A second volume, covering Austria, Chile, Colombia, Japan, the Netherlands and the United States, appeared in 1999. A third volume, covering Canada, Egypt, Israel, Mexico, Russia and South Africa, appeared in 2003. A compendium volume appeared in 2005.

species and ecosystems. Kimball produced a report that the Society published as another in its Studies in Transnational Legal Policy.[104]

9. The Demise of the Board of Review and Development, and the Rise of the Committee on Research

Even before the 1990s the Board of Review and Development had gotten away from devising new cutting-edge projects. A principal reason was that it no longer had large sums of undesignated Ford Foundation money to administer. Rather, projects had to be geared to the specific interests at any given time of granting agencies, including the Ford Foundation. In the early 1990s the B.R.D. met only once a year to review the status of existing projects and to consider new proposals originating outside the Board.

By 1993, it seemed to the Executive Committee that the B.R.D. had outlived its usefulness. Consequently the Executive Committee recommended (twice) to the Executive Council that the B.R.D. be discontinued.[105] So it came to pass, though with the recognition that the B.R.D.'s current functions would still need to be performed somehow.[106]

Edith Brown Weiss accordingly appointed a Committee on Research, initially chaired by Jonathan I. Charney and Anne-Marie Slaughter. The Committee's primary objective was to generate and refine research ideas on the forefront of international law, to be carried out under Society auspices. The hope was that the projects would attract funding.[107] Unlike the B.R.D., the committee would not formally pass on proposed research projects.[108]

The Committee sought research ideas from the Society membership. It received several proposals, and recommended some of them for prompt support by the Society. Only one of them reached full fruition: a multidisciplinary project on non-binding norms. Under the initial guidance of Edith Brown Weiss, the project explored norms in the areas of environment, arms control, human rights, and trade and finance, including the degree of compliance with the norms. The Society received a Ford Foundation grant of about USD 170,000 for the project, supplemented by funding from the National Science Foundation for a workshop in May 1996 on global change and compliance with legally

---

104 Tillar House Operations Report for Executive Council meeting of Oct. 28, 1995, at 58-60; Lee A. Kimball, *Treaty Implementation: Scientific and Technical Advice Enters a New Stage* (ASIL Studies in Transnational Legal Policy No. 28, 1996).

105 Memorandum from Louis Henkin to Members of the Executive Council, Nov. 6, 1993, in briefing book for Executive Council meeting of that date.

106 Minutes of the Executive Council, Nov. 6, 1993, at 6-7.

107 Statement from the Co-Chairs, in Report on ASIL Committees for the Executive Council meeting of Nov. 5, 1994, in briefing materials for that meeting.

108 Minutes of the Executive Council, Nov. 5, 1994, at 7.

non-binding instruments.[109] The papers presented at the workshop, emphasizing compliance with environmental instruments, were published in the Society's Studies in Transnational Legal Policy series.[110]

The larger project, directed by Dinah Shelton, came to be known as the "soft law project." It lasted three years and culminated in a ground-breaking study of compliance with non-binding norms in the international system.[111] A multinational collaborative group of twenty-seven authors – political scientists, legal scholars, lawyers in public and private practice, and an economist – contributed to the final product.

10. Interest Groups, New and Old

With the addition of new groups on arms control, the status of minorities, and international criminal law, the Society had eighteen interest groups by October 1992. The Young Members Interest Group was established in 1993. By October 1995 there were twenty-one interest groups.[112]

Several of the groups produced newsletters or even books, such as the study by the Women in International Law Interest Group (WILIG) on women and international law.[113] The WILIG study presented cutting-edge feminist analyses of international law, and went on to examine the disintegrating line between public (governmental) and private (domestic) acts against women. Public acts, but not private acts, traditionally had been regarded as appropriate subjects of international regulation, but that legal dichotomy was fading away. The study culminated with four chapters on feminist approaches to war and peace.

Interest groups sponsored a variety of programs at the Annual Meetings and elsewhere, such as a workshop on teaching international environmental law presented at McGill University in the autumn of 1992 by the International Environmental Law Interest Group,[114] a workshop on interdisciplinary approaches

---

109 Tillar House Operations Report for Executive Council meeting of Oct. 28, 1995, at 57; Minutes of the Executive Council, Mar. 27, 1996, at 2; *ASIL Newsletter*, June–Aug. 1996, at 11.

110 Edith Brown Weiss (ed.), *International Compliance with Nonbinding Accords* (ASIL Studies in Transnational Legal Policy No. 29, 1998).

111 Dinah Shelton (ed.), *Commitment and Compliance: The Role of Non-Binding Norms in the International Legal System* (Oxford Univ. Press, 2000).

112 Report of the Executive Director for the Executive Council meeting of Oct. 28, 1995, in Tillar House Operations Report for that meeting, at 1. A brief history of each interest group appears in Report on Interest Groups, in id. at 15-17.

113 Dorinda G. Dallmeyer (ed.), *Reconceiving Reality: Women and International Law* (ASIL Studies in Transnational Legal Policy No. 25, 1993).

114 Charlotte Ku, Report on Interest Groups prepared for Executive Council meeting of Oct. 24, 1992, in briefing book for that meeting.

to international economic law and a conference on institutions for international economic integration sponsored by the International Economic Law Interest Group in February 1994 and May 1996, respectively,[115] and a series of breakfasts sponsored by WILIG honoring prominent women in the international law field.[116] The Young Members Interest Group sponsored presentations on pursuing careers in private and public international law.[117] The International Economic Law Interest Group established a discussion forum on the Internet.[118]

With interest groups proliferating, revised Administrative Guidelines for Interest Groups were prepared in June 1992. The objective was to encourage formation of Interest Groups, subject to safeguards designed to ensure that there was a viable core of members in each group, there would be no significant overlap with any pre-existing interest group, and no group would outlive its usefulness.[119]

In 1992, the practice began of regularly allowing interest groups to organize panels at Annual Meetings. During each of the next four Annual Meetings, interest groups presented four panels or workshops.[120]

---

[115] Report of International Ecoonomic Law Interest Group for Executive Council meeting of Apr. 7, 1994, in briefing materials for that meeting; *ASIL Newsletter*, Jan./Feb. 1996, at 10.

[116] Minutes of the Executive Council, Nov. 6, 1993, in briefing materials for Apr. 1994 Executive Council meetings.

[117] *ASIL Newsletter*, Sept./Oct. 1995, at 19.

[118] *ASIL Newsletter*, Mar.–May 1995, at 23. The discussion group was called ASILIELG.

[119] Applications to form interest groups could be made by letter from any two or more Society members, outlining such things as the topics to be studied and the estimated number of members who might join. The Executive Director could preliminarily approve an interest group, subject to final approval by the Executive Council, if it were determined that at least twenty Society members were likely to join and there was no significant overlap with any pre-existing interest group. Any Society member could join by paying the interest group's dues. Each group needed a chair, who would prepare an annual report on the group's activities and future plans. See Administrative Guidelines for Interest Groups, June 1992, attached to Report on Interest Groups prepared for Executive Council meeting of Oct. 24, 1992, in briefing book for that meeting. The Society imposed a flat administrative charge of 50 cents per interest group member.

[120] "The Emerging New International Legal Order in the Western Pacific," 87 *ASIL Proc.* 61 (1993), "Indigenous Peoples and the Right to Self-Determination," id. at 190, "Goals of the United Nations Decade of International Law: Law Reform and National Programs," id. at 357, and "Assessing UNCED and the State of Sustainable Development," id. at 508; "Practical Aspects of Transnational Practice," 88 *ASIL Proc.* 213 (1994); "Prosecuting and Defending Violations of Genocide and Humanitarian Law: The International Tribunal for the Former Yugoslavia," id. at 239; and "Vexing Issues of Supreme Authority and Sovereign Rights Arising from Space Activities," id. at 259; Workshop on teaching international environmental law (unpublished; see *ASIL Newsletter*, Mar.–May 1994, at 20); "The Year in Review in Private International Law," 89 *ASIL Proc.* 128 (1995), "East Asian Approaches to Human Rights," id. at 146, "The UN Decade on International Law:

11. Departures from Tradition at Annual Meetings

In the mid-1990s, Annual Meeting program committees formulated overall themes and sought to organize panels that addressed specific topics clearly falling within the themes. The 1993 Annual Meeting was organized around an overall theme, "Challenges to International Governance," and four crosscutting sub-themes, with several panels addressing various aspects of each of them.[121] Examination of each sub-theme culminated in a roundtable discussion designed to focus on common issues considered by the theme panels.

The 1994 Annual Meeting modified the previous year's intense focus on themes, but did not abandon it. There were four panels explicitly focused on the central theme, "The Transformation of Sovereignty."[122] The other panels covered a wide range of topics.

The 1995 Annual Meeting was held in New York City, with a plenary session and reception at U.N. Headquarters, to commemorate the 50th anniversary of the United Nations. The theme was "Structures of World Order." The program was sprinkled with panels on aspects of the law relating to the U.N., but there were unrelated panels as well. An innovation was a series of regional theme panels addressing issues of importance to East Asia and the Pacific, Africa, the Americas and Europe, respectively, with a wrap-up session on cross-regional comparisons.[123]

The 1996 Annual Meeting returned to Washington with the theme, "Are International Institutions Doing Their Job?". Departures from past practice included increased participation by non-U.S. nationals and more input than usual by scholars and practitioners from non-law disciplines. Women and people of color were prominently represented on the panels.

Progress and Promises," id. at 172, and "The Status of Women in the UN Organization," id. at 190; "A Look at Current Action on the Conventional Weapons Convention of 1980," 90 *ASIL Proc.* 381 (1996), "International Response to Secessionist Conflicts," id. at 296, "Violence Against Women and International Law: Rape as a War Crime," id. at 605, and "Violence Against Women and the U.S. Immigration Laws," id. at 616.

121 The crosscutting sub-themes were (i) Our Changing Sense of Community: The International Legal System Following the Bipolar World (an examination of the post-Cold War international legal environment); (ii) Communities in Transition: Autonomy, Self-Governance and Independence (consideration of issues posed by the disintegration of some states and the increased integration of others); (iii) International Regimes: Progress and Problems (asking whether the end of the cold war had facilitated the development of international regimes or had opened the way to new ideological conflicts); and (iv) The Internationalization of Domestic Law: The Shrinking *Domaine Réservé* (looking at the internationalization of such formerly domestic issues as environmental law and economic law). 87 *ASIL Proc. passim* (1993).

122 88 *ASIL Proc.* 1-87 (1994).

123 89 *ASIL Proc.* 471-562 (1995).

Harold Jacobson, in his role as chair of the wrap-up panel for the 1996 meeting, noted some of the difficulties in giving an answer to the question posed. First, international institutions have many jobs, and they are constantly changing. Moreover, many criteria could be employed to assess whether they are doing their jobs. On the whole, compared with the performance of domestic institutions, he concluded that they were not doing badly.[124] Thomas Franck concurred, but pointed out a paradox: the more international institutions succeed in performing central functions formerly the province of national governments, the less benefit minority groups in multinational states perceive from remaining as subordinate entities within those states – and thus the greater the pull toward secession with all the destabilizing effects that can have.[125]

Charlotte Ku, also a participant in the wrap-up panel in 1996, observed that many non-governmental organizations, including the A.S.I.L., are international institutions. The A.S.I.L., she said, qualifies as an epistemic community that forges links among disparate groups, provides a communications network connecting individuals across national boundaries, and serves as a channel for new ideas. She gave the Society relatively high marks for its efforts along these lines, but thought it fell short of the mark in extending the expertise of its members to those outside the organization.[126] It was an issue deigned to become a central focus of the Society in the years to come.

A theme that ran through the Proceedings for these years was the rise to prominence of international humanitarian law in the context of the horrendous conflicts in the former Yugoslavia and Rwanda. As Theodor Meron observed in 1993, "This year, for the first time, international humanitarian law (IHL) assumed an essential role in international life. Also for the first time, I believe, the UN Security Council became an important factor in the enforcement of IHL."[127] At the same meeting, before the U.N. Security Council established the International Criminal Tribunal for the former Yugoslavia, a prominent panel chaired by Cherif Bassiouni addressed the prospects and problems of just such a tribunal.[128]

In 1994, after the Yugoslav Tribunal had been created, a panel revisited its prospects and problems in light of the Tribunal's Statute.[129] Remarkably, several of the quite plausible problems identified by the panel never came to pass. For example, it was said that perhaps "no one will be prosecuted because the rules

---

[124] 90 *ASIL Proc.* 583 (1996).

[125] Id. at 596-98.

[126] Id. at 584-85.

[127] 87 *ASIL Proc.* 575 (1993). Meron later became the President of the International Criminal Tribunal for the former Yugoslavia.

[128] Id. at 20.

[129] For the Statute's provisions and the U.N. Secretariat's item-by-item commentary, see U.N. Doc. S/25704 (1993), 32 ILM 1159 (1993).

could be so difficult that their requirements cannot be met. At the other extreme, there is the possibility of a rush to justice – a kangaroo court or a railroad job. Another resulting problem would be convictions of lower echelon soldiers only, where no officers are prosecuted."[130] Experience proved otherwise.

In 1995, James Crawford expressed concern about relying in the future on *ad hoc* international criminal tribunals. The International Criminal Court had not yet been created, but efforts to establish it had long been underway. He saw such a permanent court as a distinct step up from a series of *ad hoc* tribunals.[131]

In 1996, the former Yugoslavia was again on the agenda, but not in the context of international humanitarian law. Instead, the focus was on the legal aspects of the international community's response to the breakup of the Yugoslav state. There was little applause for the roles played by international law and legal principles.[132] Rwanda was also on the agenda, with a focus on the problems and accomplishments of the Rwanda Tribunal.[133]

12. Taking Substantive Positions, Revisited

As the 1995 Business Meeting drew to a close, Endicott Peabody, the former governor of Massachusetts and a Society member, proposed that the meeting adopt a resolution approving a "proposal to form a Citizens Committee for Congressional Action to preserve and invigorate U.S. participation in the United Nations, and urges its members to join said movement."[134] Governor Peabody's proposal was animated by Congressional action withholding U.S. dues from the U.N. and limiting U.S. participation in U.N. peacekeeping.

Under the procedure in what was then Article VIII of the Society's Constitution, the proposed resolution was referred to the Executive Council. On the Council's recommendation, President Edith Brown Weiss appointed an *ad hoc* committee to examine the resolution and the broader question of adopting positions on current issues.[135]

After due deliberation, including a solicitation of views of Society members, the committee concluded that the Society should not change its general practice of refraining from taking positions on matters of policy. The committee acknowledged, though, that adherence to the traditional policy would not preclude the President of the Society from making a statement expressing concern about

---

130 Remarks of Christopher L. Blakesley, 88 *ASIL Proc.* 243 (1994).

131 89 *ASIL Proc.* 301-04 (1995).

132 90 *ASIL Proc.* 471-79 (1996).

133 Id. at 333-35.

134 89 *ASIL Proc.* 588 (1995).

135 Id.; *ASIL Newsletter*, Mar.–May 1995, at 8.

Congressional action that might jeopardize U.S. participation in the United Nations and might even jeopardize the existence of the U.N. itself.[136]

13. A New A.S.I.L.–I.L.S.A. Relationship

In 1993, the Executive Director of the International Law Students Association, Brett Lorenzen, became dissatisfied with the relationship between the Society and I.L.S.A. Although I.L.S.A. remained an unincorporated association separate from the Society, with its own officers and governing bodies, in Lorenzen's view the Society had treated I.L.S.A. essentially as a program of the Society. The Society was absorbing any I.L.S.A. deficits and keeping any I.L.S.A. net profits. Contributions to I.L.S.A. were made to the Society for I.L.S.A.'s account, because I.L.S.A. did not have its own tax-exempt 501(c)(3) status. The Society was providing accounting and other services for I.L.S.A. on what Lorenzen regarded as unfavorable terms.

Lorenzen proposed that I.L.S.A.'s financial relationship with the ASIL be put on a more formal basis with regular, agreed payments for rent and services. This would give I.L.S.A. an incentive not only to be fiscally responsible, but also to turn a profit which it could retain. The Society would benefit by no longer having to absorb I.L.S.A. deficits, and could look to I.L.S.A. for regular payments.[137]

Society President Louis Henkin appointed an *ad hoc* committee in June 1993 to examine these issues and to make recommendations for improvements in the A.S.I.L.–I.L.S.A. relationship. The committee accepted Lorenzen's premise that there should be a more formal relationship between the two organizations. After several drafts and with considerable input from Steven M. Schneebaum, representing the I.L.S.A. Board of Directors, a Memorandum of Understanding acceptable to both the Society and I.L.S.A. was hammered out.[138] I.L.S.A. by that time was incorporated, and was on the verge of obtaining its own tax-exempt 501(c)(3) status.

The Memorandum of Understanding gave I.L.S.A. rent-free space in Tillar House and use of common facilities there. I.L.S.A. promised to pay the Society an agreed share of the out-of-pocket costs incurred by the Society for operating Tillar House and for common services that could not be allocated on a fee-for-use basis. The share was based on the ratio of I.L.S.A.'s space to the Society's at Tillar House.

---

[136] Report of the Ad Hoc Committee on Society Statements on Matters of Policy, Oct. 1995, in briefing book for Oct. 28, 1995, Executive Council meeting. It was also agreed that guidelines should be developed on policy statements by interest groups.

[137] Report of the Ad Hoc Committee on ASIL/ILSA Relationship, Oct. 22, 1993, in briefing book for Nov. 6, 1993, Executive Council meeting.

[138] Memorandum of Understanding between The American Society of International Law and The International Law Students Association, Mar. 1, 1995, in ASIL files.

I.L.S.A. was given sole responsibility for administering the Jessup Competition, but agreed to cooperate with the Society in planning it. The Society would continue to be a co-sponsor, with a recognized interest in the fair and efficient administration of the competition. A joint advisory committee was established and Jennifer Krieger, the Society's new Deputy Executive Director, was named as the Society's liaison with I.L.S.A.

The Memorandum of Understanding was to run for three-year renewable terms from April 1995. The arrangement worked reasonably well for about two years, but then I.L.S.A. fell substantially behind in its payments and seemed to Society leaders to be floundering in its administration of the Jessup Competition. In 1997, the Society gave I.L.S.A. notice that it intended to renegotiate the Memorandum of Understanding. Abram Chayes was appointed as the negotiator for the ASIL. By the autumn of 1998, the negotiations had turned away from preparing a new MOU, and had focused on merging I.L.S.A. into the Society.[139] But in June 1999, Steven Schneebaum, Chair of the I.L.S.A. Board of Directors, notified Chayes that I.L.S.A. did not wish to continue negotiations toward a merger.[140] The Society Executive Committee then decided to terminate the negotiations entirely, and to give I.L.S.A. ninety days to leave Tillar House (thus providing the Society with needed space for its own operations).[141] I.L.S.A. moved out of Tillar House in the spring of 2000.[142]

14. A Workshop with the Association of American Law Schools

The Association of American Law Schools (A.A.L.S.) has long had an International Law section that includes many Society members, but there had been very little collaboration between the A.A.L.S. section and the Society until 1996. In June 1996, that state of affairs changed, temporarily at least, with the presentation of a joint A.S.I.L.–A.A.L.S. Workshop on "Integrating International and U.S. Law: Environmental and Related Problems." The workshop was designed to address both teaching and scholarship. In addition to a panel on the overall theme, there were discussions of environment and trade, pollution control, and the use of natural resources.[143]

---

139 Minutes of the ASIL Executive Committee, Aug. 5, 1998.

140 Letter from Steven M. Schneebaum to Abram Chayes, June 29, 1999, attached to the Minutes of the ASIL Executive Committee, July 14, 1999.

141 Minutes of the ASIL Executive Committee, July 14, 1999, and Nov. 19, 1999.

142 *ASIL Newsletter*, May–June 2000, at 11. ILSA moved to new quarters at 1615 New Hampshire Avenue, N.W. Washington, D.C.

143 *ASIL Newsletter*, Mar.–May 1996, at 11.

15. The Newsletter Expands

Beginning with the January/February issue in 1992, the Newsletter expanded its coverage of substantive news and opinion. By August/September 1992 it had grown to twenty pages. It remained in the range of twenty to twenty-eight pages through to 1996.

The June–August 1993 Newsletter included a four-page centerfold called "ASIL Focus" on the Yugoslavia War Crimes Tribunal, written by Diane Orentlicher. It was the precursor to the ASIL Insights that appeared as centerfolds at various times thereafter.[144]

The November/December 1992 Newsletter carried a column by Paul Zarins, "What's Online in International Law."[145] The column described online data sources that would be of interest to international lawyers and academics. Under Zarins and his successors, it became a fixture in the Newsletter for several years, providing practical information about online services and internet sites.

Another fixture began in the March–May 1995 issue, with a column by Pieter H.F. Bekker on "The World Court at Age Fifty."[146] In subsequent Newsletters, his column appeared as "Recent Developments at the World Court," keeping readers informed about current I.C.J. decisions and pending cases. Eventually his commentaries on current World Court cases became part of the Insight series and were posted on the Society's web site.

With the expansion of the Newsletter to include more substantive articles as well as such practical features as "What's Online," it became marketable even to non-members of the Society. As of September 1, 1993, it became available for subscription by non-members.[147]

16. The Library Modernizes

In the 1990s, the Tillar House library continued to expand, acquiring more than 300 books a year. Jill Watson, the librarian, began building an online catalog, plus an international law articles database (INTLEX) and a database of Society publications (ASILEX). The library also contributed to the INT-LAW discussion

---

144 The first "ASIL Insight" was by Lori Fisler Damrosch, Recent Security Council Actions Concerning Internal Conflicts: Economic Sanctions, *ASIL Newsletter*, Jan./Feb. 1994, centerfold.

145 *ASIL Newsletter*, Nov./Dec. 1992, at 11-12.

146 *ASIL Newsletter*, Mar.–May 1995, at 1.

147 By autumn 1994 the Newsletter had eighty-three paid non-member subscribers. Tillar House Report for the Executive Council Meeting of Nov. 5, 1994, at 33. By the end of 1995 the number was 109. Note 5 to 1995 and 1996 Budgets, Mar. 11, 1996, in briefing materials for Mar. 1996 Executive Council meetings.

group on the Internet, for example by providing the contents of upcoming issues of A.J.I.L. and I.L.M.[148]

With the aid of a Ford Foundation grant to the Society, the library established a worldwide web home page in 1996. It provided information about Society activities, including tables of contents of current issues of the Journal and I.L.M., as well as links to sites dealing with international law and organizations.[149] Later it expanded, serving as a guide to electronic resources in international law.

17. Tillar House Renovation

In 1994, the then-dormant Committee on Tillar House was revived. With John H. McNeill as its chair, it conducted a thorough examination of the physical facilities in Tillar House and assessed its suitability as the continuing headquarters of the Society. The facilities were clearly inadequate. The building was structurally sound, but the mechanical, electrical and communications systems were at or near the end of their useful lives. Moreover, since the building was constructed as a residence, it did not function well as an office building.

The Committee considered several options, including refurbishing Tillar House, purchasing an adjacent building as an annex, moving entirely to another building, and leasing space in an office building. The most feasible option, it found, was refurbishing Tillar House. A complete renovation would cost an estimated USD 1 million in 1995 dollars.[150]

The Executive Council was quite willing to renovate if money became available. That depended on the success of the still-nascent capital fund drive.[151]

D. THE JOURNAL IN THE EARLY NINETIES

1. Changes in Composition and Selection of Board Members

The Journal's Board of Editors has faced recurring tensions between a desire for periodic turnover on the Board and a perceived need for stability. In the early nineties it focused also on diversifying the Board's membership. In 1992, the Editor-in-Chief appointed a committee of three Board members, chaired by Edith

---

148 Report on the Library, in Tillar House Report for the Executive Council Meeting of Nov. 5, 1994, at 69.

149 *ASIL Newsletter*, Mar.–May 1996, at 1.

150 Report of the Committee on Tillar House and Other Physical Resources of the Society, in briefing materials for Oct. 28, 1995 Executive Council meeting; Minutes of the Executive Council, Oct. 28, 1995, at 8-9, in briefing materials for Mar. 1996 Executive Council meetings.

151 See Chapter Thirteen, *infra*.

Brown Weiss, to consider the optimum size of the Board, the tenure of Board members, and standards for selecting them. The committee recommended that Board members serve five-year terms, with ten years maximum consecutive service followed by at least two years off the Board. This would replace the policy of four-year terms, with twelve years maximum consecutive service followed by one year off the Board. There would be twenty-five regular Board members, rather than twenty-four. The Editor-in-Chief and Editors in charge of major Journal departments would be exempt from the ten-year rule. In the committee's view, these changes would increase the rate of turnover without jeopardizing stability or quality.

As for criteria for nomination to the Board, the committee recommended that the Lillich principles, stressing scholarship, be retained. The committee thought, though, that there should be somewhat greater emphasis on intellectual diversity than had been the case in the past.

Former Board members who had reached the age of sixty-five and who had served at least ten years could be elected as (non-voting) honorary members. As in the past, regular and honorary members would be elected by the Society's Executive Council upon the recommendation of the Board itself.[152]

The Board of Editors unanimously adopted the committee's report, as did the Society's Executive Council at its October 1992 meeting.[153] The Society's Regulations were amended accordingly.[154] From 1993 through to 1996, eight new Board members were elected. Three of them were women.[155]

2. Co-Editors-in-Chief, Again

Tom Franck retired as Editor-in-Chief in 1993. In his place came the Journal's second Editor-in-Chief tandem, Theodor Meron of New York University and Detlev Vagts of Harvard.[156] Meron specialized in public international law, with an emphasis on human rights and humanitarian law, while Vagts' expertise lay primarily in international economic law and related subjects.

---

[152] Report [by the *ad hoc* committee] on Composition and Selection of Board Members, Oct. 13, 1992, in AJIL files, and summarized in *ASIL Newsletter*, Nov./Dec. 1992, at 14.

[153] Minutes of the Executive Council, Oct. 24, 1992, in briefing book for Mar.–Apr. 1993 Executive Council meetings.

[154] The revised Regulations as adopted in 1992, Sec. V.1, appear in 87 *ASIL Proc.* 626, 631-32 (1993).

[155] For the changes in Board membership during this period, see Memorandum, "ASIL History: The Journal, Its Editors and Business Practices," on file with the Society.

[156] The first tandem had been Louis Henkin and Oscar Schachter.

3. Predominant Themes and Small Changes

During this period, roughly 1993 through to 1996, three themes predominated in the pages of the Journal even though, as always, a wide range of articles and Editorial Comments appeared. The predominant themes were the law of the sea,[157] the United Nations,[158] and international economic

---

157 Lead articles: Jonathan I. Charney, "Progress in International Maritime Boundary Delimitation Law," 88 *AJIL* 227 (1994); Jonathan I. Charney, "Central East Asian Maritime Boundaries and the Law of the Sea," 89 *AJIL* 724 (1995). Editorial Comments: John R. Stevenson & Bernard H. Oxman, "The Future of the United Nations Convention on the Law of the Sea," 88 *AJIL* 488 (1994); Jonathan I. Charney, "The Implications of Expanding International Dispute Settlement Systems: The 1982 Convention on the Law of the Sea," 90 *AJIL* 69 (1996). Law of the Sea Forum: "The 1994 Agreement on Implementation of the Seabed Provisions of the Convention on the Law of the Sea," with contributions from Bernard H. Oxman, Louis B. Sohn and Jonathan I. Charney, 88 *AJIL* 687-714 (1994). Current Developments: "Panel on the Law of Ocean Uses, United States Interests in the Law of the Sea Convention," 88 *AJIL* 167 (1994); David D. Caron, "The International Whaling Commission and the North Atlantic Marine Mammal Commission: The Institutional Risks of Coercion in Consensual Structures," 89 *AJIL* 154 (1995); George Galdorisi, "The UN Convention on the Law of the Sea: A National Security Perspective," id. at 208; William T. Burke, "Implications for Fisheries Management of U.S. Acceptance of the 1982 Convention on the Law of the Sea," id. at 792; Shabtai Rosenne, "Establishing the International Tribunal for the Law of the Sea," id. at 806; Annick de Marffy-Mantuano, "The Procedural Framework of the Agreement Implementing the 1982 United Nations Convention on the Law of the Sea," id. at 814.

158 Lead articles: David D. Caron, "The Legitimacy of the Collective Authority of the Security Council," 87 *AJIL* 552 (1993); Oscar Schachter, "United Nations Law," 88 *AJIL* 1 (1994); Vera Gowlland-Debbas, "The Relationship between the International Court of Justice and the Security Council in the Light of the *Lockerbie* Case," id. at 643; Robert Y. Jennings, "The International Court of Justice after Fifty Years," 89 *AJIL* 493 (1995); Frederic L. Kirgis, "The Security Council's First Fifty Years," id. at 506; Louis B. Sohn, "How American International Lawyers Prepared for the San Francisco Bill of Rights," id. at 540; José E. Alvarez, "Judging the Security Council," 90 *AJIL* 1 (1996). Editorial Comments: W. Michael Reisman, "Preparing to Wage Peace: Toward the Creation of an International Peacemaking Command and Staff College," 88 *AJIL* 76 (1994); Frederic L. Kirgis, "The Degrees of Self-Determination in the United Nations Era," id. at 304. Notes and Comments: W. Michael Reisman, "The Constitutional Crisis in the United Nations," 87 *AJIL* 83 (1993). Current Developments: John R. Crook, "The United Nations Compensation Commission – A New Structure to Enforce State Responsibility," 87 *AJIL* 144 (1993); Virginia Morris & M.-Christiane Bourloyannis-Vrailas, "The Work of the Sixth Committee at the Forty-seventh [Forty-eighth; Forty-ninth] Session of the UN General Assembly," 87 *AJIL* 306 (1993) [88 *AJIL* 343 (1994); 89 *AJIL* 607 (1995)]; Hans Corell, "Third Legal Advisers' Meeting at UN Headquarters in New York," 87 *AJIL* 323 (1993); Barry Mawhinney & Kim Girtel, "Fourth Legal Advisers' Meeting at UN Headquarters in New York," 88 *AJIL* 379 (1994); M. Cherif Bassiouni, "The United Nations Commission of Experts Established Pursuant to Security Council Resolution 780 (1992)," id. at 784; Evan T. Bloom, "Protecting Peacekeepers: The Convention on the Safety of United Nations and

law.[159] None was surprising: the U.N. Convention on the Law of the Sea entered into force in 1994; the U.N. celebrated its fiftieth anniversary in 1995; and the Journal was under considerable pressure from the Society's influential International Economic Law Interest Group to increase its emphasis on economic law.

With the demise of the State Department's annual *Digests of United States Practice in International Law*, the Journal became an increasingly important vehicle for information about U.S. practice. The Journal had long included a department called Contemporary Practice of the United States Relating to International Law, edited for many years by Marian Nash (Leich), which summarized some of the more important current practice. In the nineties, the Journal also used its Current Developments department to present expanded information about U.S. practice.[160] Oddly, neither department gave prominence to the precursor of

---

Associated Personnel," 89 *AJIL* 621 (1995); Miguel Angel González Felix, "Fifth Legal Advisers' Meeting at UN Headquarters in New York," id. at 644; Carolyn L. Willson, "Changing the Charter: The United Nations Prepares for the Twenty-first Century," 90 *AJIL* 115 (1996).

159 Lead articles: Frédéric P. Cantin & Andreas F. Lowenfeld, "Rules of Origin, the Canada-U.S. FTA, and the Honda Case," 87 *AJIL* 375 (1993); Georges R. Delaume, "The Foreign Sovereign Immunities Act and Public Debt Litigation: Some Fifteen Years Later," 88 *AJIL* 257 (1994); George H. Aldrich, "What Constitutes a Compensable Taking of Property? The Decisions of the Iran-United States Claims Tribunal," id. at 585; Eyal Benvenisti & Eyal Zamir, "Private Claims to Property Rights in the Future Israeli Palestinian Settlement," 89 *AJIL* 295 (1995); John Y. Gotanda, "Awarding Interest in International Arbitration," 90 *AJIL* 40 (1996); Steven P. Croley & John H. Jackson, "WTO Dispute Procedures, Standard of Review, and Deference to National Governments," id. at 193; John W. Head, "Evolution of the Governing Law for Loan Agreements of the World Bank and Other Multilateral Development Banks," id. at 214; Joseph A. LaNasa III, "Rules of Origin and the Uruguay Round's Effectiveness in Harmonizing and Regulating Them," id. at 625. Editorial Comments: Andreas F. Lowenfeld, "Remedies along with Rights: Institutional Reform in the New GATT," 88 *AJIL* 477 (1994); Andreas F. Lowenfeld, "Conflict, Balancing of Interests, and the Exercise of Jurisdiction to Prescribe: Reflections on the *Insurance Antitrust Case*," 89 *AJIL* 42 (1995); Philip R. Trimble, "The Supreme Court and International Law: The Demise of Restatement Section 403," id. at 53. Notes and Comments: Larry Kramer, "Extraterritorial Application of American Law after the *Insurance Antitrust Case*: A Reply to Professors Lowenfeld and Trimble," 89 *AJIL* 750 (1995). Current Developments: Jennifer Schultz, "The GATT/WTO Committee on Trade and Environment – Toward Environmental Reform," 89 *AJIL* 423 (1995); Jack I. Garvey, "Trade Law and the Quality of Life – Dispute Resolution under the NAFTA Side Accords on Labor and the Environment," id. at 439; David K. Linnan, "APEC Quo Vadis?," id. at 824; Patrick M. Moore, "The Decisions Bridging the GATT 1947 and the WTO Agreement," 90 *AJIL* 317 (1996).

160 Report on the Publications Program, in Tillar House Report for the Executive Council meeting of Apr. 5, 1995, at 21, 22.

the 9/11 World Trade Center terrorist attack – the bombing of the World Trade Center in February 1993 by means of a van in the parking garage.[161]

With the January 1995 issue, the Journal began carrying in its Table of Contents abstracts of lead articles. The abstracts served not only as previews for potential readers, but also as useful aids in electronic searching.

E. THE FUTURE OF THE SOCIETY

1. The Short Range

When Charles Brower became President of the Society in March 1996, he focused on three areas: programs, governance and finance.

Brower, like every President before him, acknowledged the excellence of the Journal. Like every President since the inception of I.L.M., he acknowledged its excellence as well. He noted the wide variety of other Society programs, including regional meetings, interest group conferences and briefings. More could be done, though, if adequate funds were available. The emphasis, he thought, should be on continuing efforts to educate national court judges in international law; to extend that education to Congress; to address the activities of international financial institutions; to emphasize areas covered by the Society's Panel on State Responsibility; and to deal with the growing phenomenon of international adjudication and other forms of dispute resolution.[162]

Brower found the Society's governing structure curious at best and inappropriate at worst. The Vice Presidents had no prescribed function. The Executive Council – a large and unwieldy body – had only one fully substantive meeting a year, in October, with truncated meetings during the Society's Annual Meeting in the spring. Otherwise, management was in the hands of the Executive Committee, which did not include a majority of the Society's officers and did not meet regularly. Thus most of the governance fell *de facto* to the President and the Executive Director.

Brower immediately reconstituted the Executive Committee to include all seven officers of the Society plus three other members of the Executive Council. He scheduled regular monthly Executive Committee meetings by conference calls. In addition, he convened the Executive Council for a full day during the Annual Meeting as well as in October. Finally, he appointed a new Committee

---

161 The 1993 bombing was mentioned in a footnote dealing with Jordan's extradition to the United States of the person accused of driving the van into the parking garage. Marian Nash (Leich), Contemporary Practice of the United States Relating to International Law, 90 *AJIL* 79, 84 n. 3 (1996).

162 *ASIL Newsletter*, Mar.–May 1996, at 1, 4.

on Governance, under James Carter, to review the Society's Constitution and Regulations, and to recommend changes in the governing structure.[163]

Brower's major concern, though, was with the state of the Society's finances. He took note of the much-needed refurbishing of Tillar House, which would cost in excess of USD 1 million, and the need for research resources. If an average of USD 1,000 per member could be envisioned as a capital campaign goal, the Society's target for the campaign would be about USD 4.3 million.[164] He set out to figure out how to raise such a sum. A professional fund raiser was retained to provide advice.[165]

2. A Longer-Range View

As of 1996, money was indeed the crux of the matter. The Society was committed to the expanded program initiated when Chris Merillat was the Executive Director and developed significantly by his successors. Merillat had large Ford Foundation grants to work with and considerable latitude in allocating the funds. His successors had to search for more modest grants, very often limited to single projects with little or no grant funds for overhead to fuel the Society's general operations. The Seventy-fifth Anniversary Fund gave a boost to the Society's treasury, but it was inadequate to serve as a long-term source of income for ambitious research or outreach programs. Despite the obvious need for systematic fund raising, the Society in mid-1996 had no one on its staff for whom that was the primary responsibility. Brower set out to rectify the difficult situation.

The Society's flagship publications, the *American Journal of International Law* and International Legal Materials, shone as beacons of international scholarship and of timely publication of important documents, respectively. There was every indication that their predominance in their fields would continue. Both enjoyed enormous prestige internationally, and both were income-generators. But the broader research program was less solid, not only because of questions about the availability of funds, but also because of the Society's shift of emphasis toward outreach. The shift could readily be justified as comporting with one of the Society's primary purposes: "to promote the establishment and maintenance of international relations on the basis of law and justice." On a practical level, it could also be justified as bringing the Society within the current interests of the Ford Foundation and some other funding sources. Nevertheless, like most choices, it had a cost. The research program had lost some of its vitality.

If outreach had become a priority, it was fair to ask whether the Society was actually having an impact on public attitudes or on policy-making. Gone were

---

163 Id. at 4-5.

164 *ASIL Newsletter*, Mar.–May 1996, at 5.

165 Minutes of the Executive Council, Apr. 9, 1997, p. 3. See Chapter Thirteen, *infra*.

the days when sitting Secretaries of State served as Presidents of the Society or were otherwise active in its programs. Members of State Department Legal Advisers' staffs, and sometimes Legal Advisers themselves, participated in Society programs, but it was not the same as having direct access to the Secretary of State. The Society's outreach efforts, through Washington briefings, Insight bulletins and other measures, were made available to policy-makers. But whether these efforts had any real impact was impossible to ascertain.

One of the Society's weaknesses, attributable largely to lack of staff, was that it had very little follow-up capability after it held a briefing or issued an Insight bulletin. That deficiency not only made it difficult to gauge the effects, but also deprived the Society of an important means of staying in close touch with decision-makers in order to persuade them (as Louis Henkin put it) to "take international law seriously."

The Society's long-standing practice against taking positions on public policy issues also diminished its ability to influence decisions. Yet there seemed to be good reasons for the practice, including the probability that taking positions on controversial matters would split the membership and the lingering doubt that a stated Society position would in fact be taken seriously by the decision-makers – particularly if it took a long time to get consensus within the Society on a particular position.

The Society was becoming increasingly "international" rather than just "American" by the time of its ninetieth anniversary. It had established relations with similar societies in Canada, Japan, Mexico, the Netherlands and elsewhere. It was presenting programs in those countries and in others. It had a truly international roster of members, with about forty per cent of its members residing outside the United States. It remained basically American in the sense that its governing bodies were populated almost entirely by United States nationals, and in the sense that it continued to pay a great deal of attention to what the United States government did and planned to do on the international scene. Yet in outlook and in practice, it could hardly be regarded as provincial.

Strides had been taken toward enhanced diversity in the Society's inner sanctum. Women had made their mark, and continued to do so. From 1994 to 1996, women filled the posts of President, Executive Director, Deputy Executive Director and Director of Publications. People of color were represented on the Executive Council and Executive Committee. Some tensions continued to reach the surface on diversity matters, but the prognosis for accommodation of diverse interests was good.

The outlook for the future, then, was generally favorable. The Society was a heterogeneous body with an ambitious and outward-looking program. It had an abundance of intellectual resources to carry out virtually anything within its charter it wished (and could afford) to do. Its financial resources were another matter. A great deal depended on the development of an effective, ongoing fund-raising capability if the Society was to continue the dynamic pursuit of its two constitutionally mandated goals.

In addition to the need for money, there was a need to energize the membership. The freshness brought to the study of international law by the original Board of Review and Development had long since faded. In its place were individual projects, some of which were well funded and vigorously pursued. Others were less so. Research and outreach were not entirely distinct endeavors; both required adequate financial support, each could nourish the other, and each could be served by a membership that could be galvanized to investigate international law and its processes, and to try to make international law matter.

A major fund-raising campaign and an energized research/outreach effort were on the way.

Chapter Thirteen

INFRASTRUCTURE FOR EXPANDED OUTREACH

Transnational regulatory cooperation is ... a harbinger of transgovernmentalism, the core of a new international architecture for the twenty-first century.

—Anne-Marie Slaughter
Remarks, "Regulatory Cooperation for Effectiveness and Compliance: Strategies for Joint Action Among Securities, Banking and Antitrust Regulators,"
91 *ASIL Proceedings* 233 (1997).

A. AN EXPANDED RESEARCH AND OUTREACH PROGRAM

1. Getting Organized

The featured item on Charles N. Brower's agenda as President of the Society from 1996 to 1998 was building the Society's infrastructure. But infrastructure, obviously, was not a goal in itself; it had to have a real purpose. Brower had a purpose in mind: strengthening the communications and outreach programs. The effort would require planning and money.

In August 1996 the Society retained Devillier Communications, Inc. (D.C.I.), a Washington consulting firm, to assess the existing communications and outreach efforts and to suggest methods of promoting the Society's programs and increasing its visibility. A D.C.I. representative spent three weeks learning about the Society and developing recommendations.[1] In October 1996, D.C.I. submitted its Communications Plan for the Society. It outlined an ambitious program designed to invigorate the Society's communications with its members and to broaden and enliven its outreach efforts not only to members, but also to the media and the public. The plan called for more output than the Society's small staff could possibly deliver, but the overarching goals were within reach: the Society's communications with its members and others should be vibrant, relevant to current events, and designed to keep the Society prominent in the

1 Letter from Cathy M. MacFarlane to Charlotte Ku, Oct. 1, 1996.

minds of internationally oriented persons and institutions. Electronic distribution of the Society's output would be essential.[2]

2. A Frustrating Attempt at Capitol Hill Outreach

As might be expected, some efforts at outreach were more successful than others. One of the more frustrating attempts took place in 1996. Congress enacted the Helms-Burton Act, which provided that anyone who "traffics" in property that was confiscated by the Cuban government after January 1, 1959, would be liable to any U.S. national who owns the claim for money damages. In some cases a U.S. court could award treble damages.[3] Since "anyone" would include foreign nationals acting outside the United States, the Act raised troubling jurisdiction-to-prescribe issues. Even though the Act gave the President of the United States authority to suspend the right to bring an action under it (and the President did so), it engendered vigorous protests and counter-measures by foreign governments whose nationals might run afoul of it.

The Society responded to Helms-Burton by presenting a dialog on Capitol Hill, featuring three speakers who addressed the issues raised by the Act. Only five Congressional staffers attended. The lesson learned was that unless the Society could wine and dine the Congressional staff, it could not expect to attract many of them to be instructed on international law.[4]

3. The Panel on State Responsibility

The Society's Panel on State Responsibility focused primarily on the preparation of the International Law Commission's Draft Articles on State Responsibility and on the work of the Iran–United States Claims Tribunal. Richard Lillich chaired the Panel. On August 3, 1996, just as the Draft Articles were being submitted to governments for their comments, Lillich – a robust man seemingly in good health – died of a heart attack. David Bederman volunteered to fill in for him.

In the spring of 1997, the Panel met with Robert Rosenstock, the U.S. representative to the International Law Commission, and with two members of the State Department Legal Adviser's office, to provide input and to exchange ideas.[5] Individual members of the Panel then provided comments to the State Department and others on the Draft Articles. The comments were given promi-

2 Communications Plan-of-Action for The American Society of International Law, submitted by Devillier Communications, Inc., Oct. 2, 1996.

3 P.L. 104-114, 22 U.S.C. §§ 6021 et seq. (Mar. 12, 1996), 35 *ILM* 357 (1996).

4 Minutes of the Executive Committee, July 25, 1996.

5 Minutes of the Executive Committee, May 16, 1997.

nence in the U.S. government's official reactions to the Draft Articles, issued in October of that year.[6]

The Panel's interest in the Iran–U.S. Claims Tribunal gave birth to two multi-authored books: *The Iran–United States Claims Tribunal: Its Contribution to the Law of State Responsibility*,[7] and *The Iran–United States Claims Tribunal and the Process of International Claims Resolution*.[8] The former dealt primarily with substantive issues; the latter, with institutional and procedural issues. The books became staples in any law library's collection of works on state responsibility.

That was not all. The Panel continued to monitor developments at the Claims Tribunal as well as at the U.N. Compensation Commission (dealing with claims against Iraq arising out of the 1991 Persian Gulf War), as well as NAFTA Chapter 11 dispute-settlement panels and other arbitral and judicial proceedings.[9]

4. Briefings, Presentations and Workshops

The Tillar House corporate counsel briefing series, begun in 1995, peaked during Charles N. Brower's term as President. Topics included the Export–Import Bank, international commercial aviation, mitigating risks in international investment, the proposed O.E.C.D. Multilateral Agreement on Investment, and the role of the World Bank's General Counsel. By April 1997, the General Counsel of each international financial institution based in Washington had addressed a briefing session.[10]

In May 1997, the Society's Corporate Counsel Committee co-sponsored a major corporate counsel conference, along with the American Bar Association's Board of Governors and several corporate counsel organizations. The conference addressed a variety of issues facing corporate counsel, including issues raised by U.S. legislation, issues arising from the globalization of business, public service questions, and several nuts-and-bolts matters.[11] Another jointly sponsored forum for practitioners was held in Chicago in September 1999, on the proposed Hague Convention on Jurisdiction and Judgments.[12]

---

6 *ASIL Newsletter*, Mar.–Apr. 1998, at 11.

7 Edited by Richard B. Lillich and Daniel Barstow Magraw, with the assistance of David J. Bederman, and published in 1998.

8 Edited by David D. Caron and John R. Crook, and published in 2000.

9 E-mail message from David J. Bederman to Frederic L. Kirgis, July 9, 2004.

10 Minutes of the Business Meeting, April 10, 1997.

11 ABA Board of Governors, Second Annual Conf. on Corporate Counsel Issues, May 15 and 16, 1997 (leaflet).

12 The co-sponsors were the Chicago Bar Association, the ABA Section on International Law and Practice, and the American Corporate Counsel Association. *ASIL Newsletter*, July–Aug. 1999, at 11.

Public international law briefings continued as well. Just eight days after the I.C.J.'s Advisory Opinion on Legality of the Threat or Use of Nuclear Weapons[13] appeared in July 1996, the Society presented a public briefing on it. Six discussants, all of whom participated in the case, spoke before an audience of about sixty.[14] Later in that month, August Reinisch discussed issues raised when international organizations appear before national courts.[15] In December, David Scheffer, then the chief U.S. representative to the negotiations for the International Criminal Court, discussed the Administration's policy toward the creation of the Court. In all, there were nineteen Tillar House briefings in 1996 and eleven in 1997, with more to follow.

As we have seen in Chapter Twelve, the Society co-sponsored a three-day workshop in June 1996 with the Association of American Law Schools on "Integrating International and US Law: Environmental and Related Problems."[16]

In October 1997, as momentum was building toward the Rome Conference on the Establishment of an International Criminal Court, the Society co-sponsored a panel on the proposed I.C.C. at the law offices of Steptoe & Johnson, where long-time Society member Monroe Leigh was a partner. Leigh led off the program, and David Scheffer sparked a lively discussion with his presentation of the Clinton administration's position toward the Court.[17]

At the initiative of President Thomas M. Franck, the Society organized five meetings in 1998 under the heading "Meet the Lawmakers." Held in law offices in New York and Washington, the meetings were oversubscribed. Speakers included David Scheffer, Andres Rigo of the World Bank and Richard Butler, the head of the U.N. Special Commission to disarm Iraq.[18] The summer of 1998 featured a series of lectures in Tillar House for summer associates and interns in the Washington, D.C. area. Topics included international election observing, the Lockerbie Case in the I.C.J., and perspectives on the practice of international law.[19]

5. Energizing the Program

When Tom Franck became the President of the Society in April 1998, he pulled no punches in pointing out that the United States was not exactly a model

---

13 1996 *ICJ Rep.* 226, 35 *ILM* 809 (1996).

14 Minutes of the Executive Committee, July 25, 1996.

15 See *ASIL Newsletter*, Sept.–Oct. 1996, at 13-14, for a summary of his presentation.

16 See Chapter 12, Section C.14, *supra*. See also *ASIL Newsletters*, Mar.–May 1996, at 21, and Sept.–Oct. 1996, at 19.

17 See *ASIL Newsletter*, Jan.–Feb. 1998, at 4.

18 Report of the Executive Director on Administration and Finance, prepared for the March 24, 1999, meeting of the Executive Council, at 7-8.

19 *ASIL Newsletter*, July–Aug. 1998, at 4.

citizen when it came to meeting its international obligations. He noted that the United States was so heavily in arrears in paying its U.N. dues that it faced the theoretical possibility of losing its vote in the General Assembly.[20] Moreover, the Supreme Court in the first *Alvarez-Machain* case had refused to order the dismissal of an indictment against a Mexican national who – in disregard of the U.S.–Mexico extradition treaty – had been abducted in Mexico and taken to the United States to be prosecuted for his alleged participation in the murder of a U.S. agent.[21] Franck lamented the failure of the United States to seize the opportunity offered by the end of the Cold War to make law and adjudication the norm of global behavior.

He directed some of the blame toward the A.S.I.L. The Society, he said, had failed to promote fresh thinking and research; it had not sufficiently assisted its members in making their voices heard in the White House or on Capitol Hill; and it had not played a significant role in educating the American public about the importance of international law.[22] His immediate objective was to make Tillar House a center of activism, hosting a constant stream of meetings and forums on international law and current issues. Ultimately, the goal was to press the United States to respect international law consistently.[23]

He declared at the outset that his priority would be to stimulate research and outreach.[24] One of his first steps was to establish a new staff position, the Director of Research and Outreach, and to appoint Christopher J. Borgen to fill the position. He appointed a new Research Committee, chaired by Lori Damrosch, to encourage cooperative research by Society members on projects with potential for impact on policy debates, and to facilitate dissemination of their work product.[25]

Projects developed by the committee included examinations of the legal implications of new information technology on warfare and terrorism (the

---

20 U.N. Charter Art. 19 provides in part, "A Member of the United Nations which is in arrears in the payment of its financial contributions to the Organization shall have no vote in the General Assembly if the amount of its arrears equals or exceeds the amount of the contributions due from it for the preceding two years." On the U.S. arrears, see Sean D. Murphy, "Contemporary Practice of the United States Relating to International Law: Payment of U.S. Arrears to the United Nations," 94 *AJIL* 348 (2000); ASIL Insight, "United States Dues Arrearages in the United Nations and Possible Loss of Vote in the UN General Assembly" (July 1998).

21 See *United States v. Alvarez-Machain*, 504 U.S. 655 (1992).

22 *ASIL Newsletter*, May–June 1998, at 1, 12.

23 Informal notes by Frederic L. Kirgis of meeting with Thomas Franck, Charlotte Ku and Susan Karamanian, Aug. 10, 1998.

24 Minutes of the Business Meeting, Apr. 2, 1998.

25 Minutes of the Executive Committee, May 13, 1998; *ASIL Newsletters*, July–Aug. 1998, at 1, 8, and Sept-Oct. 1998, at 3.

Cyberwar project), human rights and world economic law (the H.R./W.E.L. project), e-commerce and the regulation of international business transactions, and federalism as applied to U.S. foreign relations.[26] The committee also lent its support to existing projects on soft law and on internally displaced persons.[27] Both of these projects bore fruit.[28]

Franck also formed an *ad hoc* Committee on Society Effectiveness and Outreach to examine how the Society could better make its public voice heard.[29] Keith Highet initially chaired the *ad hoc* committee. When he became ill, Rita Hauser took over. In March 1999 the committee finished its work and recommended that the Society:

- Engage the services of a media consultant to raise the Society's profile with journalists;
- Develop funding for programs directed at judges, and summer workshops for academics;
- Develop a plan for mobilizing members to make contacts with Members of Congress and to institute an A.S.I.L. Congressional information program;
- Develop the Society's electronic presence through the use of e-mail and the web site for outreach to targeted audiences; and
- Establish a speakers' bureau.[30]

The Society moved briskly to implement some of the recommendations – particularly those regarding electronic resources, programs for judges, and establishing a roster of potential speakers. But its resources were stretched, and the proposals for engaging a media consultant and developing close contacts with Capitol Hill were put on the back burner.[31]

---

26 ASIL 1999 Annual Report, page 4, in *ASIL Newsletter*, Mar.–Apr. 2000; Report of the ASIL Research Committee, Spring 1999.

27 Minutes of the Executive Council, Oct. 30, 1999.

28 See Dinah Shelton (ed.), *Commitment and Compliance: The Role of Non-Binding Norms in the International Legal System* (Oxford Univ. Press, 2000) (discussed in Chapter Twelve, *supra*); Roberta Cohen & Francis M. Deng, *Masses in Flight: The Global Crisis of Internal Displacement* (Brookings Institution Press, 2000); Walter Kalin, *Guiding Principles on Internal Displacement: Annotations* (ASIL Studies in Transnational Legal Policy No. 32, 2000, co-published with the Brookings Institution and available online at <http://heinonline.org>).

29 *ASIL Newsletter*, July–Aug. 1998, at 8, 12.

30 Report of the Ad Hoc Committee on Effectiveness and Outreach, prepared for the Executive Council meeting of March 24, 1999; see also *ASIL Newsletter*, Mar.–Apr. 1999, at 1, 5.

31 Tom Franck's vision for a visiting Chair (in Tillar House) in International Law and the Media was outlined in *ASIL Newsletter*, Jan.–Feb. 2000, at 1, 4.

6. Electronic Outreach: International Law in Brief, JSTOR and the Web Site

The seeds for some of the Hauser Committee's recommendations had already been planted. Charles N. Brower, Tom Franck's predecessor as President, had appointed an Ad Hoc Committee on Future Directions for ASIL Publications, chaired by Michael Glennon. The committee considered whether to recommend a new electronic publication tentatively called International Law Express. It would use the Internet to disseminate abstracts of documents received for possible inclusion in *International Legal Materials*. There would be electronic links from the abstracts to the source documents. At Glennon's urging, and despite reservations by some members of his Committee, the Executive Committee approved the project in June 1998 for a six-month trial period.[32]

The name was eventually changed to International Law in Brief (I.L.I.B.). David Levy, the Interim Editor of I.L.M., took charge of I.L.I.B., distributing it free of charge on a weekly basis by e-mail and posting it on the Society web site. The response from readers – including many who did not normally participate in Society activities – was overwhelmingly positive.[33] The Executive Committee decided in February 1999 to continue I.L.I.B. as a regular component of the Society's outreach program.[34] It became a fixture, sent bi-weekly to a growing list of e-mail subscribers. It summarized treaties, judicial and arbitral proceedings, and resolutions of international institutions, with links to the source documents. It continued to be archived on the web site.

Another form of electronic outreach began in 1997, when the Journal was invited to take part in the electronic archive JSTOR (an acronym for Journal Storage). On its web site, which is available to institutions, JSTOR contains the full-text contents of leading journals in the humanities and social sciences. The Journal had the distinction of becoming the first law journal included in the archive. Its JSTOR readership, affiliated with the 300-plus subscriber institutions, thus would include many scholars and teachers who would not be expected to subscribe directly to the Journal.[35]

With help from the Ford Foundation, the Society's web site continued to expand its content during the late nineties. The Insight series became a web site staple. It abandoned its previous bifurcation into regular Insights and Flash Insights. Instead, almost all Insights were of the "flash" variety: usually issued within a few days of newsworthy events (including all significant I.C.J. judgments and

---

32 Minutes of the Executive Committee, June 17, 1998.

33 Memorandum from David A. Levy to ASIL Executive Committee, Feb. 11, 1999; Memorandum from Charlotte Ku to the Executive Committee, Feb. 15, 1999.

34 Minutes of the Executive Committee, Feb. 22, 1999.

35 *ASIL Newsletters*, Sept.–Oct. 1997, at 4, and Nov.–Dec. 1998, at 6.

opinions), and offering balanced expositions of the international law issues raised by the events.[36] Insights were posted on such prominent occurrences as the conclusion in July 1998 of the Rome Conference for the International Criminal Court, the U.S. cruise missile strikes on Afghanistan and Sudan in August 1998 after the terrorist attacks on U.S. embassies in Kenya and Tanzania, the NATO bombing campaign against Yugoslavia after negotiations regarding Kosovo had broken down in 1999, and the indictment of Slobodan Milošević by International Criminal Tribunal for the former Yugoslavia. By the end of 1999, 33 Insights had appeared on the Society's web site. Their frequency would continue to grow.

I.L.I.B. and Insights were not the only web site features. Promotional information about the Society came online. Substantive messages from the Society's Presidents began to appear. For a time, the editors of the Journal, I.L.M. and the Newsletter selected items from their publications to be included on the web site. And there was more to come in the new millennium, as we will see in Chapter Fourteen.

By the end of 1997, the *ASIL Guide to Electronic Resources for International Law* had web site chapters on human rights, the United Nations, treaties, and references to then-available listserves and electronic networks.[37] By the following spring, chapters on international criminal law and environmental law had been added.[38] By mid-1999, there were new chapters on private international law and international economic law.[39] The chapters were (and are) more than compilations of links to other web sites; they include strategies on finding electronic resources in the fields they cover. The introductory chapter supplies basic information (with links) about researching international law on the internet.

In the autumn of 1998, Tom Franck, John King Gamble and Charlotte Ku began to explore ideas about a more ambitious electronic information management project. The genesis was a comment long-time Society member Paul Szasz had made to Ku shortly after she joined the staff. He said that it would be wonderful if all the major components of international law could be made accessible in one place.[40] Franck, Gamble and Ku thus set out to develop a systematized single entrance point for locating international law information on the Internet, drawing on Gamble's graduate student work on a treaty

---

36 Occasionally, Insight readers challenged the objectivity of particular Insights. See, e.g., the Comment by Edward D. Williamson in March 1998 to ASIL Insight, "The Legal Background to the Use of Force to Induce Iraq to Comply with Security Council Resolutions" (Nov. 1997), on the web at <http://www.asil.org>.

37 *ASIL Newsletter*, Nov.–Dec. 1997, at 6.

38 Report of the Executive Director for Executive Council meeting of Apr. 1, 1998, in briefing materials for that meeting.

39 *ASIL Newsletter*, July–Aug. 1999, at 6.

40 Memorandum from Charlotte Ku to Rick Kirgis, Aug. 13, 2004.

index project at the University of Washington. Initial discussions were held to explore whether the project might be carried out jointly with the Max Planck Institute for Comparative Public Law and International Law.[41] Ultimately, the Society proceeded on its own, developing the Electronic Information System for International Law (EISIL) with generous financial support from the Andrew W. Mellon Foundation. It was envisioned to become the "bookmark of choice" in the field of electronic information on international law.[42] Twelve authors were led by Jill Watson, the Society librarian and information services specialist, who was ably assisted by Marci Hoffman, then at Georgetown University and later at the University of California (Berkeley).[43]

By the autumn of 2004, EISIL had matured into an electronic database with more than 1,800 records containing information on, and links to, international law instruments, web sites and online research guides covering the entire spectrum of international law.[44]

In the month of January 1998 alone, the Society's web site received 33,049 hits from users around the world.[45] It grew from there. In September 1999 the site registered 81,829 hits.[46]

In June 1998, the *Dow Jones Business Directory* called the Society's web site "The best resource for international-law issues on the Internet."[47] The Society had come a long way from its technological infancy in 1983, when it installed its first set of computers – a Wang mainframe DEC system within Tillar House.[48] Nevertheless, at the end of the millennium the Society was chasing the developing technology rather than keeping up with it. In particular, the web site was

---

41 Proposal for a joint feasibility project for An Electronic Information System for International Law (EISIL), Jan. 14, 1999; Minutes of the Executive Committee, Jan. 29, 1999.

42 ASIL press release, Aug. 9, 2000.

43 For details regarding the development of EISIL, see Jill McC. Watson, "From Library Services to Information Services – A Chronology: 1981-2003," in briefing materials for the Executive Council meeting of Nov. 1, 2003.

44 See <http://www.asil.org/resources/index.html> and see EISIL's own web site, <http://www.eisil.org>.

45 *ASIL Newsletter*, May–June 1998, at 6.

46 Report of Jill Watson on Information Services and Website, in Report of the Executive Director for the Executive Council meeting of Oct. 30, 1999, at 21. See also Report on Development of the ASIL Web Site, at 5, prepared for the Executive Council meeting of March 24, 1999. The latter report summarizes the development of the web site from its inception in 1995 to the spring of 1999.

47 "Dow Jones Business Directory on the Internet, Your Guide to High-Quality Business Web Sites – Reviews," quoted with permission in *ASIL Newsletter*, July–Aug. 1998, at 6.

48 See Report of the Executive Director for the Executive Council meeting of Oct. 24, 1998, at 2-3.

not especially user-friendly and it was not interactive. Money, as usual, was the problem.[49]

7. Judicial Outreach

The *ad hoc* Committee on Society Effectiveness and Outreach recommended, among other things, that the Society develop programs on international legal issues for presentation to federal and state judges. Responding to this recommendation and others, the Society – with the support of a USD 300,000 grant from the Hauser Foundation and with the cooperation of the Federal Judicial Center – embarked on a program of presentations to federal Circuit Court Judicial Conferences around the country.[50] United States Supreme Court Justice Sandra Day O'Connor agreed to chair the Advisory Board of the new Program for the Judiciary.[51] The first federal circuits to sign up were the Third, Fifth, Ninth and Tenth Circuits, for the summer of 2000.[52] The program built up steam after the turn of the millennium.[53]

The Society's collaboration with the Federal Judicial Center went further than the Judicial Conference presentations. In March 1997, Keith Highet spoke at the Judicial Center on "The International Court of Justice: Yesterday, Today and Tomorrow." In April of that year, Thomas Buergenthal spoke on the Inter-American Court of Human Rights.[54] And, as has been noted in Chapter Twelve, from 1995 to 1997 the Society and the Judicial Center published the *International Judicial Observer*, a newsletter aimed at judges around the world.

B. STRENGTHENING THE SOCIETY'S COOPERATION WITH OTHER ORGANIZATIONS

Building on Edith Brown Weiss' initiative when she was the Society's President, Charles Brower and the Tillar House staff expanded the Society's contacts with international law groups outside the United States. In June 1996, the Society co-sponsored a two-day program in Mexico City with the Instituto de

---

49 Memorandum, Special Package to Maintain ASIL Competitiveness in a Changing Market, attached to Report of the Budget Committee, Sept. 15, 1999.

50 Minutes of the Executive Committee, May 19, 1999.

51 *ASIL Newsletter*, Sept.–Oct. 1999, at 1. The full initial roster of the Advisory Board appears in the Report of the Institute on International Law in Public Affairs – Judicial Outreach Program, in briefing materials for the Executive Council meeting of Oct. 21, 2000.

52 Minutes of the Executive Council, April 5, 2000.

53 See Chapter Fourteen, *infra*.

54 *ASIL Newsletter*, Mar.–Apr. 1997, at 4.

Investigaciones Jurídicas on "The Role of International Law in the Americas: Rethinking National Sovereignty in an Age of Regional Integration." Speakers included former Mexican and U.S. government officials, as well as judges, lawyers and legal scholars. Stephen Zamora and Ellen Lutz were the Society's co-chairs.[55]

The Society maintained its contacts with the Canadian Council on International Law. Brower, in his capacity as President of the Society, carried on the practice of his predecessors by addressing the meeting of the Canadian Council in the autumn of 1996.[56]

The fourth biennial joint conference with the Netherlands Society of International Law was convened at The Hague in July 1997. The topic was Contemporary International Law Issues: New Forms, New Applications. Several panels were presented, and the Foreign Ministers of The Netherlands and Poland – as well as Stephen Schwebel, then the President of the International Court of Justice – addressed the nearly three hundred attendees. Planning began almost immediately for a fifth biennial joint conference in 1999,[57] but because of coordination problems the Society did not participate in it. There were no further joint conferences in The Hague until July 2003.

The Society and the Graduate Institute of International Studies presented the second Forum Geneva in May 1998, a one-day conference on "Multilateral Treaty-Making: The Current Status of Challenges to and Reforms Needed in the International Legislative Process."[58] The organizers were Mahnoush H. Arsanjani for the Society and Vera Gowlland-Debbas for the Institute. Alain Pellet, of Université de Paris X Nanterre, gave the keynote address on codification and progressive development of international law.[59] Despite the success of the 1998 Forum, the ensuing years saw no further joint programs in Geneva.

Susan Karamanian and Hilary Charlesworth began early in 1999 to plan a joint conference in June 2000 in Australia with the Australian and New Zealand Society of International Law. The theme was "International Legal Challenges for the 21st Century." The three-day meeting, split between Sydney and Canberra, covered issues of trade and environment, Asia-Pacific regional law, international criminal law, the law of the sea, indigenous rights, East Timor and self-determination, teaching international law, and theories of international law.[60]

---

55 *ASIL Newsletter*, June–Aug. 1996, at 1, 3.

56 Minutes of the Business Meeting, April 10, 1997. The theme of the meeting was "Fostering Compliance in International Law."

57 *ASIL Newsletters*, July–Aug. 1997, at 1, and Sept.–Oct. 1997, at 11.

58 The first Forum Geneva was held in May 1995. See Chapter 12, *supra*.

59 *ASIL Newsletter*, Mar.–Apr. 1998, at 7; Forum Geneva Program (1998).

60 *ASIL Newsletter*, Mar.–Apr. 2000, at 1.

Beginning in 1991, the Society organized a panel at the annual meeting of the American Political Science Association (A.P.S.A.). The topics varied from year to year. In 1997 the panel, moderated by Charlotte Ku, dealt with teaching international law to undergraduates.[61] For the 1999 A.P.S.A. meeting, she organized a roundtable on "Exploring International Law: Opportunities and Challenges for Political Science Research."[62]

During this period the Society also maintained its active collaboration, begun in 1991, with the Academic Council on the United Nations System (A.C.U.N.S.). The two organizations co-sponsored two-week interdisciplinary summer programs on issues of international institutions and global governance.[63] Young scholars from both law and political science participated in the programs and ultimately formed a network of scholars interested in global governance issues.[64] Charlotte Ku served a term as Chair of the A.C.U.N.S. Board of Directors. She maintained a productive scholarly agenda with political scientists who had an interest in international law, including the co-editorship of an important book, *Democratic Accountability and the Use of Force in International Law,* supported by a 1997 Ford Foundation grant of USD 250,000 to the Society.[65]

C. GOVERNANCE OF THE SOCIETY

1. New Governing Instruments

When Charles Brower assumed the presidency in 1996, he observed that the Society's management was concentrated in the hands of its President and its Executive Director, without meaningful input from its other officers or from the Executive Council.[66] In search of change, he appointed a Committee on Governance, chaired by James H. Carter. The Governance Committee identified several issues:[67]

---

61 *ASIL Newsletter*, Sept.–Oct. 1997, at 9.

62 *ASIL Newsletter*, Sept.–Oct. 1999, at 2.

63 See Chapter 11, *supra*. See also *ASIL Newsletter*, July–Aug. 1997, at 2.

64 Memorandum from Charlotte Ku to Rick Kirgis, Aug. 13, 2004.

65 Charlotte Ku & Harold K. Jacobson (eds.), *Democratic Accountability and the Use of Force in International Law* (2003). See also Charlotte Ku & Paul F. Diehl (eds.), *International Law: Classic and Contemporary Readings* (1st ed. 1998; 2d ed. 2003); Charlotte Ku & Thomas G. Weiss (eds.), *Toward Global Governance: The International Law and International Relations Toolbox* (ACUNS Reports & Papers 1998, No. 2).

66 See Notes from the President, *ASIL Newsletter*, Mar.–Apr. 1997, at 1, 8.

67 Interim Report of the Governance Committee, Oct. 1996, at 1-2, submitted to the meeting of the Executive Council, Oct. 26, 1996.

- Should the President be elected for a two-year term? The Constitution in force at that time called for a one-year renewable term, subject to a limit of three consecutive terms.[68]
- Should there be a President-Elect who would serve for one year immediately preceding his or her ascension to the presidency? No such office had theretofore existed.
- Should the Executive Committee include all of the elected officers plus a limited number of other members of the Executive Council, with the aim of enabling it to function as a cabinet between Executive Council meetings? Theretofore the Executive Committee consisted of the President, Executive Vice President (in practice, the Executive Director), Treasurer, and seven other Council members.[69]
- Should the Nominating Committee report on its nominations closer to the Annual Meeting than 180 days in advance, as then required by the Constitution?[70]
- Should there be changes in the office of Honorary Vice President? At that time the Constitution placed no limit on the number of Honorary Vice Presidents and allowed them to be re-elected annually for an indefinite period.[71] They were full voting members of the Executive Council, but they had no assigned duties. The Regulations said that there "may be" twenty-seven Honorary Vice Presidents.[72]

The Governance Committee worked diligently for two years. After several drafts and after some controversy within the Executive Council particularly over the Committee's proposal to reform the office of Honorary Vice President, the Committee produced a new set of Regulations that the Executive Council approved on April 1, 1998, and a new Constitution that the Business Meeting adopted the next day. At about the same time, the Society's statutory federal charter was being recodified with some housekeeping changes that did not affect the Governance Committee's work product.[73]

---

68 Constitution of the ASIL, as amended to Nov. 6, 1993, Art. IV, in 87 *ASIL Proc.* 622, 623 (1993).

69 Regulations of the ASIL, as amended to Nov. 6, 1993, Section II(1), in 87 *ASIL Proc.* 626, 627 (1993).

70 Constitution, *supra* note 68, Art. IV.

71 Id.

72 Regulations, *supra* note 69, Section IX.

73 See Public Law 105-225, § 1, codified at 36 U.S.C. §§ 22101-22109 (Aug. 12, 1998).

The presidency was limited to a single two-year term. The new office of President-Elect was created. The President-Elect, who is preferably to be elected from among former Vice Presidents, serves in that capacity for the second year of the previous President's term. The number of Honorary Vice Presidents was set at three, who are to be the three most recent past Presidents. The officers of the Society consist of an Honorary President, the President, the President-Elect, the three Honorary Vice Presidents, four Vice Presidents, the Secretary and the Treasurer. All officers, except the President, the President-Elect and the Honorary Vice Presidents, are to be elected annually.[74]

The new Regulations designated the President, the President-Elect, if there is one, the four Vice Presidents, the Secretary, the Treasurer and three other annually elected Executive Council members as the Executive Committee, to function between Executive Council meetings.[75] In practice, under Presidents Brower, Franck, Rovine, Slaughter and Carter, the Executive Committee met regularly between Council meetings, conducting its business by conference calls.

The new Constitution shortened (to ninety days) the time between the due date for the Nominating Committee's report on its proposed candidates for office and the date of the Annual Meeting.[76] The goal was to give the Nominating Committee adequate time for its deliberations, but it was achieved at the cost of bypassing any assurance that the Executive Council would have an opportunity to vet the slate of candidates at its autumn meeting.[77]

The new Constitution also replaced the large corps of Honorary Vice Presidents with the three immediate past Presidents, who became officers as mentioned above, and twenty-four Counsellors elected to three-year renewable terms. In addition, the new Constitution designated all past Presidents who are not officers as Counsellors. Counsellors were invited to meet with the Executive Council as non-voting members.[78] They are nominated "from among Society members who have made significant contributions to the Society and to the study and development of international law."[79] Despite concerns that the new Counsellor category would unduly downgrade the status of eminent Society members

---

74 Constitution of the ASIL, as amended to Apr. 2, 1998, Art. IV, online at <http://www.asil.org>.

75 Regulations of the ASIL, as amended to Apr. 2, 1998, Section II(1), online at <http://www.asil.org>.

76 Constitution, *supra* note 74, Art. IV.

77 Minutes of the Executive Council, Oct. 25, 1997.

78 Constitution, *supra* note 74, Art. VII.

79 Regulations, *supra* note 75, Section IX.

theretofore enjoying the office of Honorary Vice President,[80] the transition to the new regime proceeded smoothly.[81]

The new Regulations formalized the status of the Society's interest groups. The Executive Council was empowered to authorize new interest groups designed to broaden interest in international law and to encourage inquiry into particular fields of international law, if twenty or more Society members express an interest in forming a group. Provision was made for Executive Council evaluation of each interest group every five years.[82] The aim was to encourage the formation of vital, active interest groups while making sure that they did not outlive their vitality.[83]

As we will see in Chapter Fourteen, ferment regarding interest groups continued in the new millennium, resulting in more changes in the Regulations.

2. Continuity in the Executive Director's Office

Charlotte Ku's three-year term as Executive Director was due to expire at the end of 1996. Charles Brower appointed an *ad hoc* committee to review her performance and make a recommendation. The committee unanimously recommended her reappointment. The Executive Council, after considering whether to offer her a renewed three-year term or a new four-year term, decided in favor of four years.[84] Dr. Ku accepted the offer.

D. THE SECOND CENTURY CAMPAIGN AND TILLAR HOUSE RENOVATION

1. The Campaign Takes Shape

Charles Brower's emphasis on fund-raising was driven by a perceived need to support expanding Society programs. If the Society was to make an impact on public opinion or on foreign relations decision-making, sustained program expansion was essential. There was no assurance that foundations could be counted on

---

80 See Minutes of the Executive Council, Oct. 25, 1997.

81 To reflect the changes in the Constitution and Regulations, the Guidelines for ASIL Nominating Committees, discussed in Chapter Ten, Section A.7, *supra*, were updated in February 2004. The updated Guidelines were made available to the Executive Council at its March 31, 2004, meeting.

82 Regulations, *supra* note 75, Section X.

83 For background information on each Interest Group (as of autumn 1999), see Report on and Redesignation of Interest Groups, prepared for the Executive Council meeting of Oct. 30, 1999.

84 Minutes of the Executive Council, Oct. 26, 1996.

to supply all the needed funds. Annual income from dues, sporadic individual contributions and return on existing investments were clearly inadequate to support significant research and outreach efforts. What was needed in the Society, to use Brower's words, was "a culture of giving."[85] The centerpiece would be an ambitious capital campaign that could provide an endowment producing the income needed to make an impact. It could also supply funds sorely needed to restore and improve Tillar House.

The Society's leaders recognized that they were not fund-raising experts. They decided to retain a professional consultant. The Executive Committee selected the firm of Marts & Lundy, represented by Elizabeth W. Gallagher.[86] She asked the Society to prepare a mission statement for the campaign and to appoint a steering committee with the mandate, at least initially, of identifying sources of large contributions to get the campaign started.[87] A steering committee was appointed and a draft mission statement was circulated to the Executive Committee. The mission statement, in its initial form, contemplated raising USD 3 million for support of working groups on emerging international legal issues, a fellows-in-residence program and an expanded use of the worldwide web; and an additional USD 1.5 million to restore Tillar House.[88]

Meanwhile, Elizabeth Gallagher conducted confidential interviews with sixteen prominent Society members to gauge their philanthropic attitudes toward the Society and to get their advice on the proposed campaign. The vast majority expressed strong support for the Society and for the idea of rehabilitating Tillar House, but they were less enthusiastic about building an endowment for programs.[89]

No pledges were sought at this point, but an eye-opening benefaction arrived on the Society's doorstep one fine autumn day in 1997. The Society's receptionist asked Charlotte Ku, Jennifer Krieger and Sandra Liebel if any of them knew anything about Lafayette Place. She said that a bank had called, wanting to know if the Society had once resided there, since a bequest in a will had been made to the Society whose address was at Lafayette Place.[90] Happily, the receptionist had not passed off the inquiry as a crank call. Happier yet, the answer was yes. Sarah Whitcraft deFord, who was virtually unknown to the Society's staff and officers, had died and left the Society about half a million dollars.

---

85 Memorandum from Charlotte Ku to Rick Kirgis, Aug. 13, 2004.

86 Minutes of the Executive Committee, Dec. 13, 1996.

87 Minutes of the Executive Committee, Mar. 14, 1997, and May 16, 1997.

88 Case statement, "The American Society of International Law: A Campaign for the Second Century" (Oct. 1997).

89 Minutes of the Executive Committee, Jan. 9, 1998; Minutes of the Executive Council, Apr. 1, 1998.

90 Memorandum from Charlotte Ku to Rick Kirgis, Aug. 13, 2004.

News of the windfall set off a bit of sleuthing for information about Ms. deFord. For many years she had been a Professor of English at Goucher College in Baltimore. In 1948 she had contacted the Society about making a planned gift, and George Finch had sent her a letter giving instructions on how to do it. She then created an *inter vivos* trust designating the Society as the beneficiary of one-third of the principal upon her death. She died in San Diego on November 17, 1996, at age 80. The half-million dollars she left the Society would become the bedrock for the new capital campaign.[91]

Elizabeth Gallagher's final report to the Society emphasized the need to hire a relatively senior development officer to articulate the mission as well as to identify needs and funding sources. She deemed the proposed USD 4.5 million goal to be unrealistic. In its place, she recommended a USD 2 million goal, with emphasis placed on funds to renovate Tillar House. She also stressed the importance of Charles Brower's continuing leadership in the campaign.[92] In April 1998 the Executive Council approved the hiring of a Director of Development, and adopted the USD 2 million goal for the campaign with the bulk of the proceeds (USD 1.5 million) to go to the renovation of Tillar House, and the rest for an endowment.[93]

At the same time, Thomas Franck, the incoming President of the Society, voiced concerns about proceeding with a new staff position for development without also addressing the Society's need to enhance its impact on how things are done in the real world. He announced plans to create a staff position for someone who would work on scholarly research and outreach to the judiciary, the media and others. Using the vacancy created by the resignation of Deputy Executive Director Jennifer Krieger, mid-level hires in both the development and the research/outreach fields could be squeezed into the budget. In January 1999, Richard LaRue was named Director of Development (later to become the Society's Deputy Director). In April of that year Christopher J. Borgen became the Director of Research and Outreach and *de facto* director of the Society's new Institute for International Law and Public Affairs – an institutional home for the Society's outreach programs. LaRue came to the Society after nearly two decades in non-profit fund-raising and management with the Urban Land Foundation, the Eisenhower World Affairs Institute, and Business Executives for

91 Minutes of the Executive Council, Oct. 25, 1997; *ASIL Newsletter*, Jan.–Feb. 1998, at 1, 8, 12. By the time the bequest was distributed later in 1998, the value was about USD 580,000. Report of the Treasurer for the Executive Council meeting of Oct. 24, 1998.

92 Feasibility Study prepared by Elizabeth W. Gallagher of Marts & Lundy, Inc., Jan. 1998; Minutes of the Executive Council, Apr. 1, 1998.

93 Draft Report of the Steering Committee for the Capital Campaign; Minutes of the Executive Council, Apr. 1, 1998; Minutes of the Executive Committee, May 4, 2000.

National Security. Borgen had been an associate with the New York law firm of Debevoise & Plimpton.[94]

James Carter joined Charles Brower as co-chair of the campaign when it progressed into its initial, "quiet" phase. They solicited potential donors who could make significant contributions before any public announcement was made. By March 2000, more than a million dollars had been given or pledged, including the large deFord bequest and a USD 150,000 contribution from the Microsoft Corporation's Rule of Law program.[95]

2. Tillar House Takes Center Stage

A new Tillar House Committee was appointed in the summer of 2000, with James G. Apple as its chair. The Committee selected Two Z, L.L.C., represented by Julia Wright, as the project manager for the renovation. The Executive Committee confirmed the selection.[96] OP.X, L.L.C., represented by Ted Oldham (who had drawn Tillar House renovation plans in 1995), was selected as the architect.

Faced with a preliminary estimated cost of slightly over USD 3 million for the entire project, including such things as relocation expenses during construction, the Executive Council in October 2000 called for preparation of alternative renovation plans with none to exceed USD 2.8 million for the entire project. The Council went on to approve the USD 2 million goal for the capital campaign, and directed that it should be used principally for renovation of Tillar House – thus, in effect, dropping the USD 500,000 endowment component that had originally been included in the campaign goal.[97]

Acting on the advice of Julia Wright and Ted Oldham, the Executive Committee and Tillar House Committee approved a design that reconfigured the first floor reception and library spaces, dedicated the second floor to flexible space for public meetings and supporting facilities, and placed all work space for Society staff on the third and fourth floors.

As a precaution brought about by cost concerns, the two committees authorized Joseph Guttentag, the Society's Treasurer, to explore alternatives to redoing Tillar House.[98] His contacts with a realtor led him to a building near Dupont Circle that would probably go on the market in the autumn of 2001. Investigation showed the building to be a viable alternative to Tillar House.[99]

---

94 *ASIL Newsletter*, Mar.–Apr. 1999, at 3.

95 Minutes of the Executive Committee, Mar. 2, 2000; e-mail from Rick LaRue to Rick Kirgis, June 28, 2005.

96 Minutes of the Executive Committee, Sept. 21, 2000.

97 Minutes of the Executive Council, Oct. 21, 2000.

98 Minutes of the Executive Committee, Nov. 29, 2000, and Dec. 13, 2000.

99 Minutes of the Executive Committee, March 14, 2001.

At that point, the inexorable law of supply and demand intervened. With the economy slowing down in the early months of 2001, demand for construction in the District of Columbia fell. The timing was serendipitous for the Society. Construction companies became interested in renovating Tillar House at prices considerably reduced from those estimated six months earlier. Two Z, the project manager, was able to get construction bids low enough to bring the total cost of renovation to roughly USD 2 million – the anticipated revenue from the capital campaign. The Executive Committee heaved a collective sigh of relief and unanimously recommended to the Executive Council that Tillar House renovation proceed according to Ted Oldham's architectural plan.[100] The Executive Council concurred.[101]

3. The Campaign in the Home Stretch

By the time of the 2001 Annual Meeting, the capital campaign had received cash and pledges totaling about USD 1,360,000, or 68 per cent of the goal.[102] The time seemed ripe to go public with the campaign. The campaign was announced at the Annual Meeting, and contacts were made with individual Society members to seek their support.[103] A sixteen-page campaign booklet was printed, illustrating and describing the planned renovation. Stephen Schwebel, the Honorary Chairman of the campaign, wrote an open letter to Society friends and colleagues, emphasizing the Society's need for a more visible public presence and influence, and a strengthened hub for sharing information in Tillar House.[104] Judge Schwebel and Messrs. Brower and Carter, with other members of the campaign committee, made countless personal contacts with potential donors as the campaign progressed. Rick LaRue coordinated the effort from beginning to successful end.

The campaign yielded sizeable grants from the Microsoft Corporation and the Hauser Foundation, but ultimately its success was ensured by contributions from Society members and friends. In all, more than three hundred contributions were received.[105] A surprising number of individual contributors gave USD 10,000 or more, thus becoming Patrons of the Society. Between June 1999 and December

---

[100] Minutes of the Executive Committee, March 30, 2001.

[101] Minutes of the Executive Council, Apr. 4, 2001.

[102] Id.

[103] Letter from Arthur W. Rovine and Charlotte Ku to ASIL members, May 23, 2001.

[104] Open letter from Stephen M. Schwebel, Oct. 2001, reprinted in *ASIL Newsletter*, Sept.–Oct. 2001, at 9.

[105] Final Report of the Second Century Campaign Committee, Oct. 22, 2002, in briefing materials for the Executive Council meeting of Nov. 2, 2002.

2002 (when the campaign ended, having raised a total of USD 2,112,000), the Society registered forty-seven new Patrons.[106]

During the renovation in 2001-2002, the ASIL staff moved to temporary quarters in a building scheduled for demolition in Chevy Chase, Maryland. The quarters were cramped, forcing the staff into a massive house-cleaning project that winnowed out old files and monographs.[107] The temporary quarters also forced the staff to become accustomed to working in an open space environment (as they would in the renovated Tillar House) rather than in individual offices.[108]

By the time the renovation was completed in the summer of 2002, Tillar House had a large and attractive lobby (named Brower Hall, in tribute to Charles N. Brower's capital campaign leadership) and the modern, state-of-the-art deFord Library and Information Center on the first floor, befitting the library's role as an international legal information provider to the world.[109] There now was the versatile Hauser Learning Center on the second floor featuring two meeting rooms that can be opened into one with seats for seventy-five or more for conferences, briefings and other presentations, as well as much-improved office space on the third and fourth floors. Gone were the "baronial chairs"[110] that had been crammed into the Tillar House board room. They were replaced by seats that could be moved easily by ordinary mortals. Gone also were the old dimly lit lamps, replaced by a modern lighting system.

Genevieve Tillar's gracious home had been transformed into an efficient, attractive venue for an institution rededicated to its goals of fostering the study of international law and promoting law and justice as an ordering force for international relations. The house was rededicated on November 1, 2002, with a symposium on The Rule of Law versus the Age of Terrorism, followed by a gala reception.[111]

---

106 Internal campaign records. For a list of Second Century Campaign contributors, see *ASIL Newsletter*, Mar.–Apr. 2003, at 7-8.

107 The space shortage led Charlotte Ku to make an arrangement with W.S. Hein Company to store and sell ASIL publications. Memorandum from Charlotte Ku to Rick Kirgis, Aug. 13, 2004.

108 Memorandum from Charlotte Ku to Rick Kirgis, Aug. 13, 2004.

109 See *ASIL Newsletter*, July–Aug. 1999, at 2 (quoting from the *Legal Times*, July 19, 1999). The library not only had upgraded technology, but also increased book capacity through the use of compact shelving. Minutes of the Executive Council, Nov. 3, 2001.

110 Jim Nafziger's term, in letter from him to Frederic L. Kirgis, Aug. 17, 2001.

111 *ASIL Newsletter*, Oct.–Dec. 2002, at 1.

E. FAMILIAR ENDEAVORS WITH SOME TWISTS

1. Annual Meetings in the Late 1990s

In September 1997, Daniel Bradlow, the Director of the International Legal Studies Program at American University, proposed that the Society join with his university to present an annual Grotius Lecture as part of the Society Annual Meeting. The lecturer would be a prominent international law scholar who normally would not attend the Annual Meeting. He or she would write a paper that would be published by A.U.'s Washington College of Law.[112] The Society went along with the plan. The first Grotius Lecture – a combined presentation by Nathaniel Berman of Northeastern University, who presented a paper, and Christopher Weeramantry, Vice-President of the I.C.J., who served as a discussant – was held on the day before the 1999 Annual Meeting.[113] The format, involving a principal presentation followed by remarks from a discussant, was replicated in the ensuing years.

The theme of the 1997 Annual Meeting was Implementation, Compliance and Effectiveness. Among the meeting's innovations were "insider briefings" on trade, public international law and private international law, and an informal conversation with Oscar Schachter. Schachter reflected on his thirty years with the United Nations and his long academic career at Columbia University, and then – in answer to questions from interlocutor Brigitte Stern – discussed the structure of international law, human rights, the role of the United Nations, and the relevance of law to decision-makers.[114]

Another, rather less scholarly, innovation at the 1997 Annual Meeting reflected Charles Brower's belief that formal speeches after cocktails and the annual dinner were a bit too stiff for the occasion. A skit inspired by *The Wizard of Oz* and written, produced and directed by Lori Damrosch for an audience of international lawyers, took the stage in place of a lecture after the annual dinner.[115] Bolstered by favorable reviews from the easily satisfied audience, plans were made for similar antics after the next annual dinner. Damrosch followed her 1997 triumph in 1998 with a musical comedy based on *The Mikado*. A cast of about ten made a valiant but ultimately unsuccessful attempt to stay on key with the music of Sir Arthur Sullivan as they belted out Damrosch's legalistic adaptation of Sir William Gilbert's libretto.

---

[112] Letter from Daniel D. Bradlow to Charlotte Ku, Sept. 12, 1997, on file with the Society.

[113] *ASIL Newsletter*, Sept.–Oct. 1998, at 7. See Nathaniel Berman, "In the Wake of Empire," 14 *Am. U. Int'l L. Rev.* 1521 (1999), and Response by Christopher Weeramantry, id. 1555.

[114] 91 *ASIL Proc.* 343 (1997).

[115] For a brief description, see *ASIL Newsletter*, Mar.–Apr. 1997, at 4.

Decorum at the annual dinner was restored in 1999, but not by going back to an after-dinner speech. Instead, Tom Franck moderated a lively exchange of views with five distinguished discussants on current international law issues. That format became the usual, but not invariable, norm for annual dinners in the years after 1999.

At the 1998 Annual Meeting, a panel chaired by Michael Glennon addressed "Legal Authority for the Possible Use of Force Against Iraq."[116] The panel contemplated not the all-out invasion that occurred five years later, but rather something on the order of the series of air strikes against Iraqi sites that occurred eight months later in Operation Desert Fox. If ever there was a timely panel at an Annual Meeting, this was it. In a debate that uncannily foreshadowed the legal debate that would take place five years later, the panel discussed the law of self-defense, the effects of U.N. Security Council Resolutions 678 and 687 (the Resolutions authorizing the use of force in the 1991 Gulf War and imposing conditions of the cease-fire after that war) and the doctrine of material breach of a treaty obligation. The discussion then turned to the constitutional question whether the President could use force against Iraq even if Congress had not authorized it – a question that was avoided in the autumn of 2002, when Congress authorized the use of force against Iraq.[117]

The planners of the 1998 Annual Meeting built on the precedent their 1997 predecessors had set with Oscar Schachter, by presenting a conversation with two giants in the international law field, Louis Henkin and Louis Sohn. The entire colloquy repays reading, but a small part of it is worth particular note. When asked by the interlocutor, José Alvarez, what were their proudest achievements, Sohn replied that it was his drafting of the articles in the U.N. Convention on the Law of the Sea on dispute settlement; Henkin replied that it was two sentences he had written: "Almost all nations observe almost all principles of international law and almost all of their obligations almost all of the time," and "Away with the 'S' word, where 'S' is for sovereignty."[118]

One can only imagine the consternation of James Brown Scott, George Finch and their contemporaries had they been able to attend the 1999 Annual Meeting. Its format was like nothing they ever contemplated. The fertile minds of the co-chairs, David Kennedy of the Harvard Law School and Berta Hernandez-Truyol of St. John's University School of Law, conceived and orchestrated a mélange of lectures and panels on a scale theretofore (and thereafter) unknown in the Society's annals. Lecturers and panelists ranged from the venerable to the unheralded, including several participants from outside the United States who

---

[116] 92 *ASIL Proc.* 136 (1998).

[117] *Public Law* 107-243 (Oct. 16, 2002), 50 USCA § 1541 Note.

[118] 92 *ASIL Proc.* 248, 249 (1998).

had not theretofore attended A.S.I.L. Annual Meetings. In all, there were 103 events with 350 panelists or speakers.[119]

The program was organized around four themes: violence (not only military conflict, but also economic coercion, human rights abuses and global poverty), money (facilitating and regulating a global market, enforcing property rights, and easing cross-border movements of goods, services, capital and persons), power (both public and private, including the relationship between law and politics), and culture (problems associated with the globalization of some local or national cultures and the localization of other cultures). In addition to a keynote address (noted below), there were five lectures and eight panels on violence, three lectures and nine panels on money, six lectures and ten panels on power, and seven lectures and eleven panels on culture, all presented within the space of three days. The resources of the Washington Monarch Hotel (not to mention the Society's staff) were stretched to the limit.

One of the innovations at the 1999 Annual Meeting was the presentation of a keynote speech before the annual reception. Louise Fréchette, the U.N. Deputy Secretary-General, spoke on the challenges facing international law if it is to be a significant instrument for order and justice in the world. The two most difficult challenges, she said, were to ensure universal acceptance of painfully negotiated international instruments, and to ensure compliance with the norms set out in those instruments. She added, pointedly, "Until the nations of this world, and especially the most powerful among them, show that they have the political will to take collective action in the global interest, rather than concerning themselves only with their own narrow self-interest and their immediate neighborhoods, the rule of international law is sure to remain very imperfect, at best."[120]

Annual Meetings after 1999 did not try to duplicate the plenitude of panels and lectures of that year, but – in contrast to the annual meetings of international law societies in Europe[121] – they continued to offer a potpourri of topics with three or four panels in each time slot. The idea of presenting a prominent keynote speaker immediately preceding the President's reception caught hold. Later years featured such luminaries as United States Supreme Court Justices.

The Society bolstered its effort to reach practitioners by organizing a one-day pre-Annual Meeting conference in April 2000 on issues international litigators often face. The conference was oversubscribed.[122]

---

119 Report of the Executive Director on Administration and Finance, prepared for the March 24, 1999, meeting of the Executive Council, at 6.

120 93 *ASIL Proc.* xiv, xix (1999).

121 French and German members of the Executive Council noted that European annual meetings concentrated on discreet subjects or issues. See the remarks of Brigitte Stern and Jochen Frowein in Minutes of the Executive Council, Oct. 30, 1999.

122 Minutes of the Executive Council, April 5, 2000.

Despite the infusion of fresh ideas and new faces at the annual meetings, subscriptions to the Proceedings dwindled in the late nineties. Libraries (from sixty-five countries) continued to be the principal subscribers. Production delays and bulky volumes took a toll on the Proceedings' usefulness.[123] From 1999 on, slimmer versions of the Proceedings were produced, containing the full text of lectures and short summaries of panel discussions.

2. It's Never Over

Speakers at Society events and authors in Society publications have always been free to express their own opinions. But, as we have seen, it has almost always been debatable – and often debated – whether the Society should go further and express institutional opinions as well. The debate, it seems, is never over.

In November 1996, Leonard Meeker, a former State Department Legal Adviser, urged the Society to take positions on important international law issues from time to time.[124] Charles Brower, the President of the Society, replied that he was inclined to concur that on certain issues, such as United States payment of its dues to the United Nations, action by the Society may be appropriate, but he wanted to seek some other views.[125]

Brower presented the matter to the Executive Committee, which declined to reconsider the long-standing policy against taking positions on substantive issues.[126] But, as we shall see in the next Chapter, the debate was merely suspended, not terminated.

3. It's Never Over, Part Two

Another recurring set of issues stems from the uneven performance of the Society's interest groups. Some have consistently been active, and some have not. The late 1990s were no exception: "What to do about interest groups" remained on the agenda for some Executive Committee and Executive Council meetings, but no significant decisions were made.

As usual, the International Economic Law Group showed its vigor. It organized a conference on "Linkages as a Phenomenon: An Interdisciplinary Approach," in December 1997.[127] In February 2000 it co-sponsored (with the Association of American Law Schools) a program on international business transactions,

---

123 Report of the Executive Director on Administration and Finance, prepared for the Executive Council meeting of March 24, 1999, at 5-6.

124 Letter from Leonard C. Meeker to Charles N. Brower, Nov. 22, 1996.

125 Letter from Charles N. Brower to Leonard C. Meeker, Jan. 6, 1997.

126 Minutes of the Executive Committee, Feb. 7, 1997.

127 *ASIL Newsletter*, Sept.–Oct. 1997, at 5.

followed immediately by its own program on the World Trade Organization-based international trading system.[128]

The Women in International Law Interest Group remained strong. It published a newsletter, sponsored panels and programs at A.S.I.L. Annual Meetings, continued its practice (begun in 1993) of making an annual Prominent Woman in International Law award, and developed its own web site.[129]

The Private International Law Interest Group co-sponsored a day-long symposium in October 1997 on the U.N. Convention on the International Sale of Goods, with presentations by American and foreign experts.[130] The Group established its own web site in 1998.[131]

4. Considering New Awards

In April 1998, Tom Franck appointed Conrad Harper as chair of an *ad hoc* committee to consider whether the Society should recognize persons for such activities as public service litigation, service to the Society and/or championing international law on Capitol Hill.[132] The committee was concerned about debasing the currency with too many awards, so it recommended against any new ones. It suggested some other ways to recognize noteworthy members, such as using plaques in Tillar House.[133]

5. The Newsletter Adds Substance

Beginning with the January–February 1997 issue, the Newsletter moved from five issues a year to a bi-monthly. With the increased number of pages came more substance. Substantive articles appeared on a wide variety of issues, including the Kyoto Protocol,[134] the workings of the Inter-American Juridical Committee,[135] the U.N. Compensation Commission's awards against Iraq,[136] and

---

128 ASIL-AALS leaflet for workshop and conference to be held on February 17-20, 2000, in Washington, D.C.; *ASIL Newsletter*, Nov.–Dec. 1999, at 9.

129 *ASIL Newsletter*, May–June 2000, at 9.

130 *ASIL Newsletter*, Jan.–Feb. 1998, at 2.

131 *ASIL Newsletter*, Nov.–Dec. 1998, at 2.

132 Minutes of the Executive Council, Apr. 2, 1998.

133 Report of the Special Committee on Awards, in briefing materials for the Executive Council meeting of Oct. 24, 1998.

134 *ASIL Newsletter*, Mar.–Apr. 1998, at 4.

135 *ASIL Newsletter*, May–June 1998, at 1.

136 *ASIL Newsletter*, July–Aug. 1998, at 1.

the pros and cons of the U.S. government's vote against the Rome Statute of the International Criminal Court.[137]

Presidents' columns dealt increasingly with substantive international law issues. Tom Franck's column in the September–October 1998 issue was particularly prescient. He noted the Pentagon's dominant influence on the U.S. government's opposition to the treaty banning land mines[138] and the Statute of the International Criminal Court,[139] and he deplored the unwillingness of others in the government to challenge the military viewpoint. He continued:

> The military mind is good at tactical engagement, but not at estimating the longer-term systemic and diplomatic costs of what, to soldiers, is essentially a logistical question. Those systemic costs, unfortunately, fall due whenever the next global crisis requires a powerful response, and the rest of the world, having adjusted their optic to ours, tells us just to keep on going it alone.
>
> During Operation Desert Storm, U.S. forces were predominant and performed magnificently. Yet, had there not been Islamic forces from the Gulf, Asia and Africa at their side, the costs of that conflict, which Iraq tried to characterize as a cultural war against Islam and the Third World, might well have been far higher. Back then, the Administration went to great pains to build and keep a common front, preventing our isolation.[140]

Less than five years later, his fears were realized when the United States, supported by the United Kingdom and a coalition of the few, invaded and occupied Iraq without U.N. Security Council authorization or support from Asia, Africa or much of Europe.

The Newsletter's new substance did not satisfy everybody. Michael Glennon, in his report as chair of the Ad Hoc Committee on Publications, opined that the Newsletter "still too often resembles assorted cut-outs from a high-school yearbook."[141] He called for outside reviewers to assess not only the Newsletter,

---

137 *ASIL Newsletters*, Sept.–Oct. 1998, at 1, and Nov.–Dec. 1998, at 1. ASIL member David Scheffer was the U.S. Ambassador-at-Large for War Crimes Issues.

138 Convention on the Prohibition of the Use, Stockpiling, Production and Transfer of Anti-Personnel Mines and on their Destruction, Sept. 18, 1997, 2056 UNTS 211, 36 *ILM* 1507 (1997).

139 Rome Statute of the International Criminal Court, July 17, 1998, 2187 UNTS 3, 37 *ILM* 999 (1998).

140 Thomas M. Franck, Notes from the President, *ASIL Newsletter*, Sept.–Oct. 1998, at 1, 4.

141 Statement of Michael J. Glennon in the Final Report of the ASIL Ad Hoc Committee on Publications, prepared for the Executive Council meeting of Oct. 24, 1998. Glennon was

but each of the Society's publications. Not all of the Committee members agreed with his approach.[142]

6. Re-examining the Society's Advisory Role in Filling I.C.J. Vacancies

Members of the International Court of Justice are elected by the U.N. General Assembly and Security Council on nominations by the national groups in the Permanent Court of Arbitration. Each national group is supposed to consult, among others, its national academies devoted to the study of law.[143] Since the Society is such an "academy," it has regularly been consulted by the U.S. national group when vacancies on the Court occur. The President of the Society has traditionally appointed an *ad hoc* committee to advise him or her as to which individuals the Society should support to fill the vacancies.

In 1996, Charles Brower appointed a committee headed by William D. Rogers. The committee supported Judge Stephen Schwebel for re-nomination to the "U.S." seat on the Court. That advice was non-controversial, but some Society members questioned whether the committee (and the Society) should recommend specific candidates to fill the foreign seats. Doubts were voiced whether the Society was qualified to judge whether foreign candidates met all of the conditions for election set forth in I.C.J. Statute Article 2. How, for example, was the Society to determine if a particular foreign candidate is a person "of high moral character" or possesses the qualifications required in his or her country "for appointment to the highest judicial offices"?

The *ad hoc* committee, the Executive Committee and the Executive Council all considered these questions, but ultimately decided essentially to continue the Society's previous practice with some tweaking reflected in newly drafted guidelines.[144] Brower noted that foreign national groups must be presumed to have found their nominees to meet the qualifications, so the Society would not pass on such things when it gives its advice regarding foreign nominees.[145]

7. The Youth Movement

Mindful of its need to serve the interests of students and other young persons, the Society in 1996 published *Internships and Careers in International Law: A Guide*

---

also critical of some other Society publications and outreach efforts.

142 See the statements of Jonathan I. Charney, Lori Fisler Damrosch, John Gamble, Mark R. Joelson and Kathleen Price, in *id.*

143 See ICJ Statute Arts. 4 & 6.

144 See Principles Concerning ASIL Advice on Nomination and Election of ICJ Judges and of Other Internationally Elected Jurists, approved by the ASIL Executive Council on October 26, 1996, and see the Minutes of that meeting.

145 See *ASIL Newsletter*, Sept.–Oct. 1996, at 1, 3-4.

for Graduate and Law School Students. It provided advice on opportunities in public and private international law, with practical suggestions for students seeking international law careers. In 1999 the Society published *Careers in International Law* with the rather pretentious subtitle, "Your Indispensable Guide to Career Paths and Internships in International Law." It was a revised version of the earlier publication, featuring a series of short essays by veterans in the various international law fields, plus a long annotated list of internship opportunities.

The Society's outreach to students was not limited to publications, but it also was not especially innovative – at least, by the standards of one of the Society's most creative members, David Kennedy, who proposed student-oriented programs that exceeded the Society's grasp.[146] Staying within its capabilities, the Society in May 1999 presented a panel on the relationship between law school and other graduate programs and on career opportunities in international law. In July 1999, about sixty students attended a Tillar House panel discussion on careers in international law.[147]

In 1996 and 1997, the Society came out with two publications on the teaching of international law. The first focused on teaching undergraduates;[148] the second addressed more broadly the approaches and techniques of teaching international law, drawing on the experiences of a several teachers in law schools and political science departments.[149]

In addition, a new Interest Group on Innovations in Teaching International Law was formed. Later renamed the Interest Group on Teaching International Law, it struggled to generate a sustained program in the ensuing years.

F. A NEW ERA FOR *INTERNATIONAL LEGAL MATERIALS*

In October 1997, Marilou Righini submitted her resignation as the Society's Director of Publications and Editor of *International Legal Materials*.[150] She had taken charge of I.L.M. in the autumn of 1968 and had been a mainstay in Tillar House ever since, not only at the helm of I.L.M., but also in the entire publications program of the Society. Through her work as the editor of I.L.M., she had

---

146 See David Kennedy's Memorandum, "Possible Student Programs," Oct. 13, 1999, in briefing materials for the Executive Council meeting of Oct. 30, 1999.

147 Christopher Borgen's "Report on Outreach," in Report of the Executive Director for the Executive Council meeting of Oct. 30, 1999, at 18.

148 *Teaching International Law to Undergraduates* (ASIL Bulletin No. 10, 1996).

149 John King Gamble & Christopher C. Joyner, *Teaching International Law: Approaches and Perspectives* (ASIL Bulletin No. 11, 1997).

150 Letter of resignation from Marilou M. Righini to Charlotte Ku and Charles N. Brower, Oct. 9, 1997.

organized and disseminated the materials that form the sources and evidence of international law to a worldwide readership, usually before the materials became publicly available elsewhere. As the Council put it in a resolution recognizing her long service, "Under her leadership International Legal Materials has become a flagship publication of the Society which is relied upon by scholars, practicing lawyers, diplomats and public and private organizations throughout the world."[151] She moved on to a new position with Transnational Publishers.

David Levy succeeded her, acting as Interim Editor of I.L.M. through the November 1999 issue. Levy was technologically savvy. He changed how I.L.M. was produced and how documents were collected. Instead of using photocopies of documents, he took many of them directly off the Internet and delivered them electronically to the printer.[152]

G. THE JOURNAL IN THE LATE NINETIES

1. Co-Editors-in-Chief Become the Norm

In the spring of 1997, Society President Charles N. Brower appointed a committee to ferret out present or past Journal editors who were interested in being considered to replace Theodor Meron and Detlev Vagts as Editors-in-Chief. There being no viable solo candidates, Jonathan I. Charney, of Vanderbilt, and W. Michael Reisman, of Yale, emerged from the pack together and were elected as Co-Editors-in-Chief in April 1998.

Because neither of the new Co-Editors was associated with a law school in New York City, Associate Editor Anna Ascher could no longer operate out of an office at Columbia or New York University. Thanks to the Internet age, she was able to reduce her commuting time to zero and function effectively from her home in the city.

2. Marshaling Scholarly Minds

Beginning in earnest with Tom Franck's tenure as Editor-in-Chief, the Journal on several occasions had bunched articles around specific subjects, particularly in Agoras, but sometimes in other formats. In the late 1990s the practice intensified, not always under a formal heading. In the latter category were the tandem of

---

151 Minutes of the Executive Council, Oct. 25, 1997; *ASIL Newsletter*, Nov.–Dec. 1997, at 2.

152 Report of the Executive Director on Administration and Finance, prepared for the Executive Council meeting of March 24, 1999, at 5. See also Chapter Fourteen, Section B.2, *infra*.

lead articles in April 1997 on international trade and the environment,[153] six relatively short articles on international criminal law and criminal tribunals assembled in January 1999,[154] and a collection of Editorial Comments in October 1999 on NATO's intervention in Kosovo.[155]

In October 1998 the Journal published "Agora: Breard."[156] The Agora assembled short pieces on the I.C.J.'s order of provisional measures in the *Breard* case,[157] to the effect that a death sentence in Virginia should not be carried out against a Paraguayan national, Angel Francisco Breard, pending a final ICJ decision on Paraguay's claim that he should be re-tried because the Virginia authorities had failed to inform him of his right to contact the Paraguayan consulate when he was arrested on a murder charge.

Steven R. Ratner and Anne-Marie Slaughter edited an innovative Symposium on Method in International Law that appeared in the April 1999 issue.[158] Contributions to the symposium included a "Prospectus for Readers" on methodology, and such wide-ranging methodological essays as one on positivism and others on international relations theory, feminist methods, and law and economics.

In the January 2000 issue, George H. Aldrich and Christine M. Chinkin put together a retrospective and prospective symposium on the areas of international

---

153 See Richard H. Steinberg, "Trade-Environment Negotiations in the EU, NAFTA, and WTO: Regional Trajectories of Rule Development," 91 *AJIL* 231 (1997); Thomas J. Schoenbaum, "International Trade and Protection of the Environment: The Continuing Search for Reconciliation," id. 268.

154 "Developments in International Criminal Law," 93 *AJIL* 1 (1999), with articles by Philippe Kirsch and John T. Holmes, David J. Scheffer, Mahnoush H. Arsanjani, Darryl Robinson, Sean D. Murphy, and Kelly D. Askin.

155 Editorial Comments: "NATO's Kosovo Intervention," 93 *AJIL* 824 (1999). The Comments were written by Louis Henkin, Ruth Wedgwood, Jonathan I. Charney, Christine M. Chinkin, Richard A. Falk, Thomas M. Franck, and W. Michael Reisman.

156 92 *AJIL* 666 (1998). After a summary of the facts by Jonathan I. Charney and W. Michael Reisman, the Agora presented short pieces by Curtis A. Bradley and Jack L. Goldsmith, Louis Henken, Carlos Manuel Vázquez, Jordan J. Paust, Lori Fisler Damrosch, Frederic L. Kirgis, and Anne-Marie Slaughter.

157 Case Concerning the Vienna Convention on Consular Relations (*Paraguay v. United States*), 1998 *ICJ Rep.* 248, 37 *ILM* 810 (1998) (Provisional Measures).

158 93 *AJIL* 291 (1999). Ratner and Slaughter not only edited the Symposium, but also wrote two of the articles – one of which performed the herculean task of tying together the disparate methodological approaches of all the others. Other contributions came from Bruno Simma and Andreas L. Paulus, Siegfried Wiessner and Andrew R. Willard, Mary Ellen O'Connell, Martti Koskenniemi, Kenneth W. Abbott, Hilary Charlesworth, and Jeffrey L. Dunoff and Joel P. Trachtman.

law addressed by the 1899 and 1907 Hague Peace Conferences.[159] The essays examined international adjudication, arms control, the laws of war on land and at sea, the Martens Clause and principles of humanity.

3. The Continuing Prominence of International Economic Law

The Journal in the late nineties continued to recognize the importance of scholarship in the field of international economic law. As before, the published articles focused more on the public law aspects of international economic transactions than on purely private law issues.[160]

4. Adding Substance to Venerable Departments

When Jonathan Charney and Michael Reisman became Co-Editors-in-Chief, they set out to add substance to the Journal's regular departments.[161] First, they sought to do more in the section on Contemporary Practice of the United States Relating to International Law than simply provide a barebones summary of what the U.S. government had done. The reinvigorated section would not

---

[159] 94 *AJIL* 1 (2000). Aldrich and Chinkin wrote an introduction and one of the essays. Other contributors were David D. Caron, Detlev F. Vagts, George H. Aldrich, J. Ashley Roach, and Theodor Meron.

[160] Lead articles: Eleanor M. Fox, "Toward World Antitrust and Market Access," 91 *AJIL* 1 (1997); Richard H. Steinberg, "Trade-Environment Negotiations," *supra* note 153; Thomas J. Schoenbaum, "International Trade and Protection of the Environment," *supra* note 153; Richard B. Lillich & David J. Bederman, "Jurisprudence of the Foreign Claims Settlement Commission: Iran Claims," 91 *AJIL* 436 (1997); David Palmeter & Petros C. Mavroidis, "The WTO Legal System: Sources of Law," 92 *AJIL* 398 (1998); Kenneth J. Vandevelde, "The Political Economy of a Bilateral Investment Treaty," id. at 621; Günther Handl, "The Legal Mandate of Multilateral Development Banks as Agents for Change toward Sustainable Development," id. at 642; Hannes L. Schloemann & Stefan Ohlhoff, "'Constitutionalization' and Dispute Settlement in the WTO: National Security as an Issue of Competence," 93 *AJIL* 424 (1999); David M. Ong, "Joint Development of Common Offshore Oil and Gas Deposits: 'Mere' State Practice or Customary International Law?," id. at 771; William W. Park, "Duty and Discretion in Commercial Arbitration," id. at 805; Daniel K. Tarullo, "Norms and Institutions in Global Competition Policy," 94 *AJIL* 478 (2000). Editorial Comments: John H. Jackson, Editorial Comment: "The WTO Dispute Settlement Understanding – Misunderstandings on the Nature of Legal Obligation," 91 *AJIL* 60 (1997); Andreas F. Lowenfeld, "Forum Shopping, Antisuit Injunctions, Negative Declarations, and Related Tools of International Litigation," id. at 314; Andreas F. Lowenfeld, "*Forum Non Conveniens* and Antisuit Injunctions: An Update," 92 *AJIL* 41 (1998). Notes and Comments: Janelle M. Diller & David A. Levy, "Child Labor, Trade and Investment: Toward the Harmonization of International Law," id. at 663; Joost Pauwelyn, "Enforcement and Countermeasures in the WTO: Rules are Rules – Toward a More Collective Approach," 94 *AJIL* 335 (2000).

[161] Minutes of the Executive Council, Oct. 24, 1998.

limit its sources to State Department materials.[162] Moreover, they contemplated producing cumulative versions of Contemporary Practice for separate publication every two or three years. In the capable hands of Sean Murphy, beginning with volume 93 (in 1999) both of these aspirations were realized.[163]

Charney and Reisman also encouraged book reviewers to provide more critical discussions of books than had theretofore appeared in the Book Review section.[164] Under Richard Bilder's steady direction as Book Review Editor, reviews became somewhat longer and considerably more analytical than they had been.

In addition, the International Decisions section, edited by Bernard Oxman, went from brief case notes to more detailed appraisals of the implications of important cases, emphasizing cases decided by tribunals outside the United States.[165]

5. Using the Available Technology

Under Charney and Reisman, Journal authors were urged to submit manuscripts electronically with endnotes that could be easily reorganized and generated. The result was a vast increase in the number of manuscripts submitted, but also a much easier editing process for manuscripts selected for publication.

With the July 1999 issue, the Journal switched to desktop publishing. The advantages included shortened production time and the ability to put the Journal online – including on LEXIS and Westlaw – more quickly than before.[166]

H. THE SOCIETY AT THE END OF THE MILLENNIUM

In the late 1990s, the Society made a commitment to outreach, including research that could have a positive effect on decision-makers. Its vision exceeded its grasp, but it made real strides toward educating judges about international law and toward developing web-based resources aimed at broad audiences. International Law in Brief and ASIL Insights became the Society's internet staples, and the Electronic Information System for International Law became more than a gleam in the eye. The Society held a variety of briefings, workshops and other meetings dealing with topics of current importance. Relationships with non-U.S. international law

---

162 Minutes of the Fall 1998 Meeting of the AJIL Board of Editors.

163 The first separate publication based on materials in the Journal was Sean D. Murphy, *United States Practice in International Law*, vol. 1, 1999-2001 (2002).

164 Minutes of the Fall 1998 Meeting of the AJIL Board of Editors.

165 See Report of the AJIL Editors-in-Chief, March 10, 2000, in briefing papers for the Executive Council meetings of April 5 and 6, 2000.

166 Minutes of the Executive Council, Oct. 30, 1999. For reasons of economy, desktop publishing was later discontinued.

societies were strengthened, particularly by way of meetings outside the United States. Nevertheless, resource limitations kept the Society from realizing all of the key goals put forth in 1999 by the Ad Hoc Committee on Effectiveness and Outreach. The Society at the end of the millennium still had no in-house media consultant, nor did it have a Congressional information program.

An impressive capital campaign produced more than USD 2 million for renovation and rejuvenation of Tillar House. A gracious old mansion meant originally to be a private dwelling was transformed after the turn of the millennium into a handsome and functional headquarters for the Society. In the process, the Society showed that it could raise a substantial sum of money for a common cause. Dedicated, energetic leaders made it happen. A perseverant staff endured cramped quarters while it happened, but emerged from exile in Maryland to reap the benefit of working in the vastly improved headquarters.

Annual meeting programs became more ambitious than ever. Noticeable, too, in the late nineties was a return to bygone days when Society annual meetings featured presentations by prominent, newsworthy persons hailing from outside academia. This time it was in the form of keynote speeches in plenary sessions held immediately before the annual receptions.

There was, in other words, new life in the old bones. Dynamic, creative Society Presidents made the Society their top professional priority while they were in office, and they got results – especially in the realms of building infrastructure and strengthening outreach. They worked closely with Charlotte Ku and her staff to develop and execute new plans. And they set the stage for their successors, who would prove to be just as dedicated and vibrant as they were.

Chapter Fourteen

APPROACHING AND CELEBRATING THE CENTENNIAL

"I ask myself, why does international law matter so much? ... The reason, of course, is globalization. No institution of government can afford now to ignore the rest of the world."

—Sandra Day O'Connor
Keynote Address,
96 *ASIL Proceedings* 349 (2002)

A. THE NEW MILLENNIUM AND THE AGE OF TERRORISM

1. The Existing International Order Disrupted

The new millennium began quietly. On January 1, 2000, computers continued to operate, despite cataclysmic predictions to the contrary. Trains stayed on their tracks. Aircraft continued to fly. Clocks still kept time. International tension was no worse than usual. There was concern about terrorism and about instability in the Middle East, but what lay ahead was barely imaginable.

A new intifada erupted in Palestine and Israel after Ariel Sharon paid a provocative visit in September 2000 to the Temple Mount/Haram al Sharif in Jerusalem. It led to suicide bombings by Palestinian militants, followed by retaliatory Israeli military strikes – a vicious circle that showed signs of abatement only with the death of Yasir Arafat in November 2004 and the election of Mahmoud Abbas as President of the Palestinian Authority in January 2005.

In April 2002, after terrorist raids against Israel had escalated, the Israeli government decided to build a barrier wall in part of the West Bank. As originally contemplated, the wall would cut off many thousands of Palestinians from the remainder of the West Bank.[1] In December 2003, the U.N. General Assembly requested the International Court of Justice to give an advisory opinion on the legal consequences emanating from the construction of the wall. After finding that it had jurisdiction to give the opinion, the I.C.J. concluded that the construc-

[1] See the U.N. Secretary-General's report pursuant to General Assembly Resolution ES-10/13, U.N. Doc. A/ES-10/248 (2003).

tion of the wall was contrary to international law and that all states are under an obligation not to recognize the resulting illegal situation.[2] In addition, the Supreme Court of Israel held that the injury that would be caused to the local inhabitants was disproportionate to the security benefits from the wall as it was originally situated; consequently the route of the wall had to be re-examined.[3] As of mid-2005, the Israeli government had scaled back the wall, but had not abandoned it.

In October 2000, terrorists attacked the U.S.S. *Cole* while it was docked in Yemen. The *Cole* attack was a prelude to the infamy of September 11, 2001, when terrorists hijacked four U.S. airliners, hurtling two of them into the World Trade Center towers and one into the Pentagon, while the other crashed in Pennsylvania. Within a week, the U.S. Congress adopted a joint resolution authorizing the President to use armed force against those responsible for the 9/11 attacks.[4] On October 7, the United States launched bombing attacks on Taliban and al Qaida targets in Afghanistan. The war on terrorism had begun in earnest. By early December the Taliban had been deposed and the on-the-ground search for Osama bin Laden was underway. It turned out to be a long and frustrating search. Bin Laden eluded capture and Afghan warlords vied for power. Nevertheless, a *loya jirga* (grand assembly) adopted a new constitution in January 2004, and a presidential election was held in October of that year.

On November 13, 2001, the President authorized the detention and trial by military commission of captured al Qaida members and any other non-U.S. citizen suspected of terrorism against the United States.[5] On March 21, 2002, the Defense Department implemented the President's order in Military Commission Order Number 1, which dealt with the jurisdiction, personnel and procedure of the military commissions.[6] A question immediately arose as to whether the detained persons were prisoners of war or – as the U.S. government asserted – unlawful combatants who would not be entitled to the protections of the Geneva Conventions of 1949. Another question arose as to whether the U.S. base at Guantanamo Bay, Cuba, where the detainees were being held, was within

---

2 Legal Consequences of the Construction of a Wall in the Occupied Palestinian Territory, 43 *ILM* 1009 (2004) (ICJ Advisory Opinion of July 9, 2004).

3 HCJ 2056/04, *Beit Sourik Village Council v. Israel*, 43 *ILM* 1099 (2004) (Supreme Court of Israel, June 30, 2004).

4 *Public Law* 107-40, 115 Stat. 224 (Sept. 18, 2001).

5 Military Order of Nov. 13, 2001, 66 Fed. Reg. 57833 (2001), 41 *ILM* 252 (2002).

6 Department of Defense Military Commission Order No. 1, Mar. 21, 2002, 41 *ILM* 725 (2002).

the United States' territorial jurisdiction and thus was within the habeas corpus jurisdiction of U.S. courts.[7]

In September 2002 the President sent to Congress "The National Security Strategy of the United States of America," asserting a right of pre-emptive self-defense to counter national security threats from rogue states and terrorists even if there is uncertainty as to the time and place of an enemy's attack.[8] This asserted right went further than the famous "instant, overwhelming, leaving no choice of means and no moment for deliberation" test for self-defense enunciated in the *Caroline* incident.[9] The pre-emptive self-defense doctrine was invoked as the United States moved toward the use of armed force against Saddam Hussein's Iraq under the apparent belief – erroneous, as it turned out – that Iraq was actively developing weapons of mass destruction. In October 2002, the Congress adopted a joint resolution in which it found that Iraq continued to possess and develop a significant chemical and biological weapons capability, and was actively seeking a nuclear weapons capability as well as supporting and harboring terrorist organizations. Accordingly, Congress authorized the President to use armed force to defend the national security of the United States against Iraq's continuing threat and to enforce all relevant United Nations Security Council resolutions regarding Iraq.[10]

The U.N. Security Council adopted Resolution 1441 in November 2002, deciding that Iraq was in material breach of its obligations under Resolution 687 (1991), which (*inter alia*) had imposed obligations on Iraq to destroy and cease developing weapons of mass destruction, and to cooperate with U.N. and I.A.E.A. inspectors. Resolution 687 also declared a cease-fire between Iraq, Kuwait and the Member States that had been authorized by Resolution 678 (1990) to restore international peace in the area after Iraq's invasion of Kuwait.[11]

In January 2003, chief U.N. inspector Hans Blix reported that Iraq had failed to give adequate answers to all the questions regarding its arms programs, but said that he had found no "smoking gun." At that point the United States and United Kingdom sought support among other Security Council members for a

---

7 The Supreme Court ultimately answered this question in the affirmative. See *Rasul v. Bush*, 124 S.Ct. 2686 (2004).

8 The National Security Strategy of the United States of America (Sept. 17, 2002), at <http://www.whitehouse.gov/nsc/nss.pdf>, reproduced in 14 *Foreign Policy Bull.*, Issue 1, at 225, 230-31 (Winter 2003). See also Sean D. Murphy, "Contemporary Practice of the United States," 97 *AJIL* 203 (2003).

9 2 J. Moore, *Digest of International Law* 409, 411-12 (1906). See also R. Y. Jennings, "The Caroline and McLeod Cases," 32 *AJIL* 82 (1938).

10 Public Law 107-243, 116 Stat. 1498 (Oct. 16, 2002).

11 See ASIL Insight, Security Council Resolution 1441 on Iraq's Final Opportunity to Comply with Disarmament Obligations (Nov. 2002).

new resolution authorizing the use of force against Iraq. When it became clear that they could not obtain the nine votes needed to adopt a resolution (if there were no veto), they withdrew their proposed resolution. President Bush told the nation that intelligence reports left "no doubt that the Iraq regime continues to possess and conceal some of the most lethal weapons ever devised,"[12] and said that the United States and its allies would rise to the responsibility to act against Iraq's threat to the peace. On March 20, 2003, the United States, the United Kingdom and other coalition forces began their invasion of Iraq. The Iraqi government fell on April 9.

The legal justification offered by the United States and United Kingdom for the invasion no longer relied on pre-emptive self-defense. Instead, the argument was made that since the Security Council had found Iraq to be in material breach of its obligations under Resolution 687, and since compliance with that Resolution was an essential premise on which the Council had declared a cease-fire, under the law of treaties the obligation of the allies to observe the cease-fire had been removed and the authority to use force under Resolution 678 (1990) had been revived.[13] Under that reasoning, so the argument went, no further Security Council resolution would be required.

A long and largely unplanned occupation of Iraq followed the invasion. Car bombs and suicide bombers became daily concerns in parts of the country. Casualties on all sides mounted. Inspectors found no weapons of mass destruction. Some coalition members pulled out, leaving the United States at the helm of a dwindling alliance seeking to restore order and rebuild infrastructure. Mistreatment of prisoners at Abu Ghraib captured world headlines and led to serious allegations of international humanitarian law violations. Despite the instability, the United States transferred formal authority to an Iraqi interim government on June 28, 2004, and elections for an Iraqi National Assembly were held on January 30, 2005. Most Sunnis boycotted the elections. Nevertheless, negotiations began among the Shiites and Kurds, leading to the formation of a government about two months later. New negotiations, in which some Sunni leaders participated, aimed at the drafting of a new Iraqi constitution. Meanwhile, sectarian violence escalated in the streets of Baghdad and other Iraqi cities and

---

[12] 39 Weekly Comp. Pres. Doc. 338-39 (Mar. 17, 2003). See also Sean D. Murphy, "Contemporary Practice of the United States," 97 *AJIL* 419, 424 (2003).

[13] For the U.S. legal position, see Letter of March 20, 2003, from the Permanent Representative of the United States to the United Nations, U.N. Doc. S/2003/351. See also Sean D. Murphy, "Contemporary Practice of the United States," 97 *AJIL* 419, 427 (2003). For the British legal justification, see the statement by a Foreign Office Minister in the House of Lords, 74 *British Y.B. Int'l L.* 787 (2003), and the legal opinion of Lord Goldsmith, the Attorney-General, 52 *Int'l & Comp. L.Q.* 811 (2003). Apparently, Lord Goldsmith told the British Prime Minister privately that the "safest legal course" would be to get a new Security Council resolution. *N.Y. Times*, Apr. 28, 2005, at A8.

towns. Despite the violence, the consitution was adopted in a referendum on October 15, and parliamentary elections were held with a large turnout on December 15, 2005.

Terrorism continued to spread. Bombings in Madrid on March 11, 2004, and in London on July 7, 2005, ostensibly were acts of retaliation against the Spanish and British governments for their support of United States policy in Iraq. Other terrorist acts, such as those in Russia, had no apparent connection with Iraq.

While the headlines in the first five years of the new millennium focused on such things as the Israel–Palestine conflict, the Iraq situation and international terrorism, less dramatic events raised international legal issues as well. Prominent among them in the United States was the frequent failure of state authorities to comply with the U.S. obligation under the Vienna Convention on Consular Relations (a) to inform the appropriate consulate when an alien is arrested and requests that the consulate be notified, and (b) to inform the alien of his or her right to communicate with the consulate.[14] These failures led to separate proceedings brought by Paraguay, Germany and Mexico against the United States in the International Court of Justice seeking to avert the execution of aliens sentenced to death as a result of murder convictions in state courts. In the first case, the I.C.J. issued provisional measures of protection calling on the United States to ensure that the Paraguayan national, Angel Francisco Breard, would not be executed pending a final I.C.J. decision.[15] The U.S. Supreme Court rejected Breard's petition for habeas corpus,[16] and the Governor of Virginia rejected the U.S. Secretary of State's request to suspend Breard's impending execution. He was executed before the I.C.J. could decide the merits of the proceedings brought by Paraguay.

In the other two cases, the I.C.J. decided on the merits that the United States had violated the Vienna Convention and was therefore obligated to allow review and reconsideration of the murder convictions and death sentences by taking account of the rights set forth in that convention.[17] In February 2005, President George W. Bush determined that the United States would have state courts give effect to the I.C.J. decision in the case brought by Mexico (the *Avena* case).[18] A

---

14 Vienna Convention on Consular Relations, Apr. 24, 1963, Art. 36(1), 21 U.S.T. 77, 596 U.N.T.S. 261.

15 Case Concerning the Vienna Convention on Consular Relations (*Paraguay v. United States*), 1998 ICJ Rep. 248, 37 *ILM* 810 (1998).

16 *Breard v. Greene*, 523 U.S. 371, 118 S.Ct. 1352 (1998).

17 LaGrand Case (*Germany v. United States*), 2001 *ICJ Rep.* 466, 40 *ILM* 1069 (2001); Case Concerning Avena and Other Mexican Nationals, 2004 *ICJ Rep.* 128, 43 *ILM* 581 (2004).

18 Memorandum for the Attorney General, Feb. 28, 2005, from George W. Bush (quoted in the Brief for the United States as *Amicus Curiae* Supporting Respondent in *Medellin v.*

week later, the United States withdrew from the Vienna Convention's Optional Protocol – the instrument that supplied the basis for the I.C.J.'s jurisdiction in the three Vienna Convention cases brought against the United States.[19] The intent was to preclude the Court from exercising jurisdiction over the United States in future cases under the Vienna Convention, unless the United States consents specifically to the Court's jurisdiction in a particular case.

The United States also emphatically declined to participate in the International Criminal Court. Although the Clinton Administration had signed the Court's Statute on December 31, 2000, the ensuing Bush Administration announced in May 2002 that the United States did not intend to become a party to it and therefore would not be bound by it. Nevertheless, the Court became a reality on July 1, 2002, when its Statute entered into force for states that had ratified it.

2. The Society's Input

In the early years of the millennium, the Society was engaged in a transformation process designed to strengthen its impact, and the impact of international law, on U.S. decision-makers in the judicial, legislative and executive branches of government. Some of its efforts were aimed directly at decision-makers, particularly judges, and others were aimed at larger audiences such as readers of the Journal as well as the media and (consequently) the public. Events like those mentioned in the section above presented the Society with plenty of opportunities for outreach to these constituencies. The Society's efforts were led in-house by its Director of Research and Outreach: Christopher Borgen from 1999 until 2002, Kathleen Wilson from 2002 until 2004, and Andrew Solomon beginning in 2004. As we have seen in Chapter Thirteen, Borgen came to the Society from private practice. Wilson came from the State Department Legal Adviser's Office, and Solomon had been Co-Director of the Rule of Law Research Office at the American Bar Association's Central European and Eurasian Law Initiative.

The Arab–Israeli conflict engendered three ASIL Insights at the outset of the millennium, each of them stemming from Israel's responses to Arab acts of terrorism.[20] Insights also appeared on the legal aspects of Israel's construction of the West Bank wall.[21] In January 2005, an A.J.I.L. Agora on the I.C.J.'s

---

Dretke, U.S. Supreme Court Docket No. 04-5928).

19 *Washington Post*, Mar. 10, 2005, p. A1.

20 See ASIL Insights, "Israeli Military Action in Gaza and the U.S. Response" (April 2001); "Israel's Intensified Military Campaign Against Terrorism" (Dec. 2001); and "Israel's Targeted Killings of Hamas Leaders" (May 2004).

21 See ASIL Insights, "The UN General Assembly Requests a World Court Advisory Opinion on Israel's Separation Barrier" (Dec. 2003); "Israeli High Court Decision on Location of West Bank Barrier" (July 2004); and "The World Court Rules that Israel's West Bank Barrier Violates International Law" (July 2004).

advisory opinion on the wall featured contrasting views by nine authors.[22] But Annual Meetings in the new millennium paid sparse attention to the Arab-Israeli conflict.[23]

* * *

One day after the attacks on the World Trade Center and the Pentagon, an ASIL Insight addressed some of the legal issues, including those related to international criminal law and to the law of self-defense in response to an armed attack. The Insight spawned fourteen comments and addenda, all of which were posted on the Society web site.[24] Related Insights appeared over the next three years.[25] The web site also opened a new resource page on the legal issues raised by these Insights, with links to the relevant documents.[26] The first issue of the Newsletter to appear after September 11 featured a discussion of the issues by Arthur Rovine, the Society's President;[27] in the next issue he focused specifically on the use of military tribunals to prosecute aliens apprehended in the war against terrorism.[28] When Anne-Marie Slaughter became President of the Society in 2002, she too employed the Newsletter to address a set of 9/11 issues, particularly those dealing with the humanitarian law of war in the new terrorist-threatened world.[29]

One month after the attacks, the Society presented a conference, "To War, To Court, To Both?," at the offices of Arnold & Porter in Washington. Presenters included the State Department Legal Adviser as well as two former Legal Advisers, other government officials and scholars. About 260 people attended,

22 Agora: "ICJ Advisory Opinion on Construction of a Wall in the Occupied Palestinian Territory," 99 *AJIL* 1 (2005).

23 Two relevant panels were: Religious and Social Ethical Perspective on International Law: The Middle East Peace Process, 95 *ASIL Proc.* 87 (2001); Is There a Role for International Law in the Middle East Peace Process?, 99 *ASIL Proc.* 213 (2005).

24 See ASIL Insight, "Terrorist Attacks on the World Trade Center and the Pentagon" (Sept. 2001), and Comments and Addenda submitted over the next three months.

25 See ASIL Insights, "Tribunals and the Events of September 11th" (Dec. 2001); "Status of Detainees in International Armed Conflict, and Their Protection in the Course of Criminal Proceedings" (Jan. 2002); "Pre-emptive Action to Forestall Terrorism" (June 2002); "United States Charges and Proceedings Against Two Guantanamo Detainees for Conspiracy to Commit Crimes Associated with Armed Conflict" (March 2004); "Distinctions Between International and U.S. Foreign Relations Law Issues Regarding Treatment of Suspected Terrorists" (June 2004); "Alleged CIA Kidnapping of Muslim Cleric in Italy" (July 2005); "The London Transportation System Bombings" (July 2005).

26 *ASIL Newsletter*, Sept.–Oct. 2001, at 2.

27 *ASIL Newsletter*, Sept.–Oct. 2001, at 1.

28 *ASIL Newsletter*, Nov.–Dec. 2001, at 1.

29 See especially *ASIL Newsletter*, July–Sept. 2002, at 1.

including several representatives of embassies.[30] In December 2001, the Society co-sponsored a panel discussion at Columbia University on human rights in the age of terrorism. That was followed by a co-sponsored public meeting on the laws of war in the war on terrorism, at the Johns Hopkins University School of Advanced International Studies, in February 2002. Briefings on international law and the war on terrorism were held in the new Hauser Learning Center in Tillar House and were open to the public, free of charge.[31]

The October 2001 release of International Law in Brief summarized the immediate post-September 11 legal developments around the world. Seeking to address the issues in greater depth, the Society formed a Task Force on Terrorism and International Law chaired by Ruth Wedgwood and Anthony D'Amato.[32] As originally conceived, the Task Force would produce a report modeled on reports of Council on Foreign Relations' task forces,[33] but instead the A.S.I.L. Task Force produced six essays. They were posted on the Society web site.[34] Also on the web site was a page with links to web-based legal resources on terrorism.

Before 9/11, the Society had scheduled programs for the Annual Meeting of the National Association of Women Judges in October 2001 and the Federal Judicial Center's National Workshop for District Court Judges in December. At the request of the judges, the Society adapted its presentations to focus on the war on terrorism.[35] Another presentation dealing with the war on terrorism was made at a second National Workshop in February 2002.[36] Later in 2002, the Society presented a program on the rule of law in the age of terrorism at the Tenth Circuit Judicial Conference.[37]

The Society also addressed the 9/11 issues in print. In September 2001, *International Legal Materials* featured a special section on terrorism-related documents related to the 9/11 attacks.[38] Subsequent I.L.M. issues reproduced more terrorism documents. The first issue of the *American Journal of International Law* to appear after 9/11 included three Editorial Comments on terrorism and

---

30 Minutes of the Executive Council, Nov. 3, 2001; roster of participants at the conference, in Report on ASIL Information Resources and Outreach, Appendix F, prepared for that meeting of the Executive Council.

31 ASIL 2002 Annual Report at 4, in *ASIL Newsletter*, Mar.–Apr. 2003. See also *ASIL Newsletter*, Oct.–Dec. 2002, at 1.

32 *ASIL Newsletter*, Jan.–Feb. 2002, at 2; ASIL 2001 Annual Report at 4, in id.

33 Minutes of the Executive Committee, Dec. 12, 2001.

34 See <http://www.asil.org/resources/terrorism.html>.

35 ASIL 2001 Annual Report at 2-3, in *ASIL Newsletter*, Jan.–Feb. 2002.

36 Christopher J. Borgen, "Outreach Update," *ASIL Newsletter*, July–Sept. 2002, at 3, discussing also the other 2001-2002 judicial outreach presentations mentioned in the text.

37 ASIL 2002 Annual Report at 3, in *ASIL Newsletter*, Mar.–Apr. 2003.

38 40 *ILM* 1254-1286 (2001).

international law.[39] Later, the Journal presented an Agora on military commissions[40] and comments on various 9/11 matters,[41] as well as summaries of the contemporary practice of the United States regarding the war on terrorism.[42]

As one would expect, the first Annual Meeting after 9/11 featured several presentations on terrorism and the conflict in Afghanistan.[43] The meeting culminated with a wrap-up panel examining some of the challenges 9/11 posed for international law and institutions. Jane Stromseth, the panel's chair, posed three of the challenges: how to respond to activities that do not fall neatly within established legal frameworks; how to respond to actions of violent non-state actors who do not share a commitment to restraint in the use of force; and how international law and institutions can address such problems as poverty and desperation around the globe. Not surprisingly, the panel reached no conclusions.[44]

* * *

September 11 and its aftermath stayed on the Annual Meeting agenda in 2003,[45] but the war in Iraq eclipsed it in 2004.

---

39 W. Michael Reisman, "In Defense of World Public Order," 95 *AJIL* 833 (2001); Jonathan I. Charney, "The Use of Force Against Terrorism and International Law," id. 835; Thomas M. Franck, "Terrorism and the Right of Self-Defense," id. 839.

40 Agora: "Military Commissions," 96 *AJIL* 320 (2002), with pieces by Daryl A. Mundis, Ruth Wedgwood, Harold Hongju Koh, Joan Fitzpatrick and Michael J. Matheson.

41 Tom J. Farer, "Beyond the Charter Frame: Unilateralism or Condominium?," 96 *AJIL* 359 (2002); Hilary Charlesworth and Christine Chinkin, "Sex, Gender, and September 11," id. 600; George H. Aldrich, "The Taliban, Al Qaeda, and the Determination of Illegal Combatants," id. 891; Steven R. Ratner, "*Jus ad Bellum* and *Jus in Bello* After September 11," id. 905; Thomas M. Franck, "Criminals, Combatants, or What? An Examination of the Role of Law in Responding to the Threat of Terror," 98 *AJIL* 686 (2004); Richard B. Bilder and Detlev F. Vagts, "Speaking Law to Power: Lawyers and Torture," id. 689.

42 Sean D. Murphy, "Contemporary Practice of the United States Relating to International Law," 96 *AJIL* 237, 255, 470, 475, 481, 731, 981 (2002); 97 *AJIL* 196, 703, 706 (2003); 98 *AJIL* 186, 188, 353, 820 (2004); John R. Crook, "Contemporary Practice of the United States Relating to International Law," 99 *AJIL* 261, 264, 479, 481, 483, 485, 486, 503 (2005).

43 "Humanitarian Law on the Conflict in Afghanistan," 96 *ASIL Proc.* 23 (2002); "American Unilateralism," id. 85; "The Judicial Response to Terror: Issues, Problems and Prospects," id. 250; "The Adequacy of International Law for Arms Control, Post-September 11," id. 273; "International Law After September 11," id. 401.

44 96 *ASIL Proc.* 401-411 (2002).

45 "Legal Responses to Terrorism: Security, Prosecution and Rights," 97 *ASIL Proc.* 13 (2003); "An Imperial Security Council? Implementing Security Council Resolutions 1373 and 1390," id. 41; "Self-Defense in an Age of Terrorism," id. 141; "Constraints on the Waging of War: *Jus in Bello* and the Challenge of Modern Conflicts," id. 193.

Even before the Bush Administration came forth in the autumn of 2002 with its National Security Strategy, the Society issued an ASIL Insight and held a public briefing in Tillar House on what would become the initial legal argument for an invasion of Iraq, as set out in the Strategy: the asserted right of pre-emptive self-defense.[46] Six weeks after the Strategy became public, the Society co-sponsored a public debate on the legality of pre-emptive self-defense in the context of an invasion of Iraq.[47]

As the Administration's legal rationale for going to war in Iraq shifted away from pre-emptive self-defense in the autumn of 2002 and toward material breach by Iraq of Security Council Resolution 687, the Society kept up with the changing scene. In November 2002 an ASIL Insight discussed Security Council Resolution 1441 (2002), which afforded Iraq a "final opportunity to comply with its disarmament obligations under relevant resolutions."[48] The Insight presented the arguments for and against use of the material breach doctrine to justify the use of armed force against Iraq. When the United States and United Kingdom failed to muster nine Security Council votes for a new resolution that, if not vetoed, would have established the legislative facts justifying the use of force, President Bush said that the United States and its allies would forcefully disarm Iraq anyway if Saddam Hussein and his sons did not leave Iraq within forty-eight hours. Another Insight appeared within that forty-eight-hour period, discussing the legal effect of the failed attempt to secure the nine votes.[49]

After the occupation of Iraq began, Insights continued to explain the legal developments as they unfolded. The post-invasion Insights dealt with U.S. legal responsibilities as an occupying power, the Security Council's role in the rebuilding of Iraq, diplomatic immunities in Iraq, obligations to protect Iraq's cultural heritage, the legal status of foreign economic interests in Iraq, the bombing of the U.N. Assistance Mission in Baghdad, venues for prosecuting Saddam Hussein, the legal status of coalition forces after the creation of an interim Iraqi administration, the mistreatment of Iraqi detainees, the request by the Interim Iraqi government for the continued presence of United States forces, prisoner

---

46 ASIL Insight, "Pre-emptive Action to Forestall Terrorism" (June 2002); "Briefing on Anticipatory Self-Defense and International Law" (Aug. 1, 2002).

47 Announcement of the debate to be held on Oct. 29, 2002, co-sponsored with The Foreign Policy Institute and International Law Program of The Johns Hopkins University School of Advanced International Studies.

48 ASIL Insight, "Security Council Resolution 1441 on Iraq's Final Opportunity to Comply with Disarmament Obligations" (Nov. 2002).

49 ASIL Insight, "Armed Force in Iraq" (March 2003). See also ASIL Insight, Addendum to Armed Force in Iraq: Issues of Legality" (April 2003).

transfers out of Iraq, and the attempt to have some American officials indicted in Germany for war crimes.[50]

Insights were not the only contemporaneous, public contributions Society members made to the debate over the legal/political issues raised by the crisis in Iraq. For example, Anne-Marie Slaughter, the President of the Society, wrote op-ed pieces (without claiming to represent the Society) for the *Washington Post* and the *New York Times*, commenting on the post-Cold War role of the United Nations as the crisis came to a head and on the potential legitimacy of the invasion.[51] She developed her views further in the *ASIL Newsletter*.[52] Other Society members commented publicly on legal issues raised by the invasion and occupation of Iraq.[53] And the Newsletter of the A.S.I.L. International Organizations Interest Group discussed the legality of the invasion and the U.S. offer to accept Saddam's exile as an alternative to the invasion.[54]

At the Annual Meeting in April 2003, Anne-Marie Slaughter in her presidential address mentioned four possible positions on the invasion of Iraq, and elaborated on two of them: that the invasion was legal but illegitimate, and that it was illegal but potentially legitimate.[55] A few panels touched on the Iraq war,[56] but concentrated discussion was left for the following year. In 2004, two panels dealt specifically with the situation in Iraq;[57] several other panels and lectures were more broadly focused, but covered issues raised by the invasion

---

50 See the Insights archive for 2003, 2004 and 2005, at <www.asil.org/insights.htm>.

51 See *Washington Post* Outlook section, March 2, 2003; *New York Times*, March 18, 2003, Section A.

52 *ASIL Newsletters*, May–July 2003, at 1, and Mar.–Apr. 2004, at 1.

53 See "ASIL Members Speak Out" (ASIL, Spring 2003), containing short excerpts from op-ed pieces and magazine articles by prominent ASIL members.

54 See the two articles by Michael P. Scharf in *International Organizations Bulletin*, Spring 2003, at 12 and 14.

55 Anne-Marie Slaughter, "An American Vision of International Law," 97 *ASIL Proc.* 125 (2003).

56 See Karima Bennoune, "'To Respect and to Ensure': Reconciling International Human Rights Obligations in a Time of Terror," 97 *ASIL Proc.* 23 (2003); Remarks by Harold Koh on the topic, "Why Obey International Law? Theories for Managing Conflicts with Municipal Law," id. 111; Remarks by Mark Drumbl and Yoram Dinstein on the topic, "Self-Defense in an Age of Terrorism," id. 141 & 147; Remarks by Gavan Griffith in the wrap-up panel on Coordination or Conflict?, id. 321.

57 "*Jus in Bello*: Occupation Law and the War in Iraq," 98 *ASIL Proc.* 117 (2004), and "Iraq, One Year Later," id. 261.

and its aftermath.[58] In 2005, Iraq and the war on terrorism were folded together in several panels.[59]

The July and October 2003 issues of the Journal featured a bifurcated Agora on Future Implications of the Iraq Conflict, examining such matters as pre-emptive self-defense, the UN role in the wake of the invasion, issues related to military occupation, and the overall implications of the war for international law and international security.[60] The Contemporary Practice section of the Journal, keeping up as always with current events involving the United States, documented the legal developments stemming from the invasion and occupation of Iraq.[61] The July segment of the Agora, and excerpts from the Contemporary Practice section and relevant Security Council resolutions, were promptly reprinted in a booklet that could be used in a variety of contexts, including international law courses.[62]

International Legal Materials reproduced Security Council Resolution 1441,[63] which declared that Iraq was in material breach of its obligations under (*inter alia*) Resolution 687. I.L.M. later published the Statute of the Iraqi Special Tribunal established by the Coalition Provisional Authority, and Security Council Resolution 1511 on the interim Governing Council of Iraq that operated under the wing of the Coalition Provisional Authority until elections were held in January 2005.[64]

---

58 Panel: Intelligence and the Use of Force in the War on Terrorism, 98 *ASIL Proc.* 147 (2004); lecture: Abdullahi Ahmed An-Na'im, Islam and International Law: Toward a Positive Mutual Engagement to Realize Shared Ideals, id. 159; Manley O. Hudson Medal Lecture: W. Michael Reisman, Why Regime Change is (Almost Always) a Bad Idea, id. 290; panel: The Bush Administration Preemption Doctrine and the Future of World Order, id. 325; remarks by Philip Alston and Brigitte Stern in the wrap-up panel, id. 368 & 369.

59 Panel discussions in 2005 included Executive Power in Wartime; Does Customary Humanitarian Law Contribute to Order or Disorder in the Regulation of Modern-Day Conflicts?; Legal Ethics and the War on Terror: The Role of the Government Lawyer; and Torture, Violence and the Global War on Terror.

60 See Agora: "Future Implications of the Iraq Conflict," 97 *AJIL* 553 and 803 (2003), with an Introduction and an Editors' Note by Lori Fisler Damrosch and Bernard H. Oxman, and contributions by William H. Taft IV and Todd F. Buchwald, John Yoo, Ruth Wedgwood, Richard N. Gardner, Richard A. Falk, Miriam Sapiro, Thomas M. Franck, Tom J. Farer, Jane E. Stromseth, Carsten Stahn, Thomas D. Grant, David J. Scheffer, and Eyal Benvenisti.

61 Sean D. Murphy, "Contemporary Practice of the United States Relating to International Law," 97 *AJIL* 419, 681 (2003); 98 *AJIL* 190, 591, 601 (2004); John R. Crook, "Contemporary Practice of the United States Relating to International Law," 99 *AJIL* 262, 265, 269 (2005).

62 See *Selections from the American Journal of International Law: Future Implications of the Iraq Conflict* (Sept. 2003).

63 42 *ILM* 250 (2003).

64 43 *ILM* 231 & 254 (2004).

A tragedy in the aftermath of the invasion of Iraq led to the creation of a new ASIL program. Arthur C. Helton, a member of the Society and a human rights advocate with a specialty in refugee law, died in a suicide bombing on August 19, 2003, in Baghdad while he was conferring with U.N. officials about the humanitarian crisis in Iraq. On the recommendation of the Society's Honors Committee, the Executive Council created the Arthur C. Helton Fellowship Program in his memory. It was conceived as a one-time program providing small grants (up to USD 1,000) for law students and young lawyers to pursue human rights work and research for one summer.[65] Six USD 1,000 grants were made for the summer of 2005, with an emphasis on action-oriented projects.[66] In May 2005 the Executive Committee decided to continue the program on a smaller scale in 2006.[67]

* * *

The Society responded also to events in the United States concerning the Vienna Convention on Consular Relations. For example, in 2004 when the I.C.J. decided in the *Avena* case that the United States was obligated to reconsider the convictions and death sentences of fifty-one Mexican nationals who had not been notified of their right to communicate with their consulate upon arrest,[68] the Society promptly came out with an Insight analyzing it.[69] When President George W. Bush determined in February 2005 that state courts would have to give effect to the I.C.J.'s decision in the *Avena* case, the Society produced another Insight discussing the legal effect of his determination.[70] When the United States then

---

65 Report of the ASIL Honors Committee for the Executive Council meeting of March 31, 2004; Minutes of that meeting.

66 Minutes of the Executive Council, March 30, 2005; ASIL 2004 Annual Report at 6, in *ASIL Newsletter*, Mar.–Apr. 2005; *ASIL Newsletter*, May–July 2005, at 3. The recipients were Anicee Van Engeland, Rosalind Evans, Elizabeth Brundige, Mark Pallis and Benedetta Lacey, and Anna Pollock.

67 Minutes of the Executive Committee, May 26, 2005. Funding from the operations budget for two Helton Fellows in 2006 was approved, if outside grants could not be obtained.

68 See text at note 18 *supra*.

69 ASIL Insight, "Consular Notification and the Death Penalty: The ICJ's Judgment in *Avena*" (April 2004). See also ASIL Insights, "World Court Consular Notification and Death Penalty Challenge Revisited: *Mexico v. United States*" (Jan. 2003) and "Consular Notification and the Death Penalty: The World Court's Provisional Measures Order in *Avena and Other Mexican Nationals (Mexico v. United States)*" (April 2003), and the ASIL Insights on other Consular Convention cases in the ICJ: "International Court of Justice Orders United States to Stay Execution of Paraguayan Nationals in Virginia" (April 1998), and "World Court Rules Against the U.S. in LaGrand Case" (July 2001).

70 ASIL Insight, "President Bush's Determination Regarding Mexican Nationals and Consular Convention Rights" (March 2005).

withdrew from the Consular Convention's Optional Protocol on compulsory dispute settlement,[71] an Addendum was attached to the 2005 Insight and was archived with it on the Society's web site. The Society posted a page on its web site with cross-references to a wide variety of resources dealing with the *Avena* case. The Journal's International Decisions and Contemporary Practice sections also reported on the case and its ramifications.[72]

After the United States announced that it would not become a party to the Statute of the International Criminal Court, the Society promulgated an Insight pointing out that nothing in international law requires a signatory to a treaty to ratify it, and outlining the legal significance of the U.S. announcement.[73] When the sixtieth country ratified the Statute, another Insight discussed some of the principal implications of its entry into force.[74] Pierre-Richard Prosper, the U.S. Ambassador-at-Large for War Crimes Issues, made a public presentation at Tillar House on the Court and the United States in September 2002. A panel at the 2003 Annual Meeting evaluated the fledgling Court and its future prospects.[75] The Journal's Contemporary Practice section kept its readers informed about the U.S. reaction to the Court,[76] and other Journal articles addressed a variety of I.C.C. issues.[77]

---

71 See text at note 19 *supra*.

72 See Dinah L. Shelton, "Case Concerning Avena and Other Mexican Nationals (*Mexico v. United States*)," 98 *AJIL* 559 (2004); Sean D. Murphy, "Contemporary Practice of the United States Relating to International Law," 97 *AJIL* 434 (2003); 98 *AJIL* 364 & 581 (2004); John R. Crook, "Contemporary Practice of the United States Relating to International Law," 99 *AJIL* 489 (2005).

73 ASIL Insight, "U.S. Announces Intent Not to Ratify International Criminal Court Treaty" (May 2002).

74 ASIL Insight, "The International Criminal Court Treaty Enters into Force" (April 2002). See also ASIL Insight, "Rome Diplomatic Conference for an International Criminal Court" (June 1998).

75 Panel: The International Criminal Court: The First Year and Future Prospects, 97 *ASIL Proc.* 259 (2003).

76 See Sean D. Murphy, "Contemporary Practice of the United States Relating to International Law," 96 *AJIL* 482, 724, 725 (2002); 97 *AJIL* 200, 710 (2003).

77 See Monroe Leigh, "The United States and the Statute of Rome," 95 *AJIL* 124 (2001); Allison Marston Danner, "Enhancing the Legitimacy and Accountability of Prosecutorial Discretion at the International Criminal Court," 97 *AJIL* 510 (2003); Daryl A. Mundis, "The Assembly of States Parties and the Institutional Framework of the International Criminal Court," id. 132; Dapo Akande, "International Law Immunities and the International Criminal Court," 98 *AJIL* 407 (2004); Hans-Peter Kaul, "Construction Site for More Justice: The International Criminal Court After Two Years," 99 *AJIL* 370 (2005); Mahnoush H. Arsanjani & W. Michael Reisman, "The Law-in-Action of the International Criminal Court," id. 385; Payam Akhavan, "The *Lord's Resistance Army* Case: Uganda's Submission of the First State Referral to the International Criminal Court," id. 403;

All told, the Society kept on top of the developing legal issues in a time of challenge to the existing international order. It did so in an informative and – at least in the pages of the Journal – a scholarly way. But if the goal was to influence decision-makers in the United States and elsewhere to give international law a meaningful, pervasive role in the shaping of foreign policy, evidence of a real impact in the first five years of the twenty-first century was not abundant.

B. THE SOCIETY'S TRANSFORMATION EFFORT

1. The New Infrastructure and Its Uses

The Society's responses to significant international events were part of its effort to transform itself into a visible player in the development of an improved international ordering system, and into a more vibrant community of informed professionals and experts in international law. The effort had other dimensions as well.

The transformation was much abetted by the remodeling of Tillar House. Improved office space and new technology gave the staff the resources they needed in order to shape and administer new programs. The new Hauser Learning Center on the second floor created a single meeting space for seventy-five persons or more, in place of two rooms that were ill-designed for any meeting of more than twenty-five. So it was that seventy-five invited guests filled the space for a panel discussion on "The Rule of Law versus the Age of Terrorism" as part of the Tillar House rededication on November 1, 2002. As soon as the panel discussion concluded, dedications of areas in Tillar House were made in recognition of major contributions of time and resources by Rita Hauser and the Hauser Foundation (the Hauser Learning Center); Charles Brower (the newly designed welcoming area on the first floor); Sarah Whitcraft deFord (the deFord Library and Information Center); William D. Rogers (the second-floor lobby); and Microsoft Corporation (the Rule of Law Reading Room in the deFord Center).

The renovated third and fourth floors were devoted to offices for senior staff and open environment working areas for the rest of the staff – many of whom had enjoyed offices in the old Tillar House. Even without separate offices, it was a step up from the old rabbit warren of offices and from the cramped Chevy Chase quarters from which the Society operated during the renovation.

Once the interior renovation was completed, attention turned to the building's exterior. A structural engineering study showed that repairs costing about USD 200,000 were needed to fix the masonry, mortar joints and window areas. The

---

Carsten Stahn, Mohamed M. El Zeidy & Hector Olásolo, "The International Criminal Court's Ad Hoc Jurisdiction Revisited," id. 421.

Executive Council approved a plan to borrow the money, with repayment to be made over five years from the designated capital account.[78] In the end, the Society was able to make the repairs by using its own funds.[79]

With the interior and exterior of the building in good shape, attention turned to what might be called aesthetic infrastructure, *i.e.* landscaping. The Tillar House Committee recommended that the Society proceed with a Centennial Garden in the front and sides of the building, with exterior lighting for the building and an irrigation system for the garden.[80] The Executive Committee approved the idea.[81]

2. New Formats and Services

In 2000 Peter Hansen, the Editor of *International Legal Materials*, and Branislav Maric, the Assistant Editor, undertook to transform I.L.M. into an international law reporter. They institutionalized the process begun in 1999, using the Internet as I.L.M.'s principal source of materials and designing computer-based macros to produce a standardized format instead of using photocopied original documents.[82] This put a dent in the appearance of authenticity, but not in the accuracy of the documents themselves or in their archival utility. The result was a more readable publication.

I.L.M. also faced questions about its role in the age of the Internet. With many documents appearing on Internet sites before I.L.M. could reproduce and disseminate them in paper copy, there was a question as to whether I.L.M. had outlived its utility. Part of the answer was a new I.L.M. focus on items not readily available on the Internet, such as decisions of some international arbitral tribunals and national courts.[83] Another point in its favor was its archival function, which gave it lasting utility to readers who could not always rely on web sites to retain

---

78 Report of the Committee on Budget and Finance and the attached recommendations of the Tillar House Committee, prepared for the Executive Council meeting of March 31, 2004; Minutes of that meeting.

79 For details, see Memorandum, "ASIL History: Details Relating to Budget, Finances and Membership" (2006), on file with the Society.

80 Report of the Tillar House Committee on Annual Inspection and Meeting, July 12, 2004, in briefing materials for the Executive Council meeting of Nov. 6, 2004. No fountains or busts would be included.

81 Minutes of the Executive Committee, Sept. 14, 2004. Funds came from the Society's capital budget, spread over the next few years.

82 For details, see the Report on ILM Office Operations in the Year 2000, prepared for the Executive Council meeting of Oct. 21, 2000.

83 Report of the ILM Managing Editor for the Executive Council meeting of April 2, 2003; and see the minutes of that meeting.

documents over the long haul. Also significant was its close tie to International Law in Brief, which had more than 4,000 e-mail subscribers.[84]

The *ASIL Newsletter* became even more substantive under the direction of Rick LaRue. It featured pieces by Society Presidents on current events, as well as printed versions of ASIL Insights and other substantive reports, along with news about the Society.

Meanwhile, the Society web site was being transformed. On May 24, 2001, the redesigned site came online. It offered expanded coverage, including links to a variety of ASIL information products such as Insights, International Law in Brief, the ASIL Guide to Electronic Resources for International Law, the ASIL Career Guide, and information about the Society and its publications and programs. It also featured an improved search engine offering users new search options.[85] In September 2001, the web site received one million hits in a single month for the first time.[86]

The web site was upgraded again on September 20, 2004, shortly after the Society's Electronic Information System for International Law (EISIL) was launched. The new site not only supplied a link to EISIL, but also offered improved navigation tools, features such as Timely Topics and Cases of Note, and interactive membership and subscription services.[87]

With its first-ever webinar, the Society demonstrated how to use EISIL to more than one hundred people from a dozen nations. The webinar involved an interactive telephone presentation with simultaneous demonstrations on the participants' personal computers.

EISIL quickly made an impact. It received the Best Web Site of 2004 award from the International Association of Law Libraries.[88] Its presence on the scene was celebrated at a reception held in connection with the annual meeting of the Association of American Law Schools on January 7, 2005.

In early 2002, the Society gave its Internet users a new medium for discussion by way of its e-mail list-serve, the ASIL Forum. It was conceived as a forum for

---

84 See the Report of Ruth Teitelbaum, Managing Editor of ILM, for the Executive Council meeting of Nov. 1, 2003, and see the minutes of that meeting.

85 See *ASIL Newsletter*, July–Aug. 2001, at 7.

86 Report on ASIL Information Resources and Outreach, in the briefing materials for the Executive Council meeting of Nov. 3, 2001.

87 See ASIL 2004 Annual Report at 4, in ASIL Newsletter, Mar.–Apr. 2005; and visit <http://www.asil.org>. Membership and subscription services were outsourced to Virtual, Inc., in Wakefield, Massachusetts. Report of the Executive Director for the Executive Council meeting of Nov. 1, 2003, in briefing papers for that meeting.

88 ASIL 2004 Annual Report at 4, in *ASIL Newsletter*, Mar.–Apr. 2005. For more on the development of EISIL, see Chapter Thirteen, Section A.6, *supra*.

replies to ASIL Insights,[89] but it quickly turned into a free-for-all discussion group. It had more than six hundred members almost immediately.[90] For reasons of practicality, it was unmoderated and thus depended for order and decorum on a set of discussion guidelines and on the cooperation of users. Order and decorum did not always prevail; every now and then the Society's Director of Research and Outreach found it necessary to remind users of what was acceptable discourse and what was not. Nevertheless, the Forum proved to be a lively Internet place used primarily by a small group of regular users who had a great deal to say to each other on topics of current interest.

IL.post, an e-mail news service for Society members only, was inaugurated in February 2005. Edited by the Society's new webmaster, Daniel Vickers, and sent out every few weeks, it featured recent ASIL Insights, Developments in International Law drawn largely from International Law in Brief, and announcements of upcoming ASIL events.[91]

In June 2005, ASIL Forum members were treated to a new e-mail service, International Law NewsWatch: a monthly compilation of significant news items, press releases, and noteworthy comments by ASIL members reported in the media.[92] The new service was linked to a page on the ASIL web site, International Law in the News, featuring electronic links to the relevant media sources.[93]

Some of the innovations fizzled out. In the autumn of 2003, the Society launched a new online calendar of international law events and an online jobs board.[94] Neither service seems to have had much impact. But most of the innovations caught on and became outreach mainstays.

3. Intensified Judicial Outreach

Outreach had been a significant item on the Society's agenda since 1991, but the results were spotty. At the beginning of the new millennium, the Society established its Institute on International Law in Public Affairs, designed to intensify its efforts to move international law toward a more central place in public discourse. Christopher J. Borgen, the Society's new Director of Research and Outreach, made outreach to the judiciary his first priority. The Hauser and MacArthur Foundations supported the judicial outreach effort with substantial grants.

---

89 Minutes of the Executive Committee, Sept. 20, 2001.

90 *ASIL Newsletter*, Mar.–Apr. 2002, at 7.

91 *ASIL Newsletter*, Jan.–Feb. 2005, at 3.

92 ASIL e-mail to asilforum members, June 8, 2005.

93 Online at <http://www.asil.org/inthenews/news.html>.

94 *ASIL Newsletter*, Sept.–Oct. 2003, at 7.

Working with the Federal Judicial Center and an advisory board chaired by Justice Sandra Day O'Connor, Borgen organized panels on various international law topics at federal judicial circuit conferences. As we have seen in Chapter Thirteen, in the summer of 2000 the Society provided programs at the Third, Fifth, Ninth and Tenth Circuit Conferences.[95] The presentations covered International Law and U.S. Immigration Policy (Third Circuit), International Arbitration and the Federal Courts (Fifth), Law Without Borders: The Increasing Impact of International Law on the Federal Courts (Ninth), and The Practice of International Law at the Dawn of the 21st Century (Tenth).[96] In the summer of 2001, the Society presented programs on International Law in the Federal Courts at the First Circuit Conference and on International Tribunals and the Federal Courts at the Second Circuit Conference.[97] As already noted, in the aftermath of September 11, 2001, the Society adapted previously scheduled programs for the judiciary to cover aspects of terrorism.[98] It also presented a program at the Seventh Circuit Conference on N.A.F.T.A. Disputes and Domestic Law.[99]

In 2003, panels were presented at the Sixth and Eleventh Circuit Conferences, and another one on treaties in civil litigation was part of a Federal Judicial Center Workshop for Eleventh Circuit judges. The Society also briefed law clerks in the U.S. District Court for the Central District of California.[100] With an eye to more lasting impact than could be achieved through brief presentations, the Society in 2003 published *International Law: A Handbook for Judges*, by David Bederman with input from Christopher Borgen and David Martin. Copies were distributed to 1,600 federal judges.[101]

In 2004, the Society returned to the Ninth Circuit Judicial Conference with a presentation on international law in U.S. Courts and another one on innovative remedies for human rights controversies in countries such as South Africa. The Society also made a presentation on international law and the federal courts at the Eighth Circuit Judicial Conference.[102] In 2005, the Society put on two

---

95 *ASIL Newsletter*, Jan.–Feb. 2001, at 1, 4.

96 ASIL 2000 Annual Report at 3, in *ASIL Newsletter*, Mar.–Apr. 2001.

97 ASIL 2001 Annual Report at 2, in *ASIL Newsletter*, Jan.–Feb. 2002.

98 See text at note 35 *supra*.

99 *ASIL Newsletter*, July–Sept. 2002, at 3.

100 The presenters at these programs and the topics are identified in Appendix 1 to Kathleen Wilson's Summary of ASIL Outreach Activities, Nov. 2002-Oct. 2003, in briefing materials for the Executive Council meeting of Nov. 1, 2003.

101 ASIL 2003 Annual Report at 2, in *ASIL Newsletter*, Mar.–Apr. 2004.

102 ASIL 2004 Annual Report at 2, in *ASIL Newsletter*, Mar.–Apr. 2005.

programs at the Eleventh Circuit Judicial Conference – one on criminal law and the other on civil law.[103]

Although most of the judicial outreach was directed at federal judges, it was not exclusively so. In particular, the program for the National Association of Women Judges in 2001 had an audience that included many state court judges.[104]

As we will see below, the Society sought and received significant grants from foundations for its expanding judicial outreach program in the early 21st century, including funds for an experimental electronic resource bank for U.S. judges and their law clerks who wish to make use of international law sources in domestic litigation.[105]

4. Media Outreach

With the help of a USD 300,000 grant from the MacArthur Foundation, the Society established a media program in 2000. The aim was to help educate the public by informing the media of the international legal implications of newsworthy international events. Initially, the plan was to retain a prominent media fellow who would provide the Society with access to practicing members of the media.[106] Unfortunately, the right person never emerged.

Another goal was to supply the media with press kits, backgrounders, special briefings and other access to the Society's resources.[107] This, too, did not come about exactly as planned, but in September 2002, the Society launched an online Media Center.[108] Its principal resource became known as "Tools for Media," posted on the ASIL web site. The tools consisted of a list covering a wide range of specific and generic international law topics and an associated list of experts, with links to them, who made themselves available to talk with the media on topics within their fields of expertise.[109]

In addition, the Society's staff fielded inquiries from the media on the international law implications of current events, directing them to Society experts whenever the staff felt the need to do so.[110] In the spring of 2003, when the invasion and occupation of Iraq began to dominate the headlines, the Society

---

103 Minutes of the Executive Committee, May 26, 2005.

104 Report on ASIL Information Resources and Outreach, in briefing materials for the Executive Council meeting of Nov. 3, 2001.

105 See text at note 141 *infra*.

106 Minutes of the Executive Council, April 5, 2000.

107 *ASIL Newsletter*, Mar.–Apr. 2001, at 3.

108 ASIL 2002 Annual Report at 3, in ASIL Newsletter, Mar.–Apr. 2003.

109 Online as of 2005 at <http://www.asil.org/inthenews/toolsformedia.html>.

110 *ASIL Newsletter*, Oct.–Dec. 2002, at 7.

often received several calls a day from journalists.[111] Members of the media were invited to some of the Tillar House briefings on current issues. And, of course, many of the ASIL Insights were designed to give unbiased guidance to the media, as well as to other laypersons, on international law issues raised by newsworthy events.

All the while, individual Society members participated in public discourse on current international events by contributing op-ed pieces to newspapers, appearing on television and radio, and expressing themselves online. The Society attempted to keep track of its members' public contributions to the understanding of international law and listed them on its web site, with links whenever possible.[112]

5. Outreach to Congress

Although plans were made to have briefing sessions and other programs for members of Congress and their staffs, the only systematic, direct contact with them came by way of sending Insights and International Law in Brief to them electronically. In part the lack of a Society presence on Capitol Hill was a problem of staffing and priorities. With just one staff member – the Director of Research and Outreach – working on all of the outreach programs, it proved impossible to do justice to them all. In part, it was a problem of getting the attention of Congress members and their staffs. The Society had no ally on Capitol Hill to match its allies on the judicial front, Justice Sandra Day O'Connor and the Federal Judicial Center, although it did collaborate with the Council on Foreign Relations to conduct roundtable discussions directed in part at law-makers.[113]

There were other hindrances as well. The Society's policy against taking positions on substantive issues made it difficult to speak the language of politicians. Finally, there was the nagging prospect of trouble with the Internal Revenue Service over the Society's tax-exempt status if the Society appeared to be lobbying Congress.

Anne-Marie Slaughter championed outreach to members of Congress indirectly, by reaching their constituents. She called for a grass-roots initiative, with Society members holding themselves available to speak to local groups on the issues of the day.[114] She appointed Steven Ratner and Laurence Helfer to

---

[111] Kathleen Wilson, Summary of ASIL Outreach Activities, Nov. 2002-Oct. 2003, in briefing materials for the Executive Council meeting of Nov. 1, 2003.

[112] As of 2005, at International Law in the News, <http://www.asil.org/inthenews/news.html>.

[113] See text at note 132 *infra*.

[114] Minutes of the Executive Committee, Oct. 18, 2001; Minutes of the Executive Council, March 13, 2002.

co-chair an *ad hoc* committee that would develop topics of interest to local foreign policy associations and come up with a roster of Society members interested in making presentations.[115] The committee produced a list of more than fifty Society members who were willing to speak to local foreign policy organizations under the auspices of the American Committees on Foreign Relations (A.C.F.R.), an association of local committees interested in foreign affairs. The A.C.F.R. did not show much interest.[116] The A.S.I.L. Committee also prepared a form letter that was sent under President Slaughter's signature to seventy state bar associations proposing presentations by Society members, but apparently no response was received.[117] All told, it was a frustrating experience.

6. Proposed Outreach to the Military and to Government Lawyers

At the Executive Council meeting in the autumn of 2002, there was extensive discussion of outreach to the military. Military lawyers seemed to be well versed in international law, but they had a problem in getting the attention of non-lawyer officers. The problem had been exacerbated by the Naval War College's abandonment of international law teach-ins. Although there was consensus in the Executive Council on the need to do more with the military,[118] other outreach priorities swallowed the available time and resources and no organized effort was made to make the Society's voice better heard in military circles.

At the Executive Council meeting in the autumn of 2003, the focus shifted to government lawyers outside the military. Following up on the Council's discussion, Michael Matheson and Sean Murphy spent several hours at the State Department Legal Adviser's Office in February 2004, talking with young attorneys in the office about customary international law. The attorneys were receptive, particularly welcoming the opportunity to tie theory to practice. Similar opportunities were offered to the Justice and Defense Departments, but the offers were not accepted.[119]

---

115 Minutes of the Executive Committee, May 23, 2002.

116 Minutes of the Executive Council, April 2, 2003; memorandum from Larry Helfer to Anne-Marie Slaughter and Charlotte Ku, March 30, 2004, in briefing materials for the Executive Council meeting of March 31, 2004.

117 Id. See also Report of the Committee on Outreach for the Executive Council meeting of Nov. 2, 2002; Minutes of the Executive Committee, Oct. 16, 2002.

118 Minutes of the Executive Council, Nov. 2, 2002.

119 Minutes of the Executive Council, Nov. 1, 2003; e-mail from Michael Matheson to Rick Kirgis, June 23, 2005.

7. Outreach to Students and Young Professionals

In January 2001 the Society took a step toward reaching a wide audience of law students, by presenting a one-day program at the annual meeting of the Association of American Law Schools on bringing international law into the first-year law school curriculum and into upper-level courses.[120]

When Anne-Marie Slaughter became the Society's President in 2002, she announced that one of her goals was to give a boost to the teaching of international law in law schools. Her claim, she said, was "that just as no educated law student should graduate without taking constitutional law, so in the 21st century no educated law student should graduate without a basic knowledge of the landscape of international law, broadly defined to include elements of public and private international law, transnational law, foreign relations law, and comparative law."[121]

She appointed a small committee to look into means of making it as easy as possible for young law teachers to enter the field and for law schools to offer, and even require, the pertinent courses. The committee gathered data on the inclusion of international legal issues in law courses not specifically devoted to international law, with an eye ultimately to stimulating the development of transnational law materials that could be used in those courses. The committee also convened roundtable discussions among teachers, addressing issues of curricula and pedagogy.[122] Other ideas included preparing a web-based international law "cookbook" that could include examples of course syllabi, unpublished teaching materials and source materials; providing a list-serve for discussion of teaching questions; and an interactive "road-map" that would guide users through specialized areas of international law at various levels of sophistication.[123]

Meanwhile, the Society launched its Career Development Partnership program. It supplied law schools with materials for distribution to students, including information on such publications as the Society's *Careers in International Law*, which reached its fifth edition in 2005.[124] By 2004, some fifty-five law schools were participating in the program.[125] In October 2003, more than sixty students

---

[120] Minutes of the Executive Council, April 4, 2001.

[121] *ASIL Newsletter*, Mar.–Apr. 2002, at 4.

[122] The program for the teaching workshop held on the Saturday afternoon of the 2004 Annual Meeting appears in the briefing materials for the Executive Council meeting of March 31, 2004.

[123] Report of the ASIL Committee on Teaching, Oct. 19, 2002, in briefing materials for the Executive Council meeting of Nov. 2, 2002.

[124] Letter from Charlotte Ku to Society members in teaching, Feb. 9, 2005.

[125] ASIL 2004 Annual Report at 3, in *ASIL Newsletter*, Mar.–Apr. 2005.

from the Washington D.C. area attended a career discussion panel and reception in Tillar House, with another 170 turned away because of space constraints.[126] At about the same time, the Society set out to identify members who would speak at career development programs put on by law schools in their regions. Member participation appears to have been spotty.[127]

Although the Society continued to keep its distance from the International Law Students Association (I.L.S.A.) during this period, it still shared Annual Meeting hotel space with the Jessup Competition final rounds and assisted in supplying judges – most of whom were Society members. In 2003, the law firm of Shearman & Sterling became the official sponsor of the Jessup international rounds and the championship trophy.

The Society reached out to young scholars by inviting them to submit abstracts of works in progress for possible presentation at the 2005 Annual Meeting.[128] Four of the nearly sixty submissions were selected for presentation in what was called a New Voices Forum, around the theme "The Role of Domestic and International Institutions in the Shaping of International Law."[129]

8. New Emphasis on Public Programs, Workshops and Conferences

Even before Tillar House was renovated, the Society launched an expanded series of public presentations and workshops. In 2000, Tillar House played host to seventeen events open to the public, ranging in scope from international trade law to international criminal law.[130] When the renovation was complete in the summer of 2002, the Society was able to use the new Hauser Learning Center on the second floor to present programs for larger groups of participants than ever before. To take advantage of the larger space and to emphasize the relevance of what would be happening there, the Society renamed the former Tillar House Briefings as the Current Issues in International Law Briefing Series. The programs sought to bring together policy-makers, diplomats, lawyers and the general public for discussions of current issues ranging from the war on terrorism to the roles of international financial institutions in post-conflict reconstruction.[131]

Tillar House hosted other public presentations as well. Noteworthy was the Society's participation in the Ralph Bunche Centenary by sponsoring two programs in 2004 – one on the Special Court in Sierra Leone and the other on the crisis in Darfur, Sudan.

---

126 *ASIL Newsletter*, Nov.–Dec. 2003, at 7.

127 Id.

128 ASIL e-mail Call for Papers, Oct. 29, 2004.

129 Program for the 99th Annual Meeting, at 35.

130 ASIL 2000 Annual Report at 2, in *ASIL Newsletter*, Mar.–Apr. 2001.

131 *ASIL Newsletter*, July–Sept. 2002, at 3, 4.

In conjunction with the Council on Foreign Relations, the Society sponsored roundtables in New York and Washington on "Old Rules, New Threats." The roundtables gave members of the executive and legislative branches, representatives of non-governmental organizations, lawyers and professors an opportunity to confer on normative issues relating to climate change, transborder financial regulation, international justice and counterterrorism. Reports relating to the sessions were posted on the web sites of the Society and the Council.[132]

Several programs were designed to be of particular interest to practitioners. Examples included pre-Annual Meeting conferences such as the ones in April 2000 on issues in international litigation, in April 2001 on international finance, and in April 2003 on annulment of I.C.S.I.D. awards, the July 2000 panel on issues in international trade, the July 2001 panel on the role of environment, labor and human rights issues in trade negotiations, and the conference in February 2005 on the relationship between trade and international security.

The series of joint conferences at The Hague with the Netherlands Society of International Law resumed in July 2003 after a six-year hiatus caused largely by coordination problems. The subject was "From Governance to Governance? The Growing Impact of Non-State Actors on the International and European Legal System."[133] The joint conference reverted to its biennial schedule in the summer of 2005, when the subject was "International Institutional Reform."[134] But coordination problems re-emerged, raising doubts about the future viability of the biennial conferences.[135]

The conference with the Australia and New Zealand Society of International Law, mentioned in Chapter Thirteen, was held on June 26, 2000, in Sydney and on June 28-29 in Canberra. The theme was "International Legal Challenges for the 21st Century." Eighteen Society members traveled from the United States to attend the conference.[136]

An ongoing collaborative effort, begun in 1991, was the Society's co-sponsorship of annual summer workshops with the Academic Council of the United

---

[132] ASIL 2003 Annual Report at 3, in *ASIL Newsletter*, Mar.–Apr. 2004; Reports of the Executive Director for the Executive Council meetings of April 2, 2003, and March 31, 2004.

[133] *ASIL Newsletter*, July–Sept. 2002, at 4.

[134] Report of the Hague Joint Conference Program Committee for the Executive Council meeting of March 30, 2005, in briefing materials for that meeting.

[135] Minutes of the Executive Committee, May 26, 2005.

[136] Susan L. Karamanian's Report on the Conference, in briefing papers for the Executive Council meeting of Oct. 21, 2000; ASIL 2000 Annual Report at 4, in *ASIL Newsletter*, Mar.–Apr. 2001.

Nations (A.C.U.N.S.). As in previous years, these two-week sessions introduced young academics and professionals to global governance issues.[137]

9. New Funds for Outreach

In 2003 Anne-Marie Slaughter set out to convince several major foundations to join forces with a USD 2.5 million grant over five years, half for operations and half for programs.[138] With the help of Rick LaRue, she brought in three significant grants by the summer of 2005. The Ford Foundation made a grant of USD 500,000 in 2004, to be spread over a three-year period. The grant was intended partly to enable the Society to continue its judicial outreach program, but also to overhaul its web site and electronic communications, and to expand its membership base.[139] The John D. and Catherine T. MacArthur Foundation followed soon after, with a USD 300,000 grant earmarked primarily for judicial outreach.[140] And in 2005, the J.E.H.T. Foundation awarded the Society USD 151,800 to develop an experimental electronic resource bank for U.S. judges and their law clerks, designed to enable them to see how international law has been regarded as relevant in prior domestic court cases.[141]

These grants reflected a significant shift in major foundations' interest in supporting Society projects. For decades grantors had supplied funds to the Society primarily for research. By the turn of the millennium, the foundations were directing their funds toward outreach projects and electronic services rather than scholarship.[142]

10. Transformation Within: Interest Groups Revisited

As we have seen in earlier Chapters, the Society's experience with interest groups has consistently been inconsistent. Some interest groups have been vibrant year after year; others have ebbed and flowed, died and been resuscitated, or died and been forgotten. The Society's leadership has sometimes focused on the role of interest groups, and sometimes has looked the other way.

---

[137] See Chapter Thirteen, Section B *supra*. For a description of the ASIL–ACUNS workshop format, see, e.g., the announcement for the 2004 summer workshop, in *ASIL Newsletter*, Nov.–Dec. 2003, at 10.

[138] Minutes of the Executive Council, Nov. 1, 2003.

[139] *ASIL Newsletter*, May–July 2004, at 3.

[140] Report of the Budget and Finance Committee for the Executive Council meeting of Nov. 6, 2004; e-mail from Richard LaRue to Rick Kirgis, June 28, 2005.

[141] Minutes of the Executive Committee, May 26, 2005; *ASIL Newsletter*, May–July 2005, at 3.

[142] Memorandum from Charlotte Ku to the Executive Committee, Sept. 18, 2000.

One interest group that has definitely been alive is the Women in International Law Interest Group, with about eight hundred members. It thrived during the first years of the new millennium, as it had before. It has presented programs at Annual Meetings, continued to make a Prominent Woman in International Law annual award,[143] offered briefings and public addresses by prominent women on a variety of topics, published a newsletter, maintained a web site, and provided a speakers and experts database.

The International Economic Law Interest Group continued to be active, presenting programs at Annual Meetings, sponsoring or co-sponsoring conferences such as the February 2005 conference on "Trade as the Guarantor of Peace, Liberty and Security?", publishing a newsletter, and maintaining a list-serve for online discussions among its members. A project begun by the Group in 1986 as a two-volume set of books, *Basic Documents in International Economic Law*, soon went online in Lexis and Westlaw. In 2003-2004 it was updated twice with commentaries on recent developments.[144]

The Human Rights Interest Group also remained quite active, publishing a newsletter twice a year, holding a business meeting annually and often presenting panels at the Annual Meeting – although, as we will see, it was frustrated in its effort to get on the program in 2005.

After several moribund years, the Francis Lieber Society, under the leadership of J. Ashley Roach, resuscitated itself in 2002 as the Society's interest group on the law of war. Like other active interest groups, it presented panels at Annual Meetings, co-sponsored conferences outside the Annual Meetings, and produced a newsletter (which it distributed electronically).[145] In 2005, the Lieber Society established the Francis Lieber Prize, to be awarded annually to an author thirty-five years of age or younger for outstanding scholarship on the law of armed conflict. The first recipient was Karen Hulme for her book, *War Torn Environment: Interpreting the Legal Threshold.*[146]

Arthur Rovine, the Society's President from 2000 to 2002, made a valiant effort to bring private practitioners into the mainstream of the Society. One of his initiatives was the creation of several interest groups that might be particularly appealing to practitioners, starting with an interest group on

[143] Annual award recipients in the new millennium were Ruth Lapidoth in 2000, Marcia A. Wiss in 2001 (presented in 2002), Judge Patricia M. Wald in 2002, Justice Sujata V. Manohar in 2003 and Judge Cecilia Medina in 2004. The award was created in 1993. For the list of recipients since then, visit the WILIG web site, which in mid-2005 was found at <http://personal.law.miami.edu/~schnably/wilig/>.

[144] Report from *International Legal Materials*, prepared for the Executive Council meeting of Nov. 6, 2004.

[145] See *ASIL Newsletters*, May–June 2002, at 9, and May–July 2003, at 7.

[146] Published by Martinus Nijhoff in 2004. See *ASIL Newsletter*, May–July 2005, at 4.

international taxation.[147] The top-down effort never got much traction, and was later abandoned.

Beginning in 2003, the Executive Committee and Executive Council addressed several issues raised by the checkered performance of interest groups. The issues ranged from size and composition of interest group membership to term limits for officers.[148]

At its meeting in the spring of 2004, the Executive Council redesignated eighteen interest groups, postponed redesignation of five others that seemed still to have some life in them, and discontinued seven others (most of them the practitioner-oriented ones). The Council also amended the Society's Regulations to require that each interest group have a minimum of two officers who may serve renewable terms of up to three years, but no longer than six years consecutively. Each interest group was required to submit an annual report to the Council, which would evaluate the group's activities every three years – or more often if circumstances call for it. No change was made in the twenty-member minimum for starting an interest group, and other issues were left unresolved.[149]

In 2004, the Society retained a consulting firm, Virtual Inc., to advise it on how to increase membership. Among other recommendations, the firm's representative emphasized eliminating barriers to participation in interest groups. He said that interest groups should be vital parts of community-building within the Society, but that would happen only if members of a group get something in return for joining the group. He viewed the minimal dues the Society was charging for membership in an interest group as a nuisance factor that did not cover the Society's costs. He suggested that those dues be eliminated.[150] The Society embarked on a pilot project designed to revive the inactive Dispute Resolution Interest Group and to test the consultant's recommendation. The Society offered A.S.I.L. members free membership in the Group for one year.[151] The results as of late 2005 were promising.

In the spring of 2000, the Society created a list-serve for interest group officers, enabling them to communicate easily with one another.[152] By 2004, the Society's new Service Center had provided a list-serve for the members of each interest group.[153]

---

147 *ASIL Newsletter*, Nov.–Dec. 2000, at 1.

148 Minutes of the Executive Council, Nov. 1, 2003.

149 Minutes of the Executive Council, March 31, 2004.

150 Minutes of the Executive Council, Nov. 6, 2004.

151 Minutes of the Executive Council, March 30, 2005; ASIL e-mail to the membership, April 11, 2005.

152 Minutes of the Executive Committee, May 4, 2000.

153 ASIL 2004 Annual Report at 7, in *ASIL Newsletter*, Mar.–Apr. 2005.

At the end of 2005, the jury remained out on the question of whether interest groups could become an engine for active membership in the Society. Two of the most energetic interest groups, the Francis Lieber Society and the Human Rights Interest Group, had voiced their frustration at having their proposals for panels at the 2005 Annual Meeting rejected by the Program Committee.[154] Some interest groups had expressed similar frustrations in other years.[155] Nevertheless, in any given year – including 2005 – several interest groups had put forward successful proposals and had carried through with them.

By 2005, inactive interest groups had been weeded out by the Society's redesignation process. The surviving interest groups seemed for the most part to be revitalized. The prognosis was guardedly good.

11. Transformation Within: Women in Multiple Leadership Roles

As we have seen in Chapters One and Two, women were not thought suitable for membership in the Society in its formative years. Only in 1920 did women become eligible for membership.

By the spring of 2004, times had changed dramatically. The Society's third female President, Anne-Marie Slaughter, was finishing her term in office; the Society's first female Executive Director, Charlotte Ku, was in her tenth year in office, and Kathleen Wilson was one of her key assistants as Director of Research and Outreach; Lucinda Low and Lucy Reed were Vice Presidents of the Society and Nancy Perkins was its Treasurer; the Journal had a female Co-Editor-in-Chief, Lori Damrosch, and seven other women were members of the Board of Editors; Ruth Teitelbaum was in the process of taking over as the Managing Editor of *International Legal Materials* (a position earlier held for many years by Marilou Righini); Jill Watson had just retired as the Director of the Library and Information Services after having guided the Society into the electronic age; Jane Stromseth was the Chair of the Nominating Committee; Lucy Reed was the Chair of the Honors Committee; Hannah Buxbaum and Janie Chuang were the Co-Chairs of the Annual Meeting Program Committee; and women were well represented on the Executive Council and the Executive Committee.

154 Minutes of the ASIL General Meeting, March 31, 2005.

155 See, e.g., Minutes of the Executive Council, April 5 and 6, 2000.

C. MINDING THE SHOP IN THE NEW MILLENNIUM

1. The Executive Directorship at the End of an Era

In 2001, as Charlotte Ku's second term as Executive Director was coming to an end, President Arthur Rovine appointed David A. Martin to chair a search committee that ultimately winnowed down the field to Dr. Ku and one other finalist. The committee recommended that Ku be appointed to a third and final term. The Executive Council agreed, appointing her for a final four-year term.[156] In the autumn of 2002, when the Council realized that the four-year term would put her out of office on the eve of the Society's centennial – a celebration and substantive feast in which she would play a major part – her final term was extended until the end of 2006.[157] She became the Executive Director with the longest service in office, dating from January 1, 1994.[158]

With the appointment of Charlotte Ku to a final term in 2001, it seemed an opportune time to do a thorough examination of how future Executive Directors would be selected, how they would be evaluated once in office, how long they could serve, and so forth. Arthur Rovine appointed Rick Kirgis to head an *ad hoc* committee to consider the issues and report back to the Council.

The committee prepared a set of guidelines intended to be binding on future search committees, and recommended that the Society's Regulations be amended accordingly. As proposed to the Executive Council, a new Executive Director's initial term would normally be for three years, with an evaluation that would begin mid-way through the first term and that would be completed by the start of the term's last year. A favorable evaluation would lead to a second term of not more than five years. Any third term would be subject to a full search. No Executive Director could serve for more than twelve years.

The committee set out a job description stressing proficiency in international law, administrative ability and experience, ability to relate to a diverse constituency, capacity to implement scholarly and outreach programs, and fund-raising ability. Each year the Executive Director would prepare a statement of goals for the coming year, to be evaluated at the end of the year by a subcommittee of the Executive Committee. An Executive Director could have a part-time appointment outside the Society if it would not interfere with his or her performance as Executive Director.

Searches for Executive Directors would be conducted somewhat more aggressively than they had been in the past. To ensure the anonymity of unsuccessful candidates, a search committee would submit to the Executive Committee and

---

156 Minutes of the Executive Council, April 4, 2001.

157 Minutes of the Executive Council, Nov. 2, 2002.

158 See Chapter Twelve, Section B.1, *supra*.

Executive Council only the names of the most highly rated candidates, even if that is only a single person.[159]

After some discussion focusing primarily on whether the committee's approach was sufficiently flexible, the Executive Council adopted the committee's report in March 2002.[160]

A couple of years later, as Charlotte Ku reflected on the role of the Executive Director, she observed that

> the institution is best served if we have an active governance and senior leadership, but where the Executive Director is fully a part of that governance and leadership. Many of the Executive Director's duties are administrative, but administration will not be effective if it does not or cannot support the mission and purpose of the organization. Therefore, the chief administrator has to be part of any long-range vision or planning.[161]

She had played that part throughout her tenure as Executive Director, though more fully under some Society Presidents than others.[162]

2. It's Never Over, Redux

In March 2001, a panel of the Second Circuit Court of Appeals notified the Society that it would accept *amicus curiae* briefs from the International Law Committee of the American Bar Association and from the Society on how, if at all, U.S. treaty obligations would bear on a specific *forum non conveniens* issue then pending in the court.[163] The Society's Executive Committee recommended to the Executive Council that the Society comply with the court's request, since it would be in keeping with the Society's outreach effort and since the Society was not being asked to take a position on the outcome of the case.[164]

---

[159] For details, see the Report of the Ad Hoc Committee on the Office of the Executive Director, Dec. 14, 2001, in briefing materials for the Executive Council meetings of March 13 & 14, 2002.

[160] Minutes of the Executive Council, March 13, 2002.

[161] Memorandum from Charlotte Ku to Rick Kirgis, Aug. 13, 2004.

[162] She noted, too, that she had called on several counselors for advice over the years, mentioning (in alphabetical order) Charles Brower, Jonathan Charney, Abram Chayes, Louis Henkin, Keith Highet, Charles Hunnicutt, Harold Jacobson, Rick Kirgis, Monroe Leigh, Nancy Perkins, Michael Reisman and Anne-Marie Slaughter. Id.

[163] The issue related to the weight a district court should give to the plaintiff's choice of a United States forum when the plaintiff's residence is elsewhere. The case was decided later that year. See *Iragorri v. United Technologies Corp.*, 274 F.3d 65 (2d Cir. 2001).

[164] Minutes of the Executive Committee, March 27, 2001.

At the Executive Council meeting a week later, there was extensive debate over whether to continue the long-standing policy against taking positions on substantive issues. At the end of the debate, Society President Arthur Rovine called for a straw vote on whether the policy should go from "rare to medium-rare." The straw vote was eighteen to ten in favor. Rovine then proposed that he appoint a committee to examine how to make that move. The Council concurred.[165]

When the Executive Council met again the next day, there was a long discussion about the Second Circuit's invitation to the Society to file the *amicus* brief on the *forum non conveniens* issue. When the dust settled, Rovine concluded that the sense of the meeting was opposed to filing the brief under the Society's auspices.[166]

The *ad hoc* "rare to medium-rare" committee reported to the autumn 2001 Executive Council meeting that it strongly favored adopting the model used by the Council on Foreign Relations: task forces could take positions that are not binding on the organization.[167] The Executive Council made no decision, but in December 2001 the Executive Committee approved Rovine's suggestion that the Society President, in consultation with the Executive Director and the Executive Committee, convene one or two task forces a year.[168] The first one was the Task Force on Terrorism, chaired by Ruth Wedgwood and Anthony D'Amato. As we have seen, it eventually posted a set of working papers on the Society web site,[169] but it did not take a position as a task force.

The subject of taking positions on some issues was raised again at Executive Council meetings in 2002 and 2004, but no action was taken.[170] After the issue was raised in 2002, President Anne-Marie Slaughter put the matter this way:

> Our mission is not to advocate any one position or set of positions, but rather to raise awareness of both the existence and the value of international law and international institutions as instruments not only for advancing the national interest of diverse nations, but also for achieving the collective goals of the international community. Those

---

165 Minutes of the Executive Council, April 4, 2001.

166 Minutes of the Executive Council, April 5, 2001. Rovine added that he would tell the clerk of the court that the Society would be glad to recommend an expert, Andreas Lowenfeld – an authority on international litigation and a prominent member of the Society. The court, however, was not comfortable with the idea. Minutes of the Executive Committee, June 28, 2001.

167 Minutes of the Executive Council, Nov. 3, 2001.

168 Minutes of the Executive Committee, Dec. 12, 2001.

169 See text at note 34 *supra*.

170 Minutes of the Executive Council, Nov. 2, 2002, and April 1, 2004.

> goals today include assuring our mutual prosperity, health, welfare, and most importantly, survival.[171]

Her admonition proved in 2004 not to be the last word on the subject, and it is safe to assume that more remains to be said.

3. Membership, Redux

When Anne-Marie Slaughter took over the presidency in 2002, the Society was stuck at about 4,000 members. She made augmenting the Society's membership a priority.[172] She appointed Jeffrey Lang to head a rejuvenated Membership Committee. He set out to do concrete things, rather than to carry out yet another study of membership trends and demographics.[173] In 2003, the two of them extracted a commitment from each Executive Council member to bring in ten new Society members.[174] That goal proved to be out of reach, but four Council members did meet the quota.[175]

As we have seen, in 2004 the Society retained a consulting firm, Virtual Inc., to study the membership situation and make recommendations as to how to increase the numbers. In addition to its suggestions about making better use of interest groups,[176] the firm's representative recommended making better use of the Internet. Specifically, he suggested an emphasis on web-based education through ongoing programs and *ad hoc* spontaneous programs.[177]

In the end, President James Carter announced that he would appoint a working group to address what should be done about the Society's membership structure.[178]

4. Human Rights and the Society's Portfolio

In April 2000, the Executive Council established a working group to examine procedures and criteria for reviewing the suitability of stocks for the portfolio of the Society, in order to screen the Society's investments on the basis of companies' compliance with human rights standards. Treasurer Joseph Guttentag reminded

---

171 *ASIL Newsletter*, Oct.–Dec. 2002, at 8.

172 Minutes of the Executive Council, March 13, 2002.

173 Minutes of the Executive Council, Nov. 2, 2002.

174 Minutes of the Executive Council, April 2, 2003.

175 Report of the Membership Committee, March 12, 2004, for the Executive Council meeting of March 31, 2004.

176 See Section B.10 *supra*.

177 For further details, see Memorandum, "ASIL History: Details Relating to Budget, Finances and Membership" (2006), on file with the Society.

178 Id.

the Council that before the end of apartheid in South Africa, the Society excluded from its portfolio stocks of companies doing business there; also, the Society currently excluded tobacco stocks.[179]

The Society's investment advisor went along with the idea of using human rights standards for investments. The working group rejected the idea of hiring a corporate monitoring firm to screen the Society's portfolio for companies that failed to respect human rights. Instead, the Society could do it simply by visiting the web sites of funds that screen for human rights relating to their own investments, and by checking a social activism web site.[180] Using these tools, the working group found no need for divestments in 2001, but recommended continued screening. The Executive Council concurred.[181] In 2002, the working group expressed some dissatisfaction with the screening mechanisms, but again refrained from advocating divestments.[182]

5. Consolidating the Awards Committees

Until 2002, the Society had separate committees each year to select the Honorary Member and the recipients of the Manley O. Hudson and Goler T. Butcher Medals. When Anne-Marie Slaughter became President, she noted the difficulty of finding qualified members of all three committees and proposed that they be consolidated into a single annual Committee on Honors. The Executive Committee concurred.[183] Lucy Reed, who chaired the first consolidated Committee on Honors, reported that it had worked very well, particularly by assuring some balance among the awards.[184]

In 2003, the Society's Regulations were amended, formalizing the President's annual discretion to appoint a consolidated Committee on Honors.[185] When James Carter took over the presidency in 2004, he continued the practice of appointing a consolidated Committee.

---

179 Minutes of the Executive Council, Apr. 5, 2000.

180 Report of the Working Group on Screening ASIL Investments for Compliance with Human Rights Standards, submitted for the Executive Council meeting of Oct. 21, 2000.

181 Report of the Treasurer for the Executive Council meeting of April 4, 2001; Minutes of that meeting.

182 Addendum to Report of the Working Group on Investments, March 12, 2002, in briefing materials for the Executive Council meeting of March 13, 2002.

183 Minutes of the Executive Committee, May 23, 2002.

184 Minutes of the Executive Committee, March 13, 2003.

185 Minutes of the Executive Council, Nov. 1, 2003, adding Paragraph 16 to Section III of the Regulations.

6. Transition in the Library

On October 24, 2003, Jill Watson retired after 22 years with the Society. She began in 1981 as the Assistant Librarian, becoming the Librarian when Helen Philos retired in 1987. In 1995 her title was changed to Director of Library and Information Services, to reflect the expanding scope of her responsibilities in the electronic age. In addition to overseeing the redesign of the library during the Tillar House renovation, she had served as co-editor of the ASIL Guide to Electronic Resources in International Law and as project manager of the Electronic Information System for International Law (EISIL).[186] In Charlotte Ku's words, she "has been a true pioneer in developing basic infrastructure for the Society's electronic activities."[187] Kelly Vinopal became the new Director of Library and Information Services.

7. Not Forgotten in the Electronic Era: Publications

In 2003, the Society published the third volumes of two sets. *Trilateral Perspectives on International Legal Issues: Conflict and Coherence* was the third volume in a series co-sponsored by the A.S.I.L., the Canadian Council on International Law and the Japanese Society of International Law. It dealt with domestic application of international law, a multilateral judgments convention, security issues, trade and environment, and the law of the sea.[188] The other was the third volume of *National Treaty Law and Practice*, examining the law and practice of Canada, Egypt, Israel, Mexico, Russia and South Africa.[189] In 2005, a consolidated and updated *National Treaty Law and Practice* volume appeared.[190] It was dedicated to Monroe Leigh, who was the guiding force behind the project.

In 2003, the Society also collaborated with the Brookings Institution and the School of Advanced International Studies to produce *The Guiding Principles on Internal Displacement and the Law of the South Caucasus: Georgia, Armenia, Azerbaijan.*[191]

In 2004, *The Methods of International Law*, number 36 in the Studies in Transnational Legal Policy series, supplied an updated and expanded version of

---

186 *ASIL Newsletter*, Sept.–Oct. 2003, at 2.

187 Memorandum from Charlotte Ku to Rick Kirgis, Aug. 13, 2004.

188 Chi Carmody, Yuji Iwasawa & Sylvia Rhodes (eds.), *Trilateral Perspectives on International Legal Issues: Conflict and Coherence* (2003).

189 Monroe Leigh, Merritt R. Blakeslee & L. Benjamin Ederington (eds.), *National Treaty Law and Practice: Canada, Egypt, Israel, Mexico, Russia, South Africa* (2003).

190 Duncan B. Hollis, Merritt R. Blakeslee & L. Benjamin Ederington (eds.), *National Treaty Law and Practice* (Martinus Nijhoff, 2005).

191 Roberta Cohen, Walter Kälin & Erin Mooney (eds.), *The Guiding Principles on Internal Dispacement and the Law of the South Caucasus: Georgia, Armenia, Azerbaijan* (2003).

the methods symposium published in the Journal in 1999.[192] Volume 5 of the *International Maritime Boundaries* series was finished,[193] and the proceedings of the 2003 Hague Joint Conference were published.[194]

Book projects still in preparation in mid-2005 included *Can Might Make Rights? Building the Rule of Law in Post-Conflict Societies*, by Rosa Brooks, Jane Stromseth and David Wippman, and the papers from the first of a series of conferences on international trade and human rights, edited by Frederick M. Abbott, Christine Breining-Kaufmann and Thomas Cottier.

D. ANNUAL MEETINGS IN THE FIRST YEARS OF THE NEW MILLENNIUM

1. Supreme Court Justices and a Secretary of State at the Podium

United States Supreme Court Justice Sandra Day O'Connor gave the keynote address at the 2002 Annual Meeting. She jump-started a remarkable string of five consecutive acceptances by Supreme Court Justices of invitations to speak at Annual Meetings. With characteristic diffidence, Justice O'Connor began by saying that she did not know enough about international law to deserve such a speaking opportunity. But she did know enough to note that although international law is seldom binding on U.S. courts, "conclusions reached by other countries and by the international community should at times constitute persuasive authority in American courts."[195] It was, of course, a view not shared by all of her Supreme Court colleagues.

Justice O'Connor concluded her remarks memorably:

> [W]e must not be tone deaf to the music of the law. ... The words you can hear to the music of the law are words of equality, justice, fairness, consistency, predictability, equity, the wrongs righted, and the repose of disputes settled without violence, without undue advantage, and without leaving either side with bitter feelings of having been cheated. It is the music sung in the world of childlike innocence in which the lion

---

192 Steven R. Ratner & Anne-Marie Slaughter (eds.), *The Methods of International Law* (2004). The earlier version is in 93 *AJIL* 291 (1999).

193 David Colson & Robert Smith (eds.), *International Maritime Boundaries*, vol. 5 (Martinus Nijhoff, 2005).

194 Wybo P. Heere (ed.), *From Government to Governance: The Growing Impact of Non-State Actors on the International and European Legal System* (2004).

195 96 *ASIL Proc.* 348, 350 (2002).

> lies down with the lamb. Perhaps it is not a world that ever was, or ever will be, but it is a world worth living toward.[196]

Justice Stephen G. Breyer was at the podium for the 2003 Annual Meeting. He addressed the reasons why he and some of his Supreme Court colleagues found international and comparative law sources to be helpful to U.S. judges in some cases. Essentially, in his view, it is a matter of learning from others without being bound by their decisions.[197]

For the 2004 Annual Meeting, ASIL President Anne-Marie Slaughter invited Justice Antonin Scalia to be the keynote speaker. Justice Scalia, never bashful, had been open about his skepticism toward the use of international and comparative law sources in U.S. courts. As Slaughter put it, she "invited Daniel to enter the lion's den, an invitation Justice Scalia well understood. In his response, he wrote: 'One act of courage deserves another,' and accepted the Society's invitation."[198]

In his address, Justice Scalia took the high ground: "It is impossible to say that [international and foreign source] materials are never relevant."[199] He noted that when a U.S. court interprets a treaty to which the United States is a party, it should give respect to the interpretation of the treaty by courts of other signatories. He expressed a similar view regarding interpretation of statutes that implement treaties and of statutes that refer to foreign law. He rather grudgingly "supposed" that foreign law could be consulted in assessing an argument that a particular construction of an ambiguous provision in a federal statute would be disastrous.

As for interpretation of the Constitution, he readily admitted consulting old English materials, most of them antedating 1791. Modern foreign materials were another matter. Not never, said the Justice; just hardly ever.[200]

At the 2005 Annual Meeting, the Society not only enticed Justice Ruth Bader Ginsburg to give the keynote address; it also persuaded Secretary of State Condoleezza Rice to introduce her. Rice was the first sitting Secretary of State to address the Society since William P. Rogers did so in 1970. She reaffirmed the United States' commitment to international norms and international mechanisms for the peaceful resolution of disputes, and acknowledged that "when we respect our international legal obligations and support an international system based

---

[196] Id. at 353.

[197] 97 *ASIL Proc.* 265 (2003).

[198] *ASIL Newsletter*, Jan.–Feb. 2004, at 8.

[199] 98 *ASIL Proc.* 305 (2004).

[200] Id. at 306-07.

on the rule of law, we do the work of making the world a better place, but also a safer and more secure place for America."[201]

Justice Ginsburg began with a Biblical reference: "Justice, justice shall you pursue, that you may thrive."[202] She focused on one aspect of that pursuit, judicial review for constitutionality. She noted, as Justice Breyer had, that American judges can learn from foreign sources, even when it comes to constitutional issues. "Judges in the United States," she said, "are free to consult all manner of commentary – Restatements, treatises, what law professors or even law students write copiously in law reviews, for example. If we can consult those writings, why not the analysis of a question similar to the one we confront contained in an opinion of the Supreme Court of Canada, the Constitutional Court of South Africa, the German Constitutional Court, or the European Court of Human Rights?"[203] The *New York Times* covered her speech, under the headline "Justice Ginsburg Backs Value of Foreign Law."[204]

Justice Anthony M. Kennedy extended the Supreme Court streak to five when he accepted the Society's invitation to deliver the keynote address at the Centennial Annual Meeting in 2006.

2. New or Revived Ways of Addressing Current Issues

At the last Annual Meeting before the terrorist attack of 9/11, the Society took a characterization devised by Oscar Schachter almost a quarter of a century earlier – "the invisible college of international lawyers"[205] – and examined whether it was still viable (and if so, whether it was still invisible). David Bederman and Lucy Reed, the co-chairs of the Program Committee, asked themselves and the rest of the Society whether international lawyers were still a college in the sense of being "a group that cuts across physical borders, national interests, and ideological divides, in pursuit of the common mission of promoting a rule of law for international affairs."[206] The answer was a qualified yes, but with a need for more visibility.

As we have seen earlier in this Chapter, the new millennium Annual Meetings responded substantively to the major issues of the day, including 9/11 and other aspects of terrorism, the situation in Iraq, and the International Criminal Court. International trade, human rights and other issues were addressed as well. The

---

201 99 *ASIL Proc.* 350 (2005).

202 *Deuteronomy* 16:20.

203 99 *ASIL Proc.* 354 (2005).

204 *N.Y. Times*, April 2, 2005, Section A, p. 10.

205 See Oscar Schachter, "The Invisible College of International Lawyers," 72 *Nw. U. L. Rev.* 217 (1977).

206 95 *ASIL Proc.* ix (2001).

United States, of course, was right at the center of most issues. Consequently, the 2002 Annual Meeting included a special Presidential Panel on the relationship of the United States, as the sole superpower, to the international legal system. President Arthur Rovine orchestrated the discussion around three observations: first, the United States has not always recognized that there are reciprocal benefits from observing common rules of international law; secondly, there was a weakening of bipartisan commitment to international law in the United States; and thirdly, the combination of the war on terrorism and the U.S. position as the world's sole superpower was unique in world history.[207]

The ensuing discussion included some trenchant remarks by Anthony D'Amato on what he perceived as the A.S.I.L.'s failure to live up to its mandate of promoting the establishment and maintenance of international relations on the basis of law and justice. In particular, he criticized the Society's policy against taking substantive positions, its policy against filing *amicus* briefs and its weak incentives to members who might otherwise put more effort into the Society.[208]

The 2002 Annual Meeting presented another innovation: the Business Meeting became the Annual General Meeting, denoting its expanded focus beyond purely business matters. The aim was to do something about the anemic attendance at Business Meetings. Accordingly, President Arthur Rovine presented a presidential address at the Annual General Meeting, discussing the role of international law in U.S. courts.[209] Attendance improved.

Later Annual General Meetings included substantive discussions as well. In 2003, there was a panel on the State of the American Society of International Law, responding in part to D'Amato's critique at the preceding Annual Meeting.[210] The 2004 General Meeting closed with a panel discussion on "Conceiving a Just World Under Law."[211] At the 2005 Annual General Meeting, James Carter gave a presidential address on "An American Society FOR International Law."[212]

In 2004, for the first time, the recipient of the Manley O. Hudson Medal gave a lecture in that capacity. The honoree, W. Michael Reisman, of Yale University, lectured to a packed house on "Why Regime Change Is (Almost Always) a Bad Idea."[213] As his title suggested, he concluded that even in exceptional cases

---

207 96 *ASIL Proc.* 159-60 (2002).

208 Id. at 161-62.

209 Minutes of the Annual General Meeting, March 14, 2002.

210 Agenda for the Annual General Meeting, April 3, 2003. The panel could also be viewed as a follow-up to the President's Round Table on The American Society of International Law, 95 *ASIL Proc.* 13 (2001).

211 98 *ASIL Proc.* 125 (2004).

212 Program for the 99th ASIL Annual Meeting (2005). (Emphasis in the original.)

213 98 *ASIL Proc.* 290 (2004); also in 98 *AJIL* 516 (2004).

where regime change by military force may be lawful, it is usually not the right thing to do. He exhorted any government considering regime change, even with the best of intentions, to "remember that not everything noble is lawful; not everything noble and lawful is feasible; and not everything noble, lawful, and feasible is wise."[214]

The 2004 Annual Meeting also featured a plenary panel composed of former Legal Advisers of the U.S. State Department. The discussion centered on the question whether they viewed the role of Legal Adviser as including advocacy of policy choices relating to international law, or simply as communicating the contents of the law to their government clients.[215] The session was so successful that in 2005 it engendered a (similarly successful) panel of former Legal Advisers to foreign offices around the world.[216]

3. A Blueprint for the Program Committee

In 2000, the Executive Committee adopted revised Guidelines on the ASIL Annual Meeting.[217] Under the Guidelines, the Program Committee has full authority to select proposals, considering scholarly merit, consistency with the overall theme, and balance among subjects and approaches. Interest groups may submit proposals, which are to be considered equally with proposals from other sources. In general, there should be no more than five concurrent events, and major events such as the Annual General Meeting and plenary lectures should have no competition. Program Committee members should not serve on panels, except perhaps in connection with opening or closing Annual Meeting sessions. Each panel should provide a diversity of presenters and views. An individual may appear on only one panel or event other than an appearance during a period reserved for interest group meetings. The Program Committee should also try to avoid having the same people appear year after year.

E. THE JOURNAL IN THE NEW MILLENNIUM

1. The Passing of an Incumbent and a Former Editor-in-Chief

On September 7, 2002, Jonathan Charney died at the age of 58. He was still serving as a Co-Editor-in-Chief with Michael Reisman, performing his duties

---

214 98 *ASIL Proc.* at 299; 98 *AJIL* at 525.

215 98 *ASIL Proc.* 378 (2004).

216 Program for the 99th ASIL Annual Meeting (2005).

217 Minutes of the Executive Committee, June 22, 2000. See also the Report of the Annual Meeting Committee for the Executive Council meeting of Oct. 21, 2000, in the briefing materials for that meeting.

until very nearly the end as he battled cancer. Reisman paid tribute to him as a scholar and as an editor, noting particularly that he had chaired or served on all the committees of the Board of Editors.[218] As a scholar, he was especially well known for his monumental multi-volume work, *International Maritime Boundaries.*

Oscar Schachter died on December 13, 2003, at the age of 88. He was a past President of the Society and a former Co-Editor-in-Chief of the Journal, as well as a celebrated scholar and teacher at Columbia University. Before he entered academia, he was a mainstay in the United Nations Office of Legal Affairs, having joined the U.N. at its inception. In the words of U.N. Secretary-General Kofi Annan, he was "one of a group of lawyers who laid the groundwork for the development of the law of the Organization as we know it to this day."[219] He authored four books and innumerable articles. His book, *International Law in Theory and Practice*, based on his General Course at the Hague Academy of International Law, was awarded the ASIL's Certificate of Merit for Creative Scholarship in 1992. Upon his passing, tributes poured in from home and abroad.[220]

2. Editors-in-Chief Designate and the Outgoing Editor-in-Chief

When there is a transition to new Editors-in-Chief, a myriad of arrangements have to be worked out – especially with the academic institutions with which the new Editors-in-Chief are associated. By 2002, it had become apparent that a smooth transition could only occur if the incoming Editors-in-Chief had time to make the arrangements and gradually work into them before they had full responsibility for reviewing manuscripts and getting the Journal published. Consequently the Board of Editors proposed a change in the Society's Regulations to provide for election of Editors-in-Chief Designate in the autumn of the last year in office of their predecessors. They would take office at the following spring meeting of the Board of Editors.[221] In November 2002, the Executive Council amended the Regulations accordingly.[222] At the same meeting the Council approved the Board of Editors' nomination of Lori Fisler Damrosch,

---

218 Minutes of the Fall 2002 Meeting of the AJIL Board of Editors. See also the tribute to him in 97 *AJIL* 80 (2003).

219 Kofi Annan, "Tribute [to Oscar Schachter]," 42 *Colum. J. Transnat'l L.* 621 (2004).

220 For commemorative pieces, see Lori Fisler Damrosch, "Oscar Schachter (1915-2003)," 98 *AJIL* 35 (2004); Kofi Annan, Hans Blix, Hans Correll, Louis Henkin, Rosalyn Higgins, Stephen Marks, Judith Schachter Modell & Stephen Schwebel, "Tributes," 42 *Colum. J. Transnat'l L.* 621 et seq. (2004); Richard N. Gardner, "Remembering Oscar Schachter," 43 *Colum. J. Transnat'l L.* 663 (2005).

221 Minutes of the Executive Council, March 14, 2002.

222 Minutes of the Executive Council, Nov. 2, 2002. See Section V, subparagraph 1(d)(4) of the Society's Regulations, as amended at that Council meeting.

of Columbia University, and Bernard H. Oxman, of the University of Miami, as Co-Editors-in-Chief Designate.[223]

Michael Reisman served as sole Editor-in-Chief from September 2002 until Damrosch and Oxman took over in April 2003. At its meeting on April 2, 2003, the Board of Editors enthusiastically adopted a good-natured Resolution of Commendation of W. M. Reisman. Lori Damrosch did not admit authorship, but it bore her indelible mark. In a cordial parody of New Haven speak, it resolved that the Board of Editors "does hereby perform the appraisal function expected of it on this solemn occasion, and it does appraise the tenure of W. Michael Reisman as Editor-in-Chief as having been marked by maximization of basic values, including *inter alia* respect, enlightenment, rectitude, and affection."[224] Myres McDougal and Harold Lasswell would have been proud.

3. *Ex Officio* Editors and New Department Editors

In 2003 the Executive Council approved the Board of Editors' recommendation that the President of the Society, in addition to the Executive Director, be an *ex officio* member of the Board of Editors, without vote.[225] The rationale was that the Board should have input from the two persons who could best contribute to discussions on issues affecting relations between the Society and the Board.[226]

With the January 2005 issue of the Journal, John Crook became the editor of Contemporary Practice of the United States Relating to International Law, replacing Sean Murphy. With the July 2005 issue, Daniel Bodansky took over from David Caron as the editor of International Decisions.[227]

4. Foreign Non-voting Editors, Revisited

As we have seen in Chapter Eleven, in 1987 the Board of Editors decided to create a board of non-voting Corresponding Editors outside the United States. No consensus as to their role ever emerged, and the idea was eventually abandoned.[228]

The Board's Nominating Committee proposed something very much like it in the spring of 2005. The Committee recommended that the Board establish

---

223 Minutes of the Executive Council, Nov. 2, 2002.

224 Resolution of the Board, attached to the Minutes of the Spring 2003 Meeting of the AJIL Board of Editors.

225 Minutes of the Executive Council, Nov. 1, 2003.

226 Memorandum from the Board's Ad Hoc Parliamentary Committee to the Board of Editors, Oct. 20, 2003.

227 Minutes of the Executive Council, Nov. 6, 2004, and March 31, 2005. For the changes in Board membership during this period, see Memorandum, ASIL History: The Journal, Its Editors and Business Practices, on file with the Society.

228 See Chapter Eleven, Section D.4, *supra*.

an Advisory Board composed of foreign scholars and practitioners who could advise on manuscripts, forward new manuscripts and advise on editorial policy. The goal would be to bring in a broad global perspective and a broadened interdisciplinary approach.[229] But when it was pointed out at the Board's spring meeting that essentially the same idea had proved unworkable in the past, no action was taken.[230]

5. Twenty-first Century Themes

As we have seen earlier in this Chapter, the Journal responded to the major world events of the new millennium – including the Arab–Israeli conflict, terrorism, Iraq, consular rights and international criminal law – with articles, Agoras, editorial comments and Contemporary Practice pieces.[231] But it did not limit itself to headline events.

The Journal continued to marshal diverse viewpoints around common themes in symposia and Agoras.[232] The January 2001 issue featured an interdisciplinary Symposium on State Reconstruction after Civil Conflict, edited by Ruth Wedgwood and Harold K. Jacobson.[233] In 2002 there were two symposia and an Agora. One symposium was on The Boundaries of the WTO, focusing on whether the World Trade Organization should concern itself not only with traditional trade issues, but also with issues relating to such things as environmental protection and labor rights.[234] The second symposium dealt with the International Law Commission's State Responsibility Articles, examining such issues as invocation,

---

229 Report of the AJIL Nominating Committee, March 14, 2005.

230 Minutes of the Spring 2005 Meeting of the AJIL Board of Editors.

231 See Section A.2, *supra*.

232 For symposia and Agoras in the years leading up to 2001, see Chapter Thirteen, Section G.2, *supra*.

233 95 *AJIL* 1 (2001). After a Foreword by Wedgwood and Jacobson, the Symposium featured essays by Payam Akhavan, Lorna McGregor, Hansjörg Strohmeyer, Jennifer Widner, Michael J. Matheson, Samuel H. Barnes, and Allan Gerson.

234 96 *AJIL* 1 (2002). José E. Alvarez organized the Symposium and wrote the Foreword, followed by essays by David W. Leebron, Steve Charnovitz, Kyle Bagwell, Petros C. Mavroidis and Robert W. Staiger, Joel P. Trachtman, Robert Howse, John H. Jackson, Jagdish Bhagwati, Debra P. Steger, and Alvarez himself.

countermeasures and remedies.[235] The Agora presented a variety of views on the use of military commissions.[236]

In 2003, two installments of a single Agora appeared, addressing the Future Implications of the Iraq Conflict.[237] The first installment focused particularly on the decision to invade Iraq; the second, on some of the ramifications of the invasion's aftermath.

An Agora in 2004 presented essays on the United States Constitution and International Law. It was inspired by two recent U.S. Supreme Court decisions in which some members of the Court looked to international practice as relevant to constitutional questions regarding the execution of mentally retarded persons and the criminalization of consensual sexual relations between persons of the same sex.[238] Views pro and con were argued on the question of whether, and if so to what extent, international and foreign practice should be considered by U.S. courts as they interpret the U.S. Constitution. It was a question distinct from the questions raised in a series of essays by conservative scholars who challenged U.S. courts' incorporation of customary international law into federal common law, and indeed questioned whether customary international law is "law" at all (in the sense of actually affecting the behavior of states).[239] The Journal did not wade into the customary international law debate until 2005, when it published a lead article by George Norman and Joel Trachtman in which they used game theory to demonstrate that custom has the capacity to affect state behavior in certain, defined circumstances.[240]

---

235 96 *AJIL* 773 (2002). Daniel Bodansky and John R. Crook wrote an analytical Introduction and Overview. The other essays were by Robert Rosenstock, Edith Brown Weiss, David J. Bederman, Dinah Shelton, David D. Caron and James Crawford. Crawford, of course, was the ILC's Special Rapporteur who brought the long-awaited Articles to fruition.

236 96 *AJIL* 320 (2002). The contributors to the Agora were Daryl A. Mundis, Ruth Wedgwood, Harold Hongju Koh, Joan Fitzpatrick, and Michael J. Matheson.

237 See note 60 *supra*.

238 98 *AJIL* 42 (2004). The cases were *Atkins v. Virginia*, 536 U.S. 304 (2002), and *Lawrence v. Texas*, 539 U.S. 558 (2003).

239 See, e.g., Jack L. Goldsmith & Curtis A. Bradley, "Customary International Law as Federal Common Law: A Critique of the Modern Position," 110 *Harv. L. Rev.* 815 (1997); Jack L. Goldsmith & Curtis A. Bradley, "Federal Courts and the Incorporation of International Law," 111 *Harv. L. Rev.* 2260 (1998); Jack L. Goldsmith & Curtis A. Bradley, "The Abiding Relevance of Federalism to U.S. Foreign Relations," 92 *AJIL* 675 (1998); Jack L. Goldsmith & Eric A. Posner, "A Theory of Customary International Law," 66 *U. Chi. L. Rev.* 1113 (1999). A revised version of the latter article appeared as Chapter 1 in Goldsmith and Posner's book, *The Limits of International Law* (2005).

240 George Norman & Joel Trachtman, "The Customary International Law Game," 99 *AJIL* 540 (2005).

In the January 2005 issue, the Journal published an Agora on the ICJ Advisory Opinion on Construction of a Wall in the Occupied Palestinian Territory – an opinion in which the Court found Israel's construction of the wall in occupied Palestinian territory to be a violation of international law.[241] The next issue included a collection of essays on Developments at the International Criminal Court.[242]

Other common themes were explored without the aid of an Agora or a symposium. In separate articles, Paul Szasz and Stefan Talmon examined the U.N. Security Council as a body exercising a newly discovered legislative role.[243] Detlev Vagts and José Alvarez focused on "hegemonic international law" – a movement away from *de jure* or *de facto* equality of states and into a system of client states operating under the protection of hegemons.[244] There was continued coverage of international economic law, in addition to the aforementioned W.T.O. symposium.[245] And the Journal did not lose sight of human rights issues.[246]

---

241 See note 22 *supra*.

242 See note 77 *supra*.

243 Paul Szasz, "The Security Council Starts Legislating," 96 *AJIL* 901 (2002); Stefan Talmon, "The Security Council as World Legislature," 99 *AJIL* 175 (2005). See also Alvarez, *infra* note 244.

244 Detlev Vagts, "Hegemonic International Law," 95 *AJIL* 843 (2001); José Alvarez, "Hegemonic International Law Revisited," 97 *AJIL* 873 (2003).

245 See note 234 *supra*. See also Joost Pauwelyn, "The Role of Public International Law in the WTO: How Far Can We Go?," 95 *AJIL* 535 (2001); Steve Charnovitz, "Rethinking WTO Trade Sanctions," id. at 792; Deborah E. Siegel, "Legal Aspects of the IMF/WTO Relationship: The Fund's Articles of Agreement and the WTO Agreements," 96 *AJIL* 561 (2002); Detlev F. Vagts, "Extraterritoriality and the Corporate Governance Law," 97 *AJIL* 289 (2003); Richard H. Steinberg, "Judicial Lawmaking at the WTO: Discursive, Constitutional, and Political Constraints," 98 *AJIL* 247 (2004); Sabrina Safrin, "Hyper-ownership in a Time of Biotechnological Promise: The International Conflict to Control the Building Blocks of Life," id. at 641; Steve Charnovitz, "Using Framework Statutes to Facilitate U.S. Treaty Making," id. at 696; Frederick M. Abbott, "The WTO Medicines Decision: World Pharmaceutical Trade and the Protection of Public Health," 99 *AJIL* 317 (2005).

246 See Christine M. Chinkin, "Women's International Tribunal on Japanese Military Sexual Slavery," 95 *AJIL* 335 (2001); Eric Stein, "International Integration and Democracy: No Love at First Sight," id. at 489; Ryan Goodman, "Human Rights Treaties, Invalid Reservations, and State Consent," 96 *AJIL* 531 (2002); Hilary Charlesworth & Christine M. Chinkin, "Sex, Gender, and September 11," id. at 600; Nsongurua J. Udombana, "So Far, So Fair: The Local Remedies Rule in the Jurisprudence of the African Commission on Human and Peoples' Rights," 97 *AJIL* 1 (2003); Paolo G. Carozza, "Subsidiarity as a Structural Principle of International Human Rights Law," id. 38; David Marcus, "Famine Crimes in International Law," id. at 245; Lee M. Caplan, "State Immunity, Human Rights, and *Jus Cogens*: A Critique of the Normative Hierarchy Theory," id. at 741; Kenneth Watkin, "Controlling the Use of Force: A Role for Human Rights Norms in

According to a web site maintained by Washington and Lee University, the Journal as of mid-2005 was the most-cited subject-matter specific law journal among 730 ranked journals in that category from both inside and outside the United States.[247]

6. An Appreciation

At the Board of Editors meeting in October 2003, a commemorative plaque and gift were presented to Anna Ascher, the Senior Associate Editor, in recognition of her twenty-five years of outstanding service to the Journal.[248] She had eclipsed the record of twenty-four consecutive years held by Eleanor Finch, who served as Assistant Editor of the Journal from 1948 to 1972.[249]

F. THE CENTENNIAL

1. The Centennial Presidents

When Anne-Marie Slaughter became the President of the Society in the spring of 2002, she was a member of the Harvard Law faculty and of the Journal's Board of Editors.[250] As we have seen, she immediately embarked on an ambitious program focusing on outreach, building the Society's membership base, and stimulating the teaching of international law. Undaunted by those challenges, she also poured herself into preparations for the centennial, building on preliminary work that had begun in 1999. She became the Chair of the Centennial Committee and in that capacity pushed forward with her quite successful fund-raising efforts on behalf of the Society.

In the spring of 2004, she was succeeded in the presidency by James H. Carter, a partner in the New York law firm of Sullivan & Cromwell. Despite the demands of an active practice in international arbitration, Carter devoted a great deal of time to the centennial. He represented the Society at a variety of meetings,

---

Contemporary Armed Conflict," 98 *AJIL* 1 (2004); Michael J. Dennis & David P. Stewart, "Justiciability of Economic, Social, and Cultural Rights: Should There Be an International Complaints Mechanism to Adjudicate the Rights to Food, Water, Housing, and Health?," id. at 462.

247 See <http://law.wlu.edu/library/mostcited/index.asp> (last visited on July 20, 2005). According to the same web site, the Journal was ranked 19th among 982 ranked law journals including general as well as specialized journals.

248 Minutes of the Fall 2003 Meeting of the AJIL Board of Editors.

249 See R.R. Baxter, Editorial Comment, 66 *AJIL* 815 (1972).

250 She later became the Dean of the Woodrow Wilson School of Public and International Affairs at Princeton University.

including meetings of international law societies outside the United States, and participated actively in the planning and fund raising for the centennial.

At the 2005 Annual Meeting, José E. Alvarez, of the Columbia University School of Law, became the Society's President-Elect, to take office as President in the centennial year.

2. The Centennial Theme

The Society's centennial theme, "A Just World Under Law," carried forward the Society's aspiration at its birth a hundred years earlier. Oscar Straus, one of the Society's founders, saw the Society's goal as securing "the peace of justice" by popularizing and developing international law.[251] Elihu Root and James Brown Scott chimed in.[252] So did Charles Evans Hughes.[253] If the aspiration had not been realized in a hundred years punctuated by armed conflicts, human rights violations, terrorism and marked quality of life disparities around the world, hardly anyone – at least not those closely associated with the Society – disputed the need to keep trying. Nor could it be denied that there had been some successes in those hundred years, as democracy replaced despotism in a good many countries, world health standards rose, human rights no longer were considered to be matters solely within the domestic jurisdiction of nation states, international trade norms were developed and implemented, and a host of new international dispute-settlement and enforcement institutions came into being. Qualified successes in some cases, to be sure, but nevertheless advances over the old order.

In significant part, the Society's transformation effort in the early years of the new millennium was aimed at a renewal of its original aspiration. The centennial would be the crown jewel in the Society's transformation, but the renewal process would not end there. The centennial, then, would not just look back at the Society's first hundred years; it would also look forward to see where life on the planet was headed and what the Society's role in it should be.

3. The Centennial Annual Meeting

Hilary Charlesworth and Donald Francis Donovan chaired the 2006 Annual Meeting Program Committee. The theme for the meeting, "A Just World Under Law," had already been selected for them. By mid-2005, U.S. Supreme Court Justice Anthony M. Kennedy and I.C.J. Judge Rosalyn Higgins had accepted the Society's invitations to be plenary speakers.

---

251 See Chapter 1, Section A.2, *supra*.

252 Id. See also Elihu Root, "The Need of Popular Understanding of International Law," 1 *AJIL* 1 (1907).

253 See Chapter 3, Section D.1, *supra*.

The Program Committee decided, for the first time in the Society's history, to solicit panel submissions from the Society's membership at large, and to use the submissions as the first pool from which to select the meeting's events. Submissions were sought under nine topics:

- environment and development;
- use of force;
- humanitarian law and international criminal law;
- human rights: civil, political, economic and social;
- post-conflict societies and transitional justice;
- international trade and investment;
- international adjudication;
- international law in national courts;
- the generation of international law, international theory and international institutions.[254]

4. The Centennial Publications

The A.S.I.L. history project was originally conceived as a history of the Society's first ninety years. When it proved difficult to find a publisher for the ninety-year volume, the project was put on hold for a few years and then was resuscitated with the centennial in mind. The result is the present volume.

From the outset, the Society's flagship publications – the *American Journal of International Law* and *International Legal Materials* – were given prominent places in the design of the centennial, but it was not clear at first just what their roles would be. Their plans developed gradually.

The Journal's Board of Editors ultimately decided to publish a set of solicited centennial essays in volume 100, squeezing as many of them as possible into the January 2006 issue.[255] The solicited topics ranged from economic law to human rights; from the law of the sea to the foreign relations law of the United States; from the use of force to peaceful dispute resolution; and from theory to practice. Some focused primarily on history; others combined a look back with a look forward.

---

[254] Charlotte Ku's Status Report for the Centennial Committee meeting, June 20, 2005; invitation to participate, sent electronically to ASIL members, July 5, 2005.

[255] Minutes of the AJIL Board of Editors Meeting, Spring 2005, and attached Update on AJIL Centennial Essays.

In addition, the Board commissioned Dinah Shelton and Arthur Rovine to prepare a volume of leading articles from the Journal's first hundred years, with an emphasis on the last forty years.[256]

On the aesthetic front, the Board decided that a facelift was in order for the Journal at age 100. It began with a redesigned cover. The January 2006 centennial cover would be unique. After that, the new Journal covers would be standard – bluish green, with a list of shortened lead article titles and Agoras. Other makeovers were planned. The goal was to make the Journal more readable and more attractive than it had been.[257]

By mid-2005, the I.L.M. Managing Editor, Ruth Teitelbaum, and her advisory committee had decided that their centennial effort would be centered on an online searchable, cumulative I.L.M. index.[258]

5. Internationalizing the Centennial

A significant feature of the centennial plan was to bolster the Society's presence outside the United States. Jim Carter led off the effort when he traveled to China and met with the Chinese Society of International Law. Next, he went with Susan Karamanian and Ved Nanda to India, where he presented a certificate from the ASIL to the Indian Society of International Law and spoke on the law of international sports disputes.[259]

The Hague Joint Conference in the summer of 2005 became one of the centennial events, focusing on international institutional reform.[260] An even more ambitious endeavor was the conference scheduled for the time of the Australia–New Zealand Society's 2006 annual meeting, around the theme of fostering a scholarly network. The conference stemmed from the combined efforts of the Australia–New Zealand Society of International Law, the Canadian Council on International Law, the Japanese Society of International Law and the ASIL.[261]

Canada was a venue for Society centennial events, as well. The Society joined forces with the International Law Association, organizing a panel to be

---

256 Id. A similar project had been undertaken in connection with the Society's sixtieth anniversary. See Chapter Nine, Section F.3 *supra*. Hence the emphasis in 2006 on the most recent forty years. The sixtieth anniversary volume is Leo Gross (ed.), *International Law in the Twentieth Century* (1969).

257 Minutes of the AJIL Board of Editors Meeting, Spring 2005; Minutes of the ASIL General Meeting, March 31, 2005.

258 Minutes of the Executive Council, March 30, 2005.

259 Id. at 3; Minutes of the Executive Committee, Feb. 3, 2005.

260 Minutes of the Executive Committee, Feb. 3, 2005. See text at note 134 *supra*.

261 Minutes of the Executive Committee, May 26, 2005.

convened at the June 2006 ILA meeting in Toronto. And the Society continued its collaboration with the Academic Council on the United Nations System, co-sponsoring its summer workshops during the centennial period – including the 2005 workshop in Waterloo, Ontario.

6. Reinvigorated Regional Meetings

Early on, the Centennial Committee decided that an element of the centennial effort would be a reinvigorated regional meeting program. Regional meetings had long been held under the Society's auspices, but – with the notable exception of those held for thirty-eight consecutive years under the leadership of Ved Nanda in Denver – they had lost steam over the years. The new effort would follow the policies and practices already in place for regional meetings, but the Society would be more proactive in encouraging potential organizers.[262]

The first Centennial Regional Meeting was held in Chicago in January 2005, focusing on reform of the United Nations.[263] Other meetings followed in venues scattered around the United States and elsewhere, on topics ranging from international criminal law to foreign investment.[264]

7. One Hundred Ways International Law Shapes Our Lives

Under the guidance of Lucinda Low, the Society included in its centennial celebration a public education project designed to bring home the many ways international law affects the lives of ordinary individuals. Called "100 Ways International Law Shapes Our Lives," the project was designed to set out, in non-technical terms, not only one hundred ways a person might be affected, but also how it would come about and the instrument or custom at the root of it. Thus: a person can fly the most direct route to international destinations pursuant to international rules and procedures developed under the Chicago Convention on

262 Report of the Centennial Committee for the Executive Council meeting of Nov. 6, 2004.

263 *ASIL Newsletter*, Jan.–Feb. 2005, at 8.

264 By mid-2005, regional meetings had been held not only in Chicago, but also in East Lansing, Michigan, on international criminal law and terrorism; in Houston on Saddam Hussein and the judicial process; in Davis, California, on foreign investment; in Palo Alto, California, on global jurisprudence; in Boston on the International Criminal Tribunal for Rwanda; in New York City on the globalization of public health; in Durham, North Carolina, on the war on terrorism; in New Orleans on trafficking in persons; in San Francisco on a just world under the rule of law; in Denver on protecting human rights; in New York City on global administrative law; in Prague, Czech Republic, on legal skills training in Central and Eastern Europe; in Washington, D.C., on the future of the Inter-American human rights system; again in Washington, on Iraqi atrocity crimes; and with more to follow.

International Civil Aviation of 1944. The Society collected examples from its members, with a view to publication in the centennial year.[265]

G. LOOKING BACK AND LOOKING FORWARD

From its inception in 1906, the Society has had a dual personality. Its constitution has said that the Society's "object" (singular) is actually plural: first, to foster the study of international law, and secondly, to promote the establishment (and, as amended, the maintenance) of international relations on the basis of law and justice. In its early years, the Society was propelled more by the second part of its single purpose than by its more scholarly aim. As a child of the American peace movement, it embodied the vision of Elihu Root, James Brown Scott and their contemporaries that international law and international arbitration could save the world from war, and could do it with justice if American constitutional law served as a model. The Society's leaders also entertained the belief that its scholarly arm, the Journal, could not only foster scholarship, but could also effectively educate the American public about international law. In turn, the public would influence government decision-makers who would choose principled arbitration over war to settle international disputes.

World War I deflated the Society's early hopes. The aftermath, when the United States declined to join the League of Nations or to become a party to the Statute of the Permanent Court of International Justice, steered the Society away from its nearly messianic mission to save the world from war, and toward the more scholarly side of its dual personality. The goal of ultimately achieving a world order based on law and justice was still there, but it was to be patiently sought by such means as the painstaking codification of international law and the production of serious scholarship not meant for direct public edification. The Journal took center stage, with Annual Meetings not far behind.

Even into its maturity between the World Wars, the Society remained solidly in the hands of (white) men, including such prominent leaders as Elihu Root, Charles Evans Hughes, James Brown Scott and Cordell Hull, and such academic stars as Manley Hudson, Edwin Borchard and Philip Jessup. Women were allowed to become members in 1920 and a woman soon was elected to the Executive Council, but power in the Society remained almost entirely masculine until well after World War II.

In the immediate post-World War II years, the Society's vision remained narrow. Its focus remained almost exclusively on the Journal and the Annual

265 *ASIL Newsletter*, May–July 2005, at 4; ASIL web site, <http://www.asil.org/Centennial/100Ways.html> as of August 2005.

Meeting. It still had no full-time Executive Director to come up with new ideas and see that they were carried out.

With the acquisition of Tillar House in 1959 and with the ascendancy in the Society of independent thinkers like Myres McDougal and Hardy Dillard, the Society's horizons broadened. Chris Merillat was brought in as the Society's first Executive Director. He brought with him a vision for expanding the Society's focus beyond traditional public international law. Under Merillat and his successors, conferences of legal advisers were organized; *International Legal Materials* was born and came of age; the Board of Review and Development became an engine for policy-oriented, interdisciplinary research; study panels were convened and books were published; new emphasis was placed on the teaching of international law; the Jessup Competition blossomed; the Society eventually entered the electronic age; and funds were raised for these and other initiatives, supplied in major part by the Ford Foundation.

Still, the Society did not seem to have much success in influencing public policy directly, or in educating the public about the importance of international law. In fact, a Ford Foundation evaluation in 1991-92 observed that the Society was not expending much effort in these directions.[266] The Society had not yet fully recognized the importance of an effective outreach effort. Moreover, its reluctance to take positions on substantive issues limited its effectiveness on the public policy playing field, even as it contributed to the Society's stature as a forum for scholarly discourse and dissemination of information.

When Louis Henkin became the Society's President in 1992, he undertook to recapture some of the founders' vision: the Society, he said, should work to make international law more relevant and to ensure that governments and peoples take international law seriously.[267] Working groups were formed and made recommendations to policy-making bodies. Briefings and other public policy-oriented meetings were held. Efforts were begun to educate judges on international law issues. Ultimately, under Charles Brower's direction, the Society's governance structure was revised and a major fund-raising campaign raised more than two million dollars. Tillar House was refurbished, providing more flexible meeting space and vastly improved information services. An endowment was created.

All of this was part of a larger transformation project designed to provide outreach to the judiciary, the media, the Congress and the public. Presentations were made to federal judicial conferences; electronic resources were developed in order to facilitate international law research and to reach the media and the public; new workshops and briefings were conducted; active interest groups were revitalized, while inactive ones were discontinued; Supreme Court Justices

[266] See Chapter Eleven, Section E, *supra*.

[267] See Chapter Twelve, Section A.1, *supra*.

and other luminaries appeared at Annual Meetings; and the Society's operating practices were streamlined.

Charlotte Ku and her staff, working with a succession of Society Presidents, guided the Society through these transformation efforts. Looking back on her long tenure as Executive Director, Dr. Ku took particular pride in developing the Society as an information network and a center to bring together groups and individuals from around the world.[268]

* * *

All the while, the Journal maintained its status as the predominant scholarly periodical in its field. In addition to publishing important lead articles, Agoras and symposia, it expanded its coverage of the contemporary practice of the United States government and deepened its analysis of important judicial decisions. Its book reviews became increasingly analytical, often amounting to self-contained essays.

Women became prominent in the leadership of the Society and of the Journal. Charlotte Ku, the first female Executive Director, served longer in that capacity than had any of her predecessors. Presidents Edith Brown Weiss and Anne-Marie Slaughter greatly influenced the direction of the Society during their incumbency and afterward. Lori Fisler Damrosch became a Co-Editor-in-Chief of the Journal. Persons of color took leadership roles on the Executive Committee and Executive Council. No longer was influence in the Society the preserve of white males. With demographic diversity came intellectual diversity. The Society in 2006 reflected a diversity of views and interests not remotely contemplated in 1906.

As the Society looked forward at its centennial, it was rededicating its effort to make the most of its dual personality. It was fostering the study of international law not only by maintaining the excellence of the Journal, but also by supporting its interest groups, commissioning scholarly books, providing gateways to Internet research, and presenting wide-ranging, probing panels and other presentations at its Annual Meetings. Some of these activities also served the purpose of promoting and maintaining international relations on the basis of law and justice. But that purpose was served in other ways as well: the Insight series explained the legal significance of current events; International Law in Brief summarized important decisions and resolutions; judicial outreach was reflected in an increasing awareness of international law in the judiciary all the way up to the U.S. Supreme Court; calls from the media came to Tillar House and often were directed to knowledgeable Society members; and the web site

268 Memorandum from Charlotte Ku to Rick Kirgis, Aug. 13, 2004. She added, "[T]he things that give me the most satisfaction are those where ideas have become operating reality and meeting stated goals."

was becoming increasingly useful, even to persons with no international law expertise.

The Society's cloudy crystal ball did not reveal how well the reinvigorated outreach program would succeed. Enough had been achieved by the centennial year to provide grounds for optimism. But much depended on continuing to bring in grants and on maintaining the energy that had been built up by 2006.

The Journal seemed destined to maintain its dominant place in the field of international law scholarship, despite the appearance of the new *European Journal of International Law* and an increasing willingness by non-specialized law reviews to publish articles on international law. Books would continue to be written and published under the Society's auspices. New voices would be heard at the Annual Meetings and in other Society forums. The Society's electronic resources would continue to develop as important vehicles for scholarship as well as for outreach and member support.

In short, the American Society of International Law in its centennial year was healthy and in a position to remain so. That is not to say that it had no issues to face. For one thing, membership numbers had remained stagnant for several years. And the question of how to influence public policy without taking positions on substantive matters remained alive. That question epitomized the Society's dual personality: one part scholarly, the other part public policy-driven. The two sides of its personality were not in irreconcilable conflict, but neither were they in perfect harmony. Perhaps, for an organism that desires to grow, it is best that way.

Appendix A

The Original Constitution of the American Society of International Law

ARTICLE I.

Name.

This Society shall be known as the AMERICAN SOCIETY OF INTERNATIONAL LAW.

ARTICLE II.

Object.

The object of this Society is to foster the study of International Law and promote the establishment of international relations on the basis of law and justice. For this purpose it will cooperate with other societies in this and other countries having the same object.

ARTICLE III.

Membership.

Members may be elected on the nomination of two members in regular standing by vote of the Executive Council under such rules and regulations as the Council may prescribe.

Each member shall pay annual dues of five dollars and shall thereupon become entitled to all the privileges of the Society, including a copy of the publications issued during the year. Upon failure to pay the dues for the period of one year a member may, in the discretion of the Executive Council, be suspended or dropped from the rolls of membership.

Upon payment of one hundred dollars any person otherwise entitled to membership may become a life-member and shall thereupon become entitled to all the privileges of membership during his life.

A limited number of persons not citizens of the United States and not exceeding one in any year, who shall have rendered distinguished service to the cause which this Society is formed to promote, may be elected to honorary membership at any meeting of the Society on the recommendation of the Executive Council. Honorary members shall have all the privileges of membership but shall be exempt from the payment of dues.

ARTICLE IV.

Officers.

The officers of the Society shall consist of a President, nine or more Vice-Presidents, the number to be fixed from time to time by the Executive Council, a Recording Secretary, a Corresponding Secretary and a Treasurer, who shall be elected annually, and of an Executive Council composed of the President, the Vice-Presidents, *ex-officio*, and twenty-four elected members, whose term of office shall be three years, except that of those elected at the first election, eight shall serve for the period of one year only and eight for the period of two years, and that anyone elected to fill a vacancy shall serve only for the unexpired term of the member in whose place he is chosen.

The Recording Secretary, the Corresponding Secretary, and the Treasurer shall be elected by the Executive Council from among its members. The other officers of the Society shall be elected by the Society, except as hereinafter provided for the filling of vacancies occurring between elections.

At every annual election candidates for all the offices to be filled by the Society at such election shall be placed in nomination by a Nominating Committee of five members of the Society previously appointed by the Executive Council, except that the officers of the first year shall be nominated by a committee of three appointed by the Chairman of the meeting at which this Constitution shall be adopted.

All officers shall be elected by a majority vote of members present and voting.

All officers of the Society shall serve until their successors are chosen.

ARTICLE V.

Duties of Officers.

1. The President shall preside at all meetings of the Society and of the Executive Council and shall perform such other duties as the Council may assign to him. In the absence of the President at any meeting of the Society his duties shall devolve upon one of the Vice-Presidents to be designated by the Executive Council.

2. The Secretaries shall keep the records and conduct the correspondence of the Society and of the Executive Council and shall perform such other duties as the Council may assign to them.

3. The Treasurer shall receive and have the custody of the funds of the Society and shall disburse the same subject to the rules and under the direction of the Executive Council. The fiscal year shall begin on the first day of January.

4. The Executive Council shall have charge of the general interests of the Society, shall call regular and special meetings of the Society and arrange the programmes therefor, shall appropriate money, shall appoint from among its members an Executive Committee and other committees and their chairmen, with appropriate powers, and shall have full power to issue or arrange for the issue of a periodical or other publications, and in general process the governing power in the Society, except as otherwise specifically provided in this Constitution. The Executive Council shall have the power to fill vacancies in its membership occasioned by death, resignation, failure to elect, or other cause, such appointees to hold office until the next annual election.

Nine members shall constitute a quorum of the Executive Council, and a majority vote of those in attendance shall control its decisions.

5. The Executive Committee shall have full power to act for the Executive Council when the Executive Council is not in session.

6. The Executive Council shall elect a Chairman who shall preside at its meetings in the absence of the President, and who shall also be Chairman of the Executive Committee.

ARTICLE VI.

Meetings.

The Society shall meet annually at a time and place to be determined by the Executive Council for the election of officers and the transaction of such other business as the Council may determine.

Special meetings may be held at any time and place on the call of the Executive Council or at the written request of thirty members on the call of the Secretary. At least ten days' notice of such special meeting shall be given to each member of the Society by mail, specifying the object of the meeting, and no other business shall be considered at such meeting.

Twenty-five members shall constitute a quorum at all regular and special meetings of the Society and a majority vote of those present and voting shall control its decisions.

ARTICLE VII.

Resolutions.

All resolutions which shall be offered at any meeting of the Society shall, in the discretion of the presiding officer, or on the demand of three members, be referred to the appropriate committee or the Council, and no vote shall be taken until a report shall have been made thereon.

ARTICLE VIII.

Amendments.

This Constitution may be amended at any annual or special meeting of the Society by a majority vote of the members present and voting. But all amendments to be proposed at any meeting shall first be referred to the Executive Council for consideration and shall be submitted to the members of the Society at least ten days before such meeting.

Adopted January 12, 1906.

Appendix B

PROSPECTUS (1906)

THE AIM AND SCOPE OF THE AMERICAN SOCIETY OF INTERNATIONAL LAW

From the very beginning of our national existence the people of the United States have been keenly interested in the common law of nations. In an ordinance of 1781, passed before the recognition of independence, Congress professed obedience to the law of nations "according to the general usages of Europe," and in the act of admission to the family of nations the new Republic recognized international law as completely as international law recognized the new Republic. Nor was this formal acceptance of international law the passing fancy of the moment. The Constitution of the United States proclaimed it as an existing system and solemnly conferred upon Congress the power to punish "offenses against the law of nations." It is therefore the law of the land by constitutional enactment, as well as by the necessities of the case, and the General Government as well as courts of justice have invariably and unhesitatingly declared that "international law is a part of our law, and must be ascertained and administered by the courts of justice of appropriate jurisdiction as often as questions of right depending upon it are duly presented for their determination." (*The Paquette Habana*, 1899, 175 U.S. 677, 700.)

If it be borne in mind that the course of recent events has not only given to our country a more prominent and influential position in the family of nations than it had previously enjoyed, but has brought Government and people into closer and more intimate relations with the Spanish-American States in the Western World and the peoples of the Eastern, it is at once evident that Government and people are fundamentally and constitutionally interested in international law, and that a correct understanding of the system as a whole is an essential element of good citizenship.

Thus to state the problem is to prove it and to make manifest to the American people the fundamental importance of a correct understanding of those principles of international law which our country is called upon to observe in its foreign relations, and to administer as municipal law in our domestic tribunals. The establishment of new and more effective agencies to promote the study of these principles and to extend their influence at home and abroad is a duty incumbent upon enlightened citizenship.

Profoundly impressed by these considerations, the American Society of International Law was organized at New York on the 12th day of January of the present year, and it is believed that the influence of an association of publicists and others organized to represent these interests of our people would count for much in the formation of a sound and rational body of doctrine concerning the true principles of international relations. It is equally certain that the publication of a journal devoted to the exposition of those principles would offer a ready and valuable means of communication between jurists and students of international law on the one hand, and the scientific and lay public on the other. The absence of any organization in the United States having for its first and sole object the promotion of these purposes, and the lack in the English-speaking world of any periodical devoted exclusively to international law indicate the need of such a society.

American publicists, such as Kent, Marshall, Story, Wheaton, Halleck, Lieber, Lawrence, Dana, Field, Woolsey, and Wharton – not to mention those among the living – have made many and varied contributions to the science of international law. It is too plain for argument that the existence of such an organization with annual and special meetings and the publication of a periodical exclusively devoted to international law will not only furnish a nucleus and incentive but also a means of communication. It would likewise seem equally clear that the Society and Journal would necessarily and directly foster the study of international law and promote the establishment of international relations upon the basis of law and justice.

Appendix C

ASIL Presidents

Elihu Root	1906-1924
Charles Evans Hughes	1924-1929
James Brown Scott	1929-1939
Cordell Hull	1939-1942
Frederic R. Coudert	1942-1946
Charles Cheney Hyde	1946-1949
Manley O. Hudson	1949-1952
Edwin D. Dickinson	1952-1953
Charles G. Fenwick	1953-1954
Philip C. Jessup	1954-1955
Quincy Wright	1955-1956
Lester H. Woolsey	1956-1957
Robert R. Wilson	1957-1958
Myres S. McDougal	1958-1959
Herbert W. Briggs	1959-1960
Charles E. Martin	1960-1961
Arthur H. Dean	1961-1962
Hardy C. Dillard	1962-1963
James N. Hyde	1963-1964
Brunson MacChesney	1964-1966
John R. Stevenson	1966-1968

Oscar Schachter 1968-1971
Harold D. Lasswell 1971-1972
William D. Rogers 1972-1974
Richard R. Baxter 1974-1976
Walter Sterling Surrey 1976-1978
C. Clyde Ferguson, Jr. 1978-1980
Alona E. Evans 1980
Monroe Leigh 1980-1982
Covey T. Oliver 1982-1984
David G. Gill 1984-1986
Keith Highet 1986-1988
Louis B. Sohn 1988-1990
Peter D. Trooboff 1990-1992
Louis Henken 1992-1994
Edith Brown Weiss 1994-1996
Charles N. Brower 1996-1998
Thomas M. Franck 1998-2000
Arthur W. Rovine 2000-2002
Anne-Marie Slaughter 2002-2004
James H. Carter 2004-2006
José E. Alvarez 2006-2008

Appendix D

MANLEY O. HUDSON MEDAL RECIPIENTS

(Not Awarded Every Year)

1956.... Manley O. Hudson

1959.... Lord Arnold McNair

1964.... Philip C. Jessup

1966.... Charles De Visscher

1969.... Paul Guggenheim

1975.... Myres S. McDougal

1978.... Eduardo Jiminez de Arechaga

1981.... Richard Reeve Baxter (posthumously) and Oscar Schachter

1982.... Hardy Cross Dillard

1984.... Suzanne Bastid

1985.... Marjorie Whiteman

1986.... Leo Gross

1993.... Robert Yewdall Jennings

1995.... Louis Henkin

1996.... Louis B. Sohn

1997.... John R. Stevenson

1998.... Rosalyn Higgins

1999.... Shabtai Rosenne

2000.... Stephen M. Schwebel

2001.... Prosper Weil

2002.... Thomas Buergenthal

2003.... Thomas M. Franck

2004.... W. Michael Reisman

2005.... Elihu Lauterpacht

2006.... Theodor Meron

Appendix E

Certificate of Merit Recipients

From 1952, when the Certificate of Merit was initiated, through 1975, a single award was available for the most distinguished work in the field of international law in the current year or in the immediately preceding years. In 1976, the single award was replaced by two awards: one for a pre-eminent contribution to creative scholarship, and one for a work of high technical craftsmanship and high utility to practicing lawyers. In 1997, a third category was added, for a work in a specialized area of international law.

1952 Hans Kelsen, *The Law of the United Nations* (1950)

1953 No award

1954 Manley O. Hudson, "The Thirty-First Year of the World Court," 47 *AJIL* 1 (1953)

1955 Charles de Visscher, *Théories et Réalités en Droit International Public* (1955)

1956 Julius Stone, *Legal Controls of International Conflict* (1954)

1957 No award

1958 No award

1959 C. Wilfred Jenks, *The Common Law of Mankind* (1958)

1960 Hersch Lauterpacht, *The Development of International Law by the International Court* (1958)

1961 Alfred Verdross, *Völkerrecht* (4th ed. 1959)

1962 Myres S. McDougal & Associates, *Studies in World Public Order* (1960)

1963 Adrian S. Fisher, Covey Oliver, Cecil J. Olmstead, I.N.P. Stokes & Joseph M. Sweeney, *Draft Restatement (2d), Foreign Relations Law of the United States* (1962)

1964 Hans-Jurgen Schlochauer (ed.), *Wörterbuch des Völkerrechts* (2d ed., 4 vols., 1960-62)

1965 Marjorie M. Whiteman, *Digest of International Law* (vols. 1-3, 1963-64)

1966 Wilhelm Wengler, *Völkerrecht* (2 vols. 1964)

1967 Angelo Piero Sereni, *Diritto Internazionale* (5 vols., last one 1965)

1968 Shabtai Rosenne, *The Law and Practice of the International Court* (1965)

1969 Richard A. Falk, *Legal Order in a Violent World* (1968)

1970 J.H.W. Verzijl, *International Law in Historical Perspective* (vols. 1 & 2, 1968-69)

1971 Rosalyn Higgins, *United Nations Peacekeeping 1946-1967: Documents and Commentary* (vols. 1 & 2, 1969-70)

1972 Elihu Lauterpacht & (posthumously) Hersch Lauterpacht, *International Law Reports* (series)

1973 Cyril E. Black & Richard A. Falk, *The Future of the International Legal Order* (4 vols, 1969-72)

1974 F.A. Mann, *Studies in International Law* (1973)

1975 Arthur Rovine, *Digest of United States Practice in International Law* (1973)

1976 Creative scholarship: Ian Brownlie, *Principles of Public International Law* (2d ed. 1973)

Technical craftsmanship: Jerome Cohen & Hungdah Chiu (eds.), *People's China and International Law: A Documentary Study* (1974)

1977 Creative scholarship: Leo Gross (ed.), *The Future of the International Court of Justice* (2 vols., 1976)

Technical craftsmanship: Peter Fischer (ed.), *Die Internationale Konzession* (1974), and *A Collection of International Concessions and Related Instruments* (1976)

1978 Creative scholarship: Charles Rousseau, *Droit International Public* (3 vols., 1970-77)

Technical craftsmanship: Blanche Finley, *The Structure of the United Nations General Assembly: Its Committees, Commissions and Other Organisms* (3 vols., 1977)

1979 Creative scholarship: No award

Technical craftsmanship: Igor I. Kavass & Michael J. Blake (eds.), *United States Legislation on Foreign Relations and International Commerce, 1789-1969* (4 vols., 1978)

1980 Creative scholarship: Jan Schneider, *World Public Order of the Environment: Towards an International Ecological Law and Organization* (1979), and R. Michael M'Gonigle & Mark W. Zacher, *Pollution, Politics and International Law: Tankers at Sea* (1979)

Technical craftsmanship: J. Gillis Wetter (ed.), *The International Arbitral Process: Public and Private* (1979)

1981 Creative scholarship: James Crawford, *The Creation of States in International Law* (1979)

Technical craftsmanship: Michael J. Glennon & Thomas M. Franck (eds.), *United States Foreign Relations Law: Documents and Sources* (2 vols., 1980)

1982 Creative scholarship: Roger Fisher, *Improving Compliance with International Law* (1981)

Technical craftsmanship: Burns H. Weston, Richard A. Falk & Anthony A. D'Amato (eds.), *International Law and World Order* (1980)

1983 Creative scholarship: Manfred Lachs, *The Teacher in International Law* (1982)

Technical craftsmanship: W.M. Bush (ed.), *Antarctica and International Law: A Collection of Interstate and National Documents* (2 vols., 1982)

1984 Creative scholarship: Kenneth W. Dam, *The Rules of the Game: Reform and Revolution in the International Monetary System* (1982)

Technical craftsmanship: J.H. Barton, J.L. Gibbs, Jr., V.H. Li & J.H. Merriman, *Law in Radically Different Cultures* (1983)

1985 Creative scholarship: Julius Stone, *Visions of World Order: Between State Power and Human Justice* (1984)

Technical craftsmanship: Hurst Hannum, *Guide to International Human Rights Practice* (1984)

1986 Creative scholarship: Thomas M. Franck, *Nation Against Nation – What Happened to the U.N. Dream and What the U.S. Can Do About It* (1985)

Technical craftsmanship: T. Alexander Aleinikoff & David A. Martin (eds.), *Immigration: Process and Policy* (1985)

1987 Creative scholarship: Theodor Meron, *Human Rights Law-making in the United Nations* (1986)

Technical craftsmanship: No award

1988 Combined award, without distinction between Creative scholarship and Technical craftsmanship: Lori F. Damrosch (ed.), *The International Court of Justice at a Crossroads* (1987), and Stephen M. Schwebel, *International Arbitration: Three Salient Problems* (1987)

1989 Creative scholarship: Barry E. Carter, *International Economic Sanctions* (1988)

Technical craftsmanship: C.F. Amerasinghe, *The Law of the International Civil Service* (1988)

1990 Creative scholarship: Edith Brown Weiss, *In Fairness to Future Generations: International Law, Common Patrimony, and Intergenerational Equity* (1989)

Technical craftsmanship: V. Coussirat-Coustere & P.M. Eisemann (eds.), *Repertory of International Arbitral Jurisprudence* (vols. I & II, 1989)

1991 Creative scholarship: Vera Gowland-Debbas, *Collective Responses to Illegal Acts in International Law: United Nations Action in the Question of Southern Rhodesia* (1990)

Technical craftsmanship: Howard M. Holtzman & Joseph E. Neuhaus, *A Guide to the UNCITRAL Model Law on International Commercial Arbitration: Legislative History and Commentary* (1989)

1992 Creative scholarship: Oscar Schachter, *International Law in Theory and Practice* (1991)

Technical craftsmanship: Alan C. Swan & John F. Murphy (eds.), *Cases and Materials on the Regulation of International Business and Economic Relations* (1991)

1993 Creative scholarship: Joaquin Tacsan, *The Dynamics of International Law in Conflict Resolution* (1992)

Technical craftsmanship: Pierre Pescatore, William J. Davey & Andreas F. Lowenfeld (eds.), *Handbook of GATT Dispute Settlement* (1991)

1994 Creative scholarship: Thomas M. Franck, *Political Questions/Judicial Answers: Does the Rule of Law Apply to Foreign Affairs?* (1992)

Technical craftsmanship: Jonathan I. Charney & Lewis M. Alexander, *International Maritime Boundaries* (2 vols., 1993)

1995 Creative scholarship: Rosalyn Higgins, *Problems and Process: International Law and How We Use It* (1994)

Technical craftsmanship: Stefan A. Riesenfeld & Frederick M. Abbott (eds.), *Parliamentary Participation in the Making and Operation of Treaties: A Comparative Study* (1994)

1996 Creative scholarship: Thomas M. Franck, *Fairness in International Law and Institutions* (1995)

Technical craftsmanship: Bruno Simma (ed.), *The Charter of the United Nations: A Commentary* (1995)

1997 Creative scholarship: Antonio Cassesse, *Self-Determination of Peoples: A Legal Reappraisal* (1995), and Sean D. Murphy, *Humanitarian Intervention: The United Nations in an Evolving World Order* (1996)

Technical craftsmanship: No award

Specialized area: Arthur Eyffinger, *The International Court of Justice, 1946-1996* (1996)

1998 Creative scholarship: Steven R. Ratner & Jason S. Abrams, *Accountability for Human Rights Atrocities in International Law: Beyond the Nuremberg Legacy* (1997)

Technical craftsmanship: Charles N. Brower & Jason D. Brueschke, *The Iran-United States Claims Tribunal* (1998)

Special mention: Robbie Sabel, *Procedure at International Conferences: A Study of the Rules of Procedure of Conferences and Assemblies of International Inter-governmental Organisations* (1997)

1999 Creative scholarship: Olivier Corten, *L'utilisation du "Raisonnable" par le Juge International: Discours Juridique, Raison, et Contradictions* (1997)

Technical craftsmanship: Virginia Morris & Michael P. Scharf, *The International Criminal Tribunal for Rwanda* (1998)

Specialized area: Brad R. Roth, *Governmental Illegitimacy in International Law* (1999)

2000 Creative scholarship: Martha Minow, *Between Vengeance and Forgiveness: Facing History after Genocide and Mass Violence* (1998)

Technical craftsmanship: Johannes Morsink, *The Universal Declaration of Human Rights: Origins, Drafting and Intent* (1999), and Arthur Eyffinger, *The 1899 Hague Peace Conference: "The Parliament of Man, The Federation of the World"* (1999)

Specialized area: Dinah Shelton, *Remedies in International Human Rights Law* (1999)

2001 Creative scholarship: Hilary Charlesworth & Christine Chinkin, *The Boundaries of International Law: A Feminist Analysis* (2000)

Technical craftsmanship: Danesh Sarooshi, *The United Nations and the Development of Collective Security: The Delegation by the UN Security Council of its Chapter VII Powers* (1999)

Specialized area: Annelise Riles, *The Network Inside Out* (2000)

2002 Creative scholarship: Martti Koskenniemi, *The Gentle Civilizer of Nations: The Rise and Fall of International Law 1870-1960* (2001)

Technical craftsmanship: Stephen C. McCaffrey, *The Law of International Watercourses: Non-Navigational Uses* (2001)

Specialized area: Simon Chesterman, *Just War or Just Peace? Humanitarian Intervention and International Law* (2001)

2003 Creative scholarship: Philip Allot, *The Health of Nations: Society and Law Beyond the State* (2002)

Technical craftsmanship: Stephanie Steinle, *Völkerrecht und Machtpolitik: Georg Schwarzenberger (1908-1991)* (2002)

Technical craftsmanship, special mention: Sean Murphy, *United States Practice in International Law: Volume 1, 1999-2001* (2002)

Specialized area: Karen Knop, *Diversity and Self-Determination in International Law* (2002)

2004 Creative scholarship: Yuval Shany, *The Competing Jurisdictions of International Courts and Tribunals* (2003)

Technical craftsmanship: M. Cherif Bassiouni, *Introduction to International Criminal Law* (2003)

Specialized area: Charlotte Ku & Harold K. Jacobson, *Democratic Accountability and the Use of Force in International Law* (2003)

2005 Creative scholarship: Gerry Simpson, *Great Powers and Outlaw States: Unequal Sovereigns in the International Legal Order* (2004)

Technical craftsmanship: Mitsuo Matsushita, Thomas J. Schoenbaum & Petros C. Mavroidis, *The World Trade Organization: Law, Practice and Policy* (2003)

Specialized area: Knut Dörmann (with contributions by Louise Doswald-Beck & Robert Kolb), *Elements of War Crimes under the Rome Statute of the International Criminal Court: Sources and Commentary* (2003)

Appendix F

GOLER T. BUTCHER MEDAL RECIPIENTS

1997 ....Thomas Buergenthal

1998 ....Gabrielle Kirk McDonald

1999 ....Baltasar Garazon

2000 ....Radhika Coomaraswamy

2001 ....Louis Henkin

2002 ....Sonia Sotela Picado

2003 ....Olara A. Otunnu

2004 ....Carla del Ponte

2005 ....Pieter Kooijmans, Nigel Rodley and Theo van Boven

2006 ....Hilary Charlesworth and Christine Chinkin

Appendix G

HONORARY MEMBERS

1959	Louis Podesta Costa	Argentina
1960	Muhammad Zafrulla Khan	Pakistan
1961	Kotara Tanaka	Japan
1962	Julius Stone	Australia
1963	Paul Guggenheim	Switzerland
1964	Walter Hallstein	Germany
1965	Louis Nwachukuwu Mbanefo	Nigeria
1966	Richardo J. Alfaro	Panama
1967	*No nomination*	
1968	Eduardo Jiménez de Arechaga	Uruguay
1969	Charles Rousseau	France
1970	Roberto Ago	Italy
1971	Edvardo Hambro	Norway
1972	Suzanne Bastid	France
1973	Taslim Olawale Elias	Nigeria
1974	Gerald Gray Fitzmaurice	United Kingdom
1975	Sigeru Oda	Japan
1976	Shabtai Rosenne	Israel
1977	Manfred Lachs	Poland
1978	Humphrey Waldock	United Kingdom
1979	Hans Blix	Sweden

1980	F. A. Mann	United Kingdom
1981	Derek W. Bowett	United Kingdom
1982	Richard Orme	United Kingdom
1983	Andre Gros	France
1984	Paul Reuter	France
1985	Nagendra Singh	India
1986	Robert Y. Jennings	United Kingdom
1987	Ian Sinclair	United Kingdom
1988	José Sette-Câmara	Brazil
1989	Rudolph Bernhardt	Germany
1990	Nicolas Valticos	Greece
1991	Krzysztof Skubiszewski	Poland
1992	Rosalyn Higgins	United Kingdom
1993	Elihu Lauterpacht	United Kingdom
1994	Rene-Jean Dupuy	France
1995	Boutros Boutros-Ghali	Egypt
1996	Ronald St. John Macdonald	Canada
1997	Mohammed Shahabuddeen	Guyana
1998	Mary Robinson	Ireland
1999	Kofi Annan	Ghana
2000	Louise Arbour	Canada
2001	Georges Abi-Saab	Egypt
2002	Ibrahim F. I. Shihata	Egypt
2003	Navanethem Pillay	South Africa
2004	Ian Brownlie	United Kingdom
2005	Florentino Feliciano	Philippines
2006	Hisashi Owada	Japan

INDEX

(Footnotes and Appendices have not been indexed.)

www.ingramcontent.com/pod-product-compliance
Lightning Source LLC
LaVergne TN
LVHW021002300926
849160LV00007B/220